Executive Self-Government and the Constitution

Executive Self-Government and the Constitution

TERENCE DAINTITH
Professorial Fellow, Institute of Advanced Legal Studies, University of London, UK

ALAN PAGE
Emeritus Professor of Public Law, School of Law, University of Dundee, UK

OXFORD
UNIVERSITY PRESS

OXFORD
UNIVERSITY PRESS

Great Clarendon Street, Oxford, OX2 6DP,
United Kingdom

Oxford University Press is a department of the University of Oxford.
It furthers the University's objective of excellence in research, scholarship,
and education by publishing worldwide. Oxford is a registered trade mark of
Oxford University Press in the UK and in certain other countries

Published in the United States of America by Oxford University Press
198 Madison Avenue, New York, NY 10016, United States of America

British Library Cataloguing in Publication Data

Data available

Library of Congress Control Number: 2024951417

ISBN 9780198863540

DOI: 10.1093/9780198937630.001.0001

Printed and bound by
CPI Group (UK) Ltd, Croydon, CR0 4YY

MIX
Paper | Supporting
responsible forestry
FSC www.fsc.org
FSC® C013604

The manufacturer's authorised representative in the EU for product safety is
Oxford University Press España S.A. of El Parque Empresarial San Fernando de Henares, Avenida
de Castilla, 2 – 28830 Madrid (www.oup.es/en or product.safety@oup.com).
OUP España S.A. also acts as importer into Spain of products made by the manufacturer.

Preface

In 1999 we published *The Executive in the Constitution*, in which we argued that the organization and management of the United Kingdom's executive government were crucial but neglected elements of our constitution, providing as they did the means through which government could respond effectively to the disciplines of parliamentary accountability and judicial control that formed the main preoccupation of constitutional law scholarship. A quarter of a century has since elapsed, in which United Kingdom governments have had to confront a degree of international, economic, and political change and instability which their late 20th-century predecessors were happily spared: the threat of a complete collapse of the financial system as a result of the global financial crisis of 2007–08; periods of coalition and minority government; the need to adjust to a fundamental change of economic and political circumstances occasioned by the unexpected (and unprepared for) referendum decision to leave the European Union (EU); the Covidpandemic; the experience of working under three different Prime Ministers in a single year (2022); and the impact, substantial even if not immediate, of war—in Iraq towards the beginning of this period, in Ukraine towards the end.

Reviewing developments in the aftermath of the EU referendum we felt that the time must be ripe to revisit our end-of-century descriptions and analyses of what we had identified as constitutionally significant features of executive organization and management. This book is the result. It does not take the form of a second edition of the 1999 volume, but of a sequel, in which we omit most of the historical and argumentative material with which we supported our case for an executive-centred account of the UK constitution, in favour of a clear focus on the events and policies of the last 25 years and the changes they have wrought in executive organization and management. Readers interested in a longer-term perspective on executive development will find it in our 1999 book, though in one area that we did not then cover, government information and communications, we start the story here a few decades earlier.

While our aim has shifted from mapping a hitherto little-explored area of the constitutional terrain to pointing out and explaining significant changes in the landscape, we have continued to employ the same methods for analysing our material and identifying what, in the vast mass of data about the operations of the executive, is relevant to our objective and what is not. As before our focus is on the UK government—we do not have the space here to deal with the devolved governments of Scotland, Wales, and Northern Ireland, which are deserving of treatment in their own right, and a fascinating subject for comparative analysis. We continue to define the constitution as 'a set of rules for obtaining, allocating, and deploying the resources required by the state for the control of its territory in the interests of the security and well-being of its people'; and the resources we focus on are people (in chapter 6 on the Civil Service), money (in chapters 7 and 8 on financial management and expenditure), law (in chapter 9 on the government's legal services and chapter 10 on legislation), and information (in chapters 11 and 12). And we continue to organize our appraisal of the constitutional position of the executive around three key features: its organization (whose development we discuss in chapters 2 and 3 on the 'centre' and departments respectively, in chapter 4 on public bodies, and in chapter 5 on devolution), its autonomy (the extent to which it can manage its affairs independently of Parliament and the courts), and its internal control. The final chapter (chapter 13) assesses the extent of change in autonomy, structure, and internal control over the last 25 years.

Like our 1999 book, this is a mixture of joint and individual efforts. The structure follows that of its predecessor with the principal differences being the expanded treatment of the machinery of government—the 'centre', departments, and public bodies—and the addition of government information and communications. Within that revised structure we have divided responsibility for drafting chapters broadly according to subject-matter. Daintith is responsible for the 'resources' chapters (except chapter 6 on the Civil Service) and has also contributed the Treasury material in chapter 2, the chapters on departments (chapter 3) and public bodies (except as below), and the conclusion (chapter 13). Page provided the Introduction (chapter 1) and the chapters on the centre of government (chapter 2, except as above), on devolution (chapter 5) and on the Civil Service (chapter 6), and the material on public appointments in chapter 4. All drafts, however, have been the subject of discussion between us, and we each accept responsibility for the whole work, and for each other's mistakes as well as our own.

We have endeavoured to state the position as at 1 August 2024, a few weeks after the return, after more than a decade, of a Labour government. The following months saw the issue of new versions of documents that play an important role in our discussion: a new Ministerial Code, separating more clearly the ethical and procedural rules to which ministers are subject, enlarging the powers of initiative of the renamed Independent Adviser on Ministerial Standards, and removing the long inoperative formal restriction on the number of special advisers each minister could appoint; a revised Code for Special Advisers; and new guidance from the Attorney General on Legal Risk, emphasizing—for the first time—the need for government lawyers to assess policy compliance with international as well as national law. These developments have come too late for discussion in our text, but we have added references to the new versions to relevant footnotes in chapters 2, 6, and 9, and in our Bibliography, so that readers may form their own view of their significance. Do they portend a change of approach to the scope or process of executive self-government? Or are they only marginal adjustments to an essentially unchanging situation?' One of the lessons of our research is that while some aspects of executive self-government may be affected by changes in the political complexion of government, most are not. Weblinks (except those for the sources mentioned above) were last accessed at 1 September 2024.

One of the changes we advert to in our chapters is the ever-increasing volume of information that the executive publishes about its work and organization. While this, coupled with freedom of information requests, has reduced the reliance we have needed to place on personal interviews, these have still been an essential source of information in a number of areas. Following a convention that is not yet outmoded, we do not name the officials who have so kindly devoted time and effort to respond to our queries and improve our understanding, but we trust that they will recognize in the pages that follow both the essential character of their contribution and our gratitude to them for providing it. We can however thank by name: Philip Larkin, Philip Rycroft, Rajiv Shah, and Nikki da Costa. We also want to express our gratitude to Will Bateman, Philip Sales, and Mike Granatt, who have reviewed and thereby improved drafts of some of our chapters. Finally, our thanks go to the Leverhulme Trust, which granted each of us an Emeritus Fellowship to assist with the costs of undertaking research for the book.

In 1999 we expressed our gratitude to our families for their forbearance. Our wives might have been excused for assuming that, by the time twenty years had elapsed since our original efforts, there was little risk that such forbearance would need to be exercised again. In this they were to be cruelly disappointed. We can only apologise.

Terence Daintith
Alan Page
Edinburgh and Dundee
November 2024

Contents

PART G. CONCLUSION

Table of Cases

Table of Statutes, Regulations, etc.

UNITED KINGDOM REGULATIONS

Prerogative Orders in Council

Statutory Instruments

COUNCIL OF EUROPE

EUROPEAN UNION

Directive

Regulations

Abbreviations

ACOBA	Advisory Committee on Business Appointments
AGO	Attorney General's Office
ALB	Arm's length body
AME	Annually Managed Expenditure
AO	Accounting Officer
ASA	Advertising Standards Authority
BCAP Code	the UK Code of Broadcast Advertising
BRE	Better Regulation Executive
BRTF	Better Regulation Task Force
CAP Code	the UK Code of Non-Broadcast Advertising and Direct and Promotional Marketing
CCS	Civil Contingencies Secretariat
CDDO	Central Digital and Data Office
COBRA	Cabinet Office Briefing Room A (the usual meeting place of the UK emergency response committee)
COI	Central Office of Information
COO	Chief Operating Officer
CPS	Crown Prosecution Service
CRAG	Constitutional Reform and Governance Act 2010
CSB	Civil Service Board
CSO	Central Statistical Office
CSPL	Committee on Standards in Public Life
CSR	Comprehensive Spending Review
CSSB	Civil Service Shadow Board
DAO	Dear Accounting Officer letter
DEA	Domestic and Economic Affairs
DEFRA	Department for Environment, Food and Rural Affairs
DEL	Departmental Expenditure Limits
DExEU	Department for Exiting the European Union
DGN	Devolution Guidance Note
DHSC	Department of Health and Social Care
DLUHC	Department for Levelling Up, Housing and Communities
DMO	Debt Management Office
DPP	Director of Public Prosecutions
DPRRC	Delegated Powers and Regulatory Reform Committee (House of Lords)
10DS	data science and analytics unit
DUP	Democratic Unionist Party
DWP	Department for Work and Pensions
EDS	Economic and Domestic Secretariat

EMO	Extended Ministerial Office
ERG	Efficiency and Reform Group
ESA	European System of Accounts
EU	European Union
F:ISC	Finance: Interministerial Standing Committee
FCDO	Foreign, Commonwealth and Development Office
FOI	freedom of information
FRAB	Financial Reporting Advisory Board
FTE	full-time employees
FTE	full-time equivalent
GCN	Government Communications Network
GCS	Government Communication Service
GDP	gross domestic product
GDS	Government Digital Service
GFC	global financial crisis
GIAA	Government Internal Audit Agency
GICS	Government Information and Communications Service
GIS	Government Information Service
GLD	Government Legal Department
GMPP	Government Major Projects Portfolio
GSS	Government Statistical Service
HMCPSI	Her Majesty's Crown Prosecution Service Inspectorate
HMRC	His Majesty's Revenue and Customs
HMSO	His Majesty's Stationery Office
IC	Interministerial Committee (time-limited)
ICT	information and communication technology
IFRS	International Financial Reporting Standards
IGR	intergovernmental relations
IMSC	Interministerial Standing Committee
IPA	Infrastructure and Projects Authority
JMC	Joint Ministerial Committee
LSAG	Legal Secretariat of the Advocate General for Scotland
MCO	Minister for the Cabinet Office
MIG	Ministerial Implementation Group
MoJ	Ministry of Justice
MoU	Memorandum of Understanding
MPM	Managing Public Money
NAO	National Audit Office
NCCC	non-corporate communications channel
nd	no date
NDPB	non-departmental public body
NMD	non-ministerial department
NSC	National Security Council
NSS	National Security Secretariat
OBR	Office for Budget Responsibility
OCPA	Office of the Commissioner for Public Appointments

ODP	Outcome Delivery Plan
OECD	Organisation for Economic Co-operation and Development
OGA	Oil and Gas Authority
OIOO	'one in, one out'
OITO	'one in, two out'
ONS	Office for National Statistics
OPC	Office of Parliamentary Counsel
OPS	Office of Public Service
OSPT	Official Solicitor and Public Trustee
OSR	Office for Statistics Regulation
PAC	House of Commons Public Accounts Committee
PACAC	House of Commons Public Administration and Constitutional Affairs Committee
PAU	Public Appointments Unit
PBL	Parliamentary Business and Legislation
PES	Public Expenditure Survey
PEX	Public Services and Public Expenditure Committee
PFO	Principal Finance Office
PIU	Performance and Innovation Unit
PMDU	Prime Minister's Delivery Unit
PMIU	Prime Minister's Implementation Unit
PSA	Public Service Agreement
QPM	Questions of Procedure for Ministers
RCPO	Revenue and Customs Prosecution Office
RIA	regulatory impact assessment
RPC	Regulatory Policy Committee
SCS	Senior Civil Service
SDP	Single Departmental Plan
SFO	Serious Fraud Office
SI	statutory instrument
SLSC	Secondary Legislation Scrutiny Committee (House of Lords)
spad	special adviser
SR	Spending Review
SRO	Senior Responsible Owner
TME	Total Managed Expenditure
TSol	Treasury Solicitor's Department
UKGG	UK Governance Group
UKSA	United Kingdom Statistics Authority
VFM	value for money

PART A
INTRODUCTION

1

The Executive in the Constitution: Forces for Change 1997–2024

I The Executive in the Constitution

> *'The Government are the people responsible for running the country . . . Parliament is there to represent our interests and make sure they are taken into account by the Government.'*[1]
>
> *'In the British constitution, the executive is the primary, general branch of government.'*[2]

These statements, the first from the website of Parliament itself, present a constitutional characterization of the executive that is very different from the one traditionally offered by most UK constitutional law writing. The emphasis in that literature on parliamentary sovereignty as the supreme, if not the only, constitutional tenet, on the lack of any limit on Parliament's power to empower or restrain executive action through legislation, and on the subjection of the executive to control by the courts, made it difficult to see the executive as a distinctive 'power' under the constitution at all, and led a senior judge to remark (albeit extra-judicially) that 'the executive cannot be one of three sovereign and equal elements of the State'.[3] Constitutional law writing instead generally presented the executive and its activity as a reflection of some other organ's concerns and functions. Departmental action was viewed through the prism of how ministers accounted to Parliament; executive action generally was observed through the distorting mirror of judicial review, with its parade of instances of bad and unlawful administration.

Events of the last 25 years have severely challenged any conception of the executive as a subordinate constitutional actor. The executive has taken us to war, in Iraq, and on other military adventures; it has navigated a global financial crisis; it has claimed the capacity to take us out of the European Union, following the 2016 referendum, regardless of the views of Parliament, and has engaged in a conflict with Parliament that was only resolved—in its favour—by the 2019 general election; and it has assumed and exercised extraordinary powers, reaching into the private life of every citizen, to deal with the Covid pandemic. It has functioned, for significant periods, within the constitutionally unusual frameworks of coalition (2010–15) and minority (2017–19) government.

[1] UK Parliament (website), *Parliament and the Government*.

[2] Timothy Endicott, *The Stubborn Stain Theory of Executive Power: from Magna Carta to Miller* (Policy Exchange 2017) 17.

[3] Stephen Sedley, 'The Sound of Silence: Constitutional Law without a Constitution' (1994) 110 Law Quarterly Review 270, 289–90.

Executive Self-Government and the Constitution. Terence Daintith and Alan Page, Oxford University Press.
 DOI: 10.1093/9780198937630.003.0001

These events have given the executive a much higher constitutional profile—some might say notoriety—but this has not necessarily entailed major change in its constitutionally significant characteristics. The idea that the executive was a distinct and autonomous element of our constitutional order—regardless of whether one might call it 'primary' or 'sovereign' or 'equal'—so that its organization and internal governance were matters of as much constitutional concern as its relations with Parliament and the courts, was what led us in 1999, in *The Executive in the Constitution*,[4] to offer a detailed analysis of the extent of the executive's capacity for self-organization and self-government. The characteristics we there identified were its capacity for autonomous action and self-organization; its institutional structure; and the manner and effectiveness of its internal control of its actions—which, we argued, was an essential support for effective external control by Parliament and courts. The extent of change in these key features of the executive over the last quarter-century is the subject of this book.

In this chapter we provide a baseline for the measurement of change by recalling the main features of the United Kingdom's executive government as they stood in 1997, when the 'New' Labour government of Tony Blair took office with a large majority on a platform of reform, before concentrating on the main forces for change in the executive over the past 25 years, as a preliminary to the analysis in the chapters that follow.

II Constitutionally Significant Features

2.1 Autonomy

The conception of the United Kingdom's executive government on which our book was based was of the executive as a self-managing or self-governing institution. As a self-governing institution the executive displayed two essential features. The first was the high value it attributed to its autonomy—i.e. to the maintenance of a self-contained normative order, insulated, so far as possible, from extraneous control. In practical terms that meant being able to govern itself without the assistance of Parliament or the courts. 'Why advise the Queen to ask Parliament to aid her to do that which she can do as effectually without their aid?', asked Sir James Stephen when the question of a statutory basis for the Civil Service was first raised in 1854.[5]

The other feature was its anti-legalism, which was founded on the belief that government was 'a system not of rules but of advice'.[6] The nature of the British constitution was not to 'circumscribe matters with rules but to rely on the more elastic safeguard of taking advice'.[7] 'Traditional civil service methods' were to be preferred to rules, which did not work:

[4] Terence Daintith and Alan Page, *The Executive in the Constitution: Structure, Autonomy and Internal Control* (OUP 1999).

[5] Sir James Stephen, letter in *Papers relating to the Re-organisation of the Civil Service*, Parl Pap (1854–55) vol 20.

[6] Christopher D Foster and Francis J Plowden, *The State under Stress: Can the Hollow State be Good Government?* (Open University Press 1996) 77.

[7] Rosamund M Thomas, *The British Philosophy of Administration: A Comparison of British and American Ideas 1900–1939* (Longmans 1978) 6–7.

> They merely stimulate ways round them, so leading to yet more rules to plug loopholes, leading to a growing climate of regulation of a kind from which the new public management saw the need to escape in the interests of efficiency. There can be no guarantee that reliance on these methods will be more effective or cheaper than relying on traditional civil service methods, based on the traditional Haldane relationship: indeed on both counts, rather the reverse.[8]

Rules were therefore to be avoided, or if unavoidable should take the form of the executive's own rules—a possibility which critics of the growth of legalism neglected.[9] Indeed by 1997 this was more than a possibility: centrally developed 'guidance' was a long established feature of Civil Service management[10] and of public expenditure control,[11] and the preference for ad hoc advice over general norms was clearly weakening. But statutory rules, which would involve both Parliament and the courts, were still in principle to be avoided, though, as we shall see, governments have since 1997 differed considerably in their readiness to subject themselves to statutory rules when policy or principle suggested this as the most effective approach.

Autonomy and anti-legalism were not merely valued as ends in themselves. They were also seen as the foundation upon which the executive's capacity for swift and effective action rested.

2.2 Structure

In terms of structure, we argued that the United Kingdom's executive government was more plural than unitary—a loose federation rather than a single entity—with the ministerial department as the 'effective unit of government'. The executive's plural character was a consequence of the practice of vesting functions in the ministerial heads of departments rather than the executive as a whole. When statutory powers first started to be conferred on government, it was accepted that the king acted on the advice of ministers and that a particular minister was responsible for advice in a particular field. It was more 'open and direct', therefore, and more in keeping with the increasing emphasis on individual ministerial responsibility for new powers and duties to be conferred, not on the king, but on the minister who would have to administer them and to take public responsibility for their performance.[12] 'In the British Constitution, government is ministerial government. Powers and duties are laid on ministers, not on the prime minister.'[13] Across much of what it did, therefore, the executive was plural rather than unitary.

[8] Foster and Plowden (n 6) 229.

[9] Daintith and Page (n 4) 387–88.

[10] Cabinet Office, *Directory of Civil Service Guidance* (2000) (2 vols), replacing Cabinet Office, Office of Public Service, *Guidance on Guidance: An Index to Useful Documents* (February 1996).

[11] HM Treasury, *Government Accounting* (1989), first circulated in 1915 as HM Treasury, *Notes for the Use of Accounts Branches of Government Departments*. The fourth edition was published by His Majesty's Stationery Office (HMSO) in 1929.

[12] Sir Norman Chester, *The English Administrative System 1780–1870* (Clarendon Press 1981) 93–94.

[13] George W Jones, 'The United Kingdom' in William Plowden (ed), *Advising the Rulers* (Basil Blackwell 1987) 64.

As the key units of management and accountability in the plural executive, departments enjoyed a high degree of autonomy. The traditional operating model of government was one of departmental autonomy, set within a spending framework determined by the Treasury at the centre.[14] As well as being reinforced by the courts,[15] departmental autonomy derived support from the underlying principle of individual ministerial responsibility. 'Ministers were always able to defend their departmental position by appealing that their accountability was to Parliament, not to Cabinet.'[16] It was also buttressed by their ministerial heads' membership of the supreme executive authority—the Cabinet. 'Whatever method was adopted to "make a reality of collective responsibility", there was the basic stumbling block that the central authority was not embodied in a single executive but in a group of ministers with shifting loyalties and views.'[17]

The other side of departmental autonomy in a plural executive was a 'centre'—the 'seamless web' of Cabinet Office, Treasury, and 10 Downing Street[18]—which, with the exception of the Treasury, possessed few powers of control over departments. The centre's powers to determine the broad structure of central government were unchallenged; it was for the Prime Minister alone, in the exercise of the power to advise the monarch on the appointment and responsibilities of ministers, to decide how functions should be divided among departments and who should head those departments. Once the structure was in place, however, the centre, with the exception of the Treasury, possessed few powers of control over the way departments exercised their functions. Departments for the most part were subject to coordination, advice, and assistance rather than direction from the centre.[19] The centre's ability to get departments to do its bidding—to bend Whitehall to its will—could not therefore be taken for granted. It was least problematic where the authority of the centre was accepted, more so where its authority was contested or open to challenge. As was said of the Coalition government's *Civil Service Reform Plan*, it was striking that the Minister for the Cabinet Office (MCO) had made more progress on 'issues with established structures and routines, where departments broadly accept the legitimacy of central control or co-ordination. The progress of other reforms which rely on persuasion and influence has been more mixed. This simply reflects the reality of the weakness of the centre.'[20]

14 National Audit Office, *The Centre of Government* (HC 2014–15, 171) para 2.

15 Daintith and Page (n 4) 30–31 and cases cited therein.

16 JM Lee, *Reviewing the Machinery of Government 1942-1952. An essay on the Anderson Committee and its successors* (Birbeck College 1977) 37.

17 ibid 28.

18 ibid 24.

19 'Because the protection and enhancement of autonomy is so important, agencies rarely try to control each other directly. The "coordinating council" is the preferred strategy for giving the illusion of mutual control, while preserving the reality of mutual independence': JQ Wilson and P Rachal, 'Can the Government Regulate Itself?' (1977) 46 Public Interest 12.

20 James Page and others, *Leading Change in the Civil Service* (Institute for Government 2014) 34.

2.3 Internal control

Internal control, the disciplines the executive applies to itself, was the starting point for our original inquiry. We argued that departmental self-discipline or self-control was the cornerstone or foundation of the executive's systems of internal control. Departmental primacy had been the central organizing principle of the executive branch since the middle years of the 19th century. Its corollary was a decentralized system of internal control for the operation of which the ministerial head of each department was responsible to Parliament. The permanent head of the department was in turn responsible to the minister for its overall organization, management, and staffing. The role of the 'centre' within this system was one of coordination, advice, and assistance rather than control. The traditional orthodoxy was that it was better to trust departments than to engage in 'a futile attempt at supervision in detail'.[21]

There were exceptions to this pattern. The most important were those in respect of expenditure and staffing, the latter being treated as part of the control of expenditure. Treasury control of money and staff in a plural executive was founded on control of access to resources, reinforced in the case of staff by a mixture of mainly prerogative and to a lesser extent statutory controls. But although the Treasury possessed important powers of control over departments, it never strayed far from an approach which treated the primary responsibility for financial as well as policy decisions as belonging to spending departments. No doubt the adoption of that approach reflected a calculation that a system in which the emphasis was on the 'conjoint and cooperative responsibility, under Ministers, of all departmental heads, including the Treasury, as opposed to the conception of an Olympian Treasury *contra mundum*',[22] was likely to be more effective than one in which the emphasis was on the Treasury's powers of control alone, but it also acknowledged the extent to which collective control in a plural executive depended on agreement among departments.[23]

The strength of the UK approach to internal control in contrast to one in which, for example, spending decisions must be approved by representatives of a central department, we suggested, was that it placed responsibility for compliance firmly on the shoulders of departments. Their sense of responsibility was not diminished by reason of responsibility being seen to lie elsewhere. Its weakness was that it was vulnerable to non-compliance. Where central systems of control had been established, reliance on the department as the primary agent of control had invariably been accompanied by some form of check on the diligence with which central disciplines were applied. So too when central management functions were later devolved to departments. Such checks on departmental action, however, were the exception rather than the rule. Across much of what the executive did the system was one of departmental

[21] Viscount Haldane of Cloan, 'An Organised Civil Service' (1923) 1 The Journal of Public Administration 8.

[22] Sir HP Hamilton, 'Sir Warren Fisher and the Public Service' (1951) 29 Public Administration 26, para 86, quoting Warren Fisher, Permanent Secretary to the Treasury and Head of the Home Civil Service 1919–39, in evidence to the Royal Commission on the Civil Service 1929–31 (Cmd 3909, 1931).

[23] Daintith and Page (n 4) 381–82.

self-discipline or self-control under the individual and collective supervision of ministers.[24]

The executive's system of internal control, we argued, was an important part of the constitution. The business of internal control might be pursued independently of Parliament or the courts, but the controls operated by Parliament and the courts depended unequivocally on the executive's own machinery for their effectiveness.

It was also a system in the process of significant change. The previous 20 or so years had seen a marked increase in the degree of control or attempted control exercised by the centre over departments. The main driving force behind this development had been the public service reforms pursued by successive governments. If burdens on business were to be reduced, if services were to be made more responsive to their users, if coordination across departmental boundaries was to be increased, the centre had to find some means of inducing departments to move in desired directions.

A striking feature of the growth of central coordination and control from our point of view was that it had not been accompanied by any increase in formal powers of direction or control over departments. Instead of taking such powers, governments had preferred to pursue their objectives through a combination of established methods of inter-departmental coordination and centrally placed 'guerilla units' such as the Efficiency Unit and the Citizen's Charter Unit, leaving the foundations of departmental autonomy within the executive branch undisturbed. The years since 1997 have, as we shall see, witnessed regular collisions between departmental expectations of autonomy and repeated initiatives, from the centre of government, aimed at improving executive performance through the adoption across government of common standards for common activities, and through breaking into departmental 'silos' to secure effective delivery of policies involving cross-departmental interests. The degree to which these initiatives have succeeded in modifying the model of central control through guidance and persuasion, rather than compulsion, is one of the questions we set out to answer in the research for this book.

III Forces for Change

3.1 Manifesto commitments

Manifesto commitments have been an important force for change in the executive in the past 25 years. 'Get Brexit Done' in the 2019 Conservative manifesto is the standout example: its result was the United Kingdom's departure from the European Union on 31 January 2020, ending almost a half-century of membership. Brexit was not just a crisis for which no preparations had been made before the 2016 referendum: it was a constitutional development of the first rank—'as significant a constitutional change as that which occurred when the UK joined the European Community [EC] in 1973'.[25] More so, arguably, because of the developments that had taken place in the intervening 47 years—the European Union the United Kingdom left was very different in terms of

[24] ibid 382.

[25] *R (Miller) v Secretary of State for Exiting the European Union* [2017] UKSC 5, [2018] AC 61 [81].

the extent of its competences and its methods of decision-making from the EC the United Kingdom joined.

In terms of 'taking back control', the UK Parliament regained its capacity to legislate without regard for obligations and constraints imposed by EU law, Acts of Parliament their status as the highest form of law known to the constitution. The executive, for its part, was freed from the constraints imposed by EU law—other than those assumed under the Trade and Cooperation Agreement, which was given legislative effect by the European Union (Future Relationship) Act 2020. A government with a stable parliamentary majority, a condition not satisfied between 2017 and 2019, also gained access to the legislative sovereignty of Parliament—reawakening a former Lord Chancellor's warning of an 'elective dictatorship',[26] a threat which the Conservatives sought to exploit in their 2024 general election campaign. And the role of the courts in the constitution was diminished with EU law ceasing to be one of the judicially enforceable restraints on legislative and administrative action.

Second in importance to Get Brexit Done in the last 25 years was the 1997 Labour government's manifesto commitment to 'the democratic renewal of our country through decentralisation and the elimination of excessive government secrecy'.[27] No less important in terms of its impact on the executive was the Conservative's deficit reduction plan, which took precedence over every other measure in the 2010 Coalition agreement.[28] Among New Labour's constitutional reforms with a direct bearing on the executive were the Human Rights Act 1998, which made rights under the European Convention on Human Rights enforceable in domestic legal proceedings; devolution to Scotland, Wales, and Northern Ireland; and freedom of information, with the 1992 Conservative government's non-statutory Code of Practice on Access to Government Information being replaced by a statutory right of access to information.[29] Other reforms bearing on the operation of the executive, which were not the subject of manifesto commitments, included Bank of England independence, with the Bank being given operational control over the setting of interest rates; and termination of the Lord Chancellor's non-executive roles, as head of the judiciary and Speaker of the House of Lords. The House of Lords was also replaced by the Supreme Court as the United Kingdom's final court of appeal.

Constitutional reform was also a priority for the Gordon Brown government which assumed office in June 2007. Revisiting its predecessor's refusal to consult on legislation to provide greater parliamentary control over the executive powers enjoyed by ministers under the royal prerogative,[30] it proposed 'surrendering or limiting' the most important prerogative powers of the Prime Minister and the executive, including

[26] Lord Hailsham, 'Elective ictatorship' *The Listener* (21 October 1976) 496–500.

[27] Labour Party, *New Labour: Because Britain Deserves Better* (1996).

[28] HM Government, *The Coalition: Our Programme for Government* (May 2010).

[29] Andrew McDonald (ed), *Reinventing Britain: Constitutional Change under New Labour* (Politico's 2007).

[30] Public Administration Select Committee, *Taming the Prerogative: Strengthening Ministerial Accountability to Parliament* (HC 2003–04, 422); Department for Constitutional Affairs, Government response to the Public Administration Select Committee's Fourth Report of Session 2003–04, *Taming the Prerogative: Strengthening Ministerial Accountability to Parliament* (Cm 6187, 2004).

those over the deployment of troops abroad, the ratification of treaties, the dissolution and recall of Parliament, and the management of the Civil Service:

> In a modern 21st century parliamentary democracy, the Government considers that basing these powers on the prerogative is out of date. It will therefore seek to limit its own power by placing the most important of these prerogative powers on a more formal footing, conferring power on Parliament to determine how they are exercised in future.[31]

The results, however, fell a long way short of the ambition. The Constitutional Reform and Governance Act 2010, which was passed in the final hours of the parliament, made provision with regard to the Civil Service and the ratification of treaties, 'but it was paltry stuff when compared to what had been promised.'[32]

New Labour's constitutional reforms were not the subject of all-party or lasting agreement. Together with the continued growth of judicial review, they were to provoke a reaction in the shape of the 2019 Conservative manifesto commitment to 're-balance' the constitution:

> After Brexit we need to look at the broader aspects of our constitution: the relationship between the Government, Parliament and the courts; the functioning of the Royal Prerogative; the role of the House of Lords; and access to justice for ordinary people... We will update the Human Rights Act and administrative law to ensure that there is a proper balance between the rights of individuals, our vital national security and effective government. We will ensure that judicial review is available to protect the rights of the individuals against an overbearing state, while ensuring that it is not abused to conduct politics by another means or to create needless delays.[33]

The Johnson government's constitutional agenda, it has been suggested, is best understood as a post-Brexit attempt to return to the traditional model of the 'political constitution', which formed the core of the British constitutional system for much of the 20th century.[34] In legislative terms its results were limited, with the Judicial Review and Courts Act 2022 having little impact on the power of the courts to check executive action, and Dominic Raab's Bill of Rights Bill eventually being dropped by the Sunak government. The prerogative of dissolution, which had been abolished by the Fixed-term Parliaments Act 2011 as part of the Coalition agreement, was revived,[35] but the

[31] Secretary of State for Justice and Lord Chancellor, *The Governance of Britain* (Cm 7170, 2007) para 17.

[32] Jack Straw, *Last Man Standing: Memoirs of a Political Survivor* (Pan Books 2012) 524. Straw, who had once advocated abolition of the prerogative, was Secretary of State for Justice and Lord Chancellor in the Brown government.

[33] *Get Brexit Done, Unleash Britain's Potential* (November 2019) 48.

[34] 'Some have suggested that the Government's agenda is some sort of authoritarian Executive power grab, but I think... Prof Colm O'Cinneide got it right when he said we are attempting to return to the political constitution model that was the orthodoxy for much of the 20th century': Robert Buckland, Lord Chancellor Speaks at UCL Conference on the Constitution <www.gov.uk/government/speeches/lord-chancellor-speaks-at-ucl-conference-on-the-constitution>, referring to Colm O'Cinneide, 'The UK's Post-Brexit "Constitutional Unsettlement"' (*Verfassungsblog*, 16 April 2021) https://verfassungsblog.de/the-uks-post-brexit-constitutional-unsettlement/

[35] Dissolution and Calling of Parliament Act 2022.

New Labour reforms survived unchanged.[36] More difficult to gauge is the impact on judicial attitudes, with the courts perhaps treading more warily than they might have in the past.

3.2 Crises

As often as not, governments do not enjoy the luxury of considered planning and preparation for change associated with carrying through manifesto commitments. They may be confronted with serious and unforeseen events, crises that demand a policy response and whose nature may be such as to demand change in the way the executive goes about its work—at least for as long as the crisis lasts. Governments in office between 1997 and 2024 have certainly had to confront their full share of such experiences. The first of these, the effects of which were to continue to be felt long after the immediate danger of a complete collapse of the financial system had passed, was the 2007–08 global financial crisis, which was followed by the Conservative-led Coalition government's programme of 'austerity'—a 'biting austerity programme that markedly shrank the size of the state' and, as we shall see, produced a lasting rebalancing of central and departmental powers over a range of activities.[37]

A crisis of a different kind was the 2014 Scottish independence referendum, an existential crisis which prompted a last-minute, hastily assembled defence of the Union.[38] Although Scotland voted No in answer to the question: 'Should Scotland be an independent country', the margin of victory was not such as to suggest that the issue had been settled once and for all—as was to prove to be the case with support for independence still running high a decade after the referendum.

The Scottish independence referendum was followed less than two years later by the referendum on the United Kingdom's continuing membership of the European Union, the unanticipated (and unprepared-for) outcome of which presented probably 'the biggest and most complex challenge the Civil Service has faced in our peacetime history'.[39] After almost four years of wrangling and division, the United Kingdom left the European Union on 31 January 2020—with many of the issues raised by withdrawal still to be resolved.

No sooner had the United Kingdom left the European Union than it was struck by Covid, a 'once-in-a-century pandemic . . . resulting in a once-in-three-centuries economic contraction via a nationwide lockdown'.[40] 'The Covid-19 pandemic was the biggest crisis our country has faced in generations and the greatest peacetime challenge in a century. It disrupted lives, separated friends and families, closed businesses, damaged livelihoods and, most tragically of all, has been associated with the deaths of

[36] For a survey, see Michael Gordon and Adam Tucker (eds), *The New Labour Constitution: Twenty Years On* (Hart Publishing 2022).

[37] Ben Riley-Smith, *The Right To Rule: Thirteen Years, Five Prime Ministers and the Implosion of the Tories* (John Murray 2023) xix.

[38] On which, see chapter 5, section II.

[39] Sir Jeremy Heywood, 'How the Civil Service is Preparing for Brexit' (*CivilService.blog.gov.uk*, 11 July 2017).

[40] Riley-Smith (n 37) xix.

over 150,000 people in the UK.'[41] It also led to the exercise, in peacetime, of the kind of all-embracing executive controls over personal and economic behaviour that we had hitherto experienced only in wartime. And then there was the energy and cost of living crisis that followed Russia's invasion of Ukraine in 2022.

After such testing experiences, 'getting back to normal' is a common and comprehensible ambition, which has driven governmental responses in the period of our analysis in the same way as it did after the 20th century's two World Wars. Nonetheless, crises may produce lasting change, and in the chapters that follow we shall try to trace their impact on the key constitutional characteristics of today's executive.

3.3 Modernization and reform

A third force for change has been successive governments' efforts to 'modernize and reform' executive government following the Thatcher and Major 'revolutions' of the previous 20 years.[42] These efforts, which we examine in more detail in the following chapters, began with the 1997 New Labour government's *Modernising Government* White Paper (October 1999) and were to continue with the Conservative-led Coalition's *Civil Service Reform Plan* (June 2012) and, after the twin crises of the vote to leave the European Union and Covid-19, the 2019 Conservative government's *Declaration on Government Reform* (June 2021). The emphasis of reform proposals differed on each occasion, but a common thread, alongside the improvement of Civil Service effectiveness, was the ambition to develop means of formulating and driving forward strategy for the government as a whole, through a better balance between the executive's 'corporate centre' and departments and the establishment of systems through which departments could be led to work together to produce 'joined-up solutions' to complex government problems. The most significant in terms of its impact was the Coalition's *Civil Service Reform Plan*, which we discuss in the next chapter.

3.4 'Democratic backsliding'

'Democratic backsliding' is a convenient shorthand expression for a final force for change: the weakening by accident or design of checks on executive power.[43] Aside from the Johnson government's efforts to rebalance the constitution, which it would be a stretch to label backsliding, two developments fit the definition.

The first is the 'sidelining' of Parliament, as a result—among other developments—of the 'ever increasing recourse to delegated legislation, in what has been described

[41] House of Commons Committee of Privileges, *Matter referred on 21 April 2022 (conduct of Rt Hon Boris Johnson): Final Report* (HC 2022–23, 564) para 7.

[42] Rodney Lowe and Hugh Pemberton, *The Official History of the British Civil Service: Reforming the Civil Service*, vol II: *The Thatcher and Major Revolutions, 1982–1997* (Routledge 2020).

[43] Stephan Haggard and Robert Kaufman, *Backsliding: Democratic Regress in the Contemporary World* (CUP 2021).

as a 'constitutionally unprincipled manner',[44] and the inappropriate 'fast-tracking' of primary legislation with, for example, the European Union (Future Relationship) Act 2020, which allowed for the ratification of the Trade and Cooperation Agreement, being passed in a single day, having been published only 24 hours before.[45] 'The risk is', one commentator wrote, 'that Covid-19, like Brexit, has reinforced the vicious cycle of decline in Westminster—in which executive disregard for parliament undermines public trust in its role, and in turn further emboldens ministers to side-line the legislature.'[46]

The second was the Johnson government's open disregard for the conventional restraints on political behaviour. 'I don't think it is a great secret to talk about the current circumstances', the Cabinet Secretary said in evidence to the House of Commons Public Administration and Constitutional Affairs Committee:

> The Government of the day are not remotely afraid of controversial policies. They believe they have a mandate to test established boundaries. They take a robust view of the national interest and of how the Government should protect and focus very much on accountability to people in Parliament, not on the unelected advisory structures.[47]

Testing established boundaries is one thing, rule breaking another. 'The prime minister and our present government not only challenge the law, but also seem to believe that they—and they alone—need not obey the rules, traditions, and conventions—call them what you will—of public life.'[48] The result was a seemingly unending succession of scandals and Boris Johnson's eventual forced departure from office.[49]

IV The Scheme of the Book

In the chapters that follow we examine the way the constitutionally significant features of executive autonomy, structure, and internal control have developed over the period since 1997. We try to show how the factors we have identified as potential drivers of change have operated on these characteristics, what change has occurred, and how and why change has been resisted. For this purpose we commence by discussing the machinery of executive government, tracing institutional developments at the centre of government—the Prime Minister's Office ('No 10'), Cabinet Office, and Treasury—in chapter 2, changes in the structure and management of central government departments in chapter 3 and, in chapter 4, developments in the organization

[44] Hayley J Hooper, 'Delegated Legislation in an Unprincipled Constitution' in Richard Johnson and Yuan Yi Zhu, *Sceptical Perspectives on the Changing Constitution of the United Kingdom* (Bloomsbury Publishing 2023) 133.

[45] Hannah White, *Held in Contempt: What's Wrong with the House of Commons?* (Manchester UP 2022) 33.

[46] ibid 26–27.

[47] Simon Case, Oral evidence to House of Commons Public Administration and Constitutional Affairs Committee, *Propriety of Governance in Light of Greensill* (28 June 2022) q 408.

[48] John Major, 'In Democracy We Trust? A keynote speech by the Rt Hon Sir John Major' (Institute for Government 10 February 2022).

[49] *Peter Hennessy, Land of Shame and Glory: Britain 2021–2022* (Haus Publishing 2023).

and management of the large population of public bodies of different types that are associated with departments. Chapter 5 on devolution completes our treatment of developments in the structure of the executive. Chapters 6–12 follow the model of *The Executive in the Constitution* and examine the development of the executive's arrangements for deploying the essential resources of government: people (chapter 6 on the Civil Service), money (chapters 7 and 8 on fiscal management and public expenditure control), laws (chapter 9 on legal services and chapter 10 on legislation and other rule-making), and information and communications (chapters 11 and 12). Governments like to be seen to be doing things and to be improving on the performance, and the institutions, of their predecessors, and these chapters show an executive engaged in a continuous process of innovation and reconsideration. How far that process has modified the executive's core constitutional characteristics—preservation of autonomy, pluralism of structure, systems of internal control—is the issue we address in our chapter 13.

PART B
THE STRUCTURE OF THE EXECUTIVE

2

The Centre of Government: Bigger and Stronger? Or Just Bigger?

I Introduction

A recurrent theme of machinery of government reform for much of the last century was the need to strengthen the centre of government—the 'seamless web' of Cabinet Office, Treasury, and 10 Downing Street—in order to better equip it to 'make a reality of collective responsibility'.[1] The corollary of departmental autonomy within the executive branch was a centre which even under the most dominant of the post-war Prime Ministers was described as 'fragmented and as lacking a single voice of authority'.[2] Despite the efforts that have been made to strengthen the centre since New Labour came to power in 1997 that criticism persists. For the Institute for Government, a 'poorly organised centre' is 'one of the core weaknesses of UK government. Successive prime ministers have found that their ability to deliver their priorities has not been helped, and has sometimes been hindered, by the way the centre of government is structured, and by failings in No.10, the Cabinet Office and HM Treasury.'[3] 'By international standards the Cabinet Office and No.10 offer limited policy and implementation support to the prime minister, meaning that the UK has the worst of all worlds: a highly centralised system of government without the capacity to organise it from the centre.'[4] In this chapter we look first at the efforts that have been made to remedy the 'hole in the centre'—'the relative weakness of the centre to determine, and ensure the implementation of, strategic priorities[5]—since 1997, before concentrating on the Downing Street-Cabinet Office complex and the Treasury.

[1] Sir John Anderson, 'The Machinery of Government' (1946) 30 Public Administration 147, 156.

[2] Efficiency Unit, *Improving Management in Government: The Next Steps. A Report to the Prime Minister* (1988) Annex B, para 38.

[3] Announcing the setting up of its Commission on the Centre of Government; for the Commission's report, see *Power with Purpose: Final Report of the Commission on the Centre of Government* (Institute for Government March 2024).

[4] Alex Thomas, *The heart of the problem. a weak centre is undermining the UK government* (Institute for Government January 2021).

[5] Rodney Lowe and Hugh Pemberton, *The Official History of the British Civil Service. Reforming the Civil Service,* vol II: *The Thatcher and Major Revolutions, 1982–97* (Routledge 2020) 5; see also Rodney Lowe, *The Official History of the British Civil Service* vol I: *The Fulton Years, 1966–81* (Routledge 2011) chs 3.2.4 and 5.3.1.

Executive Self-Government and the Constitution. Terence Daintith and Alan Page, Oxford University Press.
 DOI: 10.1093/9780198937630.003.0002

II Strengthening the Centre 1997–2024

2.1 New Labour and the centre

> The little secret of the British constitution is that the centre of government is not too powerful but too weak.[6]

Jonathan Powell, Tony Blair's chief of staff, records getting into trouble when Labour was in Opposition for suggesting that an incoming Labour government might see a move from a 'feudal system of barons to a more Napoleonic system'. 'The British system of government', he wrote later

> is traditionally a feudal system of barons (Cabinet Ministers) who have armies and funds (civil servants and budgets), who pay fealty to their liege but really get on with whatever they want to do. There is very little that the prime minister can do to make the government consistent or coherent. The only weapon he has in his armoury, a very blunt one, is hiring and firing people. My proposition was that, if the New Labour Government was going to succeed in delivering, we couldn't rely on the old ways. We needed to have greater coordination at the centre on both policy development and implementation.[7]

On becoming Cabinet Secretary in January 1998, Sir Richard Wilson was asked by the Prime Minister to review the effectiveness of the centre of government. His review saw the Cabinet Office and the Office of Public Service (OPS) merged with immediate effect and a Performance and Innovation Unit established in the Cabinet Office.[8] The incorporation of OPS into the Cabinet Office marked the final stage in the transfer of responsibility for the Civil Service from the Treasury to the Cabinet Office following the abolition of the Civil Service Department in 1981. Unlike the rest of the Cabinet Office whose main purpose was to help departments formulate policy collectively, its purpose was said to be to help departments find ways to improve the implementation and delivery of policies and services on the ground. A unified organization, so the argument ran, would thus help ensure that concerns about policy implementation were properly analysed in the process of developing policy, and help contribute to more effective follow-through when policies were agreed. The Performance and Innovation Unit (PIU), for its part, would focus on selected issues that crossed departmental boundaries, as well as the underlying question of how to get departments to work together to produce 'joined-up solutions' to complex government problems.[9]

[6] Jonathan Powell, *The New Machiavelli. How to Wield Power in the Modern World* (Vintage 2011) 29; to the same effect, see Philip Gould, *The Unfinished Revolution: How the Modernisers Saved the Labour Party* (Little, Brown 1998) xxiiii, quoted in Peter Riddell, 'Blair as Prime Minister' in Anthony Seldon (ed), *The Blair Effect: The Blair Government 1997–2001* (Little, Brown 2001) 22, 38.

[7] Powell (n 6) 78. New Labour sought 'a more formalised strengthening of the centre of government, which should not only give much-needed personal support to the prime minister . . . but provide the means of formulating and driving forward strategy for the government as a whole'. Peter Mandelson and Roger Liddle, *The Blair Revolution: Can New Labour Deliver?* (Faber & Faber 1996) 240.

[8] HC Debs 28 July 1998, vol 317, cols 132–4 (written answers).

[9] Cabinet Office, Performance and Innovation Unit, *Wiring it up: Whitehall's Management of Cross-Cutting Policies and Services* (2000). The PIU's establishment was the subject of 'an extended sparring

In his response to the review, the Prime Minister said there needed to be more emphasis on 'the corporate management of the Civil Service as a whole. My objective is to meet the corporate objectives of the Government as a whole, rather than just the objectives of individual departments.' The reorganization of the Cabinet Office, consequent upon its merger with the Office of Public Service, would give it a new focus as 'the corporate headquarters of the Civil Service'. A Management Board for the Civil Service would be established, whose membership would include a number of Permanent Secretaries, as a means of involving departments in the work of the Cabinet Office in its corporate management role.[10] The Board would be responsible for developing a more corporate approach to achieving cross-cutting goals and providing the leadership needed to drive cultural change in the Civil Service.[11]

These changes were of a piece with the 'accretive development of the Centre'.[12] A more radical plan was drawn up by John Birt, later Blair's strategic adviser, before the 2001 general election, which would have seen the Cabinet Office and No 10 merged to form a Prime Minister's department. Birt's plan was strenuously opposed by the Cabinet Secretary who feared it would undermine Cabinet government.[13] 'To Wilson, the Cabinet Office's very purpose was to support collective government and the Cabinet as a whole, and not just the Prime Minister. Such a move, he said, was a huge constitutional change and very decisive step towards the Prime Minister becoming presidential, which he thought unwise politically and administratively.'[14] A compromise was eventually reached which saw the Private Office and Policy Unit, both in No 10, merged to form a Policy Directorate after the general election, as well as three new units set up—the Prime Minister's Delivery Unit, the Office of Public Service Reform, and the Prime Minister's Forward Strategy Unit—all reporting to the Prime Minister, although they were based in the Cabinet Office, and the 'double hatting' of the heads of the Overseas and Defence and European secretariats in the Cabinet Office so that they also became advisers to the Prime Minister.[15]

For all the talk about strengthening the centre', Peter Riddell wrote:

> Mr Blair has been keen to avoid any suggestion that a Prime Minister's Department is being created—largely to avoid fuelling charges of presidentialism and in order to preserve the constitutional conventions of departmental responsibility and control. Of course, this is partly a matter of semantics. The distinction between a PM's

match' between the Chancellor, who wanted it in the Treasury, and the Prime Minister, who wanted it in the Cabinet Office. A 'messy compromise' saw it have offices in the Treasury but reporting to the Cabinet Office: Suzanne Heywood, *What Does Jeremy Think? Jeremy Heywood and the Making of Modern Britain* (William Collins 2021) 79.

[10] HC Deb 28 July 1998, vol 317, cols 132–4 (written answers).

[11] *Modernising Government* (Cm 4310, 1999) ch 2, para 12.

[12] Martin Burch and Ian Holliday, 'The Prime Minister's and Cabinet Offices: An Executive Office in All But Name' (1999) 52 Parliamentary Affairs 32, 44.

[13] Heywood (n 9) 118.

[14] Anthony Seldon with Jonathan Meakin, *Blair Unbound* (Simon and Schuster 2007) 37; Anthony Seldon with Jonathan Meakin, *The Cabinet Office 1916–2016. The Birth of Modern Government* (Biteback Publishing 2016) 248–49.

[15] HC Deb 19 October 2001, vol 372, cols 1361–62 (written answers).

> Office and a PM's Department is artificial. There is no absolute line between the two. But successive Cabinet Secretaries from Lord Hunt of Tamworth in the1970s to Sir Richard Wilson now, have been strongly opposed to crossing the line. This is both to avoid opening up broader constitutional questions about the balance between Downing Street and departments and to retain the politically neutral position of the Cabinet Office.[16]

Other changes were to follow but by the end of New Labour's time in office the 'will to have a stronger centre'[17] had not been realized.

> Despite more than a decade we spent trying, the Cabinet Office is still not a command, control and communications centre for the government as a whole, and some in the Civil Service do not accept that it should be. They think it should be a referee between departments ensuring fair play and a way of brokering agreement between departments. The trouble with this attitude is that it leads to a lowest common denominator approach. The government can only do what no department objects to, rather than the centre of government setting an objective and the Cabinet Office coordinating efforts to achieve it.[18]

2.2 The Coalition and the centre

In preparing for possible government the Conservatives disavowed New Labour's efforts to strengthen the centre. Rather than being 'man-marked' from the centre, ministers were to be left to run their own departments so long as they implemented the manifesto commitments and played ball with the new efficiency group Francis Maude, the shadow minister for the Cabinet Office, was planning to set up in the Cabinet Office.[19] The Prime Minister's Office was therefore cut back with the Strategy and Delivery Units both being abolished and the Policy Unit left with only a handful of people in it.[20] The latter was 'a Conservative decision by Mr Cameron and his advisers; in reaction to what they saw as an octopus-like No 10 operation in the Blair and Brown years interfering in the work of departments, they wanted to stand back,

16 Riddell, 'Blair as Prime Minister' (n 6) 31–32. Reflecting on the possible transformation of the Cabinet Office into a predominantly prime-ministerial entity, a colleague of Lord Hunt, Cabinet Secretary, 1973–79, is reported to have said: 'Of course it is perfectly obvious we need a Prime Minister's Department, so long as it is still called the Cabinet Office.' Hunt believed 'that may be the answer', quoted in Andrew Blick and George Jones, *Premiership: The Development, Nature and Power of the Office of the British Prime Minister* (Imprint Academic 2010) 145.

17 'There is a will to have a stronger centre', the Cabinet Secretary said in evidence to the Public Administration Select Committee, 'without encroaching on the formal constitutional position' (*The Government Information and Communication Service* (HC 1997–98, 770) evidence, q 187), the formal constitutional position being one in which powers and duties are laid on ministers, not on the Prime Minister.

18 Powell (n 6) 78; for an assessment of the position as it stood at the end of Labour's time in office, see Simon Parker and others, *Shaping Up: A Whitehall for the Future* (Institute for Government March 2010).

19 Heywood (n 9) 294–95.

20 ibid 315–16.

setting goals for Secretaries of State under the Business Plans and allowing them to get on with it without "man-marking" from the centre'.[21]

This 'hands-off' approach was not to last. One result was that some potential problems were missed 'until they had become urgent, often public, headaches'.[22] The most notorious was the Department for Environment, Food and Rural Affairs' announcement that it would meet its savings targets by selling off Forestry Commission woodlands. Another was to weaken Downing Street's ability to work out whether departments were effectively implementing the Coalition's priorities and to intervene where they weren't.[23] The size of the Policy Unit was therefore increased before prime-ministerial frustration at how slowly his policies were being implemented saw the Delivery Unit restored—and renamed the Prime Minister's Implementation Unit to distance it from its New Labour predecessor.[24]

2.2.1 The Civil Service Reform Plan

At the heart of the Coalition government's programme for government was the Conservatives' deficit reduction plan, which took precedence over every other measure in the Coalition agreement.[25] A new 'corporate centre for government', the Efficiency and Reform Group (ERG), was set up in the Cabinet Office by Francis Maude, the Minister for the Cabinet Office and Paymaster General, to give 'structure and coherence' to the policy aim of reducing spending; its purpose was to help departments make savings through improving their efficiency combined with 'stronger central oversight'.[26] New centrally managed spending controls, including mandatory restrictions on areas of spending such as consultants, marketing, and information technology (IT) were also introduced. Not surprisingly, the drive to secure efficiency savings on the scale now being sought was a source of major tension with departments, with 'an assertive centre seeking to control and, at times, override strong departmental interests embedded in the federal Whitehall structure'.[27]

21 Peter Riddell, 'The Coalition and the Executive' in Anthony Seldon and Mike Finn (eds), *The Coalition Effect 2010–2015* (CUP 2015) 113, 123; on business plans, see chapter 4.2.

22 ibid.

23 Heywood (n 9) 334–35. In evidence to the Public Administration and Constitutional Affairs Committee, Polly Mackenzie, who had worked in No 10 for Deputy Prime Minister Nick Clegg, noted the need to 'man mark' departments from No 10 to ensure they were progressing objectives that had been agreed. At times, she said, ministers from one Coalition partner could prove reluctant to progress policies that had initially been proposed by the other (*The Role and Status of the Prime Minister's Office* (HC 2021–22, 67) para 20).

24 'In opposition we got into all this "we're going to scrap all of this stuff when we get in", which we did', George Osborne the former chancellor later said. 'And then we spent years trying to recreate it but never actually calling it that': *Civil Service World* (9 November 2020). On the abolition of the Delivery Unit and its replacement by the Implementation Unit, see Oliver Letwin, *Hearts and Minds: The Battle for the Conservative Party from Thatcher to the Present* (Biteback 2017) 184–90.

25 HM Government, *The Coalition: Our Programme for Government* (May 2010).

26 National Audit Office, *The Centre of Government* (June 2014) 4. Into the ERG went the Treasury's 800-strong Office of Government Commerce, which supervised the purchase of more than £60bn of products and services each year; the Government Digital Service, which oversaw Whitehall's 750 different websites and other digital activities; and a new Major Projects Authority, which would monitor the delivery of the government's most significant projects: Heywood (n 9) 333.

27 Riddell, 'The Coalition and the Executive' (n 21) 134, adding that officials at the centre also lacked 'the necessary authority'—which was not true of Cabinet Office spending controls which operated by way of Treasury delegation of authority.

In June 2012 the Coalition published its *Civil Service Reform Plan*,[28] the Cabinet Office Minister Francis Maude having initially rejected a central reform plan in favour of 'doing stuff'. 'I think the point has been made that there has been a series of plans and blueprints and reports and White Papers over the years, but actually not all that much changes dramatically. The rhetoric has often outstripped the delivery. I am more interested in us doing stuff.'[29] The Commons Public Administration Select Committee disagreed. Without a plan, it argued, the government's agenda would fail. 'All the evidence makes clear that a coordinated change programme, including what a clear set of objectives will look like, is necessary to achieve the Government's objectives for the Civil Service. The Government's change agenda will fail without such a plan.'[30]

Acknowledging the difficulties in changing the 'culture and behaviours' in an organization that was 'dispersed and organised into separate departments and agencies', the plan made the case for 'greater clarity' in the relationship between the corporate centre and departments:

> The organisational model of the Civil Service will need to adapt if it is to successfully reform. With 17 main departments varying greatly in size, the Civil Service will need a much stronger corporate leadership model, and much more sharing of services and expertise, if it is to deliver the step change in efficiency needed . . . The demands of a smaller Civil Service together with relentless pressure to save money require greater clarity in the relationship between the corporate centre and departments.[31]

In this 'loose-tight' balance there would be 'tighter control and oversight' where collective action was needed for effectiveness and efficiency. This included development and management of leadership, talent, IT, and property infrastructure, major projects carrying financial and operational risk, and procurement of common goods and services which would 'enable the Government to harvest economies of scale and ensure that what seems like the right decision for one part of Government does not damage another'.[32]

A feature of the Coalition's Civil Service reform programme was the determination with which was pursued by the Minister for the Cabinet Office, Francis Maude. Determination alone, however, was not enough to overcome the limitations of the federal model.

> He has shown great energy and his drive and persistence have paid off in many areas. However, it is striking that he has made more progress on reform where he has been allowed to use dedicated resources in the Cabinet Office, and on issues with established structures and routines, where departments broadly accept the legitimacy of central control or co-ordination. The progress of other reforms which rely on persuasion and influence has been more mixed. This simply reflects the reality of the

[28] HM Government, *The Civil Service Reform Plan* (June 2012).

[29] Public Administration Select Committee, *Change in Government: The Agenda for Leadership* (HC 2010–12, 714) para 57.

[30] ibid para 64.

[31] HM Government, *The Civil Service Reform Plan* (n 28) 11.

[32] ibid; on the Coalition's *Civil Service Reform Plan*, see further chapter 6, section 2.

> weakness of the centre. His legacy will undoubtedly be the most significant of any recent MCO, but more ambitious reforms will require a different level of political support.[33]

An 'outsider' was brought in—in the Coalition's final year in office—to manage the Civil Service full-time with 'embedding functional leadership'—in order to realize the efficiency savings to be gained from the central delivery of cross-government professional services and to formalize the role of heads of functions in leading their profession and raising professional standards—as one of his core tasks.[34] Commenting on the appointment, the National Audit Office noted that John Manzoni, the new chief executive, had no 'extra formal powers' over departments; success in the role would therefore depend on influence and personal credibility.[35]

The importance of this point should not be overlooked. The Cabinet Office's weakness when it comes to modernization and reform, as the National Audit Office pointed out, is that it generally lacks powers to 'mandate' departments to act, and achieving its objectives often relies on 'softer influencing'.[36] As Head of the Civil Service, the Cabinet Secretary shares the same weakness, as did the chief executive officer, now chief operating officer. 'The Head of the Civil Service's only tools to drive change at present are cajolery and persuasion. These are necessary attributes for any transformation leader, along with inspiration and conviction, but they are not sufficient.'[37]

2.3 The Johnson government and the centre

The 'get Brexit done' Conservative government elected in December 2019 revived the push for a more powerful and effective centre that was the hallmark of the Blair governments at the beginning of the century. Dominic Cummings, Boris Johnson's chief adviser, was reported to want a 'smaller, more focused and more elite centre'.[38] 'A massive restructuring of the machinery of government was the Cummings-led plan . . . The centre of government was to be brought under the closer control of the Prime Minister, and the key No. 10 functions were to be transferred into a new "command centre" in the Cabinet Office'.[39] The Treasury was also to be split into finance and economics ministries 'as a way of diminishing its leverage over departments, thereby

[33] James Page and others, *Leading Change in the Civil Service* (Institute for Government 2014) 34; overcoming the limitations of the federal model, the authors argued, would require stronger and more effective leadership by both politicians and senior Civil Service leaders.

[34] Civil Service, *Civil Service Reform Plan: Progress Report* (October 2014) para 1.5. Manzoni replaced Sir Bob Kerslake, the Permanent Secretary to the Department for Communities and Local Government, who had acted as Head of the Civil Service on a part-time basis since Gus O'Donnell's retirement as Cabinet Secretary and Head of the Civil Service in December 2011. Manzoni was also responsible for project management, through the Major Projects Authority, and shared services as well as Civil Service reform.

[35] National Audit Office, *The Centre of Government: An Update* (March 2015) para 12.

[36] National Audit Office, *A Short Guide to the Cabinet Office* (September 2017) 7; the NAO added that the Cabinet Office sometimes had difficulty obtaining robust data from departments.

[37] Lord Maude of Horsham, *Independent Review of Governance and Accountability in the Civil Service* (November 2023) para 4.11.

[38] Philip Collins, 'Cummings is right about civil service failings' *The Times* (26 June 2020).

[39] Anthony Seldon and Raymond Newell, *Johnson at 10: The Inside Story* (Atlantic Books 2023) 172.

re-aligning Whitehall incentives away from parsimonious policy-making intended to balance the books in the short-term, and towards cost-effective investment which could sustain long-term growth'.[40] But by the time Cummings resigned in November 2020 there was little to show for his plan other than the setting up of a NASA-style 'mission control centre' in the Cabinet Office.[41]

III The Downing Street-Cabinet Office Complex

3.1 The Prime Minister's Office

The Prime Minister's Office is 'neither a government department in its own right, nor is it simply a Private Office'.[42] Part of the Cabinet Office but organizationally distinct from it—'you are very conscious that you are an employee of Downing Street and, by extension, of the Prime Minister rather than being an employee of the Cabinet Office'[43]—the Office helps the Prime Minister to establish and deliver the government's overall strategy and policy priorities, and to communicate the government's policies to Parliament, the public and international audiences.[44]

> Number Ten exists to protect the Prime Minister and the delivery of his agenda: officials and spads combined will push the envelope when needed. Proactively, Number Ten should be a political organ, the heart of government, pumping political oxygen into Whitehall, ensuring that policy and delivery aligns with what has been promised to the electorate.
>
> Defensively, it is a police force, with small agile teams working closely together to interrogate proposals, working though how things will play out, and ultimately stopping stupid mistakes from happening. It is the only place in government where the big political picture can be constructed, and decisions made as to where political capital should be spent.[45]

As head of the government the functions of the Prime Minister are 'nowhere authoritatively defined. His power and authority depend today, as in the past, on the fact that ministers are appointed by the King on his advice, and that the government of which he is the leader commands, for the time being, a parliamentary majority'.[46] As

[40] ibid 173.

[41] The National Situation Centre, which was intended to provide up-to-date and analysed data to ministers at the point of decision-making during a crisis (Cabinet Office, *Annual Report and Accounts 2020–21* (HC 391, 35).

[42] Public Administration and Constitutional Affairs Committee, *The Role and Status of the Prime Minister's Office* (n 23) summary.

[43] ibid para 24, quoting Patrick Diamond, a former No 10 special adviser.

[44] Public Administration and Constitutional Affairs Committee, *The Role and Status of the Prime Minister's Office: Government's Response to the Committee's First Report* (HC 2021–22, 710).

[45] Nikki Da Costa, 'The Proposed Restructuring of Number Ten Risks Mistaking a Personnel Problem for a Structural One' (*conservativehome*, 21 March 2022).

[46] Anderson (n 1) 148. The power to manage the Civil Service, which has been exercised by the Prime Minister as Minister for the Civil Service since 1968, was put on a statutory footing by the Constitutional Reform and Governance Act 2010; the power is discussed in chapter 6, section V.

well as the power to appoint and dismiss ministers and the now restored power to determine the timing of general elections, which are exercised by the King on the Prime Minister's advice, the Prime Minister's powers include control over the overall organisation of the executive and the allocation of functions between Ministers in charge of departments.[47] 'These are formidable powers which, carefully husbanded and judiciously deployed, may enable a Prime Minister to survive in reasonably good order', Ferdinand Mount wrote. 'But to drive through a coherent and sustained strategy requires a good deal more in the way of inexhaustible energy and unbreakable willpower. For the system resists coherence and co-ordination, deflects energies and fragments the will.'[48]

The resources devoted to supporting the Prime Minister have increased considerably since Mount wrote. 'The prime ministership is no longer the relatively informal man-a-boy-and-a-dog operation it used to be; it has become institutionalised.'[49] 'In terms of size, scale and range of responsibility', the Prime Minister's Office, 'is now more akin to a small Government Department than purely a dedicated Prime Minister's office'.[50] When John Major left office in May 1997 130 people were employed in No 10. By 2005 that number had grown to 226 before falling to 200 in 2010.[51] There are no official figures but under Boris Johnson it was thought to be in the region of 400—a doubling in a decade.

Behind this increase has been the desire of successive Prime Ministers to exercise greater control over the direction of their governments—what Anthony King described as 'their unending struggle to initiate policy and to steer the government in their preferred direction'.[52] 'It wasn't possible to run a modern democracy', Tony Blair's principal private secretary Jeremy Heywood believed, without the Prime Minister being 'properly briefed and able to lead strategy and monitor delivery'.[53]

As to how support was best provided, Heywood's view, which Blair's chief of staff Jonathan Powell shared, was that the Prime Minister's Office was 'missing capabilities' but should not become 'a rival bureaucracy to the Cabinet Office or a sprawling party-political machine'.[54] Some of that support has been provided by the Cabinet Office, highlighting the absence of a clear dividing line between the two offices.[55] Being

[47] *Ministerial Code* (December 2022) para 4.1. For further discussion see chapter 3, section 2.

[48] Ferdinand Mount, *The British Constitution Now: Recovery or Decline?* (William Heinemann 1992) 145.

[49] Anthony King, *The British Constitution* (OUP 2007) 21.

[50] Cabinet Office, *Investigation into Alleged Gatherings on Government Premises During Covid Restrictions—Update* (31 January 2022) para 23 vii; Gavin Barwell, *Chief of Staff: Notes from Downing Street* (Atlantic Books 2021) 48 ('the rest of the building is home to what is effectively a small government department, the office of the prime minister').

[51] House of Lords Constitution Committee, *The Cabinet Office and the Centre of Government* (HL 2009–10, 30) para 12. In 2012–13 there were 160 permanent staff and 16 special advisers employed at No 10: NAO, *The Centre of Government* (2014) para 1.6. As at 31 March 2023, 41 special advisers were working for the Prime Minister.

[52] King (n 49) 321.

[53] Heywood (n 9) 130.

[54] ibid 85; 'although I could see the argument for more muscle inside Downing Street, I was always opposed to the creation of a large prime minister's department . . . Number 10 has the advantage of small size, personal contact and nimbleness. It would be a terrible thing to sacrifice that': Powell (n 6) 81.

[55] Public Administration and Constitutional Affairs Committee, *The Role and Status of the Prime Minister's Office* (n 23) para 32.

physically located in No 10 and hence close to the Prime Minister remains important however—in the system proximity is power.

In her investigation into the 'partygate' scandal, Sue Gray, the second Permanent Secretary in the Cabinet Office, found that 'the structures that support the smooth operation of Downing Street' had not 'evolved sufficiently to meet the demands of this expansion. The leadership structures are fragmented and complicated and this has sometimes led to the blurring of lines of accountability. Too much responsibility and expectation is placed on the senior official whose principal function is the direct support of the Prime Minister.'[56] In his response to her interim report, the Prime Minister agreed that it was time to sort out what she had rightly called the 'fragmented and complicated' leadership structures of Downing Street, which would be done, 'including by creating an Office of the Prime Minister, with a permanent secretary to lead No. 10'.[57] A 're-set' of the Downing Street operation, the second in a little over a year, saw an interim Permanent Secretary and chief operating officer for No 10 appointed with immediate effect; this after current Permanent Secretaries chose not to 'take the risk' of giving up their roles while Johnson's position was so uncertain.[58]

With the collapse of the Johnson government in July 2022, work to 'further integrate' No 10 and the Cabinet Office came to an end. In its place his immediate successor Liz Truss, who was reported to be 'mildly horrified' to hear that the Prime Minister's Office had 'ballooned' to 350-plus people, sought a slimmed down Downing Street operation, which was said to reflect her desire not to have a 'presidential style' No 10. The Policy Unit, the data science and analytics unit (10DS) set up by Dominic Cummings to improve Downing Street's digital capacity, and the Delivery Unit were moved to the Cabinet Office and the number of special advisers cut, a repeat of what the Coalition had done in 2010, prompting speculation that it would only be a matter of time before the Prime Minister was driven to rebuild the Downing Street operation.[59] It was rebuilt —not by Truss, who resigned after 49 days, but by her successor Rishi Sunak. It was to take time though for the disruption involved to be overcome.

'When Truss entered No 10 one of her first acts was slash the number of policy aides working in the building—who man-mark government departments and are Downing Street's eyes and ears for what is happening in Whitehall. Sunak has reversed these decisions but that means rehiring people and going through the Cabinet Office propriety checks, all of which takes time, and at a point when No 10 needs maximum oversight. They're working through a whole list of appointments now', one government source said. 'But these things take time to arrange—so it's all a bit chaotic as Downing Street is short-staffed.'[60]

[56] Cabinet Office, *Investigation into Alleged Gatherings* (n 50) para 23 vii.

[57] HC Deb 31 January 2022, vol 708, col 23.

[58] *The Times* (11 February 2022). Samantha Jones, the interim appointee, was expected to review structures and operations in Downing Street before a competition was launched to make a permanent appointment.

[59] A former No 10 aide said: 'PMs always go in with some great new structure that will streamline things and then discover they've handed away power before spending 12 months scrabbling to get it back' (Tim Shipman, *The Sunday Times* (11 September 2022)).

[60] *The Times* (5 November 2022).

3.1.1 Accountability of the Prime Minister's Office
In its inquiry into the role and status of the Prime Minister's Office, the House of Commons Public Administration and Constitutional Affairs Committee (PACAC) was critical of the lack of accountability of the Office; 'structures of accountability' it argued 'should mirror structures of power'.[61] Rather than creating a separate Prime Minister's department, a step for which it found little support, as had the House of Lords Constitution Committee a decade earlier,[62] the Committee favoured 'greater transparency within the existing arrangements'.[63] In its response, however, the Johnson government simply said that given their close relationship and overlapping responsibilities it would be potentially misleading to separate out the work of the Prime Minister and the work of the Cabinet.[64]

3.2 The Ministerial Code

3.2.1 Introduction
'The *Ministerial Code*, issued by the Prime Minister of the day, sets out the principles underpinning the standards of conduct expected of ministers.'[65] It sets out the Prime Minister's expectations of ministers and provides guidance to ministers on how they should act and arrange their affairs in order to uphold these standards.[66] It was first issued to ministers on a confidential basis by Clement Attlee in 1945 before being made public as *Questions of Procedure for Ministers* (QPM) by John Major in 1992.[67] In 'a far more open society', the Chancellor of the Duchy of Lancaster said in 1996, 'all citizens should be able to have access to the rules by which their politicians and public servants are expected to behave'.[68] It was revised and re-issued as the *Ministerial Code: A code of conduct and guidance on procedures for Ministers* by Tony Blair in July 1997,[69] with a foreword from the Prime Minister, which stated: 'I will expect all Ministers to work within the letter and spirit of the Code.' Subsequent Prime Ministers have issued

[61] Public Administration and Constitutional Affairs Committee, *The Role and Status of the Prime Minister's Office* (n 23) para 6.

[62] The House of Lords Constitution Committee did not support calls for the creation of a separate Office of the Prime Minister, or an Office of the Prime Minister and the Cabinet, 'because we do not believe that this would significantly enhance the effective functioning or accountability of government. Instead we recommend that "Supporting the Prime Minister" should remain a core function of the Cabinet Office, so long as there is full transparency in the way in which the Cabinet Office fulfils this role, and so long as accountability mechanisms effectively reflect the importance of this function': *The Cabinet Office and the Centre of Government* (n 51) para 110.

[63] Public Administration and Constitutional Affairs Committee, *The Role and Status of the Prime Minister's Office: Government's Response to the Committee's First Report* (n 44) para 50.

[64] ibid para 7.

[65] Cabinet Office, *The Cabinet Manual: A Guide to Laws, Conventions and Rules on the Operation of Government* (October 2011) para 3.46. While this work was in press a revised version of the Code, with some significant changes which could not be reflected in the text below, was issued by Sir Keir Starmer: Cabinet Office, *Ministerial Code* (November 2024).

[66] *Ministerial Code* (December 2022) para 1.5.

[67] On the early history of the Code, see Amy Baker, *Prime Ministers and the Rule Book* (Poltico's 2000).

[68] Quoted in Terence Daintith and Alan Page, *The Executive in the Constitution: Structure, Autonomy and Internal Control* (OUP 1999) 387.

[69] It became the *Ministerial Code* with the version issued by Gordon Brown in July 2007.

their own, sometimes revised versions. The most recent was issued by Rishi Sunak in December 2022, replacing the updated Code issued by Boris Johnson in May 2022.

The Code, which states that it should be read against the background of 'the overarching duty on Ministers to comply with the law and to protect the integrity of public life',[70] consists of a foreword by the Prime Minister and ten numbered sections which span a mixture of ethical principles and procedural guidance. Annexed to the Code are the Seven Principles of Public Life and the Business Appointment Rules for Former Ministers. In the final report of its Standards Matter 2 review in November 2021 the Committee on Standards in Public Life (CSPL) recommended that the Code should be reconstituted solely as a code of conduct on ethical standards, reiterating a recommendation made in the Committee's first report in 1995.[71] Its recommendation was rejected by the Sunak government, noting the advantages of providing a single source document for all aspects of ministerial work and conduct.[72]

3.2.2 The foreword

The effect of the foreword, according to the Committee on Standards in Public Life, is 'to underline the status of the Code as the Prime Minister's document, written not only as guidance for Ministers but also as a pledge to the public.'[73] The foreword to the Code issued by Boris Johnson in August 2019 was about Brexit:

> The mission of this Government is to deliver Brexit on 31st October for the purpose of uniting and re-energising our whole United Kingdom and making this country the greatest place on earth ... To fulfil this mission, and win back the trust of the British people, we must uphold the very highest standards of propriety—and this code sets out how we must do so.
>
> There must be no bullying and no harassment; no leaking; no breach of collective responsibility. No misuse of taxpayer money and no actual or perceived conflicts of interest. The precious principles of public life enshrined in this document—integrity, objectivity, accountability, transparency, honesty and leadership in the public interest—must be honoured at all times; as must the political impartiality of our much admired civil service.
>
> Crucially, there must be no delay—and no misuse of process or procedure by any individual Minister that would seek to stall the collective decisions necessary to deliver Brexit and secure the wider changes needed across our United Kingdom.

[70] *Ministerial Code* (December 2022) para 1.3. In *R (Gulf Centre for Human Rights) v The Prime Minister* [2018] EWCA Civ 1855, the deletion of the reference in the 2010 version of the Code to 'international law and treaty obligations' was held not to involve a change of substance. The Code did not impose any free-standing duty on ministers in relation to compliance with the law, whether domestic or international. It simply referred to the 'overarching' duty which ministers already owed. The deletion was restored in the revised version of the Code issued by Sir Keir Starmer in November 2024.

[71] Committee on Standards in Public Life, *Upholding Standards in Public Life: Final Report of the Standards Matter 2 Review* (November 2021) para 3.14; *Standards in Public Life: First Report* (Cm 2850, 1995) ch 3, para 15.

[72] Cabinet Office, *Strengthening Ethics and Integrity in Central Government* (CP 900, 2023) s 7.1. The ethical and procedural elements were separated in 2005 in implementation of the Committee's recommendation in its ninth report, but the split did not survive the change of Prime Minister in 2007. The Code issued in November 2024 distinguishes the two elements more clearly.

[73] Committee on Standards in Public Life, *Reinforcing Standards* (Cm 4557, 2000) para 4.9.

After a cursory reference to its purpose—'guiding my Ministers on how they should act and arrange their affairs'—Johnson's foreword to the updated Code issued in May 2022 continued: 'As the Leader of Her Majesty's Government, my accountability is to Parliament and, via the ballot box, to the British people—not to the courts. We must show every day that we are worthy of this privilege by keeping our promises and delivering on the priorities of the British people.' No mention was made of the 'precious principles of public life'.

Rishi Sunak's foreword to the December 2022 Code restored the reference to the principles: 'And as we go about our tasks, we will uphold the Principles of Public Life, ensuring integrity, professionalism and accountability at every level.'

3.2.3 Ministerial standards

The first section of the Code sets out the standards expected of ministers. The first paragraph, in bold, provides that 'Ministers of the Crown are expected to maintain high standards of behaviour and to behave in a way that upholds the highest standards of propriety'.[74] A second paragraph, also in bold, which was added by Theresa May in January 2018, provides that

> Ministers should be professional in all their dealings and treat all those with whom they come into contact with consideration and respect. Working relationships, including with civil servants, ministerial and parliamentary colleagues and parliamentary staff should be proper and appropriate. Harassing, bullying or other inappropriate or discriminating behaviour wherever it takes place is not consistent with the Ministerial Code and will not be tolerated.[75]

Ministers are also expected to observe the Seven Principles of Public Life, which are annexed to the Code, and a set of 'principles of ministerial conduct', which were introduced on the CSPL's recommendation.[76] The principles include the requirements which Parliament has laid down in relation to the accountability and responsibility of ministers.[77]

Ministers must also comply with the Codes of Conduct for their respective Houses and also any requirements placed on them by the Independent Parliamentary Standards Authority.[78]

[74] *Ministerial Code* (December 2022) para 1.1.

[75] ibid para 1.2. Dominic Raab resigned in April 2023 after two complaints of intimidating behaviour against him were upheld by an investigation by Adam Tolley KC (Investigation Report to the Prime Minister).

[76] Committee on Standards in Public Life, *Standards in Public Life* (n 71) ch 3, paras 14–17; the principles are set out in s 1.3 of the current Code. The duty to 'be as open as possible with Parliament and the public' (s 1.3(d)) was cited by Sir Laurie Magnus in the *Zahawi* case (Investigation Report to the Prime Minister).

[77] For ministers in the Commons, these are set by Resolution (HC Deb 19 March 1997 vol 292, cols 1046–47), the terms of which are repeated at para 1.3 b. to e. For ministers in the Lords, the Resolution can be found in HL Deb 20 March 1997, vol 579, col 1057.

[78] *Ministerial Code* (December 2022) para 1.7.

3.2.4 The authority of the Code

The authority of the Code stems from its status as the Prime Minister's document. In its first report, the Committee on Standards in Public Life said of QPM that it had 'no particular constitutional status', but because it was issued by each Prime Minister to ministerial colleagues at the start of an administration or on their appointment to office, and any changes could only be authorized by the Prime Minister, it was in practice 'binding on all members of a Government'.[79]

There have been suggestions that the Code should be subject to parliamentary approval, but these were not supported by the CSPL in its Standards Matter 2 review on the grounds that that might weaken its authority.[80] The Committee recommended instead that the Prime Minister should be under a statutory duty to issue the Code; a statutory requirement, in the Committee's view, would grant the Code a 'more appropriate constitutional status' akin to that of the codes for civil servants and special advisers—which are issued under the authority of the Constitutional Reform and Governance Act 2010.[81] 'Such legislation need only specify that a code be produced and that it should be based on the Seven Principles of Public Life.'[82] In a policy statement accompanying the updated Code issued in May 2022, however, the Johnson government rejected the idea of a statutory duty on the grounds that the Code was a matter for the executive not Parliament:

> As the Prime Minister's guidance to Ministers, the Ministerial Code and its application is a matter for the Executive and—as with all matters of the Prerogative—wholly separate from the legislature. Therefore, the Government does not consider it appropriate to legislate for the Code . . . as this would undermine the constitutional settlement by conflating the executive and legislature.[83]

Its rejection of statutory backing for the Code was affirmed by the Sunak government in its subsequent response to the Committee's recommendations (below).

Statutory backing for the Code, the Johnson government went on to argue, would also provide 'an additional route where the judiciary may also be drawn into such (political) matters that the Government considers to be non-justiciable. It would not be in the public interest to further fuel politically-motivated judicial reviews.'[84] In *R (FDA) v Prime Minister and Minister for the Civil Service*,[85] which arose out of the Prime Minister's rejection of his ethics adviser's advice that the Home Secretary Priti

[79] Committee on Standards in Public Life, *Standards in Public Life* (n 71) ch 3, para 9.

[80] Committee on Standards in Public Life, *Upholding Standards in Public Life* (n 71) paras 3.18–3.19.

[81] ibid para 3.21.

[82] ibid.

[83] Cabinet Office, *Statement of Government Policy: Standards in Public Life* (27 May 2022) para 6. A decade earlier, the Coalition government rejected the suggestion that the Code should be 'owned by Parliament and controlled by Parliament' on the grounds that 'this would lead to an unacceptable blurring of the lines between the Executive and Parliament' (Public Administration Select Committee, *The Prime Minister's Adviser on Ministers' Interests: Independent or Not? Government Response to the Committee's Twenty Second Report of Session 2010–12* (HC 2012–13, 976).

[84] Cabinet Office, *Statement of Government Policy: Standards in Public Life* (n 83) para 6.

[85] *R (FDA) v Prime Minister and Minister for the Civil Service* [2022] 4 WLR 5, [2021] EWHC 3279 (Admin).

Patel had breached the Ministerial Code by bullying civil servants, the government had argued that the Code in its entirety was non-justiciable. Its argument was not accepted by the Divisional Court, however, leaving the door open to further challenges:

> We accept that the interpretation of parts, perhaps most, of the provisions of the Ministerial Code would not be justiciable because they involve political matters (such as references to collective Cabinet responsibility) or ministerial relations with Parliament. Such matters are intended to be subject to the judgement of the Prime Minister not the courts. But it does not follow that all parts of the Ministerial Code should be treated as non-justiciable.[86]

3.2.5 The independent adviser on ministers' interests

An 'independent adviser on ministers' interests' was appointed by Tony Blair in March 2006 following a recommendation in the CSPL's ninth report three years earlier.[87] The current 'ethics adviser', Sir Magnus Laurie, was appointed by Rishi Sunak for a non-renewable five-year term in December 2022. The two previous advisers both resigned: Lord (Christopher) Geidt in June 2022 after being asked to provide 'advanced cover' for a potential breach of the United Kingdom's obligations under international law[88]—but possibly also because he had concluded the job was not doable under Boris Johnson as Prime Minister;[89] and Sir Alex Allan in November 2020 after the Prime Minister rejected his advice that the Home Secretary Priti Patel had breached the Ministerial Code by bullying civil servants.

The Prime Minister is under no obligation to appoint an ethics adviser. Liz Truss in her brief tenure as Prime Minister was reported to have seen no need for an adviser, underlining the discretionary nature of the appointment. In its Standards Matter 2 review, the CSPL recommended that the appointment, together with the Ministerial Code, should be put on a statutory basis, a recommendation rejected by the Johnson government, as we have seen, on the ground that the Code was purely a matter for the executive.

'Because the role relies on a relationship of mutual trust and confidence, the appointment of the Independent Adviser is a direct appointment of the Prime Minister.'[90] For the CSPL it was critical that the adviser 'be, and be perceived to be, independent'. It therefore recommended that the adviser be appointed by open competition (chaired by the First Civil Service Commissioner, for a fixed, non-renewable

[86] ibid [39].

[87] Committee on Standards in Public Life, *Defining the Boundaries within the Executive: Ministers, Special Advisers and the Permanent Civil Service* (Cm 5775, 2003) paras 5.23–5.31. For the background to the appointment, see Public Administration Select Committee, *The Ministerial Code: The Case for Independent Investigation* (HC 2005–06, 1457) para 37 ('Although the Government had agreed in principle to CSPL's recommendation to appoint an adviser on ministerial interests, the Prime Minister finally felt moved to act by the confluence of events and bad headlines which surrounded not only the Blunkett and Jowell cases but also allegations surrounding propriety, party funding and the honours system').

[88] Email from Lord Geidt to Chair of Public Administration and Constitutional Affairs Committee (17 June 2022) at: <https://committees.parliament.uk/publications/22732/documents/167114/default/>.

[89] Sebastian Payne, *The Fall of Boris Johnson: The Full Story* (Macmillan 2022) 145 ('After his departure, Geidt told colleagues he tried his utmost but ultimately concluded Johnson would never follow the codified structures (sic) of the ministerial code').

[90] Cabinet Office, *Statement of Government Policy: Standards in Public Life* (n 83) para 8.

term).[91] Appointments have been made, however, without open competition. In its Standards Matter 2 review, the CSPL agreed that the final decision on who to appoint should be that of the Prime Minister—the adviser had to have the trust and confidence of the Prime Minister—but argued that the appointments process should have 'a greater degree of independence to improve public confidence that the Adviser will be fair and unbiased in their investigations and findings'.[92] In its report on *Propriety of Governance in Light of Greensill*, PACAC recommended that the Prime Minister's power of appointment should be balanced with 'a robust and transparent appointment process' that allowed the candidate to demonstrate their qualities for the role rather than their name being 'alighted upon', as had hitherto been the case. The adviser's appointment should also be subject to a pre-appointment hearing with the relevant select committee and should require its endorsement.[93] The current adviser, however, was appointed, as were his predecessors, through a closed recruitment process with no pre-appointment hearing. In its response to the CSPL and PACAC's recommendations, the government confirmed its belief that the adviser should continue to be a direct ministerial appointment, 'given the close relationship of trust that must exist between the Independent Adviser and the Prime Minister'.[94]

The adviser's role as it has come to be defined—in terms of reference agreed between the Prime Minister and the adviser—is twofold: to advise ministers on the management of their private interests to ensure that they do not conflict with their public duties,[95] and to investigate, at the request of the Prime Minister, alleged breaches of the Ministerial Code.[96] When the independent adviser was first appointed in 2006 it was unclear how far the adviser's investigative role would extend,[97] but when Gordon Brown became Prime Minister in 2007 the Code was revised to make clear that the adviser's role included the investigation of alleged breaches of the Ministerial Code:

> For the first time ever, the Code makes clear that if there is an alleged breach of the Code, and the Prime Minister, having consulted the Cabinet Secretary feels that it warrants further investigation, he *will* refer the matter to the independent adviser on Ministers' interests. The Government believes that this is an important development which will help to strengthen and promote public confidence in the Ministerial Code.[98]

[91] Committee on Standards in Public Life, *Defining the Boundaries within the Executive* (n 87) paras 5.30–5.31.

[92] Committee on Standards in Public Life, *Upholding Standards in Public Life* (n 71) para 3.30.

[93] Public Administration and Constitutional Affairs Committee, *Propriety of Governance in Light of Greensill* (HC 2022–23, 888) para 87.

[94] Cabinet Office, *Strengthening Ethics and Integrity* (n 72) s 2.4.

[95] *Ministerial Code* (December 2022) para 7.4.

[96] ibid para 1.4a.

[97] Public Administration Select Committee, *The Ministerial Code: The Case for Independent Investigation* (n 87) paras 38–40.

[98] Public Administration Select Committee, *The Ministerial Code; The Case for Independent Investigation: Government Response to the Committee's Seventh Report of Session 2005–06* (HC 2006–07, 1088) emphasis added; 'will' continued be used until it was replaced by 'may' in the Code issued by Boris Johnson in August 2019. See also *The Governance of Britain* (Cm 7170, 2007) para 121.

Virtue having been made of the adviser's ability to investigate allegations of ministerial misconduct, pressure grew for the adviser to be given the right to initiate investigations without first being asked to do so by the Prime Minister. The Brown government insisted, however, that 'it must be for the Prime Minister to decide whether to refer a matter to the independent adviser for investigation, and to account for his decision to Parliament and the public.'[99] The Coalition government was equally unsympathetic. 'The Ministerial Code sets out the standards that the Prime Minister expects from his Ministers, so it is appropriate that it is his decision whether a matter is referred to the Independent Adviser.'[100]

The CSPL returned to the issue in its Standards Matter 2 review.[101] In correspondence with the Prime Minister before Lord Geidt's appointment, it recommended that a new adviser should be given authority to initiate investigations where, in their judgement, this was necessary in order to establish the facts surrounding allegations that the Ministerial Code had been breached.[102] On his appointment in April 2021 Lord Geidt was given the power to advise the Prime Minister confidentially on the initiation of investigations, but not the power to initiate investigations. Defending his unwillingness to go further the Prime Minister wrote:

> The constitutional position of the Prime Minister, as having sole responsibility for the overall organisation of the Executive and recommending the appointment of Ministers, means that I cannot and would not wish to abrogate the ultimate responsibility for deciding on an investigation into allegations concerning ministerial misconduct. That ultimate responsibility is quite properly mine alone and, as an elected politician, one for which I am ultimately accountable to the electorate.[103]

For the CSPL this did not go far enough. Public confidence, the Committee argued, depended on the adviser being able to initiate investigations:

> Meaningful independence is the benchmark for any effective form of standards regulation and current arrangements still fall below this bar. Without stronger independence, the public will continue to doubt that ministers will be held to account for suspected breaches of high standards. A regulatory system that appears to be little more than self-regulation will inevitably be seen as one where party politics dominates, rather than the merits of each case.[104]

99 Public Administration Select Committee, *Investigating the Conduct of Ministers: Government Response to the Committee's Seventh Report of Session 2007–08* HC (2007–08) 1056.

100 Public Administration Select Committee, *Government Response to the Committee's Twenty Second Report of Session 2010–12* (n 83).

101 A decade earlier the Committee expressed concern that the adviser had no independent ability to initiate investigations: *Standards Matter: A Review of Best Practice in Promoting Good Behaviour in Public Life* (Cm 8519, 2013) para 7.36.

102 Correspondence between the Prime Minister and Lord Evans on the Independent Adviser on Ministers' Interests (April 2021) <www.gov.uk>.

103 ibid.

104 Committee on Standards in Public Life, *Upholding Standards in Public Life* (n 71) para 3.36.

It therefore recommended that the adviser should be able to initiate investigations and to determine whether a breach had occurred; a summary of the adviser's findings should also be published within eight weeks of a report being submitted to the Prime Minister.[105] In an 'enhanced process' put in place following discussions between Lord Geidt and the Cabinet Office, the adviser was given the power to initiate an investigation having consulted the Prime Minister and obtained his consent. Should the Prime Minister refuse his consent, the adviser would be able require the reasons for the investigation not proceeding to be made public—unless doing so would undermine the grounds for the investigation not proceeding.[106]

The changes, which Lord Geidt described as being at 'a low level of ambition',[107] met with a mixed response. The CSPL welcomed the enhanced process as an 'improvement', but remained of the view that a system in which the adviser required the Prime Minister's permission to launch an investigation was not sufficiently independent.[108] PACAC, on the other hand, saw the adviser's terms of reference as now effectively including the authority to initiate investigations. 'We would expect the requirement that Prime Ministers' consent be given beforehand to be used in extremely limited cases, such as where matters of national security or legal privilege are involved.'[109] Lord Geidt's successor did not regard the requirement of consent as a barrier to an investigation: 'if I want to initiate an inquiry and that is refused then the reasons have to be published. I think that is a very strong position to be in.'[110]

Had allegations of ministerial misconduct been investigated under the Johnson government it is unlikely the issue would have assumed the significance it did. The CSPL argued in its Standards Matter 2 review that there was a convention that

> a serious, credible allegation of a breach [of the Ministerial Code] would lead the Prime Minister to ask the Independent Adviser to launch an investigation. Yet, as has occurred on multiple occasions since the introduction of the Adviser in 2006, Prime

[105] ibid para 3.41, recommendation 8; para 3.45, recommendation 9; para 3.47, recommendation 10. The latter recommendation followed the delay in the publication of the results of the Cabinet Office's investigation into the complaints of bullying against Priti Patel. 'The bullying allegations made against the Home Secretary were investigated by the Cabinet Office but the outcome of that investigation has not been published, though completed some months ago. There may be legal complexities underlying this but those have not been made clear and this does not build confidence in the accountability of government': 'Upholding Standards in Public Life' (speech by Lord Evans, 4 November 2021) available at: <www.gov.uk/government/speeches/upholding-standards-in-public-life-speech-by-lord-evans>.

[106] *Ministerial Code* (May 2022) para 1.4b (the December 2022 version remained unchanged); Cabinet Office, *Statement of Government Policy: Standards in Public Life* (n 83) para 9.

[107] Independent Adviser on Ministers' Interests, *Annual Report 2021–22*, 3.

[108] Lord Evans' Response to Lord True (May 2022) <https://assets.publishing.service.gov.uk/media/6294dce2e90e07039f799f2a/Lord_Evans_Response_to_Lord_True.pdf>.

[109] Public Administration and Constitutional Affairs Committee, *Propriety of Governance in Light of Greensill* (n 93) para 92.

[110] Sir Laurie Magnus, *Post-appointment Hearing—Independent Adviser on Ministers' Interests*, oral evidence to Public Administration and Constitutional Affairs Committee (23 February 2023) q 22. The Ministerial Code issued by Sir Keir Starmer in December 2024 saw the adviser given the right to initiate an investigation without the Prime Minister's permission: 'Where the Independent Adviser believes that an alleged breach of the Code warrants further investigation and that matter has not already been referred to them, they may initiate an investigation after notifying the Prime Minister.'

> Ministers had been reluctant to trigger investigations which had the potential to cause political damage, even where the reported facts appear to merit investigation.[111]

But whether there ever was a convention to that effect—in the sense of practice informed by a sense of obligation—is doubtful. What there may have been was an expectation, which, as the Committee pointed out, had often not been met.[112]

3.2.6 Enforcement

The version of Questions of Procedure for Ministers published in 1992 stated that it was for individual ministers 'to judge how best to act in order to uphold the highest standards'. No mention was made of a role for the Prime Minister in enforcing those standards. In its first report the CSPL argued that ministers did not make their ethical judgements in isolation. To remain in office, they needed to retain the confidence of the Prime Minister. In relation to ministerial conduct, that would involve the Prime Minister's own judgement of the ethics of the case. It therefore recommended that the first paragraph of QPM be amended to say: 'It will be for individual Ministers to judge how best to act in order to uphold the highest standards. It will be for the Prime Minister to determine whether or not they have done so in any particular circumstance.'[113] The second sentence was rejected by the Major government because it was thought to 'go too far towards suggesting that the Prime Minister's relationship with his Ministerial colleagues is that of invigilator and judge',[114] but the Code was amended in 2001, after the Committee had returned to the issue, to make clear that the Prime Minister is 'the ultimate judge of the standards of behaviour expected of a Minister and the appropriate consequences of a breach of the standards'.[115]

In contrast to the initiation of investigations, there has been no serious challenge to the proposition that the consequences of a breach of the Ministerial Code should be a matter for the Prime Minister.[116] Instead, there has been what PACAC described as 'a broader consensus, that, given the Prime Minister's responsibility for the composition of the Government, he or she should retain responsibility for sanctioning any Minister found to have breached the Code: "a situation where any independent regulator of the Ministerial Code would effectively have the power to fire a minister would be unconstitutional". To go against this consensus would constitute a step towards a

[111] Committee on Standards in Public Life, *Upholding Standards in Public Life* (n 71) para 2.11.

[112] Ferdinand Mount contrasted the treatment of ministerial misconduct under the May and Johnson governments. 'As recently as 2017, three senior ministers had to resign instantly when they were found to have misbehaved . . . None of them was allowed to hang on for a moment. Now it seemed that the Prime Minister of the day would instinctively excuse every instance of misbehaviour, including his own': *Big Caesars and Little Caesars. How They Rise and How They Fall—from Julius Caesar to Boris Johnson* (Bloomsbury 2023) 228–29.

[113] Committee on Standards in Public Life, *Standards in Public Life* (n 71) para 3.13.

[114] *The Government's Response to the First Report from the Committee on Standards in Public Life* (Cm 2931, 1995) 3.

[115] *Ministerial Code: A Code of Conduct and Guidance on Procedures for Ministers* (July 2001) para 1.4 (see now *Ministerial Code* (December 2022) para 1.6); for the background, see Committee on Standards in Public Life, *Reinforcing Standards* (n 73) paras 4.76–4.78, recommendation 13.

[116] Not only is it a matter for the Prime Minister: it is a matter for the Prime Minister and no one else as the Code makes clear. 'It is not the role of the Cabinet Secretary or other officials to enforce the Code' (para 1.4).

very different constitutional arrangement from that which the United Kingdom has had until now.'[117]

The Prime Minister is commonly described as the 'arbiter' or the 'ultimate arbiter' of the Code. 'It is a long standing convention that the Ministerial Code is issued by the Prime Minister and that, as head of Her Majesty's Government, it is constitutionally the Prime Minister who should be the ultimate arbiter of the Code.'[118] But as the Divisional Court was careful to point out in the *FDA* case, the description of the Prime Minister as the 'arbiter of the code'—in the government statement setting out the Prime Minister's conclusions on the allegations of bullying against Priti Patel[119]—did not mean that the Prime Minister could interpret the Code as he saw fit:

> The question for this court is whether the Prime Minister proceeded on the basis that conduct would not fall within the description of bullying within paragraph 1.2 of the Ministerial Code if the person concerned was unaware of, or did not intend, the harm or offence caused. Reading the statement as a whole, and in context, we do not consider that the Prime Minister misdirected himself in that way.
>
> For completeness, we note that that view is reinforced by, but not dependent on, the reference to the Prime Minister being the 'arbiter of the code'. That is not intended to mean that it is for the Prime Minister to give any interpretation he chooses to the words used in the Ministerial Code. It reflects the fact that, ultimately, the Ministerial Code sets the standards that the Prime Minister expects of ministers and it is for the Prime Minister to determine, ultimately, whether there has been such a departure from the standards expected of ministers that he can no longer have confidence in them.[120]

Although the enforcement of the Code is a matter for the Prime Minister, there must come a point at which, as happened under Boris Johnson, the failure to enforce the Code destroys confidence in the arrangements for upholding ministerial standards. Polling of First Division Association members, one of the principal Civil Service unions, when the Association challenged the Prime Minister's decision that Priti Patel had not breached the Ministerial Code found that 85% of the Senior Civil Service and 90% of Fast Streamers had no confidence in the 'regulation of the Ministerial Code', ie in the arrangements for upholding ministerial standards, a position which the CSPL described as 'not sustainable'.[121]

In 2021 the Prime Minister agreed, in correspondence with the chair of the CSPL, to the introduction of a system of graduated penalties for breach of the Code. It was

[117] Public Administration and Constitutional Affairs Committee, *Propriety of Governance in Light of Greensill* (n 93) para 93, quoting Committee on Standards in Public Life, *Upholding Standards in Public Life* (n 71) para 3.28.

[118] Letter from Boris Johnson to Lord Geidt (31 May 2022) <www.gov.uk/government/publications/letter-from-the-prime-minister-to-the-independent-adviser-on-ministers-interests-31-may-2022--2>.

[119] 'As the arbiter of the code, having considered Sir Alex's advice and weighing up all the factors, the Prime Minister's judgement is that the Ministerial code was not breached.'

[120] *R (FDA) v Prime Minister and Minister for the Civil Service* [2022] 4 WLR 5, [2021] EWHC 3279 (Admin) [59]–[60].

[121] Committee on Standards in Public Life, *Standards Matter 2—Committee Findings* (June 2021) para 18.

disproportionate to expect resignation for what might be a minor breach of the Code.[122] Under the amended version of the Code issued in May 2022 the available sanctions include requiring some form of public apology, remedial action, or removal of ministerial salary for a period.[123]

The CSPL saw the introduction of graduated sanctions as enabling greater independence in the initiation of investigations.

> Past governments of both parties resisted granting the Adviser the power to initiate investigations independently due to the presumption of resignation, as this would have given the Independent Adviser the effective power to fire a minister—a power that only the Prime Minister should have. The introduction of a range of sanctions, with the appropriate sanction decided solely by the Prime Minister, removes this constitutional obstacle.[124]

Removal of the constitutional obstacle, however, was not sufficient to secure the adviser the right to initiate investigations.

3.3 The business appointment rules for ministers

The business appointment rules annexed to the Code govern the employment of ministers after leaving government—the so-called 'revolving door' between government and the private sector. The rules were first introduced in 1937 for civil servants and members of the armed forces before being extended to former ministers and special advisers in 1995 on the recommendation of the Nolan Committee:

> Very high standards of conduct are rightly expected from Ministers and civil servants ... There has been much concern over Ministers who, on leaving office take positions in companies with which they have had official dealings. For two years after leaving office senior civil servants have to seek clearance from an independent advisory committee before joining private companies. The same need to protect the public interest arises with Ministers and special advisers, who should be subject to a similar clearance system.[125]

The rules for former ministers seek to counter suspicion that:

[122] Correspondence between the Prime Minister and Lord Evans on the Independent Adviser on Ministers' Interests (April 2021) <www.gov.uk/government/publications/correspondence-between-the-prime-minister-and-lord-evans-on-the-independent-adviser-on-ministers-interests>.

[123] *Ministerial Code* (December 2022) para 1.7.

[124] Lord Evans' Response to Lord True (May 2022) <www.gov.uk/government/publications/lord-evans-correspondence-with-lord-true-on-the-ministerial-code>.

[125] Committee on Standards in Public Life, *Upholding Standards in Public Life* (n 71) 5; the Committee believed that a voluntary system would be sufficient to secure ministerial compliance 'without the complication of a statutory power' but did not rule out returning to the question of statutory enforcement should a voluntary system prove insufficient to sustain public confidence (para 3.30).

a. the decisions and statements of a serving Minister might be influenced by the hope or expectation of future employment with a particular firm or organisation; or
b. an employer could make improper use of official information to which a former Minister has had access; or
c. there may be cause for concern about the appointment in some other particular respect.[126]

Ministers are required to seek and abide by advice from the Advisory Committee on Business Appointments (ACOBA) about any appointments or employment they wish to take up within two years of leaving office.[127] They are also banned from lobbying government on behalf of any new employer for two years after leaving office.[128] No sanction other than the threat of negative publicity attaches to a breach of the rules.

In their application to ministers and civil servants alike the rules have long been the subject of criticism. In its Standards Matter 2 review, the CSPL found 'widespread discontent' around the operation of the rules.[129] Particular criticism was directed at the lack of effective sanctions for their breach. 'ACOBA has no formal enforcement mechanisms and no sanctions, and recent high-profile cases have shown instances where ACOBA's advice has either not been sought or ignored. The business appointments scheme is dependent on a shared assumption that ACOBA's advice should be followed, with negative publicity the only deterrent to non-compliance.'[130] 'The widespread perception that breaches of the government's Business Appointment Rules go unpunished undermines the credibility of the regulatory regime, regardless of how high compliance is in practice.'[131] The Committee recommended that the rules should be made legally enforceable through civil servants' contracts of employment, with parallel arrangements being put in place for ministers (who are office holders and not employees).[132]

[126] Cabinet Office, *Business Appointment Rules for Ministers* (December 2016) para 1.

[127] The Committee was established in 1975 in the wake of the Poulson affair to administer what were then the Civil Service business appointment rules: House of Commons Official Report, Written Answer 3rd July 1975, vol 894, cols 495–96; for a brief account of the Poulson affair, see Royal Commission on Standards of Conduct in Government 1974–76 (Cmnd 6524, 1976) paras 12–24.

[128] *Ministerial Code* (December 2022) para 7.25; the requirement to abide by the advice of the Committee was introduced by Gordon Brown in 2007: *The Governance of Britain* (Cm 7170, 2007) para 121 ('Ministers wishing to take up an outside appointment on leaving office will be required to seek the advice of the Advisory Committee on Business Appointment Rules. Former Ministers will be expected to follow the advice of the Committee. This has, until now, been voluntary.')

[129] Committee on Standards in Public Life, *Upholding Standards in Public Life* (n 71) para 4.8. For earlier criticisms, see Public Administration Select Committee, *Business Appointment Rules* (HC 2012–13, 404) and Public Administration and Constitutional Affairs Committee, *Managing Ministers' and Officials' Conflicts of Interest: Time for Clearer Values, Principles and Action* (HC 2016–17, 252).

[130] Committee on Standards in Public Life, *Upholding Standards in Public Life* (n 71) para 2.12; recent high-profile cases included those of George Osborne and Boris Johnson.

[131] ibid para 4.29.

[132] ibid; PACAC made the same recommendation as did Nigel Boardman: *Propriety of Governance in Light of Greensill* (n 93) paras 28 and 38; Cabinet Office, *Review into the Development and Use of Supply Chain Finance (and Associated Schemes) in Government Part 2: Recommendations and Suggestions* (August 2021) 18. Under Boardman's proposals, ministers would be required to sign a legally binding 'deed of undertaking' obliging them to comply with the rules and ACOBA's decisions at the end of their ministerial term.

The application of the rules by departments has also been criticized. Lord Pickles, the chair of ACOBA, characterized the approach of some departments as 'slapdash' and 'verging on negligent', while praising the approach of others.[133] A damning report by the National Audit Office in July 2017 found that the Cabinet Office had no oversight of departmental compliance with the rules, that departments were inconsistent in their application of the rules, and that transparency requirements which would reveal whether the requirements were being complied with were not being adequately enforced.[134] CSPL recommended that the Cabinet Office should ensure the rules were applied consistently across all government departments, and work with ACOBA to promote best practice and awareness of the rules.[135] In its response, the Sunak government agreed that the rules should be incorporated more effectively in civil servants' contracts, and undertook to develop a 'ministerial deed' which would make the rules enforceable against ministers.[136] But by the time it left office no action had been taken.

3.4 The Cabinet Office

> The Cabinet Office, founded to serve cabinet and its committees, has become bloated and unfocused. Despite the talent of many of its people, it is failing in its core role of supporting the prime minister and cabinet.[137]

3.4.1 Introduction

Set up as a secretariat during the First World War to serve the Cabinet and (later) its committees, the Cabinet Office's traditional role was that of ensuring the smooth working of the Cabinet system, facilitating Cabinet and collective decision-making, brokering decisions between departments, and building consensus on policies.

> It fulfils a core coordination role—supporting the Prime Minister, and facilitating Cabinet and collective decision-making across government. It brokers decisions between departments and builds consensus on policies. The department organises and runs Cabinet and Cabinet committee meetings across a breadth of policy issues, ranging from the Economic and Domestic Secretariat through to the National Security Secretariat. It also oversees and enables the delivery of the government's legislative agenda.[138]

133 Committee on Standards in Public Life, *Upholding Standards in Public Life* (n 71) para 4.33.

134 Comptroller and Auditor General, *Investigation into Government's Management of the Business Appointment Rules* (HC 2017–19, 245).

135 Committee on Standards in Public Life, *Upholding Standards in Public Life* (n 71) para 4.35, Recommendation 18.

136 Cabinet Office, *Strengthening Ethics and Integrity* (n 72) s 1.

137 Commission on the Centre of Government (n 3) 9.

138 Cabinet Office, *Cabinet Office Outcome Delivery Plan: 2021 to 2022* (July 2021). 'The enduring role of the Cabinet Office is to convene, to co-ordinate, to deal with all the contingencies as they come in and to support the Prime Minister of the day in dealing with those priorities': Alex Chisholm in evidence to PACAC (26 January 2023) q 264.

In addition to this traditional role, and its long-standing engagement in intelligence coordination, the Cabinet Office has assumed a 'much wider role' at the centre in the last 25 years, 'co-ordinating delivery and driving change across government'.[139]

3.4.2 The Secretariat

The Secretariat—the 'Cabinet Office proper'[140]—is 'the key agent of central co-ordination in the cabinet system.'[141] It exists to support the Prime Minister and the chairs of Cabinet committees in ensuring that 'government business is conducted in an effective and timely way and that proper collective consideration takes place. The Cabinet Secretariat is therefore non-departmental in function and consists of officials who are based in the Cabinet Office but drawn from across government.'[142]

Following reorganization under Mark Sedwill, Cabinet Secretary 2018–20, there are now two secretariats: the Economic and Domestic Secretariat (EDS) and the National Security Secretariat (NSS).[143] EDS supports the operation of the Cabinet and collective decision-making through 'delivery of Cabinet committees' (sic) and assuring the process for decision-making by correspondence on all economic or domestic issues.[144] Its teams include the parliamentary and business legislation team, which supports the government's legislative programme. In 2022–23 the team 'worked with every part of government to challenge and enable policy development for the delivery of a full legislative programme, which included 34 government bills, and over 1,100 pieces of secondary legislation'.[145] The NSS supports the National Security Council (NSC), a Cabinet committee, chaired by the Prime Minister, which is the primary forum for ministerial discussion and collective agreement on issues related to national security, foreign policy, defence, trade strategy, international relations, development, resilience, and resource security.[146] The Council and its sub-committees were established in May 2010 and charged with overseeing and coordinating all aspects of Britain's security, including terrorism, other security threats, hazards, resilience, intelligence policy, and the performance and resources of the security and intelligence agencies.[147] The Civil Contingencies Secretariat (CCS), which is part of NSS, is responsible for emergency planning and coordinating the government's response to major emergencies. In 2020–21, it led, coordinated and supported

[139] Cabinet Office, *Annual Report and Accounts 2020–21* (HC 391, 20). It also provides a base for units or teams working on particular policy issues. Recent examples include the Vaccine Taskforce and the Illegal Migration Taskforce. 'At the request of the Prime Minister, the Illegal Migration Taskforce was set up in November 2021 to drive forward cross-government work to tackle illegal entry to the UK through Channel crossings' (Cabinet Office, *Annual Report and Accounts 2021–22* (HC 914, 51).

[140] JM Lee, GW Jones, and June Burnham, *At the Centre of Whitehall: Advising the Prime Minister and Cabinet* (Macmillan 1998) 152.

[141] Martin Burch and Ian Holliday, *The British Cabinet System* (Prentice Hall 1996) 17.

[142] *The Cabinet Manual* (n 65) para 4.51.

[143] The EU Secretariat was disbanded after Brexit with responsibility for the United Kingdom's relationship with the European Union being moved initially to the Foreign, Commonwealth and Development Office (UIN HCWS636 24 February 2022) before being moved back to the Cabinet Office (UIN HWS19 24 July 2024).

[144] Cabinet Office, *Annual Report and Accounts 2022–23* (HC 1464, 31).

[145] ibid; on the parliamentary and business legislation team, see chapter 10, section 1.1.

[146] ibid.

[147] *The Cabinet Manual* (n 65) para 4.11.

several major responses, including the cross-government planning for EU Exit and Covidresponses.[148] A joint report from the House of Commons Health and Social Care and Science and Technology Committees found that CCS did not have adequate resources to maintain a substantial standing capability to survey the development of potential threats, and it had a limited reach into the range of departments required to respond to a pandemic.[149]

The Secretariat is headed by the Cabinet Secretary, the most senior civil servant in the United Kingdom and the principal official adviser to the Prime Minister and Cabinet. The Propriety and Constitution Group within the Cabinet Office is responsible for the operation of Cabinet government, 'working in partnership with other cabinet secretariat teams to ensure the smooth-running of the cabinet and other ministerial meetings, and to provide advice on the good running of the cabinet government. It coordinates one common set of processes and one place of expertise and advice on the operation of cabinet government, all in support of the wider cabinet secretariat.'[150]

The role of Cabinet Secretary has been combined with that of Head of the Civil Service since 1983, save between 2012 and 2014 when the two roles were split.

The Secretariat traditionally observed a convention of 'strict neutrality' in its dealings with departments. 'It is essential that we are impartial and retain the confidence of all Ministers and officials.'[151] 'We brief those who chair the meetings on handling issues and the options available. In doing so, we are bound to brief impartially.'[152] The Cabinet Manual published in 2011, however, made no mention of the convention. Nor was there any mention of the importance previously attached to avoiding any tendency to create a 'Cabinet Office view', still less a 'Cabinet Office policy'. The purpose of the Cabinet Office was to make Cabinet government work, 'not to be an *imperium in imperio*'.[153] For Jonathan Powell, Tony Blair's chief of staff, in marked contrast, it was

> important to effective administration that the Cabinet Office not become the proponent of the lowest common denominator between departments but be the driver of government. The analogy I always think of is that Number 10 should be the gear-stick in the Prime Minister's hand—light and responsive—and the Cabinet Office should be the drive shaft—making sure the wheels of government are all moving in the same direction and at the same speed.[154]

[148] Cabinet Office, *Annual Report and Accounts 2020–21* (HC 391, 35).

[149] *Coronavirus: Lessons Learned to Date* (HC 2021–22, 92) para 61; on the failures in preparation for the pandemic, see UK Covid-19 Inquiry, *Module 1; The Resilience and Preparedness of the United Kingdom* (July 2024).

[150] Cabinet Office, *Annual Report and Accounts 2021–22* (HC 914, 51–52).

[151] Cabinet Office, *Cabinet Committee Business: A Guide for Departments* (1997) 2.

[152] ibid p 8. For Robin Butler, Cabinet Secretary 1988–98, a feature of the Cabinet Office was that it was neutral on policy, and therefore more likely to have the confidence of other departments. 'I believed we could only effectively get the cooperation of the departments and ministers, and let the Cabinet operate, if they thought the Cabinet Office were honest brokers, and not just trying to manipulate things so that the Prime Minister got their own way': Seldon with Meakin, *The Cabinet Office* (n 14) 219.

[153] Harold Wilson, *The Governance of Britain* (Weidenfeld and Nicolson and Michael Joseph 1976) 94.

[154] House of Lords Constitution Committee (n 51) 180. In Machiavelli's view, according to Powell, a more Napoleonic system is much more efficient than a feudal system of barons if you want to get things done. 'It was in this sense that I wanted more central drive, and the point of the Cabinet Office was to

These competing considerations were reflected in what former Deputy Cabinet Secretary Helen MacNamara described in her evidence to the UK Covid-19 inquiry as two 'fairly distinct modes of operation: supporting the Prime Minister personally on their leadership of an issue or coordinating departments to facilitate collective agreement'.[155] She argued that it was the 'driver of government' rather than the 'facilitating collective agreement' mode of operation that had been uppermost in managing the process of exiting the European Union, and that that mode of operation had continued through into the response to Covid-19 —'the Cabinet Office is more clay than elastic; it does not spring back into shape'—with the result that the views of line departments were not necessarily sought or heard, leaving them disempowered or disregarded.[156]

3.4.3 Collective decision-making

The Cabinet is 'the ultimate decision-making body of government'.[157] 'Decisions reached by the Cabinet or [Cabinet] Committees are binding on all members of the Government.'[158] 'The Cabinet does not make suggestions. It takes decisions.'[159] Ministers also have an obligation to ensure decisions agreed in Cabinet and Cabinet committees (and in write-rounds) are implemented.[160]

Cabinet committees help to ensure that government business is processed more effectively by relieving pressure on Cabinet. The committee structure also supports the principle of collective responsibility, ensuring that policy proposals receive thorough consideration without an issue having to be referred to the whole Cabinet.[161] The structure of the Cabinet committee system, the membership of individual committees, and their terms of reference are all matters for the Prime Minister.[162] In December 2023 there were five Cabinet Committees, including the Parliamentary Business and Legislation Committee, and six sub-committees—four of the NSC and two of the Domestic and Economic Affairs Committee.[163]

The government's approach to its Brexit preparations and its Covid response saw a distinction drawn between 'strategy' and 'operations' committees—the former to handle high-level strategy decisions, the latter to drive through actions and operational outcomes or oversee operational delivery—a model which Boris Johnson, according to the Cabinet Secretary, subsequently decided to apply across what was

provide the transmission system between the will of the centre of government and what departments actually do': (n 6) 79. Machiavelli can hardly have had a view about the Napoleonic system.

[155] UK Covid-19 Inquiry. Witness Statement of Helen MacNamara (October 2023) para 10.
[156] ibid paras 11–14.
[157] *The Cabinet Manual* (n 65) para 4.1.
[158] *Ministerial Code* (December 2022) para 2.3.
[159] Clement Atlee quoted in Wilson (n 153) 60.
[160] *Ministerial Code* (December 2022) para 2.3.
[161] *The Cabinet Manual* (n 65) para 4.9. The 1997 version of the Ministerial Code offered a fuller explanation of the second purpose: committees 'support the principle of collective responsibility, by ensuring that, even though an important question may never reach the Cabinet itself, the decision will be fully considered and the final judgment will be sufficiently authoritative to ensure that the Government as a whole can properly be expected to accept responsibility for it' (para 4).
[162] *The Cabinet Manual* (n 65) para 4.10.
[163] For details, see Cabinet-Committee-List.pdf (publishing.service.gov.uk).

described as the 'waterfront of government business'.[164] The model appears to have been abandoned, however, indicating the fragility of any given committee structure.

Most issues requiring collective agreement are handled through correspondence. Under the 'write-round' procedure, ministers seeking collective agreement write to the chair of the relevant committee setting out the proposal to which agreement is sought. The initiating department is responsible for ensuring that proposals have been discussed with other interested departments and the outcome of these discussions should be reflected in the memorandum or letter submitted to the relevant committee.[165] Once all responses have been received, the chair will write to the minister confirming whether collective agreement has been reached or not and setting out any conditions to that agreement. If it is not possible to reach a decision in correspondence, the chair of the relevant Cabinet committee may decide to call a meeting to consider the issue.[166]

'[T]here is no hard-and-fast rule about what decisions must be approved by Cabinet and what may be settled by individual Ministers singly or after consulting other Ministers relevant to the decision.'[167] The Ministerial Code defines the business of Cabinet and Cabinet committees as consisting in the main of two types of questions. The first are questions which 'significantly engage the collective responsibility of the Government because they raise major issues of policy or because they are of critical importance to the public'. The Code adds that no definitive criteria can be given for issues which engage collective responsibility. The Cabinet Secretariats can advise where departments are unsure but the final decision rests with the Prime Minister.[168] The second type are questions on which there is 'an unresolved argument between departments'. When there is a difference between departments, however, it should not be referred to the Cabinet until other means of resolving it have been exhausted.[169] Matters wholly within the responsibility of a single minister and which do not significantly engage collective responsibility, on the other hand, need not be brought to the Cabinet or to a Cabinet committee 'unless the minister' wishes to inform his colleagues or to have their advice.[170]

Lord Maude's *Independent Review of Governance and Accountability in the Civil Service* (the 'Maude Review') was highly critical of what were described as the 'customs' surrounding collective decision-making, including Cabinet committees and sub-committees, describing them as 'archaic' and in need of modernization to narrow the gap between 'crisis mode' and 'business as usual'.[171] In normal times, collective decision-making typically followed a 'stately process' where decisions were taken

[164] Simon Case, Cabinet Secretary Lecture (13 October 2021) <www.gov.uk>. The strategy and operations structure, with officials sitting alongside ministers and actively contributing to discussion, is widely considered to have raised the quality of meetings: Commission on the Centre of Government (n 3) 42.

[165] *Ministerial Code* (December 2022) para 2.4

[166] *The Cabinet Manual* (n 65) paras 4.16, 4.44–4.48; see also Letwin (n 24) 233–34.

[167] Mount, *The British Constitution Now* (n 48) 118; nor, Mount added, is there any hard-and-fast rule about the manner in which approval is sought, or about the organization of committees, and the nature of the business brought before them.

[168] *Ministerial Code* (December 2022) paras 2.2 and 2.4.

[169] ibid.

[170] *Ministerial Code* (December 2022) para 2.4.

[171] Maude, *Independent Review of Governance and Accountability in the Civil Service* (n 37) para 2.4.2.

either by write-round or by discussion in a Cabinet committee or sub-committee. Some 'arcane rules, of indeterminate origin', governed these processes, the guardians of which were the Cabinet Secretariats. The rules seemed to state that Cabinet committees were to be attended only by ministers, not special advisers, and that officials, if permitted to attend, were not expected to speak. Cabinet committee minutes had a tendency to be opaque and rarely attached timelines and named individuals to action points, in the unusual event of action points appearing. Drafting was in the hands of the secretariats, who checked with departments for accuracy before distributing to the committee. No minister or special adviser saw the draft before it was circulated.[172]

In times of crisis, by contrast, the sense was that 'normal' procedures were suspended, shortcuts taken, an 'action this day' culture introduced, and a sense of urgency and immediacy prevailed. The time was right, Maude argued, for a 'more businesslike approach' to decision-making to be embedded in normal times as well as in times of crisis. It should be routine for officials to attend Cabinet committees and to speak, as happened during Covid and Brexit preparations, when 'crisis mode' was adopted.[173] The absence or silence of officials had sometimes seemed to give tacit permission for officials to ignore, delay, or later seek to reopen decisions. On one occasion, when questioned on why a Cabinet committee decision had not been implemented, an official stated that the decision had not been seen as a 'very strong mandate'. What lay behind this was that attendees at the meeting had largely been junior ministers, not necessarily well acquainted with the brief, and therefore officials felt that the decision could safely be ignored. This was exacerbated by the inconsistency of attendance of junior ministers at committees. Attendance was often an accident of whoever happened to be available. This disrupted continuity and diminished the gravitas and seriousness which committee business should attract.[174]

3.4.4 Propriety and ethics

One of the Cabinet Secretary's key roles is as the 'guardian of propriety and ethics, ministerial and Civil Service conduct'.[175] In June 2022 the core propriety and ethics team in the Cabinet Office consisted of about 20 people split across three main teams: a casework team, a policy team, and a team that provided direct support to the independent adviser when in post. The casework team did a lot of the reactive work. It was very demand-led. 'It depends what issues people are raising. I remain very encouraged that it gets so much incoming traffic from Ministers, special advisers and Permanent Secretaries, because they are asking about the right way to do stuff. That team spends a lot of its time advising people on the best way to get Government business done within the codes and rules.'[176] The emphasis on 'incoming traffic' is

[172] ibid para 8.3.

[173] Far from being 'business-like', decision-making in crisis mode could be chaotic, as demonstrated by the Covid Inquiry evidence.

[174] Maude, *Independent Review of Governance and Accountability in the Civil Service* (n 37) para 8.4.

[175] Jeremy Heywood, Cabinet Secretary 2012–18, 'The Role of the Modern Cabinet Secretary' (Institute for Government September 2015). In June 2022 the Cabinet Secretary told the Public Administration and Constitutional Affairs Committee that he was spending 'an astonishing 30% of his time on matters of propriety and ethics which former Prime Minister Rt. Hon. Sir John Major said suggests "there is a serious problem"' (*Propriety of Governance in Light of Greensill* (n 93) para 8).

[176] PACAC evidence session with Simon Case and Darren Tierney, Director General, Propriety and Ethics, Cabinet Office (28 June 2022) q 456.

revealing. The Cabinet Office's role is essentially advisory; it does not monitor departmental compliance with its codes and rules or take action when they are ignored.[177]

3.4.5 Progress assurance

The introduction of public service agreements—agreements between the Treasury and individual departments on the targets they would seek to deliver in return for the public money they received from the Treasury—in the 1998 Spending Review marked a new departure in the executive's approach to securing delivery of its priorities.[178] Their introduction was followed by the establishment of the Prime Minister's Delivery Unit (PMDU) in the Cabinet Office after the 2001 general election to provide support and scrutiny on a selection of the government's highest priority public service agreements. 'The aim was to fundamentally change the course of delivery in four departments—the Home Office, Department for Health, Department for Education, and Department for Transport—in order to meet the Government's priority objectives across 17 PSAs.'[179] The PMDU was moved from the Cabinet Office to the Treasury when Gordon Brown became Prime Minister in 2007 where it was reported to have lost its 'bite'.[180]

With the formation of the Coalition government, the Delivery Unit was abolished as part of its initial cutting back of the centre before being re-established as the Implementation Unit (later the Prime Minister's Implementation Unit (PMIU)) in the Cabinet Office to support and coordinate the delivery work of departments.

> How the Civil Service implements policies is at least as important as how it develops them. The Government has created a new Implementation unit in the Cabinet Office to focus on strengthening implementation of the policies that have been determined by the Prime Minister and Deputy Prime Minister to be of the highest strategic significance. The unit will bring together expertise from a wide range of sectors including local government, the private sector and experts from within Whitehall and internationally. It will undertake joint 'deep dive' reviews with departments on key implementation issues.[181]

The 2015 Conservative government also established 11 'implementation task forces' on key government priorities. 'Given that many of our most important implementation challenges could be met only through close cooperation between departments, what we needed was some mechanism to bring those responsible for each major project together in a setting where we could focus on action rather than policy debate.'[182] In 2017–18, task forces were operating on immigration, modern slavery,

[177] For criticism of the executive's 'advisory and light-touch' approach to enforcement, see Committee on Standards in Public Life, *Upholding Standards in Public Life* (n 71) paras 2.6–2.9.

[178] *Public Services for the Future: Modernization, Reform Accountability. Comprehensive Spending Review: Public Service Agreements 1999–2002* (Cm 4181, 1998); discussed in chapter 3, section 4.1.

[179] Nehal Panchamia and Peter Thomas, *Civil Service Reform in the Real World: Patterns of Success in UK Civil Service Reform* (Institute for Government March 2014) 49.

[180] Heywood (n 9) 199–200; on the PMDU, see Michael Barber, *Instruction to Deliver: Tony Blair, Public Services and the Challenge of Achieving Targets* (Politico's 2007).

[181] HM Government, *The Civil Service Reform Plan* (n 28) 17.

[182] Letwin (n 24) 234–35.

housing, digital, employment and skills, industrial strategy, and on rough sleeping and homelessness reduction.[183] The renamed PMIU also undertook targeted 'deep dive' reviews into 'crucial delivery challenges, identifying issues and developing solutions'.[184] One such challenge was ensuring a properly functioning statute book after Brexit.[185]

As Prime Minister, Boris Johnson initially discontinued implementation task forces before establishing four Ministerial Implementation Groups (MIGs) in response to the Covid pandemic in March 2020—on healthcare, other public services, the economy and business, and the international response to the pandemic. The PMIU was also brought back into No 10 from the Cabinet Office and renamed the Prime Minister's Delivery Unit in April 2021 following a review by Michael Barber, the architect of the original PMDU, to 'drive progress across the Prime Minister's priorities' in the aftermath of the pandemic. 'The unit became the principal innovation in domestic machinery of government under Johnson, with some solid progress on skills, health and energy to its credit. But like so much of Johnson's premiership, promising initiatives floundered because of his variable attention, and the distraction of events often of his own making.'[186]

When he first joined the Civil Service, the Cabinet Secretary said in a lecture in October 2021, the received wisdom was that it was 'good at policy and poor at delivery'. Over the course of his career, he believed this to have been 'inverted'.[187] A more cautionary note was sounded by Jonathan Powell in evidence to PACAC: 'You have no civil servants to speak of, you have almost no budget to speak of by comparison with big Departments and all you can do is persuade Cabinet Ministers who have the statutory powers to come along with you.'[188]

> As a consequence [the Committee concluded] the ability of Prime Ministers and their offices to ensure that this implementation of agreed objectives actually takes place is contingent and largely dependent on the political capital a Prime Minister can bring to bear. Where the Prime Minister feels a Secretary of State is failing to deliver an agreed policy, and if efforts at persuasion have been exhausted, the Prime Minister can replace them. However, for Prime Ministers, the freedom to do so, at least without suffering a loss of political credibility and authority, can often be limited.[189]

3.4.6 *The functional centre for government*

Among the areas on which the Coalition's *Civil Service Reform Plan* concentrated as it was implemented were departmental support functions, those 'areas of expertise that provide professional support and services to departments'.[190] One of the principles

[183] Cabinet Office, *Annual Report and Accounts 2017–18* (HC 1293, 16).
[184] ibid.
[185] Discussed in chapter 10, section 2.3.
[186] Seldon and Newell (n 39) 471.
[187] Case (n 164).
[188] Public Administration and Constitutional Affairs Committee, *The Role and Status of the Prime Minister's Office* (n 23) para 21.
[189] ibid.
[190] National Audit Office, *Capability in the Civil Service* (2017) 4.

on which the machinery of government had long been fashioned was that organization followed policy. Departments had therefore been left to develop their own specialist capability through 'ad hoc (sometimes competing) strategies. Unsurprisingly, the results were patchy.'[191] In September 2013 the Cabinet Office and the Treasury embarked on what was described as a major programme to build 'a more unified corporate centre' by centralizing eight corporate support functions: HR, legal services, communications, IT, commercial services, property, finance, and internal audit.[192] The introduction of 'strong central leadership' for cross-departmental corporate functions as was common in 'well-run' private companies and many other Organisation for Economic Co-operation and Development (OECD) governments, it was argued, would 'professionalise the Civil Service through improved decision-making, cross-departmental working, organisational capability, efficiency, resilience and control. A strong functional model would help deliver better public services and accelerate savings.'[193]

The leadership of eight of the now 13 cross-government functions is headquartered in the Cabinet Office: communication, commercial, counter fraud, grants, human resources, property, project delivery, and security.[194] Some functions are managed as a single entity, while others combine a functional centre and functional teams managed by and within departments and other organizations. The way in which the functional centres operate varies—there is no one-size-fits-all model—with some providing leadership and standards, some undertaking a few 'core' cross-government tasks, and some employing staff in departments. Together they account for much of the Cabinet Office's growth in recent years. 'We now have a headcount of 9,765 compared with 2,708 in 2016–17, reflecting our developing position as the functional centre for government.'[195]

A 'suite' of management standards sets 'expectations' for managing functions and the undertaking of functional work in departments and arm's length bodies. The standards are made up of a mixture of mandatory ('shall') and advisory ('should') elements, with the former being said to 'reflect a consensus about what is essential, including existing requirements about spending or regularity'. After a long period in which their status was unclear, the standards now derive their authority from a 2023 amendment to *Managing Public Money*, which stipulates that accounting officers 'shall also ensure they comply with the functional standards'.[196] The amendment followed a Dear

[191] Julian McCrae and Jen Gold, *Professionalising Whitehall* (Institute for Government 2017) 4; expensive and hence a target for efficiency savings as well as patchy.

[192] Civil Service, *Civil Service Reform Plan: Progress Report* (n 34) para 7.2.

[193] Cabinet Office, *The Functional Model: A Model for More Efficient and Effective Government* (March 2015). The *One Year On Report* insisted that 'tweaking' the existing model was not enough; government could not afford to continue in this way. Stronger corporate functional leadership would deliver 'potential further efficiency savings and higher quality, more resilient support for the business of government'. Civil Service, *Civil Service Reform Plan: One Year On Report* (July 2013) 32.

[194] The five other functions are: analysis; debt; finance; digital, data, and technology; and internal audit; the leadership of finance and debt is headquartered in the Treasury, internal audit in the Government Internal Audit Agency; analysis in the Office for National Statistics; digital, data, and technology in the Department for Science, Innovation and Technology. Legal, which is sometimes treated as a function, is headquartered in the Government Legal Department.

[195] Cabinet Office *Annual Report and Accounts 2020–21* (July 2021) 25–26. Staff numbers (including agencies) in June 2024 stood at 10,730 (FTE) compared with 2,950 in June 2016.

[196] HM Treasury, *Managing Public Money* (May 2023) para 4.2.1.

Accounting Officer letter (DAO 05/21), which enjoined accounting officers to 'champion the standards as drivers of coherence, consistency and continuous improvement', and to 'use them to trigger conversations about the action needed in organisations to improve the way functional work is done, to support the enduring principles and requirements set out in *Managing Public Money*'. A failure to comply, the letter warned, was an indicator of heightened risk about the underlying transactions, and of potential systemic failure. It would trigger additional scrutiny and likely corrective action through management lines, and might also lead to formal independent assurance reviews and adverse findings by internal and/or external auditors.

DAO 05/21 was issued following a review of the cross-cutting functions (and the operation of spend controls) by Lord Maude, the former Minister for the Cabinet Office, which found that the mandate of the central leadership of most of the functions had weakened significantly since 2015.[197] An earlier review had reported that Permanent Secretaries did not agree that the role of the Civil Service chief executive officer, whose lack of formal powers the National Audit Office had highlighted, should include 'overseeing delivery', illustrating, in Maude's view, the limited extent to which the functional model had been 'truly embraced by the leadership of the Civil Service in the Departments'.[198] Coordinating activity across government, he had suggested in evidence to PACAC, 'encroaches on the prized autonomy of Permanent Secretaries, which reflects the departmental structure of Whitehall and the direct accountability of departmental secretaries of state and their Accounting Officers to Parliament. Whenever you introduce any centrally driven initiative in Government, you find that there is a real interest in all of the departmental baronies to make sure it fails.'[199] What was missing in Maude's view was oversight and direction. 'I believe it is absolutely essential that the centre of government—Ministers, the [Chief Operating Officer] and the central functional leaders—must have real-time oversight and ultimately—when needed—direction over delivery'.[200]

As to how oversight and direction were to be secured, Maude's answer was collective ministerial backing. 'Generally, it will be ministers acting collectively who provide the mandate for functional leaders. Without collective ministerial leadership, official leaders (i.e. civil service leaders) are unlikely voluntarily to cede mandatory powers to the centre. Indeed if they did, because it was voluntary, they could reverse it just as easily.'[201] In the *Declaration on Government Reform*, signed by the

[197] Lord Maude of Horsham, *Review of the Cross-cutting Functions and the Operation of Spend Controls* (July 2021) 7. This is a summary of the review, which was carried out in 2020.

[198] ibid 3.

[199] Public Administration and Constitutional Affairs Committee, *The Minister and the Official: The Fulcrum of Whitehall Effectiveness* (HC 2017–19, 497) para 84. See also his September 2017 lecture: 'I Stress that I Became Disillusioned with the Service, not with Civil Servants.' (*conservativehome*) ('Imperceptibly, inch by inch, with a control dropped here or not enforced there, the old silos and departmental baronies are re-emerging, with nothing to restrain the old unreconstructed behaviours from taking hold once more.')

[200] Maude, *Review of the Cross-cutting Functions* (n 197) 3. 'One of the Aunt Sallies put up to discredit the functional model is that its advocates believe that everything should be delivered by the centre. Nothing could be further from the truth . . . most activities will be delivered by the functions in the line departments. However, it must be clearly understood that there will be oversight and direction from the centre of the function' (9). 'As I make clear elsewhere, the centre must in the last resort be able to direct departments' (9–10).

[201] ibid 4.

Prime Minister on behalf of the Cabinet and the Cabinet Secretary on behalf of the Permanent Secretaries in June 2021, the Johnson government committed itself to acting on Maude's recommendations. 'We will require all departments to meet clear standards set by the functions, backed up by strict adherence to spending controls that help ensure the government is delivering value for money for the taxpayer.'[202] Annexed to the Declaration was a list of specific actions to be taken in 2021, which included implementing 'clear standards for all functions' and ensuring 'they are used consistently across government to improve quality and efficiency'.[203] But with a government whose hold on power was already weakening collective ministerial backing was never likely to be the answer.[204] In the event it was the Treasury's powers of control that were invoked—DAO 05/21 and GovS 001 both cite the Declaration. Whether they will prove sufficient remains to be seen. Euphemistically described as being at different stages of 'maturity', which often simply reflects the lack of influence they have over the way departments operate, the functions remain a work in progress.[205]

3.4.7 *Shared services*

Running alongside the functional programme has been a shared services programme, which was first launched in 2004 with the aim of reducing the costs of administering departmental corporate functions such as human resources, finance, procurement, and payroll through the sharing of services. As had been the case in other areas, individual departments had made their own provision creating, in theory at least, scope for cutting costs and improving efficiency. Relaunched by the Coalition in 2012, the programme, according to Maude, encountered 'a great deal of resistance from departments and other entities, who typically would grudgingly offer to host another entity's activity on their system, always requiring the "guest" entity to adapt their requirements to the host's existing system'. Little progress appeared to have been made in driving forward shared services since 2015.[206] Under its 'refreshed' Shared Services Strategy the Cabinet Office's aim is for departmental back-office services to be delivered by five shared services centres by 2028.[207]

[202] *Declaration on Government Reform* (June 2021) 6.

[203] The Cabinet Office's Outcome Delivery Plan 2021 to 2022, published a month later, committed it to increasing the efficiency, effectiveness, and accountability of government through modernizing and reforming the work of the Government Functions (Priority Outcome 6). One of the functional reform agenda's objectives was for the centre of functions to have a 'strong mandate over functional activity but with discretion on how it is exercised'.

[204] Maude returned to the cross-government functions in his review of governance and accountability in the Civil Service with a series of recommendations designed to strengthen and streamline their governance: (n 37) paras 5.15–5.27.

[205] Alex Thomas and others, *A New Statutory Role for the Civil Service* (Institute for Government 2022) 23. The Commission on the Centre of Government described adherence as 'inconsistent' and departments as 'broadly choosing to follow them by consent': (n 3) 57.

[206] Maude, *Review of the Cross-cutting Functions* (n 197) 22.

[207] Cabinet Office, *Shared Services Strategy for Government* (March 2021). The Public Accounts Committee found that some progress had been made in the two years since the strategy was introduced but remained concerned about 'deliverability': *Government Shared Services* (HC 2022–23, 734).

3.4.8 Cabinet Office spend controls

A similar picture of departmental resistance to central control emerged from Maude's review of Cabinet Office spend controls—controls over 10 areas of departmental expenditure, including consultancy, information and communication technology, recruitment, marketing and property, which were introduced by delegation from the Treasury in June 2010 in response to the urgent need for fiscal consolidation. Widely expected to be temporary when they were introduced, it became clear according to Maude that they could play 'a lasting role in driving out wasteful expenditure'.[208] They had been progressively relaxed, however, with numerous exemptions being introduced and thresholds increased. Departmental compliance had also declined: 'Inevitably, over time, any organisation learns to game a control system of this type. This has plainly happened with the Cabinet Office controls. Submissions are sometimes made after the spend has been committed; there are late requests, which makes it exceptionally hard for a minister to refuse; and there are examples of projects that are sliced up and therefore escape scrutiny.'[209] Compliance, Maude insisted, could not be voluntary. 'Any failure to observe either the spirit or the letter of the controls should be a disciplinary matter for the individual official responsible, and a performance issue for the permanent secretary. It should be reported to the NAO publicly, and the attention of the PAC drawn to it.'[210] In the Declaration on Government Reform, the Prime Minister and Cabinet Secretary undertook, as we have seen, to require all departments to meet clear standards set by the functions, 'backed up by strict adherence to spending controls'.[211]

IV The Treasury

4.1 Introduction

The Prime Minister's Office and the Cabinet Office are not the whole of the centre of government. There is also the Treasury, the 'department of departments', as it has been called,[212] which manages the essential government resource that is money. This provides the Treasury with mechanisms of control of behaviour across the executive that are both pervasive and continuous and on which the Prime Minister—who retains the historic title of First Lord of the Treasury, although today this involves no day-to-day contact—must rely in order to carry through the government's overall programme and to pursue its policy priorities. While our focus here, and throughout this book, is on the Treasury's control function, it is important to remember that the Treasury is

208 Maude, *Review of the Cross-cutting Functions* (n 197) 26. Asked why Cabinet Office rather than Treasury spend controls, Maude replied: 'It could be the Treasury, but the Treasury does not do that. It does not have the capability and it is not its culture. As I say, the Treasury's culture is, "We set a budget. We let Departments get on with it," and so it is not set up to do it but there is no reason why, in other circumstances, it could not be done there': Public Administration and Constitutional Affairs Committee, oral evidence: The work of the Cabinet Office (HC 118 12 January 2021) q 636.

209 Maude, *Review of the Cross-cutting Functions* (n 197) 33.

210 ibid 33–34.

211 *Declaration on Government Reform* (June 2021) 6; see further chapter 8, section 2.4.3.

212 Maurice Wright, *Treasury Control of the Civil Service 1854–1874* (Clarendon Press 1969) 1.

also, through its roles in fiscal policy and supervision of financial services, a policy-making department. In relation to these functions, the sort of central internal control that—for the activities of other departments—is most effectively provided by the Treasury thus becomes a matter of self-discipline or self-restraint, an unusually privileged situation open to criticism on grounds both of decision-making performance and adequacy of accountability.[213] The same of course is true of the Treasury's control of its own spending.[214]

As with the powers of the Prime Minister, the constitutional and legal bases of the Treasury's powers of control and direction are poorly understood. In the case of the Prime Minister, the tendency has been to assume that any discussion of legal powers can be left to one side because of their insignificance in comparison with considerations of the incumbent's political strength or weakness. Political considerations certainly have a place in discussions of the Treasury, which have often emphasized the importance of the personal relationship between the Prime Minister and the Chancellor of the Exchequer. 'Consistent alignment between the Prime Minister and Chancellor is crucial because, as the former Cabinet Secretary and Treasury permanent secretary Andrew Turnbull explained, that relationship is the "San Andreas fault of government . . . the place where things can go most wrong".'[215] And without the Prime Minister's support Treasury rulings and rules can be overridden by Cabinet decision. Nonetheless, it is the legal and constitutional bases on which they rest that provide the foundation for the Treasury's political strength. We discussed these bases, and their historical development, in detail in our 1999 volume,[216] and in this section we provide no more than a brief recapitulation (section 4.2), before considering how the organization of the Treasury has evolved in response to 21st-century challenges and policy developments (section 4.3). Treasury decisions and requirements have been a fundamental influence on the organization and mode of operation of departments, and we address recent developments in this field in chapter 3. At the same time, the Treasury's instruments of financial control have continued to evolve over the last 25 years. We investigate this process in detail in chapters 7 and 8.

4.2 The bases of Treasury control

The United Kingdom lacks a comprehensive legal code for the management of government's financial resources. Analysing Treasury powers is an exercise in constitutional and legal geology; once one starts to probe, distinct strata of financial

[213] See eg Ian Dunt, *How Westminster Works . . . and Why It Doesn't* (Weidenfeld & Nicolson 2023) ch 5. A striking example was the exclusion from Lord Maude's review of governance and accountability in the Civil Service of 'any issues relating to taxation or the public spending accountability framework or governance processes', prompting Maude to 'merely comment on the oddity of an approach which ordains that for just one government institution the only body deemed fit to review its governance of and accountability for something so central as public expenditure is that institution itself': (n 37) para 3.2.

[214] For an example of how the Treasury 'marks its own homework' in this area, see Christopher Hood and others, *The Way the Money Goes: The Fiscal Constitution and Public Spending in the UK* (OUP 2023) 31–32, 73–77.

[215] Commission on the Centre of Government (n 3) 69.

[216] Daintith and Page (n 68) 113–23.

management and control appear, that have been laid down at different times and for different purposes. Over time they have been folded into one another in complex patterns, have interpenetrated to a considerable extent, and are by no means fully stabilized; their changing interaction is an important continuing feature of constitutional development in this area. It is useful to distinguish three control systems.

4.2.1 Treasury housekeeping

The *first* is constituted by the Treasury's 'ancient authority' within the executive, as the department to which the general management of government funds has from the earliest times been entrusted.[217] The aims which have shaped this system are those of ordinary housekeeping, albeit on the grand scale appropriate to what was once the royal household: the application of funds to their intended purposes, economy, and the avoidance of waste and fraud. While these purposes have effectively been subsumed in those of the parliamentary appropriation system, as have some of the instruments—such as audit—through which they were secured, the most basic control powers of the Treasury, notably that of prior approval of expenditure, are still grounded in this first system. The fundamental principle, as currently stated in the Treasury's *Managing Public Money*, the public expenditure rule-book, that 'Departments must have Treasury consent before undertaking expenditure',[218] rests on practice and on prerogative Orders in Council that pre-date the arrival of responsible government. In 1667 young and enthusiastic Treasury Commissioners obtained Orders requiring that they be informed of every petition which would involve a charge on the revenue, and conferring the right to give their opinion on the petition itself and the state of the revenues as a whole; and in 1668, a further Order requiring their consent for issues of warrants of expenditure. These were the precedents relied on as the basis of the 'ancient authority' of the Treasury when, from the late 18th century onwards, members of Parliament began to see themselves as having some responsibility for the supervision of the public purse, rather than just as lucky recipients of the patronage it could disburse.[219] Once that responsibility became firmly established in the course of the 19th century, we find that Treasury authority is assumed, rather than stated, in the legislation that forms the basis of parliamentary control of appropriation.[220]

217 For more detail on the history of Treasury authority, see Daintith and Page (n 68) 113–16, drawing principally on Henry Roseveare, *The Treasury: The Evolution of a British Institution* (Allen Lane The Penguin Press 1969); and *The Treasury 1660–1870* (Allen and Unwin 1973); and more recently Sir Nicholas Macpherson, 'The Origins of Treasury Control' (Lecture delivered 16 January 2013).

218 HM Treasury, *Managing Public Money* (n 196) para 2.3.1.

219 See Will Bateman, *Public Finance and Parliamentary Constitutionalism* (CUP 2020) 55, for early examples of legislation giving the Treasury specific additional expenditure control powers.

220 See Exchequer and Audit Departments Act 1868, s 27, requiring the Comptroller and Auditor General to report to Treasury any expenditure that appears to have been incurred without its authority. The contemporaneous definition of what requires authority appears in a Treasury Minute of April 1868: see Public Accounts Committee, *Epitome of Reports from the Committee of Public Accounts 1857–1937* (HC 1937–38, 154) 20–21. The current formulation of the provision appears in Government Resources and Accounts Act 2000, s 6(2).

4.2.2 Parliamentary appropriation

Such appropriation of parliamentary grants, and ensuring that expenditure complies with those appropriations, constitute the essence of our *second* system. Its bedrock is the Exchequer and Audit Departments Act 1866, as now substantially modified by the Government Resources and Accounts Act 2000, its leading personage the Comptroller and Auditor General. However, over nearly a century before the passing of the 1866 Act or the institution of that office, parliamentary concerns about the expenditure of the funds it voted were becoming increasingly congruent with Treasury concerns about housekeeping, so that the real effect of the 1860s reforms was to bring about a partial merger between two systems which up to that time had been distinct but mutually reinforcing. Consequently, after 1866 the most visible frame for the Treasury's action was the Act, and the Comptroller and Auditor General laboured (until 1983) on behalf of both Parliament and Treasury. Current constitutional doctrine still maintains that, in the absence of parliamentary restriction, the executive enjoys at common law all the capacities for action of an ordinary private individual. Legislative constraints on executive behaviour are of course important, but they are not comprehensive. If, therefore, Parliament wants to achieve any systematic oversight of government's actions outside the rather limited sphere of its coercive powers, it needs to secure at least formal control of access to the resources which make those capacities real. Legislative appropriation of funds has since the 18th century been the principal and ever-developing instrument for this purpose. Decisions as to how much may be spent, and on what, determine more effectively than anything else what may and may not be done. Transparency and regularity, assuring clarity as to what is to be spent and as to whether spending has accorded with the authorities given, are accordingly the key values of this system.

After 1866, Parliament's concerns steadily expanded so as to encompass good housekeeping as well as transparency and regularity, to the point where the congruence with traditional Treasury concerns was effectively complete. The National Audit Act 1983 formally marks this moment through its statutory recognition of value-for-money audit by the National Audit Office (NAO), while simultaneously introducing a new institutional separation between the actors in the system. The result is that while the Comptroller and Auditor General, and NAO, now answer to Parliament alone,[221] legislature and executive now profess the same concerns about the regularity and economy of public expenditure.

This second system has strengthened pre-existing Treasury controls by giving them statutory expression. Under the Exchequer and Audit Departments Act,[222] parliamentary grants are made to the Crown, that is, the government as a whole, in the form of a credit in favour of the Treasury at the Bank of England, not to the departments and other bodies to whose use they are appropriated. They are issued to each department on the authority of an order under the Royal Sign Manual countersigned by the Treasury, which is responsible for ensuring that the amounts issued are consistent

[221] NAO however continues to view departments and other audited bodies as consumers of its advice on achieving value for money, and emphasizes the importance it attaches to their awareness and opinion of the Office: see National Audit Office, *Annual Report and Accounts 2022–23* (HC 2022–23, 1515) 38–51.

[222] ss 13–15.

with the relevant legislative appropriations. Funding for services charged by legislation directly to the Consolidated Fund, by way of standing appropriations, is likewise released from the government's account with the Bank of England on a requisition from the Treasury. In other words, while Parliament *appropriates* funds for the use of particular department and services, it *grants* those funds to the Treasury. These arrangements for the issuance of funds make it impossible to suggest that there can be any departmental claim to the *ownership* of the funds they expend or, analogously, the income they receive. The importance of this was pointed out in 1957 by Beer, who noted that if appropriations were to be made not to the Crown but directly to departments, the Treasury's power of requiring its prior approval for expenditure would be gravely impaired.[223] In the field of finance, in other words, the UK executive, constitutionally, is unitary, not pluralist.

Similarly, the 1866 Act reinforced the by then established Treasury role—as gatekeeper of departments' access to Parliament to request funds via the annual estimates—by empowering it to prescribe the form of departmental accounts, with which the structure and form of their estimates would need to correspond.[224] Parliament's self-denial of any initiative in financial matters[225] means that, unlike some other legislatures,[226] it has, until very recently, seen no need to develop any institutional capacity of its own for budgetary assessment.[227] In the operation of the appropriation system, its reliance on the work of the Treasury in allocating, coordinating and controlling public spending, coupled with *ex post* review from the Comptroller and Auditor General, was in effect total—at least until the creation of the Office of Budget Responsibility provided an independent source of information through which to evaluate spending proposals.[228]

4.2.3 Public finance as economic management

A *third* system of control developed in the second half of the 20th century out of the recognition of a new economic task for the executive, and in particular the Treasury: that of influencing the operation of the national economy as a whole. While a number of instruments, such as monetary policy, have been available to government for this purpose, fiscal policy, that is to say the management of the overall relationship between public income (in the form principally of taxes and borrowing) and public expenditure, came to occupy a central place in the UK economic policy in the

[223] Samuel Beer, *Treasury Control: The Co-ordination of Financial and Economic Policy in Great Britain* (2nd edn, OUP 1957) 129.

[224] Exchequer and Audit Departments Act 1866, s 22, now replaced by Government Resources and Accounts Act 2000, s 5(2), with similar effect. See further chapter 11, section 2.1.

[225] See chapter 7, section 1.1.

[226] Such capacities were first developed in presidential systems: the United States Congressional Budget Office, established in 1974, remains the largest and most powerful example. On such offices, and other forms of what are now termed 'independent fiscal institutions', see Cal Viney and Thomas Poole, 'Independent Fiscal Institutions', in Roger Masterman and Robert Schütze (eds), *The Cambridge Companion to Comparative Constitutional Law* (CUP 2019) 441–70; Xavier Lebrun and Tidiane Kinda, 'Strengthening Post-Crisis Fiscal Credibility: Fiscal Councils on the Rise—A New Dataset' (Washington DC, 2014) IMF Working Paper WP/14/58.

[227] For the first hesitant steps in this direction (the House of Commons Scrutiny Unit), see chapter 8, n 25.

[228] Discussed in chapter 7, section 2.2.1.

course of the Second World War and the immediate post-war period.[229] Experience in the 1940s and 1950s, however, made it clear that attempting to provide economic stimulus through short-term changes to spending levels or allocations was both disruptive and inefficient.[230] Nor did the modes of accounting for public revenue and expenditure developed for the purposes of the first two systems properly reflect their impact on the economy as a whole.

After some experimentation the government's response, in 1961, was to create the Public Expenditure Survey system (PES), providing for the projection and planning of public expenditure over a period of years, having regard to the prospective development of revenue over the same period and to the impact of both public expenditure and taxation on the development of the economy.[231] While PES has changed substantially over the years, in response to the ideas of the party in power, to economic crises, to shifts in economic theory, and to new structures of government, it has always provided a framework for taking a centralized view about the government's total spending over a future period of years and about how that spending might be apportioned between the various functions for which different departments are responsible. Since 1998 the process has been referred to as the Spending Review (SR) or Comprehensive Spending Review (CSR). The Review remains wholly internal to the executive; indeed, in the early years of PES, its results were thought to be too sensitive for publication.[232] Even today Parliament hears of the results once they have been arrived at; it is not invited to approve or disapprove them, as such.[233] Nor does Parliament approve the annual budget judgement; it votes only on the resolutions, and later the legislation, renewing or changing specific taxes. The PES/SR system, superimposed on the 'parliamentary' system of estimates and accounts, has been slowly absorbing that system in much the way parliamentary appropriation gradually incorporated Treasury control in the 19th century. The presentation of information is increasingly taking place within the structures of the new system rather than the old one, and the old structures, such as supply estimates, have been reshaped to the logic of the new system.

[229] See eg JCR Dow, *The Management of the British Economy 1945–60* (CUP 1970) chs vii and viii; Roderick Floud and Donald McCloskey (eds), *The Economic History of Britain since 1700*, vol 3 (CUP 1994) 11–18; Minister of Reconstruction, *Employment Policy* (Cmd 6527, 1944), esp paras 74–79. Mark Blaug, *Economic Theory in Retrospect* (3rd edn, CUP 1978) 684, finds the earliest advocacy of public spending to smooth out cyclical fluctuations and to stabilize total economic activity in the *Minority Report* of the Poor Law Commission (Cd 4499, 1909) 1195–98 and Summary of Proposals (p 1216), paras 9–11.

[230] *Control of Public Expenditure* (Cmnd 1432, 1961) para 22.

[231] ibid paras 13–32.

[232] 'It is ... doubtful whether any Government will feel able to place these surveys before Parliament and the public. To do this would involve disclosing the Government's long-term intentions for a wide range of public expenditure; and also explaining the survey's assumptions about employment, wages, prices and all the other main elements in the national economy. It would be surprising if any Government were prepared to do this': ibid para 17. By 1969, however, the Treasury had screwed up enough courage to publish the surveys on an annual basis: Samuel Brittan, *Steering the Economy: The Role of the Treasury* (Harmondsworth, 1971) 105.

[233] For criticism of this, see Tony Prosser, '"An Opportunity to Take a More Fundamental Look at the Role of Government in Society": The Spending Review as Regulation' [2011] Public Law 596. For more detail about Parliament and Spending Reviews, see chapter 7, section 3.6.

4.3 Organization

For a department that combines the functions often distributed in other countries between a Ministry of Finance and a Ministry of Economic Affairs the Treasury is remarkably small, staff numbers in the 'core' department (excluding agencies) running at just over 2,000 in 2023. While this puts the Treasury among the smallest ministerial departments, its numbers nonetheless more than doubled over the course of the century: in 2000 they stood at 830. There was slow but steady growth thereafter under governments of all political stripes, but it was the Covid pandemic that pushed numbers up above 2,000 in 2021. Core Treasury tasks have, since the shedding of day-to-day monetary policy responsibilities to the Bank of England in 1998,[234] remained constant, and the economy with which they are discharged is explained by the Treasury's character as a compact supervisory elite, rather than as a department with executive responsibilities. In 2021 the Treasury identified its core tasks as being to

1. Place the public finances on a sustainable footing by controlling public spending and designing sustainable taxes
2. Level up the economy, by ensuring strong employment and increasing productivity across the regions and nations of the UK
3. Ensure the stability of the macro-economic environment and financial system.[235]

Reflection on the way the Treasury had performed in dealing with the financial crisis of 2007–09, coupled with the administrative economies imposed on all departments as an element of its aftermath,[236] led it to adopt in 2011 a new and more flexible management structure of 14 groups, each led by a Director accountable, for its corporate objectives and priorities and the associated discrete areas of work, to an Executive Management Board.[237] Its work on tax policy, for example, is divided between a Business and International Tax Group and a Personal Tax, Welfare and Pensions Group. So far as control of public spending is concerned, overarching public spending strategy, including the conduct of Spending Reviews, is the responsibility of the Public Spending Group. Most day-to-day contact between Treasury and departments takes place through the Treasury's spending teams, usually through departmental Finance Directors. The teams' work, and the way they are regarded by the departmental staff with whom they deal, were analysed by the Comptroller and Auditor General in the 2018 NAO report *Improving Government's Planning and Spending Framework*.[238] The Treasury has 20 spending teams, accounting for one-fifth of its staff. Their job is to advise Treasury ministers on decisions at Spending Reviews, to review and

234 Bank of England Act 1998, pt II.

235 HM Treasury, *Outcome Delivery Plan 2021 to 2022* (15 July 2021).

236 See HM Treasury, *Review of HM Treasury's Management Response to the Financial Crisis* (March 2012) esp paras 5.18–5.21.

237 For details of the groups, see HM Treasury, *Annual Report and Accounts 2022–23* (HC 2022–23, 1467) 107–08. For further discussion of performance of these tasks, see chapters 7 and 8. Organizational change up to 2013 is discussed in Richard Allen, 'Evaluating the Capability of the UK Treasury, 1990–2013' (2013) 13(3) OECD Journal on Budgeting 1–29.

238 HC 2017–19, 1679. See also discussion in chapter 7, especially at section IV. For fuller description of the system as it operated up to 2015, see Christopher Hood and others (n 214) 33–38.

approve submissions for new spending on projects and programmes, and to monitor the budgets and spending risks of the department or departments within their remit. The teams are spread across the different groups with which 'their' department's objectives are most closely related. Thus the teams dealing with the main public services like health, education, and defence are to be found in the Public Services Group, those responsible for growth-related departments (Trade, Energy Security and Net Zero, DEFRA) belong to the Enterprise and Growth Unit, while teams in the Personal Tax, Welfare and Pensions Group deal with the Department of Work and Pensions and Her Majesty's Revenue and Customs (HMRC).

Outside the core Treasury there has been considerably more movement in the course of this century, though in areas that generally bear less directly on central control of executive activity. Most high-profile, and difficult, was the merger of the two non-ministerial revenue departments with very different histories and traditions, Inland Revenue and HM Customs and Excise, effected under the Commissioners for Revenue and Customs Act 2005. The management of the new department, as of its predecessors, answers directly to the Chancellor of the Exchequer on all operational tax issues, and is the government's repository of tax expertise, but the Treasury retains a major role in tax policy, especially in the development of new taxes and the economic context and effects of taxation.[239]

Changes have also occurred in the composition of the broader group that includes the public bodies answering to the Treasury. Two new executive agencies have joined this group. The Debt Management Office (DMO) was established by the Treasury, in consequence of the establishment of the independent status of the Bank of England effected by the 1998 Act, to take over from the Bank the responsibility of managing the government's borrowings. DMO reports to the head of the Treasury's Fiscal Group. We consider the constitutional implications of this move in Chapter 7. The Government Internal Audit Agency (GIAA), reporting to the head of the Public Spending Group, represents the near-completion of a process of centralizing internal audit, which is concerned with all administrative systems in departments and operates to provide assurance that those systems are operating effectively. This was a departmental function, undertaken with guidance from a small Treasury-based team, but in 2009 concern about its quality led the Treasury to initiate a programme of consolidation, under which departments would consolidate or share internal audit services. Adopted as part of the government-wide functional programme in 2013, it culminated in the creation of GIAA in 2015.[240]

These developments could be seen as a concentration of Treasury control. Two others pointing in the opposite direction are examined in detail elsewhere in this book. The first was the transformation of the Office of National Statistics (ONS) from an executive agency reporting to Treasury ministers into the executive arm of an independent Statistics Authority established (under the name of the Statistics Board) by

[239] For background to the merger, see *Financing Britain's Future: Review of the Revenue Departments* (Cm 6163, 2004).

[240] On this process, see HM Treasury, *Review of Financial Management in Government* (December 2013) 22–23, and for the background, see Comptroller and Auditor General, *The Effectiveness of Internal Audit in Central Government* (HC 2012–14, 23) criticizing the uneven quality and varying objectives of departmental internal audit.

the Statistics and Registration Service Act 2007. The Labour government had come into office in 1997 with a commitment to make ONS independent, but it took until 2007 for it to become convinced that a statutory foundation for such independence was essential if trust in the reliability of official statistics and their protection from political manipulation was to be assured. We discuss the background to the Act, and its effects, in detail in Chapter 12.[241] The second innovation pursued a similar aim of increasing trust in the government's financial decisions. This was the creation in 2011 of the Office of Budget Responsibility, designed as an independent expert body (though still one situated within the executive branch), which would have the task of examining and reporting on the sustainability of the public finances,[242] principally by way of preparing and publishing fiscal and economic forecasts at least twice a year. These forecasts are normally adopted by the government as the official forecasts for the Budget Report, but the Treasury continues to maintain, through its Economics and Fiscal Groups, the necessary analytical and macroeconomic expertise to provide ongoing advice to the government.[243]

V Cabinet Office and Treasury—An Ill-Matched Couple?

Twenty-first-century government communications regularly present the Cabinet Office and Treasury as partner organizations forming the centre of the UK executive. 'We', said the Cabinet Office in 2023, 'are the corporate headquarters for government, in partnership with HM Treasury.'[244] Not everyone, however, is satisfied with the performance of this partnership. The Comptroller and Auditor General's Report, *The Centre of Government*, in 2014 criticized the failure of Cabinet Office and Treasury to join up their approach and avoid duplication in areas like government cost reduction, dealing with debt owed to government, promotion of cross-departmental integration of public services, and improvement of forecasting.[245] and the Public Accounts Committee (PAC) bluntly opined in the same year that '[t]he Cabinet Office and the Treasury are failing to act together as a strong corporate centre' and that,

> [a]s a result, the centre does not display strong strategic leadership and does not co-ordinate government business effectively. The Head of the Civil Service should define a new operating model for the centre of government, which includes:
>
> - control of key corporate functions—including finance, HR and IT—sitting more squarely with the centre; and
> - the centre using its strategic position more effectively to ensure government joins up its thinking and learns lessons from past mistakes.[246]

241 See also chapter 7, section 2.2.2, for discussion of the impact of statistical rules and concepts on accountability for budget decisions.
242 Budget Responsibility and National Audit Act 2011, s 4(1).
243 For more detail, see chapter 7, section 2.2.1.
244 Cabinet Office, *About Us* <www.gov.uk/government/organisations/cabinet-office/about>.
245 (HC 2014–15, 171) paras 3.5, 3.6, and figure 14.
246 Public Accounts Committee, *Civil Service Reform* (HC 2013–14, 473) conclusions para 5.

The Head of the Civil Service, with the Permanent Secretaries at the Treasury and the Cabinet Office, responded by saying in a letter to the Chair of PAC that

> the high degree of central direction and integration that you appear to recommend does not reflect the model that this government and previous governments have operated . . . [T]he Centre does not and cannot take decisions or set a strong direction on every item of the £720 billion of public expenditure. So long as the essentials—such as the controlled spending totals and collective agreement—are delivered and upheld, there is considerable freedom about implementation . . . [T]he government machine is not like a holding company dominating its subsidiaries from a corporate centre.[247]

That the centre of government should be more—though not exactly—like a holding company was in fact just what Francis Maude had been seeking in driving plans for Civil Service reform,[248] and although at that time ministers had not acquired the habit of quarrelling with their most senior civil servants in public, Maude, as Minister for the Cabinet Office, along with Danny Alexander, then Chief Secretary to the Treasury, felt moved to issue a nine-page rebuttal in the form of another letter to the PAC Chair asserting the effective exercise by the Coalition government of the centre's strategic position, and urging NAO and the Public Accounts Committee to continue its focus on the issue.[249] Issues about cooperation between the Cabinet Office and the Treasury did not start with the Coalition and its reform plans. The expansionist view of Treasury functions taken by Gordon Brown as Chancellor (1997–2007), which included leadership of social programmes and much greater involvement in the development of policy, was cited by witnesses to a House of Lords enquiry in 2009–10 as a source of 'tension' between the central institutions—though this was characterized as 'creative' rather than 'disruptive'.[250]

Part of the reason for these perceptions of an ineffective centre must surely be the mismatch between the attitudes and powers of the participants. Under Maude as Cabinet Office Minister—though not necessarily before or since—the Cabinet Office was vigorous in its pursuit of greater central control by way of the Efficiency and Reform Group and the functions programme, but completely lacking in any control levers other than the political clout of its minister and such prime-ministerial support as he enjoyed.[251] As a coordinating department, the Cabinet Office did not possess the legal or constitutional authority to make departments seek its approval for their activities. The position of the Treasury was the mirror image of this. Its varied roles

[247] Sir Bob Kerslake, Sir Nick Macpherson, and Richard Heaton, Letter to Margaret Hodge, Chair, Public Accounts Committee (24 March 2014).

[248] See section 2.2.1 and, for Maude's later views, Public Administration and Constitutional Affairs Committee, *The Work of the Cabinet Office* (HC 2020–21, 118) evidence, qq 647–49, 652.

[249] Francis Maude and Danny Alexander, Letter to Margaret Hodge, Chair, Public Accounts Committee (13 May 2014).

[250] House of Lords Constitution Committee (n 51) paras 164–76.

[251] The tone, and indeed the fact, of the Permanent Secretaries' letter strongly suggests that the Prime Minister's sympathies in this argument lay with them rather than with Maude and Alexander, which is unsurprising given his declared preference for standing back and allowing departments to pursue the goals set for them: Riddell, 'The Coalition and the Executive' (n 21) 123.

and powers that we have already sketched—housekeeping, appropriation, economic management—give it the capacity for almost total control over departmental activity. The all-embracing nature of this power has however made the Treasury, as an institution, acutely conscious of the need for restraint and discrimination in its exercise—though of course a Chancellor could use its power more aggressively, as Gordon Brown's tenure of that office demonstrated. As the regime based on the Exchequer and Audit Departments Act 1866 took effect, the Treasury renounced any intention to control 'the ordinary expenditure placed under the charge of the several departments', reserving the requirement of consent for a range of particular cases, such as additional works or new services,[252] and otherwise relying on establishing delegated spending authorities—of varying amounts depending on the nature and volume of their spending, for each department.[253] As we shall see in chapter 7, the additional opportunities to influence departmental behaviour offered by the development of the Spending Review structure, with its regular examination of departmental performance against a range of expenditure aggregates, were seen in the Treasury as permitting the relaxation of some of its more intrusive traditional controls on departmental spending, for departments with good records in financial management, in pursuance of an approach that has sometimes been labelled as 'earned autonomy'.[254] Those Spending Review opportunities have however also been used parsimoniously by the Treasury. Attempts to link the setting and monitoring of expenditure aggregates to departmental plans and performance have, under varying labels, been a constant feature of central policy since 1997, but have never produced the hoped-for capacity to shape departmental activity to the central will.[255]

[252] Treasury Minute of April 1868, reproduced in *Epitome of Reports from the Committee of Public Accounts 1857–1937* (HC 1937–38, 154) (Epitome I) 20–21.

[253] On current delegation practice, see chapter 8, section 2.4.1.

[254] HM Treasury, *Review of Financial Management in Government* (December 2013) paras 3.4–3.11.

[255] See chapter 3, section IV.

3

The Ministerial Department: Making and Breaking, Structuring, Steering

I Introduction: The Departmental System

The department is the basic building block in the structure of the UK executive. It was described in 1966 by the former head of the Civil Service as the 'effective unit of government',[1] and continues to occupy this position today. We noted in the previous chapter the continuation and intensification of efforts to 'strengthen the centre' of the UK executive during this century. Although at one time political scientists and commentators were debating the possible 'presidentialization' of the Prime Minister's position,[2] No 10 and the Cabinet Office continue to struggle to bend departments to their will. Their political strength—which in any event varies with the personal prestige of the Prime Minister—is counterbalanced by legal and administrative weakness, but that is what often matters most when coordinated action needs to be secured or common standards respected. Before we discuss the changes that have taken place in departmental structure and management in the decades since New Labour came to power in 1997, both as a result of these centre-strengthening initiatives and otherwise, let us remind ourselves of the sources of departmental strength.

First and most important is the fact that, as we emphasized in chapter 1, *legislation normally confers legal powers on individual ministers at the head of the different departments, not on the executive as a whole*. Today, while some important functions are vested in 'His Majesty in Council' or simply in 'His Majesty' (such as the appointment of the Governor and Directors of the Bank of England),[3] the vast majority are vested, via ministers, in departments. The occasional choice in legislation to empower the executive collectively, through the formula 'His Majesty in Council' or providing for delegated legislation in the form of an 'Order in Council', is commonly associated with the extra-territorial application of legislation, including its extension of legislation to Crown dependencies like the Isle of Man, and with a variety of other matters such as the drawing of electoral boundaries and the recognition of professional qualifications. It does not appear to reflect judgements about the value of collective consideration (which may happen informally but never in the Privy Council itself).

The departmental strength deriving from this legal attribution of power is buttressed by other features of our executive arrangements:

[1] Sir Edward Bridges, *The Treasury* (2nd edn, Allen and Unwin, 1966) 117.

[2] Compare Michael Foley, *The Rise of the British Presidency* (Manchester UP 1993) and Graham Allen, *The Last Prime Minister* (Imprint Academic 2003, rev edn 2017), with Martin Smith, *The Core Executive in Britain* (Palgrave MacMillan 1998).

[3] Bank of England Act 1998, s 1(2).

Executive Self-Government and the Constitution. Terence Daintith and Alan Page, Oxford University Press.
 DOI: 10.1093/9780198937630.003.0003

the absence of legal power in Prime Minister or Cabinet to override ministerial decisions;
the prestige of ministers as senior parliamentary and political figures;
the fact that the acts of departmental officials are done in the name of the responsible minister;
arrangements for civil litigation against central government;
the fact that Parliament's annual votes of funds to sustain executive activity are organized by reference to the functions of departments; and
the lengthy history of some departments.

Ministerial enjoyment of legal powers makes for strong ties between ministers and the officials who operate them and limits the scope for their decisions to be called in question by government collectively (or by the 'centre' as its controller). Indeed, the British constitution provides no legal power for Prime Minister or Cabinet to override ministerial decisions. The ability to keep ministers in line thus depends wholly on the conventions of Cabinet government as expressed, for example, in the provisions of the *Ministerial Code* enjoining collective adhesion to Cabinet decisions and stipulating when issues arising in a department should be brought before the Cabinet or its committees.[4] Failure to respect this discipline might ultimately be visited with removal or demotion in the exercise by the Prime Minister of the prerogative of ministerial appointment and dismissal, but the fact that ministers are senior parliamentary and political figures means that there are often significant constraints on the exercise of this power. Prime Ministers who win large parliamentary majorities may for a while enjoy the luxury of a subservient Cabinet—in our period one thinks of Tony Blair in 1997 and 2001, or Boris Johnson in 2019—but it is unlikely that this will last for long enough to enable any permanent shift in the balance between centre and departments. Solidarity between ministers and their officials is emphasized by the fact that, as recognized by the courts in *Carltona Ltd v Commissioners of Works*,[5] the acts of departmental officials are done in the name of the responsible minister, whose confidence they must, in the words of the Civil Service Code, 'deserve and retain'.[6]

Departmental identity is further reinforced by the fact that, since the passage of the Crown Proceedings Act 1947, civil suits in England and Wales are brought against the responsible government department,[7] and Parliament's annual votes of funds to sustain executive activity are organized by reference to the functions of departments.[8] As noted earlier, though,[9] the money, while appropriated between departments, is actually granted to the Treasury—one of the devices supporting the capacity of the Treasury, alone among the central institutions of government, to exercise direct control over departments by regulating their access to funds. Another important underpinning for departments' sense of their individual identity is longevity, permitting the

[4] Cabinet Office, *Ministerial Code* (December 2022) paras 2.1, 2.4, 2.6.
[5] [1943] 2 All ER 560.
[6] *The Civil Service Code* (March 2015).
[7] Crown Proceedings Act 1947, s 17. A list, with addresses for service, is published from time to time by the Minister for the Civil Service (aka the Prime Minister).
[8] Discussed further in chapter 8, section 2.2.
[9] Above, chapter 2, section 4.2.2.

slow development of particular ways of doing things which may produce entrenched departmental attitudes and strong contrasts between one department and another. The Home Office, for example, founded in 1782 and with functions largely undisturbed for two centuries thereafter, was identified in 2000 as being insulated from the rest of Whitehall and particularly resistant to the managerial reforms of the late 20th century.[10] Such an entrenched departmental culture, expressed in officials' attitudes to the department's remit, to the role of ministers, to their own functions, and to relations with the rest of Whitehall,[11] is however less likely to be found in a department like the Department for Energy Security and Net Zero which, since its foundation in 1942 as the Ministry of Fuel and Power, has swung between being part of a large 'industry' department (between 1970 and 1974, 1992 and 2008, and 2016 and 2023), and being a free-standing department the rest of the time. Buffeted by repeated departmental restructurings and radical policy changes, its culture and sense of corporate identity, even its periods of independent existence, were—and probably remain—weak.[12]

Together these characteristics can make departments powerful bodies with a strong sense of corporate identity. Getting them to operate in support of government-wide purposes and policies, to set collective priorities above their own concerns, to adjust their practices in line with common norms, and to accept central direction or guidance, is not easy, as the account in the previous chapter of successive initiatives to achieve a 'stronger centre' will have indicated. In the remainder of this chapter, our aim is to show how key elements of departmental structure, management, and activity have changed since the arrival in government of New Labour in 1997. Our concern here is with the ministerial departments that make up the core executive. We reserve for our next chapter consideration of changes in the broader landscape of the public bodies that surround this core—bodies which, while 'sponsored' or 'supervised' by departments, are designed to operate with a degree of independence. Their relationships with departments have always been problematic, and attempts to fix this have, as we shall see, continued to be pursued. In both chapters the focus is on general institutional and managerial issues: the deployment of the executive's resources of personnel, money, laws, and information, and the respective roles of the centre and departments in this process, will be discussed in chapters 7–12.

II The Making and Unmaking of Ministerial Departments

The ability to change structures and relationships within Whitehall by creating or abolishing departments is clearly one of the most important of a Prime Minister's powers. Some indeed would place it ahead of the power to appoint and dismiss ministers,[13] widely seen as a crucial support for prime-ministerial dominance in the setting

[10] David Marsh, David Richards, and Martin Smith, *Changing Patterns of Governance in the United Kingdom: Reinventing Whitehall* (Palgrave 2001) 65–67, 70–80.

[11] ibid ch 4.

[12] ibid 62–63, 94–98.

[13] ibid 103. Compare Peter Hennessy, *The Prime Minister: The Office and its Holders since 1945* (Allen Lane: The Penguin Press 2000) 61–90; Andrew Blick and George Jones, *Premiership: The Development, Nature and Power of the British Prime Minister* (Imprint Academic 2010) 40.

and implementation of government policy as a whole, and in relations with individual ministers and their departments. It is a power that has been substantially increased by developments over the last 75 years. Parliamentary involvement in decisions as to how the departmental core of executive government is to be organized has significantly diminished, and the corresponding increase of power and discretion has enured to the Prime Minister alone. Two factors have contributed to this shift.

First, until just after the Second World War new departments were created by legislation and major reorganizations of government likewise required it, but in 1946 the Ministers of the Crown (Transfer of Functions) Act conferred power to transfer functions between departments, and to dissolve departments, by Order in Council. While an affirmative resolution of both Houses was required for the latter step, in theory at least creating the opportunity for debate, transfers of functions required only a negative resolution. The powers are now contained in the Ministers of the Crown Act 1975.

Secondly, from the 1960s onward the practice of creating departments by statute, and giving the title of 'Minister of' to those who head them, has ceased. Since that time, most senior ministers, the ones at the head of departments, have been appointed, in the exercise of the prerogative, to the office of Secretary of State, which is in law treated as a single office that may be held by a number of persons.[14] Among Cabinet ministers only the Prime Minister, the Chancellor of the Exchequer, and the Leaders of the House of Commons and House of Lords do not now hold an office of Secretary of State, though a Secretaryship may be held in conjunction with another ministerial post, as with the Secretary of State for Justice, who is also entrusted with the remaining functions of the Lord Chancellor.

The interchangeability of Secretaries of State has not however meant that the procedures under the Ministers of the Crown Act can be dispensed with altogether. Under that Act each new Secretary of State is normally constituted as a corporation sole under a specific title (eg 'Secretary of State for Business and Trade'), so that the department, through the minister, can continue to hold property and exercise powers whatever the identity of the individual incumbent. In addition, legislation will occasionally refer to a particular Secretary of State by use of the departmental title, so that powers and duties so referenced need an Order for their transfer. The result is that when Prime Ministers reorganize their government by creating new departments (or renaming old ones) and reallocating functions, Transfer of Functions Orders may—sometimes but not always—be needed to move property and powers from one (named) Secretary of State to another.[15]

[14] Interpretation Act 1978, sch 1, re-enacting Interpretation Act 1889, s 15; and for the history of the office, AJC Simcock, 'One and Many—the Office of Secretary of State' (1992) 70 Public Administration 535.

[15] For recent examples see the Secretaries of State for Business, Energy and Industrial Strategy, for International Trade and for Exiting the European Union and the Transfer of Functions (Education and Skills) Order 2016, SI 2016/992, and the Secretaries of State for Energy Security and Net Zero, for Science, Innovation and Technology, for Business and Trade, and for Culture, Media and Sport and the Transfer of Functions (National Security and Investment Act 2021 etc) Order 2023, SI 2023/424. In addition, where other ministerial titles survive, orders may be needed for transfers to or from such ministers: see eg SI 2021/1265, transferring functions from the Minister for the Cabinet Office to the new Secretary of State for Levelling Up, Housing and Communities. More recently the minister leading the Cabinet Office has been made a Secretary of State.

In 1999 the establishment of departments in the exercise of the prerogative was described to us as 'a major expansion in the modern use of the prerogative'. Nonetheless, while it certainly moved in the opposite direction from other recent decisions about the prerogative, we thought that Parliament, being more interested in functions than in machinery, might not worry too much about this development, given that the new prerogative departments, in contrast to their statutory predecessors, reflect the reallocation of existing functions rather than the assumption of new ones.[16] In this we were proved wrong when Tony Blair's apparently ill-prepared decision to eliminate the office of Lord Chancellor, establish a Supreme Court to replace the judicial functions of the House of Lords, and modify arrangements for the appointment of judges, all announced without prior consultation as part of a ministerial reshuffle on 12 June 2003,[17] provoked widespread consternation in the judiciary and Parliament.[18] Putting this particular transfer of functions into effect eventually required primary legislation (the Constitutional Reform Act 2005) conferring broad powers to redistribute the Lord Chancellor's functions, as well as no fewer than four Transfer of Functions Orders under the 1975 Act, but the way the original decision was announced drew attention to the lack of any constitutional constraints on this prime-ministerial function.[19]

The subsequent, also controversial, decision, in 2007, to transfer prison functions from the Home Office to a new Ministry of Justice (which also took over the functions of the Department for Constitutional Affairs) provoked the Commons' Public Administration Select Committee to mount an investigation into machinery of government changes. This led to an unusually intensive dialogue between Committee and government. The Committee's principal request following its initial inquiry was that the 1975 Act should be modified so that Parliament would always have the opportunity to debate machinery of government changes. Transfer of Functions Orders should be presented simultaneously with machinery of government proposals, not months later as was commonly the case, and should be accompanied by a business case justifying the expense and disturbance which, the Committee found, commonly accompanied such changes.[20] After an initial governmental rejection of these suggestions,[21] the Committee, doubtless encouraged by the apparent openness of the new Prime Minister, Gordon Brown, to constitutional change, returned to the charge, suggesting that his forthcoming draft bill on constitutional reform should include, alongside measures to put the Civil Service on a statutory footing, measures to allow

[16] Terence Daintith and Alan Page, *The Executive in the Constitution: Structure, Autonomy and Internal Control* (OUP 1999) 33.

[17] For the text of the announcement see LGC contributor, 'Cabinet reshuffle: briefing from No 10 and summary' *Local Government Chronicle* (13 June 2003).

[18] See eg the debate at HC Deb 18 June 2003, vol 407, cols 357–72, and for an account of how the decision came to be made, House of Lords Constitution Committee, *The Cabinet Office and the Centre of Government* (HL 2009–10, 30) paras 188–217.

[19] The successive changes are chronicled in Anne White and Patrick Dunleavy, *Making and Breaking Whitehall Departments: A Guide to Machinery of Government Changes* (Institute for Government 2010) 40–42.

[20] Public Administration Select Committee, *Machinery of Government Changes* (HC 2006–07, 672) paras 35, 36, 45, 46.

[21] *Machinery of Government Changes: Government Response to the Committee's Seventh Report of Session 2006–07* (HC 2007–08, 90).

Parliament effective scrutiny of changes to the organization of government itself.[22] In this they were to be disappointed. But while yielding no ground on the Committee's requests, the government's response offered an informative analysis of the principles of executive organization, as seen from within:

> The organisation and functions of a Government Department are fundamentally a reflection of the responsibilities of the minister in charge of the Department. The allocation of functions between ministers in charge of Departments is the responsibility of the Prime Minister of the day as part of his responsibility for the overall organisation of the Executive, as set out in the *Ministerial Code*. The Prime Minister is responsible for choosing the members of the Cabinet, and determining the responsibilities that each Cabinet member should fulfil. Responsibilities of members of the Cabinet are determined according to the Prime Minister's assessment of the key challenges faced, and, as priorities shift over time, departmental structures will need to change with them. Fundamentally, the organisation of Central Government Departments cannot therefore be separated from the allocation of policy responsibilities among members of the Cabinet; so decisions on changes to Cabinet portfolios will very often bring with them changes to the structure, and sometimes the titles of Departments. Because the allocation of responsibilities by the Prime Minister and the necessary structural changes to Departments are so interlinked, the Government does not believe that giving Parliament a vote on major machinery of government changes before they happen is compatible with preserving the right of the Prime Minister of the day to organise the distribution of responsibilities among members of the Cabinet.[23]

The identity of ministerial responsibilities with departmental functions that is being invoked here is not, however, an inevitable feature of 'Westminster-model' constitutions. One alternative is close at hand: the Scottish system in which powers are conferred on 'the Scottish Ministers' collectively and exercised through a number of Directorates-General, with individual ministerial portfolios that are not necessarily coterminous with Directorate-General boundaries.[24] Further away, Australian federal legislation generally confers regulatory power not on a minister but on the Governor-General, and executive powers may simply be conferred on 'the Commonwealth Minister'. The scope of ministerial portfolios is determined by an 'Administrative Arrangements Order' made by the Governor-General on the proposition of the Prime Minister from time to time, determining which minister is to administer each department (or functions within it) and legislation for which it is responsible.[25]

With no official appetite for considering such alternatives, the mechanisms for machinery of government changes remain the same today as at the beginning of the

22 *Machinery of Government Changes: A Follow-up Report* (2007–08, 160) para 12.

23 Public Administration Select Committee, *Machinery of Government Changes: Further Report with the Government Response to the Committee's First Report of Session 2007–08* (HC 2007–08, 514) app, 4–5.

24 Scotland Act 1998, s 52; Sir John Elvidge, *Northern Exposure: Lessons from the First Twelve Years of Devolved Government in Scotland* (Institute for Government 2011) 31.

25 Terence Daintith and Yee-Fui Ng, 'Executives' in Cheryl Saunders and Adrienne Stone (eds), *The Oxford Handbook of the Australian Constitution* (OUP 2018) ch 25, 595–98.

century. Thanks though to the persistence of the Public Administration Committee, and a thorough study undertaken by the Institute for Government shortly after the Committee's engagement with government on the topic, we are much better informed about how they occur and how much—in terms of financial outlay and administrative disturbance—they cost.[26] The practice thus disclosed bears out the idea, expressed in the government's response to the Public Administration Committee cited above, that finding the right jobs for colleagues is a major driver, perhaps the major driver, for machinery of government changes. According to the Institute for Government investigation,

> [t]op officials strongly take the view that the vast majority of departmental reorganisations occur primarily as a response to political pressures at Cabinet level, including both the need to create jobs to satisfy a particularly valuable member of Cabinet as well as the need to contain the size of Cabinet—with policy and delivery requirements taking second priority.[27]

This is not to say that other factors, such as external change or administrative challenges, play no role in prime-ministerial decisions. While, for example, most machinery of government changes have respected the principle proposed in the Haldane Report of 1918 that the field of activity of a department should be defined 'according to the particular service which it renders to the community as a whole'[28] (education, defence, justice, etc), pressing needs may provoke the creation of departments with wider remits involving coordination or support across services, as when the May government created the Department for Exiting the European Union in July 2016, around a unit carved off from Cabinet Office. Today's pressing needs may however be tomorrow's organizational headaches, and within 16 months difficulties in managing negotiations with the European Union saw the Europe Unit, and that core responsibility, transferred back to Cabinet Office along with DExEU's first Permanent Secretary, changing the department's focus to coordinating domestic preparations for exit. It was wound up on 31 January 2020, as soon as formal withdrawal from the European Union took effect, and responsibility for continuing departmental coordination (on transition arrangements and implementation of post-withdrawal trading arrangements) reverted to the Cabinet Office.

The Institute for Government inquiry suggested that the haste and secrecy surrounding machinery of government changes, prompted by fear of provoking opposition or damaging morale, may be counterproductive in terms of departmental performance, as efforts continue over months or years to adjust to the demands of the new structure. The difficulty of major reorganizations, involving the transfer of significant numbers of officials from one department to another, has been significantly increased by the delegation to departments of responsibility for pay and conditions.

[26] White and Dunleavy (n 19).

[27] ibid 34.

[28] Ministry of Reconstruction, *Report of the Machinery of Government Committee (Haldane)* (Cd 9230, 1918) 7–8.

Merging departments may have radically different pay scales, leading to industrial disputes and diversion of resources to level up pay.[29]

The Coalition government returned in 2010 offered some acknowledgement of parliamentary concerns by publishing a costing on the machinery of government changes it made in its first few months, and its Conservative successor followed up by developing and publishing, in October 2015, Cabinet Office guidance on how such changes were to be carried through, identifying key roles and time periods, and highlighting issues like transfer and continuity of departmental information, and financial adjustments between 'exporting' and 'importing', or new, departments.[30] The guidance reaffirmed the pre-existing Treasury position that the cost of machinery of government changes cannot, save in exceptional circumstances, be carried through into increased departmental spending allocations.[31]

III Re-organizing the Core Department

3.1 The principle

Departmental organization, as described by the Court of Appeal in *Carltona Ltd v Commissioners of Works*,[32] is based on the notion that the decision of a government official is constitutionally that of the minister, who alone is answerable to Parliament. Public business could not be carried on, the Court thought, if the responsible minister had to personally consider every decision. The powers and duties of a minister were thus normally exercised by responsible officials in the minister's department. The obligation of the minister was to ensure that important decisions were taken by appropriately qualified officials. However, the principle that all departmental decisions, even those entrusted to junior civil servants or, for that matter, to machine intelligence, are taken in the name of the minister has as its corollary the 'preposterous fiction'[33] that the Civil Service can *only* act or speak on behalf of ministers. It is also apt to obscure the important differences that exist within departments between types of decision-maker (senior and junior ministers, Permanent Secretaries and other members of the Senior Civil Service, executive agency heads, other civil servants) and between types of activity (policy, delivery, analysis, expert advice, and so on). Over the period we are examining the general tendency has been in the direction of attenuating the fiction, and formalizing these differences, producing more complex intra-departmental structures and lines of accountability. Most of these moves have been effected purely internally, through the exercise of the executive's powers of

[29] White and Dunleavy (n 19) 50–52 on the merger producing the Department for Environment, Food and Rural Affairs (DEFRA). See also at 58–59, on the costs of creating the Department for Work and Pensions.

[30] Both documents are available as Cabinet Office, *Machinery of Government Changes: Guidance*, though the 2015 guidance was withdrawn in November 2023.

[31] Public Administration Select Committee (n 20) para 16.

[32] [1943] 2 All ER 560 (CA).

[33] Guy Lodge and Ben Rogers, *Whitehall's Black Box: Accountability and Performance in the Senior Civil Service* (Institute for Public Policy Research 2006) 68, quoting an anonymous Permanent Secretary.

self-management. Sometimes, however, Parliament may be asked to legislate, as in those cases where the *Carltona* principle is to be displaced by a requirement that only a minister can take a given type of decision.[34]

3.2 Ministerial offices

Ministers remain securely at the top of the departmental hierarchy. Since 1997 their position would appear to have been reinforced by a substantial increase in the number of special advisers they employ, from 38 at the beginning of 1997[35] to 117 in 2023.[36] Most Cabinet ministers now appoint between three and five special advisers, despite the provision in successive Prime Ministers' *Ministerial Codes* that they may appoint only two.[37] The role was well established before the turn of the century, is now enshrined in legislation,[38] and can properly pretend to constitutional status.

An attempt in 2013 by the Coalition government to carry the institutionalization of ministerial advisory roles a step further, however, was remarkably short-lived. This was the idea of building on the minister's Private Office, the small group of staff who manage the minister's time, provide support in taking decisions, communicate those decisions to others in the department and across government, and follow up on progress with their implementation.[39] This would be done by way of the 'Extended Ministerial Office' (EMO), which would contain a group of advisers, normally managed by the minister's Principal Private Secretary, drawn from among serving civil servants and special advisers but which might also include external appointees who—exceptionally—could be appointed as civil servants by the minister.[40] The idea was that this would provide wider but also more cohesive support for ministers. It was for individual Secretaries of State to decide whether they wanted to take advantage of this new possibility, and the absence of enthusiasm suggested that it was an idea whose time had not yet come: no offices were established during the tenure of the Coalition government, and only five in the first years of its Conservative successor. Part of the problem may have been that the initial Cabinet Office Guidance required approval of an EMO proposal from both Coalition partners.[41] In addition, the Civil Service Commission was suspicious of the exceptional ministerial power of direct appointment of civil servants and imposed significant limitations on it, and No 10 wanted a

34 See eg European Union (Withdrawal) Act 2018 (as amended), s 15B (only a minister can co-chair Joint EU–UK Committee under EU Withdrawal Agreement); Safety of Rwanda (Asylum and Immigration) Act 2024, s 5(2) and (4)(b) (decisions on compliance with interim orders of European Court of Human Rights).

35 Martin Stanley, *Special Advisers: Statistics.*

36 Cabinet Office, *Annual Report on Special Advisers 2023* (July 2023). Forty-four of them were employed at No 10.

37 Cabinet Office, *Ministerial Code* (2022) para 3.2.

38 Constitutional Reform and Governance Act 2010, ss 15, 16.

39 Akash Paun, *Supporting Ministers to Lead: Rethinking the Minister's Private Office* (Institute for Government March 2013).

40 Cabinet Office, *Extended Ministerial Offices—Guidance for Departments* (2013, rev June 2015). For normal appointment procedures see chapter 6, section IV.

41 This Guidance can be found at Public Administration Select Committee, *Truth to Power: How Civil Service Reform Can Succeed: Government Response* (HC 2013–14, 955) app 2.

designated member of the EMO to have a dual reporting line to its Implementation Unit as well as to the minister. The facility was withdrawn, and reference to it in the *Ministerial Code* expunged, at the end of 2016.[42]

3.3 The Permanent Secretary

3.3.1 Accountability and management of Permanent Secretaries

The civil servant with overall responsibility for the administration, finances, and personnel of each government department is its Permanent Secretary, who also functions, in ministerial departments, as policy adviser to the Secretary of State. Once this was the central role of the Permanent Secretary, but by the beginning of this century, the proportion of time that could be devoted to policy had substantially diminished as the other roles became more demanding and as other sources of advice—notably through special advisers—increased and multiplied. Management makes increasing demands also on members of the Senior Civil Service at the levels immediately below (Directors-General and Directors), with the result that policy responsibilities are lodged lower in the departmental hierarchy—commonly in Grades 6 and 7, the highest grades outside the Senior Civil Service.

As the top civil servant in the department, the role and performance of the Permanent Secretary have been the subject of regular analysis, critique, and proposals for change in the ceaseless flow of recipes for Civil Service reform (or 'better government') from parliamentary committees,[43] think tanks,[44] and government itself.[45] Over the period we are examining, the general thrust of the government's own proposals, so far as Permanent Secretaries are concerned, has been one of 'sharpening their accountability', to use the language of the 2012 *Civil Service Reform Plan*.[46] Changing rules for Permanent Secretary recruitment so as to give ministers a stronger

[42] Matt Foster, 'Existing Extended Ministerial Offices "to be dismantled", Cabinet Office confirms' *Civil Service World* (17 January 2017).

[43] See eg Public Administration Select Committee, *Making Government Work: the Emerging Issues* (HC 2000–01, 94) paras 18–43; House of Lords Constitution Committee, *The Accountability of Civil Servants* (HL 2012–13, 61) paras 20–28 (commenting on proposals to change procedures for recruitment of Permanent Secretaries); Public Administration Select Committee, *Latest Proposals for Ministerial Involvement in Permanent Secretary Appointments: PASC's Recommendations* (HC 2013–14, 1041); Public Administration and Constitutional Affairs Committee, *The Minister and the Official: The Fulcrum of Whitehall Effectiveness* (HC 2017–19, 497) (analysing Secretary of State-Permanent Secretary relationships—see esp the report of Professor Kakabadse, written evidence, CSE14).

[44] Examples are Guy Lodge and Ben Rogers, *Whitehall's Black Box: Accountability and Performance in the Senior Civil Service* (IPPR 2006) (Permanent Secretaries should become personally accountable for all department operations, including decisions over recruitment and promotion and remuneration); Alex Thomas and others, *A New Statutory Role for the Civil Service* (Institute for Government March 2022) suggesting statutory Civil Service responsibility for implementation of government programmes.

[45] Sir Richard Wilson, *Report to the Prime Minister on Civil Service Reform* (December 1999) esp para 40 (assessment of Permanent Secretaries by reference to assigned personal objectives); HM Government, *The Civil Service Reform Plan* (June 2012) (proposing a greater role for ministers in the appointment of their Permanent Secretaries); HM Government, *Declaration on Government Reform* (June 2021: jointly signed by the Prime Minister on behalf of Cabinet and the Cabinet Secretary on behalf of Permanent Secretaries); Lord Maude, *Independent Review of Governance and Accountability in the Civil Service* (13 November 2023).

[46] HM Government, The Civil Service Reform Plan (June 2012) (n 45) 19–20.

voice has been a prominent objective, but as we shall see in our chapter on the Civil Service, the Civil Service Commission has been an obstacle to achieving the desired degree of ministerial involvement.[47]

A range of other measures, introduced both before and after the 2012 Reform Plan, may be related to 'sharpening accountability', reflecting as they do a widely diffused sense among ministers that it is too difficult to get their departments to do what they want them to do, when they want them to do it.[48] In our period this perhaps began with Permanent Secretaries' commitment to accepting 'personal objectives, on which their performance will be assessed, for taking forward the Government's modernisation agenda and ensuring delivery of the Government's key targets'.[49] Under the Blair government objectives were framed, from 2002, through Performance Partnership Agreements, a form of performance contract between the Cabinet Secretary and departmental Permanent Secretaries.[50] These were discontinued when Departmental Capability Reviews, addressed to the much wider issue of the capacity of the department as a whole to carry out its assigned tasks, were initiated by the incoming Cabinet Secretary in 2005.[51] Such reviews, though widely considered to be effective, did not long survive the change of government in 2010 . . . after which the Coalition government completed the circle by reintroducing Permanent Secretaries' personal objectives. Following its Civil Service Reform Plan, objectives for the year 2012–13 were published, and this continued until 2015–16, after which the practice was abandoned. By this time the increasing vagueness of the objectives, and proliferation of the performance indicators associated with them, had led commentators to dismiss them as meaningless.[52] The 2021 *Declaration on Government Reform*, co-signed by the Prime Minister on behalf of Cabinet and the Cabinet Secretary on behalf of Permanent Secretaries, promised 'revised performance management arrangements for Permanent Secretaries that are closely aligned to the new departmental Outcome Delivery Plans'.[53]

A more significant institutional underpinning for accountability is the introduction of a five-year limit, with no necessary expectation of renewal, on the duration of a Permanent Secretary post, effected by the Coalition government in 2014;[54] and the recognition of the Cabinet Secretary's role as 'line manager' of Permanent Secretaries.[55] This role includes the making of annual performance assessments and arrangements to address inadequate performance, and involvement in processes

[47] Chapter 6, section 4.3.1.

[48] For an objective appraisal of this sentiment, and of minister/Permanent Secretary relations generally, see Andrew Kakabadse, 'Is Government Fit for Purpose?' (written evidence to the Public Administration and Constitutional Affairs Committee (n 43) (HC 2017–19, 497, CSE 14) 9–22.

[49] Wilson (n 45).

[50] Lodge and Rogers (n 44) 48, where they are described as 'effectively a self-evaluation process, with Permanent Secretaries writing letters to themselves'.

[51] Nehal Panchamia and Peter Thomas, *Capability Reviews* (Institute for Government [nd].

[52] Martin Stanley, *Permanent Secretaries' Objectives.*

[53] HM Government, *Declaration on Government Reform* (n 45) Annex, para 12. Outcome Delivery Plans are discussed in section 4.2.2 of this chapter.

[54] Maude (n 45) para 6.41. Maude notes that Blair, as Prime Minister, had decided in 2004 that all senior civil service jobs should be four-year placements, but that 'inexplicably, this decision was not implemented in any recognisable sense'.

[55] See eg Cabinet Secretary: Individual Performance Objectives 2015/16.

through which Permanent Secretaries might be moved around, whether as a result of machinery of government changes of the sort already discussed, or for other reasons. The assessment process includes feedback both from the minister and from the lead non-executive director in the department.[56]

3.3.2 *The Permanent Secretary as Accounting Officer*

There has long been a major qualification to the idea of undivided ministerial accountability for departmental action, which is to be found in the role of the Permanent Secretary as Accounting Officer for the department.

The responsibility for a department's use of public money rests not on its minister but on the Accounting Officer appointed by the Treasury. The power of appointment now derives from the Government Resources and Accounts Act 2000.[57] Once a specific responsibility for departmental accounts had been legislatively recognized in the Exchequer and Audit Departments Act 1866, the Treasury was clear that ministers were not the right people to hold it. Their tenure was too short and they were too burdened by parliamentary responsibilities to do the job properly; instead it should be undertaken by the permanent head of department. That this should be the position had been asserted by Treasury Minute as early as 1872, but it took some 70 years for it to achieve full acceptance: in 1920, when the Public Accounts Committee examined the matter in detail, 37 out of 98 Accounting Officers were not heads of department.[58] The thinking behind the Treasury view was that it was vital to the achievement of a general commitment to economy across government that financial responsibilities in the department should be lodged in its permanent head and not in some separate officer who might be seen as an emissary of the Treasury,[59] nor in Treasury officials placed in each department, as the Select Committee on National Expenditure had recommended in 1919.[60] By 1937 this approach had received the endorsement of the Public Accounts Committee, which was renewed in 1951.[61] Nowadays it is always the Permanent Secretary who is appointed.[62] The Treasury continues to hold firmly to the view that financial accountability should be concentrated in a single individual, and that that individual should be the permanent head of the department, citing Sir Warren Fisher's remark to the Public Accounts Committee of 1921:

[56] On the process as it operated in 2023, see House of Lords Constitution Committee, *Permanent Secretaries: Their Appointment and Removal* (HL 2022–23, 258), Cabinet Office written evidence (SCS0003) paras 9–17. A detailed account of arrangements operating in 2013 is in Akash Paun and Josh Harris, *Accountability at the Top: Supporting Effective Leadership in Whitehall* (Institute for Government 2013). On non-executive directors see further below, section 3.5.

[57] s 5(6). The power was previously contained in Exchequer and Audit Departments Act 1866, s 22.

[58] Public Accounts Committee, *Epitome of Reports from the Committees of Public Accounts 1857 to 1937* (HC 1937–38, HC 154) ('Epitome I') 610–20.

[59] Ian Hamilton, 'Sir Warren Fisher and the Public Service' (1951) 29 Public Administration 3, 18–22.

[60] Epitome I, 610–20.

[61] Epitome I, 760; Public Accounts Committee, *Epitome of Reports from the Committees of Public Accounts 1938 to 1969* (HC 1969–70, 187 ('Epitome II') 184, and see Treasury Memorandum at 189–95.

[62] HM Treasury, *Managing Public Money* (2023 edn) para 3.2.1.

> [I]t should not be open to any permanent head . . . to say 'please, sir, it wasn't me' . . . Pin it on him in the last resort and you have got him as an ally for economy.[63]

The extent of the Permanent Secretary's financial responsibility is not, however, recognized by statute, which simply provides that the Accounting Officer appointed by the Treasury is responsible for the preparation of the department's resource accounts, and their transmission to the Comptroller and Auditor General.[64] It is better expressed in Parliament's expectations about accountability: it is the Permanent Secretary, as Accounting Officer, who will appear before the House of Commons Public Accounts Committee to explain and justify departmental stewardship of funds. The conventional wisdom is that these appearances, in front of a Committee enjoying the support of the National Audit Office's investigatory capacities, represent a demanding discipline for Accounting Officers—and a sometimes uncomfortable one.[65] Parliament cannot, however, apply any sanctions or rewards, beyond the effect of their reports, and press releases, on an Accounting Officer's reputation. In an extreme case—such as deliberately incurring irregular or improper expenditure—an individual might be dismissed from the role of Accounting Officer and the executive responsibilities associated with it. Two chief executives of arm's length bodies (ALBs), each appointed as Accounting Officer of their ALB by the Accounting Officer of the sponsor department, have been dismissed, one in 2015, another in 2017, in the same way.[66] There is no record of any dismissal of a departmental Accounting Officer by the Treasury, but poor performances before the Public Accounts Committee would doubtless figure in any Permanent Secretary's annual performance assessment.

The nature of the Accounting Officer's responsibilities has changed radically since the initiation of the office. This is a reflection of massive increases in both the scale of government and in its institutional complexity. The Treasury's financial rulebook *Managing Public Money* (hereafter referred to as '*MPM*') still refers to the 'personal responsibility' of Accounting Officers,[67] but in an age where an Accounting Officer may have to sign off on an initiative costing billions, like the Asset Protection Scheme that formed part of the government's response to the global financial crisis, in 2009,[68] the term means something radically different from the risk of having to repay from one's own pocket any expenditure one had authorized that was found to be irregular.

The fundamental task of the Accounting Officer is to ensure that the department respects basic principles of public expenditure that have been continuously developed and elaborated since 1866: that it should be regular, proper, provide value for money, and that its objectives should be feasible.[69] We examine the contemporary application

[63] Quoted by Sir Nicholas Macpherson, Permanent Secretary to the Treasury, 'The Origins of Treasury Control' (January 2013).

[64] Government Resources and Accounts Act 2000, s 5(7).

[65] See generally, on relationships between Permanent Secretaries and the Public Accounts Committee, Josh Harris, *Following the Pound: The Accounting Officer in Central Government* (Institute for Government 2013) 20–23.

[66] The ALBs were the Office of Legal Complaints and the Student Loans Company: see references in Benoit Guerin, Julian McCrae, and Marcus Shepheard, *Accountability in Modern Government: What are the Issues?* (Institute for Government 2018) 18, notes 47, 48.

[67] See eg paras 3.3.1, 3.3.3.

[68] See chapter 7, section 2.1.2.

[69] For these principles see now *MPM* (2023) para 3.4 and box 3.2.

of these principles in detail in chapter 8 below. Since 2007, however, Accounting Officer responsibilities have been framed, in *MPM,* in considerably broader terms. As well as financial management, they are expressed to cover 'governance' and 'decision-making' quite generally. Thus Accounting Officers are expected to ensure that the department 'should support its ministers with clear, well-reasoned, timely and impartial advice' and 'make all its decisions in line with the strategy, aims and objectives . . . set by ministers and/or in legislation'.[70] It is unlikely that a published job description for a Permanent Secretary would look very different.[71]

The current approach of *MPM* is to distinguish between responsibilities for specific decisions, responsibilities for specific areas of departmental work, and responsibility for the departmental systems that are designed to ensure its correct and efficient operation. These are, respectively:

> matters requiring the Accounting Officer's personal signature—the Department's annual report and accounts and the governance statement that forms part of it—or personal approval—the Department's voted budget limits and Estimates memorandum and, since 2013 (an expression of the 'sharpening accountability' agenda) all Cabinet Committee papers and major project or policy initiatives;[72]
>
> particular areas where Accounting Officers should take personal responsibility, such as regularity and propriety; affordability and sustainability; value for money; management of opportunity and risk; and learning from experience;[73] and
>
> standards for the department or other body, in the governance and decision-making referred to above, as well as in financial management, which it is the Accounting Officer's responsibility to achieve.[74]

Since 2023 departmental compliance with functional standards also appears as an obligation of Accounting Officers—though not as a matter of 'personal responsibility'.[75]

It is not difficult to see that there is an underlying tension between the fundamental role of the Permanent Secretary to support the ministerial head of department and carry the minister's policies into effect, and the core responsibility of the same person, as Accounting Officer, for the proper management of public funds. The mechanism for reconciling these responsibilities is the right of the Permanent Secretary, as Accounting Officer, to seek a ministerial direction in a case where they appear to conflict. As requesting and issuing ministerial directions is structured by the long-established standards for public expenditure management, we deal with this issue in our discussion of these standards in chapter 8.[76]

[70] *MPM* (2023), para 3.3.1, box 3.1.

[71] The standard form of appointment letter for an Accounting Officer, however, is still of narrower, finance-related scope: see HM Treasury, *Accounting Officer Standard Appointment Letter.*

[72] *MPM* (2023), para 3.3.1.

[73] *MPM* (2023), para 3.3.3.

[74] *MPM* (2023), para 3.3.1, box 3.1.

[75] *MPM* (2023), para 4.2.1 (under 'Working methods). On the functions programme and its problems of enforcement see chapter 2, section 3.4.6.

[76] See chapter 8, section V.

3.4 Other managerial posts

Beneath Permanent Secretary level, there continues to be considerable variation in departmental management structures, a reflection of major differences in the size of departments, and in the extent of the core department's penumbra of sponsored public bodies—discussed in chapter 4—and of varying historical traditions. Some of the larger departments, for example, have a Chief Operating Officer (COO) who manages its corporate services and may also act as line manager for agency chief executives; others of similar size do not. A COO might hold the rank of Director-General, or might be a Second Permanent Secretary. There are, however, two posts below that of Permanent Secretary that are mandated by centrally imposed rules.

3.4.1 The Senior Responsible Owner

The first of these requirements stems from continuing concerns, in places like the Treasury, the Public Accounts Committee, and the National Audit Office (NAO), about excessive optimism and haste in the consideration and progressing of major spending programmes. Government has sought to address weaknesses in departmental management of large projects and programmes through expert support and supervision by an Infrastructure and Projects Authority established within the Cabinet Office in 2016 and reporting both to the Cabinet Office and to the Treasury. Its assessments of major departmental projects form an essential part of the Treasury's approval procedures.[77] Its specialists are attached temporarily to departments at key stages in project development. The Authority leads the project delivery function, and has developed the Project Delivery Standard, designed

> to set expectations for the direction and management of portfolios, programmes and projects ensuring value for money and the successful, timely and cost effective delivery of government policy and business objectives.[78]

Among the most important of those expectations, from a constitutional point of view, is the requirement that a department must appoint a 'senior responsible owner' (SRO) for all projects that qualify as 'government major projects'.[79] This person does not actually direct and manage the project—that is the role of a project director reporting to the SRO—but sponsors and steers it and is 'personally accountable' for its success both to the Accounting Officer and, since 2014, to Parliament. This latter responsibility was imposed by way of a change to the 'Osmotherly Rules' which govern the relationships

[77] Chapter 8, section 2.4.2.

[78] HM Government, *Government Functional Standard GovS 002: Project Delivery: Portfolio, Programme and Project Management* (version 2.0, 15 July 2021) para 1.1.

[79] For the definition of a 'major project' see chapter 8, section 2.4.2. For requirements relating to the appointment, responsibilities, and tenure of SROs, see generally Infrastructure and Projects Authority, *Project Delivery: Guidance. The Role of the Senior Responsible Owner* (version 2.0, April 2023) and Infrastructure and Projects Authority, *Mandate* (January 2021) 8; Comptroller and Auditor General, *Delivering Major Projects in Government: A Briefing for the Committee of Public Accounts* (HC 2015–16, 713); Public Administration and Constitutional Affairs Committee, *Delivering the Government's Infrastructure Commitments through Major Projects* (HC 2019–21, 125) paras 105–14; and see Cabinet Office, SRO appointment letter (April 2015).

between civil servants and parliamentary select committees,[80] and is reflected in the appointment letters issued to these SROs. The significance of this personal responsibility is doubtful, given the high turnover of SROs on some projects, of which the Public Accounts Committee has strongly complained in the past.[81] The Rules specify that the SRO's responsibility is only for the implementation of the project, not for the policy it reflects, but it is clear that—whatever 'personal accountability' means for the SRO—the effect of this move is to draw a line of demarcation between political and administrative responsibility for projects. Government now regularly publishes a list of all SROs for all projects and programmes falling within the Government Major Projects Portfolio. The Project Delivery Standard also envisages the appointment of an SRO for all other departmental projects and programmes, as part of a standardized governance structure.

3.4.2 The Finance Director

One of the key recommendations of the Gershon Review of public sector efficiency, commissioned by the Prime Minister and Chancellor to accompany the 2004 Spending Review, was that each department should have a professionally qualified Finance Director, responsible for advising the Permanent Secretary and members of the departmental board on the financial management of the department's operations.[82] It was already the case that every department was required to have a Principal Finance Officer (PFO) to deal with its finances and with its relations with the Treasury (in smaller departments it might be combined with responsibility for Establishments), though a requirement that departments consult the Treasury before appointing their PFOs had been removed in 1997.[83] No professional qualification was required, an omission the Public Accounts Committee noted when it appeared that at the time of an expenditure mishap the Foreign and Commonwealth Office's PFO was unqualified, 'a rising generalist'. The Committee commented:

> [A]ccounting institutes put people through years of training when generalists in the Treasury and elsewhere say 'We can do it. We have had a little experience. We have read the manual'?[84]

The qualifications and experience that Finance Directors must possess are now set out in detail in *Managing Public Money*.[85] The change can be seen as foreshadowing the drive for professionalism that lay behind the Coalition's much wider-ranging functions programme.[86]

[80] See Cabinet Office, *Giving Evidence to Select Committees: Guidance for Civil Servants* (October 2014) paras 25–30.

[81] Two projects referred to in evidence to the Committee in 2011 had, respectively, more than one SRO per year, and 10 SROs over five years: Public Accounts Committee, *Accountability for Public Money* (HC 2010–12, 740) evidence, qq 4, 8.

[82] Sir Peter Gershon, *Releasing Resources to the Front Line: Independent Review of Public Sector Efficiency* (2004) para 3.23.

[83] HM Treasury, *Government Accounting* (1989, loose-leaf), paras 6.2.40–42, removed by amendment no 7, March 1997. *Government Accounting* was the predecessor publication of *Managing Public Money*.

[84] Public Accounts Committee, *Treasury Controls* (HC 1998–99, 157) qq 65, 72.

[85] *MPM* (2023), Annex 4.1.

[86] See chapter 2, section 3.4.6.

3.5 Departmental boards

In the light of the Treasury's insistence that ultimate responsibility for the financial affairs of a department must be concentrated in a single individual, it is a little surprising to see it introducing, in 2005, a Corporate Governance Code of Practice for government departments envisaging that each department

> should be managed by an effective board which, within the strategic framework set by the minister (or, in the case of a non-ministerial department, by legislation), supports the head of the department [that is, the Permanent Secretary] by advising ministers and taking ownership of the department's performance.[87]

Such a board should include independent non-executive members

> to ensure that executive members are supported and constructively challenged in their role... that no individual or small group of individuals can dominate the board's decision-making and that the board can draw upon a wide range of experience.[88]

A structure combining a board with strategic concerns and a chief executive responsible for the day-to-day operations of the organization had long been the norm for most executive non-departmental public bodies (NDPBs), and also of public corporations and, under general company law concepts, of government-owned companies as well. The legal capacities of the latter two types of body would be vested in the board; this might also be the case with executive NDPBs, though in some, they were given to the chief executive, with the board playing an essentially advisory role. This latter model came also to be adopted for executive agencies. These developments, while they may be seen as an expression of the general ideas behind the 'New Public Management', represented a conscious attempt by civil servants to draw on private sector institutions and experience ('corporate governance') to support the efficiency and accountability of bodies that had been detached from direct ministerial responsibility.[89]

New Labour, on its accession to power in 1997, was ready to push this approach further towards the heart of government. It began with non-ministerial departments, where statutory powers and responsibilities were concentrated in an individual, normally a civil servant with Permanent Secretary rank—like the Directors-General who headed the utilities regulators set up in this form after privatization in the 1980s. Following a review of utility regulation in 1997–98, legislation was introduced transferring the regulatory powers of Directors-General to boards composed mainly of non-executive directors overseeing the activities of an executive team headed by a Chief Executive Officer.[90]

[87] HM Treasury, *Corporate Governance in Central Government Departments: Code of Good Practice* (July 2005) 7 (principle 2).
[88] ibid 11 (principle 4).
[89] Stephen Wilks, 'Boardization and Corporate Governance in the UK as a Response to Depoliticization and Failing Accountability' (2007) 44 Public Policy and Administration 652.
[90] See eg Utilities Act 2000, s 1, establishing a Gas and Electricity Markets Authority, whose executive arm is Ofgem (the Office of Gas and Electricity Markets).

Any further extension of the board model of management to ministerial departments would not require legislation, but would obviously have to take account both of the principle of ministerial responsibility and of Accounting Officer responsibilities for departmental finance. Some of the larger departments with complex structures had already experimented with the use of a departmental board. What was then the Department of Social Security, for example, had 98% of its staff working in five executive agencies delivering the department's services; it established a departmental board to oversee departmental strategy, chaired by the Permanent Secretary, comprising the heads of the agencies, along with the Head of the department's Policy Group, its Solicitor, its Principal Employment and Finance Officers, the Head of Corporate Management, and three members from outside the department.

The essential purpose of the 2005 Code seems to have been to formalize and generalize this approach. Happily for Permanent Secretaries, the Code reaffirmed their responsibility as Accounting Officers: they were to be supported (and 'challenged') by the board rather than being subject to it. The innovation thus caused little disturbance to the Accounting Officer role, and was received with some scepticism: observers within government described boards at the time as 'not actually collectively responsible for anything'; 'basically an advisory panel for the Permanent Secretary'; or 'nothing more than a vehicle for Permanent Secretary patronage'.[91] An annex tucked away at the back of the Code did however hint at more radical measures:

> A.3 . . . As management becomes increasingly professional and departmental boards assume greater responsibilities, the question of whether accountability to Parliament is best served through an unchanged Accounting Officer role deserves continuing discussion.
>
> A.4 Most radically, it is for discussion whether, under the direction of the minister, the board collectively could take responsibility for the day to day management of the department. The responsibility of the head of department to report to the Public Accounts Committee might be as the board's chair/representative.[92]

This wild talk did not reappear in the revised version of the Code issued by the Coalition government in 2011 under the joint imprint of the Treasury and the Cabinet Office, or in the latest (2017) version. Significant changes were however made. While the 2005 guidance had left discretion as to who should chair and appoint the board, the 2011 version made it clear that these were functions of the Secretary of State, not the Permanent Secretary as had been the position adopted in all departments up to that time. It also called for most non-executive members to be appointed from the commercial private sector, and for boards to be 'balanced', in that they should have roughly equal numbers of ministers, senior civil servants, and non-executives.[93] Their role, however, was to be limited to 'advice and support on the operational implications

[91] Reported in Lodge and Rogers (n 44) 70–71, and, for a comprehensive assessment of board activity and effectiveness before the Coalition changes, see Simon Parker and others, *Shaping Up: A Whitehall for the Future* (Institute for Government 2010) 43–72.

[92] HM Treasury, *Corporate Governance in Central Government Departments* (n 87) 17.

[93] A requirement repeated, since 2010, in the *Ministerial Code*: see now Cabinet Office, *Ministerial Code* (December 2022) para 3.5.

and effectiveness of policy proposals': policy itself remained the fief of ministers with official advice. At the same time non-executives were expected to play a more prominent role, leading board committees such as the Audit and Risk Committee, meeting the minister as a group without officials present, and, through a Lead Non-Executive appointed for each department, providing input to a government-wide non-executive network led by a government Lead Non-Executive. And there was a sting in the tail for Permanent Secretaries:

> As a last resort, if Non-Executive Board Members judge that the Permanent Secretary is an obstacle to effective delivery, they will be able to recommend to the Prime Minister, Secretary of State and Head of the Home Civil Service that the Permanent Secretary should be removed from his or her post.[94]

This worried the Public Accounts Committee, who felt that it might weaken the ability of the Permanent Secretary, as Accounting Officer, to stand up to the minister; the view of the government, however, was that non-executive board members were in general likely to reinforce the Accounting Officer's position vis-à-vis the minister.[95] In 2013 Lord Browne, then the Government Lead Non-Executive, told the Public Accounts Committee that no such recommendation had been made up to that time, because objectives for senior civil servants were not clear enough to use as the standard for evaluating individual performance.[96] A House of Lords inquiry in 2022–23 prompted by departures and dismissals of Permanent Secretaries did not identify any subsequent examples.[97]

Visibility and significance of the non-executive role has been emphasized by greater prominence for the Government Lead Non-Executive, who has made a number of appearances before parliamentary select committees and also presents an annual report to Parliament.[98]

The role itself has also been the subject of intensive examination from within and outside Parliament.[99] While departments have since 2011 been offered less discretion in their board arrangements, the Code still operates on a 'comply or explain' basis, enabling departments to modify its application if they can present good reasons for doing so. An exception is provided by the obligation to have a professional Finance Director as a member of the Board. The contribution of boards has varied considerably across departments. One interesting finding in the survey of non-executives conducted

[94] HM Treasury and Cabinet Office, *Corporate Governance in Central Government Departments: Code of Good Practice* (July 2011) 7. See now the April 2017 version, para 3.8.

[95] Public Accounts Committee, *Accountability for Public Money* (HC 2010–12, 740) 16, and evidence, qq 30 (Francis Maude MP, Minister for the Cabinet Office) 38 (Sir Gus O'Donnell, Cabinet Secretary).

[96] (HC 2013–14, 473) para 7. The new objectives introduced for 2012–13 (text at n 52) had not yet been applied in performance reviews.

[97] House of Lords Constitution Committee, *Permanent Secretaries: Their Appointment and Removal* (HL 2022–23, 258).

[98] See eg The Government Lead Non-Executive, *Annual Report 2021–22*.

[99] Public Administration and Constitutional Affairs Committee, *The Role of Non-Executive Directors in Government* (HC 2022–23, 318); Maude (n 45) paras 7.1–7.14, and for external analyses Robert Hazell and others, *Critical Friends? The Role of Non Executives on Whitehall Boards* (UCL Constitution Unit January 2018); Commission for Smarter Government, *Departmental Boards: Boosting Reform* (April 2021).

for the Public Administration and Constitutional Affairs Committee was that non-executives thought they contributed less through membership of the departmental board than through other activities, like chairing the Audit Committee, reviewing the arm's length bodies sponsored by the department, or advising on performance and management.[100] Though the Treasury promulgated the initial move to generalize use of boards in 2005, and the guidance to which it still puts its name says that boards, chaired by the department's lead minister, should meet at least on a quarterly basis,[101] its departmental board is among the least active, meeting only once a year.[102] Instead the Treasury delegates most functions of its board to a Sub-Committee, chaired by the Lead Non-Executive and on which the other non-executives also sit alongside its senior officials, but with no ministers present.[103] This lack of ministerial involvement has been attributed by the Treasury to the fact that it lacks the large operational responsibilities that some big spending departments have.

IV Framing Departmental Decision-Making: Planning and Performance

So far in this chapter we have described the efforts made over the years since 1997 at the centre of government to reshape the organization of ministerial departments in the interests of greater effectiveness. Despite the crises and occasional political turbulence that characterized the executive's working environment in the first quarter of this century, and regularly reiterated commitments to 'reform', organizational changes across and within departments—such as the generalized introduction of departmental boards—have left key roles and relationships largely untouched. The picture looks rather different when we turn from departmental organization to departmental decision-making: what departments decide to do, how they go about doing it, and how they account for what they have done. The basic constitutional framework for these activities is provided by the principle of ministerial responsibility. In its *individual* aspect such responsibility is expressed through the minister's position as the repository of most of the legal powers employed by the department he or she heads, and by the need to account to Parliament for their exercise. In its *collective* aspect such responsibility requires departmental loyalty, in the exercise of these powers, to the governmental policies collectively agreed at Cabinet level. Given that our primary concern in this work is with what goes on *inside* the executive, our focus in what follows is on the collective aspect, and here, sustained efforts have been made by successive 21st-century administrations to create means for shaping departmental decision-making to meet central policy priorities and performance standards.

[100] Public Administration and Constitutional Affairs Committee (n 99) para 10 and Annex A.

[101] HM Treasury and Cabinet Office, *Corporate Governance in Central Government Departments: Code of Good Practice* (April 2017) paras 2.4, 3.3.

[102] Public Administration and Constitutional Affairs Select Committee, *The Minister and the Official: The Fulcrum of Whitehall Effectiveness* (HC 2017–19, 497) para 101.

[103] HM Treasury, *Annual Report and Accounts 2022–2023* (HC 2022–23, 1467) 99. The Sub-Committee met five times in the year under report.

4.1 New Labour: The Public Service Agreement (PSA)

The return to power in 1997 of a Labour government intensely conscious of its reforming mission led to a much-strengthened focus on coherence of policy, and delivery of policy objectives, across government. This was most visibly expressed in the government's overhaul of its communication function, which we examine in detail in chapter 12, but it extended across all aspects of departmental activity. It was understood that while the government's political cohesion could be expected to ensure the alignment of departmental objectives with those expressed centrally in election manifestos and later cross-government policy statements, something more might be needed to secure that this process produced the desired results in terms of performance. New Labour's powerful Chancellor of the Exchequer, Gordon Brown, was unusual in seeing his office as a platform for promoting social as well as economic reform, which may explain why the government's chosen vehicle for driving departmental performance from the centre was the Comprehensive Spending Review (CSR), Brown's more rigorous approach to the well-established system of medium-term planning and control of public expenditure (PES) that he inherited.[104] At a late stage in the design of this system the Treasury introduced the idea of using CSR as a tool for the improvement of departmental performance. As part of the process of settling with the Treasury its total spending allocation over the three-year review period, each department would have to commit to a set of objectives, supported by a range of performance targets, aligned with the government's broad manifesto policies and promises. These commitments were described as

> detailed public service agreements between departments and the Treasury about how these overall totals will be spent, with clear objectives and output and efficiency targets that departments have agreed to meet.[105]

We remarked in 1999 that the terminology of 'agreement'

> seems to carry into the heart of government the general shift, in all areas of social and economic life, from coercive or unilateral modes of regulation to 'economic' instruments operating through 'consensual' incentives, and that it also reflected the plural character of the United Kingdom executive: if departments were not seen as distinct and in some sense autonomous there would be no sense in their making agreements with each other.[106]

The issue of enforcement of such 'agreements' was from beginning to end highly problematic. This was among the problems raised by the Treasury Select Committee as the programme was being rolled out. The Committee was not convinced that

[104] For details of the CSR and its evolution see below, chapter 7, section 3.1.

[105] Chancellor of the Exchequer, *Modern Public Services for Britain: Investing in Reform* (Cm 4011, July 1998) Foreword. See also HM Treasury, *Public Services for the Future: Modernisation, Reform, Accountability Comprehensive Spending Review: Public Service Agreements 1999–2002* (Cm 4181, December 1998).

[106] Daintith and Page (n 16) 191–92.

greater Treasury involvement in departmental spending would necessarily lead to more efficient deployment of resources; it was not clear as to how the quantitative measures targeted under the agreements would result in services being improved; and it wondered what sanctions could actually be taken against departments which did not meet the targets set out in the agreements. Would the education budget really be cut, it asked, if in two years' time class sizes and truancy rates were stable or rising instead of reducing according to the Department for Education's targets?[107]

The government's initial answer to this last question was no:

> If progress is slipping, a Cabinet Committee chaired by the Chancellor of the Exchequer will look with the relevant Minister or Ministers at ways of getting performance back on track. Should a target not be met there is no question of money being deducted from the budget for that department. Nor will additional funding over and above that already allocated be made available simply because a department is failing to meet its targets, but support and advice will be given by the committee.[108]

This statement needs to be seen in the context of the mode of preparation of the first round of Public Service Agreements (PSAs). They were produced in a hurry by recycling an existing Treasury programme, Output Performance Analyses, designed to relate reported departmental performance with objectives, and then adding targets proposed by departments—no less than 600 of them in total, a grab-bag of inputs, outputs, and outcomes, some quantified, most not. Spending allocations had already been approved while the agreements were being developed, so there was no obvious mechanism for enforcing the commitments they expressed.[109]

While the original PSAs were supposed to last as long as the CSR—three years—a first revision took place in 2000, with further remodelling in 2002 and 2004, and a completely new set of PSAs accompanied the 2007 CSR. The device was steadily refined, with far fewer but more demanding targets, down to 110 in 2004, and in 2007, only 30, all of which were cross-departmental in nature and focused on the government's most important priorities. Although from 2000 onwards the negotiation of PSAs was explicitly tied to the Spending Review process, the problem of using allocation as a lever to improve performance remained. In 1999 the government told the Treasury Committee that the PSA process would be strengthened if in presenting the results of the next review of spending it set out how key decisions about the allocation of resources in practice had been linked to outputs.[110] In response to the Committee's remark that it could see no sign of this in the 2000 review documentation, the government replied that '[o]utput information contained in the PSAs was used to judge the value for money of marginal increases in spending for one area over another', and that '[a]llocations of extra resources are linked to commitments to challenging targets'.[111]

107 Treasury Committee, *The New Fiscal Framework and the Comprehensive Spending Review* (HC 1997–98, 960) para 44.

108 HM Treasury (Cm 4181) (n 105) 2.

109 Nehal Panchamia and Peter Thomas, *Public Service Agreements and the Prime Minister's Delivery Unit* (Institute for Government [nd]) 2–3.

110 Treasury Committee, *Spending Review 2000* (HC 1999–2000, 485) para 22.

111 Treasury Committee, *Spending Review 2000: The Government's Response to the Committee's Ninth Report of Session 1999–2000* (HC 1999–2000, 941) para (k).

The absence of any reference to actual performance in this response doubtless reflects the fact that at this time the Treasury had no reliable means of relating departmental resources to departmental performance in pursuit of objectives. As we shall see, this is still the case.

Over the whole period of operation of PSAs, in fact, from 1998 to 2010, there is little sign that financial discipline was an effective support for PSA commitments. Instead, the basis of control was political. One sign of this was that as early as 2000, PSAs were no longer being described as agreements between departments and the Treasury but as 'agreements with the taxpayer, something for something, for the resources that are put in': clearly a political concept.[112] PSAs' political profile was raised in 2001 by the creation of the Prime Minister's Delivery Unit (PMDU), which supported a focus on the PSAs of four departments (Home Office, Health, Education, and Transport) whose performance was central to the achievement of the government's main social objectives. The Unit was a small but well-resourced office which monitored and rated the performance of these departments and supported a programme of regular 'stocktakes' by the Prime Minister with the responsible Secretaries of State.[113] The general principle of ministerial responsibility for achievement of PSA targets had been stated in 2000;[114] the personal involvement of the Prime Minister in these stocktakes gave it—at least in these core areas—real political weight. Elsewhere, however, there was little monitoring by the Treasury, and when the Prime Minister's attention was increasingly diverted by the Iraq War, the Unit also began to lose effectiveness. When PSAs were relaunched under the Brown government in 2007 on a cross-departmental basis, monitoring and control were entrusted to a set of Cabinet committees, again supported by PMDU, which had now become part of the Treasury.[115] Each PSA had a lead department, and was managed by a delivery board comprising senior officials from all the departments involved. Primary responsibility for delivery on PSA targets devolved upon the Secretary of State for the lead department answering to the relevant Cabinet committee. Here reliance on individual ministerial responsibility was more problematic: the Prime Minister was not directly involved, and ministers were likely to attach more importance to purely departmental objectives on which they would be judged than on being 'a good number-two or number-three player when somebody else would take all the credit for what was achieved'.[116]

4.2 Coalition and Conservative governments: from PSAs to ODPs

4.2.1 2010 to 2021: Departmental Business Plans and Single Departmental Plans

Opinions within the executive about the PSA programme varied enormously, from 'transformative of everything government did' and 'a necessary discipline' to 'a PR

[112] HM Treasury, *2000 Spending Review: Public Service Agreements* (Cm 4808, July 2000) iii.

[113] Panchamia and Thomas (n 109) 4–6.

[114] HM Treasury, *2000 Spending Review* (n 112) para 1.18.

[115] For details on the 2007 system see HM Treasury, *Meeting the Aspirations of the British People: 2007 Pre-Budget Report and Comprehensive Spending Review* (Cm 7227, October 2007) 36; Panchamia and Thomas (n 109) 7–9.

[116] Quoted from an interview with a Permanent Secretary by Panchamia and Thomas (n 109) 9.

exercise' and 'a ridiculous bureaucracy'.[117] One of the first actions of the Coalition government that took office in 2010 was to cancel the programme, which it regarded as over-complex, reliant on top-down performance management, and involving too many politically motivated targets. Another possible reason for its disappearance at this time may be that when public spending is being cut back, as the Coalition was committed to doing, output targets or numbers are more likely to reveal blame-attracting results like poorer public services than good news for voters.[118] At the same time the Coalition had to acknowledge that it still needed 'structures for ensuring departmental accountability for achieving more for less'.[119] Over the next 10 years or so the Coalition government and its Conservative successors replayed the Labour experience. The Departmental Business Plans introduced by the Coalition to replace PSAs and somehow eradicate the 'top-down' characteristics and target fetishism of that programme[120] gave way in 2015 to 'Single Departmental Plans' (SDPs) which attempted to bring together departmental resources and objectives, and a number of targets related to them, over the next two to three years. These were drawn up by departments following joint Cabinet Office and Treasury guidance, under the joint responsibility of the minister, the Permanent Secretary, and the lead non-executive director on the departmental board, and required the approval of the Minister for the Cabinet Office and the Chief Secretary to the Treasury.[121] Approval was not always initially granted: two SDPs were rejected on first submission, with the departments told to go back and do their homework again.[122] Only summaries of the plans were published, containing a list of objectives, some quantitative indicators of departmental activity, and already published Spending Review allocations—but with no attempt to link these different elements together. The Public Accounts Committee found them 'very high-level, general and unhelpful'.[123]

The government's consistent refusal to agree to the publication of the plans in full, on the ground that they might contain sensitive information—like planned workforce reductions—made it hard to judge how meaningful they were as frameworks for departmental activity, but it is clear from the history of departmental planning since 2010 that the Treasury continued to struggle to make significant progress with joining up spending, objectives, and performance, to the point where a further restructuring of the system was thought necessary in 2021. It acknowledged in 2013 that in some cases departments might have been 'gaming the system' by failing to reveal that they had no evidence of any link between increased spending and improved outcomes.[124]

[117] Reported in Christopher Hood and others, *The Way the Money Goes: The Fiscal Constitution and Public Spending in the UK* (Oxford 2023) 172.

[118] ibid 173–74.

[119] HM Treasury, *The Spending Review Framework* (Cm 7872, June 2010) para 2.7.

[120] See David Cameron, *PM's speech on Business Plans* (8 November 2010) for an account of the differences.

[121] Comptroller and Auditor General, *Government's Management of its Performance: Progress with Single Departmental Plans* (HC 2016–17, 872).

[122] Comptroller and Auditor General, *Improving Government's Planning and Spending Framework* (HC 2017–19, 1679) para 2.4.

[123] Public Accounts Committee, *Improving Government Planning and Spending* (HC 2017–19, 1556) para 22.

[124] Public Accounts Committee, *Managing Budgeting in Government* (HC 2012–13, 661) para 11.

In 2016 it could not provide a single example of a department's changing or dropping a commitment as a result of the supposedly improved planning processes provided by the Plans, many of which failed to assign any budgets to departmental objectives.[125] A 2018 survey of senior departmental officials by the NAO indicated only qualified acceptance of SDPs as a framework for action, with only 58% of respondents agreeing that the Plan was used by senior management for decision-making.[126] No less strikingly, it disclosed that the Treasury's own spending teams generally did not refer routinely to departmental SDPs in performing their work.[127] The NAO's assessment was bleak:

> Recent spending reviews have been characterised by bilateral deal-making between departments and HM Treasury, and incentives to meet short-term spending targets . . . This creates a risk that departments and HM Treasury are complicit in agreeing over-optimistic delivery or spending reduction plans that have no realistic chance of being delivered. Departments have their short-term funding needs met; and HM Treasury gets the savings it needs to meet its fiscal targets. Performance problems that begin to appear can be patched up with short-term funding boosts, when the fiscal position makes this possible. Meanwhile the long-standing lack of transparency around performance and value for money has made it extremely difficult for Parliament or citizens to hold government to account for failure to deliver.[128]

In 2018 the Treasury was offering the same bromides as in 2000: 'The Treasury is working with the Cabinet Office on how to use SDPs to challenge bids and inform allocations at the next Spending Review.'[129]

4.2.2 2021–: Outcome Delivery Plans

From 2021 to 2022 SDPs were replaced by ODPs—Outcome Delivery Plans. The 2020 one-year Spending Review, it was claimed, 'included a greater focus on the intended outcomes of spending bids, as well as plans to monitor and evaluate progress towards them'.[130] The switch to 'outcomes' was inspired both by the notion of a 'Public Value Framework' designed to maximize the social value harnessed by public spending,[131] and by perceived defects in the SDP system: excessive focus on inputs and outputs at the expense of real-world outcomes (such as educational attainment, crime, or life expectancy); ineffectiveness in coordinating cross-cutting outcomes; and failure to

[125] Public Accounts Committee, *Managing Government Spending and Performance* (HC 2016–17, 710) 6.

[126] Comptroller and Auditor General (n 122) 34 (figure 8).

[127] On the composition and work of the spending teams see above, chapter 2, section 4.3.

[128] Comptroller and Auditor General (n 122) para 4.13.

[129] Public Accounts Committee (n 123) para 12. On the position subsequent to the Comptroller and Auditor General's 2018 report (n 122) see HM Treasury, *The Government Financial Reporting Review* (CP 67, April 2019) 105–06, noting that from the 2018–19 planning year, departments were required to submit quarterly performance reports against their single departmental plan objectives to Cabinet Office and the Treasury. On departmental reporting generally see below, chapter 11, section 2.2.

[130] Letter from the Cabinet Office and HM Treasury to the Chair of the Public Accounts Committee, 'Outcome Delivery Plans' (16 March 2021).

[131] HM Treasury, *Delivering Better Outcomes for Citizens: Practical Steps for Unlocking Public Value* (17 November 2017).

integrate financial management in the Treasury with the wider oversight of government performance in No 10 and the Cabinet Office. Departments were accordingly required to propose priority outcomes and metrics for measuring progress in their delivery, and these were agreed with the Treasury as part of the Spending Review process. Associated with this as part of a revised performance framework were a greater emphasis on deliverability, improved monitoring and reporting procedures, more extensive joint working through cross-departmental priorities, and centrally driven dissemination of best practice in the processes and culture of planning and performance management. Thanks to all this, 'the new ODPs and their corresponding performance information will be used to inform future Spending Reviews.'[132] 'Ownership' of the programme was however now clearly shared between Treasury and Cabinet Office, with input also from the Prime Minister's Office.[133]

Unfortunately the advancement of the programme into 2022–23 was overtaken by the government's decision in May 2022 to make very large cuts in Civil Service staffing, after departments had already prepared their draft 2022–23 ODPs. The programme of cuts was not proceeded with by the Sunak government that took office in October, but the updating of plans that had already been commenced was still necessary, and the decision was taken that there should be no publication of the 2022–23 plans, with progress in that year being reported in the annual departmental reports and accounts. Subsequently Treasury and Cabinet Office ministers jointly announced that publication would not be required for 2023-24 either, public accountability for performance again being limited to reporting on the delivery of ODPs in 2023–24 reports and accounts. Apparently preparing summary plans for publication would make it too difficult for departments to focus on delivering the Prime Minister's policy priorities.[134]

Departments have now been producing plans, multi-year or single year, in accordance with centrally stipulated designs, over almost the entire period since 1997. It would, however, be rash to assume that such planning has become embedded in our constitutional practice. We shall argue, in chapter 7, that this might now be the position in relation to Spending Reviews and the fiscal rules associated with them, but those processes involve interactions—albeit weak ones—with Parliament. Defining and pursuing departmental objectives is still, as the 2023 decision to draw a veil of secrecy over the process demonstrates, regarded as falling wholly within the sphere of executive autonomy, and is best regarded as supported by practical necessity without any associated constitutional obligation or, indeed, expectation. At the same time, its links with departments' reporting and accounting obligations, which have a firm basis in statute, provide an avenue for continued external scrutiny. We examine these obligations, and 21st-century developments in relevant practice, in chapter 11 below.

132 The original 2020–21 ODPs are collected at <www.gov.uk/government/collections/outcome-delivery-plans>.

133 Rhys Clyne and Nick Davies, *Outcome Delivery Plans: The Case for Keeping and Improving the Government's Performance Framework* (Institute for Government September 2022) 24.

134 Letter from the Chief Secretary to the Treasury and the Minister for the Cabinet Office to the Chair of the Public Administration and Constitutional Affairs Committee (6 July 2023).

V Framing Departmental Decision-Making: Guidance on Decision-Making

5.1 In general

Departmental officials do not lack for advice on how to do their job. One of the most striking features of the operation of the executive in this century is the extraordinary expansion of the mass of rules, guidance, and advice furnished by the centre to departments and other bodies. There now seems to be a guidance document on virtually any activity or process that is common to departments across government. While some such documentation represents new central policy, much may have previously existed in a shape that was either less formal, or was confidential within the executive, or both. Much of this guidance is considered in this book as part of our discussion of particular areas or aspects of executive government. In relation to structural issues, we have already noted in this chapter the Cabinet Office guidance on *Machinery of Government Changes* and the *Corporate Governance Code of Practice.* In particular subject areas, requirements imposed by *Managing Public Money*, for example, are extensively analysed in chapter 8 below on expenditure discipline, the Cabinet Office's *Guide to Making Legislation* is treated in chapter 10 on legislation and regulation, while chapter 12 offers analysis of the content and significance of *Government Communication Service Propriety Guidance* addressed to departmental communications services.

Some of the general guidance on decision-making has been in circulation for decades. The Treasury first produced a manual of guidance on departmental accounting—in effect the ancestor of *Managing Public Money*—in 1915, covering everything from parliamentary supply procedure to the working of punched card machines and the choice of envelopes for payments.[135] The Treasury *Green Book*, the government's guide to policy, programme, and project appraisal and evaluation, was first issued in the 1970s; recent reviews of its content occurred in 2020 and 2022.[136] Other related guidance is of more recent vintage. We now have a guidance rainbow: a *Magenta Book* (2020, first published 2011) ('a comprehensive overview of evaluation in government: its scoping, design, management, use and dissemination');[137] an *Aqua Book* (2015), designed to ensure that the policy process is underpinned by high-quality analysis;[138] and an *Orange Book* (2023, first published 2020), setting out principles for risk management in government.[139] While several of these appear under

[135] Apparently first generally published as HM Treasury, *Notes for the Use of Accounts Branches of Government Departments* (4th edn, HMSO 1929).

[136] See now HM Treasury, *The Green Book: Central Government Guidance on Appraisal and Evaluation* (2022), and, for an idea of the range of associated and supplementary literature issued by the Treasury and user organizations, HM Treasury and Evaluation Task Force, *Collection: The Green Book and Accompanying Guidance and Documents* <www.gov.uk/government/collections/the-green-book-and-accompanying-guidance-and-documents>.

[137] HM Treasury, *Magenta Book: Central Government Guidance on Evaluation* (March 2020). 'Evaluation' is defined (at 5) as 'a systematic assessment of the design, implementation and outcomes of . . . any policy, programme or other government activity meant to elicit a change'.

[138] HM Treasury, *The Aqua Book: Guidance on Producing Quality Analysis for Government* (2015).

[139] UK Government, *The Orange Book: Management of Risk—Principles and Concepts* (2023).

a Treasury rubric, preparation may involve input from a number of other organizations. A key source of the more recent publications has been the cross-departmental structures established under the functions programme, and the associated Civil Service professions.[140] The analysis function, for example, provided input to the revision of the *Magenta Book*; the *Orange Book* 2023 update was produced by the Head of the Government Risk Profession and Risk Centre of Excellence, a unit within the Government Finance Function. The functions have also set out to rationalize 'how to do it' guidance to departments by way of the standards they produce, with the aim of creating

> a coherent, effective and mutually understood way of doing business within government organisations and across organisational boundaries, and [providing] a stable basis for assurance, risk management and capability improvement.[141]

These commonly include provisions on the way the function should be organized within the department (or other body), how tasks should be identified and allocated, who answers to whom, and so on. They also provide reference lists of the guidance documents on which they draw: the Property Standard (GovS 004), for example, lists 66 of these, while the Digital Standard (below) has 35. The standards purport to distinguish mandatory requirements from advice, though they do not indicate the specific sources of authority for mandatory provisions. According to a Treasury 'Dear Accounting Officer' letter issued in September 2021, '[t]he mandate for use of functional standards is provided by *Managing Public Money (MPM)* and endorsed by ministers through the *Declaration on Government Reform*.'[142] Functional standards, in other words, like Cabinet Office controls, rely for their constitutional support on Treasury authority.[143]

5.2 A case study: e-government

Standards, guidance, and advice together represent only one of the ways in which the functions programme sought to lift executive performance. The other way is for the task itself, or some crucial element of it, to be centralized. This might normally be through its leadership by a Cabinet Office unit, but it can also be done through the transfer of departmental specialists to bodies with executive-wide competence, like the Government Internal Audit Agency or the Government Legal Department. To understand the possibilities of interplay between centralization of activity and guided departmental competence, it is instructive to look at how the executive has confronted the major contemporary challenge to its decision-making practice presented by the

[140] See chapter 2, section 3.4.6.

[141] Cabinet Office, *Collection: Functional Standards* (updated October 2021) <www.gov.uk/government/collections/functional-standards>.

[142] HM Treasury, DAO letter, 'Mandating Functional Standards from end September 2021' (DAO 5/21) (30 September 2021) Annex A; and see now *MPM* (2023), para 4.2.1. For the *Declaration* see chapter 2, section 3.4.6.

[143] On these controls see chapter 8, section 2.4.3.

development of digital technology—both by exploiting its opportunities and managing its risks.

Departments, and the centre of government, have long been using such technology to communicate with citizens. The first online website for central government as a whole—open.gov.uk—was established by the Government Information Service in 1994. Development of this public-facing aspect of e-government, which we discuss in chapter 12 below, has been paralleled by the digitization of a wide range of government functions and services. Unfortunately, the use by departments of information technology systems to facilitate their work has in recent years often come to public attention through expensive system failures. Consequent financial losses and inefficiencies have been a recurring concern of the NAO[144] and a major driver for the development of the Treasury's current system of control of spending on major projects.[145] Such systems may relate in a variety of ways to departmental decision-making, from supporting civil servants' and ministers' decisions through the provision of background data, through identification of the data on which a specific decision is based, to delivery of the decision itself, as where an online application for provision of a service is automatically processed: an example might be the renewal of annual motor vehicle licences by the Driver and Vehicle Licensing Agency. The greater the reliance placed on information technology as a component of the production of the actual decision, the wider the range of risks that need to be assessed and managed, as system malfunctions and failures become capable of producing not just financial losses and wastage for government but also increasingly serious consequences for the individuals, businesses, or other actors to whom decisions are addressed. One doubts if there could ever be a clearer illustration of the dangers of such reliance than that provided by the Post Office's willingness to pursue over 15 years a campaign of recoveries from and prosecutions of innocent sub-postmasters on grounds of theft and false accounting, in the face of evidence that the problems lay with malfunctions in its IT accounting system.[146]

Primary responsibility for the proper deployment and operation of information technology rests, like other decision-making functions, with the management of the relevant departments. Central involvement over the current century has taken two forms. The *first* has been the development of a centre of expertise to provide services on which all departments might draw. This has been the role of the Government Digital Service (GDS), created in 2011 by the merging of directgov[147] with the Cabinet Office Digital Delivery and Digital Engagement teams. Originally based in the Cabinet Office as part of the Efficiency and Reform Group, the Service both ran the programme for bringing the many separate departmental internet interfaces onto the single site that is now gov.uk, and built common platforms to help departments

[144] See eg Comptroller and Auditor General, *The Challenges in Implementing Digital Change* (HC 2021–22, 575).

[145] See chapter 8, section 2.4.2.

[146] See generally Nick Wallis, *The Great Post Office Scandal* (Bath Publishing 2022). For other aspects of the scandal see chapter 4, sections I and 3.2 on lessons for the supervision of arm's length bodies, and chapter 9, text at nn 142–45 on powers of private prosecution.

[147] This was a cross-government internet interface that had replaced uk.online, itself the successor of open.gov.uk (above), and had been managed by the Department of Work and Pensions.

improve their digital services. From the time of its creation until 2020 GDS was also tasked with the *second* form of central involvement, developing and monitoring standards for the provision of digital services across government. In this role GDS produced a wide range of advice and standards to guide departmental activity, based on a Government Digital Strategy published in 2012. This was the forerunner of the current *Government Functional Standard GovS 005: Digital*.[148]

This role of guidance and advice was split off from GDS in January 2021 and handed to a new Cabinet Office body, the Central Digital and Data Office (CDDO).[149] It is to that Office that departments would now look for guidance on matters ranging from employment of IT contractors to the use of artificial intelligence (AI) in the development and operation of policies and services. The Office is also responsible for cross-government digital and data performance and assurance, and for operating Cabinet Office spend controls as they apply to digital and technology expenditure.[150] GDS continues to operate as central government's centre of in-house IT products and services: it had 750 employees distributed across several centres in 2023. Both GDS and CDDO were transferred by the incoming Labour government in July 2024 from the Cabinet Office to the Department of Science, Innovation and Technology.

Like other functional hubs CDDO faces the problem of securing commitment from departments whose activity in the function area it can guide but not direct. Its functional standard places heavy emphasis on effective and accountable management of digital services within departments. Thus it identifies both roles specific to digital activity, such as Chief Digital Officer, and also linked and overlapping roles such as Chief Data Officer, Chief Technology Officer, and the service owners responsible for the delivery of individual departmental services (involving both their digital and non-digital elements), to whom digital service managers should be accountable for the development and day-to-day operation of the digital aspects of their assigned service.[151] CDDO's *Roadmap for Digital and Data*, developed by the Digital and Data Board, a forum of Permanent Secretaries, seeks to reinforce departmental commitment to its strategy for improving the effectiveness of the function across government by installing the Permanent Secretaries of the departments with the most important digital activities as sponsors of the strategy's different work streams. Further reinforcement is sought from work with departments and the Treasury to align criteria for spending controls approval to the roadmap, in the hope that newly approved spend will support delivery of both the strategy missions and departmental priorities.[152]

Specialized guidance in the form of an *Ethics, Transparency and Accountability Framework* has been produced for departments considering the use of AI to assist

[148] Central Digital and Data Office, *Government Functional Standard GovS 005: Digital* (November 2023).

[149] For the background to this change see Digital Economy Council, *Organising for Digital Delivery* (9 September 2020).

[150] On these controls see below, chapter 8, section 2.4.3.

[151] See generally s 4.5 of the standard (n 148).

[152] Central Digital and Data Office, *Transforming for a Digital Future: 2022 to 2025 Roadmap for Digital and Data* (updated September 2023).

with or take over elements of their decision-making.[153] The guidance distinguishes between 'solely automated decision-making'—decisions that are fully automated with no human judgement—and automated assisted decision-making—automated or algorithmic systems that assist human judgement and decision-making. While the former may be used in a scenario that is often repetitive and routine in nature, the latter are more complex, often with more serious implications for citizens. While the guidance is expressed to apply in its entirety to both types of application of AI, it notes that the use of solely automated decision-making is restricted by article 22 of the General Data Protection Regulation,[154] under which a solely automated decision that has legal or similarly significant effects on an individual can only be made when it is necessary for the entry into or performance of a contract, is authorized by law, or is based on the individual's explicit consent. Article 22, along with parallel provision in the Data Protection Act 2018,[155] also requires that the arrangements safeguard the individual's rights and freedoms and legitimate interests, including the right to obtain human intervention on the part of the controller, to express his or her point of view, and to contest the decision. These constraints apply quite generally, not just to government, and further guidance on how to operate within them has been provided by the Information Commissioner's Office.[156] The *Ethics, Accountability and Transparency Framework* also emphasizes the need to respect government equality obligations by dealing with the risk that algorithms may incorporate human and societal biases and forms of prejudice, particularly those related to sensitive characteristics. It requires ministerial sign-off for every process or service that involves an algorithm or system making a significant decision; and suggests that all major processes and services, subject to automation consideration, should have a senior owner, and that government legal advisers should be involved from the start in the development process.[157]

[153] Cabinet Office, Central Digital and Data Office, and Office for Artificial Intelligence, *Ethics, Transparency and Accountability Framework for Automated Decision-Making* (2021, updated 29 November 2023).

[154] Regulation (EU) 2016/679 of the European Parliament and of the Council, as amended and applied by the Data Protection, Privacy and Electronic Communications (Amendments etc) (EU Exit) Regulations 2019, SI 2019/419.

[155] s 14, applying in the case where automated decision-making is authorized by law. See also the special regimes for law enforcement data processing and intelligence service data processing provided by pts 3 and 4 of the Act.

[156] Information Commissioner's Office, *Rights relating to Automated Decision making Including Profiling* [nd].

[157] (n 153) ss 2, 3, and 6.

4

Public Bodies: Creation, Culling, Classification, and Patronage

I Introduction: The Landscape

While the ministerial department, as a mode of organization of executive functions, has occupied the high ground of executive policymaking in the United Kingdom for the last 150 years or so, it has never wholly supplanted other governance devices, detached both from local government organization and from direct lines of accountability through ministers and Parliament. Dominant until the middle of the 19th century, the independent board of officials charged with carrying out specific functions, in fields like taxation, transport, social welfare, or foreign trade, began from that time onwards to be replaced by ministerial departments (though these continued to be called 'Boards')[1] or to be brought under ministerial control, in response to the idea that ministerial responsibility was crucial to the effective democratic control of administration. Nonetheless, some of the older boards survived, and new 'independent' boards and commissions, not under direct ministerial control, continued to be created.

As that process has carried on throughout the 20th century, non-departmental public bodies have swelled in numbers and importance. Despite prime-ministerial fondness for making and remaking departments to suit their political and policy requirements, the number of ministerial departments has remained remarkably stable for the past 50 years at around 20.[2] Around this stable executive core swirls an unstable mass of these other bodies, bodies that by reason of their attachments to departments are considered to be part of the executive. Within this mass there is a subset of bodies with defined characteristics now officially referred to as 'arm's length bodies' (ALBs). In 2020, the last year for which the government has published comprehensive data on ALBs, there were 293 of these, accounting for annual expenditure of £223.9bn.[3] They employed 318,714 full-time equivalent staff, as opposed to an estimated 182,860 in ministerial departments.[4] Yet bodies classified as ALBs by the Cabinet Office in fact represent only a minority of all the bodies identified by the Office for National Statistics (ONS) as falling under the heading of central government in accordance with the international and European classification systems applied by the Office: in

[1] Examples are the Board of Agriculture and the Board of Education, both created in 1889.

[2] Anne White and Patrick Dunleavy, *Making and Breaking Whitehall Departments: A Guide to Machinery of Government Changes* (Institute for Government 2010) 16–17.

[3] Cabinet Office, *Public Bodies 2020* (15 July 2021). More than half of this expenditure (£124.8bn) was accounted for by National Health Service (England).

[4] *Public Bodies 2020*, figure 3; Office for National Statistics, *Public Sector Employment* (March 2020) table 9.

Executive Self-Government and the Constitution. Terence Daintith and Alan Page, Oxford University Press.
 DOI: 10.1093/9780198937630.003.0004

2019 these numbered 830.[5] The basic test for this classification is one of control: 'the ability [of government] to determine the general policy or programme of the body.'[6] Today, however, we cannot even say what proportion of central government public bodies is represented by ALBs. No Cabinet Office listings of ALBs have been published for the years subsequent to 2020. In addition, ONS has changed the presentation of its *Public Sector Classification Guide* so that it no longer provides separate lists of central government bodies and other kinds of public sector bodies such as local government bodies. A single table, also including bodies formerly classified as part of central government, now includes more than 3,300 bodies, and lumps together all bodies that fit the European System of Accounts 'central government' classification, with no distinction between ALBs and others.[7] In consequence we now know less about the composition of the public bodies sector than at any time since the beginning of this century.

The label 'ALB' was not in use at the time New Labour came to power in 1997, but the classes of body it includes now were all then in existence. These are three: executive agencies; non-departmental public bodies (NDPBs); and non-ministerial departments (NMDs). The characteristics that distinguish them have not changed over the period since 1997. Only in 2016, however, did the Cabinet Office articulate a general principle to indicate which sort of body should be created when it appeared that a job should be done by government but without direct political oversight. This principle is that the classification of an ALB should be determined by the degree of freedom that body needs from ministerial control to perform its functions.[8] In terms of degrees of freedom, executive agencies are conceived of as being on the lowest level, with NDPBs and then NMDs above. This approach should perhaps eventually bring to an end the confusion engendered by the fact that some public bodies were attributed to more than one class simultaneously: thus the Treasury Solicitor's Office, and the Government Legal Department as its successor, have since 1996 been both an NMD and an executive agency, with the odd result that the Treasury Solicitor is appointed by the Prime Minister as head of the department but by the Attorney General as head of the agency.[9]

In 1999 we described *executive agencies* as 'the most significant development to have taken place in the machinery of government this century.'[10] The *Next Steps* programme of separating the service delivery functions of central government departments from

[5] Comptroller and Auditor General, *Central Oversight of Arm's Length Bodies* (HC 2021–22, 297) paras 1.5, 1.6. Included in the larger total were bodies falling within the purview of the Scottish, Welsh, and Northern Irish devolved administrations, but some other bodies linked with departments were still excluded, such as public corporations (see below).

[6] European System of Accounts (ESA 2010), Regulation 549/2013 of 21 May 2013 [2013] OJ L174/1, Annex A, paras 2.35–2.39. For the detailed tests applied by the Office for National Statistics see Office for National Statistics, *UK Economic Statistics Sector and Transaction Classifications: The Classification Process* [nd], esp s 3.1. Advice to Departments on classification is provided by the Treasury: HM Treasury, *Class (2013) 1: Sector Classification* (August 2013).

[7] Office for National Statistics, *Public Sector Classification Guide and Forward Work Plan* (29 February 2024).

[8] Cabinet Office, *Classification of Public Bodies: Guidance for Departments* (Public Bodies Handbook—Part 1) (April 2016) 3.

[9] See further chapter 9, section 2.1.2.

[10] Terence Daintith and Alan Page, *The Executive in the Constitution: Structure, Autonomy and Internal Control* (OUP 1999) 37.

policy functions, hiving them off into agencies which, while still forming part of the department, had their own objectives, funding, and management structure, had by 1998 produced a situation in which three out of four civil servants were working in an agency or a 'department operating on Next Steps lines';[11] 138 agencies had been created. Over this century there has been a remarkable reduction in the number and significance of executive agencies, only 40 being listed in the government's list of 'Departments, agencies and public bodies' in early 2024.[12] Only one or two, like the Prison and Probation Service attached to the Ministry of Justice, continue to perform high-profile functions. Part of the reason for this shrinkage is that a number of agencies, including very substantial ones like the Passport Office and Border Agency (Home Office) and Jobcentre Plus (Department of Work and Pensions) have over time been reabsorbed into their parent departments. Others have been merged, privatized, or have changed status, for example to become public corporations. While this process has been unspectacular, overall it may represent as significant a change in executive organization in this century as the creation of the programme did in the last. Possible drivers for the process have been identified as the difficulty of separating policy and operational activities, loss of agency autonomy as basic services come to be shared across the whole department, and duplication of effort involved in operating effective agency sponsorship and control functions.[13] Executive agencies have no separate legal existence, and their staff form part of the Civil Service personnel of the parent department.

Non-departmental public bodies form the second, the largest and the most diverse group of ALBs. Two categories of NDPBs are currently recognized: *executive NDPBs*, which have decision-making power to deliver public services ranging from industrial conciliation and arbitration to the provision of museums and galleries, though there are some that have the kind of regulatory powers often entrusted to non-ministerial departments;[14] and *advisory NDPBs*, groups of experts and others set up to provide advice in defined areas, usually to government but sometimes to other bodies or to the courts. *Tribunal NDPBs*, performing judicial functions, once formed a third category, but the Cabinet Office policy is now that all new tribunal functions must be delivered within HM Courts and Tribunal Service, an executive agency within the Ministry of Justice, and not as separate NDPBs.[15] Some tribunals established earlier continue to carry the 'Tribunal NDPB' label. Save in a few exceptional cases NDPBs do not enjoy

[11] At that time those departments were Customs and Excise, Inland Revenue, the Crown Prosecution Service, and the Serious Fraud Office. The first two are now merged into HMRC.

[12] At <www.gov.uk/government/organisations>.

[13] Thomas Elston, 'Principles meet Practicalities: Challenges of Accountability Reform in the British Civil Service' in Tom Christensen and Per Lægreid (eds), *The Routledge Handbook to Accountability and Welfare State Reforms in Europe* (Routledge 2017) ch 17, citing the difficulty of separating policy and operational activities, loss of agency autonomy as basic services shared across whole departments, and duplication of effort involved in operating effective agency sponsorship and control functions. See also Colin Talbot and Carole Talbot, 'One step forward, two steps back? The rise and fall of government's Next Steps agencies' *Civil Service World* (23 September 2019), noting the weakening of agency independence over the period of Labour government.

[14] Examples from different fields are the Oil and Gas Authority (which now calls itself the North Sea Transition Authority), the Environment Agency, the Regulator of Social Housing, or the Care Quality Commission.

[15] Cabinet Office (n 8) 12.

Crown status and their employees are not civil servants. Most executive NDPBs have been established by statute with a specific legislative mandate, but as we shall see, this has not always been the case, and a number of such bodies have been created as companies under the Companies Acts, which may raise issues of both classification and accountability.

Non-ministerial departments are exactly that: central government departments that are not headed by a minister. Like ministerial departments they are funded by their own annual vote in the Supply and Appropriation Acts,[16] and their employees are civil servants. In 2024 there were 20 such departments. Generally speaking they cover areas that are at the core of government, but for which a measure of independence from political influence is considered desirable—though the extent of that independence varies considerably. This is a highly varied group of bodies, with headcounts ranging from 63,000 at His Majesty's Revenue and Customs (HMRC) to 60 at the Supreme Court, and one whose member bodies were established at different times for different reasons, though regulatory bodies form a significant sub-group of such departments.[17] NMDs we shall encounter later in this book include the Government Legal Department, the Crown Prosecution Service, and the UK Statistics Authority. The NMD classification is now reserved for 'exceptional cases'.[18]

If we subtract the 295 ALBs identified by the Cabinet Office from the 830 central government bodies identified by the Office for National Statistics, there appear to be no fewer than 535 bodies that in 2019 fell outside the ALB category. What are these? A substantial number of them are executive agencies or NDPBs that operate within the jurisdiction of the Welsh, Scottish, and Northern Ireland governments. This still leaves a large number of miscellaneous bodies that for one reason or another the Cabinet Office is content to leave unclassified. Some of these are of major importance, such as the United Kingdom's main financial regulator, the Financial Conduct Authority, and communications regulator, Ofcom; financing bodies such as the British Business Bank; and energy market managers like the Electricity Settlements Company and the Low Carbon Contracts Company.

A further group of bodies falls outside both the ALB category and the statistical definition of central government used by ONS. These are public corporations. The traditional use of this term in public law served to describe public bodies incorporated by statute; historically it has been closely associated with the nationalized industries that ran public utilities and other basic industries, created by the 1945–51 Labour government and largely dismantled through privatization by the Conservatives between 1979 and 1997. As applied by both the Cabinet Office and ONS, 'public corporation' now signifies a public body that operates on market principles, recouping more than

[16] An exception is the Forestry Commission, an NMD funded through the DEFRA vote; there may be others.

[17] It has been suggested that the utility regulators first established following privatization in the 1980s took this form because NMDs were not at that time listed as public bodies so that the official 'quango count' was not thereby increased: Matthew Flinders, *Delegated Governance and the British State: Walking without Order* (OUP 2008) 77. On the incoherence of the NMD category see Jill Rutter, *The Strange Case of Non-Ministerial Departments* (Institute for Government 2013).

[18] Letter from Alex Chisholm, Civil Service Chief Operating Officer and Cabinet Office Permanent Secretary to Chair of Public Accounts Committee (23 June 2021).

50% of its production costs through sales revenues at economically significant prices over a period of three years or more. A body meeting this criterion will be identified as either a 'financial' or 'non-financial' public corporation depending on its sector of activity and will be treated differently for accounting purposes from public sector bodies generally.[19] Currently active public corporations include the Post Office, the British Broadcasting Corporation, Ordnance Survey, the Civil Aviation Authority, and the National Physical Laboratory. It is difficult to generalize where these bodies might be situated in terms of the criterion of 'the degree of freedom that body needs from ministerial control to perform its functions' used by the Cabinet Office to classify ALBs. Ministerial and departmental oversight of the Post Office, for example, was called into question by their long-continued lack of any response to the Post Office's remarkable record of prosecutions of its sub-postmasters, but the framework document detailing the relationship between the department and the Office suggests that the department was interested in little beyond the Post Office's financial performance.[20] BBC management might well be envious.

In the remainder of this section we use 'public bodies' to refer to the full range of non-ministerial central government bodies, and reserve 'ALB' for the bodies that fit the official definition.

II Proliferation, Culling, and Classification

2.1 New Labour's inheritance and 'institutionalitis'

Since the beginning of the 20th century there has been intermittent concern about the proliferation of central government bodies falling outside the reach of the direct individual ministerial responsibility to Parliament that was the lodestone of late 19th century reforms. A succession of reviews and reports have warned against the possibly adverse effects on accountability of this proliferation and have commented on the confusion and disorder in governance arrangements that have resulted.[21] These reviews start with the report of the Royal Commission on the Civil Service in 1914[22] and continue right through to the Cabinet Office Structural Reform Plan 2010,[23] announced very shortly after the arrival in power of the 2010–15 Coalition government and initiating a series of Public Bodies Reform Programmes running until 2025.[24]

Little progress had been made in arresting the growth in the numbers of these bodies by the time New Labour came to power in 1997. Nor had any government developed overarching principles to determine when such bodies should be created

[19] Cabinet Office, *Classification of Public Bodies* (n 8) 31; Office for National Statistics, *UK Economic Statistics Sector and Transaction Classifications* (n 6) paras 3.1.2, 3.1.3.

[20] Cabinet Office, *Classification of Public Bodies* (n 8). On the approach to departmental oversight and control of the Post Office see this chapter, text at nn 69–70; on the Post Office prosecutions see chapter 9, text at nn 142–45.

[21] See generally Flinders (n 17) 68–98, covering the period 1900–2007, from which the material in the following paragraphs is drawn.

[22] Cm 7748 (1914).

[23] Cabinet Office, *Draft Structural Reform Plan* (June 2010) 4.

[24] Section 3.3 of this chapter.

and what attributes and relationship with ministerial departments they should have. There had not even been a serious attempt to maintain an account of how many there were at any given time. The Bowen survey in 1975–78 identified 776 'quangos', as they were then called; this prompted a promise to abolish quangos in the Conservative election manifesto of 1979, but their victory led only to the identification of 436 bodies for abolition, almost all advisory and often dormant anyway. The subsequent Pliatzky Review disclosed that more than 1,500 advisory bodies, 67 'tribunal systems', and nearly 500 executive bodies were nonetheless still in existence, but led to the abolition of only 30 such executive bodies. That review did however result in an attempt to bring some order to the landscape by formally identifying a class of 'non-departmental public bodies', the official synonym for quangos, but this had the perverse result that because the government was committed to reducing the number of quangos, new bodies started to be created in forms that escaped the NDPB classification, like the NMD or government-owned company. This problem persists, as we shall see.

The professed Conservative distaste for quangos did not prevent its adoption of the principle of separating departments' policy and delivery functions, leading to the creation of executive agencies as a further class of bodies outside the direct lines of ministerial responsibility, albeit still operating within departments. Its New Labour successors accepted this change, and largely abandoned the sport of quango-hunting, switching their focus to improving the management and accountability of NDPBs. At the same time they allowed the steady expansion of the numbers of NDPBs and other public bodies to continue. Flinders has remarked that in its early period, the Labour government 'appeared to be suffering from "institutionalitis"—the tendency to respond to every problem by setting up another organization', listing nearly 300 bodies created by the Blair governments between 1997 and 2007.[25] Many of these were NMDs, NDPBs, or executive agencies, but many were not, so that the diversity (or disorder) of the sector continued to grow, with adverse effects on the accountability the government had promised to improve.[26] Only at the very end of the Brown government's tenure did the Treasury announce new controls on the creation of ALBs, such as a requirement that a value-for-money assessment be published in advance of start-up.[27]

2.2 Progress under the Coalition

In 2010 the incoming government, this time a Conservative/Liberal Democrat Coalition, reacted against its predecessor's approach, announcing as the second of its Cabinet Office priorities, after Civil Service reform, 'Quango reduction: abolish/bring into departments the majority of quangos and enforce new standards for the

[25] Flinders (n 17) 84–85 and app 2.

[26] Gordon Brown's government did however undertake a review in 2009, announcing in its 'Smarter Government' programme that the number of arm's length bodies would be reduced by 120: Lucinda Mair and Feargal McGuinness, *Public Bodies Bill (HL)* (House of Commons Library Research Paper 11/50) 9.

[27] HM Treasury, *Reforming Arm's-Length Bodies* (March 2010) 11, cited in Mair and McGuinness (n 26) 17.

remaining'.[28] This particular cull was approached in a more scientific manner than its predecessors, on the basis of three criteria:

1. does it undertake a precise technical operation?
2. is it necessary for impartial decisions to be made about the distribution of taxpayers' money?
3. does it fulfil a need for facts to be transparently determined, independent of political interference?

Satisfying at least one of these tests was presented as essential if a body was to survive the review.[29] These continue to be the basic tests applied by the Cabinet Office to departmental proposals to create new public bodies.[30] The reduction process encountered the usual initial problem of ascertaining what the current population of public bodies actually was, eventually arriving at the figure of 901. When the review—which did not cover executive agencies—was completed in October 2010, 192 bodies were earmarked for elimination as public bodies (though some were expected to continue outside government), a further 118 for mergers to reduce their number to 57, and 211 proposed for substantial reform or under continuing review.[31]

Government determination to carry through the reform was signalled by the introduction of broadly expressed legislation to permit the abolition or modification of bodies created or otherwise structured by statute. No such legislation had been provided in relation to earlier culls, which could thus not touch statutory public bodies unless specific amendments to their founding legislation were passed. The powers the government considered it needed to carry through the review results were presented, initially to the House of Lords, in the Public Bodies Bill of 2011. The Bill was not well received. Ministers may have thought they had made a sufficient obeisance to parliamentary democracy by proposing that the order powers they were asking for—to abolish, merge, or modify the functions or funding of the public bodies listed in a number of schedules—should be subject to affirmative resolution procedure in both Houses. Parliament did not see this as an adequate safeguard for the very wide powers being taken. The House of Commons does not always debate such resolutions and never rejects them, and the House of Lords was to find itself the subject of governmental excoriation a few years later for daring to do this on a single occasion.[32] Noble Lords had harsh things to say,[33] and inserted additional controls on the government's powers:[34] a consultation requirement, an enhanced scrutiny procedure

[28] Cabinet Office, *Draft Structural Reform Plan* (n 23) 2, 4.

[29] See HC Deb 9 June 2010, vol 511, col 313 (Francis Maude, Minister for the Cabinet Office).

[30] Cabinet Office, *The Approvals Process for the Creation of New Arm's-Length Bodies: Guidance for Departments* (Public Bodies Handbook—Part 2) (2018) 6.

[31] Mair and McGuinness, above (n 26) 5–7. Results of the review updated to December 2011 can be found at [Cabinet Office], *Public Bodies Reform—Proposals for Change* (14 December 2011).

[32] For the story see Edward Scott and Heather Evennett, *Strathclyde Review and the Primacy of the House of Commons* (House of Lords Library, December 2015). For later controversy on similar issues relating to executive powers to modify legislation, see chapter 10, sections 1.3, 2.3.

[33] '[T]his is a bad Bill. It is badly thought out, badly structured, badly executed, bad for the constitution, bad for public bodies and bad for government': Baroness Royall at HL Deb 9 November 2010, vol 722, col 68.

[34] Public Bodies Act 2011, ss 10–12.

for the exercise of order powers, and a time limit within which any scheduled changes must be carried out. They also deleted its longest schedule, listing 150 bodies that the government thought it might want to do something about sometime but for which it had no current proposals.

The Coalition reform programme was successful in reversing the trend of relentless increase in numbers of public bodies, though again, advisory bodies formed the easiest targets. By the end of its life in 2015, the programme was expected to reduce the number of ALBs to 598, 306 fewer than in 2010. Other reductions were achieved mainly by merging existing bodies and by taking functions previously delivered in arm's length bodies back into departmental structures. At the same time new executive NDPBs, like the Office of Budget Responsibility, continued to be created, and the NHS was reconstituted as NHS England, an enormous executive NDPB.[35] Only 23 abolition orders and two merger orders were made under the Act, so that the great majority of abolitions and mergers appear to have been capable of accomplishment without the need for resort to statutory powers.[36]

2.3 Control through classification

With the achievement of relative stability in the population of ALBs, the government's focus shifted to a preventive approach: an attempt to secure tighter central control over the creation of new public bodies; a much-needed effort to bring some order into the field by establishing a more rigorous approach to the classification of public bodies; and measures to get better results, in terms of efficiency and accountability, from existing public bodies.[37] Even while pushing the Public Bodies Bill through Parliament, the Minister for the Cabinet Office had confessed that,

> even at the end of the process that we are currently proposing, that [public bodies] landscape will still be quite muddled, but it will at least have been cleared up to some extent.[38]

Relevant guidance had already been developed by the preceding Labour government in *Public Bodies: A Guide for Departments*, originally published in ten 'chapters' in 2006 and offering a comprehensive guide to the management of a public body, from conception to abolition.[39] Its provisions on creation and classification of bodies were replaced by the *Public Bodies Handbook*, whose Part 1, published in 2016, dealt with classification, while Part 2 (2018) covered approvals processes.[40] There is a notable

[35] Jonathan Pearson, Tom Gash, and Jill Rutter, *Out of the Ashes: Priorities for Reforming Arm's-Length Government in the UK* (Institute for Government 2015) 3.

[36] Some abolitions and other changes will have been made through amendments to legislation specific to given public bodies and their functions.

[37] For these latter measures see section III.

[38] HC Deb 12 July 2011, vol 531, col 218 (12 July 2011) (Francis Maude).

[39] Cabinet Office, *Public Bodies: A Guide for Departments* (June 2006).

[40] Part 3 of the Handbook deals specifically with the creation and management of executive agencies. There is no equivalent specialist treatment of the other types of ALB: NMDs and NDPBs.

difference of tone between the 2006 document and their replacements. The former reads as a helpful centrally produced guide for the people who are taking the decisions in this field—that is, departments. The *Handbook* is much more directive. Thus, while much of Part 2—*The Approvals Process for the Creation of New Arm's-Length Bodies: Guidance for Departments*—is still couched as advice on intra-departmental design and other processes, central control is firmly asserted:

> Formal approval for setting up a new ALB must be sought and received from Cabinet Office ministers and the Chief Secretary to the Treasury, before any decision or announcement about a new ALB is made.[41]

A prerequisite for such approval is prior submission to the Cabinet Office and Treasury of a full business case setting out the rationale for the proposal in detail, including consideration of alternative delivery options for further assessment. If establishment is approved, the relationship between the department and the ALB, as expressed in a framework document or equivalent, must also be agreed with the Treasury.[42] In practice, however, Cabinet Office and Treasury have proved to be feeble watchdogs: none of the 24 business cases submitted between 2016 and 2020 included all of the details requested by the Cabinet Office, and about a third omitted basic elements like consideration of alternatives to an ALB, but many of them were still approved.[43]

Another limitation on the control is that it only applies to ALBs, and ALBs, as noted at the beginning of this chapter, occupy only a part of the landscape of public bodies associated with central government.

Since 2010, the policy of the government has been that new ALBs should be set up 'only as a last resort, when consideration of all other delivery mechanisms have *[sic]* been exhausted'.[44] We should therefore not find it surprising that over recent years departments wishing to create a new public body should have looked for possibilities outside the ALB sector. One such possibility exists in the shape of the public corporation, but, as already noted, such a corporation needs to operate on market principles, which excludes bodies funded through grants and levies. For some years there appeared to be a belief—in some departments at least—that an answer could be found in creating a publicly owned company, established under the Companies Acts, to do the job, on the assumption that this too was a separate category from ALBs. Taking this route might thus dodge the 'no more ALBs' policy, as well as offering other advantages like easy incorporation and a more flexible management and pay regime than was available to NMDs and NDPBs. Thus in an echo of the earlier use of MNDs as vehicles for economic regulators to avoid swelling the ranks of NDPBs,[45] we find departmental functions of regulation of oil and gas production being hived off in 2016 to such a company, the Oil and Gas Authority (OGA).[46] At least 50 other government-owned

[41] Cabinet Office, *The Approvals Process for the Creation of New Arm's-Length Bodies* (n 30) 11.

[42] ibid 13. On framework documents see section 3.2 of this chapter.

[43] Public Accounts Committee, *Government's Delivery through Arm's-Length Bodies* (HC 2021–22, 181) para 8.

[44] Cabinet Office, *The Approvals Process for the Creation of New Arm's-Length Bodies* (n 30) 3.

[45] Flinders (n 17).

[46] This took place in two stages. Created in 2015 as an executive agency within the Department of Energy and Climate Change pending the enactment of the Energy Act 2016, OGA was in 2016 constituted

or -controlled companies have been created since the beginning of the century to perform a variety of tasks, only a few of which have market functions and can thus be classified as public corporations.

In 2016, therefore, the Cabinet Office felt it needed to disabuse departments of the belief that creating a company was a simple way of escaping ALB controls. In its revised classification guidance it pointed out that

> [t]here has been a general misconception that companies (that are owned by the government) and ALBs are alternatives to one another. This is incorrect as the two are not mutually exclusive, . . . These descriptors refer to different attributes of an organisation. 'Arm's length body' or 'public body' signifies that government controls the general corporate policy of the organisation, while 'company' signifies that it is incorporated under and is subject to the Companies Act 2006. The government provides guidance for departments about public bodies . . . which applies equally to those public bodies that are companies as to those that are not.[47]

The *Report on the Outcome of the Classification Review* that underpinned the revised guidance also promised that '[i]n future there will only be three main categories of bodies—Executive Agency, Non-Departmental Public Body and Non-Ministerial Department—which will be comparable, mutually exclusive and comprehensively cover the landscape' and that '[a]ny new bodies should be set up within this framework'.[48] These statements seemed to portend an energetic effort to bring these free-floating public bodies within the ALB categories. Yet neither the 2020 Public Bodies listing nor the ONS 2022 *Public Sector Classification Guide*,[49] the last to indicate the administrative classification of central government bodies, evidences any significant shift of government companies into the ranks of ALBs. Only a handful, such as the Student Loans Company, possess this status. It appears that arguments for an orderly landscape and consistent treatment continue to be overridden by departmental claims of special circumstances. The provisions of *Classification of Public Bodies: Guidance for Departments* leave plenty of scope for this, allowing lack of classification to be justified by the small or temporary nature of the body, by the fact that ONS classification has been sought but is still awaited, the fact that the body is awaiting significant structural change, or—an open invitation to special pleading—the fact that

> for reasons associated with function or services, [the body] cannot be classified into one of the main [ALB] categories without adversely impacting on the body's ability to fulfil of *[sic]* those functions / deliver those services.[50]

as a company under the Companies Act and received a range of powers under the Act. For the issues of accountability and control presented by the use of companies, as opposed to bodies constituted by statute, to perform regulatory functions, see Terence Daintith, 'Government Companies as Regulators' (2019) 82 Modern Law Review 397. OGA has since adopted the 'trading name' of 'North Sea Transition Authority'.

[47] Cabinet Office, *Classification of Public Bodies* (n 8) s 7.3.

[48] Cabinet Office, *Report on the Outcome of the Classification Review* [nd but 2016]. The review was commissioned by the Coalition government.

[49] Office for National Statistics, *Public Sector Classification Guide* (November 2022).

[50] Cabinet Office, *Classification of Public Bodies* (n 8) s 7.2.

Cabinet Office success in this endeavour can be judged from the fact that, more than a decade after his comments on his Public Bodies Bill, Lord Maude still thought that

> [t]he landscape of Arm's Length Bodies (ALBs) is confused and confusing . . . There should be a sustained programme to map the landscape of ALBs accurately and on a consistent basis; categorise them on the basis of the appropriate governance and accountability arrangements (the 'length of the arm'); and introduce a consistent approach across government for reporting in to the sponsoring department and the way in which appointments to their boards are made.[51]

III Managing Public Bodies

3.1 Control and accountability

When a department establishes a public body, whether it falls within or outside the ALB categories, this does not mean that the department can wash its hands of the matter and leave the body to perform its assigned tasks in whatever way it thinks fit. Even if the function is one that calls for a significant degree of independence from political control, it remains within the department's area of concern; the body remains public and in most cases will depend in some measure at least on public funding; and Parliament will continue to view the minister in charge as the most convenient channel of accountability for the activities of bodies associated with the department. Management of the department's activities must accordingly be so designed as to cope with the need for an appropriate and effective measure of control of, and accountability for, the activities of the varied and often numerous bodies associated with it. Since an essential part of the rationale for establishing any public body is that the performance of its tasks requires a degree of separation from direct political supervision, such control is necessarily problematic.

A key lesson to be drawn from the experience of attempting to control the scope, and numbers, of non-ministerial public bodies since 1997 is the need for some effective central constraint on departmental tendencies towards disorderly diversity, along with promotion of effective delivery of the policies creation of these bodies was designed to support. The problem here is that while the language adopted in recent years is more directive than before, it remains the case that the Cabinet Office has no formal power to tell ministers how to manage 'their' public bodies. We shall see that the Treasury is better equipped in this respect by reason of its traditional and comprehensive powers over public expenditure, some of which have been delegated to the Cabinet Office, and that these can be made to bear directly on the behaviour of individual bodies; but the traditional and strong preference remains one of seeking to achieve central steering of the public body sector through the intermediary of the responsible departments.

[51] Lord Maude of Horsham, *Independent Review of Governance and Accountability in the Civil Service* (November 2023) para 2.4.5.

3.2 Framework documents

The key elements of the relationship between an ALB and the department with which it is associated will usually be set forth in what is now known as a framework agreement or framework document. This terminology was introduced with the creation of executive agencies to describe an agency's relations with its minister and its accountability, both for its finances and its performance, to the minister and to Parliament.[52] At the time Labour came to power in 1997 the documentation of the functions, control, and accountability of other ALBs was managed differently, focusing on accounting for the funds provided by the department to the ALB to support its operations (its 'grant-in-aid'), by way of a financial memorandum and/or management statement.[53] The term 'framework document' has now been extended to cover the entire universe of ALBs—and indeed, some other public bodies as well. Such documents are officially described as 'a core constitutional document of the ALB' and 'a guide to govern the collaborative relationship between the ALB, the sponsor or shareholder department and the rest of government'.[54] These relationships may vary considerably: MNDs, for example, normally have their own Vote in the Supply and Appropriation Act and so are not financially dependent on a sponsoring department, and public corporations, some of which also have framework documents, are likewise normally financially independent by reason of their commercial activities. In consequence the Treasury, in *Managing Public Money (MPM)*, now provides no fewer than seven framework document templates[55] to cover a range of cases: executive agencies, NDPBs, government companies, public corporations, NMDs, NDPBs with charitable status, and statutory office-holders.[56]

These templates supplement rules about this documentation presented in the latest edition of *MPM* in terms that assert strong Treasury control.[57] When creating new bodies, or revising the framework documents for existing ones,[58] departments must clear the documentation with their own Corporate Governance Team or Financial Governance Team or equivalent, before clearance with the relevant Treasury spending team and the Treasury Officer of Accounts. It may also be appropriate to share the framework documents for new public bodies or where there are complex governance arrangements with the Cabinet Office Public Bodies Governance Team for their views.[59] In settling relationships with their public bodies, departments are expected to choose the appropriate template, if necessary with Treasury advice, and

[52] HM Treasury, *Government Accounting* (1989, rev 3/94) para 16.1.3.

[53] Recommended contents for this were set out in *Government Accounting* (1989) Annex 13.1: Grants in aid: financial memorandum: subjects to be covered.

[54] HM Treasury, *Framework Documents: Collection* <www.gov.uk/government/collections/framework-documents-collection>.

[55] HM Treasury, *Managing Public Money: Framework Documents* (July 2022).

[56] Examples of such office-holders are the Public Trustee appointed under the Public Trustee Act 1906 and the Official Solicitor appointed under the Senior Courts Act 1981, in each case by the Lord Chancellor. The offices are now combined in a single person, who heads a function employing about 135 civil servants.

[57] See *Managing Public Money* (*MPM*) (2023) ch 7, esp ss 7.2, 7.7–7.10; Annexes 7.1 and 7.2.

[58] The Treasury stipulates that the document be reviewed and updated at least every three years: *MPM* (2023) Annex 7.1, para A7.2.10.

[59] *MPM*, paras A7.2.7, A7.2.9.

to explain, and secure Treasury agreement for, any departures from it.[60] The resulting framework documents are public documents which are to be published online and added to the Treasury's collection page for framework documents, and deposited in the libraries of both Houses of Parliament.[61]

The successive editions of *MPM* (2007, 2013, 2023), like the Cabinet Office Guidance discussed earlier,[62] express a continuing attempt to tighten central control in this area and reinforce a consistent approach. At the end of 2023 there was still quite a long way to go. Only 10 out of the 18 ministerial departments sponsoring public bodies had entries on the Treasury's collections page. Some of these were incomplete, including the Treasury's.[63] In the absence of individual inquiries, it was impossible to know whether these omissions simply represented failure to publish, or the absence of any document expressing the department-public body relationship. Concentrating on the central disciplines for managing the extended department can make it easy to forget that the process of reaching agreement between department and public body can be an arduous one, as we shall see when discussing relationships between the NMDs that run the government's legal services (Government Legal Department, Crown Prosecution Service, and Serious Fraud Office) and the Attorney General's Office as their ministerial 'sponsor'.[64]

The move to multiple templates from the single example that had been offered since the days of *Government Accounting* can however be seen as an acknowledgment of the necessary variety of arrangements appropriate to bodies that vary massively in size, that have different kinds of functions which may or may not be stipulated in legislation, that may or may not be financially dependent on their sponsoring department, and that may need, for the proper discharge of their functions, varying degrees of independence from departmental control. Use of particular legal forms for public bodies may also demand the use of specialized provisions: on the use of the minister's powers as a shareholder, for example, in the case of a government-owned company, or to recognize the board's obligations as trustees under charity law where an NDPB has charity status. Nonetheless, across all templates it is possible to recognize the core concerns which the relationship is likely to address. These are

The body's purpose, powers and duties, whether legislatively specified or otherwise
How its accountability to Parliament will be secured
The responsibilities of the sponsor department AO and of the body's AO
The responsibilities of the body's board, chair, and individual board members
Essential publications of the body, including annual report and accounts
Internal and external audit arrangements

[60] *MPM*, para A7.2.6.

[61] *MPM*, para A7.2.4. The collections page is at <www.gov.uk/government/collections/framework-documents-collection>.

[62] Text at nn 39–44.

[63] Its list had no entries for the Office for Budget Responsibility (a Treasury NDPB) or the Debt Management Office (a Treasury executive agency).

[64] Chapter 9, sections 2.1.4, 3.1. The 2019–20 stewardship accounts of the Official Solicitor and Public Trustee (December 2020) anticipated the conclusion of a new framework agreement with the sponsor department, the Ministry of Justice (MoJ), in 2020–21. At the end of 2023 it was still 'awaiting approval' at MoJ: information from OSPT (23 December 2023).

Obligation to abide by the requirements of *MPM*
Corporate governance arrangements, including risk management, corporate plan and its revision, budgeting procedures
Reporting to the sponsor department: including frequency, main activities, financial performance, expenditure
Activities of, and changes within, the body requiring clearance from the sponsor department, including delegated limits for new activities and capital projects
Staff
Reviews
Procedures for winding up.

How varied may be the ways in which these concerns are dealt with may be judged from viewing some framework documents of bodies whose activities we deal with elsewhere in this work.[65]

Negotiating a satisfactory framework document and getting it past the Treasury does not, as noted earlier, put an end to a department's responsibilities vis-à-vis its ALBs. Continuing, effective, but also sensitive supervision is expected. The Public Accounts Committee, supported by reports from the Comptroller and Auditor General, reviewed departments' performance in managing their public bodies in 2016–17 and again in 2020–21. In 2016 the Committee noted that the quality of oversight by departments was inconsistent, and it renewed this criticism in 2020–21. Consistency had not been achieved through the promulgation by the Cabinet Office of a Code of Good Practice in 2017; the Cabinet Office did not monitor whether departments followed the Code or how they oversaw their ALBs.[66] Promises to do better were renewed, through the 2021 *Declaration on Government Reform* ('24. . . . increase the effectiveness of [ALBs'] departmental sponsorship, underpinned by clear performance metrics and rigorous new governance and sponsorship standards'),[67] which was followed up by a revised Cabinet Office Sponsorship Code of Good Practice. The 'metrics' were however limited to counting the number of departments 'adopting' the new Code and to departmental self-reporting, by reference to criteria in the Code, on the adequacy of their own sponsorship arrangements.[68] Further review of the adequacy and appropriateness of departmental approaches to sponsorship responsibilities can hardly be avoided following disclosure of the apparent lack of interest exhibited by the successive sponsoring departments of the Post Office in its behaviour in relation to its defective Horizon IT system, including legal oppression of hundreds of sub-postmasters. The list of issues identified for investigation by the Horizon public

65 See eg the framework documents for the Government Internal Audit Agency, since 2015 a Treasury executive agency (chapter 2, section 4.3); the Office for Budget Responsibility, a Treasury NDPB (chapter 7, section 2.2.1); the Crown Prosecution Service, an NMD sponsored by the Attorney General's Office (chapter 9, section 3.1); and the Statistics Authority, an NMD (chapter 12, section 3.5.2), described as a 'Memorandum of Understanding', doubtless to emphasize the limited competence of the Cabinet Office as sponsoring department.

66 See generally Public Accounts Committee, *Government's Delivery through Arm's-Length Bodies* (HC 2021–22, 181) and Comptroller and Auditor General, *Central oversight of arm's-length bodies* (HC 2021-22, 297).

67 HM Government, *Declaration on Government Reform* (June 2021).

68 Cabinet Office, *Arm's Length Body Sponsorship Code of Good Practice* (May 2022) 11.

inquiry includes the adequacy of mechanisms for government oversight in relation to the performance of Post Office Limited and its compliance with its legal and ethical obligations.[69] No specific consideration is given to such obligations in the Post Office's 2020 framework agreement, and while the agreement requires the Post Office to keep the department's representative informed about actual or likely litigation, such information must be treated as confidential.[70]

3.3 Reviews of public bodies

Another expression of central policy has been a succession of review programmes for public bodies. This stream was initiated in July 2011 with a Cabinet Office requirement that each department conduct a triennial review of each of its NDPBs, initially focusing on the NDPB's appropriateness as a policy delivery vehicle, and expanded in 2014 to give greater emphasis to its efficiency and its governance.[71] This programme was replaced in 2015 with the Tailored Review Programme (2015–20),[72] which slightly relaxed the frequency of reviews ('once in the life of each Parliament') while extending the scope of the programme to include executive agencies and NMDs as well as NDPBs, and to consideration of the effectiveness of the relationship between the body being reviewed and its sponsoring department. Reviews remained departmental, but arrangements were made for a tiering system to identify 'priority reviews' with enhanced Cabinet Office supervision, such as sign-off on terms of reference and the final report. The NAO report on the programme suggested that it had had only limited success: only one-third of the intended tailored reviews were completed by 2020, and in a pendulum swing from the preceding programme, reviews now tended to focus too narrowly on governance arrangements, failing to address wider priorities such as overall delivery and effectiveness.[73] The government's third attempt at improvement through review was presented as the Public Bodies Review Programme (2020–25).[74] This saw the Cabinet Office stepping back somewhat from supervision, though still claiming a voice, with the Treasury, on each department's prioritization of its reviews. Instead it introduced the requirement for an 'independent' lead reviewer—though the appointment was still left to departmental ministers. No general rule as to frequency of reviews was imposed. A possible further enlargement of the scope of the programme was signalled by a provision 'strongly encouraging' departments to use the programme guidance when reviewing public bodies outside of the formal ALB classification with the aim of identifying an appropriate administrative classification where possible, and requiring them to set out why any high-risk unclassified bodies

[69] Post Office Horizon IT Inquiry, *Completed List of Issues 17-11-21*, Governance and Oversight, nos 206–10.

[70] Department for Business, Energy and Industrial Strategy, *Post Office Limited: Shareholder Relationship Framework Document* (March 2020), cll 13.3, 13.4.

[71] On the initial reviews in this programme, and their results, see Comptroller and Auditor General, *Progress on Public Bodies Reform* (HC 2013–14, 1048) 26–36.

[72] Cabinet Office, *Tailored Reviews of Public Bodies: Guidance* (March 2016).

[73] Comptroller and Auditor General (n 5) paras 3.20, 3.22.

[74] Cabinet Office, *Public Bodies Review Programme* (2022, updated to October 2024).

had not been reviewed.[75] A total of 40 bodies were programmed for review in 2022–23 across 15 departments, 44 across 17 departments in 2023–24.

3.4 From accountability for decisions to accountability for systems

If you looked at the government's online list, 'Departments, Agencies and Public Bodies',[76] in early 2024 you would have seen that the 24 ministerial departments had no fewer than 373 public bodies attached to them, an average of more than 15 per department. We have shown just how varied these bodies are and also what a mass of expenditure and personnel they account for. These characteristics impinge upon the very nature of departmental management. As the Committee of Public Accounts put it in 2016:

> Over the years, government has increased in complexity. Changes to the way that government implements policies and delivers services include: increased devolution to local areas and delivery bodies, greater outsourcing, use of government companies, cross-cutting programmes across departments and delivery through central initiatives. These developments have increased the complexity of delivery relationships and responsibilities within government, and also challenged the traditional model of accountability through the AO [Accounting Officer] (which relies on AOs being solely and personally accountable to Parliament for all spending under their remit). AOs now commonly delegate, devolve or share implementation responsibilities, which means a departmental AO must operate at the head of a *system* of accountability for delivery.[77]

The most obvious manifestation of the systemic character of responsibility for public money is the fact that, in most departments, the Permanent Secretary, as departmental AO, presides over a group of AOs, each responsible for the spending of a public body falling within the departmental accounting boundary or for a discrete function within the department. AOs for government trading funds established under the Government Trading Funds Act 1973 are appointed by the Treasury.[78] For other types of arm's length body, the permanent head of the body will be appointed as its AO by the principal AO of the responsible department.[79] AOs may also be appointed in this way for specific functions within a department:[80] thus in the Treasury itself, its First Permanent Secretary acts as Treasury AO and also as AO for the Consolidated Fund and the National Loans Fund, and has appointed senior officials as additional

[75] ibid para 11.
[76] At <www.gov.uk/government/organisations>.
[77] Public Accounts Committee, *Accountability to Parliament for Taxpayers' Money* (HC 2015–16, 732) para 5. See also *Accountability for Public Money* (HC 2010–12, 740); *Accountability for Public Money—Progress Report* (HC 2010–12, 1503).
[78] *MPM*, para 3.2.2.
[79] *MPM*, para 3.2.3.
[80] *MPM*, para 3.2.3. While this states that such appointments are at the discretion of the principal AO, the Treasury is itself empowered to make such appointments by Government Resources and Accounts Act 2000, s 5(8).

AOs for the Contingencies Fund, the Exchange Equalisation Fund, and the Whole of Government Accounts.[81]

The central response to the concerns of the Public Accounts Committee was based on recommendations made by the then Permanent Secretary to the Department for Communities and Local Government, which was very much at the leading edge of implementation of the relevant reforms. He proposed that AOs should draw up, and publish, concise 'Accountability System Statements' setting out, for each major decentralized funding stream, the system through which they would provide the necessary assurances to Parliament. These statements would both provide a means through which departments could think through the systems proposed to be put in place and help inform scrutiny of the systems and their performance.[82] Initially limited to describing accountability for departmental grants to local government, schools, and the NHS, this device was, following the 2016 Public Accounts Committee report referred to above, generalized to cover all departments, and renamed the 'Accounting Officer System Statement'. As the Treasury's guidance on the coverage and form of such statements defined it, this was 'a single statement setting out all of the accountability relationships and processes within a department, making clear who is accountable for what, from the Principal Accounting Officer down'.[83] The Statement should ensure accountability for all of the public money and other public resources which fall within a single AO's responsibilities, including funding for:

> the activities of the core department;
> activities of its arm's length bodies;
> delivery through local partners, private and voluntary sector bodies, and other third party arrangements; and
> major contracts and outsourced services, and any financial investments or commercial joint ventures.[84]

Statements are published 'alongside', but not as part of, each department's annual report and accounts. They should be reviewed annually as each year's accounts are being prepared, and re-published if there are any material changes.[85]

Responsibilities of AOs in ALBs and in discrete departmental functions are essentially similar to those undertaken for departmental spending by the departmental AO. AOs in ALBs do, however, have to work both within the legislative or other structure establishing their ALB and within the provisions of the ALB's framework document, which will allow the sponsor department to exercise meaningful oversight of the ALB's strategy and performance, pay arrangements, or major transactions. This may involve

[81] HM Treasury, *Annual Report and Accounts 2019–2020* (HC 2019–21, 746) 76. A list of AOs appointed for the Treasury's executive agencies and other ALBs appears at 238.

[82] Department for Communities and Local Government, *Accountability: Adapting to Decentralisation* (September 2011) para 51.

[83] HM Treasury, *Accounting Officer System Statements: Guidance* (April 2017) para 1.7.

[84] ibid para 1.9.

[85] Statements in force are collected at <www.gov.uk/government/collections/accounting-officer-system-statements>.

regular returns, standard delegations, and reporting of exceptions.[86] Such oversight is something for which the departmental AO is responsible.

IV Public Appointments

One consequence of the growth of public bodies of one kind or another over the course of the last century was the emergence of new 'spoils' system in the shape of a substantial increase in the patronage available to ministers.[87] In contrast to appointments to the Civil Service, which had been regulated since the Northcote-Trevelyan reforms of the mid-19th century, appointments to public bodies were to remain unregulated until the end of the last century. Under the system then introduced ministerial appointments to a prescribed list of public bodies are 'regulated' by a Commissioner for Public Appointments. Not all appointments to the bodies discussed in the preceding sections of this chapter are so regulated.[88]

4.1 The Nolan reforms

The catalyst for reform was the Committee on Standards in Public Life (CSPL, or the Nolan Committee after its first chair), which was appointed by John Major in response to the allegations of 'sleaze' which dogged the 1992 Conservative government. The abuse of ministerial powers of appointment did not feature among the allegations, but in its first report the Committee found much public concern about appointments to 'Quango Boards' and a widespread belief that they were not always made on merit.[89] Departments were responsible for making their own appointments, with the role of the central departments being limited to issuing guidance and maintaining a list of potential candidates.[90] An interdepartmental review of these arrangements, coordinated by the Public Appointments Unit (PAU) within the Cabinet Office, had found that, 'despite the common central guidance, actual procedures varied widely. There were many areas of good practice, but other areas and departments where procedures were less thorough.' The review recommended the 'strengthening of the guidance, and the promotion of good practice to bring all procedures into line with the best.'[91]

The Nolan Committee recommended that public appointments remain a ministerial function—accountability to Parliament was an important constitutional principle which the Committee had no wish to weaken[92]—but it was not persuaded that the existing or proposed safeguards were sufficiently robust. In the Committee's view,

[86] *MPM*, para 3.8.2. See also Treasury Officer of Accounts, *The Accounting Officer's Survival Guide* (December 2015) paras 32–36.
[87] Ivor Jennings, *Cabinet Government* (3rd edn, CUP 1959) 132–33.
[88] For a classification of different types of government appointment, including unregulated appointments, see Matthew Gill and Grant Dalton, *Reforming Public Appointments* (Institute for Government August 2022) 10.
[89] Committee on Standards in Public Life, *Standards in Public Life: First Report* (Cm 2850, 1995) 6.
[90] ibid para 4.13.
[91] ibid para 4.16.
[92] ibid para 4.29.

the main weakness both in the current arrangements and those proposed in the PAU Review was the absence of effective external scrutiny. The PAU appeared to have little role in monitoring the working of its central guidance beyond that necessary to produce its annual report, which was largely a statistical summary of appointments. There was no mechanism for the regular review of the work of individual departments and no means of identifying failures of system or practice. An independent body was needed to undertake the continued standard setting and monitoring that would enhance and sustain public confidence in the appointments process.[93] The Committee's recommendations—for the extension of the merit principle to public appointments (to which the government was already committed); for appointments to be made after advice from a panel or committee which included an independent element; and for an independent commissioner for public appointments to monitor, regulate, and approve departmental appointments procedures—were implemented by prerogative Order in Council in November 1995,[94] illustrating the speed and ease with which reform based on the prerogative could be introduced. While it might be appropriate in due course for the arrangements for the Commissioner to be put on a statutory footing, there was no need to wait for legislation to make the necessary administrative arrangements.[95]

In its assessment of the system a decade later, CSPL was in no doubt that it was an improvement on the system of unrestricted ministerial patronage it had replaced. There were weaknesses that needed to be addressed but the suspicion of cronyism in public appointments had been removed.

> In summary, we were told about a 'rather sensible system' which acts as 'a badge of reassurance' for probity. And a system which, despite flaws, works . . . As [the Commissioner] herself explained, 'If I remember why my office was set up in the first place, it was set up to ensure that cronyism was not the order of the day and it was set up to ensure people who were appointed were fit for appointment' . . . Significant steps have been made towards these goals.[96]

4.2 The Grimstone Review

The Grimstone Review of the system of public appointments was commissioned by the 2015 Conservative government shortly after the general election.

> We are now twenty years on, and this provides a suitable opportunity to review the role of the Commissioner and the processes around public appointments. In the light of the range and diversity of public appointments, it is important to ensure that the

[93] ibid paras 4.52–4.53.

[94] Public Appointments Order in Council 1995. As originally introduced the Nolan reforms applied only to executive NDPBs and NHS trust boards. In 1998 their scope was extended to include advisory NDPBs, public corporations, and certain utility regulators.

[95] Committee on Standards in Public Life, *Standards in Public Life: First Report* (n 89) para 4.58.

[96] Committee on Standards in Public Life, *Getting the Balance Right: Implementing Standards of Conduct in Public Life* (Cm 6407, 2005) para 2.24.

> procedures are both effective and proportionate and to review whether procedures as practised fit within the intentions of the Nolan principles.[97]

The review recommended significant changes to the system. The Commissioner's Code of Practice for Ministerial Appointments to Public Bodies should be replaced by a government code—the government rather than the Commissioner should set the rules—and the Commissioner's role should be confined to ensuring that appointing authorities acted in accordance with the rules. Commissioners had become 'increasingly involved in the running of competitions as opposed to regulating them. The effect of this was to increase consistency but at the expense of creating complex bureaucratic processes that blurred the lines between the regulator and departments.'[98] The Commissioner's role should be correspondingly reduced.

> It is the role of ministers and departments to inspire public confidence by demonstrating through their actions that they are complying with the [rules]. It is the role of the Commissioner for Public Appointments to provide independent assurance that they have done so. To ensure that the independence of the regulatory role is maintained, the Commissioner should not play a direct part in recruitments.[99]

The proposals, which were warmly welcomed by the government, met with fierce criticism from the outgoing Commissioner, Sir David Normington:

> Taken together, Grimstone's proposals would enable ministers to set their own rules; override those rules whenever they want; appoint their own selection panels; get preferential treatment for favoured candidates; ignore the panel's advice if they don't like it; and appoint someone considered by the panel as not up to the job. The main check on these powers is transparency, but transparency has its limits when there is no-one with the power to intervene if the rules are broken.[100]

The Commissioner's criticisms were widely shared:

> Many distinguished observers of the appointments system have expressed considerable concern about Grimstone's proposals—these must not be dismissed. The system of public appointments must be seen to ensure that appointments are being made on merit. Given the criticisms that have been made, it is clear that, without extensive amendment, the Grimstone proposals will not and cannot sustain public confidence.[101]

97 Written Ministerial Statement UIN HCWS82 (2 July 2015).

98 Cabinet Office, *Better Public Appointments: A Review of the Public Appointments Process* (March 2016) para 2.14.

99 ibid conclusions and recommendations, para 30.

100 Sir David Normington, 'The five reasons I'm concerned about plans to overhaul the public appointments process' *Civil Service World* (21 March 2016).

101 Public Administration and Constitutional Affairs Committee, *Better Public Appointments? The Grimstone Review on Public Appointments* (HC 2015–16, 495) para 70.

The government was unmoved. Like the Nolan reforms 20 years earlier, the reforms were implemented by prerogative Order in Council,[102] illustrating the ease with which a system based on the prerogative could be altered—'by a stroke of the pen and a nod of the Privy Council' as the outgoing Commissioner later put it in evidence to CSPL.

4.3 The current system

The bodies to which the public appointments system applies are listed in the Public Appointments (No 2) Order in Council 2023. Appointments to public bodies or public offices not listed are not regulated by the Commissioner for Public Appointments. The appointments to which it applies are ministerial appointments of non-executive chairs and directors of public bodies, statutory office-holders, and members of advisory committees. It does not apply to the appointment of an employee of a public body or public office except so far as specified in the Order.

The Minister for the Cabinet Office is required by the Order in Council to prepare, publish, and keep under review a Governance Code which sets out the principles of public appointments, and guidance on the practices to be followed in relation to making public appointments.[103] The Governance Code on Public Appointments 2016, which replaced the Commissioner's Code of Practice for Ministerial Appointments to Public Bodies, significantly increased the ability of ministers to shape the appointments process, in line with the recommendations of the Grimstone Review, giving ministers the right to determine panel composition and advise panels on preferred candidates at all stages of a competition. It also gave ministers powers to overrule assessment panels, either by asking that the recruitment process be re-run with a new panel, or by appointing someone a panel had not deemed 'appointable'. No person who has not been deemed 'appointable' has been appointed since the Code was introduced.

The Order in Council provides that the Commissioner's functions must be exercised 'with the object of ensuring that appointing authorities act in accordance with the Governance Code, including the principles of public appointments'.[104] The Commissioner must also, in the manner the Commissioner thinks fit, carry out an audit of the procedures and practices followed by appointing authorities in making public appointments, including the interpretation and application by them of the Governance Code including the principles of public appointments.[105] 'The aim is not to find fault but to identify good practice, challenges, and to encourage improvement.'[106] The Commissioner may also conduct investigations and inquiries, the latter into the procedures and practices followed by an appointing authority in relation to any public appointment whether in response to a complaint or otherwise.[107]

[102] Public Appointments Order in Council 2016, which came into effect on 1 January 2017. Some concessions were secured in negotiations between the Cabinet Office and Normington's successor, Peter Riddell.

[103] Public Appointments (No 2) Order in Council 2023, art 3(1).

[104] ibid art 4(1).

[105] ibid art 4(2).

[106] Commissioner for Public Appointments, *Annual Report 2020–21*, Commissioner's Foreword.

[107] Public Appointments (No 2) Order in Council 2023, arts 4(3),(4) and 6.

As important as the Grimstone changes in procedures, the Commissioner said in correspondence with PACAC before the new system came into operation, would be the spirit in which they were interpreted and implemented by ministers and departments.[108] It was perhaps little surprise therefore that the Johnson government should have attempted to manipulate the system to its advantage:

> Over the past 18 months, the present Government has actively sought to appoint allies to the boards of public bodies. This is not the first time this has happened. Such attempts tend to go in waves. And there is nothing in the Code, or, indeed, past practice, against appointing people with political links . . . It is perfectly understandable that ministers want to appoint allies and those who agree with their goals to executive arms length bodies. Past Labour as well as Conservative Governments have appointed people with clear party backgrounds and ties. What is different now is the breadth of the campaign and the close engagement of 10 Downing Street.[109]

Ministers were in 'a strong even dominant position in public appointments' but some were 'now seeking to tilt the process even further to their advantage'. There had been leaks that 'Number 10 favours certain candidates even before a competition starts. This matters mainly because it deters good candidates from putting their names forward—and there is anecdotal evidence of such a chilling effect. Ministers insist that they deplore such leaking but it has not stopped some of their advisers.' Ministers had tried to undermine the independence of interview panels, including by trying to appoint Conservative members of the House of Lords as senior independent panel members. There had also been cases of ministers seeking to pack interview panels, including 'by appointing non-executive members of their departmental boards who are political allies'.[110]

The Johnson government's abuse of the system aside, the Grimstone reforms effectively saw ministers and departments regain control over public appointments, subject to the external oversight seen as critical by the Nolan Committee.[111] A key question therefore was whether departments would perform any better than they had 20 years before. On the evidence of the Commissioner's most recent annual report it would seem not. Among the 'offenders' were the Treasury and the Cabinet Office, with the latter able to provide little of the data requested during the annual audit. Both had yet to establish central teams to manage public appointments as recommended by the Governance Code.[112] The writ of the Minister for the Cabinet Office, whose code after all it was, it would seem, did not run to the Cabinet Office.

108 Public Administration and Constitutional Affairs Committee, *Better Public Appointments? Follow-up and the Government Response to the Committee's Third Report, Better Public Appointments?: The Grimstone Review on Public Appointments* (HC 2016–17, 1062) app 2.

109 Peter Riddell, *Pre-Valedictory speech to the UCL Constitution Unit on Public Appointments* (April 2021).

110 ibid; see also Commissioner for Public Appointments, *Annual Report 2020–21* (n 106).

111 The Grimstone Review was equally insistent on the importance of external oversight: Cabinet Office, *Better Public Appointments* (n 98) para 3.10 ('It is essential that public confidence is maintained in the system of appointments. A strong control framework driven by a combination of self-regulation, and robust external scrutiny and regulation is the best way to ensure this, backed up by full transparency').

112 Commissioner for Public Appointments, *Annual Report 2022–23*, 13.

4.4 Prospects

CSPL's assessment of the public appointments system's prospects in its Standards Matter 2 Review was pessimistic:

> Though the public appointments system has generally worked well in recent years, it is highly dependent on informal mechanisms, including the willingness of ministers to act with restraint and the preparedness of the Commissioner to speak out against breaches of the letter or the spirit of the code. It is unlikely that a system so dependent on personal responsibility will be sustainable in the long term.[113]

The Committee made a number of recommendations for reform, some of which—including that non-executive directors should become regulated appointments—were accepted by the Sunak government in its response almost two years later. The government however declined to accept the Committee's recommendation that the Commissioner should be put on a statutory basis. It believed that the current constitutional position was the correct one, and that placing scrutiny bodies into primary legislation risked drawing the courts into political matters.[114] Whether its belief is shared by a Labour government elected on a manifesto commitment to establish an independent Ethics and Integrity Commission to ensure probity in government remains to be seen.[115]

[113] Committee on Standards in Public Life, *Upholding Standards in Public Life: Final Report of the Standards Matter 2 Review* (November 2021) 10, paras 5.8–5.9. The Public Accounts Committee's assessment was that the current process 'does not give confidence that it is efficient, transparent and fair'; its criticisms were levelled at the Cabinet Office, which among other things did not check whether its Code was being followed across government: Committee of Public Accounts, *Government's Delivery through Arm's-Length Bodies* (HC 2021–22, 181) Conclusions and recommendations, para 6.

[114] Cabinet Office, *Strengthening Ethics and Integrity in Central Government*, CP 900 (July 2023) 6.

[115] Labour Party, *Change: General Election Manifesto 2024* (June 2024) 107.

5

Devolution: From 'Devolve and Forget' to 'Protect and Respect'

I Introduction

One of the 1997 New Labour government's major achievements was its programme of constitutional reform. Devolution to Scotland, Wales, and Northern Ireland was at the heart of that programme; Scottish devolution its 'flagship . . . and the centrepiece of the legacy of John Smith'.[1] In contrast to the failed devolution initiative of the 1970s it was achieved 'extraordinarily quickly and with apparent ease', in part because of the size of the government's majority.[2] It was also eased by the relatively limited nature of the adjustments involved: most of the functions devolved were already administered separately in Scotland, Wales, and Northern Ireland, the devolved administrations continued to be funded as before, and the Home Civil Service (serving the UK government and the Scottish and Welsh governments) remained unified (Northern Ireland retained the separate civil service it had had since 1922). The Scotland, Wales, and Northern Ireland Offices were also retained as a link between the UK government and the devolved administrations.[3]

The powers of the devolved institutions of government have been significantly increased since devolution.[4] Those of the Scottish Parliament were increased by the Scotland Acts of 2012 and 2016, the latter in implementation of the recommendations of the cross-party Smith Commission following the 2014 independence referendum, making Holyrood, it was claimed, 'one of the most powerful subnational parliaments in the world'.[5] Having initially been limited to subordinate law-making, the Welsh Senedd acquired primary law-making powers in 2011, following a referendum, and further powers under the Wales Acts of 2014 and 2017 in implementation of the recommendations of the Silk Commission.[6] The powers of the Northern

[1] Kenneth Mackenzie, 'How the Reforms Came about' in Andrew McDonald (ed), *Reinventing Britain: Constitutional Change and New Labour* (Politico's 2007) 103, 115.

[2] Sir Richard Wilson, Portrait of a Profession Revisited, Speech 26 March 2002. The Belfast/Good Friday Agreement sat outside the main constitutional reform programme. 'British policy-makers of all parties had long conceived of Northern Ireland as a special case, deserving of particular treatment. Northern Ireland was, quite simply, different and the resolution of its plight took place in a distinct political space, far removed from talk of Lords reform, PR or, even, devolution to Scotland and Wales': Andrew McDonald, *Changing States, Changing Nations: Constitutional Reform and National Identity in the Late Twentieth Century* (Bloomsbury Publishing 2021) 67.

[3] Akash Paun and Robyn Munro, *Governing in an Ever Looser Union* (Institute for Government 2015) 10.

[4] Cabinet Office, *Review of UK Government Union Capability* (November 2019) 12.

[5] HM Government, *Scotland in the United Kingdom: An Enduring Settlement* (Cm 8890, 2015).

[6] Commission on Devolution in Wales, *Empowerment and Responsibility: Financial Powers to Strengthen Wales* (November 2012); *Empowerment and Responsibility: Legislative Powers to Strengthen Wales* (March 2014).

Executive Self-Government and the Constitution. Terence Daintith and Alan Page, Oxford University Press.
 DOI: 10.1093/9780198937630.003.0005

Ireland Assembly have also been increased, most notably in respect of policing and criminal justice and corporation tax,[7] but the concern has been more with the stability of the power-sharing system of government than the Assembly's powers.

The devolution of further powers to the Scottish Parliament after the 2014 independence referendum prompted criticism that this had been done with scant regard for the implications for the Union. In its 2016 report on *The Union and devolution*, the House of Lords Constitution Committee criticized successive governments for having 'taken the Union for granted'. Power had been devolved in 'an ad hoc, piecemeal fashion' without 'proper consideration of the cumulative impact of devolution on the integrity of the Union itself'. 'An inattentive approach to the integrity of the Union cannot continue', the Committee warned. 'While the constitution should reflect the wishes and interests of the nations and regions, that must not be at the expense of the stability, coherence and viability of the Union as a whole.'[8]

Not only had the Union been 'forgotten', the Committee suggested, but so too had the devolved nations:

> One thing that has struck us a lot . . . has been the sense within Whitehall particularly, although also in Westminster, that says, 'Right. Scotland, Wales and Northern Ireland are looking after their own affairs. We don't have to think about them' . . . Psychologically, people post-1999 were almost saying, 'Oh well, we've done devolution'.[9]

For the Committee, this attitude of 'devolve and forget' had become 'entrenched and widespread to the detriment of effective relations and the interests of the people of the devolved nations'.[10] What was needed, it argued, was:

> a new mindset throughout the UK Government and Civil Service with regard to relations with the devolved nations. The mechanisms by which the UK Government manages relations with the devolved administrations must strengthen, rather than weaken, the Union. The UK Government must recognise that it retains an overarching responsibility for ensuring that the governance of the UK operates effectively. Instead of a 'devolve and forget' attitude they should be engaging with the devolved

[7] The Northern Ireland Act 1998 (Devolution of Policing and Justice Functions) Order 2010, SI 2010 976; Corporation Tax (Northern Ireland) Act 2015.

[8] House of Lords Constitution Committee, *The Union and Devolution* (HL 2015–16, 149) Summary. The Committee had raised the issue earlier in its response to the government's proposals. 'We recognise the political imperatives behind these proposals, but they continue a pattern of ad hoc, piecemeal change to the devolution settlements which could well destabilise the Union as a whole in the longer term. We question how any process that does not consider the future of the Union as a whole could provide for an "enduring" settlement' (*Proposals for the Devolution of Further Powers to Scotland* (HL 2014–15, 145) Summary. In its report on *Inter-governmental Relations in the United Kingdom*, the Committee recorded its 'deep concern' at the 'lack of central coordination and oversight of the devolution settlements and of the minimal consideration given to the effect of devolution in one area of the UK on other areas, and on the Union as a whole' (*Inter-governmental Relations in the United Kingdom* (HL 2014–15, 146) para 133).

[9] House of Lords Constitution Committee, *The Union and Devolution* (n 8) para 294, quoting Peter Riddell in evidence.

[10] ibid para 295.

> administrations across the whole breadth of government policy: not interfering, but co-operating and collaborating where possible and managing cross-border or UK-wide impacts that may result from differing policy and service delivery choices. The UK Government should work to reach an agreement with the devolved administrations to ensure a constructive approach to this engagement is introduced and maintained for the long-term on all sides.[11]

Far from a new mindset, however, the outcome of the EU referendum a month later, was to precipitate a breakdown in relations between the UK and Scottish governments after Theresa May rejected the Scottish First Minister Nicola Sturgeon's call for a second independence referendum, Scotland having voted to remain. 'Now is not the time', the Prime Minister said.[12] With the renewed threat of the break-up of the Union, the Cabinet Office's strategic objectives were redefined with 'Maintain the integrity of the Union' (December 2017) replacing 'Create a more united democracy' (February 2016). And on becoming Prime Minister in July 2019, Boris Johnson styled himself 'Minister for the Union'—working 'to ensure that all of government is acting on behalf of the entire United Kingdom: England, Northern Ireland, Scotland, and Wales'—and established a Union Unit within the Prime Minister's Office, with 'ensuring the benefits of the Union are clear, visible and understood' as its core aim.[13]

While the difficulties have not been entirely of the United Kingdom government's own making, the general picture 25 years on is one of a system of government that has yet to adjust to devolution.

The chapter proceeds as follows. We begin with the multiple changes in the allocation of responsibility for the Union and devolution within central government over the last 25 years and the criticism that continuous reorganization has impeded its capacity to manage the devolved system of government.[14] We then examine the arrangements for managing relations between the UK government and the devolved governments, before ending with the efforts that have been made to build 'devolution capability' in Whitehall.

[11] ibid para 305; in evidence to the Committee it was said the culture of the Civil Service had yet to adapt to devolution: 'The more important issue is to get a different culture within UK Government departments, to recognise and build on what has been achieved in the devolution model rather than somehow, if not fighting against it, being slightly grudging in celebrating what goes on': para 293, quoting former Scotland Office Director Alun Evans.

[12] Northern Ireland also voted to remain, but power-sharing collapsed in January 2017, leaving it without a devolved government until power-sharing was restored in January 2020, only to collapse again in February 2022 when the Democratic Unionist Party (DUP) First Minister withdrew in protest at the Northern Ireland Protocol. It was to be another two years before it was restored.

[13] Anthony Seldon and Raymond Newell, *Johnson at 10: The Inside Story* (Atlantic Books 2023) 170–71; the Unit was headed by Luke Graham, a Conservative Scottish MP defeated at the 2019 general election. Graham was replaced by Oliver Lewis, a protégé of Dominic Cummings, in February 2021, who quit a fortnight after his appointment after being accused of briefing against Michael Gove.

[14] House of Lords Constitution Committee, *Respect and Cooperation: Building a Stronger Union for the 21st century* (HL 2021–22, 142) para 280.

II The Machinery of Government and Devolution

For some observers the first decade of devolution was the decade of the 'missing' or 'hollow' centre.[15] During that time, departmental responsibility for overseeing the working of the devolved system of government had been 'divided and unsettled'. It had involved the Cabinet Office; 10 Downing Street; the Ministry of Justice; the former Department for Constitutional Affairs; the former Office of the Deputy Prime Minister; and the Scotland, Wales, and Northern Ireland Offices. What was lacking, the House of Commons Justice Committee argued, was 'any one department which is clearly charged with taking a holistic view of the infrastructure of government across the United Kingdom and the constitutional and policy issues involved'.[16]

The Scottish independence referendum was 'a challenge for which the machinery of government was distinctly unprepared'.[17] The response within Whitehall

> involved an uncomfortable amalgam of teams and individuals from the Treasury, No 10, the Cabinet Office and the Scotland Office, corralled through a series of working groups organised by the Deputy Prime Minister's office, and given overall political direction by the Scotland Cabinet sub-committee. Buffeted by internal political pressures within the Whitehall machine, this arrangement unsurprisingly began to fray as the campaign wore on ...
>
> [Departments for their part] were badgered to manage their own communications and announcements in ways that were sensitive to Scottish interests, and to send a minister on an occasional foray north of the border. But, for the most part, ministers and central government departments were no more visible in Scotland than in normal times—a striking reflection of the inability of the centre to make even an existential threat to its territorial integrity its main strategic priority.[18]

After the referendum, efforts were made to address the weaknesses that had been revealed—principally by bringing the Scotland and Wales Offices, the 'orphan children of Whitehall',[19] into the Cabinet Office. Acknowledging that, 'historically, Whitehall hadn't paid much attention to Scotland or to the details of the devolution settlement',[20] the UK Governance Group (UKGG) was established within the Cabinet Office in June 2015 to lead the UK government's work on the constitution and devolution.[21]

The Group brought together, under one Civil Service command, the Cabinet Office's Constitution Group, the Scotland Office, the Office of the Advocate General for Scotland, and the Wales Office—but not the Northern Ireland Office for a mixture

[15] House of Commons Justice Committee, *Devolution: A Decade On* (HC 2008–09, 529) para 31.
[16] ibid para 63.
[17] Michael Kenny, Philip Rycroft, and Jack Sheldon, *Union at the Crossroads. Can the British State Handle the Challenges of Devolution?* (The Constitution Society 2021) 15.
[18] ibid 17.
[19] ibid 15.
[20] Suzanne Heywood, *What Does Jeremy Think? Jeremy Heywood and the Making of Modern Britain* (William Collins 2021) 431.
[21] Responsibility for constitutional issues had moved from the Ministry of Justice to the Cabinet Office with the formation of the Coalition government in 2010.

of personal and policy reasons.[22] Led by a Second Permanent Secretary in the Cabinet Office, reporting directly to the Cabinet Secretary, the Group gave the Scotland and Wales Offices, for the first time since devolution was introduced, as well as the government's broader constitutional and devolution agenda, a voice at the weekly meetings of Permanent Secretaries.[23] They also gained greater heft in Whitehall by reason of being part of the Cabinet Office. The Secretaries of State also got to keep their offices and better support.

Further consideration was given to the machinery of government by the Dunlop Review of UK Government Union Capability, which was commissioned by the outgoing Prime Minister, Theresa May, in July 2019 to consider 'whether UK Government structures are configured in such a way as to strengthen the working of the Union, and to recommend changes where appropriate'.[24] Lord Dunlop's review reiterated the criticisms of the House of Lords Constitution Committee three years earlier. Not enough attention had been paid to the implications of the devolution of significant powers 'for the way our Union runs'; the focus had been on the devolution of powers to the neglect of the machinery and arrangements which 'enable the UK Government to discharge sensitively its own unique duties to people across all parts of the country, and to work constructively with devolved governments where responsibilities overlap'—machinery and arrangements which were 'an essential part of the glue that binds together our United Kingdom'.[25] The creation of the UKGG had 'greatly enhanced the way in which the centre and three Secretary of State offices worked together and given the UK Government a greater presence in Scotland, Wales and Northern Ireland. It had provided a more powerful collective voice within the upper echelons of the government for issues related to Scotland, Wales and Northern Ireland and the Union'.[26] But there was still some way to travel to reach 'a consistent and systematic consideration of how the UK Government delivers for the whole of the UK, with robust actionable plans'.[27] More needed to be done 'to embed the Union at the heart of UK Government policy development and decision-making'.[28]

The review made a number of recommendations 'aimed at deepening Whitehall's engagement with the devolved parts of the UK, the most eye-catching of which was establishment of a new, senior cabinet post with responsibility for managing intergovernmental relations and constitutional policy'.[29] As Minister for the Union, Lord Dunlop argued, the Prime Minister needed to be supported by the establishment of 'an operational arm, in ministerial terms, with day-to-day oversight of matters related to Scotland, Wales and Northern Ireland and the constitution'.[30] A new senior Cabinet position—a 'Great Office of State'—should be formally recognized within

[22] A Northern Ireland team was subsequently added: Cabinet Office, *Review of UK Government Union Capability* (n 4) 16.
[23] Kenny, Rycroft, and Sheldon (n 17) 22.
[24] Cabinet Office, *Review of UK Government Union Capability* (n 4); the Review was completed in 2019 but not made public until March 2021.
[25] ibid 7.
[26] ibid 16.
[27] ibid 14.
[28] ibid 8.
[29] Kenny, Rycroft, and Sheldon (n 17) 39.
[30] Cabinet Office, *Review of UK Government Union Capability* (n 4) 15.

the machinery of government with specific responsibility for the constitutional integrity of the United Kingdom. The new role, with the suggested title 'Secretary of State for Intergovernmental and Constitutional Affairs', should have a status akin to the Chancellor of the Exchequer, Foreign Secretary, or Home Secretary. The new Secretary of State would speak in Cabinet for the constitution and would take a holistic view across the United Kingdom, arbitrating between other ministers. Just as the Lord Chancellor was responsible for defending judicial independence, the new Secretary of State would have a duty to uphold the integrity of the constitution, including intergovernmental relations.[31]

The new Secretary of State should be supported by a Cabinet sub-committee which would be responsible for preparing cross-government strategic priorities to enhance the Union and ensuring their effective delivery. As well as the new Secretary of State, its membership should include the Chancellor of the Exchequer . . . and the Secretaries of State for Scotland, Wales and Northern Ireland. Other Cabinet ministers would be invited to attend depending on the agenda, not least to ensure effective accountability for the development and delivery of their Union plans.'[32]

It was time to 'fully realise the benefits of the UKGG'. A single permanent secretary head of UKGG should be established to lead the three offices of the Secretaries of State for Scotland, Wales and Northern Ireland as well as the relevant Cabinet Office teams, supporting the new senior minister and three Secretaries of State. This would give Union strategy 'a coherent voice within government', for example at the weekly meeting of Permanent Secretaries chaired by the Cabinet Secretary.[33]

The Northern Ireland Office should also be brought into the UKGG fold. This would better enable a more joined-up approach to devolution issues, while protecting the unique features of the individual devolution settlements.[34] The three territorial Secretaries of State, should remain, however, because there was 'great value in continuing to have ministers of Cabinet rank, providing a distinct voice and collective conscience for the interests of Scotland, Wales and Northern Ireland within the UK Government'.[35] The aim was 'the optimum balance between the representational value of the offices of the Secretaries of State for Scotland, Wales and Northern Ireland, and the convening power of the Cabinet Office'.[36]

Little of this had happened by the time the review was published in March 2021, almost two years after it had been commissioned. Nor was it to happen. In September 2021, six months after the review was published, responsibility for UK governance and devolution policy was transferred from the Cabinet Office to the freshly rebranded Department for Levelling Up, Housing and Communities (DLUHC), formerly the Ministry of Housing, Communities and Local Government, with Michael Gove as Secretary of State for Levelling Up, Housing and Communities *and* Minister

[31] ibid 9; in similar vein, Alun Evans (head of the Scotland Office 2012–15) proposed a deputy prime minister with responsibility for the nations and regions: *The Times* (3 May 2021).

[32] Cabinet Office, *Review of UK Government Union Capability* (n 4) 18.

[33] ibid 19.

[34] ibid.

[35] ibid 17.

[36] ibid 8.

for Intergovernmental Relations.[37] With the transfer of responsibility, 'maintaining the integrity of the Union' was dropped from the Cabinet Office's priority outcomes, and 'ensuring the benefits of the Union are clear, visible and understood' (formerly the 'core aim' of the Union Directorate established in the Cabinet Office in early 2020) added to those of DLUHC.[38]

Two Cabinet committees were also established, on the model of the Brexit strategy and operations committees: a Union Strategy Committee chaired by the Prime Minister and charged with considering 'matters relating to strengthening the Union of the United Kingdom', supported by a Union Policy Implementation sub-committee, chaired by the Levelling Up Secretary, to deliver the government's priorities relating to the Union.[39]

Welcoming the combined responsibility for the devolution arrangements across the United Kingdom, the House of Lords Constitution Committee expressed the hope that they would become a settled part of the machinery of government. 'We believe that Whitehall's capacity to manage a fundamental part of the United Kingdom's governance arrangements would be at risk of being undermined if this combination continues to be vulnerable to frequent and significant restructuring.'[40] Within a year, however, it was undone by Liz Truss as Prime Minister with the appointment of Nadhim Zahawi as Chancellor of the Duchy of Lancaster and Minister for Intergovernmental Relations in September 2022, only to be restored by her successor Rishi Sunak seven weeks later with the reappointment of Michael Gove, who had been sacked by Johnson in one of his last acts as Prime Minister, as Levelling Up Secretary and Minister for Intergovernmental Relations in October 2022.

The two Cabinet committees were also abolished by Liz Truss before being replaced by her successor with a single Domestic and Economic Affairs (Union) Committee, 'to consider matters relating to the Union of the United Kingdom', chaired by the Prime Minister and including the Chancellor of the Duchy of Lancaster, the Levelling Up Secretary and Minister for Intergovernmental Relations, and the three territorial Secretaries of State among its members.

Lord Dunlop had recommended that the new Secretary of State should remain within the Cabinet Office, taking advantage of that department's 'convening power' and 'overall responsibility for the implementation of government policy'.[41] The

[37] UIN HCWS309 (23 September 2021): 'I am making this statement to bring to the House's attention the following Machinery of Government change. Responsibility for driving forward the levelling up agenda and elections and UK governance and devolution policy is being moved to create a new Department for Levelling Up, Housing and Communities. This change will embed levelling up commitments and policy on governance in the United Kingdom and elections within a single department which already manages relationships with local communities, local government and the housing sector. Bringing these responsibilities together will allow the Secretary of State to embed ever closer working with the Territorial Offices and lead coordination with the devolved administrations on my behalf.'

[38] In May 2023, the UK governance team was moved from the Cabinet Office into the Union and Devolution team in DLUHC: (UIN HCWS803, 23 May 2023).

[39] House of Lords Constitution Committee, *Respect and Cooperation* (n 14) para 289. Established in February 2021, the Union Strategy Committee replaced the short-lived Union Unit in the Prime Minister's Office; Michael Gove took responsibility for all Union policy after the resignation of the Unit's head, Oliver Lewis, in February 2021.

[40] ibid para 285.

[41] Cabinet Office, *Review of UK Government Union Capability* (n 4) 16–17.

political importance of levelling up together with Gove's abilities as a minister doubtless explain the Prime Minister's decision to appoint him Levelling Up Secretary and to add the Union and devolution to the responsibilities of the rebranded department. The transfer of responsibility to the former Ministry of Housing, Communities and Local Government, however, was widely regarded as a retrograde step:

> For the devolution settlement to work as well as it needs to, it is important that there is a senior Minister at the centre of Government . . . who can take that overview. If you hive it off to any single Department, however committed and well-intended a particular Minister might be, it seems to me that you lose something. Also, that Minister is not going to be there forever, and you do not get that same institutional commitment from Housing and Local Government any more than you would from putting devolution in with DEFRA [Department for Environment, Food and Rural Affairs] or the Home Office.[42]
>
> Let's not forget that Whitehall is an intensely hierarchical place. If you are a line Department . . . you might reluctantly take instruction from the Cabinet Office, the Treasury or No. 10, but you will be very reluctant to do the bidding of another line Department. Putting responsibilities in a line Department signals to the rest of Whitehall that this set of issues is a lower order priority than the things that the centre wants to concentrate on.[43]

Appearing before the Public Administration and Constitutional Affairs Committee (PACAC) as Chancellor of Duchy of Lancaster, three months before his appointment as Levelling Up Secretary and Minister for Intergovernmental Relations, Michael Gove described 'the work of coordinating the roles of the Scotland Office, the Wales Office and Northern Ireland Office with other UK Government Departments' as 'a natural fit in the Cabinet Office'.[44] After the July 2024 general election responsibility for devolution outside England returned to the centre, with the Chancellor of the Duchy of Lancaster also becoming Minister for Intergovernmental Relations.[45]

[42] Public Administration and Constitutional Affairs Committee, oral evidence, *Devolution Capability in Whitehall* (HC 200, 16 January 2024) q 53 (Sir David Lidington). 'Were I to do the report again, given what has happened, I would go with what a lot of people have said: that what was the UK Governance Group and is now the Union and Devolution Directorate located in DLUHC should be returned to the centre of Government' (ibid q 83 Lord Dunlop).

[43] Public Administration and Constitutional Affairs Committee, oral evidence, *Devolution Capability in Whitehall* (HC 1438 13 September 2023) q 6 (Philip Rycroft).

[44] Public Administration and Constitutional Affairs Committee, oral evidence, *The Dunlop Review and the UK Government's Union Capability* (HC 39 20 May 2021) q 56.

[45] 'Responsibility for Union and devolution policy across Scotland, Wales and Northern Ireland will move from the Ministry of Housing, Communities and Local Government to the Cabinet Office. This change will support cross-government coordination and engagement with the devolved governments which will be led by the Chancellor for the Duchy of Lancaster as Minister for Intergovernmental Relations. Responsibility for devolution policy in England and engagement with Mayors and local government will remain with the Deputy Prime Minister and Ministry of Housing, Communities and Local Government': (UIN HCWS71, 5 September 2024).

III Intergovernmental Relations

> *'All complex, multi-level constitutional systems have had to develop tools to co-ordinate the exercise of powers distributed amongst various decision-making entities.'*[46]

The need for some liaison machinery and 'administrative conventions' of cooperation and joint working between the four administrations was recognized early on and addressed in a series of multilateral and bilateral agreements. Among the things that went through 'virtually on the nod' in the preparation of the devolution White Papers was 'the adoption of administrative concordats to regulate dealings between the Scottish and Welsh departments and their UK or English opposite numbers in London rather than have a formal code of conduct enshrined in statute law'.[47]

The principal agreement continues to be the Memorandum of Understanding (MoU) between the four administrations, which set out the 'shared understanding' of the UK government and the devolved administrations of the principles, drawn from pre-devolution practice, on which relations between them were to be based.[48] Separate overarching 'concordats' applied broadly uniform arrangements to three areas where a common approach was felt necessary: the handling of matters with an EU dimension, financial assistance to industry, and international relations touching on the responsibilities of the devolved administrations. Bilateral concordats between individual Whitehall departments and the devolved administrations made more detailed provision in relation to individual policy areas. Their aim and purpose was 'to preserve existing good working relationships and ensure that the business of government [was] conducted smoothly and efficiently under devolution'.[49]

The agreements made clear that they were not intended to be legally binding. The MoU is 'a statement of political intent and should not be interpreted as a binding agreement. It does not create legal obligations between the parties.'[50] The overarching concordats were likewise 'not intended to be legally binding, but to serve as working documents',[51] while the purpose of bilateral concordats was '*not* to create legal obligations or restrictions on any party; rather they will set the ground rules for administrative cooperation and exchange of information'.[52]

A Joint Ministerial Committee (JMC), made up in its plenary format of the Prime Minister as chair and the First Ministers from Scotland, Wales, and Northern Ireland,

46 Johanne Poirier, *The Functions of Intergovernmental Agreements: Post-Devolution Concordats in a Comparative Perspective* (The Constitution Unit, UCL 2001) 7.

47 Mackenzie (n 1) 111–12.

48 Cabinet Office, *Memorandum of Understanding and Supplementary Agreements between the United Kingdom Government, the Scottish Ministers, the Welsh Ministers and the Northern Ireland Executive Committee* (October 2013). *The Review of Intergovernmental Relations* (below) sets out new structures and ways of working in place of those set out in the MoU.

49 Devolution Guidance Note (DGN) 1, *Common Working Arrangements*, Annex A.

50 Cabinet Office, *Memorandum of Understanding and Supplementary Agreements* (n 48) para 2.

51 ibid para 3.

52 Devolution Guidance Note 1, *Common Working Arrangements*, Annex A, original emphasis. DGNs set out advice on working level arrangements; these, too, are 'not legally binding but are designed to set out principles to which all officials can adhere': Cabinet Office, *The Cabinet Manual. A Guide to Laws, Conventions and Rules on the Operation of Government* (October 2011) para 8.17.

was also established as a 'forum for engagement' between UK ministers and their devolved counterparts—'mainly as an act of statesmanship but with the potential for serving as a court of appeal if the going got rough'.[53] The model was the Cabinet committee with the addition of ministers from the devolved administrations ('some devolved ministers initially thought existing Cabinet committees might just become joint between the different governments').[54] Its terms of reference were:

- to consider non-devolved matters which impinge on devolved responsibilities, and devolved matters which impinge on non-devolved responsibilities;
- where the UK government and the devolved administrations so agree, to consider devolved matters if it is beneficial to discuss their respective treatment in the different parts of the United Kingdom;
- to keep the arrangements for liaison between the UK government and the devolved administrations under review, and to consider disputes between the administrations.[55]

As a consultative body the JMC had no power to make binding decisions. 'It may not bind any of the participating administrations, which will be free to determine their own policies while taking account of JMC discussions.' Nevertheless, the expectation was that participating administrations would support positions the JMC had agreed.[56]

Outside the JMC framework other forums for engagement were established, including in respect of finance, which the Treasury continued to regard 'as uniquely its business'.[57]

During the early years of devolution this machinery was little used. With Labour in power in London, Edinburgh, and Cardiff, intergovernmental relations were mainly handled on an informal basis through well-established party channels.[58] The exception was Europe, where the JMC machinery was used to agree the 'UK line' before EU Council meetings. With seemingly little to do, the Constitution Secretariat in the Cabinet Office, which had policed the liaison system 'in a quasi-executive role', was wound up after the 2001 general election.[59] There were also no checks on the quality of engagement at the all-important departmental level, despite some departments being seen as more 'devolution hostile' than others.[60]

In its 2003 report on *Devolution: Inter-Institutional Relations in the United Kingdom*, the House of Lords Constitution Committee recommended greater use be made of the formal mechanisms,

[53] Mackenzie (n 1) 116.

[54] Jim Gallagher, 'Intergovernmental Relations: Two Decades of Co-operation, Competition and Constitutional Change' in Michael Keating (ed), *The Oxford Handbook of Scottish Politics* (OUP 2020) 565, 572.

[55] Cabinet Office, *Memorandum of Understanding and Supplementary Agreements* (n 48) para A1.2.

[56] ibid para A1.10.

[57] Gallagher (n 54) 573.

[58] Cabinet Office, *Review of UK Government Union Capability* (n 4) 31.

[59] Mackenzie (n 1) 116.

[60] Alan Trench, 'Washing Dirty Linen in Private: The Processes of Intergovernmental Relations and the Resolution of Disputes' in Alan Trench (ed), *Devolution and Power in the United Kingdom* (Manchester UP 2007) 161, 189–90.

even if they seem to many of those presently involved to be excessive. Formal mechanisms, such as the Joint Ministerial Committee (JMC), are not intended to serve as a substitute for good relations in other respects, or for good and frequent informal contacts, but rather to serve as a framework for such relations and to act as a fall-back in case informal personal relations cease to be sufficient. Such mechanisms are likely to become increasingly important when governments of different political persuasions have to deal with each other.[61]

The formation of an SNP (Scottish National Party) government at Holyrood in 2007 saw the JMC meet in plenary format (in June 2008) for the first time in six years. A campaign was also launched to raise Whitehall awareness of devolution.[62] The Calman Commission, which had been set up by the opposition parties in the Scottish Parliament, with the UK government's support, as a rival to the SNP's *National Conversation*,[63] found 'a good deal of effective cooperative working, some of it simply a continuation of pre-devolution arrangements'. Overall, however, intergovernmental relationships were 'under-developed': the overarching machinery had not operated in 'any systematic way', the systems in place for working-level discussions to clarify issues often 'failed to do so before they escalated to more senior and political forums', and the regularity of JMC meetings was 'insufficient and too ad hoc'.[64] What was needed, the Commission concluded, was a 'much better developed and more robust framework . . . to ensure that where developed and reserved responsibilities overlap or impinge on one another, proper coordination and joint working are more fully encouraged and supported, with appropriate scrutiny by the parliaments to which the governments are accountable'.[65]

That prescription was to be repeated five years later by the cross-party Smith Commission, which was set up to deliver 'the vow' after Scotland voted No in the independence referendum, little having changed in the meantime.[66] The Commission called for 'the current intergovernmental machinery between Scottish and UK Governments, including the Joint Ministerial Committee (JMC) structures' to be reformed 'as a matter of urgency and scaled up significantly to reflect the scope of the

[61] House of Lords Constitution Committee, *Devolution: Inter-Institutional Relations in the United Kingdom* (HL 2002–03, 28) para 29.

[62] Cabinet Office, *Annual Report and Accounts 2008–09* (HC 442, 59).

[63] Scottish Government, *Choosing Scotland's Future: A National Conversation* (August 2007); the *National Conversation* was to have been followed by a referendum on independence, which the SNP government was eventually forced to drop when it became clear that it could not secure a majority for the referendum legislation in the Scottish Parliament.

[64] Commission on Scottish Devolution, *Serving Scotland Better: Scotland and the United Kingdom in the 21st Century* (June 2009) paras 4.119–4.120.

[65] ibid para 4.128. In its first report the Commission expressed surprise that none of the recommendations of the Constitution Committee five years earlier appeared to have been acted upon; the evidence it had received appeared to indicate that little had changed and that therefore an early opportunity to put intergovernmental relations on a more robust footing might have been missed: Commission on Scottish Devolution, *The Future of Scottish Devolution within the Union: A First Report* (December 2008) para 7.57.

[66] In the final days of the referendum campaign, with the polls suddenly narrowing, the leaders of the three main political parties at Westminster 'vowed' to deliver 'extensive new powers' for the Parliament, 'by the process and according to the timetable agreed and announced by our three parties': *Daily Record* (16 September 2014).

agreement arrived at by the parties'.[67] 'Throughout the course of the Commission', the chair of the Commission Lord Smith of Kelvin wrote,

> the issue of weak intergovernmental working was repeatedly raised as a problem. That current situation coupled with what will be a stronger Scottish Parliament and a more complex devolution settlement means the problem needs to be fixed. Both Governments need to work together to create a more productive, robust, visible and transparent relationship. There also needs to be greater respect between them.[68]

At the plenary meeting of the JMC in December 2014, ministers agreed to commission work on a revised MoU. They also discussed ways in which their respective Parliaments and Assemblies could be 'kept informed' of the work of the JMC. The proposals that came out of this work were 'fairly modest in scope, but they pointed the way towards the possibility of converting the JMC into a more meaningful and important forum for collective discussion across the different administrations'.[69] They were to have been signed off at Theresa May's first JMC meeting as Prime Minister in October 2016, only to be 'vetoed at the very last moment by Sinn Féin's Martin McGuiness, who objected to the proposal that, in return for UK government support for their overseas visits, ministers from the devolved administrations should respect the UK government line in their discussions with other governments'.[70]

The outcome of the EU referendum provided a renewed spur to reform.[71] At its plenary meeting on 14 March 2018, the JMC commissioned a review of the existing intergovernmental structures, including the MoU, 'to ensure they were fit for purpose in the light of the UK's exit from the EU'. Lord Dunlop's unsurprising conclusion a year later was that there was a broad consensus that the United Kingdom's intergovernmental relations machinery was 'no longer fit for purpose and in urgent need of reform'.[72] It was important, however, to be realistic about what reform could achieve. 'No IGR [intergovernmental relations] machinery, however perfect', was capable of resolving 'fundamentally different political objectives', particularly where these involved 'very different visions for the UK's constitutional future'. It was, however, realistic to expect 'serviceable and resilient working relationships, based on mutual

[67] Smith Commission, *Report of the Smith Commission for Further Devolution of Powers to the Scottish Parliament* (November 2014) para 28.

[68] ibid Foreword.

[69] Kenny, Rycroft, and Sheldon (n 17) 21; the proposals included regularizing the timetable for the holding of JMC plenary meetings, rotating the venue where it was held, allowing for the commissioning of joint work to report back to the JMC, and providing the opportunity for more informal discussions between ministers.

[70] ibid. 'This was often a vexed issue due to the tension between the expectation of devolved ministers to receive support for their overseas engagements from the UK government, usually the Foreign Office, and their occasional reluctance to toe the UK government line in their interaction with foreign governments.'

[71] A Joint Ministerial Committee on EU Negotiations (JMC (EN)) was established in October 2016 to facilitate collaboration between the UK government and the devolved administrations on the United Kingdom's exit from the European Union but it offered few opportunities to influence the process.

[72] Cabinet Office, *Review of UK Government Union Capability* (n 4) 31; see also Public Administration and Constitutional Affairs Committee, *Devolution and Exiting the EU: Reconciling Differences and Building Strong Relationships* (HC 2017–19, 1485) ch 8.

respect and far greater levels of trust'.[73] A 'more transparent, predictable and robust system' should be put in place. 'The machinery supporting intergovernmental relations should act as a stimulus for more mutually beneficial working relationships rather than as a platform for public dispute or grievance.'[74] What had become 'a forum largely for airing grievances and managing disputes needed to evolve into a forum for fostering more effective collaboration . . . The JMC machinery must look and feel like a joint endeavour.'[75]

It was to take the best part of another four years for the review to reach a conclusion.[76] A set of principles for intergovernmental relations provided the starting point for the review: :

- maintaining positive and constructive relations, based on mutual respect for the responsibilities of the governments and their shared role in the governance of the UK;
- building and maintaining trust, based on effective communication;
- sharing information and respecting confidentiality;
- promoting understanding of, and accountability for, their intergovernmental activity; and
- resolving disputes according to a clear and agreed process.[77]

The expectation was that all ministerial engagement would be conducted in accordance with these principles (para 5).

Agreement was also reached on the replacement of the JMC machinery by a new three-tier structure:

1. a first tier of portfolio engagement at official and ministerial level. The general principle, which is carried over from the original arrangements, is that intergovernmental business should be conducted through normal official-level channels wherever possible (para 4). Ministerial oversight is however regarded as essential to promote effective collaboration and to provide political accountability. Ministerial forums should therefore be in place to consider and, where appropriate, reach agreement on issues of mutual interest across policy areas (para 5).[78]
2. two middle-tier forums, an Interministerial Standing Committee (IMSC), for cross-cutting and strategic issues, and a Finance: Interministerial Standing Committee (F:ISC) for finance and funding matters; with provision for further time-limited Interministerial Committees (ICs) should the need arise; and

[73] Cabinet Office, *Review of UK Government Union Capability* (n 4) 31.
[74] ibid.
[75] ibid 33. 'Despite the breakdown in relations between the UK and Scottish governments a substantial measure of cooperation was achieved at official level over the need to ensure a properly functioning statute book after the UK's withdrawal and, latterly, the possibility of a "no deal" Brexit': Kenny, Rycroft, and Sheldon (n 17) 28–29.
[76] Cabinet Office and Department for Levelling Up, Housing and Communities, *The Review of Intergovernmental Relations* (January 2022).
[77] ibid para 1. The principles were first published in July 2019: Cabinet Office, *Agreement on Joint Working* (July 2019).
[78] For an up-to-date list of Interministerial Groups, see Intergovernmental relations—<www.gov.uk>.

3. a Prime Minister and Heads of Devolved Governments Council, chaired by the Prime Minister, which is responsible for overseeing intergovernmental relations in the United Kingdom. 'All middle-tier and portfolio engagement is accountable to this forum' (para 17).

The new arrangements (the Council, IMSC, and ICs) are supported by a standing IGR Secretariat, consisting of officials from all four governments. The Secretariat, which is accountable to the Council rather than to individual sponsoring governments, promotes the efficient and effective maintenance of relations at each tier, facilitates prompt handling and resolution of disputes, and provides administrative support (para 19). The F:ISC is supported by a separate secretariat led collectively by officials from its members (para 20).

Decision-making under the new arrangements continues to depend on agreement. 'Intergovernmental decisions will continue to work on the basis of agreement by consensus. The default position will remain that a joint approach will not be taken in the absence of such agreement' (para 6). The revised machinery does not have the power to bind any of the participating governments, including crucially the UK government in respect of reserved matters.

Critical to the success of the new arrangements will be the attitude of the participants. For the House of Lords Constitution Committee strengthening the intergovernmental structures would achieve only so much. 'The success of the new arrangements will depend on how the Government and devolved administrations operate them and whether they are committed to using the new structures to cooperate on achieving shared objectives, rather than simply managing—or taking opportunities to accentuate—their differences.'[79]

In its election manifesto the incoming Labour government undertook to 'protect and respect' devolution, 'reset' relations with the devolved governments, ensure the structures and institutions of intergovernmental working, 'improve relationships and collaboration on policy', and to set out a new MoU outlining how the nations will 'work together for the common good'. It would also establish a new Council of the Nations and Regions.[80]

Looking back over the immediate past history of IGR, it is striking that the response to the Covidcrisis was not handled through the JMC machinery. The initial response saw 'unprecedented coordination' through a 'four-nations approach'.[81] It was handled through COBRA, the United Kingdom's emergency response committee (so called after Cabinet Office Briefing Room A, its usual meeting place), and then by four

[79] House of Lords Constitution Committee, *Respect and Cooperation* (n 14) para 182; a view reiterated by the Committee in its most recent report in which it urged the incoming Labour government to 'fully embed' the new structures into the day-to-day business of government, and the devolved governments to demonstrate their commitment to engaging with them: *The Governance of the Union: Consultation, Co-operation and Legislative consent* (HL 2024–25, 13) para 73.

[80] Labour Party, *Change: Labour Party Manifesto 2024* (June 2024). The first meeting of the Council of the Nations and Regions took place on 11 October 2024.

[81] Scottish Affairs Committee, *Coronavirus and Scotland: Interim Report on Intergovernmental Working* (HC 2019–21, 314) para 4. The approach saw the adoption of a joint action plan and devolved agreement to the Coronavirus Act 2000. The Act was framed, as was the response to the pandemic more generally, on the basis that the devolved administrations would lead on the devolved aspects of the emergency, laying the basis for the subsequent divergences in response between the four governments.

Ministerial Implementation Groups (MIGs)—on healthcare, other public services, the economy and business, and the international response to the virus—in which the devolved governments were invited to take a full part. The MIGs were subsequently replaced by two Cabinet committees—one for Covid strategy, the other for Covid operations—membership of which was restricted to a small number of senior UK government ministers. Whether the removal of devolved representation was a factor or not, the 'four-nations approach' quickly broke down once the immediate threat had passed and attention turned to emergence from lockdown.[82]

A persistent criticism of intergovernmental relations has been that they are

> predominantly conducted behind closed doors, limiting the involvement of other branches of government and the public in decision-making. The secrecy and complexity of IGR tends to blur lines of responsibility, leaving citizens less able to call government to account as each order blames the other for policy problems and failures. IGR are often beyond the reach of the traditional mechanisms for executive accountability through parliamentary and judicial oversight.[83]

In advance of the conclusion of the IGR review, the UK government announced measures to improve the transparency and accountability of its relations with the devolved administrations, recognizing that 'effective transparency, accountability and parliamentary scrutiny of the Government's participation in intergovernmental structures will support relationships between the Government and devolved administrations so that we work together effectively on behalf of citizens across the UK.'[84] The measures announced, which mirrored the approaches taken by the Scottish and Welsh governments in reporting to their legislatures, included increased reporting and a dedicated webpage,[85] together with a commitment to strengthened parliamentary engagement through regular ministerial statements and appropriate appearances before select committees. The review committed all four governments to increased transparency through enhanced reporting to their legislatures, while the intergovernmental forums were encouraged to produce communiqués on their meetings and activities and publish these online.[86]

[82] For Martin, Kan, and Fink the removal of devolved representation appeared mistaken as did the unwillingness of the UK government to make clear that new measures it announced applied only to England. Ciaran Martin, Hester Kan, and Maximillian Fink, *Crisis Preparation in the Age of Long Emergencies. What Covid-19 Teaches Us about the Capacity, Capability and Coordination Governments Need for Cross-Cutting Crises* (Blavatnik School of Government 2023) 123.

[83] Johanne Poirier and Cheryl Saunders, 'Conclusion' in Johanne Poirier, Cheryl Saunders, and John Kincaid (eds), *Intergovernmental Relations in Federal Systems. Comparative Structures and Dynamics* (OUP 2015) 482.

[84] UIN HCWS564 (10 November 2020).

[85] <www.gov.uk/government/collections/intergovernmental-relations>.

[86] Cabinet Office and Department for Levelling Up, Housing and Communities (n 76) paras 22–23. The first annual report recorded 227 intergovernmental ministerial meetings in 2022, down from over 440 the previous year, which it attributed to 'the UK government's leadership changes and suspension of the Northern Ireland Executive': Department for Levelling Up, Housing and Communities, *Intergovernmental Relations Annual Report 2022* (CP 826, 2023). There were 210 intergovernmental ministerial meetings in 2023: Department for Levelling Up, Housing and Communities, *Intergovernmental Relations Annual Report 2023* (CP 1064, 2024).

Like the arrangements they replaced, the revised arrangements are entirely non-statutory. 'The following reforms of intergovernmental structures and processes . . . provide a statement of political intent, but are not intended to create new, or override existing, legal relations or obligations, or to be justiciable.'[87] The Dunlop Review opposed putting the arrangements on a statutory basis:

> While the Review . . . agrees there should be a far greater role for Parliament in scrutinising discussions which take place in an IGR setting, to put their basis in statute risks dragging the courts into what fundamentally should be a political and parliamentary realm. In order to build respect and trust around IGR it is therefore important political differences are handled in a political, not legal, space. Indeed, statute could also prevent the necessary flexibility required in the system to respond to changing circumstances. Moreover, increasing the scope to involve the courts to resolve disagreements could militate against reaching timely agreement on contentious issues. Greater transparency and more robust scrutiny by the UK Parliament and the devolved legislatures is a more appropriate means of encouraging the right types of collaborative behaviours.[88]

Having previously suggested that the UK government should consider whether the framework of intergovernmental relations should be set out in statute,[89] the House of Lords Constitution Committee had second thoughts about statutory backing:

> However, on reflection, the downsides of such an approach are worth considering. Depending on how any statutory provisions were drafted, if they are too high-level the courts may decline to make these justiciable, as per the statutory form of the Sewel convention; if they are too detailed there is a risk of political disputes becoming legal ones. It may therefore be better to resolve political differences in the enhanced dispute avoidance and resolution process agreed by the UK Government and devolved administrations as part of the joint review of intergovernmental relations.[90]

Attitudes and behaviours needed to change to make the new arrangements a success. If that did not happen, there might be a stronger argument for placing intergovernmental relations on a statutory footing. 'However, we are alive to the potential downsides of detailed statutory provisions resulting in political disagreements being settled in court rather than through political dialogue.'[91]

[87] Cabinet Office and Department for Levelling Up, Housing and Communities (n 76) para 2.

[88] Cabinet Office, *Review of UK Government Union Capability* (n 4) 34.

[89] House of Lords Constitution Committee, *Inter-governmental Relations in the United Kingdom* (n 8) para 86; see also Public Administration and Constitutional Affairs Committee, *Devolution and Exiting the EU* (n 72) para 132.

[90] House of Lords Constitution Committee, *Respect and Cooperation* (n 14) para 198.

[91] ibid para 199; see also House of Lords Constitution Committee, *The Governance of the Union* (n 79) para 193.

IV Devolution Capability

'One of the major challenges for the newly established UK Governance Group was to confront the relative ignorance of, and considerable indifference towards, devolution right across Whitehall. Very few officials understood how these reforms had altered the nature of power relations within the UK, and few ministers were inclined to accord the Union political priority even after the shock of the Scottish referendum.'[92]

> The MoU, DGNs and concordats provide clear explanations on how the Governments should communicate with each other on various matters, including the legislative process. However it is clear from the evidence we have received that a number of Whitehall departments are either not always aware of these basic documents or do not always apply them when developing and implementing policy or during the legislation (sic) process itself.[93]

A second strand of the UK Governance Group's work was thus directed to building or strengthening the 'devolution capability' of departments by raising general awareness of the devolution settlements and encouraging early engagement with the devolved administrations on the formulation and implementation of legislation and policy.

In July 2015 the Cabinet Secretary launched *Devolution and You*, a programme (of learning) designed to improve Civil Service knowledge and skills on the devolution settlements for Scotland, Wales, and Northern Ireland.[94] Departments were also required to produce devolution capability plans and report on them to the Cabinet Secretary.

> A basic grasp of how the devolution settlements work is essential. But it goes deeper than that. We need an appreciation of the political dynamic in the different parts of the UK. We need to learn how to manage the political objectives of whichever government we work for, when collaboration might be essential, but the politics hotly contested . . . The need to 'get' devolution will intensify, not diminish. That is why all departments now have a devolution capability plan; these are an important statement of ambition as to how each department will meet the devolution challenge.[95]

While welcoming the work being undertaken by the UKGG, PACAC regarded it as unacceptable 17 years after the advent of devolution that Whitehall departments were not better at involving and consulting the devolved administrations, so that their views and interests were positively engaged at the outset, rather than as an

[92] Kenny, Rycroft, and Sheldon (n 17) 22–23.

[93] Commission on Devolution in Wales, *Empowerment and Responsibility: Legislative Powers to Strengthen Wales* (n 6) para 5.2.9.

[94] On *Devolution and You*, now the Civil Service Devolution Capability Programme, see House of Commons Scottish Affairs Committee, *The Relationship between the UK and Scottish Governments* (HC 2017–19, 1586) ch 5, and *Devolution: Guidance for Civil Servants*. Although the programme had been in operation since 2015, the House of Lords Constitution Committee noted continuing concerns about civil servants' knowledge of devolution, *The Governance of the Union* (n 79) para 127.

[95] Philip Rycroft and Russell Barnes, 'Getting to Grips with the Devolution Challenge' (5 February 2016).

afterthought. To supplement the progress departments had made in engaging relevant officials from devolved administrations in UK policy formation, the Committee recommended that departments should 'implement procedures to ensure such engagement takes place. A senior official should also be appointed within each department to review successful and failed examples of inter-administration engagement at official level. The UK Governance Group should ask departments to report on reviews and lessons learned every year.'[96]

Changing the culture of departments was always going to be a struggle, however, and with the outcome of the EU referendum there was little prospect of it being accorded the priority it would have needed:

> On a day-to-day basis, Whitehall departments continued to interact with their devolved counterparts as good administrative order required. Where the interface was close, for example on agriculture and fisheries and some aspects of transport, co-operation could be effective. But for most departments, dealing with devolution was one among many subsidiary objectives, and never a main strategic goal. Even without the advent of Brexit, turning round the culture in Whitehall in this area was an uphill struggle. Following the referendum of June 2016, there was little chance of it being accorded the priority it deserved.[97]

The Cabinet Office's May 2018 single departmental plan adopted as its primary objective 'maintaining the integrity of the Union', to which end it would increase devolution capability and engagement by holding departments to account on agreement and implementation of their devolution engagement and capability plans and improving the capability of the Civil Service to understand devolution and sustain and strengthen the Union. But when the plan was updated a year later devolution engagement and capability plans did not feature, leaving *Devolution and You* as the principal means of improving devolution capability.

The subsequent Dunlop Review examined the capability of departments to 'deliver policies for the whole of the United Kingdom, cognizant of where this has implications for devolved areas'.[98] Each department, the Review found, had its own 'Devolution Team', some sizeable, others as little as one full-time equivalent, responsible for straddling both devolution capability and ensuring, where appropriate, that UK-wide delivery was embedded in policy development. Some teams had specific policy responsibilities, others operated much more as a guidance service. All aimed to improve the department's overall capability to engage with devolved governments across the United Kingdom and act as catalysts for change. Where teams 'owned' specific policy in departments, the Review heard this could have the effect of insulating the rest of the department from the need to develop the skills necessary to operate UK-wide. In extreme cases this had created a perception that teams absolved the wider department of responsibility for understanding the context in Scotland, Wales, and

96 Public Administration and Constitutional Affairs Committee, *The Future of the Union, Part Two: Inter-Institutional Relations in the UK* (HC 2016–17, 839) paras 111–12.
97 Kenny, Rycroft, and Sheldon (n 17) 23.
98 Cabinet Office, *Review of UK Government Union Capability* (n 4) 21.

Northern Ireland. To address this, some departments had created a network of 'champions' to help improve capability in different teams. However there seemed to be considerable inconsistency in the effectiveness of this approach.[99]

Departments also had a senior civil servant responsible for devolution who represented the department at meetings of the Devolution Leaders Network, which was the Cabinet Office's principal means for discussing departments' Union priorities. The effectiveness of this network—in spite of attempts to test different structures and agendas—had been questioned, however, as evidenced by the frequency with which attendance was delegated. As a result, the network had 'struggled to significantly support efforts to improve outcomes'.[100] 'Union plans' had also been created 'as a means of understanding what departments were doing to deliver UK-wide'. However these were often 'a brigading of existing policy'. Most lacked 'hard-edged metrics' to monitor improvements and it was not always clear how they related to the Cabinet's wider Union ambitions and strategy.[101]

System-wide reforms to the structure of departments, the Review argued, were needed to equip them with the necessary Union and devolution capability. Each department should have a senior civil servant board member with lead responsibility for the department's devolution capability and Union strategy. Departments should also have a nominated non-executive board member with specific responsibility to lead on advising and challenging the department on its Union strategy and devolution capability. Devolution teams should not be peripheral within departments but should be located at the heart of strategy and policy development. The Cabinet Office should ensure there were outcome-based metrics to continually assess departmental capability.[102] It should also be a condition of the appointment of civil servants to the higher levels of the service that they should have 'significant experience working in or with one of the devolved administrations or [on] a Union-related issue'.[103] There should also be more opportunities for loans and secondments between the UK, Scottish, and Welsh governments, and also greater interchange with the Northern Ireland Civil Service.[104]

How much of this had happened by the time of the 2024 general election is unclear. Writing to Lord Dunlop after publication of his review in March 2021, the Chancellor of the Duchy of Lancaster Michael Gove said that all departments had made structural adjustments that would help ensure that 'UK-wide issues are properly considered and sit at the heart of policy making'. Every UK government department had, for example, made a member of their board and also a non-executive director responsible for coordinating work across all parts of the United Kingdom. Departments and civil servants would also be better equipped to look after the interests of all their fellow citizens in the United Kingdom thanks to 'our revamped approach to Government knowledge and skills, with its renewed commitment to devolution and intergovernmental working in training and policy development'.[105] In written evidence to PACAC

99 ibid 22.
100 ibid.
101 ibid.
102 ibid.
103 ibid 25.
104 ibid 10.
105 Letter from Michael Gove to Lord Dunlop (24 March 2021).

three years later, the Institute for Government agreed that devolution awareness had improved, but warned of a 'continual need to monitor devolution capability to ensure that central government can coordinate across policy areas'.[106] In its most recent report, the House of Lords Constitution Committee urged the new Labour government 'to ensure that every department has a properly equipped team—and a Ministerial lead—with the knowledge and skills necessary to address, anticipate and engage with devolution matters as they arise, providing an identified point of contact for the devolved administrations'.[107] Looking at the picture in the round, it is difficult to avoid the conclusion that the system of government has yet to adjust to devolution.

[106] Institute for Government, written evidence from the Institute for Government (DWC21) <committees.parliament.uk/written evidence/127350/pdf/>.
[107] House of Lords Constitution Committee, *The Governance of the Union* (n 79) para 126.

PART C
THE RESOURCES OF THE EXECUTIVE: PEOPLE

6
The Civil Service: The Continuing Failure of Reform

I Introduction

'What is internationally unusual and often envied is the [UK civil] service's ability to preserve its impartiality so that it can transfer seamlessly its expertise, commitment and loyalty to a government of a different political make-up tomorrow.' So wrote the Minister for the Cabinet Office and the Cabinet Secretary and Head of the Civil Service in their foreword to the 2010–15 Coalition government's final report on its *Civil Service Reform Plan*.[1] The need to preserve its impartiality so that it can transfer its loyalty to a government of a different political make-up stems from the fact that the UK Civil Service is a largely permanent service whose members are not liable to lose their jobs on a change of government. The United Kingdom never developed a spoils system of the kind found in the United States, where the senior echelons of the administration are liable to be replaced on a change of government by the new government's own supporters.[2] Instead the tradition that developed was of 'an efficient body of permanent officers, occupying a position duly subordinate to that of the Ministers who are directly responsible to the Crown and to Parliament, yet possessing sufficient independence, character, ability, and experience to be able to advise, assist, and to some extent, influence those who are from time to time set over them'.[3]

The usual justification offered for a non-political, permanent Civil Service is that it secures continuity through changes in government.[4] It is also said to be a more 'efficient' means of securing continuity than the alternative, which would involve some sort of ministerial *cabinet* system. 'We believe intensely that a non-political Civil Service such as ours makes for a more efficient system of government than one in which changes in the top posts have to be made whenever a Government of a different political complexion takes over.'[5] Be that as it may, there are no constitutional

[1] Civil Service, *Civil Service Reform Plan—Progress Report* (October 2014). The Maude Review of governance and accountability in the Civil Service proceeded on the basis that the United Kingdom's current system of a permanent and politically impartial Civil Service would be maintained. 'For around 150 years there has been a broad consensus that the UK is best served by a permanent Civil Service that is politically impartial, in the sense of being capable of serving governments of any political persuasion with the same high level of capacity and commitment' (Lord Maude, *Independent Review of Governance and Accountability in the Civil Service* (November 2023) para 3.4).

[2] Henry Parris, *Constitutional Bureaucracy: The Development of British Central Administration since the Eighteenth Century* (Allen and Unwin 1969) ch 1; contrast public appointments where a spoils system did develop: see chapter 4, section IV.

[3] Stafford Northcote and CE Trevelyan, *The Organisation of the Permanent Civil Service*, Parl Pap, vol XXVII, 1854.

[4] Cabinet Office, *The Civil Service: Continuity and Change* (Cm 2627, 1994) para 2.2.

[5] Sir Edward Bridges, quoted in Richard Chapman, *Ethics in the British Civil Service* (Routledge 1988) 94. As to ministerial cabinets, see Institute for Public Policy Research, *Accountability and Responsiveness in the*

Executive Self-Government and the Constitution. Terence Daintith and Alan Page, Oxford University Press.
 DOI: 10.1093/9780198937630.003.0006

guarantees of the principle of permanence. In the absence of statutory backing, the principle depends on the forbearance of an incoming administration, and the 'accepted wisdom' that the potential victims of a purge are possessed of 'a peculiarly British conception of neutrality which involves the chameleon-like ability to identify with successive governments of quite different political complexions'.[6]

The notion of an impartial or non-partisan Civil Service, capable of serving successive governments, was the more important of what traditionally were regarded as the UK Civil Service's two distinguishing features. The other was that it was said to present 'a unique combination of unity and diversity. It is a single unified service, but its members serve under some scores of separate and partially independent employing authorities, and the duties which they perform are of almost limitless variety.'[7] It was only after the end of the First World War that it became accepted that the service 'should be organised and staffed more as a unit than as a collection of heterogeneous departments each with its own way of handling and grading its employees'.[8] Before then the 'service' was made up of a group of independent departments over which the Treasury exercised 'only an uneasy suzerainty'.[9] An important part of the Northcote-Trevelyan prescription had been for measures to mitigate the evils resulting from the fragmentary character of the service, as well as for the replacement of patronage by competition, but it took 70 years for their prescription to be realized.

The orthodoxy that emerged after the end of the First World War—that the service should be organized and managed as a single organization—was to survive effectively unchallenged for the next 50 years. As Greaves presciently observed, however, no description of the service 'can be realistic which overlooks either the historical fact that there were once as many services as there were establishments and that it is on these that the principle of integration has been superimposed, or the political fact of the continuing powerful pulls in the direction of maintaining or reverting to the principle of severalness'.[10] In the closing decades of the last century it was the principle of severalness that was uppermost. For the Efficiency Unit, the service was too big and diverse to be run as a single rigid organization with common rules for financial and personnel management. Centralized rule-making was criticized for being insufficiently discriminating and for denying managers the flexibility they needed in order to manage. 'Many managers told us that central rules were acting as a constraint on good management and taking away their scope to do things which would be sensible in terms of their own organisation.'[11] With the setting up of Next Steps agencies,

Senior Civil Service: Lessons from Overseas (Cabinet Office 2013). The Coalition government agreed in 2013 to the establishment of extended ministerial offices (EMOs), made up of civil servants, special advisers, and external policy experts, to increase the support available to ministers: see chapter 3, section 3.2.

[6] Treasury and Civil Service Committee, *Civil Servants and Ministers: Duties and Responsibilities* (HC 1985–86, 92) para 5.10.

[7] Sir Thomas Padmore, 'Civil Service Establishments and the Treasury' in William A Robson (ed), *The Civil Service in Britain and France* (The Hogarth Press 1956) 124–25.

[8] Eunan O'Halpin, *Head of the Civil Service: A Study of Sir Warren Fisher* (Routledge 1989) 25.

[9] Kingsley Bryce Smellie, *A Hundred Years of English Government* (Duckworth 1937) 262.

[10] HRG Greaves, 'The Structure of the Civil Service' in Robson (n 7) 103.

[11] Efficiency Unit, *Improving Management in Government: The Next Steps. A Report to the Prime Minister* (1988) paras 10–11; Annex B, paras 40–45.

therefore, came pressure for the devolution of central management functions to departments and agencies. Devolution was effectively completed in 1996 when responsibility for the pay and grading of staff below senior levels was delegated to departments and agencies.

When New Labour took office in 1997 Civil Service numbers stood at 475,000, on a full-time equivalent (FTE) basis, having declined steadily during the previous 18 years of Conservative government. Hitting a low of 384,000 in June 2016 after six years of Coalition and Conservative government, numbers then steadily rose again, mostly through recruitments to deal first with repatriated competences after Brexit, and then with the needs of the Covid emergency. In June 2024, despite various plans to reduce numbers, there were more civil servants than in 1997 (513,000 FTE).[12]

II Civil Service Reform 1997–2024

> *'A sceptic might remark that nothing persists except the persistent drive to reform.'*[13]

In July 2022 Lord Maude, Minister for the Cabinet Office and Paymaster General in the 2010–15 Coalition government, was appointed to undertake a review of Civil Service governance and accountability following commitments made in the Conservative government's *Declaration on Government Reform* a year earlier. His report published in November 2023 was highly critical of the results of the efforts that had been made to reform the Civil Service over the previous almost half-century.

> There has been a failure over decades to implement or sustain agreed and uncontroversial reforms and improvements—the 'stewardship obligation'. Failings identified by the Fulton Committee in 1968, for example the dominance of 'generalists', 'churn' whereby officials move from post to post in an apparently unplanned and uncontrolled manner, and an excessively closed culture and lack of interchange with external sectors, all constantly recur in reviews of and commentaries on the Civil Service.[14]

No one seriously contested that these criticisms were real, nor did anyone dispute that the failings needed to be remedied. Yet the necessary changes had either not been attempted, or been abandoned before completion, or not been sustained after completion.[15]

12 See Martin Stanley, Key Facts (June 2024) <www.civilservant.org.uk/information-numbers.html> for a useful historical survey, and for quarterly updates, Office for National Statistics, Public sector employment time series (table C9KQ) <www.ons.gov.uk/employmentandlabourmarket/peopleinwork/publicsectorpersonnel/datasets/publicsectoremploymenttimeseriesdataset>.

13 Paul Fawcett and Roderick AW Rhodes, 'Central Government' in Anthony Seldon (ed), *Blair's Britain 1997–2007* (CUP 2007) 79.

14 Maude Review (n 1) para 2.2.1; the stewardship obligation was defined as 'the obligation to see through to completion reforms to the Civil Service that are uncontroversial. These reforms are required to drive continuous improvement and to maximise organisational health and effectiveness' (para 4.2).

15 ibid para 4.4.

Maude's criticism did not exclude the efforts that had been made to reform the Civil Service since 1997, including those of which he was among the principal architects. The first such effort was *Civil Service Reform* (December 1999), the Civil Service leadership's answer to what New Labour's *Modernising Government* White Paper (March 1999) meant for the Civil Service.[16] In their report, which was drawn up at the request of the Prime Minister, the Cabinet Secretary Richard Wilson and his Permanent Secretary colleagues 'pledged themselves personally' to drive forward 'a new agenda of Civil Service reform', both corporately, ie across the Civil Service as a whole, and in modernizing their own departments. The action they had agreed to take would be based on six key themes: stronger leadership with a clear sense of purpose; better business planning from top to bottom; sharper performance management; a dramatic improvement in diversity; a service more open to people and ideas, which brought on talent; and a better deal for staff. Departments, overseen by the newly formed Civil Service Management Board made up of the Cabinet Secretary and his colleagues, would 'drive through' action in these six areas, integrating this work with other change programmes to deliver the government's objectives.[17]

One reason why Civil Service reform programmes have had limited impact is because of a lack of commitment on the part of politicians and Civil Service leaders. The Prime Minister was said to have been 'hardly involved' in the reforms.

> He approved what Sir Richard was doing and gave his nod to the detailed plans after an hour long session in Downing Street in late 1999. After Sir Richard and his fellow permanent secretaries had made their presentation . . . he asked Lord Simon [of Highbury] his opinion as a former chairman of BP about how the proposals looked from a private sector perspective. He duly approved and that was enough for Mr Blair.[18]

Departmental 'change programmes' were subsequently introduced as part of the 'culture-changing' efforts of the reform programme—in the words of Richard Wilson's successor Andrew Turnbull 'with varying degrees of success'.[19]

The limited success of the programme raised the question of whether reform should be left to the Civil Service. There was a feeling in some quarters, the Public Administration Select Committee reported, that the Civil Service 'has once again absorbed attempts at reform. A possible conclusion may be that the service is incapable of effectively changing itself and that reform must be imposed from outside.' The Committee agreed with the Cabinet Secretary that reform should not damage the Civil Service's 'core values', but suggested that, 'thirty years or more after Fulton', the time was

[16] *Modernising Government* (Cm 4310, 1999). Later dismissed as 'platitudinous and lacking real bite' (Michael Barber, *Instruction to Deliver: Tony Blair, Public Services and the Challenge of Achieving Targets* (Politico's 2007) 45), it was overtaken by the shift in focus to delivery after the 2001 general election.

[17] *Civil Service Reform: Report to the Prime Minister from Sir Richard Wilson* (October 1999).

[18] Peter Riddell, 'Blair as Prime Minister' in Anthony Seldon (ed), *The Blair Effect: The Blair Government 1997–2001* (Little, Brown 2001) 38; contrast the Prime Minister's much greater degree of commitment to the delivery agenda.

[19] House of Commons Research Paper 03/49 *Whither the Civil Service?* (May 2003) 20.

'ripe for a new Royal Commission to take comprehensive stock of the Civil Service and map out a more comprehensive strategy for change'.[20]

The Prime Minister returned to the need for 'radical reform' in a speech to mark the launch in February 2004 of *Civil Service Reform: Delivery and Values*, a document which the Cabinet Secretary Andrew Turnbull said was intended 'to remind ourselves of the strengths of the Civil Service, to recognise how much we have changed, and to identify the work going forward for the future, and to put it all in context'.[21] The world had changed, and the Civil Service must change with it, the Prime Minister said. The purpose of change was not to alter the service's ethos and values but, on the contrary, to protect them by making them work in a way more relevant to the modern age. In practical terms this meant: a smaller, strategic centre; a Civil Service with professional and specialist skills; a Civil Service open to the public, private, and voluntary sectors and encouraging interchange among them; more rapid promotion within the Civil Service and an end to tenure for senior posts; a Civil Service equipped to lead, with proven leadership in management and project delivery; a more strategic and innovative approach to policy; government organized around problems, not problems around government.[22]

Civil Service Reform was followed by the Coalition's *Civil Service Reform Plan*, published in 2012, the idea of a plan having initially been rejected by Maude as we have seen in favour of 'doing stuff'.[23] Under the plan the service would become smaller and more strategic, its policymaking capability would be improved, its capability increased, and a modern employment offer created for staff that 'encouraged and rewarded a productive, professional and engaged workforce'.[24] As Maude later realized, the plan was little different from Blair's proposals nearly a decade earlier:

> a civil service with professional and specialist skills; a civil service open to the public; a more strategic and innovative approach to policy. The world had changed and the civil service must change with it. That was nearly 10 years ago; but today the diagnosis remains pretty similar. When I was sent Blair's 2004 speech some months after we had published our reform plan I was struck by the deja vu. I found I had been echoing his concerns, indeed his very phrases.[25]

Resisting the temptation to put 'a rosy glow' on progress, the *One Year On* report made clear that progress in implementing the plan had been limited.[26] The reform programme was 'a significant undertaking'—perhaps one that had been 'initially

[20] Public Administration Select Committee, *Making Government Work: The Emerging Issues* (HC 2000–01, 94) para 20.

[21] Cabinet Office, *Civil Service Reform: Delivery and Values* (2004); Civil Service Reform Event—24 February 2004, Opening remarks by Sir Andrew Turnbull <www.civilservant.org.uk/library/2004-CSR_Conference_Opening_Remarks.pdf>.

[22] Speech given by the Prime Minister on the subject of Civil Service Reform—24 February 2024 <http://www.civilservant.org.uk/library/2004_PM_CSR_Delivery_Speech.pdf>.

[23] Chapter 2, section 2.2.1.

[24] HM Government, *The Civil Service Reform Plan* (June 2012).

[25] Francis Maude, Ministers and Mandarins: Speaking Truth unto Power (Lecture, 4 June 2013) <www.gov.uk>.

[26] Cabinet Office, *Civil Service Reform Plan: One Year On Report* (July 2013).

underestimated'—and had itself 'illustrated the challenges of becoming more corporate within a federated structure'. 'Despite the very best endeavours of many people', delivery of the plan had been 'held back by some of the very things that it was designed to address—weaknesses in capability, lack of clear accountability, and delivery discipline.'[27] The final report a year later offered a more reassuring picture of 'real progress towards the Government's vision of a more skilled, less bureaucratic and hierarchical, and more unified' Civil Service.[28] On a more cautionary note it warned that there was 'much more to be done' and that constant improvement was needed to avoid 'slipping back'.[29] With Brexit and the Covid pandemic , however, Civil Service reform ceased to be an immediate priority.

The Coalition's *Civil Service Reform Plan* was followed a decade later by the Johnson government's *Declaration on Government Reform*. In the Declaration, which was signed by the Prime Minister on behalf the Cabinet and the Cabinet Secretary on behalf of the Permanent Secretaries, the Cabinet and Permanent Secretaries committed themselves to a 'collective vision for reform' in which they aimed to have the best people leading and working in government, to sharpen up how government prioritized and evaluated its work, and to make sure that politicians and officials acted as a single united team to deliver for citizens.[30] The Declaration and the accompanying (internal) 'vision for a Modern Civil Service' had barely begun to be implemented however before the Johnson administration collapsed. In a subsequent statement on Civil Service reform the Cabinet Office announced in July 2023 that its vision for a Modern Civil Service would now focus on five key 'missions for reform'—capability, place, delivery, digital and data, and innovation—'areas where we can support departmental priorities and really drive forward change to unlock improvements across the Civil Service'.[31]

There is no question that commitment (or its lack) and crises are factors in the success or otherwise of efforts at Civil Service reform. But for the Maude Review the continuing failure to fulfil the stewardship obligation highlighted two systemic weaknesses: a lack of authority to 'drive reform through the whole Service' and the accountability arrangements for the implementation of reform, which the review described as 'gravely deficient'.[32] 'It is hard to escape the conclusion that—almost alone among state institutions—there is no organised scrutiny of the way the Civil Service is managed.'[33] Maude's solution would have seen the Prime Minister's power to manage the Civil Service under the Constitutional Reform and Governance Act 2010 delegated to a head of the Civil Service, a separate appointment from that of the Cabinet Secretary, who would be accountable to a reformed Civil Service Commission for the implementation of an agreed programme of reforms. There was no indication, however,

[27] ibid Introduction.

[28] Civil Service, *Civil Service Reform Plan Progress Report* (October 2014).

[29] National Audit Office, *Departmental Overview; the Performance of the Cabinet Office 2013–14* (November 2014) para 2.16.

[30] Cabinet Office, *Annual Report and Accounts 2020–21* (HC 391, July 2021) Foreword.

[31] Cabinet Office, *A Modern Civil Service: The Next Steps on our Journey* (July 2023).

[32] Maude Review (n 1) para 3.22.1.

[33] ibid para 3.7. See also to the same effect, *Power with Purpose: Final Report of the Commission on the Centre of Government* (Institute for Government March 2014) 56–62. The proposed remedies differ but the analysis is the same.

of Maude's recommendation finding favour before the Sunak government left office. As to why that might be, a sceptic might remark that it is because it is in no-one in government's interest for authority and accountability for reform to be as clearly defined as Lord Maude recommended.

III From the Prerogative to Statute: The Legal Basis of Control

For more than 150 years the management of the Civil Service was 'one of the aspects of the Prerogative which [was] exercised by Ministers on behalf of the Crown', from which it followed that it was 'for Ministers alone to issue instructions concerning the management of the Civil Service, and that they [did] not require Parliamentary authority to do so'.[34] That all changed with the Constitutional Reform and Governance Act 2010, which put the management of the service on a statutory footing.

That the Civil Service should be managed by Orders in Council issued under the Royal Prerogative was, in the beginning at least, a matter of accident rather than design. Fearing the effects of departmental opposition to their proposals, Northcote and Trevelyan recommended that they be implemented by legislation:

> It remains for us to express our conviction that if any change of the importance of those which we have recommended is to be carried into effect, it can only be successfully done through the medium of an Act of Parliament. The existing system is supported by long usage and powerful interests; and were any Government to introduce material alterations into it, in consequence of their own convictions, without taking the precaution to give those alterations the force of law, it is almost certain that they would be imperceptibly, or perhaps avowedly, abandoned by their successors, if they were not even allowed to fall into disuse by the very Government which had originated them. A few clauses would accomplish all that is proposed in this paper.[35]

In the event parliamentary legislation was beyond the reach of the government. It was therefore compelled to rely on its inherent powers, a course urged upon it by those who, while by no means favouring the Northcote-Trevelyan proposals, were nevertheless opposed to any further erosion of the prerogative. 'Why add yet another to the many recent sacrifices of the royal prerogative? Why advise the Queen to ask Parliament to aid her to do that which she can do as effectually without their aid?', asked Sir James Stephen.[36] The extent of the opposition to the Northcote-Trevelyan reforms was underlined when the House of Commons declined to back the Order in Council implementing the Report. Undeterred the government went ahead.[37] The

[34] Cabinet Office, *The Civil Service: Taking Forward Continuity and Change* (Cm 2748, 1995) para 2.15.
[35] Northcote and Trevelyan (n 3)
[36] *Papers relating to the Reorganisation of the Civil Service*, Parl Pap (1854–55) vol 20, 79.
[37] Maurice Wright, *Treasury Control of the Civil Service 1854–74* (Clarendon Press 1969) 64; rejection by the legislature would of course have been fatal to parliamentary legislation.

foundations were thus laid for a 'tradition' of the regulation of the Civil Service in the exercise of the royal prerogative, which was to be maintained for the next 150 years.

What then prompted the change?

The origins of the shift to parliamentary legislation as the basis for the management of the service may be traced to the fear that its essential character was in danger of being altered by the reforms to the organization and management of government pursued by successive governments in the closing decades of the 20th century. The argument, as it was to be summed up later, was that the fundamental values of the Civil Service 'cannot be assured when the arrangements for upholding them are laid down in prerogative Orders in Council that can be amended by the Executive without the involvement and scrutiny of Parliament'. They should therefore 'be enshrined in statute to put beyond doubt the impartiality and political neutrality of the permanent Civil Service and to maintain public trust in central government and public office holders'.[38]

In 1994 the Treasury and Civil Service Committee called for statutory backing to be given to its proposals for strengthening the essential values and standards of the Civil Service. The Committee was not convinced of the case for 'a wide-ranging Civil Service Act as a mechanism for either furthering or delimiting reforms of the Civil Service'. It did, however, believe that there would be

> considerable value in a much narrower statute, principally designed to provide statutory backing for [the] new mechanisms (in the form of a Civil Service Code and a direct line of appeal to the Civil Service Commissioners in cases of alleged breaches of the Code) for maintaining the essential values of the Civil Service . . . We believe the time has come to implement the last recommendation of the Northcote-Trevelyan Report and establish a new Civil Service Commission on a statutory basis.[39]

In its response, the Conservative government acknowledged that statutory entrenchment 'if based on cross-party consensus could be an effective means of expressing and entrenching general agreement on the non-political nature of the Civil Service'. It was, however, 'cautious about the prospect of opening up the possibility of change in the constitutional position of the Civil Service, and thereby risking its politicisation'. Before introducing a Civil Service bill it would need to be satisfied that there was 'a broad measure of agreement on legislation which sustained rather than altered the existing constitutional position of the Civil Service, retained the flexibility of the existing arrangements for regulating the terms and conditions of civil servants, and did not change the position of civil servants under general employment law'.[40] In the event no legislation was forthcoming.[41]

New Labour came to power in 1997 with a commitment to a Civil Service Act,[42] but it was to be more than a decade before that commitment was

[38] Cabinet Office, *A Draft Civil Service Bill: A Consultation Document* (Cm 6373, 2004) para 17.

[39] Treasury and Civil Service Committee, *The Role of the Civil Service* (HC 1993–94, 27) para 116.

[40] Cabinet Office, *The Civil Service* (n 34) paras 2.16–2.17.

[41] Cabinet Office, *A Draft Civil Service Bill* (n 38) para 16.

[42] Labour Party, *Report of the Joint Consultative Committee on Constitutional Reform* (March 1997) paras 83–84.

fulfilled.[43] The problem, as was explained to the Committee on Standards in Public Life, was that the Act 'lacked a champion'.[44] That changed in July 2007 when it became part of the new Prime Minister, Gordon Brown's programme of 'constitutional renewal'.[45] 'To reinforce the neutrality of the civil service, the core principles governing it will no longer be set at the discretion of the executive but will be legislated by Parliament—and so this Government have finally responded to the central recommendation of the Northcote-Trevelyan report on the civil service made more than 150 years ago in 1854.'[46] It was to be another three years, however, before the legislation was enacted—as Part 1 of the Constitutional Reform and Governance Act 2010.

IV Selection for Appointment

4.1 The principle of selection on merit

The fundamental principle on which Civil Service recruitment has been based for more than 150 years is selection for appointment on merit on the basis of fair and open competition (the 'merit principle').[47] As an internal review of recruitment responsibilities in 1994 pointed out, the language had changed over the years, but the underlying intent had remained the same since Northcote-Trevelyan: 'to guard against patronage, political or otherwise; to render jobs in the civil service accessible to those who may wish to apply for them; and to ensure that people appointed to those jobs are competent to do them'.[48] The review saw no cause to abandon a principle which had provided the foundation of an 'effective, non-political' Civil Service for more than a century. On the contrary, the devolutionary trends now affecting the service made it all the more important that it be reasserted and maintained.[49]

The Constitutional Reform and Governance Act (CRAG) gave statutory expression to the merit principle in essentially the same terms as those used in the Civil Service Order in Council it replaced. Whereas the Order in Council provided that 'no person shall be appointed to a situation in the Service unless the selection for appointment is made on merit on the basis of fair and open competition',[50] the Act now

[43] A consultation document with a draft bill was published in November 2004 (Cabinet Office, *A Draft Civil Service Bill* (n 38)), following pressure from the House of Commons Public Administration Select Committee (*A Draft Civil Service Bill: Completing the Reform* (HC 2003–04, 128) and the Committee on Standards in Public Life (*Reinforcing Standards: Review of the First Report of the Committee on Standards in Public Life* (Cm 4557, 2000)).

[44] 'In fact one of the things that is often not said about the Civil Service Act is that one of the reasons it has not happened is not because anyone is particularly against it, but because up until now it has lacked a champion. When the Queen's speech is written there are not many members of the Cabinet saying, "Hang on, I think you should drop that Education Bill and we should have a Civil Service Act"': Committee on Standards in Public Life, *Defining the Boundaries within the Executive: Ministers, Special Advisers and the Permanent Civil Service* (Cm 5775, 2003) para 10.17, quoting Pat McFadden.

[45] Anthony Seldon and Guy Lodge, *Brown at 10* (Biteback Publishing 2010) 17–18.

[46] HC Deb 3 July 2007, vol 462, col 817.

[47] The Civil Service Order in Council 1870 established open competition as the normal method of entry to the Service.

[48] Cabinet Office, *Responsibilities for Recruitment to the Civil Service* (1994) para 4.1.

[49] ibid paras 2.1 and 4.6.

[50] Civil Service Order in Council 1995, art 2(1)(a).

provides that selection for appointment to the Civil Service 'must be on merit on the basis of fair and open competition'.[51]

The merit principle as enshrined in the Act applies only to 'the selection of persons who are not civil servants for appointment to the civil service'.[52] It does not apply to the appointment, promotion, and lateral moves of existing civil servants. As regards such internal appointments, the Civil Service Management Code (below) provides that departments and agencies must ensure that 'all promotions and lateral transfers follow from a considered decision as to the fitness of individuals, on merit, to undertake the duties concerned',[53] a less onerous requirement than that which applies to external appointments. The Maude Review recommended that the Civil Service Management Code merit requirement be revised to bring it much closer to the statutory requirement for external appointments, and the Civil Service Commission's remit extended to include the oversight of internal as well as external appointments.[54]

4.2 The Civil Service Commission

The Civil Service Commission, a non-departmental public body sponsored by the Cabinet Office, is responsible for overseeing the application of the merit principle; it 'regulates selection for appointments to the Civil Service to provide assurance that appointments are made on merit on the basis of fair and open competition'.[55]

Civil Service Commissioners were first appointed in 1855 to test the qualifications of candidates nominated for appointment to departments.[56] For much of their history they served as 'a central recruiting, examining and certifying body under Treasury regulation'.[57] With the delegation of the bulk of recruitment functions to departments and agencies they were recast as the custodians of the merit principle as part of a series of reforms aimed at 'revitalizing' the principle in Civil Service recruitment.[58] They were also given responsibility for hearing appeals under the new Civil Service Code, a 'very different' role from their traditional responsibilities but one which the commissioners said fitted well with the 'regulatory body' they had now become.[59]

The Constitutional Reform and Governance Act reconstituted the Commissioners as a statutory body, the Civil Service Commission, with the same regulatory and appellate functions as before.

The Commission consists of a minimum of seven members, one of whom is the First Civil Service Commissioner.[60] The First Civil Service Commissioner is appointed by the King on the recommendation of the Minister for the Civil Service (the

[51] CRAG 2010, s 10(2); the requirement does not apply to the appointment of special advisers (s 10(3)(b)).
[52] CRAG 2010, s 10(1).
[53] Civil Service Management Code (November 2016) para 6.3.2.
[54] (n 1) para 6.9 (recommendation 19).
[55] Civil Service Commission, *Annual Report and Accounts 2018–19* (HC 2414) 10.
[56] Civil Service Commissioners Order in Council 1855.
[57] Greaves (n 10) 103.
[58] Cabinet Office, *Responsibilities for Recruitment to the Civil Service* (n 48) para 3.24.
[59] Civil Service Commissioners, *Annual Report 1994–95*, 6.
[60] CRAG 2010, sch 1, para 1.

Prime Minister) following consultation with the leaders of the main opposition parties.[61] The obligation to consult the leaders of the main opposition parties, which was introduced in response to a recommendation of the Committee on Standards in Public Life,[62] is intended to ensure that all the main political parties, and not just the party or parties in power, are confident that the First Commissioner will uphold the impartiality of the Civil Service; without that shared confidence the likelihood of the principle of a permanent Civil Service surviving a change of government is diminished.

The other members are appointed by the King on the recommendation of the Minister for the Civil Service, made with the agreement of the First Commissioner.[63] Appointments (of the First Civil Service Commissioner and the other Commissioners) are for a single non-renewable term of not more than five years,[64] which is intended to ensure that they cannot be influenced, or be seen to be influenced, by the prospect of not being reappointed. They may be removed from office, but only on limited grounds, including being unfit or unable to carry out the functions of the office.[65]

The Commission's two main functions are to oversee the application of the merit principle by departments and agencies;[66] and to hear appeals under the Civil Service Code.[67] It may also be given additional functions in relation to the Civil Service, by agreement between the Commission and the Minister for the Civil Service.[68] It currently has two such functions: Commissioners chair *internal* competitions at Director General and Permanent Secretary level under the Senior Appointments Protocol agreed with the Head of the Civil Service, and it supports departments and agencies in promoting the Civil Service Code. It also provides secretariat support to the Advisory Committee on Business Appointments (ACOBA) and the Office of the Commissioner for Public Appointments (OCPA).

The Memorandum of Understanding which governs relations between the Commission and the Cabinet Office provides that the Commission 'in discharging its functions, is independent of the Government and the Civil Service'.[69] The Maude Review, however, saw the Commission as

> set up in such a way that its independence from the Civil Service hierarchy is limited. It is viewed as a Cabinet Office 'arm's length body'; but its budget is set by the Cabinet Office; its chief executive is a career civil servant line managed by the head of propriety and ethics; its staff are all civil servants; and its last two First

[61] CRAG 2010, sch 1, para 2; the First Ministers of Scotland and Wales must also be consulted.

[62] Committee on Standards in Public Life, *Defining the Boundaries within the Executive* (n 44) paras 6.69 and 10.26.

[63] CRAG 2010, sch 1, para 3.

[64] CRAG 2010, sch 1, paras 2 and 3.

[65] CRAG 2010, sch 1, para 5.

[66] CRAG 2010, ss 11–14.

[67] CRAG 2010, s 9.

[68] CRAG 2010, s 17.

[69] Cabinet Office and Civil Service Commission, *Memorandum of Understanding between the Cabinet Office and the Civil Service Commission* (11 November 2010) para 2.1.a <https://civilservicecommission.independent.gov.uk/wp-content/uploads/2019/03/01b_Memorandum-of-Understanding.pdf>.

Commissioners before the current incumbent were both former Civil Service permanent secretaries.[70]

As to whether the Commission might provide a means of redressing the lack of accountability for Civil Service reform, the Review saw its current institutional arrangements as militating

> strongly against its ability to operate as an independent regulator of the Civil Service. Indeed, historically it has seen its role less as a regulator of the Civil Service than as its protector; and with its sole specified responsibility for overseeing external recruitment it has tended to focus on guarding the perimeter. Its role has largely been a passive one, primarily to prevent 'bad things' happening—principally 'politicisation' and the dilution of the merit principle.[71]

It would need to be reformed therefore if it was to meet the need.

The Memorandum of Understanding, which has not been revised since it was adopted in 2010, is currently being updated. According to the Cabinet Secretary, the revised document will continue to make clear that the Constitutional Reform and Governance Act 'allows the Commission to assert greater independence should it wish to (for example by directly recruiting its own staff from outside the Civil Service)'.[72] The Commission's triennial review thought it 'surprising' that its staff were all seconded from the Civil Service. The Commission had the power to employ its own staff and its management should not all be, or have been, senior civil servants.[73] The Maude Review recommended that the staff of a reformed Commission should be independent of the Civil Service and include at most a small minority of civil servants.[74]

4.3 The recruitment principles

While the Constitutional Reform and Government Act was to make no difference to the power to manage the Civil Service, which continued to be vested in the Prime Minister as Minister for the Civil Service as before, its significance in terms of recruitment to the service was considerably greater. As well as putting Civil Service Commissioners on a statutory basis it gave the Commission control of the principles which govern recruitment to the service. When therefore the Coalition government wanted to give ministers a greater say in senior Civil Service appointments, it found that it could not simply replace the Commission's principles with its own, as its

[70] Maude Review (n 1) para 3.11; 'the Commission operationally is heavily dependent on the Civil Service. Its independence is accordingly truncated' (para 2.1.2). See also Benjamin Barnard, *Open, Meritocratic and Transparent: Reforming Civil Service Appointments* (Policy Exchange November 2021).

[71] Maude Review (n 1) para 4.30.

[72] House of Lords Constitution Committee, *Permanent Secretaries: Their Appointment and Removal* (HL 2022–23, 258) para 27.

[73] Cabinet Office, *A Better Civil Service: Triennial Review of the Civil Service Commission* (December 2014) paras 3.23–3.24; on the then operative arrangements for the review of public bodies see chapter 4, section 3.3.

[74] Maude Review (n 1) para 2.3.3.

Conservative successor was to do with the Commissioner for Public Appointment's Code of Practice for Ministerial Appointments to Public Bodies, but had to secure the Commission's agreement, which was only forthcoming when the Commission was satisfied that there was all-party support for the change.[75] The Constitutional Reform and Governance Act requires the Commission to publish a set of principles to be applied for the purposes of complying with the merit principle.[76] The Commission's long-held view has been that 'an overly prescriptive approach to compliance . . . would be counterproductive for government departments. Our principles-based regulation provides departments with the flexibility to design resourcing solutions which suit them, while still meeting the core requirements of an appointment on merit, after fair and open competition.'[77]

The principles were first introduced in 2009, in anticipation of the Act, when they replaced the Recruitment Code issued by the Commissioners under the 1995 Order in Council. Revised versions were introduced in 2014 and 2018, with the latter putting greater emphasis on the importance of seeking to attract a strong and diverse pool of candidates for every selection competition and introducing changes to the exceptions regime.[78] (The 2014 revision, which followed extensive public consultation, was described as 'much clearer than previously', enabling the Commission to dispense with five separate documents of guidance. 'They are drafted with all recruiters to the Civil Service at all levels in mind, not just those recruiting senior staff.'[79])

The Recruitment Principles explain the legal requirement for merit, fairness, and open competition and set out the rules and procedures which departments and agencies (and the devolved administrations) must follow in selecting people for appointment. Among the issues the principles address are: ministerial involvement in appointments, approvals for selections, and exceptions.

4.3.1 Ministerial involvement

Guidance first issued by the Civil Service Commissioners in 1994 acknowledged ministers' 'legitimate interest' in a small number of very senior posts of considerable importance for the 'setting and delivery of their policies', but sought to accommodate that interest 'within a system which produces appointments which can last into other Administrations and are free from personal or political bias'.[80] While ministers were to be consulted (about the job and person specification, the criteria for selection, and the composition of the selection panel), they were not to participate in the selection

[75] On the replacement of Commissioner for Public Appointment's Code of Practice see chapter 4, section 4.2.

[76] CRAG 2010, s 11; the Commission must consult the Minister for the Civil Service before publishing the principles.

[77] Civil Service Commission, *Annual Report and Accounts 2021–22* (HC 525) 22.

[78] Civil Service Commission, *Annual Report and Accounts 2018–19* (n 55) 20–21.

[79] Civil Service Commission, *Annual Report and Accounts 2014–15* (HC 251) First Civil Service Commissioner's Foreword.

[80] Civil Service Commissioners, *Annual Report 1994–95*, 7; for the background see Terence Daintith and Alan Page, *The Executive in the Constitution: Structure, Autonomy and Internal Control* (OUP 1999) 81. Lord Maude thought it 'unlikely that this formulation would pass muster today. Most Ministers would consider that they have a "legitimate interest" in the appointment of every single individual for whose activities they can be held accountable' (n 1) para 6.3, fn 17.

process, a principle which, for the Committee on Standards in Public Life, was 'fundamental to the maintenance of a service which is, and is perceived to be, politically impartial'.[81] Invited to consider giving ministers a choice in appointments, the Civil Service Commissioners initially concluded there was no reason for changing their approach before agreeing to an amendment to the Recruitment Code in 2004 whereby a panel might revise its recommendation at the minister's request, but only with the agreement of all the Commissioners.[82] Under renewed pressure from the 2010 Coalition government, following publication of its *Civil Service Reform Plan* in which it sought a 'strengthened role' for ministers in senior appointments,[83] the Civil Service Commission subsequently agreed to the government's 'long-standing wish that the Prime Minister should have a degree of choice in selecting Permanent Secretaries'.[84]

The Recruitment Principles accordingly distinguish between Permanent Secretary appointments and other senior appointments. For the latter, the Principles provide for ministers to be 'fully involved' but continue to stop short of giving them a choice of candidate. A minister with an interest in an appointment should thus be consulted on and agree the final role and person specification and the terms of advertisement. The minister should also agree the composition of the selection panel. The minister may meet each of the shortlisted candidates, to discuss their priorities and the candidates' approach to the role, and feed back to the panel views on any issues the minister wants the panel to test at interview. Meetings between the minister and candidates must however be attended by a representative of the Civil Service Commission. The minister may not be a member of a selection panel and may not add or remove candidates from a competition. The panel must assess the merits of the candidates using the best possible evidence and testing any issues raised by the minister. The panel must recommend the best candidate for appointment. If not satisfied with the panel's recommendation the minister may ask the panel to reconsider, setting out the reasons. The panel may revise its order of merit, but the reason for this must be recorded, and the panel must obtain the approval of the Board of the Commission before any appointment can be made.[85]

For Permanent Secretary appointments, the final choice of candidate, assuming more than one candidate is appointable, lies with the Prime Minister, in consultation with the Head of the Civil Service and the First Civil Service Commissioner. Before making the final selection, the Prime Minister may meet the appointable candidates. If the Prime Minister does so, he or she must meet all the appointable candidates and must do so with the First Civil Service Commissioner (or nominee) present.[86] Described as 'controversial' when it was introduced in 2014, this process, in the former First Civil Service Commissioner's judgement, was 'both compliant with

[81] Committee on Standards in Public Life, *Defining the Boundaries within the Executive* (n 44) para 6.39.

[82] Civil Service Commissioners, *Recruitment Code* (5th edn, 2004) paras 2.56–2.57; Civil Service Commissioners, *Annual Report 2003–04*, 39 and app D; for the Commissioners' initial response, see Civil Service Commissioners, *Annual Report 2002–03*, 25.

[83] HM Government, *The Civil Service Reform Plan* (n 24) 21.

[84] Civil Service Commission, *Annual Report and Accounts 2014–15* (HC 251) 6–7 ('We decided to make the change only when we believed there was a consensus, including a cross party political consensus, for doing so').

[85] Civil Service Commission, *Recruitment Principles* (April 2018) paras 39–43.

[86] ibid para 47.

the Constitutional Reform and Governance Act 2010, and works well in practice, balancing the need for politicians to make clear their expectations for the role, while protecting the impartiality of the Civil Service'.[87]

Giving ministers a choice of candidate, the Commissioners had argued, would erode the principle of selection on merit and the concept of a permanent Civil Service: 'Ministers moved on whereas the permanence, professionalism and impartiality of the Civil Service ensured it could serve any government of the day.'[88] A minister would be less likely to accept an appointment for which their predecessor had pressed. The force of the second objection for Permanent Secretary appointments was weakened by the Coalition government's introduction of fixed-term appointments for Permanent Secretaries in 2014, with appointments coming to an end after five years unless they are extended.[89] The introduction of fixed-term appointments for senior posts, including those of Permanent Secretaries, had been announced by Tony Blair in 2004 but for reasons that are unclear this did not happen.[90]

The Johnson and Truss premierships saw the resignation or dismissal of several Permanent Secretaries, including most notoriously that of the Permanent Secretary to the Treasury who was sacked on Truss's appointment. Under Johnson the Cabinet Secretary was ousted amid briefing that he had 'failed to grip' the coronavirus emergency.[91] The House of Lords Constitution Committee took the view that their removal was not 'indicative of a trend' but that some departures and appointments had been 'conducted in the public eye and might be seen to reflect a desire on the part of ministers to personalise appointments and assert their authority'. This practice, the Committee said, should be avoided. 'It risks senior civil service turnover coinciding with ministerial churn, creating a perception of politicization and damaging institutional knowledge.'[92] The Sunak government welcomed the Committee's conclusion that there was no evidence of a trend towards the removal of civil servants on political or ideological grounds.

The Committee also found that the selection routes for very senior appointments were 'convoluted and unclear' and had evolved significantly since the Senior Appointments Protocol was agreed in 2011 and the most recent Recruitment Principles published. It recommended that both be updated, in particular to reflect the 'external by default' policy (below) and the Prime Minister's role in approving director general appointments as well as those of Permanent Secretaries. The Committee welcomed the commitment of the Cabinet Secretary and First Civil Service Commissioner to ensure both were updated.[93]

87 Civil Service Commission, *Annual Report and Accounts 2019–20* (HC 455), 10.

88 Civil Service Commissioners, *Annual Report 2003–04*, 39.

89 Cabinet Office (n 26) 31.

90 'When we introduced a five-year fixed term for Permanent Secretaries, this was putting into effect, very belatedly, what a Prime Minister thought he had introduced eight years previously' (Public Administration and Constitutional Affairs Committee, 12 January 2021, q 652 Lord Maude).

91 Other Permanent Secretaries who resigned, were sacked, or whose contracts were not extended included Rutnam HO, Moriarty DExEU, Heaton MOJ, McDonald FO, Dawes MHCLG, and Slater DfE. The turnover of Permanent Secretaries was not unprecedented: only three of the 2010 cohort of Permanent Secretaries were still in post in 2015.

92 House of Lords Constitution Committee, *Permanent Secretaries* (n 72) para 136.

93 ibid para 89.

4.3.2 Commission approval

The Constitutional Reform and Governance Act provides that the Commission may require its approval to be obtained for selections for appointment which are subject to the merit principle.[94] Commission approval serves as 'a form of guarantee that the normal principles have been observed where an appointment is seen to be susceptible to Ministerial influence'.[95] Where its approval is required the Commission may participate in the selection process, the manner of its participation being up to the Commission.[96] The principles provide that Civil Service Commissioners must chair all competitions for posts at SCS Pay Band 4 (Permanent Secretary) and SCS Pay Band 3 (Director General) level. Under the Senior Appointment Protocol, this requirement applies both to open (external) competitions and to Civil Service-wide (internal) competitions, an 'important additional safeguard' which gives the Commission 'oversight of the competitions for all the top jobs, however they are filled'.[97] Commissioners normally also chair competitions for open (external) competitions at SCS Pay Band 2 (Director) level.[98]

4.3.3 Exceptions

The Commission may also except selections for appointment from the merit principle, but only where it is satisfied that the exception is justified by the needs of the Civil Service or is necessary to enable the Civil Service to participate in a government employment initiative.[99] The Recruitment Principles currently set out 10 exceptions, including for temporary appointments, support for government employment programmes, and highly specialist skills.[100] The Commission may, in exceptional circumstances, except other appointments or classes of appointments from the requirement where it believes this is justified by the needs of the service.[101] Extensive use was made of this power in preparing for Brexit and in responding to the pandemic.[102] Certain appointments by exception require the Commission's prior approval, including appointments where the Commission considers there is a risk the Recruitment Principles may be breached.[103] The Commission has been keen to reduce departments' reliance on exceptions, following a necessary period of high-volume, time-limited appointments during the pandemic.[104]

94 CRAG 2010, s 12(1)(a).
95 Cabinet Office (n 48) para 5.20.
96 CRAG 2010, s 12(2),(3).
97 Civil Service Commission, *Recruitment Principles* (n 85) para 50; Civil Service Commissioners, *Annual Report 2007–08* (Letter from the First Civil Service Commissioner).
98 Civil Service Commission, *Recruitment Principles* (n 85) para 51.
99 CRAG 2010, s 12(1)(b) and (4).
100 Civil Service Commission, *Recruitment Principles* (n 85) Annex A.
101 ibid para 100.
102 'The Commission was quick to recognise government's need to recruit and redeploy senior and specialist people in bulk on a short-term basis to deliver Brexit, and so we created a protocol to enable them to do it. When COVID-19 struck, requiring a response on a much bigger scale, the Commission enabled the rapid mobilisation of people to roles across the Civil Service without losing the integrity of appointments' (Civil Service Commission, *Annual Report and Accounts 2020–21* (HC 465) 8.
103 Civil Service Commission, *Recruitment Principles* (n 85) paras 62–63.
104 Civil Service Commission, *Annual Report and Accounts 2022–23* (HC 95) 24. On 30 August 2024, the First Civil Service Commissioner announced a short review of appointments made by exception at delegated grades, which do not require the Commission's prior approval, between 1 July and 31 August 2024. This followed criticism of a number of appointments made by the incoming Labour government.

4.3.4 'External by default'
The Civil Service Commission's oversight is limited as we have seen to external recruitment to the Civil Service. It has no power to oversee or investigate internal moves and promotions. Following a commitment made in the *Declaration on Government Reform*, the Johnson government announced in May 2022 that all senior appointments would be opened to public competition by default, advertised in such a way as to ensure the widest possible pool of applicants, which would widen the range of appointments subject to Commission oversight. Data subsequently disclosed by government departments under the Freedom of Information Act revealed that a third of all jobs for the country's most senior civil servants had not been advertised externally—151 of the 457 jobs filled between May 2022 and January 2023—despite the government commitment to do so,[105] prompting the Minister for the Cabinet Office to write to all Secretaries of State to reinforce the importance of the 'external by default' policy and to ask for continued support in its full implementation.

4.4 Compliance monitoring

The Civil Service Commission is responsible for auditing departmental compliance with the merit principle. It is under a statutory duty to carry out whatever reviews of recruitment policies and practices it thinks are necessary to establish that the merit principle is being upheld and not being undermined in any way (apart from non-compliance).[106] Under its previous strategy it employed a 'comprehensive compliance regime' in auditing organizations' recruitment policies and practices, following which it published a compliance rating based on in-year performance (good, fair, or poor) and likely trajectory (at risk, static, likely to improve) for each organization. In its 2021–22 annual report it described overall compliance with the Recruitment Principles as 'broadly good and improving', with a number of organizations having maintained or improved their rating and/or trajectory since the previous year.[107]

Following the introduction of external by default the Commission is revising its strategy to focus on departments with poor practice. 'Our aim is to focus regulatory effort and support on departments with poor practice, allowing departments to earn greater autonomy where practice and understanding of the Commission's recruitment principles is strong.'[108] The audit cycle will move from annual to triennial, which means that every department within the Commission's regulatory remit will be audited at least once every three years. It is also moving from its current nine ratings to four (good, fair, requires improvement, and requires regulatory intervention), bringing it in line with other regulators. Departments with lower ratings (eg 'requires regulatory intervention') will be audited annually until their score becomes 'fair' or

[105] *The Times* (20 April 2023).
[106] CRAG 2010, s 14; other ways in which it might be undermined include by abuse of the exceptions (short-term appointments, secondments).
[107] Civil Service Commission, *Annual Report and Accounts 2021-22* (n 77) 10.
[108] Civil Service Commission, *Annual Report and Accounts 2022–23* (n 104) 10.

'good'. This approach will ensure that the Commission's resources are continually focused on where we can have the most impact.[109]

Departments are required to retain sufficient information on their recruitment to provide evidence that they have complied with the Recruitment Principles and to provide the Commission with any information it reasonably requires. The Commission may require departments to change their recruitment procedures, and it may publish details of departments which breach the Principles.[110]

The Commission's triennial review was told that the operation of the Principles in practice by some departments left 'something to be desired' and was 'not always in line with best practices elsewhere'. It was important to be alert that 'form does not substitute for substance' which was why regular monitoring by the Commission was important to ensure that the Principles were being adhered to. The review recommended that departments which 'consistently and materially do not adhere to the Principles should be reported by the Commission to the Head of the Civil Service and the Minister for the Cabinet Office for appropriate action to be taken'.[111] In its 2021–22 annual report, the Commission announced that it had agreed with the Cabinet Secretary and the Government Lead Non-Executive that the Commission's audit of departments' performance against the Recruitment Principles and Civil Service Code complaints would be part of each Permanent Secretary's annual performance review.[112]

4.5 Complaints

A person who has reason to believe that a selection for an appointment has been made in contravention of the merit principle may complain to the Commission.[113] The Commission only accepts complaints about open (external) competitions (all grades) and Civil Service-wide (internal) competitions (SCS Pay Band 3 and above only).[114] After considering the complaint, the Commission may make recommendations about how the matter should be resolved.[115] The Commission is the 'final decision-maker' in respect of complaints.[116] No appeal lies against its 'recommendation'. In 2022–23, 167 Recruitment Principles complaints were received, 37 of which were referred back to departments for investigation and initial decision.

[109] ibid 19.
[110] Civil Service Commission, *Recruitment Principles* (n 85) paras 65–66.
[111] Cabinet Office, *A Better Civil Service* (n 73) paras 3.28 and 3.36.
[112] Civil Service Commission, *Annual Report and Accounts 2021–22* (n 77) 6.
[113] CRAG 2010, s 13(2); Civil Service Commission, *Recruitment Principles* (n 85) paras 67–72.
[114] Civil Service Commission, *Recruitment Principles* (n 85) para 68.
[115] CRAG 2010, s 13(3)(c).
[116] Civil Service Commission *Annual Report and Accounts 2018–19* (n 55) 10.

V The Management of the Civil Service

5.1 The power to manage the service

The Constitutional Reform and Governance Act vests the power to manage the Civil Service in the Minister for the Civil Service.[117] The Prime Minister has been the Minister for the Civil Service since the office was created in 1968 when responsibility for the management of the service was transferred from the Treasury, of which the Prime Minister is First Lord, to the Civil Service Department.[118] The Prime Minister's responsibility for the management of the Civil Service is intended to underline its importance to the government as a whole as well as to individual departments. The Fulton Committee was 'strongly of the opinion that it is in the interests of the Service for the Prime Minister to be seen to be ultimately responsible . . . for the total task of managing the Service. No other Minister can assert the needs of the government service as a whole over the sectional needs of powerful departmental Ministers.'[119] The Prime Minister is supported in carrying out his or her responsibilities as Minister for the Civil Service by the Chancellor of the Duchy of Lancaster, the most senior minister in the Cabinet Office after the Prime Minister, and the Paymaster General and Minister for the Cabinet Office.

In exercising the power to manage the Civil Service, the Prime Minister must have regard to 'the need to ensure that civil servants who advise Ministers are aware of the constitutional significance of Parliament and of the conventions governing the relationship between Parliament and His Majesty's Government'.[120] That obligation is mirrored in the Civil Service Code, which provides that civil servants advising ministers should 'be aware of the constitutional significance of Parliament, and of the conventions governing the relationship between Parliament and the government'.[121] No explanation is offered of the constitutional significance of Parliament or of the conventions governing the relationship between Parliament and government. Perhaps none was thought necessary; or that any explanation would only raise more questions than it answered.

The Maude Review was critical of the lack of an overall scheme of delegation setting out how the statutory power to manage the Civil Service was to be exercised in practice, whether by ministers or by civil servants.[122]

> It is obvious that no Prime Minister can expect to exercise this power personally—for nearly all purposes that power would be expected to be delegated. However, it has been exceptionally difficult to piece together how (and in many cases whether) such formal delegation has occurred, and through what instruments of delegation.

[117] CRAG 2010, s 3(1); the power does not extend to the diplomatic service, which is managed by the Secretary of State.

[118] Minister for the Civil Service Order 1968, SI 1968/1656.

[119] Committee on the Civil Service, *The Civil Service: Report of the Committee 1966–68* (Cmnd 3638, 1968) para 261.

[120] CRAG 2010, s 3(6).

[121] Cabinet Office, *Civil Service Code* (2010, rev 2015).

[122] Maude Review (n 1) para 2.1.1.

> No comprehensive scheme exists, and the picture can only be loosely sketched out by examining a variety of documents—in particular letters delegating powers directly to ministers (never made public or revealed to ministers themselves) and the published Civil Service Management Code.[123]

For Maude, as we saw, the lack of any clear authority to drive reform was a key factor in the failure 'to implement or sustain agreed and uncontroversial Civil Service reforms and improvements'. It was essential therefore that a single comprehensive scheme of delegation should emerge from consideration of his review. If acted on, his recommendation—a comprehensive delegation to the Head of the Civil Service who would in turn be accountable to a reformed Civil Service Commission for the implementation of an agreed programme of Civil Service reforms—would radically alter the relationship between the centre and departments. There is no indication, however, that this might happen.

5.2 The Civil Service Management Code

The management of the Civil Service, responsibility for reform aside, has been largely delegated to departments and agencies under the Civil Service (Management Functions) Act 1992.[124] The delegations are set out in the Civil Service Management Code, issued under the authority of the Constitutional Reform and Governance Act, which sets out regulations and instructions to departments and agencies regarding the terms and conditions of service of civil servants and the delegations which have been made under the Civil Service (Management Functions) Act to ministers and office-holders in charge of departments, and the Scottish and Welsh First Ministers, together with conditions attaching to those delegations.[125]

Under the Code, ministers and office-holders in charge of departments, and the Scottish and Welsh First Ministers, have been given the authority:

a. to prescribe the qualifications (so far as they relate to age, knowledge, ability, professional attainment, aptitude and potential, health and coping with the demands of the job) for the appointment of home civil servants (with the exception of the Fast Stream Development Programme) in departments; and
b. to determine the number and grading of posts outside the Senior Civil Service in departments and the terms and conditions of employment of civil servants relating to:

    - the classification of staff (with the exception of the Senior Civil Service);
    - remuneration (with the exception of the Senior Civil Service);

[123] ibid para 3.9.

[124] Civil Service (Management Functions) Act 1992, s 1. An 'old' Act put to a new purpose.

[125] Cabinet Office, *Civil Service Management Code* (n 53) Introduction, para 2; the Code was first issued in 1993 with the aim of providing a clear and accurate statement of the terms and conditions of service of all civil servants, regardless of the department or agency in which they worked, in which respect it has been superseded by the delegation of authority to departments and agencies.

- allowances; expenses; holidays, hours of work and attendance;
- part-time and other working arrangements;
- performance and promotion;
- retirement age (with the exception of the Senior Civil Service);
- redundancy; and
- the re-deployment and lateral transfer of staff within the Civil Service.[126]

Delegation is subject to the condition that recipients comply with the provisions of the Code as amended from time to time (para 4). Departments and agencies are reminded that the government is committed to maintaining the reputation of the Civil Service as a good employer. The terms and conditions of civil servants must be determined with regard to: the general practice of large employers; value for money; and the provisions of *Government Accounting*—now *Managing Public Money*, which is in fact silent on the matter (para 4).[127] Departments and agencies must comply fully with legislation which binds the Crown or which ministers have undertaken to apply as if it were binding on the Crown. They must define clearly the terms and conditions of service of their staff and make these available to staff, for example in departmental or agency handbooks. Where departments and agencies have delegated powers or discretion, they must make clear to their staff how these will be applied by setting out the relevant rules and procedures in their handbooks (para 5).

Compliance with the Code does not relieve departments and agencies of the obligation to submit to the Cabinet Office proposals or arrangements which are 'contentious, or raise questions of propriety' (para 4). This obligation reflects the Cabinet Office's continuing responsibility for the oversight of the service, enabling it to consider difficult cases and if necessary to revise the central framework in the light of them. The Cabinet Office also retains the right to inspect and monitor observance of the Code in departments and agencies, but the aim is to keep such inspection and monitoring to 'the minimum level consistent with central responsibilities' (para 7).

5.3 The Government People Group

The Government People Group, formerly Civil Service HR, is one of the cross-government functions. Its purpose is to 'lead and manage human resources activity across government, ensuring people are recruited, developed and deployed to meet the government's needs'.[128]

The Human Resources Functional Standard sets expectations for the leadership and management of human resources across government.[129] The function is led by the Government Chief People Officer, who is accountable to the Chief Operating

[126] ibid para 3; where departments have agencies, the presumption is that delegated functions will be exercised by agency chief executives, but the precise extent to which ministers may wish to allow the exercise of their powers by chief executives is a matter for them to determine (para 2).

[127] Given that the Code was revised in 2016, the continued presence of this reference is surprising—an illustration of communication failure within the 'centre'.

[128] Government functions <www.gov.uk>.

[129] HM Government, *Government Functional Standard GovS 003: Human Resources* 2.0 (July 2021).

Officer for the Civil Service for: setting a cross-government human resource 'governance and management framework'; defining, communicating, and implementing a cross-government human resource 'vision, strategy and policy'; and managing strategic relationships with professional associations and internal and external service providers with a focus on human resource management (4.5.2). Responsibilities for the leadership and management of human resources within departments and agencies, however, remain unchanged. The Accounting Officer, in the case of a department the Permanent Secretary, thus continues to be responsible for 'human resource activities' in their organization (4.5.5) as part of their responsibility for its overall organization, management, and staffing, with the senior officer accountable for human resources in turn being accountable to the organization's accounting office for 'people issues', including: defining and delivering the department's overall human resources strategy and objectives, aligned to [its] business strategy; defining and implementing the organization's human resources governance and management framework; overseeing delivery of human resource services to employees, line managers, and business leaders in line with quality standards defined by the management framework; and compliance with the standard by entities for which the organization is the sponsor or for which the organization's Accounting Officer is accountable (4.5.6).

In his earlier review of the cross-cutting functions, Lord Maude welcomed the appointment of a Chief People Officer at a senior level to oversee HR across the government. A new and much more unified approach was essential, which would start to rectify clear deficiencies in skills and capabilities, and by doing this on a much more whole of government basis would be able to make substantial reductions in cost. It was clear that there were significant variations in HR practice in different parts of government. The time was right therefore for a significant strengthening of the Chief People Officer's mandate. Civil Service HR should adopt the common employment model in which senior executives in the functions in the departments would be directly employed by the central function rather than by the departments, and the Chief People Officer should have the power to insist on the standardization of definitions, data, and HR practices across government.[130] It is not clear, however, whether this has happened.

The functional standard obliges those engaged in human resource management to ensure that they comply, and guide their organizations to comply, with 'prevailing employment law' and, among other obligations, the Civil Service Code and the Civil Service Commission's Recruitment Principles (4.6).

5.4 The Civil Service Governance Boards

The Civil Service Board (CSB), formerly the Civil Service Management Board, is responsible for 'the strategic leadership of the Civil Service, to make sure it works as a coherent and effective whole and has the capability both now, and in the future, to respond to any challenges'. Chaired by the Chief Operating Officer for the Civil Service,

[130] Lord Maude; *Review of the Cross-cutting Functions and the Operation of Spend Controls* (July 2021) 19–20; Maude Review (n 1) paras 5.26–5.27.

it is made up of a cross-section of Permanent Secretaries from Civil Service departments. The People Board, a sub-board of the CSB, oversees strategic people-related issues across the Civil Service. There is also a Civil Service Shadow Board (CSSB), made up of civil servants from the departments represented at the CSB. CSSB members are drawn from grades below the Senior Civil Service to provide different perspectives and views on the issues discussed at the CSB.

VI Standards of Conduct

6.1 Introduction

The UKCivil Service tradition relied heavily on unwritten rules. 'Much had been left unsaid previously which was made explicit when the Service grew large, but the "code" (if such it can be called) still le[ft] a great deal to personal honour and common sense.'[131] The Board of Enquiry in the *Francs* case was strongly of the view that 'practical rules for the guidance of social conduct depend as much upon the instinct and perception of the individual as upon cast-iron formulas', adding its hope that the 'surest guide' would always be found in 'the nice and jealous honour of Civil Servants themselves'.[132] According to the former Establishments Officers' Guide, the 'distinctive character' of the British Civil Service depended largely on 'the existence and maintenance of a general code of conduct which, although to some extent intangible and unwritten, is of very real influence'.[133] Of real influence or not, the Civil Service has not escaped the 'codification of what might once have been assumed to be common ground',[134] with the introduction of a Civil Service Code in 1996 as a means of strengthening the existing arrangements for upholding its essential values and standards.

The standards of conduct expected of civil servants are set out in the Civil Service Management Code and the Civil Service Code. Departments and agencies are responsible for defining the standards of conduct they require of their staff, but the standards they require must 'fully reflect' the Civil Service Code and central framework outlined in the Civil Service Management Code.[135]

6.2 The Civil Service Management Code

The central framework outlined in the Civil Service Management Code is designed to deliver, through departments and agencies, 'the standards expected of civil servants

[131] William JM Mackenzie and JW Grove, *Central Administration in Britain* (Longmans 1957) 8.
[132] Board of Enquiry, *Report of the Board of Enquiry appointed by the Prime Minister to Investigate Certain Statements affecting Civil Servants* (Cmd 3037, 1928) para 59.
[133] Establishments Officers' Guide (1976) para 4060, reproduced in *Report of the Royal Commission on Standards of Conduct in Government* (Cmnd 6524, 1976) app 11.
[134] Committee on Standards in Public Life, *Standards in Public Life: First Report* (Cm 2850, 1995) para 3.11.
[135] Civil Service Management Code (n 53) para 4.1.2.

individually and of the civil service as a whole'.[136] It 'derives from the need for civil servants to be, and to be seen to be, honest and impartial in the exercise of their duties. They must not allow their judgement or integrity to be compromised in fact or by reasonable implication.'[137] The Code provides that civil servants must not:

- misuse information which they acquire in the course of their official duties, or disclose official information without authority;
- seek to frustrate the policies, actions, or decisions of government (either by declining to take, or abstaining from, action which flows from ministerial decisions or by unauthorised, improper or premature disclosure outside the government of any information to which they have had access as civil servants);
- take part in any political or public activity which compromises, or might be seen to compromise, their impartial service to the government of the day or any future government;
- misuse their official position or information acquired in the course of their official duties to further their private interests or those of others; or
- receive gifts, hospitality, or benefits of any kind from a third party which might be seen to compromise their personal judgement or integrity.[138]

These principles are amplified by rules in respect of confidentiality and official information, standards of propriety, and political activities.

Those in respect of confidentiality and official information require departments and agencies to remind staff on appointment, retirement, or resignation that they are bound by the provisions of the criminal law, including the Official Secrets Acts, since 1989 significantly narrowed in scope, and by their duty of confidentiality owed to the Crown as their former employer.[139] Departments and agencies must also ensure that civil servants do not, without relevant authorization, disclose official information which has been communicated in confidence within government or received in confidence from others; or seek to frustrate the policies or decisions of ministers by the use or disclosure outside the government of any information to which they have had access as civil servants.[140]

The rules in respect of standards of propriety cover such matters as the letting of contracts to departmental and agency staff, and the employment of staff who are bankrupt or insolvent on duties which might permit the misappropriation of public funds, as well as the acceptance of gifts, hospitality, or benefits in kind.

They also include the business appointments rules for civil servants, which aim to avoid any reasonable concerns that:

a. a civil servant might be influenced in carrying out his or her official duties by the hope or expectation of future employment with a particular firm or organisation, or in a specific sector; or

136 Cabinet Office, *The Civil Service* (n 34) para 2.35.
137 Civil Service Management Code (n 53) para 4.1.3.
138 ibid.
139 ibid para 4.2.1.
140 ibid paras 4.2.2 and 4.2.6.

b. on leaving the Civil Service, a former civil servant might improperly exploit privileged access to contacts in Government or sensitive information; or
c. a particular firm or organisation might gain an improper advantage by employing someone who, in the course of their official duties, has had access to:

i. information relating to unannounced or proposed developments in Government policy, knowledge of which may affect the prospective employer or any competitors; or
ii. commercially valuable or sensitive information about any competitors.[141]

The rules apply for one or two years depending on seniority. The most senior civil servants (typically Directors General and Permanent Secretaries) are required to obtain the approval of the Advisory Committee on Business Appointments (ACOBA) before accepting an appointment or employment within two years of leaving the Civil Service. They are also in principle banned from lobbying government on behalf of a new employer within the two years. Depending on their seniority, other civil servants to whom the rules apply[142] are required to obtain the approval of their department before accepting an appointment or employment within one or two years of leaving the service. Unlike the ministerial rules, the Civil Service rules are contractually binding, but no sanction, contractual or otherwise, currently attaches to their breach other than the threat of negative publicity for civil servants whose subsequent employment requires the approval of ACOBA.[143]

As we saw in chapter 2, the business appointment rules in their application to ministers and civil servants alike have been heavily criticized in recent years. Reforms have been proposed but have yet to be implemented.[144]

The purpose of the political activities rules is to maintain public confidence in the political impartiality of the service. They are intended to avoid public identification of individual civil servants with a party political stance that could call into question an individual's impartiality, or more generally the neutrality of the service as a whole; and to avoid criticism that people paid from public funds are being used for party political purposes.[145]

[141] ibid s 4.3, Annex A, para 3.

[142] ibid para 13.

[143] The Salmon Commission did not see how any penalty could be devised: 'The civil service rules are not supported by any formal sanctions. A civil servant who left the service to take a business appointment for which permission had been refused by the Government would not be in jeopardy of any penalty. We do not see how any penalty could be devised. It would be wrong to attempt to apply the criminal law to such situations. Nor would it be in keeping with current ideas to make provision for a civil servant who disobeyed the Government's instructions in this way to forfeit any part of his pension rights' (*Report of the Royal Commission on Standards of Conduct in Government* (Cmnd 6524, 1976) para 204).

[144] Chapter 2, section 3.3.

[145] Cabinet Office, *Guidance on Guidance* (1996) *Political Activities* (*Guidance on Guidance* was replaced by Cabinet Office, *Directory of Civil Service Guidance* (2000), which refers to the Civil Service Management Code without the explanation).

6.3 The Civil Service Code

The Civil Service Code is the 'ethical code' of the Civil Service. It was first issued in 1996 on the recommendation of the House of Commons Treasury and Civil Service Committee, which saw a code as a means of strengthening the existing arrangements for upholding the essential values and standards of the Civil Service.

> It would enable civil servants themselves and those they serve—both Ministers and the public—to know what was expected of the Civil Service. It would strengthen the hands of those who sought to maintain essential values in the face of perceived threats to those values. It would make more tangible the values which civil servants hold in common.[146]

The Conservative government accepted the Committee's recommendation 'in the interests of maintaining public confidence in the impartiality and integrity of the Civil Service'—the purpose of the Code would be to set out 'with greater clarity and brevity than existing documents the constitutional framework within which all civil servants work and the values which they are expected to uphold'.[147]

Originally issued under the prerogative,[148] the Code is now issued under the Constitutional Reform and Governance Act, which requires the Minister for the Civil Service to publish a code of conduct for the Civil Service.[149] Separate codes may be, and in practice are, published for civil servants working for the Scottish and Welsh governments, who are part of the 'Home' Civil Service.[150] The Code must be laid before Parliament, as must the Scottish and Welsh codes before the Scottish Parliament and the Welsh Senedd, but there is no requirement for their parliamentary approval.[151] The current version of the Code, which forms part of civil servants' terms and conditions of service,[152] was laid before Parliament in November 2010, with an amended version laid in March 2015 (requiring ministerial authorization for contact with the media).

The Act sets out the minimum requirements that must be included in the Code and its devolved equivalents. There are two requirements: the Code must require civil servants 'to carry out their duties for the assistance of the administration as it is duly constituted for the time being, whatever its political complexion'; and it must require them to do so 'with integrity and honesty, and with objectivity and impartiality'.[153]

146 Treasury and Civil Service Committee, *Civil Servants and Ministers* (n 39) para 105.

147 Cabinet Office, *The Civil Service* (n 34) paras 2.6–2.8.

148 Civil Service (Amendment) Order in Council 1997; strictly speaking there was no need for prerogative authorization to issue the Code, but it was felt desirable to have a reference to the Code on the face of the Order in Council.

149 CRAG 2010, s 5(1); a parallel obligation lies on the Foreign Secretary to publish a code for the diplomatic service (s 6).

150 CRAG 2010, s 5(2); the Scottish and Welsh First Ministers must be consulted before the codes for civil servants serving their administrations are published (s 5(3)).

151 CRAG 2010, s 5(5)–(7); the Committee on Standards in Public Life recommended that the Code should be contained in secondary legislation subject to affirmative resolution of both Houses, thereby 'ensuring that flexibility is joined with scrutiny': (n 134) para 3.55.

152 CRAG 2010, s 5(8).

153 CRAG 2010, s 7(2),(4).

(Special advisers (below) are also required to carry out their duties with integrity and honesty but need not be required to so with objectivity and impartiality.[154])

The Code, which was rewritten in 2006 to make it shorter and more accessible, describes the Civil Service as 'an integral and key part of the government of the United Kingdom', which 'supports the government of the day in developing and implementing its policies, and in delivering public services' (para 2). Civil servants are expected to carry out their role 'with dedication and a commitment to the Civil Service and its core values: integrity, honesty, objectivity and impartiality' (para 3). The Code explains what is meant by each of the core values and sets out the standards of behaviour expected of civil servants in upholding them, explaining both what they must do as well as what they must not do in order to meet the expected standards.

Integrity is defined as putting the obligations of public service above personal interests. It requires that civil servants must: fulfil their duties and obligations responsibly; always act in a way that is professional and that deserves and retains the confidence of all those with whom they have dealings; make sure public money and other resources are used properly and efficiently; deal with the public and their affairs fairly, efficiently, promptly, effectively, and sensitively; ensure they have ministerial authorization for any contact with the media; keep accurate official records[155] and handle information as openly as possible; and comply with the law and uphold the administration of justice;[156] and that they must not: misuse their official position, accept gifts or hospitality or receive other benefits from anyone which might reasonably be seen to compromise their personal judgement or integrity, or disclose official information without authority (paras 6–7).

Honesty is defined as being truthful and open. It requires that civil servants must set out the facts and relevant issues truthfully, and correct any errors as soon as possible, and use resources only for the purposes for which they are provided; and that they must not deceive or knowingly mislead ministers, Parliament, or others, or be influenced by improper pressures from others or the prospect of personal gain (paras 8–9).

Objectivity is defined as basing advice and decisions on rigorous analysis of the evidence. It requires that civil servants must: provide information and advice, including advice to ministers, on the basis of the evidence, and accurately present the options and facts, take decisions on the merits of the case, and take due account of expert and professional advice; and that they must not: ignore inconvenient facts or relevant considerations when providing advice or making decisions, or frustrate the implementation of policies once decisions are taken by declining to take, or abstaining from, action which flows from those decisions (paras 10–11).

Impartiality is defined as acting solely according to the merits of the case and serving equally well governments of different political persuasions. In *general terms* it requires that civil servants must carry out their responsibilities in a way that is fair, just, and equitable and reflects the Civil Service commitment to equality and diversity,

[154] CRAG 2010, s 7(5).

[155] On record keeping, see chapter 11, section IV.

[156] In *R (FDA) v Minister for the Cabinet Office* [2024] EWHC 1729 (Admin), the Divisional Court held that the duty to comply with the law did not require or enable civil servants to decline to implement a ministerial decision on the basis that to do so would or might be a breach of the United Kingdom's obligations under international law.

and that they must not act in a way that unjustifiably favours or discriminates against particular individuals or interests (paras 12–13). In *political terms* it requires that civil servants must: serve the government, whatever its political persuasion, to the best of their ability in a way which maintains political impartiality and is in line with the requirements of the Code, no matter their own political beliefs, act in a way which deserves and retains the confidence of ministers, while at the same time ensuring that they will be able to establish the same relationship with those whom they may be required to serve in some future government, and comply with any restrictions that have been laid down on their political activities; and that they must not: act in a way that is determined by party political considerations, or use official resources for party political purposes, or allow their personal political views to determine any advice they give or their actions (paras 14–15).

6.3.1 Complaints

Civil servants who believe that they are being, or have been, required to act in a way that conflicts with the Code, or that another civil servant is acting, or has acted, in a way that conflicts with the Code may complain to the Civil Service Commission.[157] It is normally only where it has not been possible to resolve the matter at departmental level that a civil servant may complain to the Commission, although it will consider taking complaints directly. After considering the complaint, the Commission may make recommendations to resolve the matter.[158] No appeal lies against the Commission's recommendation. If the matter cannot be resolved on a basis the civil servant is able to accept, they must either carry out their instructions or resign from the service.[159] In 2022–23, the Commission received 85 'appeals' from civil servants, 16 of which were referred back to departments for investigation and initial decision.[160]

With the support of the Committee on Standards in Public Life, the former Civil Service Commissioners sought a reserve power to initiate an investigation without a complaint being made by a civil servant, but this was opposed by the 2007 Labour government, which did not believe such a power was necessary or that it should be for the Commission alone to initiate an inquiry.[161]

6.3.2 Promoting the Code

As well as hearing complaints from civil servants where it has not been possible to resolve these at departmental level, the Commission works with departments to promote the Code and help ensure its effective operation. The annual Civil Service People Survey includes three questions relating to the Code. In its 2021–22 annual report, the Commission described the results for general understanding of the Code, how to raise a concern, and confidence that a concern would be investigated properly as 'worrying'. The Commission would be reviewing departments' individual People Survey results

157 CRAG 2010, s 9(3); for the background, see Daintith and Page (n 80) 98–101; 'another civil servant' would include a special adviser.

158 CRAG 2010, s 9(5).

159 The Civil Service Code (March 2015) para 19.

160 Civil Service Commission, *Annual Report and Accounts 2022–23* (n 104) 11.

161 Ministry of Justice, *The Governance of Britain—Constitutional Renewal* (Cm 7342, 2008) para 183; Civil Service Commissioners, *Annual Report 2007–08* (n 97) paras 32–33.

and, where an organization's response shows signs of weakness, it would offer further support and training.[162] In its most recent annual report, the Commission reported that while awareness of the Code was embedded across the Civil Service, the results for how to raise a concern and confidence that a concern would be investigated properly were 'of concern'. The Commission would continue to monitor them.[163]

VII Special Advisers

7.1 Introduction

First appointed as an experiment by the February 1974 Labour government,[164] special advisers had become an established feature of the system of government—the third side of a triangle of ministers, civil servants, and special advisers—by the time Labour regained power in 1997. They are employed as temporary civil servants 'to help ministers on matters where the work of government and the work of the party, or parties, of government overlap and where', in the words of the Cabinet Manual, 'it would be inappropriate for permanent civil servants to become involved';[165] inappropriate because it would make it difficult if not impossible for them to gain the confidence of a government of a different political complexion. 'They are an additional resource for the minister, providing assistance from a standpoint that is more politically committed and politically aware than would be available to a minister from the permanent Civil Service.'[166]

The rules governing special advisers were added to and amended by the 1997 New Labour government before being put on a statutory basis by the Constitutional Reform and Governance Act. As they stood when Labour came to power in 1997 the rules were to be found in three instruments: Questions of Procedure for Ministers, which was re-issued as the Ministerial Code, which made provision for the appointment of up to two special advisers by each Cabinet minister subject to the approval of the Prime Minister; the Civil Service Order in Council 1995, which exempted their appointment from the requirement of selection on merit; and the Civil Service Code issued in 1996. To these were added a model contract for special advisers in 1997 and a separate code of conduct for special advisers in 2001, the latter on the recommendation of the Committee on Standards in Public Life.[167] The legislation placing the Civil Service on a statutory footing, the government said in the *Governance of Britain*

[162] Civil Service Commission, *Annual Report and Accounts 2021–22* (n 77) 33.

[163] Civil Service Commission, *Annual Report and Accounts 2022–23* (n 104) 28.

[164] Harold Wilson, *The Governance of Britain* (Weidenfeld and Nicolson and Michael Joseph 1976) app II (The 'political advisers' experiment).

[165] *The Cabinet Manual: A Guide to Laws, Conventions and Rules on the Operation of Government* (October 2011) para 7.11.

[166] ibid; 'an extra pair of hands, ears and eyes and a mind more politically committed and more politically aware than would be available to a Minister from the political neutrals in the established Civil Service': Wilson (n 164) 204.

[167] Committee on Standards in Public Life, *Reinforcing Standards* (n 43) para 6.70; the Committee described the 1997 arrangements as a 'useful advance on previous informal arrangements for the employment of special advisers' (para 6.58).

Green Paper, would 'clarify the legitimate and constructive role of Special Advisers within government', before going on to reiterate that having special advisers 'allows Ministers to get the political advice they need, and reinforces the political impartiality of the permanent Civil Service by clearly distinguishing the sources of political and non-political advice'.[168]

7.2 The Constitutional Reform and Governance Act

The Constitutional Reform and Governance Act makes provision with regard to the appointment of special advisers. Those working for the UK government must be appointed to assist a minister of the Crown after being selected for appointment by that minister personally; their appointment must also be approved by the Prime Minister, as must their terms and conditions of appointment, which must provide for their appointment to end either when the appointing minister ceases to hold office or, if earlier, immediately following the next parliamentary general election.[169] 'Spads are hired by their minister and they expire with their minister.'[170] The same requirements apply to special advisers in the Scottish and Welsh governments, save that they are selected for appointment by the First Minister personally, rather than by individual ministers, and their appointment comes to an end when the First Minister ceases to hold office.[171]

As personal appointees of ministers, the appointment of special advisers is not subject to the merit principle.[172] 'Special adviser appointments are personal appointments made by the Minister and in view of the personal and temporary nature of their role they are exempt from the principle of recruitment on merit through fair and open competition.'[173]

The 1995 Order in Council defined the appointment of special advisers for the purpose of their exemption from the requirement of selection on merit as being 'for the purpose only of providing advice',[174] a definition at variance with the subsequent Code of Conduct, which described their role as including such matters as 'preparing speculative policy papers which can generate long-term policy thinking within the Department, including policies which reflect the political viewpoint of the Minister's party', and 'representing the views of their Minister to the media including a Party viewpoint, where they have been authorised by the Minister to do so'.[175] Rather than attempt a definition of what special advisers could do, the Committee on Standards in

168 Secretary of State for Justice and Lord Chancellor, *The Governance of Britain* (Cm 7170, 2007) para 45.

169 CRAG 2010, s 15(1); the Ministerial Code (December 2022) para 3.2, provides that appointments require 'the prior written approval of the Prime Minister, and no commitments to make such appointments should be entered into in the absence of such approval'.

170 Ian Dunt, *How Westminster Works... and Why it Doesn't* (Weidenfeld & Nicholson 2023) 130.

171 CRAG 2010, s 15(2),(3).

172 CRAG 2010, s 10(3)(b).

173 Ministry of Justice (n 161) para 190.

174 Civil Service Order in Council 1995, art 3; this restriction was first added in 1991 (see below).

175 The Civil Service (Amendment) Order in Council 2005 redefined the purpose of their appointment as being for the provision of 'assistance' rather than 'advice'.

Public Life recommended that 'a clear statement of what special advisers cannot do should be set out in primary legislation'.[176]

The Act accordingly sets out restrictions on special advisers' activities which must be included in the Code. There are three restrictions. The Code must provide that a special adviser may not: authorize public expenditure, 'exercise any power in relation to the management of any part of the civil service of the State' (except in relation to other special advisers), or otherwise exercise any statutory or prerogative power.[177] The restriction on the management of the Civil Service had its origins in a 1997 amendment to the Civil Service Order in Council to allow the appointment of a maximum of three special advisers in the Prime Minister's Office with 'executive powers', ie with civil servants working directly for them.[178] The Prime Minister's chief of staff and his chief press secretary were appointed in the exercise of this power.[179] It was revoked when Gordon Brown became Prime Minister in 2007,[180] with the restriction subsequently being made permanent by the Constitutional Reform and Governance Act.[181]

The Act sets no limit on the number of special advisers who may be appointed, the Labour government having rejected the notion of a cap in favour of an annual report to Parliament of their number and costs.[182] The most recent report showed 117 (115.35 FTE) special advisers working across the whole of government at a cost of £15.96m, 41 of whom worked for the Prime Minister.[183] Under the then Ministerial Code Cabinet Ministers might each appoint up to two special advisers, but ministers commonly appointed more.[184]

Special advisers' terms and conditions of appointment are set out in the Model Contract for Special Advisers and the Code of Conduct for Special Advisers.[185]

[176] Committee on Standards in Public Life, *Defining the Boundaries within the Executive* (n 44) para 7.29.
[177] CRAG 2010, s 8(5).
[178] Civil Service (Amendment) (No 2) Order in Council 1997.
[179] 'Apart from ministers of the Crown, no non-civil servants had ever been in a position, formally, to tell civil servants what to do (although several had done so in practice). Powell and Campbell were thus the most special of special advisers': Anthony King, *The British Constitution* (OUP 2007) 231.
[180] Civil Service (Amendment) (No 2) Order in Council 2007.
[181] In a revealing observation on the development of the special adviser regime, a former Cabinet Secretary told the Committee on Standards in Public Life: 'I had not realised until recently that the qualification [that special advisers may only advise] was only added in 1991 . . . throughout the 1980s special advisers had no limits on what they could do in law . . . What the recent Order in Council actually does is just to remove the restriction on advice—in relation to the three so called executive posts—that was introduced in 1991, and put those three posts back to where all special advisers were before 1991 . . . we have been improvising over a period of years': Committee on Standards in Public Life, *Defining the Boundaries within the Executive* (n 44) para 9.20, Sir Richard Wilson.
[182] CRAG 2010, s 16; the devolution statutes did impose a cap, which was replaced by the requirement of an annual report under the Constitutional Reform and Governance Act. '[T]he Government does not believe that it is necessary to continue with the arrangement whereby a cap on numbers is specified for appointments in Scotland and Wales. Transparency [is] ensured through the publication of the annual statement' (Ministry of Justice (n 161) para 192).
[183] Cabinet Office, *Special Adviser Data Releases: Numbers and Costs, July 2023.*
[184] *Ministerial Code* (December 2022) para 3.2. This restriction was omitted from the Ministerial Code issued by Sir Keir Starmer in November 2024.
[185] ibid.

7.3 The Code of Conduct for Special Advisers

A code of conduct for special advisers was first published in 2001 on the recommendation of the Committee on Standards on Public Life, which concluded that the Model Contract and the Civil Service Code, which had hitherto been relied on, did not 'set out with sufficient clarity the specific obligations of special advisers. In the interests of accountability, there needs to be a single code that guides special advisers and sets out for their departments and the wider public the rules that they should observe.'[186] The Code is now issued under the Constitutional Reform and Governance Act, which requires the Minister for the Civil Service to publish a code of conduct for special advisers.[187] As with the Civil Service Code, separate codes are published for special advisers working for the Scottish and Welsh governments.[188]

The Code describes special advisers as 'a critical part of the team supporting Ministers. They add a political dimension to the advice and assistance available to Ministers while reinforcing the political impartiality of the permanent Civil Service by distinguishing the source of political advice and support.'[189] They should be 'fully integrated into the functioning of government. They are part of the team working closely alongside civil servants to deliver Ministers' priorities.'[190] Ministers' priorities, however, are not their only consideration. In an amendment made by David Cameron in 2010, the Code adds that special advisers are appointed 'to serve the Prime Minister and the government as a whole, not just their appointing Minister'.[191] This was no doubt prompted by the Prime Minister finding himself in coalition, but as Yong and Hazell note, 'the tension between serving the minister and serving the government is built into the Whitehall model'.[192]

In accordance with the recommendation of the Committee on Standards in Public Life,[193] the Code continues to list the sorts of work a special adviser may do at the request of their minister. Among other things, they may: give assistance on any aspect of departmental business, and give advice (including expert advice as a specialist in a particular field); undertake long-term policy thinking and contribute to policy planning within the department; write speeches and undertake related research, including adding party political content to material prepared by permanent civil servants; liaise with the Party, briefing party representatives and parliamentarians on issues of

186 Committee on Standards in Public Life, *Reinforcing Standards* (n 43) para 6.70.

187 CRAG 2010, s 8(1); the Code is laid before Parliament but is not subject to any form of parliamentary approval (s 8(8)).

188 CRAG 2010, s 8(2); the Scottish and Welsh First Ministers must be consulted before the codes are published or revised (s 8(3)).

189 Cabinet Office, *Code of Conduct for Special Advisers* (December 2016) para 1. A new version of the Code was published while this work was in press: Cabinet Office, *Code of Conduct for Special Advisers* (September 2024). The substance of the Code remains unchanged.

190 Cabinet Office, *Code of Conduct for Special Advisers* (n 189) para 2.

191 ibid; see also to the same effect para 10 ('They are employed to serve the objectives of the Prime Minister, the Government and the Minister(s) for whom they work') and the *Ministerial Code* (December 2022) para 3.3 ('All special advisers must uphold their responsibility to the Government as a whole, not just to their appointing Minister').

192 Ben Yong and Robert Hazell, *Special Advisers: Who They Are, What They Do and Why They Matter* (Bloomsbury Publishing 2014) 136.

193 Committee on Standards in Public Life, *Defining the Boundaries within the Executive* (n 44) para 7.30.

government policy; represent the views of their minister to the media (including a party viewpoint), where they have been authorized by the minister to do so; and liaise with outside interest groups (including those with a political allegiance).[194]

In working with other civil servants, they can, on behalf of their minister: convey to officials ministers' views, instructions, and priorities, including on issues of presentation. In doing so, they must take account of any priorities ministers have set; request officials to prepare and provide information and data, including internal analyses and papers; hold meetings with officials to discuss the advice being put to ministers; and review and comment on—but not suppress or supplant—advice being prepared for ministers by civil servants.[195] They must not however ask civil servants to do anything which is inconsistent with their obligations under the Civil Service Code or behave in a way which would be inconsistent with standards set by their employing department.[196]

As temporary civil servants, special advisers are also bound by the Civil Service Code, save that they are not required to carry out their duties with objectivity or impartiality,[197] recognizing their allegiance is to the governing party or parties and that they are not expected to retain the confidence of future governments of a different political complexion.[198]

7.4 Management and conduct

Under the Ministerial Code, as amended in 2005, following the Jo Moore affair,[199] the appointing minister is responsible for the management and conduct, including discipline, of special advisers.[200] Before then formal responsibility for disciplining special advisers lay with the departmental Permanent Secretary but was complicated by the close personal relationship between ministers and special advisers. In its amended form, the Ministerial Code provides that individual ministers 'will be accountable to the Prime Minister, Parliament and the public for their actions and decisions in

194 *Code of Conduct for Special Advisers* (December 2016) para 3.

195 ibid para 4.

196 ibid para 5; the prohibition on asking civil servants to do anything inconsistent with their obligations under the Civil Service Code was included on the recommendation of the Committee on Standards in Public Life, *Reinforcing Standards* (n 43) para 6.72 ('one specific omission needs to be corrected when the new code is drawn up. There is no reference, in either the Civil Service Code or the Model Contract, to any duty on special advisers to refrain from asking civil servants to act in ways which threaten the impartiality of those civil servants. Ministers are obliged to refrain from such action . . . special advisers should be required to observe similar restraint').

197 CRAG 2010, s 7(5).

198 *Code of Conduct for Special Advisers* (December 2016) para 8.

199 *Ministerial Code: A Code of Ethics and Procedural Guidance for Ministers* (July 2005) para 2.12; for the Jo Moore affair, see Public Administration Select Committee, *These Unfortunate Events': Lessons of Recent Events at the Former DTLR* (HC 2001–02, 303). The affair had two aspects. One was her grotesque and well-publicized email on the afternoon of the September 11 attacks ('today is a very good day to get out anything we want to bury': see Daintith [2002] Public Law 13–21). Second, and more significant, was her attempt to order a Civil Service information officer to brief against a report on the future of London underground commissioned by Bob Kiley (Peter Riddell, *The Times* (2 November 2001)).

200 *Ministerial Code* (December 2022) para 3.3; *Code of Conduct for Special Advisers* (December 2016) para 9.

respect of their special advisers', before adding that '[i]t is, of course, also open to the Prime Minister to terminate employment by withdrawing his consent to an individual appointment'.[201] For the Public Administration Select Committee, however, the responsibility of ministers had proved 'more theoretical than real. We cannot recall any minister ever resigning over the conduct of a special adviser, despite some astonishing cases.'[202] While Permanent Secretaries did not have any direct responsibility for the management and conduct of special advisers they were nonetheless responsible for the management of the department as a whole, and they would inevitably have a role in overseeing and monitoring the activities of special advisers, arising from their status as temporary civil servants.[203] It was imperative that they be ready to give advice and support on matters of propriety to special advisers and ministers. They should be made responsible for ensuring that any potential problems were addressed without delay. 'They must take this responsibility seriously, be vigilant and proactive, and ensure that they are aware what the special advisers are doing in the name of their Minister and the department. They should refer any continuing concerns which the Minister fails to address to the Cabinet Secretary.'[204]

The Johnson government saw an attempt to centralize the management of special advisers by the Prime Minister's chief adviser, Dominic Cummings.[205] Cummings was able to play a leading role in their management and recruitment because he wielded the power of the Prime Minister, the employment of special advisers being conditional on the Prime Minister's consent,[206] and because the Act excepts the management of special advisers from the restriction on managing civil servants.[207] The Public Administration Select Committee had earlier rejected the idea that special advisers should be accountable to No 10. 'It would not be appropriate for Number 10 or the Cabinet Office to have an explicit role in directing or appraising special advisers appointed by ministers of other departments.'[208] After Cummings left government his approach was said to have continued, 'albeit with less zeal'.[209]

[201] *Ministerial Code* (December 2022) (n 200) para 3.3.

[202] Public Administration Select Committee, *Special Advisers in the Thick of it* (HC 2012–13, 134) para 91.

[203] ibid para 93.

[204] ibid para 99; in its response the government agreed that Permanent Secretaries had 'an important role to play in providing support and advice to both Ministers and their special advisers': *Special Advisers in the Thick of it: Government Response to the Committee's Sixth Report of Session 2012–13* (HC 2013–14, 515) para 14.

[205] Dunt (n 170) 134–36; a policy which saw Sonia Khan, an adviser to the Chancellor, Sajid Javid, marched out of Downing Street by armed police officers after being fired by Cummings, and Javid's resignation after he refused to accept the Prime Minister's insistence that he dismiss all his advisers.

[206] *Ministerial Code* (December 2022) para 3.3 ('It is, of course, also open to the Prime Minister to terminate employment by withdrawing his consent to an individual appointment').

[207] CRAG 2010, s 8(6).

[208] Public Administration Select Committee (n 201) para 107; in its response the government agreed that ministers were accountable for the management and conduct of their special advisers. However, the Prime Minister approved all special adviser appointments, and it was therefore entirely appropriate for appraisals to be conducted on his behalf, and for Downing Street to take an active interest in the conduct of special advisers and to direct them: (n 204) para 15.

[209] Dunt (n 170) 136.

PART D
THE RESOURCES OF THE EXECUTIVE: MONEY

7

Fiscal Responsibility and Expenditure Planning and Control

I Introduction: Gordon Brown's Inheritance

1.1 The Treasury-Parliament nexus

Governments can do nothing without money. Parliament's constitutional supremacy is built on its successful assertion of control of the government's access to money: first through the control of taxation, then by way of appropriation—the determination of the purposes for which government might spend its money, whether raised by taxation or otherwise. The argument over taxation may fairly be seen as closed in Parliament's favour by the Revolution Settlement of 1689.[1] From that time Parliament also stipulated how the tax revenues it granted should be spent, but comprehensive appropriation had to wait until the government's other stream of revenue, from borrowing, also became subject to parliamentary control.[2] The fact that government can neither tax the citizen, nor expend any of its funds, without parliamentary approval of the rules and levels of taxation on the one hand, and of the broad purposes of expenditure, and the amounts to be applied to such purposes, on the other, remains the fundamental support for the central position of Parliament within our constitution. What matters here is the need for approval: the fact that government has to come to Parliament to get its money, so that Parliament must meet at least as often as grants need renewal. The duration and timing of legislative grants of taxes and authorizations of expenditure are thus more central to sustaining parliamentary democracy than whether government's requests for those taxes and authorizations are approved—as, thanks to the strength of our party system, they (almost) always are.

If one pillar of UK arrangements for taxing and spending is that government must ask Parliament for money, the other is that Parliament cannot provide it unless government asks. This is a self-denying ordinance of Parliament itself, first enacted as a House of Commons resolution of 1706 after a brief period of unhappy experiences dealing with private petitions for the grant of funds.[3] Originally dealing only with such

[1] Bill of Rights 1689, art 4.

[2] On how and why this happened, see Will Bateman, *Public Finance and Parliamentary Constitutionalism* (CUP 2020) 42–51.

[3] See now House of Commons Standing Order 48: 'This House will receive no petition for any sum relating to public service or proceed upon any motion for a grant or charge upon the public revenue, whether payable out of the Consolidated Fund or the National Loans Fund or out of money to be provided by Parliament, or for releasing or compounding any sum of money owing to the Crown, unless recommended from the Crown': *House of Commons Standing Orders as at 6 November 2019* (HC 2019–20, 314). For its history see Gordon Reid, *The Politics of Financial Control: The Role of the House of Commons* (Hutchinson 1966) 35–45; Bateman (n 2) 51–52.

Executive Self-Government and the Constitution. Terence Daintith and Alan Page, Oxford University Press.
 DOI: 10.1093/9780198937630.003.0007

petitions, the wording of what became a Standing Order in 1713 was broadened in the second half of the 19th century so as to debar members of Parliament not only from introducing proposals for new taxes or spending but even from increasing the amounts or levels requested by government, a constraint copied in other 'Westminster' parliamentary systems but otherwise highly unusual among national fiscal regimes.[4] While Parliament devotes considerable time and effort to debating the details of tax legislation, it has for well over a century treated spending proposals, and the revenue aggregates needed to pay for them, in a quite different way. Its efforts are directed not to the discussion of legislative authorizations but to making the government accountable for decisions that are implicitly acknowledged to be the government's own. An Australian regulator recently described the essence of his job as being to 'test, challenge and expose' the performance of the firms he regulated,[5] and this seems a good description of what Parliament is trying to do through its financial procedures.

There is, however, no way Parliament can do this job satisfactorily unless government itself possesses properly functioning systems for relating overall revenue and expenditure needs, determining how revenue is to be raised, setting limits on expenditure, allocating it between functions, and ensuring that those limits and functions are respected and that, so far as possible, expenditure is effective and not wasteful. With us, responsibility for such systems has, even since pre-democratic times, been the province of the Treasury. In relation to these basic requirements, there is a large overlap between the interests of Parliament in financial control and those of the people within government entrusted with these tasks. In consequence, there is a long-standing alliance between Parliament and Treasury—albeit one whose significance to the parties has varied with their respective enthusiasms for economy in public expenditure—directed toward the proper management of such expenditure and grounded in a mutual dependence. The Treasury has depended on Parliament for the public ventilation of its control problems and the marshalling of political pressure in favour of the adoption of more effective systems of control. Parliament has in its turn depended on the Treasury to deliver systems which, as well as being effective, are transparent: that is to say, they incorporate the specific virtue of generating sufficiently detailed and consistent information about financial decisions to enable a body outside the administration to maintain a genuine process of supervision.[6]

4 For an analysis of fiscal powers of 28 legislatures in different types of system (presidential, parliamentary, Westminster etc) see Ian Lienert, 'Who Controls the Budget: The Legislature or the Executive?' (2005) IMF Working Paper WP/05/115, 22–23 (Annex 2).

5 Paul Fearon, Chief Executive, Energy Safety Victoria, *Energy Safety Regulation: Prescriptive versus Goal-based Approaches* (presentation, University of Melbourne, 21 March 2016: on file with author).

6 This dependence may not always be acknowledged. In 2013 the House of Lords Constitution Committee objected to the Treasury's representing itself as the 'guardian' of Parliament or as subject to 'an ancient convention' that it 'should strive to look after parliament's interests in Whitehall': *The Pre-emption of Parliament* (HL 2012–13, 183) paras 18–26.

1.2 The fiscal constitution: challenge and change in the 21st century

In our discussion in chapter 2 of the powers of the Treasury as part of the 'centre of government', we identified the three systems of financial management and control that it operates, laid down at different times and for different purposes. First came the housekeeping function of management of the monarch's own resources; next the implementation of the system of parliamentary appropriation of funds granted to the executive; and finally the management of public financial resources as an element of the management of the national economy. Together these interlocking systems furnish the United Kingdom's fiscal constitution, and in this chapter and the next we examine its evolution over the course of the current century. Over that period its levers have been operated by governments from across the political spectrum—including that rarity in British constitutional history, a formal coalition—and it has been subjected to the major economic shocks represented by the financial crisis of 2007–09, the Covid-19 pandemic of 2020–21, and the fuel cost crisis exacerbated by the Ukraine war—and to the depressing effects of exit from the EU single market. Possible further shocks flowing from Brexit may still be to come. At the same time, it has functioned within a framework of ideas and practices regarding executive government in general that continues to change.[7]

To understand this evolution, we need to start in 1997, the year that the 'New Labour' government dominated by Tony Blair and Gordon Brown returned to power. The economic and fiscal policies they brought with them represented the most far-reaching change in the financial management system since the introduction of the Public Expenditure Survey, and have proved to be of lasting constitutional significance. In pursuit of an overriding objective of stability in economic policy, responsibility for the conduct of monetary policy was devolved, within broad annual targets to be set by the Chancellor, to an 'independent' Bank of England and its expert Monetary Policy Committee.[8] Fiscal policy, which would in consequence be the principal tool for steering the economy left in the hands of elected politicians, was subjected to the overriding discipline of published fiscal rules; and the structure for the planning and control of public expenditure over the medium term was considerably reinforced. (It was also, as something of an afterthought, explicitly linked to procedures for improving efficiency, and we have already examined the operation of these in chapter 3.) These innovations, and the further developments that have come in their train, have substantially modified all three of the control systems we have identified. In the remainder of this chapter we focus on the 'macro' aspects of fiscal discipline—fiscal rules and the new institutions associated with their operation, and the recent evolution of the Spending Review system. In the next chapter we look at recent developments in the operation of central controls over departmental expenditure and financial management, examining its links with parliamentary processes,

[7] For a detailed account of public expenditure policy over the period 1992–2015, drawing extensively on interviews with officials and ministers and internal Treasury documentation, see Christopher Hood and others, *The Way the Money Goes: The Fiscal Constitution and Public Spending in the UK* (OUP 2023).

[8] For analysis from a constitutional standpoint see Tony Prosser, *The Economic Constitution* (OUP 2014) ch 6. For an 'official' explanation and justification see HM Treasury, *Reforming Britain's Economic and Financial Policy: Towards Greater Economic Stability* (Palgrave 2002) chs 3 and 7.

its key principles, its location—Cabinet Office now exercises extensive financial control powers under a delegation from the Treasury—and its interaction with the mechanisms of external control operated by the National Audit Office (NAO) and by the courts.

II Fiscal Stability and Budgetary Responsibility

2.1 Fiscal rules

During their long years in Opposition under the Thatcher and Major governments, Labour leaders became convinced that re-election depended on shedding the 'tax and spend' reputation of their party.[9] Prudence, stability, and transparency became the watchwords of Gordon Brown as shadow Chancellor in 1992, underpinned by an intellectual commitment to the idea that while discretion was essential to effective economic and financial policy, it had to be constrained by appropriate rules and structures if the credibility crucial to its effective deployment was to be maintained.[10] In fiscal policy, 'New Labour' thinking was signalled by Brown's announcement in 1995, as Shadow Chancellor, of the two fiscal rules he would follow in government: the so-called 'golden rule', that over the economic cycle, the government would borrow only to invest and not to fund current spending; and the 'sustainable investment rule', that public sector net debt as a proportion of gross domestic product (GDP) would be held over the economic cycle at a stable and prudent level.[11] Commitment to these rules was restated in Labour's 1997 manifesto and in Brown's first Budget speech as Chancellor.[12]

The United Kingdom was certainly not the first country to adopt the notion that some rule-based constraint on budgetary discretion would produce positive economic results. Japan and Germany have had budget-balancing provisions written into law since 1947 and 1967 respectively, and New Zealand was the first among UK-style parliamentary democracies to introduce a fiscal stability law in 1994.[13] It was not to be assumed, however, that if a UK government accepted the idea of such rules it would seek to express them in legislation. After all, the executive's traditional posture, in budgetary matters as in many others, has been to prefer self-discipline to legislative discipline where a choice was available, so that one might have expected that a public announcement of the new rules would be seen as sufficient. This would have been enough to permit Parliament to use the rules as an instrument for accountability and criticism, as occurred when John Major decided to put *Questions of Procedure for*

[9] For an account of this intellectual journey see William Keegan, *The Prudence of Mr Gordon Brown* (Wiley 2003) chs 2–6.

[10] For more detailed explanation of this idea see HM Treasury, *Reforming Britain's Economic and Financial Policy* (n 8) 30–42.

[11] Speech to Labour Finance and Industry Group 17 May 1995, cited in Keegan (n 9) 145. As applied from 1998–2010, the 'stable and prudent level' was set at 40%, to be achieved each year: Treasury Committee, *The 2007 Comprehensive Spending Review: Prospects and Processes* (HC 2006–07, 279) para 15.

[12] HC Deb 2 July 1997, vol 297, col 303.

[13] See generally Ian Lienert, 'Should Advanced Countries Adopt a Fiscal Responsibility Law?' (IMF 2010) Working Paper WP/10/254.

Ministers (now the *Ministerial Code*) into the public domain in 1992.[14] In addition, the absence in the United Kingdom of any concept of a budget law, in which Parliament would formally approve the government's annual taxation and spending proposals as a whole, leaves us without the kind of legislative base on which such constraints have been erected elsewhere.[15]

2.1.1 The Code for Fiscal Stability

In the event the Labour government decided that the importance of its new fiscal regime should be signalled by grounding it in legislation—while avoiding any legislative expression of its operative rules. The 1998 Finance Act thus required the government to promulgate a Code for Fiscal Stability. The Code was to be laid before Parliament and would become operative on approval by a resolution of the House of Commons. It was to set out 'the Treasury's understanding of what each of the key principles'—identified as transparency, stability, responsibility, fairness, and efficiency—'involves in relation to fiscal policy and policy for the management of the National Debt'.[16] The reader who thought that this understanding might appear in the Code in the form of Mr Brown's two rules was in for a disappointment. The Code restated and elaborated on the five principles (indicating, for example, that transparency had some rather closely drawn limits) before requiring that in each Budget, 'the Government . . . state and explain its fiscal policy objectives and the rules by which it intends to operate fiscal policy over the life of the Parliament'. Provision was then made for modifying the objectives and rules, or temporarily departing from them.[17] The fiscal rules, in other words, were situated at not just one, but two removes from any possible legislative obligation, on the ground that 'to embed the Government's two fiscal rules in the Code. . . would be unduly restrictive'. The rules, it was said, might need to be supplemented over time, and it was for the government of the day to say what rules, consistent with the Code, it intended to abide by.[18] Unsurprisingly, Opposition MPs took exception to this omission, suggesting that it made the Code 'vacuous' and 'meaningless'—but since they also characterized the rules themselves as 'obscure' and 'meaningless' it is not obvious that including them would have won bi-partisan support.[19]

It is important to notice that the legislative provision for the Code was accompanied by obligations on government to provide Parliament each year with a Financial Statement and Budget Report, an Economic and Fiscal Strategy Report, and a Debt Management Report.[20] Requirements as to the contents of these documents, and as to

[14] Chapter 2, section 3.2.

[15] From 1993 to 1996 the government had moved in the direction of a unified (but not legislative) Budget by transferring the Budget Statement to November, when outline spending proposals were traditionally made in the Autumn Statement: see eg Chancellor of the Exchequer, *Financial Statement and Budget Report 1997–98* (HC 1996–97, 90). The Labour government reverted to a Spring Budget, splitting tax and spending proposals again.

[16] Requirements relating to the Code appear in s 155 of the Act.

[17] Code for Fiscal Stability (December 1998) paras 3–12. The Code was laid before Parliament on 3 November and approved by resolution of the House of Commons on 9 December: HC Deb vol 322, cols 430–51.

[18] Chancellor of the Exchequer, *Budget 1998: The Code for Fiscal Stability* (March 1998) 17.

[19] See HC Deb vol 322, cols 434, 441, 449, 450.

[20] Finance Act 1998, s 156.

the economic and fiscal projections they might contain, were elaborated in the Code, which also required their submission to the Treasury Select Committee.[21] Provision was also made in the Act for the Comptroller and Auditor General to report to the House of Commons on the conventions and assumptions underlying the Treasury's preparation of those documents,[22] but this function was limited by a provision in the Code restricting such examination to cases where there were 'changes' to 'key' assumptions and conventions.[23] There is plenty of room for doubt as to whether this was an effective guarantee of the integrity of the Treasury forecasting process, by reason of the NAO's lack of expertise in the field of macroeconomic forecasting.[24]

Writing about the Code shortly after its promulgation, we took the view that the Finance Act and the Code did little to impinge on the substantive discretion that surrounds spending decisions, and that it was 'too early to say whether this new emphasis on codes and rules signals any consensus on the principles of fiscal policy strong enough to put their content beyond day-to-day politics and hence to justify a claim that they might have any "constitutional" value'.[25] Those remarks were directed to the Code and its broad principles rather than to Mr Brown's fiscal rules, but it is clear that even at the level of the rules, the most specific level of commitment, the obligations were so framed as to afford ample scope for discretion and for conflicting interpretations of essential criteria. The obligation of result imposed by the two rules was to be assessed 'over the economic cycle', but determining when a cycle begins and ends is a matter of arcane and contested economic judgement, as became clear when the Treasury suggested in 2006 a change in the projected end-date of the current cycle from 2008–09 to 2007. This was strongly criticized by the Treasury Select Committee as making compliance with the 'golden rule' easier, at the cost of storing up difficulty for next cycle; the Committee also recorded disagreement about when the current cycle might have started.[26] In addition, the question of whether compliance with the rules was being achieved depended heavily on the accounting practices operated by government. Meeting a restrictive expenditure target is clearly made easier if one can classify the expenditure in a way that keeps it outside the scope of the target or, indeed, outside the definition of public expenditure altogether. This was certainly not a new issue in 1998—the Public Expenditure Survey (PES) system had included expenditure totals representing targets and instruments of control since 1976—but the adoption of the rules and of the transparency obligations of the Code provided a powerful new springboard for criticisms of government accounting practice.[27] We shall see that

[21] Code for Fiscal Stability, paras 15–25, 30.

[22] Finance Act 1998, ss 156(5)(6), 157.

[23] Code for Fiscal Stability (n 21) para 26.

[24] Hood (n 7) 187–90.

[25] Terence Daintith and Alan Page, *The Executive in the Constitution: Structure, Autonomy and Internal Control* (OUP 1999) 153, 145.

[26] Treasury Committee, *The 2006 Pre-Budget Report* (HC 2006–07, 115) paras 27–35. The NAO registered no serious objection to the change in cycle dates: Hood (n 7) 189.

[27] '[S]ince May 1997, we have seen a consistent and deplorable manipulation of figures and the presentation of public accounts. The most notorious example is the misclassification of the working families tax credit as a negative tax with flagrant disregard for the Office for National Statistics and all international conventions': Philip Hammond, HC Deb 6 December 1999, vol 340, col 639 (Government Resources and Accounts Bill, second reading).

the quest for fiscal credibility that drove the adoption of the rules also led to significant institutional changes responding to such criticisms.[28]

While drawing attention to these and other problems, a 2004 assessment by the independent Institute for Fiscal Studies concluded that up to that date the Code had generally worked well. The government's belief that the advantages of fiscal credibility would outweigh the loss of a completely discretionary fiscal policy had been 'largely fulfilled: the Code has raised standards, particularly with respect to the disclosure of information, without causing a deterioration in those areas where the government's current practice exceeds the Code's minimum requirements.'[29] The Report summarized what we might regard as a constitutional case for a Code, based on accountability:

> Setting out an explicit code of conduct can serve to focus the debate on fiscal policy to within parameters that can be judged more easily and coherently than undertaking an overall assessment of a government's record on fiscal policy on an ongoing basis. It can reduce the scope for both the government to focus selectively on aspects of policy that reflect more favourably on it in retrospect and for only selective aspects of fiscal policy to make it into the public debate. Also, it can focus debates between the party in government and the opposition on aspects of policy that are seen as being key, making the arguments made on both sides more directly comparable to each other and therefore understandable.[30]

This was not to say, of course, that a Code incorporating relatively precise rules would necessarily produce positive economic results or survive economic shocks. The authors' suggestion that 'it might be very difficult for a future government to remove or substantially loosen the Code without significant loss to its economic credibility'[31] might have appeared over-optimistic as the United Kingdom was drawn ever deeper into the problems of sustaining the banking system during the crisis of 2007–09.[32]

2.1.2 The impact of the 2007–2009 crisis

The most dramatic difficulties faced by the government were those of maintaining confidence in the stability of the banking system. Initially manifested, in 2007, as a liquidity crisis at a small Newcastle-based bank, Northern Rock, they spread in autumn 2008, via the contagion of multiple financial failures in the United States and elsewhere, to some of country's largest retail institutions, such as Halifax Bank of Scotland, Lloyds Bank, and Royal Bank of Scotland. The combined balance sheets of the latter two banks amounted to a sum three times as large as the country's GDP. To meet the crisis government drew both on its legal and its financial resources. An

[28] In section 2.2 of this chapter.

[29] Carl Emmerson, Christine Frayne, and Sarah Love, *Updating the UK's Code for Fiscal Stability* (WP04/29) (Institute for Fiscal Studies 2004) 2.

[30] ibid 7.

[31] ibid 8.

[32] See generally Julia Black, 'The Credit Crisis and the Constitution' in Dawn Oliver, Tony Prosser, and Richard Rawlings (eds), *The Regulatory State: Constitutional Implications* (OUP 2010) 92–128; HM Treasury, *Review of HM Treasury's Management Response to the Financial Crisis* (2012); Colin Thain, 'A Very Peculiar British Crisis?: Institutions, Ideas and Policy Responses to the Credit Crunch' (2009) 4 British Politics 434.

initial guarantee of Northern Rock's deposits in August 2007 had to be followed by its nationalization in February 2008 because no private buyer could be found. That step required legislation, the Banking (Special Provisions) Act 2008, which was framed in general terms so to as to authorize the compulsory transfer of bank shares or assets in circumstances such as those that had arisen in relation to Northern Rock (that is, where the Treasury had assumed liabilities or offered guarantees), or where the Treasury considered it essential to maintain the stability of the UK financial system.[33]

Problems were seen to be more general in autumn 2007 and spring 2008, when it became apparent that mortgage-backed securities held by UK banks could not be sold or used to secure borrowing, thus restricting their own ability to lend. This was met by a Bank of England scheme (the Special Liquidity Scheme) for the temporary exchange of these assets for tradeable Treasury bills, a scheme that required a Treasury guarantee with a potential exposure of some £287bn (as at January 2009)—though in the event, by the time the scheme was wound up in January 2012, no Treasury liability had been incurred.[34] A situation of acute crisis re-emerged in October 2008, following the collapse of Lehmann Brothers in the United States. This time the Exchequer was not to escape unscathed. Measures announced on 8 October included, alongside extension of the Special Liquidity Scheme, a new Treasury recapitalization scheme allowing it to purchase £25bn of capital in eight eligible institutions including Halifax Bank of Scotland and the Royal Bank of Scotland, the provision of a further £25bn for Treasury purchase of preference shares, and a £250bn credit guarantee scheme for new and short-term debt issuance by banks for up to three years. Later measures included an Asset Protection Scheme, protecting financial institutions against losses incurred by holding assets affected by the credit crunch;[35] the Asset Purchase Facility, guaranteeing Bank of England purchases of high-quality private sector assets to improve liquidity; and further share acquisitions. By the end of the acute phase of the crisis, at the end of 2009, the Treasury had incurred a total bill for bank share purchases of £75bn, had granted loans totalling £53bn, had issued guarantees amounting to £764bn, and had other contingent commitments amounting to £63bn.[36]

It seems safe to assume that compliance with the fiscal rules was not uppermost in the minds of ministers and Treasury officials as they struggled, over these months, to avert a financial Armageddon. The sustainable investment rule had been breached by the very first important move, the guaranteeing of Northern Rock's deposits, classified by the Office for National Statistics as a government liability, which pushed net public sector debt beyond 40% of GDP, the figure set by Gordon Brown in 1997 as representing the 'stable and prudent' level required by the rule.[37] As the crisis went

[33] Banking (Special Provisions) Act 2008, s 2(2). The powers, which expired after a year, were later used for the partial nationalization of the Bradford and Bingley Building Society and to transfer UK deposits of a failed Icelandic bank to a safe home. The Act was replaced by comparable permanent provision made by the Banking Act 2009.

[34] On the operation of the scheme see generally Sarah John, Matt Roberts, and Olaf Weeken, 'The Bank of England's Special Liquidity Scheme' [2012] *Bank of England Quarterly Bulletin* Q1.

[35] This scheme was the subject of a request by the Permanent Secretary to the Treasury for a ministerial direction: see further chapter 8, section V.

[36] Figures from Comptroller and Auditor General, *HM Treasury: Maintaining the Financial Stability of UK Banks: Update on the Support Schemes* (HC 2010–11, 676) 7 (Figure 1).

[37] Miles Costello, 'Northern Rock blows a hole in government's debt pledge' *The Times* (7 February 2008); Treasury Committee, *Financial Reporting and the National Accounts*, oral evidence (HC 2007–08,

on and the interventions multiplied, any hope of adhering to the rules, even over the medium term, vanished completely, but the Code and rules were not abandoned. Instead, the Chancellor announced in November 2008 that while the principles and objectives under the Code continued to apply, there would be a 'temporary departure' from the rules,[38] in the shape of a 'temporary operating rule' which, when taken with the measures planned for its implementation, would represent a real and continuing constraint:

> to set policies to improve the cyclically adjusted current budget each year, once the economy emerges from the downturn, so it reaches balance and debt is falling as a proportion of GDP once the global shocks have worked their way through the economy in full.[39]

Whether, and if so when, this temporary rule might expire was not made clear, but this question became academic when the Labour government lost to the Conservative-Liberal Democrat coalition in the general election 18 months later. By that time, however, the government itself had denatured the Code by securing the passage of the Fiscal Responsibility Act 2010, which provided that the Treasury must reduce government borrowing as a percentage of GDP year by year so as to halve that percentage by 2014, and ensure that public sector net debt, again as a percentage of GDP, was less in 2016 than in 2015.[40] For subsequent years the Act required the Treasury to impose fiscal duties on itself in binding fiscal plans framed as statutory instruments to be approved in draft by Parliament.[41] Despite the language, one hesitates to describe these obligations as 'legal', in light of a further provision stipulating that failure to comply with these and other duties imposed by the Act 'does not affect the lawfulness of anything done, or omitted to be done, by any person'.[42] Nonetheless, this rigid and constricting formulation was precisely what the careful architecture of the Code was designed to avoid, and it is not surprising that the Chancellor of the day should later acknowledge that it was introduced 'to almost universal derision'.[43]

2.1.3 From Code to Charter

Despite these crisis and post-crisis vicissitudes, and its own opinion that even prior to the crisis, fiscal rules had lost credibility as a meaningful constraint on policy,[44] the

397-I) (4 March 2008) qq 54–71 (suggesting some pressure from the Treasury to present the debt figures in a way that made it clear that the Northern Rock liabilities were responsible for the overrun: q 61).

38 As provided for by the Code, para 11.

39 Treasury Committee, *Pre-Budget Report 2008* (HC 2008–09, 27) paras 49–57. For the Chancellor's own account see Alistair Darling, *Back from the Brink: 1000 days at Number 11* (Atlantic Books 2011) 179–80.

40 s 1.

41 s 2.

42 s 4(3). For internal guidance indicating that Law Officers are likely to advise against such legislation not having legal effect see chapter 10, text at nn 44–50.

43 Darling (n 39) 268. For a selection of the epithets applied to the Bill at its Commons second reading ('load of nonsense', 'financial figleaf', 'dangerously wrong-headed', 'a rhetorical substitute for action', 'profoundly pointless', 'a fiscal straitjacket'), see HC Deb 5 January 2010, vol 503, cols 63–120.

44 Robert Chote and others, *The IFS Green Budget: January 2009*, 81.

Institute for Fiscal Studies' prediction that abandoning fiscal rules would be problematic proved to be correct: the incoming government adopted a remarkably similar regime in the shape of the Charter for Budget Responsibility. This had its legislative base in the Budget Responsibility and National Audit Act 2011, which also established an independent monitoring and forecasting body, the Office for Budget Responsibility (OBR), discussed in the next section. The Charter, which has been updated a number of times but retains its broad shape, takes a more direct approach to fiscal rules than its predecessor. Under the 2011 Act, it is to be laid before Parliament and approved by the House of Commons. The annual documentation to be presented to Parliament is however limited to the traditional Financial Statement and Budget Report.[45] The design also departs from that of the Code in that it substitutes a statement of objectives for the Code's principles. In the original (2011) Charter these were stated as being:

> to ensure sustainable public finances that support confidence in the economy, promote intergenerational fairness, and ensure the effectiveness of wider Government policy; and to support and improve the effectiveness of monetary policy in stabilising economic fluctuations.

The new government's fiscal rules for the current Parliament were then presented in the guise of 'Treasury mandates':

> a forward-looking target to achieve cyclically-adjusted current balance by the end of the rolling, five-year forecast period; and
> a target for public sector net debt as a percentage of GDP to be falling at a fixed date of 2015–16, ensuring the public finances are restored to a sustainable path.[46]

By inserting the fiscal rules into the document to be approved by the House of Commons, the Charter arguably gave them greater democratic legitimacy than the rules referred to, but not included in, its predecessor Code: a step that received bipartisan approval.[47] It also, of course, made them more rigid, since departure from them entailed presentation and approval of a revised Charter.[48] A further element of flexibility was removed by acceptance of the Treasury Committee's earlier strictures on the room for manipulation offered by the 'economic cycle' basis of Gordon Brown's 'golden rule',[49] with the adoption, for deficit reduction, of a rolling five-year target.

We should not be surprised, then, that the Charter has undergone much more frequent revisions than the Code, and that these revisions have been politically controversial. An updated Charter, adding a 'welfare cap' to the Treasury mandates, accompanied by a complex monitoring procedure, was presented for House of Commons approval by the Coalition government in March 2014.[50] That government

[45] Budget Responsibility and National Audit Act 2011, ss 1, 2.

[46] HM Treasury, *Charter for Budget Responsibility 2011* (April 2011) paras 3.1–3.3. These rules bore a remarkable resemblance to those in the Fiscal Responsibility Act 2010, which had been described by the then shadow Chancellor as 'complete nonsense': HC Deb 5 January 2010, vol 503, col 73.

[47] HC Deb 11 May 2011, vol 527, col 1310.

[48] HM Treasury, *Charter for Budget Responsibility 2011* (n 46) para 3.4.

[49] See Treasury Committee, *The 2006 Pre-Budget Report* (n 26) and related text.

[50] See HC Deb 26 March 2014, vol 578, cols 374–405. On the 'welfare cap', see further below, section 3.3.3.

changed the Treasury mandates again following the 2014 Autumn Statement. The incoming Conservative government presented another revised Charter in October 2015; a further updating was made in January 2017. On both occasions the Opposition divided the House.[51] Yet further fiscal rules, representing a significant loosening of the Charter mandates, were set out in the Conservative manifesto for the December 2019 general election and guided the policy decisions in the spring 2020 Budget, but were not incorporated in a revised Charter.[52] That Budget was presented just before the full force of the Covid-19 pandemic became apparent; a year later, with the country still in lockdown, the Chancellor's position was that 'the current level of uncertainty means it is not yet the right time to set new medium-term fiscal rules' and that the current Charter remained in force pending the setting of new rules.[53] New fiscal mandates were eventually announced with the 2021 Autumn Budget and Spending Review,[54] and incorporated in an updated Charter approved in January 2022.

One significant change in this version was that all the mandates were now couched in terms of three-year rolling targets, rather than fixed periods, which offered more flexibility. But as the OBR pointed out,

> the fact that the date for meeting [rolling targets] never arrives means that the fiscal position can progressively deteriorate. History tells us that Chancellors tend to take advantage, over successive Budgets, of the additional year to meet their targets by loosening fiscal policy, while planning a sufficiently large fiscal tightening to hit the target in the target year.[55]

Otherwise the mandates were similar in many respects to those announced in the spring 2020 Budget,[56] despite the fact that the government's measures to control the pandemic (massive purchases of protective personal equipment, vaccine development and administration, contact tracing) and to alleviate its economic effects (furlough schemes, financial assistance to businesses and local authorities) had required the deployment of public funds, and consequent borrowing, on a scale dwarfing the impact of the 2007–09 financial crisis. In June 2022 the NAO reported estimated government outlays of £376bn (of which £321bn were known to have actually been spent), with a further £132bn in loans and guarantees.[57] Nonetheless OBR took a positive view of the government's chances of meeting its 2021–22 fiscal mandates, reasoning that its expenditure measures had in fact limited the structural damage to the fiscal position

[51] See the debates at HC Deb 14 October 2015, vol 600, cols 427–56; HC Deb 24 January 2017, vol 620, cols 234–56.

[52] Conservative and Unionist Party Manifesto 2019, 7; Chancellor of the Exchequer, *Budget 2020* (HC 2019–20, 121) para 1.34. The impact of these changes is discussed in Office for Budget Responsibility, *Economic and Fiscal Outlook*, CP 230 (March 2020) 159.

[53] Chancellor of the Exchequer, *Budget 2021* (HC 2019–21, 1226) para 1.61.

[54] Chancellor of the Exchequer, *Autumn Budget and Spending Review 2021: A Stronger Economy for the British People* (HC 2021–22, 822).

[55] Office for Budget Responsibility, *Economic and Fiscal Outlook*, CP 545 (October 2021) para 4.31.

[56] ibid para 4.9.

[57] National Audit Office, *Covid-19 Cost Tracker*. Compare the Comptroller and Auditor General's figures for the financial crisis (n 36), showing much smaller expenditures but very large contingent liabilities that did not, in the event, materialize.

over the medium term, and that it was reasonable to anticipate a more modest degree of economic scarring from a pandemic than from a financial crisis: 'the economy did not enter the pandemic with financial imbalances that needed to be unwound.'[58]

OBR's optimism could not, of course, take into account the disastrous market impact of the proposals for tax reductions, increased domestic and commercial energy subsidies, and additional borrowing, announced in September 2022 by Kwasi Kwarteng, Chancellor of the Exchequer in the short-lived government formed by Liz Truss.[59] Negative market sentiment was exacerbated by the impression that the Prime Minister and Chancellor had deliberately chosen to ignore their official sources of advice. The Permanent Secretary to the Treasury was dismissed on the Chancellor's first day in office, and the government initially refused to allow OBR to conduct its usual evaluation of what it claimed was 'not a Budget': an evaluation which, as we note below, would have included an assessment of the extent of its compatibility with the fiscal mandates.[60] Within a week the latter decision had been reversed and a medium-term fiscal plan, accompanied by a full OBR forecast, had been promised for 23 November, later brought forward to 30 October. By that time, however, the markets had responded with higher borrowing costs and lower exchange rates, Kwarteng had been sacked, and his successor as Chancellor had reversed most of his measures.[61] The new Chancellor subsequently published a further updating of the Charter—approved by Parliament in January 2023—with new and less ambitious fiscal mandates contemplating continuing budget deficits over the next five years and a reduction in public sector net debt as a percentage of GDP only by 2027–28.[62]

Over the period 1998–2010, therefore, there were just two modifications to the original fiscal rules; from 2010 to 2023 there were seven sets of fiscal mandates under a Charter that has been updated five times. There must be doubt as to whether the rules now provide the assurance of fiscal stability that was said to justify their introduction. The post-crisis change of nomenclature from 'Fiscal Stability' to 'Budget Responsibility' has proved to be significant. But the Charter structure, even if unstable, still offers at least some of the accountability benefits identified by the Institute for Fiscal Studies in 2004.

[58] Office for Budget Responsibility, *Economic and Fiscal Outlook* (n 55) 148–50 (box 3.1).

[59] The proposals can be found at Chancellor of the Exchequer, *The Growth Plan 2022*, CP 743 (September 2022). The Truss government's tenure was the shortest in British history, lasting from 7 September to 20 October 2022.

[60] Truss had already shown distaste for OBR during her leadership campaign: Warner, 'The OBR has been a triumph of transparency—little wonder Truss wants rid' *The Telegraph* (24 August 2022). The first piece of legislation introduced by the incoming Labour government in July 2024 was a Bill to make reference of 'fiscally significant' measures to OBR compulsory and to enable OBR to cost such measures on its own initiative if no such reference was made: see now Budget Responsibility Act 2024.

[61] Matthew Keep, *The 17 October 2022 Fiscal Statement: Summary and Background* (House of Commons Library 17 October 2022).

[62] HM Treasury, *Charter for Budget Responsibility: Autumn 2022 Update* (January 2023). For the OBR assessment of the likelihood that government would be able to adhere to these mandates see Office for Budget Responsibility, *Economic and Fiscal Outlook*, CP 804 (March 2023) ch 5.

2.2 Institutional change

2.2.1 Economic forecasting and assessment: the Office for Budget Responsibility

Market reactions to the Truss government mini-budget suggested that what matters today is not so much the stability of the fiscal mandates as the availability of their independent assessment by OBR. The creation of the Office was designed to address a 'lack of transparency' in the government's accounts and to 'put the Government at one remove from the forecasting business, with all the temptations to fiddle the forecasts that can come with that', by providing Parliament and the markets with an independent assessment of the sustainability of the government's budget judgement and overall spending plans.[63]

The Office was created by the Coalition government's Budget Responsibility and National Audit Act 2011, at a time when numerous institutions with broadly similar missions were being created around the world.[64] Its core duty is 'to examine and report on the sustainability of the public finances'.[65] To perform this duty it must prepare fiscal and economic forecasts at least twice a year, along with an assessment of the extent to which the fiscal mandate has been, or is likely to be, achieved; and also prepare, at least once a year, an assessment of the accuracy of its previous fiscal and economic forecasts, and an analysis of the sustainability of the public finances.[66] The Act guarantees to the Office complete discretion in performing—objectively, transparently, and impartially—its main duty, while having regard to any relevant government policies (but OBR is not to consider what the effect of any alternative policies might be).[67] It must also act 'economically and efficiently' and has a statutory right of access to all government information that it may reasonably require.[68] The powers and functions of OBR represent a very large step forward from the highly constrained opportunities for the Comptroller and Auditor General to comment on Treasury economic projections under the Finance Act 1997,[69] and the opening to public scrutiny and use of the Treasury's forecasting model (but not its assumptions) mandated by the Industry Act 1975.[70]

While OBR has been designed to provide external and objective assessment of the government's fiscal judgements, it is not, structurally, independent of the executive. Unlike the Comptroller and Auditor General, who is an officer of Parliament, and the National Audit Office, which is funded via the Parliamentary Accounts Commission, OBR is, formally speaking, an executive, not a parliamentary, body. It is constituted as a non-Departmental Public Body (NDPB) whose sponsoring department is the Treasury; it exercises its functions on behalf of the Crown; and its staff are civil

[63] HC Deb 5 January 2010, vol 503, cols 92–95 (Mr Andrew Tyrie, who also claimed the paternity of the notion, expressed in his 1996 proposal for an 'independent fiscal projection committee').

[64] Cal Viney and Thomas Poole, 'Independent Fiscal Institutions' in Roger Masterman and Robert Schütze (eds), *The Cambridge Companion to Comparative Constitutional Law* (CUP 2019) 441–70.

[65] 2011 Act, s 4(1).

[66] s 4(3)(4).

[67] s 5.

[68] s 9. This is subject to any enactment or rule of law restricting disclosure: s 9(4).

[69] See text at nn 22–24.

[70] s 27 and sch 5 (repealed by the 2011 Act). The Treasury was required to produce its own twice-yearly forecasts using the model.

servants—though the members of the Office, who direct its work, are not.[71] OBR is a small organization, with five members and a staff of around 30. As an NDPB, it is highly unusual in that the appointment of three of its members, including the Chair, by the Chancellor of the Exchequer requires the approval of the House of Commons Treasury Committee.[72] The approval of that Committee is likewise required before the Chancellor can exercise the limited powers of dismissal the Act gives him.[73] These three members of OBR form the Budget Responsibility Committee and lead the Office's work. The two remaining members, appointed on the nomination of that Committee, are non-executive, and with the Committee members constitute an Oversight Board.

Can OBR, as a body within the executive, really be independent? The key provisions of the Act, and the appointment arrangements, are clearly designed to achieve this, but at the same time the government has sought to ensure that the Office operates in a way that is useful to it: hence there is quite elaborate provision, in the Charter, as to the minimum necessary content of OBR's economic and financial forecasts, and of its annual report on the sustainability of the public finances—all this against the background of assurance of OBR's complete discretion as to its methodology, its judgements, the content of its publications (subject to the minimum content requirements above), and its work programme.[74] Most unusually among the many independent fiscal institutions recently established in different countries,[75] OBR's fiscal and economic forecasts are adopted by the government as the official forecasts for the Budget Report—though the government retains the right to disagree with OBR's forecasts and, if this is the case, will explain why to Parliament.[76] The Treasury continues to maintain the necessary analytical and macroeconomic expertise to provide ongoing advice to the government.[77]

Activities of the Office are also regulated, as is normal for NDPBs, by a framework document jointly subscribed by the Office and the Treasury as its sponsoring department. The document adds further detail to the Charter on issues like the respective responsibilities of the OBR's Budget Responsibility Committee and Oversight Board, and of its Chair as accounting officer, and provides for OBR's funding over a period of several years.[78] Yet another document governing OBR activity is the Memorandum of Understanding between the Office, the Treasury, the Department for Work and Pensions (DWP), and HM Revenue and Customs (HMRC).[79] This reflects the fact

[71] On the latter two points see 2011 Act, sch 1, paras 7 and 8.

[72] 2011 Act, sch 1, para 1. Compare the provision, also in the Act, for the appointment of the Comptroller and Auditor General: by Her Majesty on an address of the House of Commons, to be moved by the Prime Minister with the agreement of the Chair of the Public Accounts Committee: s 11.

[73] 2011 Act, sch 1, para 6.

[74] See HM Treasury, Charter for Budget Responsibility, Autumn 2016 update (January 2017) s 4, esp paras 4.4, 4.8–4.12, 4.15–4.18.

[75] Viney and Poole (n 64).

[76] This arrangement continues to attract criticism as being responsible for an excessively close relationship between OBR and the Treasury: see HC Deb 6 February 2023, vol 727, cols 732–33.

[77] HM Treasury, Charter for Budget Responsibility (n 74) para 3.12.

[78] Office for Budget Responsibility and HM Treasury, *Framework Document* (7 March 2019).

[79] Office for Budget Responsibility, HM Treasury, the Department for Work and Pensions and HM Revenue and Customs, *Memorandum of Understanding* (8 March 2017). Separate Memoranda govern the relationships between the Office and the devolved administrations (5 April 2019 for Wales, 8 January 2019 for Scotland).

that OBR's forecasting underpins the preparation of crucial government documents such as the Financial Statement and Budget report, and that in order to prepare its forecasts, OBR needs to draw on forecasting and analytical resources across government, notably public spending outturns and forecasts from the Treasury, and forecasts of benefit payments from DWP and of tax returns from HMRC. The Memorandum organizes the necessary cooperation, including the creation of steering groups involving all four entities, exchanges of information, and timetabling of release of information by OBR. It also provides that officials from the Treasury, DWP, and HMRC must attend 'challenge meetings' as required by OBR to explain their forecasts, long-term projections, and other analysis (para 4.13). This dependence on the work of departmental officials (about 100 were involved in 2010) has been described as essential,[80] but has worried the Treasury Committee,[81] and the Memorandum can be seen as an attempt to assuage these fears.

Concerns about independence were further sharpened by press disclosure in 2015 that the Treasury had profited from its right, under the Memorandum, to limited pre-release access to OBR reports, in order to offer not just factual corrections (as envisaged by the Memorandum then in force) but also drafting suggestions, including one from a minister. This was strongly condemned by the Treasury Committee.[82] The temptation to fiddle with the presentation of material that may be critical of crucial government policy decisions is certainly one that ministers and officials may find it hard to resist.[83] To protect OBR's potentially fragile independence from such pressure, the Memorandum now provides for greater transparency in the pre-release access process. OBR reinforces this by maintaining and publishing a log of its substantive contacts with Treasury ministers, their special advisers, and their private office staff. Most unusually, too, the Memorandum now contains an explicit warning to officials, in their interactions with OBR, not to be economical with embarrassing truths, such as data relating to areas where ministers have policy targets that are not on track to be met; where the department does not want to be seen to be making a forecast; or where there is commercially sensitive information, or politically sensitive negotiations.[84]

Despite these concerns, a review of OBR by the Organisation for Economic Co-operation and Development (OECD) in 2020 reported that it had scored highest for independence among 26 comparable institutions assessed according to variables drawn from the OECD Principles and data from the OECD International Fiscal Institutions Database, and that its peers throughout the OECD had consistently looked to OBR as a model of independence and operational credibility.[85]

[80] See Treasury Committee, *Office for Budget Responsibility* (HC 2010–11, 385) para 70, noting that according to the first (interim) Chair of OBR, these posts could not simply be taken out of the Treasury, nor duplicated in the OBR: 'Not only would it be a waste of money, Chairman, they could not do it because so many of these 100, the people I think of as the expert analysts, are only able to do it because they work in the departments and help produce the policies and monitor the forecasts. They are part of these departments and that is where they gain their knowledge, so if they were not there they would not be able to perform that role.'

[81] ibid paras 67–73.

[82] Treasury Committee, *Reviewing the Office for Budget Responsibility* (HC 2015–16, 514) paras 14–38.

[83] On issues of pre-release access to statistics more generally, see chapter 12, section 3.5.3, at end.

[84] Memorandum of 8 March 2017 (n 79) Annex, para A.4.

[85] OECD Independent Fiscal Institutions Review, *Office for Budget Responsibility (OBR) of the United Kingdom* (OECD 24 September 2020) 45. On early attitudes to OBR see Hood (n 7) 190–92.

2.2.2 Public finance and national accounts: the role of the Office for National Statistics

These rather surprising injunctions to be honest offer a measure of the tension that exists between the desire of politicians to look good in the eyes of the electorate and the objective of providing accurate and useful information to Parliament and people about the state of public finances. The temptation to muddle or massage the figures for the sake of some perceived political gain has been yielded to often enough to create a real credibility problem around government financial information. This problem was, if anything, exacerbated by the promulgation of fiscal rules in 1997: the heavy political costs of publishing figures that show you have breached, or are likely to breach, your own rules create an additional temptation to manipulation. One solution, represented by the creation of OBR, is to have your figures prepared by an independent body with limited and transparent engagement with the Treasury. Another is to seek to improve the pedigree of the figures themselves.

When he introduced his fiscal rules Gordon Brown sought to guarantee the objectivity and reliability of the government's figures by adopting, for the presentation of budgetary information, the concepts and definitions used in the system of national accounts—the statistics representing the whole performance of the UK economy, including the public sector, which had been produced annually since 1952.[86] The constraint represented by this reference to detailed published standards was reinforced by the decision to align the national accounts with the European System of Accounts (ESA).[87] Regular reporting of national economic data according to this system was required, under the European Union's Stability and Growth Pact, concluded in 1997, to permit monitoring of member states' adherence to the deficit and debt limits established by the Maastricht Treaty.[88] For internal use member states remained free to use ESA, or not, as they preferred, but because of the obvious costs and other disadvantages of using different systems for different audiences, the UK national accounts were recast from 1998 to accord with the ESA. This alignment has continued after Brexit. Until 2024 it was needed in order to ensure that UK gross national income statistics remained comparable with those of EU member states pending finalization of UK contributions to the EU budget.

The consequence of the government's adoption of national accounts definitions and conventions as the basis for its fiscal policy framework was that classification decisions made by the Office for National Statistics (ONS) for purposes of the national accounts define the organizations and institutions which are within the public sector; classify transactions according to the type of expenditure or revenue they represent (examples being whether something is a tax, a subsidy, a transfer, or a social benefit); and identify the financial assets and liabilities which are to be recorded in financial accounts and balance sheets and those which are to be excluded (an example

[86] Chancellor of the Exchequer, *Stability and Investment for the Long Term: Economic and Fiscal Strategy 1998*, Cm 3978 (1998) 39–40 (para 4.3.2). Michael Kell, *An Assessment of Fiscal Rules in the United Kingdom* (2001) IMF Working Paper WP/01/91, 8–9, sees this as an acknowledgment of the risk of future manipulation of the current/capital spending distinction under the 'golden rule'.

[87] The current version of the ESA is Eurostat, *ESA 2010* (Publications Office of the European Union, Luxembourg 2013).

[88] The key provisions are now to be found in the Treaty on the Functioning of the European Union [2012] OJ C326/98, arts 121, 126, 136, and Protocol 12 on the excessive deficit procedure (C326/279).

of an area of exclusion being contingent liabilities).[89] These decisions, fundamental to government's budgeting and its ability to comply with its fiscal self-discipline,[90] are now further regulated by much more detailed guidance on public sector definition and other issues in the Eurostat *Manual on Government Deficit and Debt* (2016), an 'indispensable complement to ESA 2010',[91] which is likewise relied upon by ONS.

While the linkage of fiscal documentation and national accounts statistics has been seen as an example of government's 'tying its hands' in order to 'limit definitional slippage',[92] there was still enough flexibility around in 1998 to prompt suggestions of 'fiddling the figures' on a range of issues: whether the effect of the new Working Families Tax Credit was properly treated as a reduction in tax income as opposed to an increase in public expenditure; whether a Private Finance Initiative project which results in increased debt should be regarded as government or private sector debt; whether the ONS definitions of capital and revenue were too loose to be useful.[93] These concerns strongly influenced the process, described in chapter 12, that led to stronger guarantees of independence for ONS's work in general, and eventually to its transformation into the executive arm of an independent, legislatively established UK Statistics Authority. So far as the interaction between national accounts classifications and fiscal documentation is concerned, current arrangements emphasize the independence of ONS in making classification decisions and their non-political nature. The ONS has stressed

> that ESA 2010 does not allow for consideration of political or commercial significance when making classification decisions and that as an independent statistics office, ONS ensures that classification decisions are robust and fully consistent with the rules of ESA 2010 and additional relevant statistical guidance.[94]

As with OBR, keeping the balance between independence and efficiency is not necessarily easy. While ONS, acting through its own Economic Statistics Classification Committee, has the final say on classification decisions, which are notified in ONS's monthly *Public Sector Classification Guide*, its programme of work in this area is driven in part by classification requests from the Treasury, either transmitting enquiries from departments (for example, as to the classification of a new body), or raising its own queries (eg about classification issues raised by a projected new policy). Devolved administrations also participate in framing the programme of work. The Treasury maintains its own classification capability, and issues general guidance—agreed with ONS—directly to departments to help them classify their activities for national

[89] Office for National Statistics, *Clarifying how Public Sector Finances classification Decisions Are Made* (July 2016) s 3.

[90] For a detailed explanation of a classification decision (student loans), see Office for National Statistics, *New Treatment of Student Loans in the Public Sector Finances and National Accounts* (17 December 2018). See also text at n 37, and Martin Kellaway, *Public Sector Interventions in the Financial Crisis—Statistical Classification Decisions* (Office for National Statistics 2009).

[91] Eurostat, *Manual on Government Deficit and Debt* (2016) 1.

[92] Kell (n 86).

[93] For detailed discussion of these issues see Hood (n 7) 68–82.

[94] Office for National Statistics, *UK Economic Statistics Sector and Transaction Classifications: The Classification Process* (28 June 2018) para 2.

accounts purposes. The expectation is that most cases in departments will be settled by reference to the guidance without the need for any consultation.[95] Identifying cases where this departmental discretion may have been used incorrectly depends on effective Treasury oversight. Departments may push back against inconvenient ONS decisions[96] and the attitude of the Treasury in any such dispute will clearly be important.

There is particularly close cooperation between ONS and Treasury in the application of classification decisions to the recording of public finance statistics,[97] which form the bridge between the national accounts and fiscal documentation. Occasionally classification decisions in this area require a judgement to be made on how to treat an institution, transaction, or an asset or liability level that is not clearly or specifically covered by the national accounts' guidelines and rules. In such cases ONS convenes an expert group, the Public Sector Finances Technical Advisory Group. Concerns raised in 2013 about whether the composition and remit of this group threatened the independence of ONS decision-making led to a revision of membership and advice arrangements to ensure that ONS members would always be in a majority and that high-profile issues would be referred back for decision to the relevant ONS Director.[98]

2.2.3 *Managing the public debt: the Debt Management Office*

There is one area of activity relevant to the Budget judgement and fiscal responsibility that has moved towards concentration, rather than diffusion through the involvement of bodies outside the Treasury. This is debt management. The announcement of the independence of the Bank of England with the devolution of interest rate decision-making to its new Monetary Policy Committee was accompanied by two other institutional changes. The first was a rearrangement of responsibilities for financial regulation between the Bank, the Treasury, and what was then the Financial Services Authority—a rearrangement tested in the fire of the 2007–09 financial crisis, found to be wanting, and later partially reversed.[99] More successful if less spectacular was the transference of responsibility for managing the government's borrowing from the Bank to a new executive agency of the Treasury, the Debt Management Office (DMO). This task is not an insignificant one. In December 2019, even before the massive borrowings in 2020 and 2021 needed to defray the costs of supporting the economy through the Covid pandemic, total central government debt stood at £1,560.8bn and the expected borrowing requirement over the next five years averaged some £150bn per year.[100] By end-2022 these figures had risen to £2,174.2bn and £228bn respectively.[101]

95 For the current guidance, see HM Treasury, *Class (2013) 1: Sector Classification* (August 2013).

96 For an example (ONS's classification of the Financial Reporting Council to the public sector) see Terence Daintith, 'Government Companies as Regulators' (2019) 82 Modern Law Review 397, 413–15.

97 Released monthly under the title *Public Sector Finances: UK*.

98 Office for National Statistics, *Clarifying how Public Sector Finances Classification Decisions Are Made* (n 89) ss 4–5.

99 See authorities cited at n 32.

100 HM Treasury, *Debt Management Report 2020–21* (March 2020) 15–16.

101 HM Treasury, *Debt Management Report 2023–24* (March 2023) 22, 23.

The Bank's role as the government's agent for the management of the national debt had developed gradually over the course of the 19th century, supported by annual financial legislation but had never—except in relation to the issuance of Treasury Bills, the government's short-term borrowing instrument[102]—been the subject of explicit statutory provision.[103] The Bank's functions in relation to Treasury Bills were transferred to the Treasury by the Finance Act 1998,[104] which also provided for the creation of a debt management account under the control of the Treasury.[105]

Unlike taxation, government borrowing is a consensual commercial transaction and as such, can be undertaken without parliamentary consent as an exercise of the common law capacities that the Crown shares with the ordinary citizen. Parliament, however, became involved, because by the end of the 17th century the Crown's own credit rating was so poor. From 1692 onwards, we find legislation authorizing borrowing and securing repayment by linking it to particular streams of revenue. In the next three centuries legislation regularly authorized Treasury borrowing of defined amounts on both a long-term and a short-term basis.[106] Extant legislation of this kind was in 1968 swept away by the National Loans Act, which provided both a general authority for the Treasury to borrow, and a specific regime for the regulation of the process of government borrowing.[107] However, the level of the annual public sector borrowing requirement, and its cumulated expression in the form of the national debt, has never been the subject of parliamentary authorization either in legislation or in a House of Commons resolution. In successfully rebuffing an attempt to impose a requirement for such authorization during debates on what became the National Loans Act 1968, ministers pointed out that the requirement simply represented the difference between government receipts from all sources (other than from borrowing) and government expenditure and lending, and that both receipts (in the form of proceeds of taxation, fees, and other charges) and expenditure (through the Appropriation Act and specific lending statutes) were subject to legislative control.[108] To assess what any Budget meant for borrowing, MPs just had to do their subtraction sums.

This was a cynical response: the necessary calculations involve assessment of probable tax yields, projections about the cost (and yields) of future debt financing, and assembly of spending figures from a range of sources. The 1998 changes, however, offered Parliament some real improvements. Bringing management of the government's vast borrowings under the control of the Treasury meant that debt management was henceforward operated under an annual published remit given by the Treasury to DMO, which accounts for its performance to Parliament—in particular, to the Treasury Committee. Second, debt management has been integrated into the publicity and control arrangements instituted by the Code for Fiscal Stability and continued under the Charter for Budget Responsibility. Each version of the two documents has included a debt management objective: since 2016,

[102] Treasury Bills Act 1877.
[103] Bateman (n 2) 46–49.
[104] s 159.
[105] s 160, inserting a new sch 5A in the National Loans Act 1968.
[106] Bateman (n 2) 42–46.
[107] National Loans Act 1968, s 12.
[108] See HC Deb 19 February 1968, vol 759, cols 160–66.

> to minimise, over the long term, the costs of meeting the government's financing needs, taking into account risk, while ensuring that debt management policy is consistent with the aims of monetary policy.[109]

The Treasury is also obliged by the Charter to publish a debt management report each year. The overall effect has been a major increase in accountability for this function, notably through the Treasury Committee's inquiries,[110] NAO investigations,[111] and the DMO's own annual report.

III The Evolution of the Spending Review Process

3.1 Introduction

Fiscal rules and central bank independence were key elements of the 1997 Labour government's plan to achieve fiscal stability and market credibility. Another was a more rigorous approach to the well-established system of medium-term planning of public expenditure initiated in pursuance of the Plowden Committee's recommendations in 1961. Conceived of simply as a tool for observing and planning the share that public expenditure would take in the process of economic growth (1961–76), the Public Expenditure Survey (PES) was subsequently transformed into a means of bringing public expenditure growth under control (1976–80), and then of linking public expenditure levels to government revenue levels and holding down public expenditure as a percentage of GDP (1980–97). Ever since 1976 the emphasis has been on setting totals which will represent targets and instruments of control, and not merely projections—both of public expenditure overall, and of the shares to be allotted to different activities within government.

One of the things incoming governments like to do is to denounce the ineptness of their predecessor's spending policy, but in 1997 Labour stuck by the outgoing government's spending plans for two years while it formulated its new approach. Its centrepiece was a Comprehensive Spending Review (CSR), completed in July 1998,[112] involving departments in 'scrutinising their programmes and producing recommendations for change, to refocus their policies and spending on the government's key priorities, as set out in its Manifesto'.[113] The aim was to conduct a more radical review of activities and their expenditure implications than occurred within the PES cycle, in which annual review of the three-year expenditure horizon had enabled departments to renegotiate their spending allocations each year in order to accommodate to

[109] Charter for Budget Responsibility (autumn 2016 update) (2017) para 3.15.

[110] See Treasury Committee, *Government's Cash and Debt Management* (HC 2000–01,154); and most recently oral evidence: *The Work of the Debt Management Office* (HC 2017–19, 2082).

[111] A comprehensive recent discussion, also covering retail borrowing through National Savings and Investments (a non-ministerial department), can be found in Comptroller and Auditor General, *Managing Government Borrowing* (HC 2022–23, 1658). See also National Audit Office, *The Debt Management Office—Borrowing on Behalf of Government* (January 2007).

[112] HM Treasury, *Modern Public Services in Britain: Investing for Reform. Comprehensive Spending Review: New Public Spending Plans 1999–2002* (Cm 4011, July 1998).

[113] Chancellor of the Exchequer, *Stability and Investment for the Long Term* (n 86) s 4.1.

changing circumstances, weakening incentives to achieve value for money and to engage in long-term planning.[114] The CSR system had several aims: to serve as a framework for setting overall public sector spending levels over the next three years, within the discipline imposed by the fiscal rules; to be the means of allocating that spending between department and functions; and to furnish an instrument for regulating departmental spending, in supplementation of the long-established regulatory capacities of Treasury control and parliamentary supervision. At a late stage in its initial development, a further function was added to the system. The expenditure settlement reached through the Review was to incorporate undertakings by each department and its agencies to meet a set of performance targets in pursuit of defined governmental objectives. As we saw in chapter 3, it has not been easy to use Spending Reviews as an instrument of control for this purpose.

In the remainder of this chapter we describe the essential elements of this system and trace its evolution down to the present, including the process of blending it with the older system of parliamentary appropriation of expenditure through the establishment of a common basis for PES and estimates calculations. While parts of the system have been changed or abandoned, its core features have survived several changes of government and continue to provide the overall framework for the executive's expenditure allocation decisions.

3.2 Reviews under the Blair and Brown governments

3.2.1 Key features of the system

Under the CSR, spending plans were set covering the whole public sector, using a new aggregate, Total Managed Expenditure (TME), split into separate current and capital budgets, at levels consistent with the government's fiscal rules. The split was carried over into distinct departmental budgets for capital and current expenditure, with a view to ensuring that longer term capital investment would not be squeezed out by short-term pressures on current spending, now termed resource spending. Capital and resource spending were further divided into two types: spending subject to Departmental Expenditure Limits (DEL), and other spending, referred to as Annually Managed Expenditure (AME).

Departmental Expenditure Limits were fixed for three years, covering about half of TME. They were fixed in cash terms, covering both the costs of programmes and of departmental administration, but were accompanied by greater flexibility than previously to carry unspent cash over from one year to the next. In this way the system integrated and rationalized the experience of imposing cash limits on some parts of departmental expenditure introduced in 1976 and refined over the next decade.[115] Similarly the distinction drawn between programme expenditure and administration expenditure absorbed into the system the device of running costs control instituted

[114] For more detail on pre-1998 arrangements see Daintith and Page (n 25) 143–51, and for an official critique, and explanation of the new system, see HM Treasury, *Reforming Britain's Economic and Financial Policy: Towards Greater Economic Stability* (n 8) ch 12.

[115] Daintith and Page (n 25) 183–86.

in 1986.[116] Annual negotiation of departmental running costs limits had enabled the Treasury to maintain its pressure for economy in administration despite delegation to departments of responsibilities for pay and grading of staff and the formal transfer of the Treasury's establishments function to the Minister for the Civil Service in 1995. The total allocated to DEL also included a small reserve, set at a little under 1% of the total, to deal with emergencies, genuine contingencies, and inter-departmental budgets.[117]

AME represented spending whose variability meant that it could not reasonably be given firm multi-year limits: examples were social security benefits, local authority self-financed expenditure, debt interest, and EU payments. The promise was to subject such expenditure to 'tough annual scrutiny . . . as part of the annual budget process'.[118] In 1998 AME accounted for about half the expenditure total; the split remained broadly similar in 2019, just before Covid-19 struck. But while before 2010 AME was simply estimated, from that date it was constrained by being included in the overall total of managed expenditure, so that overall totals for AME and DEL were traded off against one another in Spending Reviews from 2010 onwards.[119]

3.2.2 *Later reviews*

While the original CSR envisaged that successive reviews would each cover three years, but overlapping with previous reviews by a year, with the result that reviews would occur at two-year intervals, in fact no further zero-based CSR took place until 2007. Reviews in 2000, 2002, and 2004 were titled simply 'Spending Reviews' and were not zero-based. The 2007 review, the last under the Labour government, incorporated significant changes to performance and efficiency arrangements.[120] It was also notable for the fact that the process of reaching departmental settlements as to funds that would be available in the review period (2008–11) was spread out over time, with a substantial number of departments reaching early settlements, in some cases more than 18 months before the formal announcement of the results of the Review in October. This had happened in a few cases in earlier reviews, but the effect in this case was that the allocation of about 30% of DEL had already been fixed six months before the Review announcement.[121] Agreeing early did not necessarily result in a better deal, though it did mean a longer period of assured funding. Some of the early settling departments accepted cuts of up to 5% over the three years, as well as having to make efficiency gains over the review period of 3% per year, a figure imposed across the board.[122]

[116] For details see Daintith and Page (n 25) 188–90. On the history of administration costs control up to 2015, and the difficulty of dispensing with it, see Hood (n 7), ch 8.

[117] The size of the reserve has remained broadly the same over the years. The Reserve is not to be confused with the Contingencies Fund: see chapter 8, section 2.3 and Daintith and Page (n 25) 186–88.

[118] HM Treasury, *Modern Public Services in Britain* (n 112) Annex B.

[119] Hood (n 7) 94.

[120] See chapter 3, section 4.1.

[121] Treasury Committee, *The 2007 Comprehensive Spending Review* (n 11) paras 11–13.

[122] ibid paras 44–59, 66–71.

3.3 Reviews under Coalition and Conservative governments

3.3.1 The Coalition government's approach

The Spending Review process has been continued by the Coalition government of 2010–15 and the five Conservative governments in power since then. The Coalition's 2010 Review, presented in October 2010 but preceded by an 'emergency' June Budget in which some major immediate spending decisions were announced, was carried out against the background of the damage to the public finances caused by the 2007–09 financial crisis and of a general election in which the extent and timing of expenditure cuts had been a major issue. It sought to deploy a radical reappraisal of public expenditure priorities in the service of a substantial reduction of government debt.[123] This presented particularly difficult challenges for departments that had already absorbed negative settlements and efficiency savings from the 2007 review. Cuts in departmental allocations were unprecedented: 8.3% in overall DEL over the period to 2015, with variations ranging between a 29% cut for the Department for Environment Food and Rural Affairs (DEFRA) and a 37% increase for the Department of International Development.[124] As with the Coalition's fiscal rule structure, the Review was in some respects more ambitious than those of its predecessor government, in that it covered four years' spending (2011–15).

3.3.2 The 'equalities' obligation

A new element in this Review responded to the statutory 'equalities' obligation on public authorities under the Equality Act 2006. Applicable at the time of the Review to functions in relation to race, disability, and gender, the obligation was by the Equality Act 2010 later extended so as to create a general 'public sector equality duty', requiring authorities to have due regard to the need to eliminate discrimination and promote equality of opportunity across the whole range of protected characteristics recognized by the Act.[125] The equality issue was acknowledged in the Review by a brief note, along with an analysis of the distributional effect of the Review allocations,[126] and by an accompanying Treasury 'equalities overview document' indicating the role it saw itself playing in achieving respect for the equality duty. The document, and the processes it described, were examined in a subsequent report by the Equality and Human Rights Commission, prepared in the exercise of its statutory power to assess the extent to which a person (in this case the Treasury) has complied with the public sector

[123] For detailed discussion of the Review see Tony Prosser, '"An Opportunity to Take a More Fundamental Look at the Role of Government in Society": The Spending Review as Regulation' [2011] Public Law 596.

[124] HM Treasury, *Spending Review 2010* (Cm 7942, October 2010), 81 (Annex A, table A.5).

[125] See ss 4–12 (protected characteristics), 149–57 (public sector equality duty). The Act had been passed under the previous Labour government; these provisions were brought into force in April 2011. A further provision of direct relevance to public expenditure, s 1(1), provides that '[a]n authority to which this section applies must, when making decisions of a strategic nature about how to exercise its functions, have due regard to the desirability of exercising them in a way that is designed to reduce the inequalities of outcome which result from socio-economic disadvantage'. This provision has however so far been brought into force only in Scotland, in 2017, and Wales, in 2021.

[126] HM Treasury, *Spending Review 2010* (n 124) 31 (Box 1.4), 89–100 (Annex B).

equality duty.[127] The Commission's review, focused on nine case studies from a variety of areas, found the procedure to have been satisfactory in most cases.[128]

This development subjected the Spending Review process to an additional normative control—a 'soft' one certainly, insofar as the equality obligation was only to 'have due regard' to certain desiderata, but one with a clear legislative base, and one whose requirements had already been the subject of judicial interpretation.[129] The effect was to open up the process to judicial review. When the Department for Education cut its programme of assistance for school building in preparation for the Review it was the subject of a successful judicial review by a number of affected local authorities on the ground, among others, that it had not given due regard to equalities considerations in framing its cutback policy.[130] More recently the Treasury's own involvement in the review process has been scrutinized in *Simone, McFinnigan and Riddell v Chancellor of the Exchequer and Secretary of State for Education*,[131] where the claimants, who were parents of disabled children, attacked the decision of the Chancellor to postpone consideration of a specific bid from the Department of Education to the planned 2019 spending round, rather than funding it in his 2018 autumn Budget. They alleged that he had failed, in breach of the 'equality obligation' to have due regard to the children's disability. The Court found that in reaching his decision the Chancellor had fully satisfied the requirements of the obligation, but the case makes it clear that high-level political decisions with macroeconomic effects, such as those taken in the spending rounds, are not exempt from searching examination.

3.3.3 The welfare cap

In a spending round in 2013, providing a bridge to the next CSR period, the government announced a new allocation element, the introduction of a so called 'welfare cap' with effect from 2015.[132] Most welfare spending has been treated as falling into AME, rather than DEL, because driven by cyclical factors determining benefit application rates, and often involving payments mandated by permanent legislation. This was not something that relevant departments could restrain through minor economies. The cap was an attempt to reinforce control over such spending, following indications that its growth over the period since Spending Reviews started had significantly outstripped that of DEL. Elaborate rules for its definition and monitoring were set out for

[127] Equality Act 2006, s 31.

[128] Equality and Human Rights Commission, *Making Fair Financial Decisions: an Assessment of HM Treasury's 2010 Spending Review conducted under Section 31 of the 2006 Equality Act* (May 2012). a further report was made in February 2015 reviewing the progress made on the Commission's original recommendations, including changes in the approach to the 2013 Spending Round: Equality and Human Rights Commission, *Future Fair Financial Decision-Making* (February 2015). See also Women and Equalities Committee, *Equalities Analysis and the 2015 Spending Review and Autumn Statement* (HC 2016–17, 825), and the government's response at (HC 2016–17, 974), resisting the requested disclosure of aspects of the Spending Review process.

[129] See in particular *R (Brown) v Secretary of State for Work and Pensions* [2008] EWHC 3158 [90]–[96].

[130] *R (Luton Borough Council and Nottingham City Council) v Secretary of State for Education* [2011] EWHC 217.

[131] [2019] EWHC 2609 (Admin). Discussion of the equalities aspect of the Chancellor's decision will be found at [56]–[70].

[132] HM Treasury, *Spending Round 2013* (Cm 8639, June 2013) paras 1.45–1.50.

the first time in the March 2014 revision of the Charter for Budget Responsibility.[133] The basic idea was that the Treasury would set limits for relevant welfare expenditure over each of the next five years, with a small margin above to provide for pressures on, and fluctuations in, capped welfare spending; and that OBR should assess each year whether forecast welfare expenditure was likely to fall within these limits. OBR said in 2016 that,

> [o]f the assessments that Parliament has tasked us to make via the Charter for Budget Responsibility, the welfare cap assessment is by some margin the most complex. We need to make judgements in two grey areas: the distinction between policy changes and forecast changes (where operational changes that might or might not be considered part of the business-as-usual delivery of policy come up quite frequently); and identifying classification changes.[134]

These judgements might determine whether the cap was 'breached' in the sense that forecast relevant spending for a given year would be above the capped figure, and hence whether, under the terms of the Charter, the Secretary of State for Work and Pensions must go to Parliament with a motion either to approve measures to reduce spending to comply with the cap; or to accept that the breach is justified.[135] Such motions, to accept the government's justification for welfare cap breaches, were presented to Parliament in 2015 and 2016 in respect of every one of the years from 2016 to 2021.[136] This does not say a lot for the significance either of the cap itself or of the fact of parliamentary involvement. The cap has, however, been maintained and updated despite unplanned-for changes to social security benefits to palliate damage caused by the Covid pandemic.[137]

3.3.4 *Conservative government reviews*

The Conservative governments in power since 2015 have conducted three further reviews: a multi-year review in 2015, and single-year spending rounds in September 2019 and November 2020; a full-scale review was scheduled for 2019 but was postponed to 2020 because of uncertainty about the terms on which the UK would withdraw from the European Union. Covid-19 subsequently intervened, with the result that the 2020 Review likewise covered only a single year. A full multi-year review, to 2024–25, was finally organized in 2021,[138] with adjustments announced in the Autumn Statement 2022 after the crisis provoked by the Truss government's *Growth Plan 2022*.[139]

[133] HM Treasury, *Charter for Budget Responsibility, March 2014 update* (March 2014) paras 3.4, 3.20–3.32.

[134] Treasury Committee, *Spending Review and Autumn Statement 2015: Government and Office for Budgetary Responsibility Responses to the Sixth Report from the Committee, 2016–17* (HC 2016–17, 683) app 2, 16.

[135] *Charter for Budget Responsibility, Autumn 2021 update* (January 2022) para 3.35.

[136] HC Deb 15 December 2015, vol 603, cols 1633–50; HC Deb 12 December 2016, vol 618, cols 570–83.

[137] HM Treasury, *Spending Review 2020* (CP 330, November 2020) Annex D. See Table 1.1 for relevant spending decisions.

[138] HM Treasury, *Autumn Budget and Spending Review 2021* (HC 2021–22, 822).

[139] Chancellor of the Exchequer, *Autumn Statement 2022* (CP 751, November 2022).

3.4 Review procedures

Over time the procedures for conducting Spending Reviews have varied widely, as has the amount of information government has disclosed about them. We know more about the procedure employed to reach the results of the 2010 Review—in the remarkably short time of five months from the date of the general election—than about earlier or more recent reviews. In introducing CSR in 1998 Labour did not change the formal mechanism it had inherited for determining the allocations to be made at the Review. This continued to be a small Cabinet committee chaired by the Chancellor, now titled the Public Services and Public Expenditure Committee (PSX, later PEX).[140] Other members were the Chief Secretary to the Treasury, the minister with immediate responsibility for government spending, another senior minister, and two Cabinet Office ministers. This 'official' structure continued in much the same form right through to the end of the Coalition government in 2015. Procedure, however, varied greatly over time. In 1998 the Prime Minister and the Chancellor 'just called in ministers and told them how much they were getting'.[141] '[T]he public spending committee rarely met and played a much lighter touch role'.[142] By contrast in 2010 a formal process started with Treasury guidance to departments in early June, followed by a meeting of PEX providing indications of the scale of spending reductions for different departments (which varied considerably).[143] Treasury–department dialogue over the summer then led to allocation decisions, either by PEX, in relation to smaller and medium-sized departments, or, in relation to the larger departments and the Review as a whole, by the so-called 'Quad'—the quadrilateral of Prime Minister, Deputy Prime Minister, Chief Secretary to the Treasury, and Chancellor of the Exchequer). PEX worked its way through the allocations at a series of meetings. As it did so, its membership grew, since once a department settled, its Secretary of State was invited to join the Committee. Thus on 2 September early settlements were reached with six departments, including the three (Foreign and Commonwealth Office, Treasury, and Cabinet Office) already represented. The other three departmental ministers then joined. By the end of the process PEX had 10 members.[144]

This procedure, which met with general approval,[145] was seen as a move towards more formal, collective, decision-making. The 2010 arrangements were repeated in the 2013 'Spending Round', undertaken to carry expenditure planning forward for a further year, to the end of the 2015–16 financial year. Again, early settlement following negotiations with the Treasury was rewarded with a departmental seat on PEX for the remainder of the process. The fact that this was coalition government may, perhaps

[140] For arrangements prior to the creation of this Committee in 1992, see Daintith and Page (n 25) 148–49.

[141] David Lipsey, *The Secret Treasury: How Britain's Economy is Really Run* (Viking 2000) 165. See also Hood (n 7) 67.

[142] Treasury Committee, *Spending Review 2010* (HC 2010–12, 544) para 30 (quoting a Treasury official).

[143] Equality and Human Rights Commission, *Future Fair Financial Decision-Making* (n 128) 23.

[144] ibid 19–20, and apps 7 and 11.

[145] Treasury Committee, *The 2007 Comprehensive Spending Review* (n 11) para 30—though other procedural aspects, like the mode of public consultation, were received with some scepticism: see para 38 and Prosser, '"An Opportunity to Take a More Fundamental Look at the Role of Government in Society"' (n 123) 608–10.

paradoxically, have facilitated the apparently smooth operation of the review process in 2010 and 2013. The 'Quad' was part of the Coalition apparatus. The Chancellor and the Chief Secretary were from different parties, as were the Prime Minister and Deputy Prime Minister. Balancing their interests and influence led to a more formal approach.[146]

The process of the Conservative government's reviews is much less clear. PEX was used in 2015, but only to consider 'cross-cutting spending and policy issues', as opposed to individual departmental settlements.[147] These resulted from bilateral negotiations between the Chief Secretary and Secretaries of State. Theresa May's government conducted a cull of Cabinet committees in 2016. PEX seems to have disappeared at this time, and no public expenditure committee has been listed among those announced since. In subsequent rounds and reviews (2019, 2020, and 2021), allocations have continued to be settled bilaterally, with cross-governmental linkages limited to coordination at official and ministerial level between the Treasury and the Prime Minister's Office. In the 2021 Review allocations were based at least in part on proposals generated through cross-governmental discussion of the results of a Savings and Efficiency Review designed to achieve greater efficiencies and to adjust medium-term priorities.[148] The Review also innovated in this area by explicitly setting out the priority outcomes that departments were to deliver with their agreed funding and the metrics to be used to measure progress towards them.[149] According to the Treasury, this facilitated selection of lower priority programmes that departments could cut when squeezed by the inflation induced by the Covid recovery and the energy price fallout from the Ukraine war.[150] The economic upheavals associated with Brexit and the Covid pandemic may have favoured the traditional, bilateral approach, but the way these reviews have been carried out strongly suggests that the more structured approach to Spending Review in 2010–14 was an idiosyncrasy of coalition government.

3.5 The scope of reviews

One notable feature of the evolution of the review process is its diminishing scope. Use of the word 'comprehensive' in 1998 signalled that the whole of government spending should be looked at together, and that departments had no vested rights in the level of their historic allocations. Of course some departments *did* have certain vested rights, reflecting obligations under permanent legislation and other long-term commitments, but these were not such as to protect any department from scrutiny. As time went on, however, such protection became an issue. While the 2007 Review

[146] Treasury Committee, *The 2007 Comprehensive Spending Review* (n 11) oral evidence, qq 209–13 (Chancellor of the Exchequer). For detail on the substance of the Review see Hood (n 7) 95–98.

[147] HM Treasury, *Spending Review and Autumn Statement 2015* (Cm 9162, November 2015) para 1.68.

[148] HM Treasury, *Autumn Budget and Spending Review 2021* (n 138) para 1.92.

[149] paras 1.85–1.89. Priority outcomes are summarized, department by department, in chapter 4 of the Review. They were to form the basis of Outcome Delivery Plans for 2022–25 (para 1.88). These, while prepared in draft, were superseded by later financial developments and were not published as planned: see chapter 3, section 4.2.2. For the detailed listing of outcomes and metrics, see HM Treasury, *Spending Review 2021: Priority Outcomes and Metrics* (October 2021).

[150] Treasury Committee, oral evidence: *Work of the Treasury* (HC 2022–23, 137) qq 124–29.

was also labelled 'comprehensive', the spreading out of the departmental settlements over time meant, as we have noted, that the allocation of 30% of DEL had already been fixed six months before the announcement of the review results. Within certain limits, this spreading out of decision-making is no more than a reasonable reflection of the fact that discussion of spending is a continuous ongoing process between department and Treasury public expenditure teams; the fact that some discussions may lead more quickly to agreement than others does not mean that the Treasury has no overall view of the spending picture. The radical review undertaken by the Coalition in 2010, however, was conducted in pursuance of a 'Coalition Agreement' that committed the government to guaranteed levels of expenditure for budgets like health—guaranteed to rise each year in real terms—pensions—protected by the 'triple lock' of rising in line with the higher of earnings, prices, or 2.5%—and overseas aid:[151] all of which, against the background of the overriding policy of reducing TME and hence borrowing, meant larger cuts for 'unprotected' departments exposed to the review process.

The Conservative government of 2015 did not have to work within a confining Coalition Agreement, but it continued and enlarged this 'ring fencing' approach, extending it to include defence, counter-terrorism, and child benefit, with the result that the 2015 Review covered only 23% of departmental expenditure.[152] This situation was severely criticized in evidence to the Treasury Committee taken in 2010 and in 2015, both on the ground that the long-term effect of protecting particular budgets was to cause major shifts in the balance of public expenditure—which meant major shifts in what government actually did—and that protecting budgets disincentivized any attempt to operate them more efficiently.[153] The government's response that it was still allocating spending in accordance with priorities published and explained at 'fiscal events'[154] was close to an admission that its medium-term spending plans and discipline now resulted not from a concentrated across-the-board review, but from a bundle of decisions taken at different times and under different constraints.

Since 2015 some multi-year growth commitments have been maintained or reinforced: in the case of the National Health Service, the government dramatized this commitment by securing the passage of 'permanent' legislation that set minimum resource spending on the service in England until 2024.[155] More generally, the succession of economic disturbances occasioned first by Brexit, then Covid, then the Ukraine war and energy price crisis, produced some major variations in departmental settlements which were not always favourable to traditionally protected functions like defence and overseas aid. The scope of the 2021 Spending Review, setting departmental allocations to 2024–25, was thus effectively increased beyond the very constrained perimeter of 2015.

[151] HM Government, *The Coalition: Our Programme for Government* (May 2010) 24, 26, 22.

[152] Treasury Committee, *Spending Review and Autumn Statement 2015* (HC 2015–16, 638) paras 46–56.

[153] ibid, and for a chorus of criticism of the practice, Treasury Committee, *Spending Review 2010* (HC 2010–12, 544-ii) written evidence) ev w13, 19, 21, 29, 39, 42.

[154] Treasury Committee, *Spending Review and Autumn Statement 2015: Government and Office for Budgetary Responsibility Responses to the Sixth Report from the Committee, 2016–17* (HC 2016–17, 683) para 11.

[155] NHS Funding Act 2020: this was enacted before the seriousness of the Covid pandemic was appreciated.

3.6 The Spending Review in Parliament

3.6.1 An executive preserve?

In 1999 we concluded that the Public Expenditure Survey system, the forerunner of Spending Reviews, 'is wholly internal to the executive'.[156] As a result of what was called the 'alignment' or 'clear line of sight' project, a judgement on the Spending Review system today needs to be a little more nuanced, but it remains the fact that the reviews have never provided a platform for parliamentary discussion of the range of spending policy choices facing government. Governmental practice from beginning to end has been to present Parliament with the results of the review, at a moment when there is clearly no scope to influence its content, whether hammered out in Treasury–department negotiations, rationally discussed in PEX, or simply announced to departments by a Prime Minister-Chancellor duumvirate. The distancing of Parliament from the actual process of decision-making has been expressed by the denial of any possibility of parliamentary discussion of the options, as to spending levels and allocation, among which government will choose in the course of the review. Members of Parliament have been asking for this ever since 1998; ministers have consistently brushed off these requests.[157] While the Treasury Committee has done sterling work over the years in examining the reviews once presented and providing informative bi-partisan reports, the presence of Spending Reviews in Hansard's record of Commons proceedings is limited to brief discussions of the ministerial statements presenting the reviews, and a small number of short follow-up debates, which have proceeded along predictable party political lines. And despite the appearance of Parliament as an occasional actor in fiscal rules arrangements, there seems to be no reason to expect any change in this respect.

In thinking about democratic control we should keep in mind that Spending Review decisions have been superimposed upon the traditional system of parliamentary authorization and appropriation of central government expenditure. They do not replace that system. In terms of formal constitutional ordering, they are indeed subordinate to that system, in that the planned allocations of spending determined in the reviews cannot be realized unless Parliament provides the necessary legislative spending authorizations, either annually, as part of the parliamentary supply cycle, or by way of a standing appropriation—the charging of defined expenditure directly to the Consolidated Fund, the government's general expenditure fund. In practice, of course, this formal subordination does not mean that Parliament can, through the mechanisms of annual supply procedure, intervene in the Spending Review process. As we have already seen, the House of Commons' ceding of all financial initiative to the Crown means that the content of the estimates and of the Appropriation Acts is entirely determined by the government. The role of Parliament is simply to approve, and to approve, moreover, with minimal debate.[158]

[156] Daintith and Page (n 25) 142.

[157] See HC Deb 21 April 1998, vol 312, col 1101; Treasury Committee, *Spending Review 2000* (HC 1999–2000, 485) para 5; for later attempts see Prosser, '"An Opportunity to Take a More Fundamental Look at the Role of Government in Society"' (n 123) 605–08.

[158] Since 1982 the time available for considering the main estimates has been restricted, under Standing Orders 54 and 55, to three days, chosen for debate on estimates selected for this purpose by the House of Commons Liaison Committee established under Standing Order 145, between the presentation of the

3.6.2 The alignment project (or 'Clear Line of Sight')

Against this background the value that parliamentary discussion could add to the public expenditure process was defined by the House of Commons Liaison Committee in 2008:

> Improving financial scrutiny is not about finding ways to force through major changes to the Government's overall revenue-raising and spending plans. [. . .] What [it] *is* about is making the Government, individual Departments and other public bodies accountable for their financial decisions—in other words, requiring them to justify their revenue-raising and spending plans and, later, to explain whether the expenditure achieved its objectives and, if not, why not.[159]

A prerequisite for such accountability is that Parliament should receive accurate and meaningful information about government's expenditure planning and performance. Within this framework, the key information vehicle is the documentation associated with the government's annual estimates and accounts.

The shaping of this documentation is characterized by real interdependence between Parliament and Treasury. Parliament cannot get the reliable and useful information it needs to call departments to account unless the Treasury can exercise control over the information they provide;[160] the Treasury, for its part, can use Parliament's demands for information to buttress its internal budgeting and planning disciplines. The result has been a continuing dialogue between the Treasury and the relevant Committees about the estimates and accounts, with the Comptroller and Auditor General offering independent expert advice. The fruits of that dialogue have been a gradual convergence between Spending Review figures and the estimates, essentially through modification of the scope and basis of estimates calculations. Dialogue has been assisted by what the Treasury Committee perceived, at the outset of the process in the 1990s, as 'the wholly cooperative manner in which the exercise [was] conducted', and

> the apparent determination of the senior Treasury officials involved to ensure that a sensible timetable should be established for the introduction of resource accounting which meets the needs of the Government service as a whole, and is not tailored to the immediate political imperatives of Ministers.[161]

estimates and the summer recess. The remainder of the estimates are put to the vote without the possibility of debate. The Appropriation Acts, which translate the main elements of the estimates resolutions into legislative form, are not debated at all.

[159] Liaison Committee, *Parliament and Government Finance: Recreating Financial Scrutiny* (HC 2007–08, 426) paras 8–9.

[160] For developments in Treasury control over estimates and accounts, see chapter 8, section 2.2 and chapter 11, section 2.1.

[161] Treasury and Civil Service Committee, *Simplified Estimates and Resource Accounting* (HC 1994–95, 212) paras 5, 27.

This approach has been maintained through a number of stages. The first was the simplification of estimates in the 1990s, with much detail removed to the annual reports produced at that time by departments as part of the Public Expenditure Survey process. At the same time, the government initiated a switch from cash accounting to a resource or accrual basis,[162] carried out gradually over the years from 1995 onwards and completed with the passage of the Government Resources and Accounting Act 2000, making the legislative changes necessary to support the replacement of appropriation accounts, on a cash basis, with resource accounts. By the 1990s there was general agreement that cash estimates and accounts were of little use as an instrument of accountability. Their simplicity and immediacy had long been prized by Parliament, but as the Comptroller and Auditor General pointed out to the Procedure Committee, 'they are so straightforward . . . they tell you essentially nothing'.[163] For example, cash figures, in themselves, gave no information about contractual commitments which a department might have taken on and which might extend over many years. Nor did they distinguish between current and capital expenditure. Most critically for the Treasury, they gave little sense of the true cost of activities—notably, the cost of holding capital assets such as buildings and equipment.

The final stage, which has brought some aspects of the Spending Review process within Parliament's purview, has been the elimination of the 'misalignment' in the bases on which financial information is presented to Parliament in the government's different financial documents—the budgets presented as part of the Spending Reviews, the annual estimates, and the resource accounts—along with the differences in the format and timing of this information. Following very soon after a Treasury Committee recommendation, Gordon Brown's new government undertook, in the *Governance of Britain* Green Paper presented in 2007, to

> simplify its reporting to Parliament, ensuring that it reports in a more consistent fashion, in line with the fiscal rules, at all three stages in the process; on plans, Estimates and actual expenditure outturns.[164]

If the response was rapid, the process of achieving a 'clear line of sight' across government's different financial statements was a laborious one, which took three years to complete, including a consultation process involving no fewer than five House of Commons Committees.[165]

Essentially the form and bases of the estimates were brought into line with the Spending Review figures and the departmental budgets set by those reviews. The loss of some formal approval powers that this entailed, over some sources of departmental

[162] For the initial proposals see HM Treasury, *Better Accounting for the Taxpayer's Money: Resource Accounting and Budgeting in Government* (Cm 2626, July 1994), and for the definitive plans HM Treasury, *Better Accounting for the Taxpayer's Money, The Government's Proposals: Resource Accounting and Budgeting in Government* (Cm 2929, July 1995).

[163] Procedure Committee, *Resource Accounting and Budgeting* (HC 1997–98, 438) Evidence, q 22.

[164] Secretary of State for Justice and Lord Chancellor, *The Governance of Britain* (Cm 7170, July 2007) para 111, following Treasury Committee, *The 2007 Comprehensive Spending Review* (n 11) para 110.

[165] For the detailed Treasury proposals see HM Treasury, *Alignment (Clear Line of Sight) Project* (Cm 7567, March 2009) para 1.8.

income from outside the Appropriation Act, was compensated for by the use of the Spending Review aggregates—TME, DEL, AME, and the split between current and capital expenditure and programme and administration expenditure—as the main elements of the estimates framework. That framework was also extended, by way of the amendment of the Government Resources and Accounts Act 2000,[166] so as to bring non-departmental public bodies and other bodies classified to the central government sector within departmental estimates and accounting boundaries. The Treasury calculated, using 2008–09 figures, that if the estimates changes were made, the amount of funding in Departmental Spending Review budgets that did not appear in the estimates would be reduced from £129bn to almost zero, while the disparity between resource accounts figures and those for both budgets and estimates would be reduced to £19bn.[167]

The result of the 'clear line of sight' project is that the same figures provide the baseline both for Treasury control of executive expenditure and parliamentary supervision of its employment. Adherence to departmental spending settlements is now not just a matter of internal control in the framework of Treasury–departmental relations. Through their translation into the estimates, respect for the Spending Review figures becomes a matter of regularity of departmental expenditure, subject to the scrutiny of the Comptroller and Auditor General and Public Accounts Committee. Indeed, for those aggregates that figure in Part I of a department's estimate and are reproduced in the annual Appropriation Act, respect becomes a matter of legal obligation.

A further result of the project has been that the definitions and concepts developed within the Spending Review framework are no longer a matter for the executive alone. In accordance with long-standing constitutional practice,[168] important changes in the customary form of the estimates require the prior approval of the relevant Committees of the House of Commons (and, if those Committees so propose, of the House as a whole). If estimates and budgets are to remain aligned, any significant changes to budgets that would impact on the format or content of the estimates need to be agreed with the Commons in advance of implementation. Accordingly the Treasury, with the agreement of the House of Commons Liaison Committee, has established a protocol to regulate the process of change.[169] It distinguishes changes that will not go ahead without parliamentary approval (movements into or out of the budgeting boundary or other significant changes to the budgeting framework); changes to the treatment of spending within the boundary (such as from DEL to AME), of which Parliament would be notified in advance, and which it could refuse—in relation to estimates—at the cost of introducing a new misalignment; and other changes whose importance, and whose appropriate treatment, would be discussed in

[166] This was done by a provision in the Labour government's Constitutional Reform and Governance Act 2010 (s 43), which its Coalition successor brought into effect in November 2010. For further discussion of the position of NDPBs see chapter 4.

[167] HM Treasury, above (n 165) tables 3.A, 3.B, and 5.A. For the explanation of the latter figure see Annex F, paras F.4–F.7.

[168] Erskine May, *Treatise on The Law, Privileges, Proceedings and Usage of Parliament* (25th edn, 2019) para 34.9, states that this is a parliamentary 'expectation' based on 'established usage'.

[169] The agreed version is to be found in HM Treasury, *Supply Estimates: A Guidance Manual* (July 2011) paras 2.6–2.10.

advance between the Treasury and parliamentary authorities (primarily the NAO, the Public Bill Office, and the House of Commons Scrutiny Unit, as appropriate). The protocol also provides for the establishment of an Alignment Review Committee to consider proposed changes before any recommendations are put to ministers and Parliament. The Committee is managed by the Treasury and consists of representatives from the Treasury, other departments, NAO, House of Commons Scrutiny Unit, Financial Reporting Advisory Board, and ONS.

IV Conclusion: Effects on Executive Autonomy and Internal Control

The key driver for the introduction of the fiscal responsibility reforms, including reinforcement of medium-term expenditure planning, was the concern of a new government with untried leaders to establish the credibility of its economic policies. The package was the government's idea: developed in opposition, set out in its manifesto, and owing nothing to parliamentary pressure beyond the political bonus of action in sympathy with Parliament's long-term quest for improved financial accountability (though not necessarily with the interests of back-benchers looking for more generous public spending outlays). Securing and maintaining the confidence of the international bond markets might have been seen as the crucial credibility issue, at least if the Chancellor was to avoid the fate of which a Swedish Prime Minister complained in the 1990s: spending more time in the City of London giving presentations to young bond market traders than talking to the Swedish people about the fiscal problems the country faced.[170]

What if any positive economic effects flowed from this commitment to stable and transparent policies is a question for economists and political commentators to answer. Our concern is with how the commitment affected the executive's constitutional relationships and internal structure. What seems undeniable is that the Code, the Charter, and the roles played by ONS and OBR have all contributed significantly to greater transparency of executive action in this area, and hence to greater accountability to Parliament and public. Their combined effect has been to change the nature of public accountability for Budget judgements. This had relied entirely on non-normative control: 'answerability to a body (a Parliamentary assembly, the electorate itself) which may examine and censure regardless of any established norms, and also regardless of their absence.'[171] The adoption of the fiscal rules added to this the norm-based control and accountability that we associate traditionally with the activity of courts, but which may be deployed by any kind of body, including Parliament and its agencies. It would be naive in the extreme to imagine that from 1998 public critique of government fiscal policy would be pursued *only* by reference to whether the fiscal rules and mandates were being adhered to—non-normative accountability is still alive and kicking—but the rules enabled evaluation and criticism to be more sharply

[170] Quoted by the shadow Chancellor at HC Deb 5 January 2010, vol 503, col 80.

[171] Terence Daintith, 'Between Domestic Democracy and an Alien Rule of Law? Some Thoughts on the "Independence" of the Bank of England' [1995] Public Law 118, 125.

focused and less easily deflected by arithmetic manipulations. Actual and projected performance could be judged, by the independent OBR and external commentators, against the government's own rules as well as by reference to critics' own pet policies, while the increasingly independent ONS guaranteed the integrity of the numbers on which such performance would be assessed. In this respect it is hard to exaggerate the importance of the other decision of Gordon Brown, to use the ESA definitions and classifications as the basis of the government's financial documentation.

Has the addition of this normative apparatus diminished the autonomy of executive action in this field? Certainly, a legislative underpinning for such action was furnished first by the 'fiscal rules' provisions of the Finance Act 1998, followed by the Statistics and Registration Service Act in April 2008—whose effects we consider more generally in chapter 12—and then the short-lived Fiscal Responsibility Act 2010 and its more durable Coalition successor, the Budget Responsibility and National Audit Act 2011. This formal change, however, probably mattered little by comparison with the effect of creating publicly visible rules and institutions to which governments would be expected to have regard, irrespective of their constitutional status. The rules of the Budget Responsibility and National Audit Act did not stop the Truss government from announcing a dramatic economic policy shift in September 2022 without the accompaniment of an OBR forecast. Indeed the failure to ask for a forecast arguably did not even breach the Memorandum of Understanding between the government and the OBR. Nonetheless, a perception of government refusal to be guided by expert advice was enough to drive a market reaction that precipitated its rapid collapse and the subsequent disowning of its policies by its successor.

It should also be remembered that the rules and institutional oversight generated by the 2011 Act operate only at the level of the broadest aggregates of taxation, borrowing, and expenditure, and that while the debt mandates constrain borrowing, the rules do not touch such crucial choices as whether to favour higher taxes or lower public expenditure. These are much more likely to reflect the personal style and interests of different Prime Ministers, and the political strength of the Chancellor of the day.[172] Again, the rules do not touch the major decisions about prioritization of policies and expenditures that government takes in its multi-year Spending Reviews. The Reviews have never provided a platform for parliamentary discussion of the range of spending policy choices facing government, and the decision process is still purely internal. The alignment project patiently pursued by the Treasury and by House of Commons Committees has arguably given a new constitutional status to the *results* of the reviews by building their departmental allocations into the estimates, appropriation and accounting procedures that constitute the formal apparatus of parliamentary supervision of public expenditure. It is not clear, however, how this might translate into greater departmental accountability to Parliament for the use they make of these allocations, given that value for money in employment of appropriated funds has long been subject to NAO and Public Accounts Committee scrutiny.

[172] For a general discussion of the relations between post-World War II Chancellors and their Prime Ministers, see Richard Holt, *Second among Equals: Chancellors of the Exchequer and the British Economy* (Profile Books 2001) 115–40. For a specific example see Darling (n 39) 183–84, and for the general discussion of budget preparation David Lipsey (n 141) 119–32, suggesting a tendency towards greater openness.

Otherwise, have the fiscal responsibility programme and the Spending Reviews modified the system of control within the executive in any constitutionally significant way? To take Spending Reviews first, we have seen that the Treasury has had limited success in utilizing this machinery as an instrument of control of departmental priorities and performance.[173] Respect for spending limits does not always mean value for money. As the Comptroller and Auditor General has put it,

> there are occasions when we see value for money being compromised by the needs of short-term spending control. Unrealistic, over-optimistic budgets are kept within the spending envelope by short-term unplanned cuts, which can damage long-term programmes and drive suppliers to distraction.[174]

The Treasury has also had to be constantly on the alert to respond to departmental efforts to manipulate or 'game' the system when it produces uncomfortable constraints, and has not always managed to stay one step ahead.[175] So far, however, as its primary purpose is concerned, of setting limits to public sector expenditure aggregates and seeing to it that they are respected, there is no doubt that the Spending Review system has been highly effective. Over the years between 2000 and 2015 the United Kingdom was by some distance the best performer among European countries at meeting its spending forecasts: the difference between outturn and forecasts made a year in advance were minimal as a percentage of GDP.[176] Whether the fiscal rules have made any contribution to this is open to question. Alastair Darling, as Chancellor when introducing the ill-fated Fiscal Responsibility Act, emphasized the value to him of 'the discipline created by rules, so the Chancellor can tell Departments that they cannot have any more funds because it would breach a particular rule'.[177] The frequency with which fiscal rules have been changed in response to the economic shocks of recent years suggests scepticism, however, as to whether they can add any significant constraint to that provided by Spending Review controls, and the other controls that we shall examine in the next chapter.

[173] Chapter 3, section IV.
[174] Comptroller and Auditor General, *Improving Government's Planning and Spending Framework* (HC 2017–19, 1679) 15 (para 25).
[175] Hood (n 7) 3–6, 202–23.
[176] See International Monetary Fund, *United Kingdom—Fiscal Transparency Evaluation* (November 2016) IMF Country Report No 16/351, 37, cited in Comptroller and Auditor General (n 174) 47.
[177] HC Deb 5 January 2010, vol 503, col 65. He was less enthusiastic about the Act in his memoirs (n 39, 267–68): 'Legislation is no substitute for sound judgement.'

8
Spending Responsibly: Expenditure Principles and Treasury Control

I Introduction

1.1 The Spending Review and established controls

When the new Spending Review system was established, Treasury officials were hopeful that it would not only function to set appropriate and enforceable limits on departmental spending, but would also improve expenditure management generally, providing the means of securing that departments operated more economically, more efficiently (doing more with less resource), more effectively (in terms of achieving policy objectives), and with better coordination (in relation to policy goals that cut across departmental boundaries). The Treasury hoped that these objectives could be advanced with a lighter and more sensitive touch than under its traditional system of control, with its reliance on a structure of Treasury rules, consents, and delegations developed around the principle of prior consent. In 1998 it invited the Public Accounts Committee to accept a degree of relaxation in the operation of its consent requirements, arguing that its continuing dialogue with departments in the context of the Comprehensive Spending Review was its best source of intelligence about the way departments were run, and that concentrating on the big things like the Review, rather than getting bogged down in micro-issues,[1] would mean

> better relations between the Treasury and departments because, while departments accept the need for the Treasury to be involved in strategic decisions affecting public expenditure control and overall value for money, they tend to regard Treasury involvement in less important decisions as unnecessary meddling, and inconsistent with trends in other areas (such as pay and grading) where delegation to departments has already taken place. Moreover, it is difficult to argue that departments should delegate responsibility within their own organisation (e.g., to agencies) and empower more junior staff while insisting that the Treasury should retain detailed controls over minor spending decisions.[2]

We have already seen that the use of the Spending Review system as a performance discipline has had a chequered history,[3] and that while its record in keeping spending

[1] Public Accounts Committee, *Treasury Controls* (HC 1998–99, 157) oral evidence, qq 53, 54, and written evidence, Treasury Memorandum 97–98/35, para 17.
[2] Written evidence, Treasury Memorandum 97–98/35, para 17.
[3] Chapter 3, section IV.

Executive Self-Government and the Constitution. Terence Daintith and Alan Page, Oxford University Press.
 DOI: 10.1093/9780198937630.003.0008

out-turns close to planned figures has been very good, critics have argued that this has been achieved by short-term unplanned cuts to keep over-optimistic budgets within the spending envelope, at the cost of damage to long-term programmes.[4] This chapter will explain how the Treasury's traditional controls over public expenditure have continued to operate and evolve over the period of operation of Spending Reviews. In particular it will consider how far the Treasury has carried the process of relaxation suggested in 1998, and how (if at all) this process affects the interaction between internal control and the external controls on public expenditure operated by the Comptroller and Auditor General, Parliament, and the courts.

The expenditure disciplines to which central government departments are subject are the product of a process of cooperation, extending over some 160 years, between the Comptroller and Auditor General, Parliament, in the shape of its Public Accounts Committee, and the Treasury. The first audits the government's accounts, the second calls government to account for any failings demonstrated by the audit, the third lays down the rules to be followed by departments in the management of their expenditure and in reporting on it. We devote most of this chapter to the detailed rule-book for departmental expenditure, *Managing Public Money (MPM)*, a 230-page tome most recently updated in 2023,[5] which forms the most basic element of a library of Treasury requirements and guidance on departmental finance. At the core of *MPM* are basic expenditure standards which officials with financial responsibilities must respect. At the turn of the century these were three: regularity, propriety, and value for money. Now there are four: respect for the principle of 'feasibility' appeared as an additional obligation in the 2013 version of *MPM*. These standards are seen as key to meeting parliamentary expectations as to the proper use of funds, along with the rules for reporting on departmental finances, likewise the domain of the Treasury.

1.2 Expenditure standards and Treasury supervision

In the remainder of this chapter we examine, in sections II–IV, each of the expenditure standards in turn, identifying its basis in legal rules, general accounting principles, and Treasury authority. We also show how the exercise of the Treasury's powers has affected the application of the standards, and how their operation has responded to the crises and challenges confronted by the executive in the current century. We continue (in section V) by looking at how they bear upon the relationship between Permanent Secretaries, as departmental accounting officers, and their ministers. Finally, we consider briefly in section VI whether this century has brought any significant changes in the operation of the external disciplines, parliamentary and judicial, that might support or otherwise affect the exercise of Treasury spending controls.

[4] Chapter 7, text at n 173.

[5] This is the successor to HM Treasury, *Government Accounting: A Guide on Accounting and Financial Procedures for the Use of Government Departments*, a loose-leaf compilation last updated in 1989.

II Expenditure Standards: Regularity

2.1 Introduction

MPM currently defines ***regularity*** as

> [t]he principle that resource consumption should be compliant with the relevant legislation and wider legal principles such as subsidy control and procurement law, delegated authorities and following the guidance in this document.[6]

This understanding of regularity has not changed since 1999. While legality (as expressed, for example, in the provisions of a Supply and Appropriation Act) provides its core, its scope is wider. Its content is now indicated by the Government Resources and Accounts Act 2000, which sets out the matters on which the Comptroller and Auditor General must seek to satisfy himself in relation to departmental accounts submitted to him:

(a) that the accounts present a true and fair view,
(b) that money provided by Parliament has been expended for the purposes intended by Parliament,
(c) that resources authorised by Parliament to be used have been used for the purposes in relation to which the use was authorised, and
(d) that—
(i) the financial transactions of the department, and
(ii) the financial transactions of any body that is a designated body under section 4A in relation to the department for the year in question,[7]

are in accordance with any relevant authority.[8]

The Comptroller and Auditor General reports to the House of Commons if he is not satisfied as to any of these matters.[9] 'Relevant authority' includes compliance not just with specific legislative requirements for Treasury consent, but also with general Treasury powers to consent to expenditure, as expressed in *MPM* itself, based on its 'ancient authority'.[10] Thus 'if resource accounts appear to the Comptroller and Auditor General to suggest that a material use of resources required but did not receive the authority of the Treasury', he is to inform the Treasury, which may give retrospective authorization, whereupon the use is to be treated as regular.[11]

Breach of legal rules may not always entail irregular expenditure. Departments are subject to general regulations, on matters like occupational health and safety and equal opportunities. They may breach such regulations, but this is unlikely to have a

[6] *MPM*, 225 (Glossary) 225. See also *MPM*, para 2.4.1 (box 2.4).

[7] These are the arm's length bodies (ALBs) sponsored by the department that were brought within the scope of departmental resource accounts as part of the alignment project (chapter 7, text at n 165).

[8] s 6 (1), as amended by Constitutional Reform and Governance Act 2010, s 43. This repealed and replaced Exchequer and Audit Departments Act 1921, s 1(1).

[9] s 6(3).

[10] *MPM*, paras 2.3.1–2.3.7.

[11] s 6(2).

material impact on the regularity of expenditure which supports the offending activities, because those regulations do not provide authority for financial transactions of the department. Other regulations—fixing the criteria for social security payments, for example—do provide such authority. Overpayments may thus be irregular; underpayments will not.

2.2 Estimates and Supply and Appropriation Acts

'Parliament', says the Treasury, 'looks to the Treasury to make sure that departments use their powers only as it has intended, and that revenue is raised, and the resources so raised spent, only within the agreed limits.'[12] Supervision of the estimates and appropriation process is thus a key element of the Treasury's concern with regularity. One effect of the alignment project has been that a department's budget totals (of the Departmental Expenditure Limit (DEL) and Annually Managed Expenditure (AME)) for the year derived from the Spending Review are now imported into its estimate and vote,[13] so that those totals, originally binding only within the executive, now form part of the financial order policed by the Comptroller and Auditor General.

Since 2003 Parliament passes two 'Supply and Appropriation' Acts each year. A Supply and Appropriation (Main Estimates) Act is passed near the end of each parliamentary session, normally in July, giving legal force to the estimates authorizing the majority of the government's spending in the current financial year (1 April to 31 March). A further Supply and Appropriation (Anticipation and Adjustments) Act is passed in February or March, appropriating the additional sums granted by the winter and spring supplementary estimates, retrospectively authorizing departmental expenditure in excess of estimates (Excess Votes), and also giving legislative force to the Vote on Account for the next financial year.[14] The content of these Acts, and of the estimates on which they are based, is controlled by the Treasury. This is both a corollary of its statutory power to determine the form of departmental accounts, now conferred by section 5(2) of the Government Resources and Accounts Act 2000 but supported by statute since 1866,[15] and a reflection of a still older parliamentary expectation, based on custom rather than any formal rules,[16] that it is for the Treasury, not the individual departments, to present the government's spending proposals.

While the alignment project, and other significant recent improvements in the information presented to Parliament through and alongside the estimates, may have made it easier for the House of Commons and its committees to call departments to

[12] *MPM*, para 1.4.1.

[13] Chapter 7, section 3.5.2.

[14] This Vote authorizes the proportion of that year's expenditure to be incurred between the beginning of the year in April and the approval of the Supply and Appropriation (Main Estimates) Act. The amount voted is generally based on a standard proportion (45%) of the amount so far voted for the corresponding services in the previous year; it does not, therefore, imply any decision as to the level of funding in the year to which it relates. For the background to the change, see Procedure Committee, *Estimates and Appropriations Procedure* (HC 2003–04, 393) para 8 and, in more detail, app 2, paras 28–32.

[15] Exchequer and Audit Departments Act 1866, s 23.

[16] Henry Roseveare, *The Treasury 1660–1870* (Allen and Unwin 1973) 68–74; Norman Chester, *The English Administrative System 1780–1870* (Clarendon Press 1981) 205–06.

account for their spending performance, it remains the case that only the Treasury is in a position to exercise *ex ante* control so as to ensure that departmental estimates are in line with their Spending Review allocations and, if not, whether the departures are justified. Estimates may be 'owned' by departments[17] but they are presented to Parliament by the Treasury, and the Treasury scrutiny that this entails is described in detail in its *Supply Estimates: A Guidance Manual*—which, for example, makes explicit the responsibility of Treasury spending teams to ensure that departmental estimates are 'taut and realistic'.[18]

In addition, Treasury control of the format of estimates and of the Supply and Appropriation Acts means that it determines the degree of legal constraint on spending imposed by these elements of the supply cycle. The estimates organize grants of expenditure into large blocks (Votes) which are then divided into smaller blocks (sections and sub-heads). Over the years the general tendency of change has been to concentrate authorization for supply expenditure into ever fewer and larger Votes and sub-heads, with the idea of making control less detailed but more meaningful in economic and policy terms. The number of Votes reached a peak in 1946, at 196; in 1996–97 there were 110; and over the period which interests us the number has further declined to stand in 2021 at 52—basically, one Vote for each department, including non-ministerial departments like HM Revenue and Customs and the Competition and Markets Authority, and a miscellany of other bodies including public service pension schemes.[19] Each Vote has a Part I that splits the total amount granted into resource and capital DEL and AME, indicates any non-budget expenditure (eg payments to be made under permanent authorities direct from the Consolidated Fund), and sets the total cash requirement for the department. It also includes a description of the activities to be funded from the Vote (the 'ambit'). Detailed guidance on how this description is to be written has been issued by the Treasury.[20] As part of the estimate, it is subject to Treasury approval.[21] The sums can be considerable: the total cash requirement for the Department for Work and Pensions in the 2020–21 estimates was £114.5bn, and the smallest component of its Vote was £175m for capital DEL. Only Part I is transposed to the corresponding Supply and Appropriation Act so as to have legislative effect.

A more detailed breakdown appears in Part II of each Vote, where the overall totals for resource and capital DEL and AME are broken down by reference both to the different activities under the Vote, each of which occupies a separate line and is referred to as a 'section', and to their components of administration expenditure (the running costs of the department or service) and programme expenditure (the costs of the programmes themselves), referred to as 'subheads'. For each of these kinds of expenditure, as well as capital expenditure, on a defined activity, Part II also shows a gross figure and a figure for any income received. All these Part II figures, while not given

[17] HM Treasury, *Supply Estimates: A Guidance Manual* (2011) para 6.33.

[18] See generally ibid Annex G (paras 6.31–6.41).

[19] Terence Daintith and Alan Page, *The Executive in the Constitution: Structure, Autonomy and Internal Control* (OUP 1999) 161; HM Treasury, *Central Government Supply Estimates 2020–21: Main Supply Estimates* (HC 2019–20, 293), which is the source for data referred to.

[20] HM Treasury, *Supply Estimates* (n 17) paras 3.8–3.12.

[21] para 1.28.

legal effect through incorporation in the Supply and Appropriation Act, are nonetheless binding in the sense that spending which exceeds them without authorization will be irregular and will need retrospective parliamentary authorization by way of an Excess Vote.

Since 2004, an additional support for accountability has been provided by accompanying each departmental estimate with an explanatory memorandum.[22] This was introduced as a requirement by the Treasury in response to parliamentary concerns about the usability of estimates information. According to the *Estimates Manual*, it should indicate the purpose and expected outcome of the planned spending, say what has changed since the last estimate, specify any efficiencies being achieved, and explain how the planned spending relates to the department's overall aims, priorities, and business plan.[23] After the Procedure Committee of the House of Commons expressed, in 2017, continuing dissatisfaction with estimates procedure and information, including the uneven quality of Estimates Memoranda,[24] the House of Commons Scrutiny Unit,[25] which had drafted this part of the *Manual*, produced a detailed critique of current practice, along with proposed new guidance.[26] This has not (yet) been incorporated into the Treasury's *Guidance Manual*, but departments are now presenting their memoranda according to the improved template that it offered.

Estimates procedure affords departments some flexibility to move resources within Part II of their Vote so that underspending in one area can be applied to relieve pressure in others, a practice known as *virement*, but only subject to Treasury rules or supervision. This is a form of control that has become less restrictive over the years. Spending has been concentrated into fewer and larger sections and sub-heads, and relaxations in 1996 and 2009 have enabled *virement*, without Treasury consent, between both sections and sub-heads.[27] Treasury consent is however still needed for certain *virements*, such as moving funds from programme to administration subheads (where it will only be granted if this does not increase the administration budget beyond that set in the department's Spending Review allocation); or moving funds into a new section not included within the last estimate approved by Parliament (but there can be no *virement* to support a function not covered by the ambit of the estimate, which has legislative force).[28] Likewise there can be no *virement* between the main headings in Part I: this would require a supplementary estimate to be reflected in a Supply and Appropriation (Anticipation and Adjustments) Act. The Treasury spending teams

[22] Memoranda and related correspondence can be found through <https://committees.parliament.uk/publications>.

[23] HM Treasury, *Supply Estimates* (n 17) Annex F, paras 6.19, 6.21.

[24] Procedure Committee, *Authorising Government Expenditure: Steps to More Effective Scrutiny* (HC 2016–17, 190) paras 103, 107.

[25] The Unit was established in 2002 to provide the House, through its Select Committees, with expert analysis and advice on government information for Parliament, in particular on draft bills and estimates material. See House of Commons Liaison Committee, *Annual Report for 2004* (HC 2004–05, 419) app 4, and the Unit's webpage at <www.parliament.uk/mps-lords-and-offices/offices/commons/scrutinyunit/>.

[26] Procedure Committee, *Review of Estimates Memoranda by the House of Commons Scrutiny Unit: Response to the Committee's Fifth Report of Session 2016–17* (HC 2017–19, 1156) app.

[27] See HM Treasury, *Alignment: (Clear Line of Sight) Project* (Cm 7567, March 2009), Annex G: Proposed new virement rules under alignment.

[28] HM Treasury, *Supply Estimates* (n 17) para 2.75.

operate these rules and provide any advice a department might seek on the propriety of *virement*.

Since the practice of *virement* makes for economy in the estimates, the Treasury does not view *virement* requests negatively, though they have to be supported by justification. However, even where a specific consent requirement does not apply, departments are warned by the Estimates Manual that *virement* is not allowed where the amount involved is significant in relation to the estimate as a whole; where the spending it supports might be viewed by Parliament as either novel or contentious; or where it would imply significant liabilities for further spending in future years.[29] Since the 1996 changes it is for departments themselves, rather than the Treasury, to judge if one of these prohibitions might apply. Misjudgement might, however, lead to irregularity.

2.3 Spending without appropriation: the Contingencies Fund

Unforeseen emergencies—like the Covid-19 pandemic—and other major events may call for government expenditure that falls outside the year's appropriations and that cannot await the approval of a supplementary estimate. Such expenditure will be irregular unless the department defrays it by seeking and obtaining an advance from the Contingencies Fund, under the supervision of the Treasury. The Fund was established by Treasury Minute in 1862, at the very beginning of the operation of the current system of parliamentary appropriation, and is currently supported by the Miscellaneous Financial Provisions Act 1946—which defines the circumstances in which it may be used—and the Contingencies Fund Act 1974—which defines its size. Neither Act, however, authorizes its creation or maintenance, and the legality of the operations of the Fund has been called into question—though not in recent years.[30] The Fund is used to make advances to a department for urgent expenditure ahead of the approval—or indeed, sometimes, the presentation—of the estimate or supplementary estimate that would ordinarily be needed to authorize it (or if there is no further opportunity to present a supplementary estimate during the year, of an Excess Vote included in the Supply and Appropriation (Anticipation and Adjustments) Act). These are strictly temporary advances, to be repaid from the relevant estimate or Vote once granted. The size of the Fund has had to be steadily increased over the years and in 1974 was fixed by reference to the level of authorized supply expenditure for the previous financial year. The Act limits the outstanding capital of the Fund to 2% of this figure.[31] That amount was sufficient to cope with the emergency spending entailed by the 2007–09 financial crisis. In 2008–09, the year of maximum government outlays to support banks and other institutions, the 2% limit gave the Fund a capital of £8.17bn. Over the year, the Fund disbursed £10.96bn to departments, but repayments within

[29] ibid para 2.73.

[30] For discussions up to 1988 see John F McEldowney, 'The Contingencies Fund and the Parliamentary Scrutiny of Public Finance' [1988] Public Law 232.

[31] Contingencies Fund Act 1974, s 1.

the year as supplementary estimates were approved meant that the capital limit was not breached.[32]

The detailed rules for the operation of the Fund are set out in the Treasury's *Estimates Manual*.[33] As resort to the Fund enables money to be spent without appropriation, those rules are strict, both as to how authorization is to be obtained and how Parliament is to be informed about resort to the Fund. Arrangements for approval and parliamentary information vary according to the nature of the call on the Fund. The *Manual* identifies six categories of request. The commonest is where a department has used up the cash granted in its main estimate and needs more to continue services in advance of the approval of a supplementary estimate. Another is where cash is needed for a service that is authorized by legislation, but for which no estimates provision has been made: here, payment can only be authorized by the senior Treasury official who is the Accounting Officer for the Fund.[34] The same is true of the most problematic category, to provide cash for an urgent service that requires specific legislative authorization which has not yet been given. The Treasury has said that such a use of the Fund is 'particularly exceptional', and that 'an advance from the Fund should never be made until the legislation has had a Second Reading in the House of Commons (i.e., there is a parliamentary expression of support for the principle of the Bill)'.[35] The Treasury will normally only accept a request to draw on the Fund after Parliament has been notified, by a note attached to the relevant estimate request, a written ministerial statement, or both, unless this is impracticable by reason of urgency or a parliamentary recess.[36]

When the Covid pandemic took hold in early 2020, the lessons of the previous crisis, notably the risk of inadequacy of the Contingencies Fund in the face of outsize emergency requirements, were taken on board. The main estimates to cover departmental spending in 2020–21 were not due to be passed until the summer, and the Vote on Account already approved was likely to fall short of departments' immediate emergency spending requirements by considerably more than the £10.7bn that would be available under the 2% limit. In addition, the constraints on behaviour that might be needed to control the virus created the risk that Parliament might not be in a position to pass the main 2020–21 estimates according to the planned timetable. Just before the end of the 2019–20 financial year, therefore, the government secured the passage of the Contingencies Fund Act 2020, raising the percentage from 2% to 50% with immediate effect, but only until 1 April 2021. Parliament was asked to expedite passage of the bill, which was debated only at second reading stage.[37] In the event the main

32 HM Treasury, *Contingencies Fund Account 2008–2009* (HC 2008–09, 892) 2.

33 HM Treasury, *Supply Estimates* (n 17) paras 5.5–5.33.

34 On the role and responsibilities of Accounting Officers, see below, section V.

35 HM Treasury, *Supply Estimates* (n 17) para 5.7 and box 5.A. For further information on management of the Fund see comments by its Accounting Officer in HM Treasury, *Contingencies Fund Account 2019–20* (HC 2019–21, 764) esp at 9: 'The Estimates Clerk, with authority delegated by me, or staff with authority delegated by the Estimates Clerk in the Treasury's Public Spending Group authorise most advances from the Contingencies Fund. I approve advances considered to be novel or contentious. The Treasury's Exchequer Funds and Accounts (EFA) Team administers the account.'

36 Detailed rules, including suggested forms of wording, are set out in paras 5.18–5.26.

37 HC Deb 24 March 2020, vol 674, cols 261–97. Later stages were taken in the Commons on the same day.

estimates were duly approved in July and the consequent appropriations given legal effect as from the beginning of the financial year by the Supply and Appropriation Act 2020. While requirements for emergency Covid-related spending before the end of the 2019–20 financial year were managed within the 2% limit then operative, the 2020–21 situation was very different. The Vote on Account was insufficient to sustain spending in several departments up to the passage of the Supply and Appropriation Act, and a number of new Covid-related services were initiated, together leading to published requests for cash from the Contingencies Fund up to that time amounting to £116.65bn, approximately half of the sum available as a result of the increase of the limit to 50%.[38] Over the year to March 2021, the Fund paid out over £210bn.[39]

The pandemic was still producing unusual spending needs at the time the 2020 Act was due to expire, and a further ad hoc enlargement of the fund for 2021–22 was accordingly authorized by the Contingencies Fund Act 2021. This time the stipulated ceiling was fixed at 12% of authorized supply expenditure (£104.95bn). Of this sum, £35.6bn was actually paid out.[40] The Opposition used the debate on the Act to propose an amendment requiring a report to Parliament on the nature of each Contingencies Fund request to the Treasury, by reference to the *Estimates Manual* categories. Although supported by the Chair of the Public Accounts Committee, this was rejected by the government as unnecessary in the light of existing requirements, notably the obligation on departments to notify Parliament of their requests.[41] A classification of the year's Fund expenditures by category and by department is provided in each year's Contingencies Fund Accounts, and since 2003 an increasing proportion of requests have been the subject of ministerial statements to Parliament, available through a search of Hansard. While some of these statements provide a bare minimum of information, others are detailed enough to provide some indication of the degree of rigour with which the Treasury applies its tests for access to the Fund, notably its definition of 'genuine urgency in the public interest':

> This public interest test cannot be met by reference to ministerial or official commitments having been made or to administrative convenience. Issues such as cost benefits, other efficiencies, health and safety, etc, are what count in this respect.[42]
>
> The Treasury judges applications for access to the Contingencies Fund cautiously and on their merits. It is important to note that neither political imperative nor ministerial preference is relevant to making this assessment.[43]

While one can agree that this test was easily passed by the request for funding for the government's energy price guarantee domestic scheme in November 2022,[44] it is

[38] This figure is calculated from ministerial statements to Parliament between the beginning of the financial year and the passage of the Supply and Appropriation Act. No additional requests notified by way of footnotes to estimates were found.

[39] See HC Deb 11 March 2021, vol 690, col 1024.

[40] HM Treasury, *Contingencies Fund Account 2021–22* (HC 2022–23, 329) 3.

[41] HC Deb 11 March 2021, vol 690, cols 1040, 1047–48, 1053–54.

[42] HM Treasury, *Supply Estimates: A Guidance Manual* (2011) para 5.10.

[43] *MPM*, Annex 2.4, para A2.4.12.

[44] Contingencies Fund Advance: Energy Price Guarantee (Domestic), HC Deb 30 November 2022, vol 723, col 39WS (HCWS328).

much harder to convince oneself of the presence of the relevant indicia of urgency in the Department of Education's request in September 2022 for £6.68m from the Fund to meet set-up costs for a new government-owned company which will 'support teachers in delivering excellent curriculum content as part of world-class lessons'.[45] In 2013, however, the Treasury did provide the House of Lords Constitution Committee with a list of cases in which requests for funds for use in relation to legislation still in progress were accepted, as well as examples of requests not proceeded with, apparently on the ground that the Treasury was not convinced of their urgency in the public interest.[46]

2.4 Treasury delegations and consents

Even if departmental expenditure is within its budgetary envelope as determined by the Spending Review, is within the limits set by its Vote and the relevant estimate subheads, and fits within the ambit provisions of Part I of its Vote, it may still be irregular if it is not covered by a Treasury delegation or consent.

Times have changed since Tony Benn, as Secretary of State for Industry, complained that 'I can't blow my nose without asking the Treasury'.[47] The basic principle of prior authorization, asserted by the 17th-century Treasury Commissioners, still appears in a prominent place in *MPM*: 'Departments must have Treasury consent before undertaking expenditure or making commitments which could lead to expenditure'.[48] But ever since a comprehensive system of management of government spending was initiated in the 1860s, the Treasury's constant preoccupation has been to define the expenditures on which to concentrate its efforts, excluding smaller and more routine expenditures by a system of delegations of spending discretion to departments, and identifying the expenditures whose significance or sensitivity is such that—whatever their size—they merit specific consideration by the Treasury. Developments since Tony Benn wrote, and in particular developments in this century, have both facilitated the enlargement of departmental spending delegations and restricted the need for individual Treasury consents—though, as we shall see, other changes may possibly leave Mr Benn's successors with the same feeling of being subject to onerous external constraints.

2.4.1 Delegations

The Treasury has always avoided any across-the-board system of spending delegation. Delegation ceilings reflect the spending profile of departments. Thus in 2013 the Ministry of Defence had a delegated limit of £100m, and the Foreign Office one of £15m.[49] In addition to the delegated limit below which consent is delegated to the

[45] Contingency Fund Application: Departmental Update, 719 HC Deb 5 September 2022, vol 719, col 9WS (HCWS277).

[46] Constitution Committee, *The Pre-emption of Parliament* (HL 2012–13, 183) evidence, HM Treasury, supplementary evidence, Annex 1.

[47] Tony Benn, *Against the Tide: Diaries 1973–76* (Arrow Books 1990) 328.

[48] *MPM* para 2.3.1 (box 2.2).

[49] HM Treasury, *Review of Financial Management in Government* (December 2013) para 2.3.

department,[50] and above which spending proposals still require specific Treasury consent, delegation arrangements may include objective criteria for exceptions requiring specific Treasury scrutiny or approval, or a sampling mechanism to allow specimen cases to be examined. Delegations are settled in detail with each department, and confirmed by a lengthy delegation letter, which may set limits by reference to different categories of expenditure.[51] In this process the Treasury, in coordination with the Cabinet Office, consider a range of factors: the nature and quality of departmental internal governance, capability and leadership; past limits and forecast expenditure; significant changes in departmental structure, size, spending or responsibility; and departmental financial management. The detail with which delegations are stipulated, and the review provisions they incorporate, mean that the system certainly does not amount to unsupervised departmental discretion within their delegation limits.[52] Moreover, the fact that delegations can be limited or withdrawn operates as a reinforcement for other controls, such as spending limits. Breach of a DEL limit or repeated applications by a department for funding from the Spending Review Reserve might lead the Chief Secretary to the Treasury to reduce its delegated authorities, as one of a number of possible sanctions envisaged for department actions that do not comply with spending control expectations.[53]

The operation of delegated authorities is also affected by the structure of departments, and, in particular, the degree to which their activities are carried on through executive agencies and other arm's length bodies, or consist in the administration of grants to other public bodies, such as non-departmental public bodies and local authorities, or the supervision of contracted-out services. Delegated authorities for these bodies and services are to be set out in delegation letters that are reviewed regularly and shared with the Treasury, and need Treasury consent if their limits do not fall within the department's own delegations.

2.4.2 Prior consent

Expenditures that are not covered by departmental delegated authorities must necessarily receive prior Treasury consent if they are to be regarded as 'regular'. Most of these expenditures are likely to be for major projects and programmes. Repeated experience of cost over-runs and project failure have led the Treasury to develop a detailed approvals process,[54] involving passage of the proposal through a number of checkpoints and the involvement, alongside Treasury and Cabinet Office teams, of the Infrastructure and Projects Authority (IPA) established within the Cabinet Office in 2016 to support departmental initiation and management of major projects with specialist expertise. IPA reports both to the Cabinet Office and to the Treasury. Its assessments of major departmental projects form an essential part of the Treasury's approval procedures, and its specialists are attached temporarily to departments at key stages in project development. Particularly complex programmes and projects

[50] Though subject now to any relevant Cabinet Office controls, this chapter section 2.4.3.
[51] For the form of the letter, which runs to 14 pages, see HM Treasury, *Template Delegated Authority Letter* (2023).
[52] See generally *MPM* Annex 2.2.
[53] HM Treasury, *Consolidated Budgeting Guidance 2023–2024* (March 2023) paras 2.96, 2.97.
[54] HM Treasury, *Treasury Approvals Process for Programmes and Projects* (March 2022).

with a multi-year life span will form part of the Government Major Projects Portfolio. Inclusion in the Portfolio, which is subject to intensified control and reporting, is determined by Treasury and Cabinet Office ministers, on the advice of the IPA. In 2023 there were 244 projects in the Portfolio with a total whole life cost of £805bn, being delivered by 21 departments and their arm's length bodies (ALBs).[55] These and some other projects must have a Senior Responsible Owner within the department with direct accountability to Parliament.[56]

The fact that a proposed expenditure falls within departmental delegated authority does not, however, automatically mean that prior Treasury consent need not be sought. The approvals process just described will also apply to a spending proposal which

> could create pressures leading to a breach in Departmental Expenditure Limits, administration cost limits, or Estimates provision;
>
> would entail contractual commitments to significant levels of spending in future years for which plans have not been set;
>
> could set a potentially expensive precedent;
>
> is novel, contentious, or could cause significant repercussions, posing risks to the public sector;
>
> requires primary legislation, or where Treasury consent is a statutory requirement.[57]

Managing Public Money offers some examples of spending in the 'novel, contentious or repercussive' category: ephemeral ex gratia payment schemes such as payments to compensate for official errors; extra statutory payments similar to but outside statutory schemes; unusual financial transactions, for example imposing lasting commitments or using tax avoidance; or unusual schemes or policies using novel techniques.[58] While this may give an impression that the range of sensitive expenditures is now a very small subset of overall spending, the general description of spending needing prior approval is however still couched in vague enough terms ('transactions which set precedents, are novel, contentious or could cause repercussions elsewhere in the public sector'[59]) to discourage any department from hazarding a unilateral interpretation of the consent requirement in preference to a frank exploration with its spending team of whether an approval might be necessary.

Until recently a further common basis for a requirement of Treasury consent was the insertion of an express provision to this effect in legislation. This was usually framed as a qualification of a ministerial power to incur expenditure, but might also be attached to powers to approve schemes under which moneys become payable to departments and other agencies, for example through levies and fees. The Treasury's ability to secure the insertion of such provisions is protected by the consultation

55 Infrastructure and Projects Authority, *Annual Report on Major Projects 2022–23* (2023).
56 Chapter 3, section 3.4.1.
57 HM Treasury, *Treasury Approvals Process for Programmes and Projects* (n 54) para 1.10 and box 1A.
58 *MPM* para 2.3.6 and box 2.3.
59 *MPM*, para 2.3.4.

requirements enjoined on departments by the Cabinet's procedures for scrutiny of legislative proposals,[60] and the fact that any bill requiring a money resolution or a ways and means resolution must be approved by the Chief Secretary to the Treasury.[61] Broadly speaking, the Treasury is to be consulted as part of the process of preparing any proposed legislation that authorizes public expenditure, borrowing, or the imposition of fees and charges, but inclusion of a Treasury consent provision in the legislation will normally only be required[62] where the relevant departmental is empowered to modify such financial arrangements—for example, by changing rates of grant or coverage of fees and charges. While the provisions in *MPM* to this effect have not changed since 1997, the number of new consent requirements has diminished substantially in recent years. There were 42 of them in legislation passed in 1996, on matters ranging from the Humber Bridge to schools inspection, but over the five years ending in 2022 we find only eight in total. The relative absence of new permanent legislation authorizing spending schemes may account for a part of this decline, but more important reasons may be the view now taken at the Office of Parliamentary Counsel that internal rules requiring one minister to consult another or to obtain Treasury consent are not matters of law that should be reflected on the face of primary legislation,[63] along with confidence that the Treasury interest is adequately protected by other controls, like those over major infrastructure projects noted above. Notice, however, that where the Treasury does obtain the insertion of a consent provision in legislation, proceeding without it will be unlawful, not simply irregular, and the defect cannot be repaired by giving a ministerial direction.[64]

2.4.3 Cabinet Office controls

Any movement since 1998 towards more light-handed central regulation of spending was abruptly reversed when the Coalition government came into office in 2010 on a platform of reduction of public expenditure. Departments found themselves subjected to a new and onerous set of requirements for prior consent to certain kinds of spending. These were not concerned with the major projects or with the exotica identified by *MPM*, but with bread-and-butter items like advertising, commercial contracts, leases, facilities management, digital services, and consultancy. The controls, most of which were still in operation in 2024,[65] focus on expenditure exceeding certain thresholds: currently, for example £100,000 per annum for any advertising, marketing, and communications campaign; £500,000 for a firm lease commitment or freehold; £10m for commercial contract commitments (or £20m if the project is part of a departmental 'pipeline'—see below). These controls are not operated by the

[60] Described generally, chapter 10, section 1.2, and see *MPM*, Annex 2.2 para A2.2.1 for the Treasury's own statement of the position.

[61] Cabinet Office, *Guide to Making Legislation* (July 2017), paras 19.5, 19.6. See also *Cabinet Manual: A Guide to Laws, Conventions and Rules on the Operation of Government* (October 2011) para 4.32.

[62] Exceptions still occur: see eg Energy Act 2023, s 287 (financial assistance to companies to achieve fuel sector resilience).

[63] Discussed further in chapter 10, text at nn 44–50.

[64] On directions see further this chapter, section IV.

[65] The control on consultancy spending was removed in February 2023.

Treasury, but by the Cabinet Office under a Treasury delegation.[66] Lord Maude, who as Minister for the Cabinet Office introduced these controls, explained this choice:

> [F]inance ministries the world over tend to look at what the budget is for a particular spending entity—ministry, Department, agency, whatever—and if a particular piece of expenditure comes within a particular budget line, then it gets a tick and is okay ... [T]he Treasury ... does not have the capability [to run spending controls] and it is not its culture. As I say, the Treasury's culture is, 'We set a budget. We let Departments get on with it.'[67]

While the general trend of Treasury policy over our period has indeed been to move away from detailed control, it seems unlikely that it would have endorsed this reductionist view of the work of its spending teams. In fact the operation of the controls, at least in their first years when they were managed by the Efficiency and Reform Group (ERG) in the Cabinet Office,[68] were the source of considerable friction between Cabinet Office and Treasury. One reason was that ERG and the spending teams often found themselves examining the same departmental proposals. Another was the profound contrast between Treasury and Cabinet Office approaches to control. Internal Treasury documents criticized ERG's approach as narrow and counterproductive, and argued for a more strategic risk- or capability-based approach to the controls and for incentivizing departments to 'take ownership' of the agenda.[69] Maude's view, as the responsible minister, was (and remains) exactly the opposite. For him, spend controls represent a deliberate incursion into the operational independence of departments: 'the ability of the centre to tell departments how they can and can't spend money ... is at the heart of what spend controls were set up to do.' But under our constitution the centre—in the shape of the Cabinet Office—has no ability to tell departments how they can and can't spend money. For this, the authority of the Treasury is needed, and the controls are operated by the Cabinet Office as its delegate. Departments are warned that breaches of the controls are serious and may be considered as irregular spend, with the exposure to censure by the Comptroller and Auditor General and Public Accounts Committee that might flow from this. No such sanctions are available to the Cabinet Office.

It was widely assumed when the controls were introduced that they would be temporary. To quote Lord Maude again:

> Nobody believed when we introduced the spend controls that they would continue. It was meant to be a bit of tokenism. I think the way David Laws put it—he was Chief Secretary when we introduced it—is that it was to send a shockwave through the system, but then everyone assumed that we would pack up because, as we know,

[66] See generally Cabinet Office, *Cabinet Office Controls*, at <www.gov.uk/government/collections/cabinet-office-controls>.

[67] Public Administration and Constitutional Affairs Committee, *The Work of the Cabinet Office* (HC 2019–21, 118) oral evidence session, 12 January 2021, qq 629, 636.

[68] Above, chapter 2, sections 2.2.1, 3.4.8. ERG was wound up in 2014.

[69] Referenced in Christopher Hood and others, *The Way the Money Goes: The Fiscal Constitution and Public Spending in the UK* (OUP 2023) 103–05.

> politicians have short attention spans and they get bored and move on to something else.[70]

In fact the controls were put on a continuing basis in July 2012. The document introducing the government's functional programme in 2015 claimed that the controls had served to stop wasteful spending, to implement cross-government strategies, and to facilitate more joined-up delivery of public services, and that they had 'helped' to deliver a significant proportion of the government's efficiency and reform savings.[71] They could be seen as the cutting edge of the programme. In the early phases of the programme Cabinet Office sought to use it as a vehicle for advancing specific policies across government in particular control areas, with a focus on reduction of spending. Up to 2023, for example, its *Guidance: Advertising, marketing and communications spend controls* stated that advertising expenditure would only be approved

> where government has a legal duty to provide people with information, such as changes to legislation or public services; where marketing and advertising is critical to the effective running of the government; and where there is robust evidence that marketing and advertising delivers measurable outcomes that meet government objectives.[72]

These restrictive criteria have now been replaced by the less demanding requirement that such expenditure be 'cost-effective, coordinated and reflect functional standards and professional best practices'.[73] On the same lines, property spending was subject to a policy requiring organizations to exit leased properties as break options and expiries occurred, unless operational necessity was demonstrated.[74] Today the controls are designed to support more general objectives whose expression varies from area to area but which have a common focus on value for money, cooperation across government, and more strategic and rigorous decision-making.

The effectiveness of the controls has also, Lord Maude has alleged, been impaired by a decline in departmental compliance.

> Inevitably, over time, any organisation learns to game a control system of this type. This has plainly happened with the Cabinet Office controls. Submissions are sometimes made after the spend has been committed; there are late requests, which makes it exceptionally hard for a minister to refuse; and there are examples of projects that are sliced up and therefore escape scrutiny.'[75]

[70] Public Administration and Constitutional Affairs Committee (n 67) q 640.

[71] Cabinet Office, *The Functional Model: A Model for More Efficient and Effective Government* (March 2015).

[72] Cabinet Office, *Guidance: Advertising, Marketing and Communications Spend Controls* (9 April 2014): this text is no longer visible on gov.uk.

[73] Cabinet Office, *Guidance: Advertising, Marketing and Communications Spend Controls* (5 January 2023) para 1. See further chapter 12, section 3.2.

[74] Cabinet Office, *Guidance: Property Spend Controls* (25 April 2019). This element no longer figures in the current control arrangements.

[75] Lord Maude of Horsham, *Review of the Cross-cutting Functions and the Operation of Spend Controls* (July 2021) 33.

If we remember that the Treasury told the Public Accounts Committee in 1997 that 'departments . . . tend to regard Treasury involvement in less important decisions as unnecessary meddling',[76] it seems unlikely that they would view Cabinet Office involvement any differently. The 2015 assessment perhaps acknowledged this feeling in stressing that 'the emphasis of the programme was shifting from spending controls to more positive standards and frameworks of delegation operating along a functional axis'.[77] As we have seen, the development of professional functions within government has been a major priority in recent years and has significantly influenced expenditure decision-making, and in two areas where centralized functional capacity is highly developed, commercial and digital/technology spend, central approvals for individual commitments have been replaced by a process of departmental and central assessment and review of a so-called 'pipeline' of contract commitments of the relevant size planned to be entered into over a defined period.[78] But it was stated in 2015 that 'spending controls [would] remain in place until the government builds the necessary capability, standards, behaviours and governance within the functions'.[79] Apparently this has yet to happen. In the Declaration on Government Reform, the Prime Minister and Cabinet Secretary undertook to require all departments to meet clear standards set by the functions, 'backed up by strict adherence to spending controls'.[80] The controls, however, do not cover the full range of functional requirements, and the expedient actually adopted was to treat *MPM* as 'mandating' adherence to the standards and then to revise it accordingly.[81]

2.4.4 Transparency

At much the same time as these tighter controls were introduced, the government also imposed on departments and on the great majority of ALBs a further obligation, to publish all items of expenditure over £25,000, in order to allow government to be held to account and to drive down costs. Compliance with this obligation is supervised directly by the Treasury, rather than the Cabinet Office, and is the subject of Treasury guidance detailing, among other things, the items that may be withheld or redacted on grounds of national security, personal security, foreign relations, or legal prohibitions such as the Data Protection Act. Departments are advised to use the Freedom of Information (FOI) Act rules as a guideline, and are warned that '[t]he credibility of transparency reporting would be seriously undermined if expenditures redacted for the purposes of £25k transparency were subsequently published under FOI'.[82]

[76] Public Accounts Committee, written evidence, Treasury Memorandum 97–98/35, para 17 (n 2).
[77] Cabinet Office, *The Functional Model* (n 71).
[78] For details of how this works, see Cabinet Office, *Guidance: Digital and Technology Spend Controls (Version 5)* (21 July 2023; *Commercial Spend Controls (Version 7)* (1 February 2023).
[79] Cabinet Office, *The Functional Model* (n 71).
[80] *Declaration on Government Reform* (June 2021) 6.
[81] See chapter 2, section 3.3.5, and references at chapter 13 (n 50).
[82] HM Treasury, *Guidance for Publishing Spend Over £25000* (November 2017) para 2.14. FOI is discussed in chapter 11, section III.

III Expenditure Standards: Propriety

3.1 A broadening concept

MPM now offers a significantly broader conception of the notion of ***propriety*** than that contained in *Government Accounting*, which referred only to dealing with expenditure and receipts in accordance with parliamentary intentions and principles of parliamentary control.[83] As explained in *The Executive in the Constitution*,[84] until the end of last century the key application of 'propriety', as something distinct from 'regularity', was to determine the circumstances in which expenditure could properly be incurred on the basis of the Supply and Appropriation Acts alone, without the support of, or in anticipation of, specific permanent legislation. While it is of continuing importance to the preservation of both parliamentary accountability and legal certainty, this issue has become submerged in the serious and more general concerns about probity in public life that prompted the appointment of the Nolan Committee and its promulgation of 'seven principles of public life' (selflessness, integrity, objectivity, accountability, openness, honesty, and leadership).[85] Adoption of these principles as central to public financial operations has led to a definition of propriety as

> [t]he principle that patterns of resource consumption should meet high standards of public conduct and robust governance and respect Parliament's intentions, conventions and control procedures, including any laid down by the P[ublic] A[ccounts] C[ommittee].[86]

Parliament's intentions must be taken to include that 'funds should be managed with impartiality, honesty, the avoidance of personal gain, waste, and extravagance'.[87] This wider concept of propriety overlaps largely with concepts of good public governance, and addresses patterns of expenditure as well as individual decisions.

It would be worrying if this broader concept of propriety needed to be regularly invoked to guide the behaviour of government officials. It appears, from published information on accounting officers' requests for ministerial directions to engage in spending which they feel may not satisfy one or more of the basic expenditure standards,[88] that most of the invocations of the propriety standard continue to address the issue of spending in anticipation of the passage of legislation.

[83] para 6.2.14.
[84] Daintith and Page (n 19) 173–74.
[85] Committee on Standards in Public Life, *Standards in Public Life: First Report* (Cm 2850, 1995) 14.
[86] *MPM*, 224–25 (Glossary). See also *MPM*, 15 (box 2.4).
[87] Treasury Officer of Accounts, *Regularity, Propriety and Value for Money* (November 2004) para 5.10. This document has been withdrawn because the examples in it, drawn from a 1993 Public Accounts Committee report, *The Proper Conduct of Public Business* (HC 1993–94, 154), were seen as outdated, but its elaboration of Parliament's intentions still seems sound. Proposals for applying the Nolan Principles to arm's length bodies were set out in Cabinet Office and HM Treasury, *Spending Public Money: Governance and Audit Issues* (Cm 3179, March 1996).
[88] Discussed in section V.

3.2 Propriety and the form of legislative authority

3.2.1 The 'Concordat'

In any event, the core meaning of 'propriety' continues to have a constitutional significance that exceeds the impact of any recent enlargement, in that it embodies the criterion determining what legislative authority is needed for departmental spending. Its source is not an historic judicial decision, nor a legislative statement of principle, but rather one of those mysterious 'understandings' that crop up from time to time in UK constitutional organization. This is the 1932 'Concordat' between the Treasury and the House of Commons Public Accounts Committee. Technically this is no more than one of the regular exchanges between the Committee and the Treasury, taking the form of a Committee recommendation and a Treasury Minute in response, but it is one to which particular weight was attached at the time because it was seen as settling a very long-running issue between the Committee (and the Comptroller and Auditor General) and the government.[89] It sets out their shared understanding of the criteria which should determine when a department should bring forward legislation to support and regulate the provision of a new public service or function, as opposed to relying on the minister's common law powers and the financing of the service on an annual basis by means of provision in the Appropriation Act. In the language of the Treasury Minute:

> [P]ractice should normally accord with the view expressed by the Committee that, where it is desired that continuing functions should be exercised by a government department (particularly where such functions involve financial liabilities extending beyond a given year) it is proper that the powers and duties to be exercised should be defined by specific statute. The Treasury will, for their part, continue to aim at the observance of this principle.[90]

The wording is anodyne, but it is hard to overestimate the importance of this statement. We regard parliamentary sovereignty as perhaps the most basic principle of our constitution, but this is a rule that operates to determine whether, in cases that do not involve modification of existing legal rights and duties, Parliament actually gets to exercise it.

The translation of the Concordat's principles into operational rules is to be found in *MPM*, which sets out the exceptions to the basic rule that expenditure must be supported by permanent legislation. These are:[91]

> routine matters covered by common law (such as routine administration costs, purchase contracts, and prerogative spending);
>
> projects or services which are modest or temporary.[92]

[89] For some references to the historical background see Terence Daintith, 'The Legal Effects of the Appropriation Act' [1998] Public Law 552, 553, and *MPM*, Annex 2.3.

[90] *MPM*, Annex 2.3, para A2.3.6.

[91] *MPM*, paras 2.5.3, 2.5.4.

[92] *MPM*, para 2.5.3 also mentions Consolidated Fund standing services as an exception, which seems unnecessary as permanent charges on the Consolidated Fund all have their origins in permanent legislation: see eg Administration of Justice Act 1973, s 9(5).

This latter category may cover *either* services or initiatives lasting no more than two years, such as a pilot study or one-off intervention, *or* expenditure of no more than £1.75m a year, provided that there is no specific legislation covering these matters before Parliament and existing statutory restrictions are respected. Use of either of these exceptions requires prior Treasury consent.[93] Under these rules the Treasury agreed (one assumes) to a non-statutory scheme for payments to civilian internees in Japan in World War II which was estimated to cost £167m, involving one-off payments of £10,000 to an estimated 16,700 people.[94] By contrast, a proposal to make loans to Ireland with a limit of £3.25bn over a period of five years was made the subject of specific legislation.[95]

A further exception is provided by the so-called 'new services' rules, under which departments may in certain circumstances draw on the Contingencies Fund to defray expenditure on such services in anticipation of getting the necessary permanent legislation through Parliament—for example for the purpose of hiring a chief executive-designate for a new ALB—where the expenditure does not fit within the other exceptions. Parliament is particularly anxious about such spending by reason of the risk that it pre-empts, or could be seen to pre-empt, consideration of the content of the legislation.[96] Treasury rules for such use of the Contingencies Fund are consequently highly restrictive.[97]

What might happen in the event of a serious difference of opinion between Treasury and department as to the availability of an exception to the general requirement for legislation is far from clear. In the general scheme of *MPM*, proceeding without Treasury consent in a case where it is required—as with the 'modest or temporary' category above—would entail possible breach of the regularity as well as of the propriety standard, 'regularity' being defined as 'compliant with the relevant legislation . . . , delegated authorities and following the guidance in this document'.[98] A determined minister might well be prepared to accept such risks, but if the proposal is sufficiently novel reliance on the Supply and Appropriation Act might also require a change in the description of the purposes of the expenditure it covers contained in the so-called 'ambit' of the departmental Vote; this too would require the approval of the Treasury.[99] The likeliest outcome might be settlement of the matter at Cabinet level.[100]

[93] *MPM*, para 2.5.4 (box 2.6).

[94] See *R (on the application of Association of British Civilian Internees (Far East Region)) v Secretary of State for Defence* [2002] EWCA Civ 473 [15].

[95] Loans to Ireland Act 2010. Such government bills, introduced with the principal or sole purpose of giving effect to this rule, are sometimes referred to as 'Concordat' or 'Baldwin Convention' bills: Erskine May, *Treatise on The Law, Privileges, Proceedings and Usage of Parliament* (25th edn, 2019) para 33.11.

[96] Constitution Committee (n 46) paras 10–48.

[97] See text at n 54, and in relation to the specific case of anticipating the passage of legislation, *MPM*, Annex 2.4, box A2.4D.

[98] *MPM*, box 2.4 and para 2.4.5.

[99] HM Treasury (nn 20, 21).

[100] And see *Cabinet Manual* (2011) para 4.32, under which Treasury consent is normally needed to bring forward proposals with expenditure implications: a rule formerly stipulated in the Ministerial Code (see for example the Blair government's Code (1997), printed in Amy Baker, *Prime Ministers and the Rule Book* (Politico's 2000) 149–92, para 10).

3.2.2 Forms of specific legislative authorization

The requirement for permanent legislation means that the department must win a place for it in the government's legislative programme—which may constitute a significant hurdle[101]—and ensures that Parliament has the opportunity for substantive debate on the policy. It does not necessarily lead to legislative expression of details of the expenditure scheme, such as would represent a serious constraint on the department's spending discretion. The legislation may be confined to authorizing expenditure for a defined purpose, with little or nothing by way of qualification or conditions save a reporting obligation and a requirement for Treasury consent.[102] While the extraordinary sums disbursed by government during the Covid-19 pandemic were often payable under existing powers, like those in the Industrial Development Act 1982, billions were distributed on behalf of the Treasury by Her Majesty's Revenue and Customs, under section 76 of the Coronavirus Act 2020, which was worded with striking economy:

> Her Majesty's Revenue and Customs are to have such functions as the Treasury may direct in relation to coronavirus or coronavirus disease.

The directions to HMRC under this power, published in the Gazette, required them to be responsible for the payment and management of amounts to be paid under the Job Retention Scheme (April 2020), the Self-Employment Income Support Scheme (May 2020), and the Eat Out to Help Out Scheme (July 2020), and subsequent renewals and extensions.[103] Schedules to the directions set out in detail the conditions of eligibility for payments. Neither the Act nor the directions say anything about the total amounts to be spent in this way, but there is nothing unusual in this: unless permanent spending legislation charges payments directly on the Consolidated Fund, payments under it may only be made on the authority, and within the limits, of the annual Appropriation Act.

At least the need to mount these schemes produced a specific—if hardly constraining—legislative authority. Elsewhere the existence of broad and long-standing permanent expenditure powers may mean that while the Concordat is a useful control instrument in the Treasury's armoury, it provides little or no assurance of parliamentary involvement in major spending decisions of the sort that a requirement of permanent legislative authority might be assumed to secure. In 2021, for example, the government unveiled its Net Zero Strategy,[104] in pursuance of Parliament's instruction, in the Climate Change Act 2008, to prepare and present proposals for meeting the carbon budgets set under the Act.[105] This relies heavily on government assistance and investment as an incentive for the private investment needed to move the economy away from carbon. The size of the funds being set up for specific purposes within the Strategy, like the Future Nuclear Enabling Fund (£120m), the Industrial

[101] On legislative programming see further chapter 10, section 1.1.

[102] See eg the High Speed Rail (Preparation) Act 2013.

[103] Coronavirus directions published in the Gazette are collected at <www.thegazette.co.uk/coronavirus-notices/>.

[104] HM Government, *Net Zero Strategy: Build Back Greener* (October 2021).

[105] ss 13, 14.

Energy Transformation Fund (£315m), the Boiler Upgrade Scheme (£450m), and many others, dwarfs the thresholds for the requirement of permanent legislation under the Concordat and *MPM*. Only in one or two cases where specific new legislation is projected, however, does the Net Zero Strategy documentation make any reference to the permanent legislation that presumably underpins these commitments. The relevant authority is to be found in general legislation like the Science and Technology Act 1965 (for the vast majority of spend),[106] the Public Contracts Regulations 2015 (for support services and procurement of research),[107] and the Higher Education Research Act 2017 (where UK Research and Innovation, the umbrella body for the UK Research Councils. is the delivery partner).[108] Equipped with such general and permanent powers to distribute public largesse across wide swathes of the economy, government is unlikely to need to frame its many schemes, funds, and competitions for finance in new permanent legislation and to offer Parliament the opportunities for detailed examination that that may entail.[109]

Despite the Concordat and the steady increase in the transparency of governmental decision-making in this century, the question of what legislative authority supports the government's many major spending schemes is shrouded in mystery. To check respect for the Concordat, the Treasury requires only that departments provide a note in their estimate of any planned expenditure that is supported by the Supply and Appropriation Acts alone.[110] There is no positive requirement to identify the legislation that supports all other expenditure. The relevant supervisory bodies seem unconcerned by this. The Treasury discourages departments from referring in the ambit of their estimates to the legislative basis of items it contains;[111] the House of Commons Scrutiny Unit has not suggested that this information should figure in Estimates Memoranda; and neither the Public Accounts Committee nor the Comptroller and Auditor General has drawn attention to the question. A step towards remedying the omission has however been provided by the practice adopted since 2017 of publishing

[106] See s 5(1): 'The Secretary of State . . . may defray out of moneys provided by Parliament any expenses which, with the consent of the Treasury, they may respectively incur—

(a) in carrying on or supporting scientific research or the dissemination of the results of scientific research;
(b) in furthering the practical application of the results of scientific research; . . .'

[107] SI 2015/102.

[108] s 101 of the Act provides for grants to UK Research and Innovation 'of such amounts, and subject to such terms and conditions, as the Secretary of State considers appropriate'.

[109] For an example of slightly more restrictive terminology see Industrial Development Act 1982, s 8: 'For the purposes set out in subsection (2) of section 7 above the Secretary of State may, with the consent of the Treasury, provide financial assistance where, in his opinion—

(a) the financial assistance is likely to benefit the economy of the United Kingdom, or of any part or area of the United Kingdom; and
(b) it is in the national interest that the financial assistance should be provided on the scale, and in the form and manner, proposed; and
(c) the financial assistance cannot, or cannot appropriately, be so provided otherwise than by the Secretary of State': s 8(1).

The purposes in s 7(2) are broad and include promoting the development, modernization, or efficiency of an industry.

[110] HM Treasury, *Supply Estimates* (n 17) para 1.12.

[111] ibid para 3.12.

summaries of the assessments of compliance with the key expenditure standards of regularity, propriety, value for money, and feasibility that Accounting Officers prepare.[112] Such assessments are required to be produced for all projects or programmes forming part of the Government Major Projects Portfolio (GMPP), which means that major grant programmes, at least, are likely to be covered. Some, but not all, of these summaries identify the legislation supporting the programme as a way of providing evidence of its regularity; others simply assert the Accounting Officer's satisfaction that adequate legislative cover exists.

3.3 Propriety and the effect of the Supply and Appropriation Act

The complaints of the Public Accounts Committee that produced the Concordat were based not only on the absence, in certain cases, of permanent legislation to support continuing spending, but also on the practice of using the Appropriation Act to override spending restrictions in existing permanent legislation. On this latter point, Committee and Treasury agreed that while it was

> competent to Parliament, by means of an annual vote embodied in the Appropriation Acts, in effect to extend powers specifically limited by statute, constitutional propriety requires that such extensions should be regularised at the earliest possible date by amending legislation, unless they are of a purely emergency or noncontinuing character.[113]

This statement continues to appear in *MPM*, but the government's approach to several recent cases in which expenditure decisions were challenged by judicial review raises doubts about whether this possibility of extension has any practical significance. The question of the relation between an Appropriation Act provision and permanent spending legislation is one not only of propriety but also of law, and the leading judicial authority is hostile to the notion of implied repeal of spending restrictions by an Appropriation Act. In the New Zealand case of *Auckland Harbour Board v R*, an Appropriation Act provision was claimed to override a condition attached by an Act of 1912 to a payment to the Harbour Board. Though the condition had not been satisfied, the money had been paid by the government under a subsequent Appropriation Act, with the endorsement of the Comptroller and Auditor General, but it later changed its mind and came to court to get it back. The Privy Council dealt with the relationship between the two Acts in a single but telling sentence: 'Their Lordships . . . are unable to agree . . . that there is evidence of any later appropriation made by Parliament which dispensed with the condition imposed in 1912.'[114] An Appropriation Act override, in other words, would need to be in express terms in order to be effective.

[112] For details see text at nn 154–56.
[113] *MPM*, Annex 2.3, paras A2.3.4, A2.3.6.
[114] [1924] AC 318 (PC) 326. See further Charles Mitchell, 'Recovery of Ultra Vires Payments by Public Bodies' [2010] Public Law 747, 756–63, and for a similarly restrictive Australian authority, *Fisher v R* (1901) 26 Victoria LR 781; sustained on appeal in *R v Fisher* [1903] AC 158 (PC).

In recent years the government's approach appears to have been one of maintaining the assumption underlying the Concordat while trying to avoid giving the courts any occasion to rule in a way that might restrict the effect of the Appropriation Act. In the *Pergau Dam* case in 1995[115] counsel for the Crown apparently did not even think it worthwhile to argue that the coverage of the disputed payment in the Overseas Development Administration Vote under the Appropriation Act might 'override' the restrictions which the court, to the Administration's surprise, found to inhere in section 1(1) of the Overseas Development and Co-operation Act 1980. Yet after the decision, it proceeded on this basis. Examination of the aid budget disclosed two other continuing projects which might, in terms of the court's decision, be *ultra vires* the 1980 Act, and which could not be funded under other permanent legislation. Since funding was not expected to be needed beyond 1997–98,

> [t]o provide statutory authority for this expenditure in 1994–95 and in subsequent years the Administration chose to introduce a new sub-head in a Supplementary Estimate and seek Parliamentary approval to extend the ambit of the External Assistance Vote through the Appropriation Act. The Administration's legal advice was that this would be an acceptable course of action provided that Parliament was clearly informed in advance of what it was being asked to approve.[116]

In other words, the Appropriation Act's broader definition of lawful expenditure was used to override, for the continuing duration of these projects, the 1980 Act's narrower one. The government's legal advice was not tested by further judicial review.

The government took similar evasive action in the *Fire Brigades Union* case,[117] in which the House of Lords found it to be unlawful for the Home Secretary to bring forward a new scheme for criminal injuries compensation under common law powers, supported like the old scheme by the Appropriation Act alone, at a time when a statutory scheme had been enacted, but not yet brought into force. Lord Justice Hobhouse pointed out at some length in the Court of Appeal, that the new, allegedly unlawful scheme had been funded by a Vote in the Appropriation Act 1994, based on an estimate explicitly referring to that scheme,[118] but the House dismissed this argument on the basis of a concession by the Lord Advocate, who led the argument for the government. He accepted that if the decision to introduce the tariff scheme was unlawful, the fact that Parliament had voted funds for it in the Appropriation Act could not cure the invalidity. This approach, identifying the validity of proceeding on a non-statutory basis as the primary issue, and treating the Appropriation Act as relating purely to the availability of funds, has been confirmed by later decisions and dicta.

[115] *R v Secretary of State for Foreign Affairs, ex p World Development Movement Ltd* [1995] 1 WLR 386, [1995] 1 All ER 611.

[116] Comptroller and Auditor General, *Report, in Appropriation Accounts 1993–94, Vol 2 Class II—Foreign and Commonwealth Office* (HC 1994–95, 100-II) para 34.

[117] *R v Secretary of State for the Home Department, ex p Fire Brigades Union* [1995] 2 All ER 243 (HL), [1995] 1 All ER 887 (CA).

[118] [1995] 1 All ER 887, 903–06.

Fire Brigades Union is an early example showing claimants exploiting the extension, to the executive's common law or prerogative powers,[119] of the general grounds of judicial review, for the purpose of challenging their treatment under non-statutory payment schemes.[120] If payments are not to be irregular, such a scheme requires both Appropriation Act cover and possibly prior Treasury approval also: 'extra statutory payments similar to but outside statutory schemes' is the first of the examples given in *MPM* of expenditure that always requires Treasury consent.[121] Some bold claimants, pointing to the similarity of their situation to that of persons covered by a statutory scheme that excluded them, have indeed recently asserted a right to such payments, on grounds such as discrimination contrary to the Human Rights Act 1998, irrationality, and the equalities obligation.[122] Viewed through the lens of the Concordat, it might appear that if such payments could be covered by the ambit of a Vote in the Appropriation Act, the restrictive provisions in the permanent legislation would thereby suffer a temporary implied repeal, clearing the way for payment to the claimants. This however ignores the need, recognized by *MPM*, for the minister to point to common law or prerogative powers that support any action of his that is without legislative authority.[123] This, rather than the possible effect of the Appropriation Act, has been the primary issue to which the courts have addressed themselves. In the *Hooper* case, the Court of Appeal unanimously held that the purported use of common law powers to make payments to persons that Parliament had plainly intended to exclude would be an abuse of power and unlawful, and that this would be so even if Parliament had authorized the issue of funds for that purpose in an Appropriation Act.[124] Two members of the House of Lords agreed with the first of these propositions;[125] the other three held that it was not necessary to express a view on this point in order to decide the case. The Court in *CC's* case decided, on the same basis as in *Hooper*, that the Secretary of State had no power at common law to make the payment sought by the claimant. The claimant here had invoked *MPM* and the Concordat, presumably to support in some way an extension of the minister's powers, but the Court responded:

> The Concordat does not purport to describe the existence of any executive power, but only to describe circumstances in which public funds will be available to meet the cost of the exercise of the executive powers which are otherwise available. Thus, neither the Treasury document nor the Concordat provides a source of power that

119 Following *Council of Civil Service Unions v Minister for the Civil Service* [1985] AC 374.

120 See eg *R (on the application of Association of British Civilian Internees (Far East Region)) v Secretary of State for Defence* [2002] EWCA Civ 473 (allegation of irrational operation of scheme of *ex gratia* payments for civilian internees in Japan in World War II).

121 para 2.3.4, box 2.3.

122 *R (on the application of Hooper) v Secretary of State for Work and Pensions* [2005] UKHL 29, [2005] 1 WLR 1681, [2006] 1 All ER 487; *R (on the application of CC) v HM Treasury and Secretary of State for Work and Pensions* [2020] EWHC Admin 2817.

123 *MPM*, para 2.5.3 (box 2.5).

124 *R (on the application of Hooper) v Secretary of State for Work and Pensions* [2002] EWCA Civ 813 [133]–[134].

125 [2005] UKHL 29 [95] (Lord Scott); [123] (Lord Brown) ('an obvious abuse of power'). Of the other three judges, Lord Nicholls explicitly reserved any ruling on this issue [6]; Lord Hoffman, at [46]–[47], felt the contrary argument had 'a good deal of force'; while Lord Hope appears to have assumed the existence of a common law power to make payments.

would enable the Secretary of State (or for that matter the Treasury) to make the payment claimed by the Claimant.[126]

This *Fire Brigades* line of cases appears to have been ignored by those who advised the Permanent Secretary and the Secretary of State at the Department for Work and Pensions when in 2021 it became apparent that the benefit of payments from certain schemes for compensating victims of institutional sexual abuse would effectively be lost if they were taken into account in calculating means-tested benefits. The department planned to introduce new regulations to change scheme rules so as to avoid this in January 2022, but wanted also to leave out of account payments already made. This involved a breach of propriety, because Parliament would not have had an opportunity to consider the proposed disregard, and because reliance could not be placed on the Supply and Appropriation Act alone—among other reasons, because current regulations made it clear that, unless specifically disregarded, compensation payments must be treated as part of a benefit claimant's capital. The Permanent Secretary therefore invited the minister to direct him to disregard the payments in the relevant benefits calculations by relying on her common law powers; and this is what she duly did.[127] But if the views of the majority of the judges who ruled in the *Hooper* and *CC* cases were to be applied, this represented an unlawful use of power; and as *MPM* makes clear, 'a direction does not permit unlawful action and does not protect against a court finding unlawfulness.'[128] Given the remoteness of the possibility that any public-spirited skinflint would seek judicial review of this small act of generosity, we may speculate that the department's lawyers felt that the lack of a ruling at Supreme Court level, coupled with the low risk of challenge, meant that giving and following the direction did not incur unacceptable legal risks.[129]

IV Expenditure Standards: Value for Money and Feasibility

A third key concept is '***value for money***' (VFM). As with regularity and propriety, *ex post* audit of expenditure is an essential mechanism for assessing compliance with this principle. 'Value for money examination' is the second main branch of public audit, now carried out by the Comptroller and Auditor General in pursuance of his statutory power to examine 'the economy, efficiency and effectiveness with which any department, authority or other body . . . has used its resources in carrying out its functions'.[130] VFM is also, however, one of the principal preoccupations of Treasury spending teams in their interactions with departments: its importance to the Treasury is attested by the fact that the phrase appears nearly a hundred times in *MPM*. At the same time the notion has clearly proved difficult to define. In setting out the personal

[126] *R (on the application of CC) v HM Treasury and Secretary of State for Work and Pensions* [2020] EWHC Admin 2817 [14].

[127] Department of Work and Pensions, *Treatment of Historical Institutional Abuse Payments in Means-Tested Benefits* (December 2021).

[128] para 3.6.7. This warning does not appear in earlier versions of *MPM*.

[129] On legal risk see chapter 9, section 2.2.1.

[130] National Audit Act 1983, s 6(1).

responsibilities of Departmental and other Accounting Officers, *MPM* describes VFM in high-level terms, as

> ensuring that the organisation's procurement, projects and processes are systematically evaluated to provide confidence about suitability, effectiveness, prudence, quality, good value judged for the Exchequer as a whole, not just for the accounting officer's organization.[131]

Later, focusing on procurement, it is defined as meaning 'securing the best mix of quality and effectiveness for the least outlay over the period of use of the goods or services bought', as opposed to 'minimising up front prices'.[132]

Vital as VFM is to the achievement of general Treasury objectives, the Treasury cannot simply rely on the Comptroller and Auditor General's VFM audit. This is carried out as a distinct procedure on behalf of Parliament, not the Treasury, with the programme of investigations determined by the Comptroller and Auditor General on the basis of information obtained through the NAO's continuous monitoring of the bodies it audits. The Public Accounts Committee is given the opportunity to comment on the draft programme, but the Treasury has no formal role in drawing it up, though NAO keeps the Treasury updated on its workplans, and the Treasury may offer its views—though the Comptroller and Auditor General retains complete discretion as to the areas he investigates. While the risk of becoming the subject of a critical VFM audit, with attendant criticism from the Public Accounts Committee, may be a stimulus to departments to strive to achieve value for money, the occasional nature of such investigations, and the Treasury's lack of any VFM audit capacity of its own, have meant that a range of other mechanisms, besides audit, have been deployed, as described in this work, in support of VFM, from specialist government contracting and project development services, through centralized prior approval systems, to support for departmental internal audit services and incentives to economy, efficiency, and effectiveness through the Spending Review system.

These were the three key concepts at the beginning of the century, but since 2011 public spending authorities have had to take account of a fourth: ***feasibility***. This is defined as 'the principle that proposals with public expenditure implications should be implemented accurately, sustainably and to the intended timetable'.[133] While assessment of feasibility of alternative courses of action had already been identified as part of good internal decision-making and risk management,[134] its promotion to 'key concept' status dates only from 2011,[135] after a Treasury review in response to Public Accounts Committee concerns that money had been wasted because Accounting Officers failed to stand in the way of over-optimistic departmental

[131] para 3.3.3.
[132] Annex 4, para A.4.6.3.
[133] *MPM*, 221 (Glossary).
[134] *MPM* (2007) paras 4.2.1 (box 4.2) and 4.3.3.
[135] It was introduced, after consultation with departmental Accounting Officers, by a 'Dear Accounting Officer' letter of April 2011: DAO(GEN) 01/11; see now *MPM* paras 1.4.3 and box 3.2.

decision-making[136]—an issue figuring regularly in NAO reviews.[137] A particular factor that appears to have influenced the introduction of the new criterion was the unworkable complexity of some payments schemes, such as tax credits, said to have been described by the then Permanent Secretary at the department as 'unimplementable'.[138] Review of the directions sought and granted since 2011 shows that reference to the feasibility criterion has been rare. It has been invoked on only three occasions, in each case in conjunction with a reference to value for money, by far the most common basis on which Accounting Officers ask for a ministerial direction. This of course does not exclude the possibility that on other occasions worries about feasibility have deterred ministers from proceeding with a scheme, so that no direction needed to be sought.

V Expenditure Standards, the Accounting Officer, and the Minister

In each department, the responsibility for ensuring compliance with these financial standards rests with the Accounting Officer appointed by the Treasury. As we saw in chapter 3, for the past hundred years or so the job of Accounting Officer has always been undertaken by the Permanent Secretary. As Permanent Secretary, however, the Accounting Officer is at the orders of the minister as the politically responsible head of the department. What if these orders conflict with the requirements of regularity, propriety, value for money, or feasibility, issues that engage the personal responsibility of the Accounting Officer? *MPM* distils the results of a century and a half of practice and debate in this area,[139] which began with a Treasury decision of 1877. Following findings of irregularities in the operation of Post Office and telegraph services, the Treasury ruled that an Accounting Officer receiving orders to make payments for which he had no legally applicable funds would not incur personal responsibility if he could show that he was obeying written instructions from his superior officer (normally the minister), and had advised the minister, again in writing, that no funds were legally available for such a service.[140]

Today, according to *MPM*, the right course for the Accounting Officer who believes that a ministerial policy or proposal fails to meet the public expenditure tests is to discuss the matter with the minister with a view to modifying it so as to achieve compliance. If this cannot be done and the minister still wants to proceed, the Accounting Officer should ask for a formal written direction. If the minister fails to give it, the proposal can proceed no further. If a direction is given, the papers should be copied to the

[136] See Public Accounts Committee, *Accountability for Public Money* (HC 2010–12, 740) evidence, q 4 (Sir Nicholas Macpherson).

[137] See eg National Audit Office, *Over-Optimism in Government Projects* (December 2013); *The Art of Spending Public Money Wisely* (September–October 2015); *Survival Guide to Challenging Costs in Major Projects* (June 2018).

[138] See Josh Harris, *Following the Pound: The Accounting Officer in Central Government* (Institute for Government [nd]) 13, quoting Richard Bacon MP, in Public Accounts Committee, *Accountability for Public Money* (HC 2010–12, 740) evidence, q 38. Bacon cites other over-complex schemes at q 37.

[139] paras 3.6.1–3.6.8.

[140] Public Accounts Committee, *Epitome of the Reports from the Committee of Public Accounts 1857–1937* (HC 1937–38, 154) 47, 69.

Public Accounts Committee, the Comptroller and Auditor General, and the Treasury Officer of Accounts; the direction implemented forthwith; and arrangements made to ensure that it is promptly published—unless the matter has for some reason to be kept confidential—on the government website. These rules reflect a much more open attitude to directions than prevailed in the past. Prior to a critical report by the Public Accounts Committee on the Pergau Dam affair,[141] only ministerial directions sought on grounds of regularity or propriety, as opposed to value for money, gave rise to an obligation to inform the Treasury and to communicate the papers to the Comptroller and Auditor General. Thereafter these obligations were made general; and when the official guidance for ministers was reissued at the outset of the Blair government as the *Ministerial Code*, it was thought worthwhile, for the first time, to summarize the terms of the minister-Accounting Officer relationship, including the directions procedure.[142] The current rules requiring routine publication of directions stem from a Treasury decision in 2011.[143]

Openness to the idea of publication may reflect a recognition within government that there have been changes in the relationship between ministers and Permanent Secretaries in this century. Not that long ago, for an Accounting Officer to request a direction was described as a 'nuclear option'[144] or 'very rare',[145] and even in 2016 the Public Accounts Committee could still characterize the procedure as 'an extreme step' that is 'seldom used'.[146] In the period 1997–2010 there were 37 directions, the majority of them (24) invoking 'value for money' as a ground of concern.[147] From 2011 to mid-2023 there were 51, again with a majority (36) involving value for money.[148] Over the period of our concern this averages out at something more than three per year across the whole of government, which suggests that while unusual, a request for a direction need not indicate a situation of crisis or breakdown within a department. Averaging however can be deceptive: in a number of years, notably 2011–14, when the Coalition government was in office, there were no directions, while there were 17 in 2008–10 and eight in 2015. Since then the number of reported directions each year has varied between none in 2017 and 18 in 2020. In evidence to the Public Accounts Committee in 2016, the Cabinet Secretary and the Permanent Secretary to the Treasury suggested

[141] *Pergau Hydro-Electric Project* (HC 1993–94, 155).

[142] Cabinet Office, *Ministerial Code: A Code of Conduct and Guidance on Procedures for Ministers* (1997) paras 57–59. See now Cabinet Office, *Ministerial Code* (2022) paras 5.3–5.5, in similar terms.

[143] Information about published directions is collected at <www.gov.uk/government/collections/ministerial-directions>. As noted above, publication may be withheld on grounds of confidentiality.

[144] Lord Butler of Brockwell (Cabinet Secretary 1988–98) evidence to House of Lords Constitution Committee, *The Accountability of Civil Servants* (HL 2012–13, 61) oral and written evidence, 18 July 2012, q 303.

[145] Tony Benn (n 47) 296, quoting his Permanent Secretary, Sir Anthony Part, at the Department of Industry.

[146] Public Accounts Committee, *Accountability to Parliament for Taxpayers' Money* (HC 2015–16, 732) 5.

[147] House of Lords Constitution Committee, *The Pre-emption of Parliament* (HL 2012–13, 183) evidence, HM Treasury, supplementary evidence, Annex 2. The same table can be found in Harris (n 138) 32–33. For earlier directions see Comptroller and Auditor General, *Accountability to Parliament for Taxpayers' Money* (HC 2015–16, 849) para 1.19, counting 14 directions (two per year) from 1990 to 1996.

[148] Figures derived from <www.gov.uk/government/collections/ministerial-directions>.

that such variations may reflect the economic and political context.[149] 2008–10 were the years of the financial crisis, when the government was taking urgent and unusual steps to support the banking system; this may have led Accounting Officers to seek the shelter of ministerial directions. In contrast, the Coalition government was elected on an austerity platform which meant that ministers would be unusually sensitive to value-for-money issues and unlikely to insist on spending in the face of Accounting Officer objections.[150]

The Covid-19 pandemic has had an even more dramatic effect on numbers of directions. Of the 18 directions in 2020 14 were related to expenditure responding to the pandemic, involving not only value-for-money issues, but also questions of regularity and propriety created by the need to bring schemes of payment into operation in advance of the necessary legislative authority. On a smaller scale, four of the seven requests for directions in 2017 were prompted by pressures of preparing for Brexit, raising the same propriety issue. In these cases the relevant spending had effectively been pre-authorized by the Treasury: the Chief Secretary had 'advised that ministers should issue technical directions to enable urgent spend when delaying would jeopardise our readiness for EU exit'.[151]

Numbers of directions actually issued may not be the most reliable indicator of the significance of the procedure. Serving and former Permanent Secretaries have asserted that the threat of needing to issue a direction was enough to persuade most ministers to adapt their plans to provide assurance of compliance with the standards, and it appears that use of the directions process is contemplated far more frequently than it is actually used.[152] Nonetheless, one of the concerns of the Public Accounts Committee and the Comptroller and Auditor General has been that Accounting Officers may be too reluctant to take the final step of actually requesting a direction, leading to the acceptance of projects that turn out to be financially disastrous. In 2016 the Comptroller and Auditor General listed a number of factors that he thought were putting the relationship between minister and Permanent Secretary (and Accounting Officer) under strain, and hence creating 'a climate where AOs lack the confidence or incentive to challenge ministers on the feasibility and value for money of their policies':

> 'the demarcation between ministerial responsibility for policy and accounting officer responsibility for implementation has blurred, as ministers in successive administrations have taken a closer interest in how their policies are delivered . . . which can mean officials are held responsible for implementation decisions not directly under their control';

[149] Public Accounts Committee, *Accountability to Parliament for Taxpayers' Money* (n 146) oral evidence, qq 45–48.

[150] Some respondents to the Institute for Government inquiry offered more cynical explanations: that the incidence of directions increased towards the expected change of government in 2010 as civil servants sought to protect themselves from criticism by a successor government, and that their absence in 2010–14 was because new Permanent Secretaries did not wish to undermine their relationships with ministers: Harris (n 138) 18.

[151] See letter of 7 February 2018 from the Permanent Secretary at the Department of Transport to her Secretary of State.

[152] Harris (n 138) 15, 20.

a perception among some ministers 'that civil servants sometimes obstruct implementation of government policies';

'growth in the use of special advisers over several decades' and the risk that special advisers might function 'as an interposed layer of authority between the Minister and his or her civil servants'.[153]

The official response to this concern was to point to Treasury encouragement to Accounting Officers to prepare formal written assessments of significant policy proposals, and of novel or contentious transactions, from the point of view of regularity, propriety, value for money, and feasibility—'accounting officer assessments'.[154] These help to decide whether to seek a ministerial direction or to inform design or redesign of the policy or proposal to meet the standards; provide an audit trail for any NAO value-for-money report on the policy or proposed action; and help to deal with challenges to the decision, for example from the Public Accounts Committee.[155] The Public Accounts Committee wanted to see these assessments made available to Parliament to strengthen transparency and accountability.[156] The government, however, took the view that as the value of these assessments lay in their frank examination of possibly sensitive issues, including the essence of the policy, its purposes and its prospects, it was important to preserve their confidentiality. It did, however, agree that Accounting Officers should always make assessments of projects in the GMPP and that summaries of these should be provided to Parliament; and that Accounting Officers might choose to publish similar information from assessments made in other circumstances at their discretion.[157] Current practice regarding the making and publication of assessments reflects Public Accounts Committee recommendations issued in 2022.[158]

This further step towards transparency still leaves one area in surprising obscurity. This is the role of the Treasury in the process. *MPM* insists that the ultimate judgement as to whether a proposal complies with the expenditure standards is that of the Accounting Officer. A proposal that prompts concern from an Accounting Officer may however often also require Treasury consent, either because it exceeds the department's delegated authorities or because it is a type of spending identified in *MPM* as requiring Treasury approval even if within delegation limits: 'transactions

[153] Comptroller and Auditor General, *Accountability to Parliament for Taxpayers' Money* (n 147) paras 1.23–1.29. He did not mention threats to the health of AOs: in *Against the Tide* (n 47), his 1973–76 diaries, Tony Benn, then Secretary of State for Industry, recounts with some pride that his fierce response to a memorandum by his Permanent Secretary, Sir Anthony Part, regarding a ministerial direction in connection with the funding of the Kirkby Engineering workers' cooperative, left Part 'white as a sheet' (297). Three weeks later we find Benn recording, without further comment, a visit to see Sir Anthony in hospital, where he was recovering from a heart attack (311).

[154] See now *MPM*, paras 3.4.1–3.4.12.

[155] For the current guidance see HM Treasury, *Accounting Officer Assessments: Guidance* (2017, rev May 2023).

[156] Public Accounts Committee, *Accountability to Parliament for Taxpayers' Money* (n 146) 6.

[157] Treasury Minute on Public Accounts Committee Report 39 of 2015–16 (Cm 9389, December 2016) paras 3.4–3.8.

[158] Public Accounts Committee, *Improving the Accounting Officer Assessment Process* (HC 2022–23, 43). The summaries can now be found, organized by department, at <www.gov.uk/government/collections/accounting-officer-assessments-collection>.

which set precedents, are novel, contentious or could cause repercussions elsewhere in the public sector.'[159] *MPM* advises Accounting Officers to discuss the matter with the Treasury, and to obtain its consent, if needed, before finalizing a direction request. Other Treasury guidance evokes the possibility that it might identify an activity as appearing inconsistent with the standards and 'challenge' the proposal in question.[160] Treasury consent powers, therefore, may reinforce Accounting Officer resistance, and may facilitate the 'dialogue' with the minister that, 'more often than not', leads to the 'reconfiguring' of a contested proposal.[161] At the same time the Treasury says that it 'does not routinely second guess in detail' how Accounting Officers run their organizations,[162] and its Permanent Secretary has stated, of a particular case raising value-for-money issues, that if 'the accounting officer took a decision in good faith not to seek a direction. That has to be his decision. The Treasury can't second-guess that.'[163] This seems to suggest that even if there were doubts about whether a project requiring Treasury consent met expenditure standards, the Treasury would not refuse approval if the Accounting Officer decided against seeking a direction. Indeed, *MPM* contemplates the case where consent is granted even where the Accounting Officer decides that a direction is needed, noting that 'Treasury consent does not remove the need for a direction if the requirements of box 3.2 [which lists regularity, propriety, value for money and feasibility] are not met'.[164] And as the *Accounting Officer's Survival Guide* puts it:

> 61. If a ministerial direction is required which includes novel or contentious spending, the necessary Treasury financial consents can only be supplied by a Treasury minister, usually the Chief Secretary, as officials cannot sanction any proposed transaction or activity which breaches the accounting officer standards. If the Treasury minister does consent, he or she will normally do so only on condition that the departmental minister primarily responsible directs his or her accounting officer.

Treasury ministers, in other words, are not bound by the expenditure standards, and can like their departmental colleagues take account of other factors. Ultimately, therefore, in the face of a minister determined to follow a particular course of action, the vaunted standards of regularity, propriety, value for money, and feasibility rest on no stronger basis than the willingness and ability of Treasury ministers to fight for them in Cabinet—and win.

Conflicts between respect for expenditure standards and policy initiatives can also occur at the level of ALB decision-making. Here things may be more complicated for Accounting Officers. This is because the legal power of decision-making in such bodies may be vested not in their chief executive—who will be the Accounting

159 *MPM* para 2.3.4 and box 2.3.

160 Treasury Officer of Accounts, *The Accounting Officer's Survival Guide* (December 2015) para 60.

161 Public Accounts Committee, *Accountability for Public Money* (HC 2010–12, 740) evidence, q 3 (Sir Nicholas Macpherson, Permanent Secretary, HM Treasury).

162 *The Accounting Officer's Survival Guide*, para 29.

163 Public Accounts Committee, *Accountability for Public Money* (n 161) evidence, q 4 (Sir Nicholas Macpherson).

164 para 3.6.3.

Officer—but in the body's board, either by the legislation creating the body or, where the ALB is a company constituted under the Companies Acts, as the consequence of the ordinary rules of company law. This is not a problem for executive agencies. Such agencies may or may not be equipped with a management board including external non-executive members, depending on the size and desired degree of independence from the department to be enjoyed by the agency. But even where there is such a board, final decisions (and the responsibility and accountability for them) continue to rest with the chief executive.[165] With other ALBs, however, where the board has the final say, the approach to be followed by the chief executive as Accounting Officer is set out in *MPM*. If a proposal before the board appears to conflict with personal Accounting Officer responsibilities, he or she should vote against it. If the board requires the Accounting Officer to proceed in a way that might be contrary to any of the key principles for managing public money, the Accounting Officer should follow the procedure set out in the organization's framework document. This process is similar to that for seeking directions in departments but will be tailored to reflect the position of the organization's board, which is often appointed under statute.[166] There is no publication of any such ALB directions.

VI The Links with External Control

6.1 Parliamentary institutions

A direction on grounds of regularity or propriety does not make the spending in question regular or proper. It may therefore be the subject of adverse comment or a qualified 'regularity opinion' in the Comptroller and Auditor General's report on the departmental accounts,[167] and of inquiry by the Public Accounts Committee. Nor does a direction permit unlawful action or protect against a court finding unlawfulness.

The general pattern of relationships between departments, Treasury, the Comptroller and Auditor General and NAO, and the Public Accounts Committee has remained stable since the beginning of the century, and the broad lines of the account we offered in 1999 remain accurate.[168] It does not appear to have been much affected by the changes to the structure of NAO effected by the Budget Responsibility and National Audit Act 2011. A review of the corporate governance of the Office, initiated by the House of Commons Public Accounts Commission in 2007, proposed, in line with arrangements being widely adopted within the executive, that the Comptroller and Auditor General, while retaining absolute discretion as to the carrying out of the

165 Cabinet Office, *Executive Agencies: A Guide for Departments* (2018) 6–8.

166 *MPM* paras 3.10.5, 3.10.6. On framework agreements see chapter 4, section 3.2.

167 See eg Department of Health and Social Care, *Annual Report and Accounts 2019–20* (HC 2019–21, 1077) 127–29 (Comptroller and Auditor General's comments on scheme to compensate consultants for adverse tax consequences of personal pension contribution limits: irregular as contrary to *MPM* (para 5.6.1) as constituting a form of tax planning).

168 Daintith and Page (n 19) 193–99. On 21st-century developments at NAO see David Dewar and Warwick Funnell, *A History of British National Audit: The Pursuit of Accountability* (OUP 2017) ch 10, and on recent PAC practice see Harris (n 138) 20–23.

professional functions of the Office, should cease to be solely responsible for its management and finances. Instead, these should be placed in the hands of a board with an independent chairman. The proposals were very largely accepted by the Commission and carried into effect by the 2011 Act. The independence of the Comptroller and Auditor General, who remains an officer of the House of Commons and chief executive of NAO (though not an employee) is recognized and preserved. NAO becomes a corporate body, whose relationship with the Comptroller and Auditor General is regulated by schedule 3 of the Act. This requires it, for example, to provide the resources required for the Comptroller and Auditor General's functions.[169] More detailed provision is made by a Code of Practice promulgated under the schedule.[170] There is no evidence that these changes have affected the role of the Comptroller and Auditor General and NAO as an external supervisor of respect for the expenditure standards.

More significant in this context was something that did not happen. As part of its 1998 proposals for switching the emphasis of expenditure control towards Spending Review discipline, the Treasury suggested that responses to Public Accounts Committee (PAC) reports should no longer take the form of Treasury Minutes, save where the Treasury's own business was concerned, but should be submitted directly over the signature of the departmental minister. This attempt to distance itself from parliamentary accountability for departmental spending was roundly rejected by the Committee. There was, it said, 'a continuing need for an independent oversight within Government of departments' replies to this Committee's reports', a responsibility embodied in the Treasury's central responsibility for financial relations, and the proposal risked weakening, rather than enhancing, departmental accountability.[171] The Treasury took this view to heart and since 2012 has reinforced its support for the Committee's recommendations by providing reports, generally twice a year, to set out progress with implementing outstanding recommendations that government has accepted, and in 2020 issued a formal 'Dear Accounting Officer' letter chiding departments for playing fast and loose with promised implementation dates for Committee recommendations and requiring prompt and reasoned announcements of postponements.[172]

6.2 Judicial review

While parliamentary mechanisms of accountability have thus continued, with Treasury support, to function as a significant discipline for the enforcement of expenditure standards, the judicial role in assuring even the more limited demands of legality of expenditure remains at best marginal. With the passage of the Exchequer and Audit Departments Act 1866, the policing of compliance with public expenditure

[169] See generally Dewar and Funnell (n 168) 251–57.

[170] National Audit Office, *Code of Practice Dealing with the Relationship between the National Audit Office and the Comptroller and Auditor General* (HC 2021–22, 1230).

[171] Public Accounts Committee, *Treasury Controls* (n 1) paras 21–25.

[172] HM Treasury, DAO letter, 'Revision of Target Dates for Implementing Public Accounts Committee Recommendations' (12 June 2020).

law was collapsed into the broader notion of regularity, policed not by the courts but by the Comptroller and Auditor General. In recent cases where challenges to spending decisions have been brought via judicial review, outcomes have depended heavily on the terminology of the relevant statutory spending authorities, so that nothing resembling a coherent body of doctrine on legal aspects of public expenditure has emerged. In cases on local authority spending, the existence of budgetary constraints has sometimes been held to be a relevant consideration in the exercise of spending discretion; but in other cases, where duties involving expenditure have been couched in more specific terms, it has not.[173]

At the same time it is clear that courts are listening to a wider range of arguments in public spending cases than might have been available in the last century. Essentially this is the effect of developments in judicial review: the currently relaxed view on standing requirements; the comprehensive extension of review to non-statutory powers, which has opened up to review spending based purely on the Supply and Appropriation Acts; and the appearance of new grounds of review, notably legitimate expectation and breach of equalities obligations. Arguments on such grounds have seldom been successful, but they have led courts to examine aspects of the public expenditure process that would once have been hidden from judicial view.

In *R (People and Planet) v HM Treasury*,[174] for example, we find a judge looking carefully at the Treasury Green Book, a document which sets out the tests and procedures to be followed by departments in preparing and presenting significant spending projects. He was willing to hear arguments about the Green Book's requirements in relation to a policy adopted under common law powers, on the ground that,

> although there was no obligation upon HM Treasury to carry out a Green Book assessment before it adopted the policy, it is arguable that because it decided that a Green Book assessment should be carried out it came under an obligation to carry out that assessment properly.[175]

He concluded that the Green Book left the Treasury with a very wide discretion to decide what factors to treat as relevant or weighty or not for the purposes of formulating its policy, a discretion that it had not exceeded.[176] The finding is unsurprising; but the possibility that a Green Book assessment may be open to judicial review could greatly increase the public visibility of processes of expenditure decision-making within the executive.

Again, the equalities obligation has opened up to judicial review the kind of general spending decisions, including those taken in the budget and Spending Review process, that might formerly have been thought to be immune from this kind of scrutiny.[177]

[173] Compare *R v Gloucestershire County Council, ex p Barry* 1997 [1997] AC 584 (lack of resources justifying reduction of benefits) with *R v Sussex CC, ex p Tandy* [1998] AC 714 (lack of resources an irrelevant consideration).

[174] [2009] EWHC 3020 (Admin).

[175] At [8].

[176] See at [22], [25], [36].

[177] See *R (Luton Borough Council and Nottingham City Council) v Secretary of State for Education* [2011] EWHC 217, and *Simone, McFinnigan and Riddell v Chancellor of the Exchequer and Secretary of State for Education* [2019] EWHC 2609 (Admin), discussed in chapter 7, section 3.3.2.

Barriers to successful review in relation to such processes, however, still remain high. A few months after the successful challenge in the *Luton* case,[178] a failure to consult on a policy to cut assistance to local authorities planning waste diversion plants was held in *R (Cheshire East Borough Council) v Secretary of State for Environment Food and Rural Affairs and HM Treasury*,[179] to be not unreasonable when Treasury pressure for cuts in anticipation of the 2015 Comprehensive Spending Review compelled a particular level of reduction in the departmental budget.

Notwithstanding the enlarged range of decisions and materials that might be subject to judicial examination, it seems unlikely that the courts could find themselves playing a significant role as a support for, or external control upon, the Treasury's public expenditure disciplines, simply because individuals seldom want to challenge the expenditure of funds by departments, while non-governmental organizations and pressure groups tend to use judicial review to impugn policies, rather than the spending that supports them.[180] As seen in our discussion above of propriety and the Concordat, the work of the courts has consequently been focused on challenges to the legality of refusals or failures to spend public funds, determined according to general principles of judicial review. Where payment is refused the Treasury's own controls may be presumed to have worked. Where payment is made, perhaps they have not, but in such cases the likelihood of litigation is low.

178 Above n 177.
179 [2011] EWHC 1975 (Admin).
180 The *Pergau Dam* case (n 115) provides an exception.

PART E
THE RESOURCES OF THE EXECUTIVE: LAW

9

How Government Lawyers Advise Ministers and Manage Prosecutions

I Introduction: The Legal Environment 1997–2023

1.1 The executive: a legal subordinate?

Law fulfils two principal roles in connection with the functioning of the executive. In the first place, it provides support and legitimation for executive action. For any executive decision, our constitution assumes that the relevant minister or officials will be able to point to some legal authority that underpins it, whether this be specific legislative provision, common law powers or capacities, spending authority in the Supply and Appropriation Acts, or the special and steadily shrinking powers conferred by the royal prerogative. This assumption, which flows directly from our continuing and recently reasserted commitment to the rule of law as a basic constitutional principle,[1] makes law an essential resource of government. Law's second role is to operate as a constraint on executive action which, to be valid and effective, needs to respect the limits expressed or implicit in the law that authorizes it. Under our constitution the management of how law performs these roles is not entrusted to the executive itself. Rather, the executive is formally subordinated to Parliament in matters of legislative ordering, and to the views of the courts as to the interpretation, and the application in practice, of both parliamentary legislation and common law.

So far as legislative ordering is concerned, subordination is indeed little more than formal.[2] The reason lies in the key distinguishing feature of the Westminster model of parliamentary democracy: the linkage of legislature and executive, through Cabinet government, which, in conjunction with a strong party system, means that—save under the most exceptional circumstances like those of autumn 2019 when the Johnson government lost control of the Commons agenda—the legislative activity of Parliament is very largely controlled by the same body of people as control the activity of the executive branch of government. The executive can thus largely shape its own legal powers through the legislation it promotes. That legislation may in turn give it extensive powers of law-making through delegated legislation, and as we shall see, its control in practice over delegated legislation is even more complete. UK constitutional doctrine accepts that legislation may contradict the country's international legal obligations, such as those stemming from treaties like the Energy Charter Treaty

[1] Constitutional Reform Act 2005, s 1.

[2] Indeed, even the formal position of the executive is stronger than is generally recognized: in relation to legislation having any financial implications its right of initiative in proposing both taxes and spending makes it the partner, not the subordinate, of Parliament (chapter 7, section 1.1).

Executive Self-Government and the Constitution. Terence Daintith and Alan Page, Oxford University Press.
 DOI: 10.1093/9780198937630.003.0009

or the European Convention on Human Rights; or may reverse unattractive judicial decisions.[3] Indeed it can do both at once. The Safety of Rwanda (Asylum and Immigration) Act 2024 negates the effect of the Supreme Court's finding that Rwanda is not a safe country for the reception of certain would-be migrants to the United Kingdom,[4] and the government was unable to affirm its compatibility with rights conferred under the European Convention on Human Rights.[5] Constraint has been most acute where international obligations entail the transfer by Parliament of legislative power to other bodies like the European Union. That particular fetter was, of course, broken by our withdrawal from the Union at the end of 2020.

The executive however lacks any analogous influence over judicial decisions;[6] the locus of authority for the interpretation and declaration of the law has since 1689 been firmly established outside the executive, in the King's courts, not just in form but in fact. Maintaining, even temporarily, departmental interpretations of legal powers that are at odds with judicial rulings is apt to be visited with vigorous judicial disapproval.[7] The matter is seen in the same light from within government. In the words of a former Treasury Solicitor, 'if a declaration is made against the government or a minister as to the position in a particular case, the government will comply with that without being compelled to do so'—though sometimes with reluctance.[8]

1.2 The 'iron triangle'

1.2.1 Executive–judicial tensions

At different times in the period since the end of the Second World War these relationships of subordination have engendered tensions between the executive and the other powers under the constitution. Ministers, and sometimes civil servants also, have resented the constraints on their ability to make and carry through policy represented both by restrictive rules, of international and—much more acutely—of EU law, and by restrictive judicial interpretations of their legal powers, normally articulated in the framework of judicial review proceedings. Along with the increasing influence

[3] *R (Reilly) v Secretary of State for Work and Pensions* [2013] UKSC 68, [2014] AC 453 [33]–[42], where the Supreme Court did not criticize the retrospective validation, by the Jobseekers (Back to Work) Schemes Act 2013, of regulations ruled by the Court of Appeal to be *ultra vires*, only remarking that the executive's conduct in maintaining an appeal against that ruling after the Act had rendered it moot was 'rather unattractive'.

[4] *R (AAA(Syria)) v Secretary of State for the Home Department* [2023] UKSC 42; Safety of Rwanda (Asylum and Immigration) Act 2024, s 1(2)(b): 'this Act gives effect to the judgement of Parliament that the Republic of Rwanda is a safe country.'

[5] See the statement to this effect by the Home Secretary on the face of the bill, as required by Human Rights Act 1998, s 19(1)(b): HC Bill (2023–24) [38].

[6] Or at least, any overt influence: see Robert Stevens, *The Independence of the Judiciary: The View from the Lord Chancellor's Office* (Clarendon Press 1993) 92–96.

[7] See, for a recent example, *R (JZ) v Secretary of State for Foreign, Commonwealth and Development Affairs* [2022] EWHC 771 (Admin) [31] (Lieven J), applying *R (Majera) v Secretary of State for the Home Department* [2021] UKSC 46, [2021] 3 WLR 1075; and for discussion of earlier examples, Terence Daintith and Alan Page, *The Executive in the Constitution: Structure, Autonomy and Internal Control* (OUP 1999) 327–29.

[8] Constitution Committee, *The Roles of the Lord Chancellor and the Law Officers* (HL 2022–23, 118) oral evidence (23 March 2022) q 34 (Sir Jonathan Jones).

of pressure groups, these constraints were characterized by one minister in 1997 as an 'iron triangle' imprisoning the executive.[9] In the last quarter of the 20th century there were continual rumblings of discontent, within both major parties (Labour discontents predominating in the seventies and early eighties, Tory discontents thereafter), about the United Kingdom's membership of the European Union, though it is difficult to assess the part played in this by chafing within the executive at the restriction of policy choices. So far as the courts were concerned, the sense of disruption of executive activity stemming from judicial review—in particular, from the unpredictability of its results[10]—had by the mid-eighties become sufficiently strong for a broad-ranging inquiry to be launched within government. Instead of any attempt at restriction of judicial review, however, the inquiry identified a need for better education of administrators as to the legal parameters of their activity. This led the Treasury Solicitor's Department, the forerunner of the Government Legal Department, to prepare a simple guide to judicial review for the use of administrators: *The Judge over Your Shoulder*.[11] While this was doubtless a valuable development, it did not stem a rising tide of ministerial resentment as the volume and reach of judicial review decisions continued to grow in the last decade of the century, leading to overt criticism of judges from ministers—like the Home Secretary—who found themselves particularly exposed, by reason of the areas of policy for which they were responsible, to an unremitting barrage of judicial reviews and to many unexpected reversals.[12]

In the first decade of this century, with the Labour governments of Blair and Brown in power, a relative calm descended upon these relationships. While the volume of judicial review applications continued to rise inexorably, the increase was driven by immigration and asylum applications. Other applications increased by only some 17% over the 10-year period,[13] and publicly expressed irritation seems to have been limited to the Home Office, whose judicial review caseload continued to dwarf that of other departments.[14] The government's own policies and legislation were in fact calculated to promote enlarged judicial scrutiny of executive action, notably through the adoption in domestic law, by the Human Rights Act 1998, of the rights guaranteed by the European Convention of Human Rights. As for its legislative restructuring of institutional relations between the executive and the judiciary through the Constitutional Reform Act 2005, involving the dismemberment of the multiple functions of the Lord Chancellor and the creation of the Supreme Court in place of the Appellate

[9] David Willetts, 'The Perils of Political Power' *Financial Times* (30 January 1997) 18.

[10] Sir Michael Kerry, 'Administrative Law and the Administrator' (1983) 38 Management in Government 168 and 'Administrative Law and Judicial Review—The Practical Effects of Developments over the Last 25 Years on Administration in Central Government' (1986) 64 Public Administration 163; HF Rawlings, 'Judicial Review and the "Control of Government"' (1986) 64 Public Administration 135.

[11] Treasury Solicitor's Department, *The Judge over Your Shoulder* (Cabinet Office 1987).

[12] Andrew Le Sueur, 'The Judicial Review Debate: from Partnership to Friction' (1996) 31 Government and Opposition 8.

[13] Report of Independent Review of Administrative Law (Lord Faulks, Chairman) (CP 407, March 2021) paras D12, D13.

[14] For references to criticism of judges by Labour Home Office ministers, see Lord Dyson, *Criticising Judges: Fair Game or Off-Limits* (Third Annual BAILI Lecture, 27 November 2014). From 2007–13, the Home Office and the Ministry of Justice accounted for 95–98% of claims for judicial review involving central government departments: see Catherine Haddon, Raphael Hogarth, and Alex Nice, *Judicial Review and Policy-Making: The Role of Legal Advice in Government* (Institute for Government April 2021) 6.

Committee of the House of Lords, prefaced by the legislative commitment to the rule of law to which we have already referred, this seems to have had no direct connection with the concerns we have been describing: anyone who saw it as a pathway to a more deferential judiciary will have been disabused by a reading of later Supreme Court jurisprudence.

1.2.2 Conservative discontents

Since 2010 and the arrival of the Conservative-dominated coalition in power, followed by no fewer than five Conservative governments between 2015 and 2024, these tensions have become steadily more acute. Though the general level of judicial review applications has declined rather than increased over the period of Conservative governments,[15] the place it occupies in executive consciousness has expanded mightily: *The Judge over Your Shoulder*, originally published as a slim pamphlet, extended in its sixth (2022) edition to 112 pages.[16] The expanding scope of judicial review has also given rise to a campaign of academic criticism, mostly under the banner of the Judicial Power Project run from the Policy Exchange think-tank.[17] Ministers in particular seem to be more resentful of its effects than were their predecessors. By the time of the 2019 general election such feelings had reached the point where the Conservatives thought it appropriate to campaign on an undertaking to 'look at the broader aspects of our constitution, including the relationship between the Government, Parliament and the courts', by setting up a Constitution, Democracy & Rights Commission to 'examine these issues in depth, and come up with proposals to restore trust in our institutions and in how our democracy operates'.[18] Such a Commission never saw the light of day: instead, the government set up independent reviews of administrative law and of the operation of the Human Rights Act. The first of these concluded that judicial review was generally working well, the second reached a broadly similar conclusion regarding the Human Rights Act.[19] The government did not much like either result. On judicial review it made the minor legislative changes recommended by the Faulks Committee while consulting on more far-reaching reforms.[20] Its reactions to the human rights review were prefigured by the commitment to replace the Human Rights Act with a British Bill of Rights that had already appeared in the 2010 and 2015 Conservative manifestos,[21] but had been put on hold while the government worked its way through the process of leaving the European Union. It introduced a Bill of Rights Bill proposing much more

[15] Haddon, Hogarth, and Nice (n 14) 7.

[16] Government Legal Department, *The Judge over Your Shoulder* (6th edn, 2022).

[17] For the Project's publications, see <https://judicialpowerproject.org.uk/>. For a critical view of the Project, see Maximilien Steinbeis, 'Right-Wing Crits' (*Verfassungsblog*, 15 November 2019).

[18] Conservative Party (Great Britain), *Get Brexit Done: Unleash Britain's Potential: The Conservative Party and Unionist Party Manifesto 2019* (2019) 48.

[19] Report of the Independent Review of Administrative Law (above, n 13); Report of the Independent Human Rights Act Review 2020–21 (Sir Peter Gross, Chair) (CP 586, December 2021).

[20] See Judicial Review and Courts Act 2022, ss 1 and 2; Lord Chancellor and Secretary of State for Justice, *Judicial Review Reform: The Government Response to the Independent Review of Administrative Law* (CP 408, March 2021); *Judicial Review Reform Consultation: The Government Response* (CP 477, July 2021).

[21] The Conservative Manifesto 2010, *Invitation to Join the Government of Britain* (2010) 79; Conservatives, *The Conservative Party Manifesto 2015* (2015) 73.

radical—and restrictive—changes to human rights law than had been recommended by the Independent Review or supported in its subsequent consultation exercise.[22] A major aim of the bill was to diminish the influence on UK courts of the decisions of the European Court of Human Rights, viewed with suspicion and distaste over the whole period of Conservative rule since 2010 as the expression of improper 'foreign' judicial interference with democratic decision-making.[23]

Following a change in the identity of the responsible minister, the bill was withdrawn in June 2023 before it reached second reading stage. The government continued, however, to encounter difficulties in reconciling its preferred policies for managing illegal migration—notably 'stopping the boats'—with its obligations under the European Convention on Human Rights and other international instruments, leading to its invitation to Parliament, in the Safety of Rwanda (Asylum and Immigration) Act 2024 to legislate in explicit contravention of such obligations.

It was hardly surprising that the more chauvinistic elements in the government's majority should turn their fire on the European Convention on Human Rights once the government had 'got Brexit done' through completing the arduous legislative marathon necessary for withdrawal from the European Union. That process produced a constitutional turmoil in which the performance of judicial and parliamentary roles in these relationships became indelibly associated with presumed attitudes or effects regarding the basic issue of withdrawal from the European Union. Save in those cases where it was instigated by those accusing the government of weakness in negotiating with the European Union,[24] the assertion of judicial or parliamentary powers of control of executive action was construed as political opposition to the result of the referendum. The Brexit experience also had a corrosive effect on relationships within the executive. Not only Conservative party members and backbenchers, but also ministers, began to treat it as acceptable to make public criticisms of their civil servants.[25] In the broader political arena—though not with attribution to serving ministers—aspersions were cast not just on civil servants' efficiency but also on their impartiality and their alleged lack of sympathy with the Brexit project, with the dehumanizing term 'the blob' being employed to spread the slander as broadly as possible.[26]

The lawyers employed by central government are civil servants and there is no reason to assume that their work, and their relationships with ministers, should not have been affected by these changes in atmosphere alongside that of their administrative colleagues. Indeed, their position has been particularly delicate and exposed in a

22 See Bill of Rights Bill HC Bill (2022–23) [117]; Deputy Prime Minister, Lord Chancellor, and Secretary of State for Justice, *Human Rights Act Reform: A Modern Bill of Rights. A Consultation to Reform the Human Rights Act 1998* (CP 588, December 2021).

23 A catalyst for this was the Court's decision in *Hirst v United Kingdom (no 2)* [2005] ECHR 681, 19 BHRC 546, [2006] 1 Prison LR 220, (2006) 42 EHRR 41, holding that the blanket disenfranchisement of all convicted prisoners under the Representation of the People Act 1983 was contrary to the Convention's Protocol 1, art 3.

24 As by the Conservative and Democratic Unionist Party members of Parliament who voted down the May Government's initial withdrawal agreement with the European Union in January 2019: see HC Deb 15 January 2019, vol 652, cols 1122–25.

25 See section 2.2, text above n 77, for an example from the legal field.

26 For a vigorous official condemnation of criticism in this style, see Public Administration and Constitutional Affairs Committee, *The Work of the Cabinet Office* (HC 2022–23, 950) evidence (12 July 2023) qq 418–22 (Simon Case, Cabinet Secretary).

period during which ministers, as we have seen, have been ready to invite Parliament to pass legislation that is inconsistent with international law obligations and whose implementation may involve civil servants acting in breach of international law.[27] The Civil Service Code requires all civil servants to 'comply with the law':[28] government lawyers are both subject to this obligation and charged with advising on what it means.

Over the period we are examining, however, the principal challenge for government lawyers has been the sheer volume of legal work that has been created by policies like withdrawal from the European Union—for which there had been no preparation prior to the referendum result—and crises like those presented by the Covid pandemic and, earlier, the near-collapse of major elements of the banking system. We shall see that the organization of government legal work looks very different in 2024 from the way it did at the beginning of the century, and one objective of this chapter and the next is to tease out the relationships between this organizational change and these developments in the volume of work, and the changes in the political environment in which it is conducted. Writing in 1999, we described the structure of government legal services as 'untidy and piecemeal'.[29] Since that time the general direction of change has been towards centralization and rationalization. In attempting to understand the process of change, its limits, and its effect, we need to keep in mind that some of this untidiness stems from basic characteristics of our constitution: notably the separate system of Scots law and jurisdiction preserved by the Treaty of Union, which accounts for the existence of a Scottish structure of legal administration within the executive that is separate from that operating in England and Wales and that is distinctive in many respects.[30] Another enduring reason for diversity is to be found in the fact that legal work in government encompasses a range of tasks and that differences between them may call for different modes of organization. The most recent comprehensive review of government legal work identified, as distinct roles of lawyers in government: legal advice, preparation of legislation, civil litigation, conveyancing, criminal prosecution, international affairs, and law reform.[31] Differences between these roles have been reflected in institutional specialization, in the form of bodies such as the Treasury Solicitor's Department (legal advice and civil litigation, since the 17th century); the Office of Parliamentary Counsel (legislative drafting, since 1869); the Crown Prosecution Service (prosecutions in England and Wales,[32] since 1986); or the Law Commissions (law reform, since 1965). Accordingly, we need to give separate consideration to developments in three broad areas: legal advice and civil litigation

[27] As with the Safety of Rwanda (Asylum and Immigration) Act 2024: see text at nn 5–6 above, and for an earlier example, the Northern Ireland Protocol Bill HC Bill (2022–23) [12], disapplying aspects of the Northern Ireland Protocol annexed to the UK-EU Withdrawal Agreement, which was not proceeded with after its committee stage in the House of Lords.

[28] *The Civil Service Code* (updated 16 March 2015).

[29] Daintith and Page (n 7) 214.

[30] The Northern Ireland system is likewise separate and distinctive, albeit with very different historical roots.

[31] Sir Robert Andrew, *Review of Government Legal Services* (Cabinet Office 1989) 10 (para 2.4).

[32] In Scotland, prosecution has long been a centralized function, placed in the hands of Procurators-Fiscal organized within the Crown Office, headed by the Crown Agent under the direction of the Lord Advocate, the senior Scottish Law Officer.

(section II below), criminal prosecution (section III), and the preparation of legislation (chapter 10).

II Legal Advice and Civil Litigation

2.1 The Government Legal Department

2.1.1 Creation

There has since 1999 been a major change in the way that core civil legal work is carried out in England and Wales. Between 2011 and 2017, the teams of legal advisers hitherto maintained as part of the departmental establishment by most of the major departments of state were brought together in a Government Legal Department (GLD), alongside the existing staff of the Treasury Solicitor's Department (TSol). GLD, headed by the Treasury Solicitor, now undertakes all advisory and civil litigation work for central government, with the exception of legal advice and international litigation for the Foreign, Commonwealth and Development Office, and legal advice for Her Majesty's Revenue and Customs.

The feeling, at the centre of government, that there might be substantial advantages in moving towards a unified legal service seems first to have been expressed back in the 1870s, when the Chancellor of the Exchequer, according to the Treasury Minute establishing the Jessel Committee,

> apprehend[ed] that . . . there may be reason to doubt whether so many separate [legal] departments are necessary, and whether it might not be better to suppress some of them, and to give their business to the Treasury Solicitor, with liberty to employ agents, as the business from time to time might require.[33]

At that time, in fact, the Treasury Solicitor was already acting for 16 departments outside the Treasury. Only eight other departments had their own solicitor.[34] The Chancellor's doubts were not shared by the Committee, which recommended against the establishment of a single office for legal work despite acknowledging the effectiveness of the Treasury Solicitor's Office. More than a century later a similar vision of unification was evoked by the next major review of government legal work, Sir Robert Andrew's *Review of Government Legal Services* in 1989: a vision of

> a unified legal service whose members are paid from a single Vote and can be deployed by a central authority to the areas of greatest need. Only in this way . . . can parochial barriers be broken down and the most effective use made of scarce resources. Complete centralisation of the Government Legal Service would be a culmination of a process begun in the 19th century and would make possible the effective

[33] *First, Second and Third Reports of the Departmental Committee to Inquire into the System under which the Legal Business of Government is Conducted* (Sir George Jessel, MR, Chairman) (HC 1876–77, 199) 1877 Parl Pap XVIII (folio) 51.

[34] *Third Report* (n 33) 63, 86.

> management of the Service, which the various co-ordinating committees proposed in the past have signally failed to do. It would also reinforce the independence of government lawyers by detaching them slightly from the departments they advise.[35]

The immediate effects of the Andrew Report were limited to the formal recognition of the Treasury Solicitor as the head of a Government Legal Service made up of lawyers in the majority of central government departments, with responsibility for the career structure of lawyers throughout the Service and with the support of a Lawyers' Management Unit, created in 1989 and formally incorporated into the TSol.[36] That service has gone under the name of the 'Government Legal Profession' since 2020. But over the next 20 years there was little change in the organization of substantive legal work. While TSol was by the beginning of this century providing civil litigation services to the great majority of departments except Customs and Excise and Inland Revenue; Agriculture, Fisheries and Food; Health; and Social Security, it was giving legal advice to a far smaller proportion of departments than in 1875;[37] the century-long growth in the extent, intensity, and complexity of administrative action had led almost all the large departments to develop and reinforce their own legal services.

Against this background, bringing virtually all of central government's civil legal work into one department in the space of a single decade seems nothing short of revolutionary. What made it possible was a happy combination of successive Treasury Solicitors' ambitions for a more efficient and effective government legal service, with the implementation of the executive-wide functional programme developed by the Coalition government (2010–15), based on the idea that government would work better if certain services of the sort used by a number of departments were brought together in groupings or units able to achieve economies of scale, dissemination of best practice, and enhancement of the expertise of the civil servants performing the relevant roles. This agenda, described in detail in chapter 2 above,[38] provided powerful political support for the advancement of the ambitions nurtured by the then Treasury Solicitor and his senior team.

With the great majority of civil litigation work already concentrated within TSol, its additional role as a hub for developing legal careers and expertise made legal services an area in which early progress in the Coalition's Civil Service reform agenda might be demonstrated. Thus they were identified as the first of the cross-government professional services being developed under the Coalition's 'Functional Leadership' programme, 'delivering efficiency savings through centralised service delivery and improving professional capability with the Heads of Function taking a leadership role in relation to the whole of the professional community across the Civil Service'.[39]

[35] Andrew (n 31) 34 (para 510).

[36] Daintith and Page (n 7) 216, 218.

[37] In 2001, only the Cabinet Office; the Treasury; the Ministry of Defence; and the Departments for International Development, Education and Skills, and Culture, Media and Sport were being advised by TSol: *Treasury Solicitor's Annual Report and Accounts 2001–02* (HC 2002–03, 252) 8. The Ministry of Defence appears to have established its own in-house team in 2003. For the position in 2012, see Ben Yong, *Risk Management: Government Lawyers and the Provision of Legal Advice within Whitehall* (Constitution Society 2013) 43.

[38] See section 3.4.6.

[39] Civil Service, *Civil Service Reform Plan—Progress Report* (October 2014) 22–23. Curiously, however, legal services are not recognized as a 'function' to which any of the government's functional standards

Progress towards centralization of advisory services in fact started as early as 2011, when the legal team of the Department of Environment, Food and Rural Affairs transferred to TSol. By 2015, when the conversion of TSol into GLD was announced, all departmental advisory teams with the exception of those at HM Revenue and Customs; the Foreign, Commonwealth and Development Office (FCDO); Business and Innovation and Skills; and Energy and Climate Change, had migrated to GLD. Lawyers from the latter two departments followed in 2016 after their merger to form the Department for Business, Energy and Industrial Strategy.

The creation of GLD within such a short period was undoubtedly assisted by the support not only of the Minister for the Cabinet Office and of the then Cabinet Secretary, but also that of two successive Attorneys General, Dominic Grieve and Jeremy Wright; and by the adoption of a step-by-step policy in which the order of approach was determined in part by the attitudes of departmental legal advisers and administrators.[40] It is however important to stress that the creation of GLD is very far from representing a complete unification of central government legal services within a single organization. As we have already noted, certain types of legal work are undertaken by other bodies. Most important among these is criminal prosecution, the responsibility of the Crown Prosecution Service (CPS) and the Serious Fraud Office (SFO). Separate arrangements have always applied to lawyers in Scotland, and to lawyers working for FCDO who are, like the rest of its staff, not members of the (home) Civil Service but of the Diplomatic Service.

2.1.2 Organization

It was improvement of the quality of legal service across the whole range of central government that provided the main driver for bringing departmental advisory teams together. As the Treasury Solicitor who oversaw most of the process put it:

> [T]he purpose of the changes we are making includes an opportunity to get more systematic control over the quality of legal work... It stands to reason that if you have lots of relatively separate individual legal teams, some will be better than others. If you do not have a system for crossfertilisation and sharing between them, you are less likely to bring the poorer ones up to the standard of the best... There is some reinventing the wheel in individual teams, because they are all basically trying to do the same kind of work.[41]

The absorption of virtually all the departmental advisory teams has made it possible for GLD to organize its work in a way that better reflects the need for specialized expertise within general government legal work. GLD's structure combines departmental advisory teams with specialist groups dealing with particular types of work

apply: HM Government, *Government Functional Standard GovS001: Government Functions* (15 June 2022) para 1.2.

[40] Interview with Sir Jonathan Jones, Treasury Solicitor 2014–20 (10 March 2022).

[41] House of Lords Delegated Powers and Regulatory Reform Committee, *Inquiry into Delegated Powers Memoranda* (HL 2014–15, 39) oral evidence (25 June 2014) qq 24, 30 (Jonathan Jones).

across government, and divisions dealing with common administrative needs.[42] Since the 1970s the litigation services provided by TSol for the whole of central government have been separated from the advisory teams. Under the current structure the advisory teams provide legal advice to departments and other public bodies on the development, design, and implementation of government policies and decisions; draft secondary legislation; and work with Parliamentary Counsel on primary legislation. Teams have been formed, merged, or reconstituted to reflect changes in departmental organization. For example, the European Division of Cabinet Office Legal Advisers, which coordinated legal advice and conducted EU litigation, disappeared with Brexit and was succeeded by a team created to serve the Department for Exiting the European Union, whose members were redistributed again after the demise of that department in 2020. Alongside them are three large groups whose remit is cross-governmental in character: the Litigation Group; the Employment Law Group, which handles all the government's employment litigation and the vast majority of its employment advisory work, and a Commercial Law Group, established in June 2014, operating as a specialist commercial litigation and dispute resolution team, and also supporting individual departments in their commercial arrangements. A further cross-governmental element of the structure is the Statutory Instrument Hub, a specialist unit for handling and advising on delegated legislation, created in 2015, whose work is described in more detail in chapter 10.[43] A specialized function is that of the Bona Vacantia division in administering unclaimed estates, and assets of dissolved companies and failed trusts, undertaken on behalf of the Treasury Solicitor as Crown nominee.

These groups and divisions are supported by administrative divisions dealing with such matters as finance and operations, and 'Knowledge and Innovation', which works with legal divisions to professionalize legal knowledge and learning activity and supports a network of 'Centres of Excellence' on particular topics relevant to GLD's work, ranging from artificial intelligence, through human rights, to subsidy control. Members are drawn from divisions and group across GLD. This enables specialized lawyers to make their expertise available across the whole range of GLD's work as and when it is needed by providing support at the request of advisory teams.[44] The Attorney General's Office now regularly invites GLD legal advisers to consider consulting a Centre of Excellence, if relevant to the problem, before making a reference to the Law Officers.[45]

The result of this century's developments is a very substantial organization. GLD in 2022–23 had 2,822 staff of whom about 75% were qualified as solicitors or barristers.[46] Growth has been fuelled both by transfers into TSol, and the GLD, from

[42] The following description is based on Government Legal Department, *Annual Report and Accounts 2022–23* (HC 2022–23, 1279) 15.

[43] See section 2.3.

[44] The Centres thus provide some of the internal coordination function previously discussed in Daintith and Page (n 7) 319–22.

[45] *Guidance on Letters of Request for Law Officer Advice*—a joint note from AGO and the Legal Secretariat to the Advocate General for Scotland—is available to government lawyers through the LION intranet, but has not been more widely published.

[46] Government Legal Department, *Annual Report and Accounts 2022–23* (n 42) 55.

departments—TSol's complement in 2010–11, the last year before this migration started, was 858—and by growth of the demand from across the executive for GLD's legal services, with staffing rising by 19.5% in the four years from 2018–19 to 2022–23.[47] However, most advisory teams, though part of GLD, continue to be located alongside the staffs of the departments they serve.[48] In consequence, the structure through which lawyers deliver their advice and their litigation services has changed radically since the beginning of the century. The aim was, as we have seen, to improve the quality of legal services and the efficiency with which they are delivered, and the official message was that this should and could be done without affecting the essential character of the legal function in central government. In particular, it would leave untouched the relationships between lawyers and the departmental administrators and ministers whom they served; and it was apparently not expected to affect the division of roles between the main body of government lawyers, now grouped in GLD under the Treasury Solicitor, and the Law Officers, among whom the Attorney General continues to be described as the government's 'Chief Legal Adviser'. In later sections of this chapter we consider whether this century's structural changes are really consistent with maintaining these relationships on their traditional basis.

2.1.3 Contracting out

The concentration of legal resources in GLD, and the accompanying reinforcement of specialist competences within it, has not led to complete self-sufficiency in the provision of legal services to central government. One of the things Sir Robert Andrew's review was asked to consider in 1989 was the scope for privatization or contracting out of legal services. He concluded that there was little if any scope for privatization, and that while contracting out was 'a more promising method to pursue',[49] it was ordinarily unsuitable for any of the functions we have been discussing other than conveyancing and litigation, and even there it was likely that in-house lawyers would usually provide a cheaper service. He was not referring here to appearances in court. GLD administers, on behalf of the Attorney General, panels of junior counsel to undertake government representation. There are currently about 400 counsel on these panels. Sitting above the panels are First Treasury Counsel who are the main advocates for the government in civil litigation affecting the Crown. While panel counsel are encouraged to maintain both a public and private practice, including acting against government, on the argument that 'it is beneficial to government if counsel have had experience of acting against government', First Treasury Counsel must do exclusively government work for the duration of their appointment.

Given the attention paid to developing specialist competences in GLD over recent years, other needs for contracting out would seem small. Andrew did however recommend that departments should be ready to contract out legal work if the necessary expertise did not exist in government, if government did not have the resources to

[47] Treasury Solicitor, *Annual Report and Accounts 2010–11* (HC 2010–12, 1053) 58; Government Legal Department, *Annual Report and Accounts 2019–20* (HC 2019–21, 310) 51.

[48] But the move to GLD's current premises in Petty France involved the transfer of 1,300 centrally located staff, out of a then total of 2,500: Government Legal Department, *Annual Report and Accounts 2019–20* (HC 2019–21, 310) 58.

[49] Andrew (n 31) 25.

do the work without undue delay, or if it were more cost-effective for the work to be done in the private sector.[50] These considerations were reflected in guidance to departments issued by the Attorney General in 1991.[51] This guidance is still in effect, but now forms part of an elaborate set of documentation developed by GLD jointly with the Crown Commercial Service explaining to departments and 'other enabled Central Government customers' how to procure legal services from the private sector using the General Legal Services Panel Agreement.[52] For the purposes of this agreement the Crown Commercial Service has established a panel, currently comprising 18 law firms qualified to supply a range of defined legal advice services covering elements of public, private, and commercial law, to assist with complex and often specialized legal issues and projects. Departments and executive agencies that wish to procure private legal services otherwise than from a panel firm must justify this choice in an 'exceptions process' which is run by GLD's Commercial Law Group, by showing that there is a specialist requirement that cannot be met through the General Panel, or by demonstrating that significantly better value for money can be obtained through an alternative arrangement.

The Attorney General's guidelines repeat Andrew's criteria for determining when departments and agencies should be 'ready to contract out legal work': lack of expertise (where there is no long-term value in growing it), avoiding undue delay, and cost-effectiveness. They also identified a concept of 'core governmental work', not appropriate for contracting out even where other criteria might be seen as satisfied. 'Core governmental work' is currently described as 'an area where the government's interests are likely to be best served by a continuing relationship of close confidence between ministers and departmental legal advisers who, as specialists in public law, understand both the cross-government implications of policy options and the public interest factors in play'.[53] It includes, but is not restricted to

> work with national security or other especially sensitive implications;
> work relating to major policy or constitutional issues;
> government-to-government and other international non-commercial work;
> work affecting the long-term interests of more than one Department, such as public interest immunity; and
> work where Cabinet Office co-ordination is necessary.

These matters, as we shall see, bear a strong resemblance to those on which departments may be expected to seek legal advice from the Law Officers.[54] 'Customers' are

[50] ibid 92.

[51] Attorney General, *Use of the Private Sector for Government Legal Work: Guidance* (mimeo, 1991). Similar guidance for work in Scotland was issued by the Lord Advocate: Lord Advocate, *Use of the Private Sector for Government Legal Work in Scotland: Guidance by the Lord Advocate* (London, Lord Advocate's Department 1993).

[52] This is collected at Crown Commercial Service, *General Legal Advice Services* <www.crowncommercial.gov.uk/agreements/RM3786>. The Attorney General's guidelines form part of the 'Customer Guidance Document'. Separate Panels, and Panel Agreements, exist for Rail Legal Services (for the use only of the Department for Transport), for Finance and Complex Legal Services and, since 2021, for Trade Law.

[53] Crown Commercial Service, *General Legal Advice Services: Customer Guidance Document* (n 52) para 1.4.

[54] This chapter, section 2.2.

also reminded by the guidance that Cabinet Office consultancy controls may also apply, as may internal departmental procedures for seeking external legal advice, and that the department's legal adviser must be consulted and kept informed about the procurement.

2.1.4 Control and accountability

GLD has inherited the status, and the position in the structure of the executive, held by TSol as its predecessor. Like the Crown Prosecution Service and the Serious Fraud Office, GLD is a non-ministerial department, but the powers and responsibilities of the Treasury Solicitor, as its head—and as its Permanent Secretary—are not conferred by legislation. The Treasury Solicitor has however been legally constituted as a corporation sole by the Treasury Solicitor Act 1876, essentially for the purpose of the functions of the office with respect to unclaimed estates. Since 1876 the office has been conjoined with that of HM Procurator General, which has a number of specific responsibilities in matrimonial, admiralty, and international matters. The situation is complicated by the fact that in 1996 TSol was established as an executive agency, a status retained by GLD alongside its position as a non-ministerial department. At the time, this was seen as the most appropriate way of recognizing TSol's role in providing services for departments across government, and the expectation that in performing it TSol would meet key performance indicators such as full recovery of costs, increase of chargeable hours, and reduction of hourly costs, and would enjoy control over the pay and grading of its staff and the management of all property occupied.[55] The Treasury Solicitor is the chief executive of the agency and is appointed to this position by the Attorney General; but appointment to the office of Treasury Solicitor, and as Permanent Secretary of GLD, is by the Prime Minister.

As we have seen, the process leading to the creation of GLD was propelled in part by the support of successive Attorneys General. Ministerial responsibility for the wide range of legal work undertaken on behalf of the UK government rests on the shoulders of the Law Officers:[56] the Attorney General[57] and Solicitor General,[58] the Advocate General for Scotland (in relation to non-devolved matters affecting Scotland), and the Advocate General for Northern Ireland, a post concurrently held by the Attorney General. Within the Attorney General's remarkably varied set of tasks and powers, ranging from intervention in charity matters to referring sentences considered unduly lenient for further judicial consideration, the two major areas of activity are criminal prosecution, and legal advice and services to government in civil matters.

[55] Lord Chancellor's and Law Officers' Departments, *Departmental Report: The Government's Expenditure Plans 1996–97 to 1998–99* (Cm 3209, March 1996) paras 37–38.

[56] Except in so far as the legal advisers to FCDO and HM Revenue and Customs continue to be departmental employees: see section 2.1.1.

[57] For comparison of the Attorney's position with that of other Law Officers in the United Kingdom, including the Law Officers of the devolved administrations in Scotland, Wales and Northern Ireland, see Conor McCormick, *The Constitutional Legitimacy of Law Officers in the United Kingdom* (Hart Publishing 2022).

[58] As the Solicitor General, unlike holders of the office of the same name in countries like the United States and Australia, has no distinct functions but simply supports the Attorney by sharing the workload, we say nothing further about the office here. See Daintith and Page (n 7) 232–33, and for more detail, McCormick (n 57) 44–45.

In both areas the position of the Attorney as a responsible minister is unusual because the Attorney, unlike most other ministers, does not exercise direct political control over a segment of executive activity, but is charged with functions of 'superintendence and sponsorship' of the three non-ministerial departments (GLD, CPS, and SFO) that carry out the vast majority of government legal activity. As we shall see, the independence of CPS and SFO in their operational decision-making has been the subject of extensive parliamentary debate in this century and has been formally recognized as crucial to the integrity of the criminal prosecution system.

One might have expected that the concentration of legal advisory services in TSol and its transformation into GLD would have prompted debate about its unorthodox relationship with the Attorney General. A recent annual report of HM Procurator General and Treasury Solicitor describes the Law Officers as having 'sponsorship responsibilities' in relation to GLD and being 'answerable in Parliament for its operations'.[59] According to the (separate) annual report from GLD, 'as Chief Legal Adviser to government, the Attorney has a close interest in the legal advice and legal services being provided to government by GLD and the wider Government Legal Profession'.[60] One would not expect to see the Chancellor of Exchequer described as having 'a close interest' in the Treasury's management of the economy, or the Secretary of State for Defence described as having 'a close interest' in the maintenance of the United Kingdom's armed forces: the formulation points to a certain distance between the Attorney and day-to-day civil legal work which is not necessarily identical in nature with the more formal limitations on the Law Officers' engagement with prosecutions that we examine in section III. In terms of financial accountability the situation of GLD is also unusual. The Treasury Solicitor is the accounting officer not just for TSol, now GLD, but also for the Attorney General's Office (AGO), the small team of lawyers and administrators that directly supports the Law Officers' work, including the exercise of the role of oversight and accountability to Parliament in respect of GLD. This produces the odd result that the principal official of AGO reports in respect of its financial performance to the head of a department subject to his minister's 'supervision and sponsorship'.

The process of centralization of advice pursued between 2011 and 2015 meant that over a very broad area of central government, legal advisers ceased to be responsible to departmental ministers and funded from departmental budgets, and instead became answerable for their performance to the Treasury Solicitor and funded via the fees charged by TSol, and then GLD, to departments. Before this happened, the Attorney General's relationship with departmental legal advisers responsible to different ministers had been, at best, indirect.[61] Now virtually all the government's civil legal staff

[59] HM Procurator General and Treasury Solicitor, *Annual Report and Accounts 2021–22* (HC 2021–22, 189) 8. The annual report of HM Procurator General and Treasury Solicitor is a separate publication from the annual report of GLD, and covers both GLD and the other bodies for which the Treasury Solicitor is financially responsible—the Attorney General's Office (AGO) and Her Majesty's Crown Prosecution Service Inspectorate (HMCPSI).

[60] Government Legal Department, *Annual Report and Accounts 2022–23* (n 42) 34.

[61] Though at the time of the Andrew Inquiry, the then Attorney General, Sir Patrick Mayhew, argued strongly and persistently with ministerial colleagues and the Treasury in favour of improved pay and recognition for lawyers across the Civil Service: see correspondence and minutes collected in The Andrew Review of Government Legal Services—Lawyers' Pay, National Archives file PO-CH/NL/0207, Part A (1988).

worked for an executive agency responsible to the Attorney. This produced a situation very close to Sir Robert Andrew's 1989 vision of 'a unified legal service whose members are paid from a single Vote', which he envisaged as being organized as a department under the direct ministerial responsibility of the Law Officers.[62] In 1989 this radical proposal was quietly ignored by government.[63] By 2015, however, the most difficult change, persuading large departments to give up their own legal services, had already been accomplished. Could this have been the moment to relaunch the notion of a legal service under the direct ministerial control of the Law Officers? Did the nature of GLD's work of legal advice and civil litigation require the same degree of independence of political control as was considered essential in the prosecution field?

It appears that it was not until the tenure of Geoffrey Cox as Attorney General (2018–20) that this possibility was given serious consideration. We have noted that framework agreements, invented in the 1980s for the management of executive agencies, have since become the normal means through which most arm's length bodies' relationships with their sponsoring department are organized, objectives determined, financial accountability arrangements stipulated, and so on.[64] Having settled framework agreements with SFO and CPS in 2019 and 2020,[65] Cox initiated a similar process in relation to GLD. There had been a succession of such agreements between the Attorney and the Treasury Solicitor. The one in force at the time of creation of GLD has been characterized as 'relatively formal' and replacing it with an agreement offering closer oversight appears to have been difficult. It may have been derailed—at least temporarily—by a proposal by Cox that GLD should be absorbed into an Attorney General's Department so as to be subject to ministerial control, rather than mere superintendence and sponsorship.[66] One can feel some sympathy with this move. The Attorney is, after all, customarily described as the government's 'Chief' legal adviser,[67] and it is perhaps surprising for newly appointed Attorneys to find themselves Chief but with very few Indians—only the 65 staff of the AGO, while the 2,822 at the GLD have a different leader: the Treasury Solicitor.[68] There are also basic differences between the situation of GLD and that of the other bodies over which the Attorney exercises 'superintendence'. CPS and SFO decisions are executive while GLD's activity is principally advisory; CPS and SFO activities are funded through the parliamentary supply cycle, while GLD is almost entirely funded by the fees paid by its departmental and other clients. The advisory role may be thought to weaken any need in the organization of GLD for the sort of distance between Law Officers and individual

[62] Andrew (n 31) 31–33.
[63] Daintith and Page (n 7) 216.
[64] Chapter 4, section 3.2.
[65] This chapter, section 3.2.
[66] Interview with Sir Jonathan Jones, Treasury Solicitor 2014–20 (10 March 2022).
[67] The suggestion, by a former First Parliamentary Counsel, that the Attorney General and Solicitor General are the government's 'only' legal advisers and that any other legal advice is tendered as a 'delegate' of the Law Officers, or is conditional on express or implied adoption by them, is unsupported by authority and wholly at odds with the historical evolution of the legal advice function in government: Stephen Laws, *The Treasury Devil and the Scandal that Never Was* (Policy Exchange 20 June 2022), cited in Richard Ekins, Stephen Laws, and Conor Casey, *Government Lawyers, the Civil Service Code and the Rule of Law* (Policy Exchange 2023) 14, n 7.
[68] Figures from HM Procurator General and Treasury Solicitor, *Annual Report and Accounts 2022–23* (HC 2022–23, 1320) 48.

decision-making that has shaped their relationship with CPS and SFO. At the same time, however, that role means that departmental ministers, as the fee-paying clients GLD lawyers are organized to serve, may be suspicious of any reform that might create a possibly conflicting relationship of subordination for those lawyers. Geoffrey Cox's plans may well have run aground on the rock of such suspicions.

The 2019–20 review of the work of the Attorney General's Office simply referred to activity in 'exploring options for formalising the governance relationship' with GLD,[69] and despite the work of a review group with members from GLD, AGO, the Treasury, and the Cabinet Office, a new framework agreement between GLD and the Attorney General (covering governance structures and accountability arrangements) remains, at the time of writing, on an 'interim' basis. A ministerial strategy board has however been set up and has held several meetings, and the then Attorney (Suella Braverman)[70] signalled her 'close interest' and desire for active engagement by initiating, in October 2020, an internal review of GLD's work. A further step that brought the Attorney General's position closer to that of other departmental ministers was the appointment by Ms Braverman of the first political advisers (spads) to serve in AGO. The question of whether the Law Officers should have such an adviser had apparently cropped up regularly on the appointment of a new Attorney, and at least one Treasury Solicitor had advised strongly against it because it suggested that politics might colour the Attorney's opinions. Not having a spad, however,

> sometimes caused slight problems, because people would say, 'Hasn't your special adviser told you about this?', because there was a whole nexus, and I would say, 'I don't have one'. You could be a bit out of the loop.[71]

While Ms Braverman took at least one of her spads with her to her next posting at the Home Office, subsequent Attorneys have followed her example: AGO had two spads in March 2023. Within AGO, the post is apparently seen as having value in ensuring political information and context and in providing alternative channels through which Law Officers' advice to ministers, and reactions to it, can travel to and fro.

2.2 Legal advice

2.2.1 Legal advice and legal risk

It is clear that considerable efforts were deployed, over the period when departmental legal teams were being brought into the ever-growing TSol, to reassure departments and their ministers that the transference of responsibility for the organization and

[69] Attorney General's Office, *AGO Business Plan 2020–21*, 13.

[70] Since 2018 Attorneys General have succeeded one another in bewilderingly rapid sequence: Geoffrey Cox (July 2018–February 2020), Suella Braverman (February 2020–March 2021), Michael Ellis (acting) (March–September 2021), Suella Braverman (September 2021–September 2022), Michael Ellis (September–October 2022), Victoria Prentiss (October 2022–).

[71] Dominic Grieve, former Attorney General: Constitution Committee (n 8) oral evidence (6 July 2022) q 106. Nonetheless, he thought that appointing a spad was 'a strange thing for an Attorney General to do'.

salaries of lawyers from departments to GLD would *not* affect the attitude of those lawyers to the interests of the departments that they continued to advise—and in which, physically, they normally continued to be located. Most government lawyers interviewed for a 2013 research project thought that ministers and administrators would see little change: their assumption tended to be that the lawyers in their department were their department's lawyers, even when those lawyers technically belonged to TSol. There were, however, some government lawyers who were concerned that there might be a ministerial perception that lawyers who technically came from outside the department might view priorities and issues differently: they were not 'one of us'.[72] There are indications that the position of departmental legal advisers within their client department may have changed somewhat. We no longer find such advisers serving on departmental boards, as was the case with several departments in the past, and a senior GLD lawyer from outside the departmental advisory teams told us that the relationship of advisers with policymakers in departments was now 'less intimate'. Efforts to retain the confidence of departmental clients appear however to have been rewarded by the maintenance of levels of client satisfaction at GLD similar to those recorded for TSol before enlargement.

At the same time some officials have expressed the view that government lawyers are much more exposed than in earlier periods to internal criticism, whether from ministers, administrators, other lawyers, or standing or ad hoc reviews of executive action.[73] Such criticism is not new: earlier research presenting the results of interviews with government lawyers and administrators back in 2002–03 showed that then too, some administrators, at least, stereotyped government lawyers as excessively conservative and obstructive.[74] Officials did not link recent perceived growth of critical attitudes to centralization, but to a number of other contextual changes over the years: more prolific use of legislation by government, more proactive approaches by courts, substantial increases in the numbers of government lawyers, constitutional change, and the greater prominence of lawyers in policy formulation.[75] The increase in ministerial readiness to challenge legal advice was seen as in many ways a positive development, in some cases illustrative of ministers engaging fully with the legal advice they received, and such challenge could assist government lawyers to understand better their ministerial clients' objectives, risk appetite, and perspectives. It was a bipartisan phenomenon, but it was also clear that Brexit represented a watershed in this general critical tendency, with a step change in the level of ministerial pushback against legal advice. Indeed government lawyers have now become the target of the sort of public criticism from ministers previously reserved for judges, with Suella Braverman, as Attorney General, announcing that her 2020 review of GLD had produced the 'overwhelming' conclusion that government lawyers were too cautious in

[72] Views recorded by Yong (n 37) 44–45.

[73] Official interview, 28 September 2022.

[74] Philip Lewis and Linda Mulcahy, 'Government Lawyers: Technicians, Policy Shapers and Organisational Brakes' (2021) 28 International Journal of the Legal Profession 23.

[75] On this last point see in more detail Yong (n 37) ch 3, noting, at 51, that most of the government lawyers he interviewed thought that there had been a noticeable decline in the legal literacy and/or policy capacity amongst administrators, which might be a reason for the greater, and earlier, involvement of lawyers in policy development.

their advice and that this had needlessly hampered the achievement of ministerial policy objectives.[76] The review, and its aftermath, demonstrate how the creation of GLD has, even in the absence of formal institutional change, increased ministerial influence over government lawyers; it is hard to see how an Attorney General could have offered this sort of criticism of lawyers employed by other departments.

The more fundamental issue raised by the review, however, was about the very nature of government legal advice work in a period of all-embracing judicial review. There was a time—a century ago—when government lawyers, noting that 'the departmental adviser is called on to assist the department with his advice in the many cases where the question of pressing the rights of the Crown is one of discretion', whether because of financial or other obstacles to litigating against the Crown, or the lack of a judicial remedy, could assert 'the almost judicial nature of the discretion which the official lawyer is compelled to exercise'.[77] This idea that the government lawyer might function as an internal judge of executive action, applying standards of justice as well as of strict legality, is not reflected in contemporary official guidance. Instead, government lawyers are instructed that their advice should focus on the level of legal risk presented by proposed executive action and on options for mitigating or avoiding risk. This approach was only formalized in GLD guidance in 2015, revised and reissued as 'Attorney's General's Guidance' in 2022,[78] but Yong, in his study of government lawyers conducted in 2012–13, reported that all the government lawyers he interviewed were 'adamant' that it would be rare to see the provision of advice in terms of whether something was 'legal' or not, unless the law was clear-cut; it was more about understanding and managing legal risk. The 2015 *Guidance Note* seems to have been mainly directed to ensuring consistency of measurement and vocabulary among lawyers when advising on legal risk, by identifying different types of risk (of whether litigation would occur, of adverse findings if it did, and of seriousness of impact of any such findings) and different levels (low: <30%; medium low: 30–50%; medium high: 50–70%: and high: >70%). Interviewees accepted, however, that the risk focus represented a change from earlier practice under which 'lawyers might give advice in the nature of a quasi-"judgment", setting out preferred options and providing definitive answers to those options'.[79] Later research (2020–21) 'found that, in general, policy officials did not think that government lawyers took an "obstructive" approach to legal advice. Many lawyers we spoke to emphasized that their role was to advise on risk; it was then for the "policy client" to decide what risk to take.'[80]

76 Tevye Markson, 'Attorney General accuses "overcautious" government lawyers of "hampering ministers"' *Civil Service World* (2 August 2022). Comments on the review from other sources, however, suggest that Ms Braverman may be more easily overwhelmed than others who have longer experience of government legal work.

77 Alfred H Dennis, 'The Legal Departments of the Crown' (1926) 4 Public Administration 141, 153.

78 Government Legal Department, *Guidance Note on Legal Risk* (2015); *Attorney General's Guidance on Legal Risk* (2 August 2022) para 15. A further revision appeared while this work was in press: Attorney General, *Attorney General's Guidance on Legal Risk* (November 2024), which adds new material on compliance with international law and replaces the minimum requirement, for advising that a proposal is not unlawful, of a 'respectable' legal argument in its favour with that of a 'tenable' argument.

79 Yong (n 37) 52–53.

80 Haddon, Hogarth, and Nice (n 14) 11.

There has been much emphasis in recent years on the importance to good administration of getting lawyers—and indeed other professional specialists—involved at an early stage in policy formation. Such involvement means that lawyers in advisory teams have more chance of influencing the shape of policies while these still possess some political flexibility. As a result, it has perhaps become less likely that a position will be reached where a lawyer might feel compelled to express a negative opinion on the legality of the action proposed. Indeed, GLD's 2015 *Guidance Note* suggested that it was likely to be 'highly exceptional' for a lawyer to need to advise that proposed action was unlawful. We should stress that the reference here is to *final* legal advice, given at the point of ministerial decision; advice given at earlier stages might regularly steer a department away from policies or procedures which it had not perceived as going beyond its powers. And the bar for finding a proposal 'unlawful' is set pretty high: that 'no respectable legal argument could be put to the Court'. An argument could be 'respectable' even if the lawyer rated its chances of succeeding at less than 30%—in which case he or she was expected to advise that action was 'high risk', but ministers might 'legitimately decide to proceed'.[81]

This approach seems a world away from the concerns expressed in the 1920s about the wisdom and justice of pressing the rights of the Crown. Instead, as policy officials have noted, it provides support and legitimation 'when the government is consciously seeking to push policy as far as is permissible within the constraints of the law' or where, 'as with certain Home Office decisions, politicians would find it more politically palatable to be forced to abandon a policy or action by a court than to abandon it themselves'.[82] Formulating the task of advising in terms of risk also offers comfort to ministers mindful of their 'overarching duty' under the Ministerial Code 'to comply with the law'.[83] All that is needed, no matter how improbable an eventual finding of legality might be, is a 'credible argument the government could properly run in court'.

But what if there is no court, as may be the case where the matter is one of international law? Diametrically opposed views appear from the evidence given at the Chilcot Inquiry into the Iraq War, on the question of whether UN Security Council Resolution 1441 required a second resolution as a precondition for an invasion of Iraq.[84] Sir Michael Wood, the legal adviser to the Foreign Office, was firmly of the opinion that it did. For the Foreign Secretary, the fact that international law was an uncertain field with 'no international court for resolving such questions in the manner of a domestic court' and that 'the issue is an arguable one capable of honestly and reasonably-held differences of view' entitled him to reject Sir Michael's advice as being

[81] At least in relation to the use of force, the 'respectable argument' approach has been rejected by a former Lord Chancellor, Lord Mackay of Clashfern, in evidence to the House of Lords Constitution Committee in 2022: (HL 2022–23, 118) 8 June 2022, q 76, where he disagreed with the idea that 'a respectable argument that something is legitimate . . . is sufficient to justify the particular course . . . If you are faced with the question as to whether this is lawful or not, I regard it as my responsibility to reach a view as to what the law is on that or whether it was justified.'

[82] Haddon, Hogarth, and Nice (n 14) 11, 12. See also Joe Tomlinson, Naoise Coakley, and Roisin Gambroudes, 'It's a trap! The Changing Dynamics of Executive Engagement with Judicial Review' (*UK Const L Blog*, 28 July 2022).

[83] Cabinet Office, *Ministerial Code* (as revised November 2022) para 1.3.

[84] Report of the Iraq Inquiry (Chilcot Inquiry) oral evidence (26 January 2010).

'very dogmatic'.[85] For Sir Michael, the absence of the possibility of judicial resolution worked to the opposite effect:

> As part of giving advice and the client accepting the advice, the absence of a court, I think, is a reason for being more scrupulous in adhering to the advice, because it cannot be tested. It is one thing for a lawyer to say, 'Well, there is an argument here. Have a go. A court, a judge, will decide in the end'. It is quite different in the international system, where that's usually not the case. You have a duty to the law, a duty to the system. You are setting precedents by the very fact of saying things and doing things.[86]

Against this background the Attorney General's claim that her review of GLD advice activity in 2020–21 had reached the 'overwhelming' conclusion that government lawyers were too cautious in their advice and this had needlessly hampered ministerial policy objectives seems highly surprising. There was, she claimed, 'a clear trend of lawyers advising negatively, only to be proven wrong in court'.[87] While blaming the lawyers is easy—if unexpected in the mouth of an Attorney General—it would seem, in line with the findings of the 2013 and 2021 investigations of government legal advice, that what hampers ministerial policy objectives is a weak risk appetite on the part of some ministers and their officials, while others, recipients of 'negative' legal advice, appear to go boldly forward and seek the judgment of the courts. Certainly if we look at the modified legal risk *Guidance Note* that emerged after this inquiry and after lengthy discussion between GLD and AGO, we find that while there is a lot more verbiage, the basic risk matrix remains unchanged, while the possibility of finding that projected action or policy is unlawful has been slightly widened: from 'highly exceptional' to 'exceptional'.[88]

2.2.2 Whose advice? The position of the Law Officers

Discussions of formalizing the Attorney General's relationship with GLD, and reconsideration of GLD's advice function, do not appear so far to have impinged upon the respective roles of the Law Officers, and of GLD and other government lawyers, in providing legal advice on specific issues. The detailed official guidance as to when it would be 'appropriate' to seek the Law Officers' advice has not changed over this century. It has however disappeared from the Ministerial Code, which mentions only the general rule that 'the Law Officers must be consulted in good time before the Government is committed to critical decisions involving legal considerations'.[89]

[85] ibid 32–33. He also reminded Sir Michael that 'when he had been at the Home Office, . . . he had often been advised things were unlawful and he had gone ahead anyway and won in the courts' (31).

[86] ibid 34. He received support from the Attorney General, who responded to the Foreign Secretary's rebuke to Wood by saying, 'if a government legal adviser genuinely believes that a course of action is unlawful, then it is his or her right and duty to say so. I support this right regardless of whether I agree with the substance of the advice which has been given.' Report of the Iraq Inquiry (Chilcot Inquiry) oral evidence (26 January 2010).

[87] As reported in Markson (n 76). cf the Foreign Secretary's 2003 remark reported at n 85.

[88] *Attorney General's Guidance on Legal Risk* (n 78) para 15.

[89] Cabinet Office, *Ministerial Code* (as revised November 2022) para 2.10.

Instead the guidance has been inserted in the *Cabinet Manual*, prepared in 2010–11 and not since updated.[90] According to the *Manual*:

> 6.6 The Law Officers must be consulted by ministers or their officials in good time before the Government is committed to critical decisions involving legal considerations. It has normally been considered appropriate to consult the Law Officers in cases where:
>
> the legal consequences of action by the Government might have important repercussions in the foreign, EU or domestic fields;
>
> a departmental legal adviser is in doubt concerning:
>
> - the legality or constitutional propriety of proposed primary or subordinate legislation which the Government proposes to introduce;
> - the powers necessary to make proposed subordinate legislation; or
> - the legality of proposed administrative action, particularly where that action might be subject to challenge in the courts;
>
> ministers, or their officials, wish to have the advice of the Law Officers on questions involving legal considerations that are likely to come before Cabinet or a Cabinet committee;
>
> there is a particular legal difficulty (including one that arises in the context of litigation) that may raise sensitive policy issues; or
>
> two or more government departments disagree on legal questions and wish to seek the view of the Law Officers.

In an era when the possibility of administrative action's being challenged in the courts is an everyday fact of executive life, the idea of 'doubt' as to legality as the trigger for reference to the Law Officers looks, taken by itself, to be a recipe for a flood of references. As discussed above, however, it now needs to be seen in the context of the development by TSol, GLD, and AGO of an explicitly quantitative approach to the estimation of legal risk. Guidance has also been circulated by AGO on the procedure for making a reference, laying emphasis on the need for adequate preparation, and on the existence of other sources of advice—such as counsel, or legal colleagues within one of GLD's Centres of Excellence—that might be more appropriate, at least in the first instance, for cases where there is a gap in the law, or the legal position is novel, complex, or uncertain.[91] We heard suggestions that a feeling that outside counsel should be consulted en route to the Law Officers was becoming widespread, and that this was producing the idea that, notwithstanding the specialist expertise of GLD legal advisers, counsel could somehow provide a 'higher' level of legal advice—which was unfortunate.

Among the triggers for a reference to the Law Officers is a case where 'two or more departments disagree on legal questions and wish to seek the view of the Law Officers'. One purpose of creating GLD was to secure better communication of information across the government legal service, and more contact and movement

[90] Cabinet Office, *Cabinet Manual* (2011) para 6.6, and see Daintith and Page (n 7) 303 for the almost identical formulation operative in 1997.

[91] See n 45.

between departmental legal teams; and, as we have seen, specialist functions like employment and commercial matters are now organized on a cross-departmental basis. Unsurprisingly, therefore, issues that might previously have come to the Law Officers as the subject of inter-departmental legal arguments may now frequently be resolved by discussion within GLD—though a minister who is dissatisfied with the result continues to have the option to move the issue up to the Attorney for an authoritative opinion. The creation of GLD has not had the effect of introducing any kind of filtering of requests for Law Officers' advice. While the scope for settling issues within GLD might mean that fewer issues of this kind have been referred to the Law Officers in the last few years, the overall volume of references may have been sustained by a greater number of cases in which departments or their ministers sought the comfort of a Law Officer's opinion, for example by reason of the political salience of the issue. The convention that the content, and also the fact, of a Law Officer's advice is not to be disclosed without that Law Officer's agreement—which is accorded with great rarity[92]—means that no information is available about individual opinions, and aggregated information is also lacking: advice may be formal or informal in nature; the propensity to consult the Law Officers may vary between ministers and departments and, within departments, over time; and even AGO itself still does not maintain a single database collecting all Law Officers' advice.[93] The latest parliamentary inquiry into the work and status of the Law Officers has endorsed, once more, the convention of non-disclosure, with a possible exception for opinions relating to the use of armed force.[94]

The greater strength and scope of GLD legal advice has certainly done nothing to weaken the principle that the Law Officers' opinions are final and binding, even if they run counter to the weight of specialist opinion within GLD, or other departments like FCDO, and regardless of the degree of expertise and authority that underlay their preparation. Curiously, perhaps, the Constitution Committee's observation that in recent years Attorneys General have been appointed with less legal experience than was previously the case, four of the six appointed since 2010 not having attained the rank of Queen's or King's Counsel prior to appointment,[95] did not lead it to reflect on the possible diminution of the authority their advice might carry within government. Political status, character, and independence of mind seemed to count more heavily in this respect than legal reputation and experience.[96] Such reputation and experience must, however, be sufficient to support the Attorney's personal responsibility for her advice, even if she herself receives advice from a range of sources within or outside the Government Legal Profession. One former Attorney General insisted that while, in framing her opinions, the Attorney might herself be drawing on advice, possibly from a range of sources, those opinions must be her own. Any suggestion that the Attorney

[92] McCormick (n 57) 205–08; Conor McCormick and Graeme Cowie, *The Law Officers: A Constitutional and Functional Overview* (House of Commons Library Briefing Paper, May 2020) 51–55.

[93] For the similar position at the turn of the century, see Daintith and Page (n 7) 302–09.

[94] Constitution Committee (n 8) paras 150–56.

[95] para 234.

[96] paras 232, 238.

General is 'the person who commissions advice for the Government' would represent 'a subtle, but worrying, shift in where the Law Officers' responsibilities lie'.[97]

III Criminal Prosecution

3.1 The Law Officers, CPS, and SFO

When GLD came into being the public prosecution function in England and Wales had already been centralized for 30 years. The CPS was established in 1986, under the Prosecution of Offences Act 1985, to take responsibility for most public prosecutions in England and Wales, on a pattern already long established in Scotland. It is headed by the Director of Public Prosecutions (DPP), an office dating back to 1879 which has always had close links with the Attorney General.[98] The creation of CPS radically changed the role of the DPP, from a specialized office dealing with serious and sensitive crime, either in general or by virtue of special statutory competences, to one of managing the entire criminal prosecution system. Special arrangements were made under the Criminal Justice Act 1987, Part I, for the prosecution of serious fraud, and the SFO, with its own Director, was set up in that year. Its remit extends to England and Wales and Northern Ireland (but not Scotland). The DPP and the Director of SFO are both appointed by the Attorney General, and CPS and SFO are both 'Law Officers' Departments', but the role of the Attorney General is one of statutory superintendence rather than hierarchical authority on the usual departmental pattern. As already noted, their status is that of non-ministerial departments.[99]

The position of the Attorney General, at one and the same time a politically responsible government minister (and member of Parliament), and a lawyer sitting at the apex of the government's various legal functions, has been the object of intermittent concern among constitutional and political commentators for at least a century. While the tension between political partisanship and legal objectivity extends across the whole range of the Attorney's very varied functions,[100] it has been most acute in relation to the function of prosecuting crime. Public controversies on this score erupted at intervals during the 20th century, starting with the *Campbell* prosecution in 1924, in which allegations of political interference brought down the Labour government of the day.[101] These tensions did not suddenly cease with the arrival of the new millennium, but in recent years some significant moves to address them have been made, notably by clarifying the relationship between the Law Officers, CPS, and SFO in making prosecution decisions.

[97] Dominic Grieve, former Attorney General: Constitution Committee (n 8) oral evidence (6 July 2022) q 114.

[98] Prosecution of Offences Act 1879, s 2; John LlJ Edwards, *The Attorney-General, Politics and the Public Interest* (Sweet and Maxwell 1984).

[99] See generally chapter 4, section I.

[100] For these, see generally Daintith and Page (n 7) 231–36; House of Commons Constitutional Affairs Committee, *Constitutional Role of the Attorney General* (HC 2006–07, 306) paras 10–24; McCormick and Cowie (n 92) 10–21; McCormick (n 57) ch 3; and see further below, section 3.2.

[101] John LlJ Edwards, *The Law Officers of the Crown* (Sweet and Maxwell 1964), 199–225.

The relationship between the Law Officers and CPS and SFO is set out in some detail in these organizations' framework documents. As we have seen, framework documents or agreements were introduced as an element of the Next Steps programme of devolving departmental service delivery to executive agencies.[102] They describe the role of the agency and its general relationship with the department of which it forms an appendage, and are filled out by regularly revised corporate and business plans. This arrangement has since been extended to cover also many non-departmental public bodies, which may also operate under the close supervision of a department but which, unlike executive agencies, have a separate legal existence. Non-ministerial departments (NMDs) like CPS and SFO, however, do not normally operate in this way. The desire to recognize their independence, which may have statutory expression, and their financial status—they enjoy their own Vote in the annual estimates—may be thought to make assimilation to executive agencies and NDPBs inappropriate, though as has been forcibly pointed out, different NMDs have quite inconsistent views of how close their relationship should be with the ministers who answer for their activities in Parliament, and some NMDs, among them GLD, also have the status of executive agencies.[103]

Framework agreements were, however, concluded between the Law Officers and SFO,[104] and the Law Officers and CPS,[105] in January 2019 and December 2020 respectively.[106] They incorporate material commonly found in the general run of framework documents, such as matters of general governance, financial discipline, and accountability. In pursuance of the Attorney General's acknowledged accountability for the general operation of both CPS and SFO,[107] they reinforce the instruments through which the strategy of these services may be shaped. A strategy board chaired by the Attorney has been established for each of CPS and SFO. These boards have been described by a subsequent Attorney as 'candid' and 'effective' fora for probing and challenging them on their performance, strategy, and plans.[108] The Attorney's influence over strategy is doubtless also supported by her role as 'the Minister who is going to go in to bat for their budgets'.[109]

The arrival of the 21st century did not herald the sudden cessation of the concerns about such independence which, as we have noted, had existed for many years. In 2007 the Constitutional Affairs Committee of the House of Commons reviewed the constitutional situation of the Attorney General. Its decision to do so was prompted in part by the change in the role and status of the Lord Chancellor, who under the Blair government's constitutional reform[110] ceased to take a judicial oath of office and

[102] Chapter 4, section 3.2; Daintith and Page (n 7) 37–46.

[103] Jill Rutter, *The Strange Case of Non-Ministerial Departments* (Institute for Government 2013).

[104] Attorney General's Office and Serious Fraud Office, *Framework Agreement between the Law Officers and the Director of the Serious Fraud Office* (21 January 2019) (SFO Framework Agreement).

[105] Attorney General's Office and Crown Prosecution Service, *Framework Agreement between the Law Officers and the Director of Public Prosecutions* (18 December 2020) (CPS Framework Agreement).

[106] See, for more detail, Justice Committee (HC 2017–19, 1887) qq 3, 18–20 (Geoffrey Cox QC).

[107] See the recent evidence sessions before the House of Commons Justice Committee on the work of the Attorney General: Jeremy Wright QC (HC 2015–16, 409); Geoffrey Cox QC (HC 2017–19, 1887); Suella Braverman QC (HC 2019–21, 462); (HC 2021–22, 962).

[108] Suella Braverman QC (HC 2019–21, 462) qq 70, 74, 75.

[109] *Per* the Chair of the Justice Committee, Sir Robert Neill (HC 2019–21, 462) q 76.

[110] Constitutional Reform Act 2005.

saw his multiple roles reduced to that of a departmental minister, responsible for the Ministry of Justice, leaving the Attorney General and Solicitor General as the only members of government required to be legally qualified. Against the background of the greater salience of the Attorney's legal responsibilities, the Committee noted the recurrence of controversies highlighting concerns about potential conflicts between the Attorney's political duties as a minister and his or her functions of providing independent legal advice and superintending the prosecution services in England and Wales. The most egregious of these controversies, arising out of the Iraq war, raised questions about the Attorney's independence in offering advice to the Cabinet on international law issues,[111] but two others related directly to the Law Officers' prosecution functions: consideration of whether there should be prosecutions under the Honours (Prevention of Abuses) Act 1925 in respect of allegations that loans to the Labour Party to fight the 2005 general election had been induced by promises of peerages; and discontinuance by the Director of SFO of investigations of bribery charges against British Aerospace in connection with a Saudi Arabian contract.[112] The so-called 'cash for honours' scandal ended after a lengthy police investigation with a decision by CPS to drop the case on finding that the available evidence would not support a realistic prospect of convicting any person for any offence under the 1925 Act.[113] The *British Aerospace* case saw the Prime Minister making representations to the Attorney General that the investigation should be stopped, following Saudi government threats to suspend anti-terrorism cooperation if possible corruption by Saudi officials were further investigated. In neither case, it would appear, did the Attorney General take the relevant decision or even seek to influence it,[114] but for the House of Commons Constitutional Affairs Committee, the fact that there may have been 'perceptions' of a lack of independence and of political bias on the part of the Attorney General was sufficient to justify radical change in the nature and responsibilities of the office. They recommended that the Attorney's legal policy functions be transferred to the Minister of Justice and that legal decisions in prosecutions and the provision of legal advice should rest with someone who was appointed as a career lawyer, and was not a politician or a member of the government.[115]

Gordon Brown's government was more than ready to listen to propositions for change, announcing a consultation exercise on the Attorney's position, among a number of other issues, in its White Paper on the *Governance of Britain*,[116] published in the same month as the Committee's report. On the key issues of whether

[111] Rebecca Moosavian, 'Power/Knowledge Dynamics in the Attorney General's Iraq War Advice' [2020] Public Law 72.

[112] Constitutional Affairs Committee, *The Constitutional Role of the Attorney General* (n 100) paras 35–46.

[113] For its reasoning, see Public Administration Select Committee, *Propriety and Peerages* (HC 2007–08, 153) paras 46–51.

[114] On the 'cash for honours' investigation, see n 113; the Director of the SFO's decision in *British Aerospace* was challenged by judicial review, and the judgment of the House of Lords sustaining the decision furnishes exhaustive detail on the exchanges that led to it: *R (on the application of Corner House Research) v Director of the Serious Fraud Office* [2008] UKHL 60.

[115] Constitutional Affairs Committee, *The Constitutional Role of the Attorney General* (n 100) paras 54, 105.

[116] Secretary of State for Justice and Lord Chancellor, *The Governance of Britain*, (Cm 7170, July 2007) paras 52–56.

the government's chief legal adviser and person ultimately in charge of prosecutions should continue to be a minister, substantial majorities among consultees—with lawyers and legal organizations prominent among them—rejected the proposals of the Constitution Committee and favoured the status quo.[117] The influence over other members of government thought to be conferred by the Attorney's ministerial status trumped concerns about perceptions of lack of independence. Nonetheless, in the draft bill responding to the consultation, the government brought forward some significant measures designed to guarantee that the prosecution function would, so far as possible, be untainted by perceptions of political influence.[118] These provisions would have

> made it clear that the Attorney's statutory role of 'superintendence' did not encompass a power of direction of prosecutors on individual cases save where legislation required the Attorney's consent to a prosecution (cl 2);
>
> provided for a protocol governing the Attorney's involvement with CPS and SFO, to be laid before Parliament (cl 3);
>
> introduced 5-year fixed term appointments for the heads of the public prosecution services (cll 4–6);
>
> provided for the modification of certain consent functions of the Attorney (cll 7–10);
>
> abolished *nolle prosequi*, the common law writ through which the Attorney can stop any prosecution in England and Wales (cl 11);
>
> defined the Attorney's power to intervene in prosecutions on security-related issues (cll 12–15); and
>
> required an annual report to Parliament on the exercise of the Attorney General's functions (cl 16).

When the bill was brought back to Parliament in 2009 as the Constitutional Reform and Governance Bill, these provisions had been taken out.[119] The Joint Committee of Lords and Commons that had examined the draft bill had questioned the need for legislation in this area,[120] favouring the current status of the Attorney and doubting even whether changes like the removal in most cases of the power of direction were appropriate. The result was that changes requiring legislation, like the abolition of *nolle prosequi* or the power of selective removal of statutory consent functions, were lost, and that a non-statutory protocol was relied upon for the expression of the most significant remaining reforms.

[117] Lord Chancellor and Secretary of State for Justice, *The Governance of Britain—Constitutional Renewal* (Cm 7342-3, 2008) paras 32–98.

[118] Lord Chancellor and Secretary of State for Justice, *The Governance of Britain—Draft Constitutional Renewal Bill* (Cm 7342-2, 2008).

[119] On the differences between the draft Bill and the 2009 Bill and the resulting Constitutional Reform and Governance Act 2010, see Mark Ryan, 'The Constitutional Reform and Governance Act 2010: The Evolution and Development of a Constitutional Act' (2014) 35 Liverpool Law Review 233.

[120] Joint Committee on the Draft Constitutional Renewal Bill, Vol I: Report, (2007–08) HL 166-I, HC 551-I, p 7 and, for detailed commentary, paras 77–133.

The 2019 and 2020 framework agreements between the Law Officers and the head of SFO and the DPP replaced the protocol and are now the vehicles for these protections of prosecutorial independence. They incorporate the idea that it is the DPP and the Director of SFO who, in the exercise of their independent and quasi-judicial decision-making function, determine whether to prosecute, except in cases where the Attorney's consent to a prosecution is required by statute.[121] But where the 2008 legislative proposals would have made it clear that 'superintendence' did not permit Law Officer directions on individual cases, the framework agreements suggest the opposite in certain limited circumstances. In regard to national security, the agreement states:

> Exceptionally, and only where in the Attorney General's opinion it is necessary to do so for the purposes of safeguarding national security, the Attorney General will consider the exercise of their *power to issue a direction that a prosecution is not started or not continued.* (emphasis supplied)[122]

The agreements also preserve, for 'a few very exceptional cases', the so-called 'Shawcross exercises' of the sort undertaken in the *British Aerospace* case. Under this procedure the Directors of SFO or CPS, as advised by the Attorney, or (in a statutory consent case) the Attorney herself, may 'seek wider ministerial representations' for the purpose of 'identifying particular public interest considerations which may be relevant to the prosecution decision'.[123]

It is, consequently, impossible to see in the framework agreements any reflection of the concerns that prompted the proposed 2008 legislative reforms. It is the *status quo ante* applicable at the beginning of the century that is being formalized in the casework sections of the agreements and that continues to underpin the Attorney General's position. *Nolle prosequi* continues to exist; the Attorney General does not provide an annual report to Parliament of the type envisaged by the bill; the Directors of CPS and SFO enjoy no statutory guarantees of tenure. Curiously, the only significant innovation is the explicit exclusion of the Law Officers from any involvement in prosecutions concerning parliamentarians, ministers, political parties or elections, or their personal interests, which was a matter that did *not* figure in the 2008 bill.[124]

3.2 Control of other prosecuting authorities

The creation of CPS and SFO was not accompanied by the transfer to them of the prosecution powers that numerous central government departments were accustomed to exercise in relation to offences under legislation for which they were specifically responsible. In relation to those prosecutions, the Attorney General did not and still does not possess the rights of superintendence conferred by statute in relation to

[121] See SFO Framework Agreement (n 104) paras 42–48; CPS Framework Agreement (n 105) paras 46–52.
[122] SFO Framework Agreement (n 104) para 49; CPS Framework Agreement (n 105) para 53.
[123] SFO Framework Agreement (n 104) paras 53–55; CPS Framework Agreement (n 105) paras 57–59.
[124] SFO Framework Agreement (n 104) para 64; CPS Framework Agreement (n 105) para 68.

CPS and SFO prosecutions.[125] After the passage of the 1985 Act, the Attorney General described his position in this respect as one of 'overall purview',[126] hardly a position of strength and effectively one that was supported only by his ability either to stop the prosecution through the issue of a *nolle prosequi*[127] or by inviting the DPP to take it over and stop it using his statutory powers. Proceedings in the 'Supergun' and *Matrix Churchill* cases in the 1990s, both of them prosecutions by HM Customs and Excise arising out of suspicions that British companies were engaged in forbidden arms exports to Iraq, demonstrated the difficulty of the Attorney General's position when confronted with a department that apparently did not view its prosecution powers as subject to his control. Customs and Excise did not even consult him before launching the *Matrix Churchill* prosecution.[128]

Continuing problems with Customs and Excise prosecutions cast their shadow into the 21st century. The collapse in 2002, as a result of the non-disclosure of the involvement of an unpaid Customs informant, of the *London City Bond* trial for evasion of tens of millions of pounds of excise duties led to a review, jointly commissioned by the Treasury and the Attorney General, of the circumstances leading to this result. The review, by Mr Justice Butterfield, also considered developments in Customs and Excise prosecution practice following an earlier review by a former Treasury Solicitor and another QC, which had taken the view that while Customs and Excise should continue to be a prosecuting authority, solicitors at the department should, in the interest of independence, be accountable in respect of prosecutions to the Attorney General, not to the Commissioners.[129] Unsurprisingly in the light of Butterfield's finding that there had been major failings in the investigation into and prosecution of the *London City Bond* cases, the government accepted his recommendation that the Customs and Excise Prosecuting Office should become an entirely separate prosecuting authority accountable to the Attorney General on lines similar to CPS and SFO.[130]

The newly constituted office came into being simultaneously with HM Revenue and Customs, the body resulting from the merger of the two historic revenue departments, Customs and Excise and the Inland Revenue, effected under the Commissioners for Revenue and Customs Act 2005.[131] The Act established, as an independent entity, the Revenue and Customs Prosecution Office (RCPO), under the superintendence of the Attorney General, with the function of instituting and conducting Revenue and Customs criminal proceedings. A memorandum of understanding laid out the boundaries between the work of the RCPO and HMRC. Within five years, however, the new organization had been incorporated into the CPS, by means of appointing the DPP to the separate statutory post of Director of RCPO, a step hopefully described by RCPO

[125] Prosecution of Offences Act 1985, s 3(1); Criminal Justice Act 1987, s 1(2).

[126] Trade and Industry Committee, *Exports to Iraq* (HC 1991–92, 86) evidence, q 3436 (Sir Patrick Mayhew).

[127] For more detail on the use of *nolle prosequi*, see Crown Prosecution Service, *Termination of Proceedings (including Discontinuance)* (November 2019).

[128] See generally Daintith and Page (n 7) 290–95; Sir Richard Scott, *Report of the Inquiry into the Export of Defence Equipment and Dual-Use Goods to Iraq and Related Prosecutions* (HC 1995–96, 115).

[129] See the Solicitor General's written answer at HC Deb 12 March 2001, vol 364, col 416W.

[130] See the Attorney General's written answer at HL Deb 4 December 2003, vol 655, cols WA32–33.

[131] For the official review making the case for the merger, see Gus O'Donnell, *Financing Britain's Future: Review of the Revenue Departments* (Cm 6163, 2004).

as 'a merger not a takeover', under which 'HMRC work will be given appropriate priority and serviced within a ring-fenced division where established expertise can be preserved and new talent grown'.[132] The final nail in the coffin of the revenue departments' prosecution powers was driven in 2014, when the post of Director of Customs Prosecutions was abolished, and its functions transferred to the DPP, by means of a statutory instrument made under the Public Bodies Act 2011.[133]

While there have been fundamental changes in relation to 'revenue' prosecutions, there remain a large number of public authorities outside CPS and SFO which have statutory powers to prosecute but whose actions are not regulated by the parameters of the Law Officer/CPS/SFO relationships.[134] The Food Standards Agency, for example, has its own Legal Services Group to which Agency officials may refer serious or repeated breaches of regulations with a view to prosecution. The organization of prosecutions depends on the nature of the contravention, with some types (such as contraventions of hygiene rules in abbatoirs) investigated and prosecuted wholly internally, with no CPS involvement (though the prosecutor will proceed according to the Code for Crown Prosecutors),[135] while others, falling under the jurisdiction of the Department for Environment, Food and Rural Affairs (DEFRA), will be investigated by the Agency's Investigation Officers but prosecuted by CPS, as provided for, since 2011, by DEFRA's Enforcement Policy Statement.[136] Comparable differences in practice also exist elsewhere. The Insolvency Service (an executive agency of the Department of Business and Trade)[137] and the Maritime and Coastguard Agency (an executive agency of the Department of Transport)[138] continue to run their own prosecutions. Indeed, the latter agency, while noting that its prosecution activity, 'although not subject to direct managerial control by the Attorney General is subject to his oversight and as such the Maritime and Coastguard Agency make regular reports to him', departs from the principle of the independence of prosecutors by putting the decision whether or not to prosecute in the hands of its Director of Finance and Audit. In contrast, health and welfare fraud are investigated by Department of Work and Pensions and Department of Health staff, but since 2012 'the decision to prosecute and charge is made by a CPS prosecutor in all welfare and health fraud cases'.[139]

[132] Revenue and Customs Prosecutions Office, *Annual Report and Resource Accounts 2008/09* (HC 2008–09, 658) 6.

[133] Public Bodies (Merger of the Director of Public Prosecutions and the Director of Revenue and Customs Prosecutions) Order 2014, SI 2014/834. The two posts had been identified as a possible target for merger by sch 2, group 3 of the Act. On the Act see generally chapter 4, section 2.2.

[134] Authorities listed as linked with CPS by a 'Prosecutors' Convention', designed to avoid conflicts and overlaps, include the Civil Aviation Authority; Department for Business, Energy and Industrial Strategy; Department for the Environment, Food and Rural Affairs; Department of Work and Pensions; Environment Agency; Food Standards Agency; Gambling Commission; Health and Safety Executive; Information Commissioner's Office; Maritime and Coastguard Agency; Office of Rail Regulation; and Service Prosecuting Authority: see Crown Prosecution Service, *Relations with other Prosecuting Agencies and the Prosecutors Convention* (updated to October 2023).

[135] Food Standards Agency, *Manual for Official Controls: Legal Requirements and Standards for Approved Meat Establishments* (January 2022) ch 7, Annex 2, para 32.

[136] DEFRA, *Enforcement Policy Statement 2015*.

[137] Insolvency Legal Services Directorate webpage.

[138] Maritime and Coastguard Agency, *Guidance: MCA Enforcement Policy Statement* (16 November 2021) para 2.

[139] CPS, *Prosecuting Welfare and Health Fraud Cases* (September 2019).

In addition, the prosecution (and persecution) of large numbers of sub-postmasters by the Post Office, a limited company wholly owned by government, was a reminder that the right of private prosecution continues to exist and can be used by public bodies no less than by private individuals, with minimal central control.[140] While the DPP may take over any private prosecution under section 6(2) of the Prosecution of Offences Act 1985, there is no obligation on a private prosecutor to inform the CPS of a prosecution, and if the CPS learns of such a prosecution (eg through press reports) then unless it is specifically requested to intervene (eg by the defendant), no action will generally be taken unless there are exceptional circumstances.

The House of Commons Justice Committee conducted an inquiry into private prosecutions in 2020–21 following a request from the Chair of the Criminal Cases Review Commission, following the Commission's assessment of the unprecedented scale of the Post Office's misuse of its prosecution powers. The Committee noted that the Post Office was an untypical private prosecutor, by reason of its investigatory capacities and possession of an in-house team of prosecution lawyers. It was concerned about the general growth in the incidence of private prosecutions and issues of fairness as between prosecutors and defendants, and recommended that the government establish a central register of private prosecutions and provide for the CPS to be notified of all such prosecutions, and for defendants to be informed of a right to seek review by the CPS.[141] Government accepted the first of these recommendations, but rejected the others on the ground that they would in effect require CPS to investigate all such prosecutions, a task which, it said, CPS lacked the resources to carry out.[142] The terms of reference of the public inquiry into the Post Office prosecutions appear to have been deliberately drawn so as to exclude any consideration of the conduct of CPS, stating that 'the engagement or findings of any other supervisory or complaints mechanisms, including in the public sector, are outside the Inquiry's scope'.[143]

In the course of this century there has clearly been some movement, in England and Wales, towards more centralized decision-making on prosecutions, impelled partly by failures in prosecuting authorities but also, perhaps, echoing the programme of functional specialization promoted under the Coalition government and most clearly expressed in the creation of GLD. Nonetheless, the maintenance of some important independent prosecution powers means that the UK Law Officers still have less control over parts of the prosecution domain ('purview') than over others ('superintendence'), and nothing like the competences of management and direction taken for granted by their ministerial colleagues.

[140] See for a general account Nick Wallis, *The Great Post Office Scandal* (Bath Publishing 2021).
[141] Justice Committee, *Private Prosecutions: Safeguards* (HC 2019–21, 497) 30, 31.
[142] Justice Committee, *Private Prosecutions: Safeguards: Government Response* (HC 2019–21, 1238).
[143] Post Office Horizon IT Inquiry, *Terms of Reference*. No appearances by CPS witnesses appear to have been scheduled at the Inquiry.

10
Shaping Legislation, Exploiting Delegated Legislation, Reining in Regulation

I Preparing Primary Legislation

1.1 The legislative programme

1.1.1 The development of central control

The functions of legal advice and prosecution that we discussed in the previous chapter are areas where any attempt at central control or even coordination has to cope with the essential plurality of the UK executive and its departmental structure. Legal services and legal powers exist to support departmental policies and regulations. Of course there are government-wide policies and concerns, but executive legal organization tends to treat these as a specialized issue, attracting the specific mechanism of references to the Law Officers. Departments might be inclined to think in the same proprietorial way about the legislation they need to provide the legal basis for the policies they want to pursue, but obtaining such legislation requires access to the scarce resources of parliamentary support and parliamentary time. In the 19th century, when the executive was still in the process of developing its dominance over the legislative functions of Parliament, departments did indeed act independently in seeking to obtain and use such resources, introducing bills that were not necessarily mutually consistent and which might, indeed, create unexpected financial burdens.[1]

Such a free-for-all could hardly persist into the century of the welfare state, with the exponential expansion of both the functions of government and the legislation needed to sustain them. From 1918 there existed a committee of Cabinet, the Home Affairs Committee, that reviewed and classified departmental proposals for legislation and made recommendations to Cabinet. From 1935, access to the drafting services of Parliamentary Counsel was made available only for bills that had been identified as the main items in the government's legislative programme.[2] At the start of the present century the job of settling the programme was being done by a Queen's Speeches and Future Legislation Committee, whose terms of reference were 'to prepare and submit to the Cabinet drafts of the Queen's Speeches to Parliament, and proposals for the Government's legislative programme'. A separate committee, the Legislation Committee, had the task of keeping the agreed programme for the current session under review, including giving approval for the introduction of bills into Parliament once drafted.[3] These Committees were merged in 2000 to form the Committee on

[1] Sir Courtenay Ilbert, *Legislative Methods and Forms* (Clarendon Press 1901) 83–84.

[2] Stephen S Wilson, *The Cabinet Office in 1945* (HMSO 1975) para 521.

[3] For more details on these committees see Terence Daintith and Alan Page, *The Executive in the Constitution: Structure, Autonomy and Internal Control* (OUP 1999) 242–45, 256–58.

Executive Self-Government and the Constitution. Terence Daintith and Alan Page, Oxford University Press.
 DOI: 10.1093/9780198937630.003.0010

the Legislative Programme, with terms of reference combining those of the two pre-existing Committees.

Under its current title of 'Parliamentary Business and Legislation' (PBL), this Committee continues to exist today with simplified terms of reference: to consider matters relating to the government's parliamentary business and delivery of its legislative programme. Its membership reflects the idea articulated by Herbert Morrison, as Leader of the House of Commons in the first post-war Labour government, that the then Future Legislation Committee should be a 'small and impartial planning tribunal' which would decide between competing departmental claims, so that departmental ministers should be excluded, as being 'possible competitors for places in the programme'.[4] Ministerial titles have varied over the years, but the key members are those responsible for getting the government's business through Parliament: the Lord President of the Council and Leader of the House of Commons, who chairs the Committee; the Lord Privy Seal and Leader of the House of Lords; and the Chief Whips for Commons and Lords. Other current members are the Secretaries of State for Northern Ireland, Scotland, and Wales, who will be concerned with issues of territorial scope of bills and devolution impacts; the Chief Secretary to the Treasury, with an eye to financial impacts of legislation; the senior minister at the Cabinet Office; and for legal advice, the Attorney General and the Advocate General for Scotland. The Committee is supported by a Cabinet Office Secretariat, the Parliamentary Business and Legislation Secretariat.

This institutional structure does not incorporate any express role for the Prime Minister or No 10, despite their dominant position in the shaping of the political programme underlying the government's legislative proposals.[5] The absence of clear and direct channels through which advice and information from the Whips, the PBL secretariat, and the Office of Parliamentary Counsel (OPC) could be transmitted to, and receive responses from, 10 Downing Street was a source of difficulty until the May government that took office in 2017 established the post of Director of Legislative Affairs at No 10, recognizing the special importance of links with Parliament at a time when the government had to rely on the support of the Northern Ireland Democratic and Unionist Party to maintain a tiny majority.[6] This is a special adviser post, not a Civil Service appointment. The key task of the post-holder is to ensure that the political implications of the legislative programme and of the progression of legislation through the drafting and parliamentary stages, as perceived at No 10, are constantly kept in view. The role may assume particular importance in periods where the Leader of the House of Commons, in this role and as Chair of the PBL Committee, is not a particularly close colleague of the Prime Minister. The Director attends the Prime Minister's daily briefing meeting and has a weekly meeting with the PBL Secretariat.[7]

[4] Lord Morrison, *Government and Parliament: A Survey from the Inside* (OUP 1964) 234.

[5] John Ludlow, 'The Queen's Speech 2005: How Government Laws are Initiated in the United Kingdom' (2005) 31 Commonwealth Law Bulletin 61, 64.

[6] Gavin Barwell, *Chief of Staff: Notes from Downing Street* (Atlantic Books 2021) 42–43, noting that the proposal for a legislative affairs team at No 10 had already been developed by the Cabinet Secretary.

[7] Information from official interviews, 21 February 2023, and 17 March 2023.

1.1.2 Procedures and criteria

The key element in the procedures through which the legislative programme is settled[8] is a bidding round conducted by the PBL Committee some 9–10 months before the opening of the relevant parliamentary session, in which departments are invited to submit proposals. The PBL Secretariat, in consultation with No 10, parliamentary business managers, and Parliamentary Counsel, produces proposals for the Committee, whose recommendations form the basis of a provisional Cabinet decision on the programme—which is subject to review over the whole period up to the King's Speech, so that more urgent proposals may be inserted as necessary. Cabinet ministers disappointed by the Committee's recommendations can of course carry the fight for their bill into Cabinet itself, sometimes with success.[9] The provisional decision provides authority for departments to proceed with the drafting of approved bills.

Factors influencing the proposal's chances of success in a competition in which, currently, only one bill in two is likely to be accepted[10] include: the possibility of using alternative means of implementing the policy; political content, or urgency; advancement of work on the proposal, for example progress in agreeing the policy content of the bill; previous publication in draft for consultation and pre-legislative scrutiny; handling issues (presumably a euphemism for the possibility of difficulties in getting the bill through); and devolution issues and their handling.[11] Further hints as to favourable factors emerge from the bidding template provided by the PBL Committee to departments for the purpose of setting out the broad policy objectives, the need for legislation, and provisional timelines or deadlines. The content has varied over time: the 2023 template invites the department to say if its bill fulfils a manifesto commitment, a Spending Review commitment, an existing commitment to legislate, or a prime-ministerial priority—failing which it asks what is the driver for the measure. It requests ministers or special advisers to briefly set out the political narrative/driver or political imperative for the bid, and asks what backbenchers thought of the proposal, if already debated, and how (in fewer than 50 words) the government might 'sell' the bill.

The listed factors reflect changes to the legislative landscape noticeable since the beginning of the century. One is the government's commitment 'to publishing more of its bills in draft before they are formally introduced to Parliament, and to submitting them to a parliamentary committee for parliamentary pre-legislative scrutiny where possible'.[12] A bill that has been so published and considered will be favoured for a place in the programme in the following session. Although a high proportion of bills originally presented in draft reach the statute book via this route, and there is a broad parliamentary consensus that pre-legislative scrutiny significantly improves the quality of legislation,[13] it should not be assumed that the draft legislation route is

[8] Described in some detail in Daintith and Page (n 3) 242–45; see currently Cabinet Office, *Guide to Making Legislation* (2022) ch 5 (hereinafter '*Guide*').

[9] Daintith and Page (n 3) 245.

[10] *Guide*, para 2.4.

[11] *Guide*, para 5.8.

[12] *Guide*, para 21.1.

[13] See Richard Kelly, *Pre-legislative Scrutiny under the Coalition Government: 2010–2015* (House of Commons Library Briefing Paper no 05859, 13 August 2015) 14.

an easier pathway towards selection and passage of a bill proposal. Departments may not wish to subject their bills to select committee scrutiny, which is likely to be more searching and less politically manageable than ordinary legislative procedure; they may be impatient of the delays built into the procedure; and even if they are ready to proceed, it is the PBL Committee that takes the decision whether a bill should go forward in this way.[14] Despite the apparent commitment to increase the use of the procedure, the number of draft bills has been in decline since Conservative governments came to power in 2015: they offered 22 draft bills over the period 2015–23, fewer than three per year, as opposed to an average of just under six per year under Labour (1997–2010) and seven per year under the Coalition (2010–15).[15]

Another obvious change is the appearance of separate legislatures for Scotland and Wales alongside that for Northern Ireland, which may raise questions about the appropriate coverage of the UK bills with which the Committee is concerned, and about coordination of the content of such bills with legislation that might be passed by the devolved legislatures in pursuance of their own competences. Programming issues might, for example, arise where a bill is likely to deal with matters devolved under the Scotland Act so as to bring into operation the Sewel Convention under which the consent of the Scottish Parliament would normally be required.[16] While refusal of consent does not prevent Parliament from passing the legislation, provision will still need to be made for seeking the consent of the Scottish Parliament in the course of the bill's passage. Bills that have found a place in the programme may also turn out, once drafted, to raise devolution-related issues to which the Committee will need to give attention.[17]

A third, less obvious, change may be enhanced governmental appreciation of Parliament's capacity to derail the legislative implementation of its policies, reflected in the emphasis on 'handling strategies' in the process of selecting and preparing legislative proposals. There has been much argument in recent years among political scientists about the effectiveness of Parliament as a legislature. Parliament has been characterized as 'much of the time, either peripheral or totally irrelevant' as a legislative assembly,[18] or as 'the emblematic example . . . of [the] weak Parliament'.[19] '[T]he parliamentary decline thesis dominated accounts of political behaviour and dynamics throughout the 20th century'[20] and has survived into the 21st. Another strand of writing, however, fortified by extensive empirical research,[21] seeks to falsify this

[14] *Guide*, para 21.5.

[15] For details of the period 2010–15 see Kelly (n 13) 6–12. Statistics for the period 1997–2010 appear at 16–17. Not all promised bills were actually presented.

[16] Scotland Act 1998, s 28(8) (added by Scotland Act 2016, s 2). Similar procedures for seeking the consent of the devolved legislature exist in relation to Wales and Northern Ireland. For recent practice under the Convention see Akash Paun and others, *Sewel Convention* (Institute for Government February 2022).

[17] For details of the quite complex consultation and programming issues that may arise, see *Guide*, ch 14.

[18] Anthony King and Ivor Crewe, *The Blunders of Our Governments* (Oneworld 2013) 361.

[19] Amie Kreppel, 'Typologies and Classifications' in Shane Martin, Thomas Saalfeld, and Kaare Strom (eds), *Oxford Handbook of Legislative Studies* (OUP 2014) 95.

[20] Matthew Flinders and Alexandra Kelso, 'Mind the Gap: Political Analysis, Public Expectations and the Parliamentary Decline Thesis' (2011) 13 British Journal of Politics and International Relations 249, who see the thesis as 'deeply flawed'.

[21] In particular the work of Meg Russell and her colleagues: see Meg Russell and Daniel Gover, *Legislation at Westminster: Parliamentary Actors and Influence in the Making of British Law* (OUP 2017); Meg Russell, Daniel Gover, and Kristina Wollter, 'Does the Executive Dominate the Westminster Legislative

analysis by showing how Parliament has been influential in shaping legislation, most obviously by securing government agreement to proposed amendments but also, and arguably more significantly, through the 'anticipated reactions' of both Chambers, and in particular of government backbenchers, to executive proposals. Government, it is argued, pays keen attention to these reactions and designs legislation accordingly.[22] This concern is evidenced by the introduction of the 'handling strategy' as an element of the departmental material requiring approval by the PBL Committee as part of the process of prioritization and progression of bills. Introduced after 1997 by the first Blair government in relation to passage through the Lords, it has since been extended and generalized. Reference to backbench views in the template for a bid for a place in the programme is followed up and elaborated, in the *Guide to Making Legislation*, in the requirements for the parliamentary handling strategy to be presented to PBL Committee with the draft bill.[23] This is to be 'a living document, updated throughout the passage of the bill and crucially always looking and planning ahead to the next parliamentary stage and beyond', and one which sets out '[p]ossible concessions and fall-back positions, and the handling these will require'.) A 'stakeholder and media handling strategy' is also now required by the *Guide*.

1.2 The content of legislation

1.2.1 In general

The process through which a department wins a slot in a session's legislative programme for its proposals is distinct from that of obtaining collective approval of the content of those proposals. Here the relevant forum for initial approval is not the PBL Committee but the relevant Cabinet policy committee, which will also need to approve any amendments to be offered in Parliament that represent a significant change in policy.[24] Preparing the path towards such approval will entail timely consultation with other departments whose interests are likely to be affected. Areas flagged by the *Guide* include national security, impacts on the regulation of digital technologies, effects on competition, and effects on the areas within the remit of the Scottish, Welsh, and Northern Ireland Offices.[25] Some issues and interests enjoy more vigorous protection. Thus it may be necessary for a department to show that specific consents have been obtained from other departments: from the Treasury for any tax proposals or implications, and likewise for any implications for public expenditure or public service

Process?: Six Reasons for Doubt' (2016) 69 Parliamentary Affairs 286; Meg Russell and Philip Cowley, 'The Policy Power of the Westminster Parliament: The "Parliamentary State" and the Empirical Evidence' (2016) 29 Governance 121. See also Flinders and Kelso (n 20).

22 Russell and Cowley (n 21) 124–28.

23 paras 19.1–19.6.

24 *Guide*, para 3.5. Numbers, names and functions of Cabinet Committees vary considerably over time reflecting the preferences of Prime Ministers. For the position under the Sunak government see Cabinet Office, *List of Cabinet Committees and their Membership* (December 2023).

25 *Guide*, ch 4. These differ significantly from those picked out in its 1996 precursor, Office of Public Service, *Guide to Legislative Procedures* (4th edn, 1996): see Daintith and Page (n 3) 246–50.

manpower;[26] and from Cabinet Office and Treasury Ministers for the creation, abolition, reclassification, or merger of arm's length public bodies (ALBs).[27] Some interests and policies are protected by specific legislative requirements that need to be referenced in the bill, such as compliance (or lack of it) with the European Convention on Human Rights,[28] and compatibility with data protection regulation;[29] or that must be respected in its preparation, such as consideration of the impact on groups protected by equalities legislation.[30]

The PBL Committee continues to exercise supervision over departmental legislative proposals once they have been admitted to the programme. Admission provides drafting authority and enables the department to give formal drafting instructions to OPC, though the *Guide* advises departments to make contact with OPC as soon as it decides to pursue a bill, so that the resources needed for preparation, both in the department and in OPC, can be estimated. The department will have constituted a bill team—the *Guide* now provides highly detailed advice on this subject—to prepare instructions, maintain liaison with the drafter at OPC, and see the bill through all its stages. Its consent is also required for

> publishing a bill or clauses in draft, as noted above;
> announcing the intention to legislate to a specific timetable, or in a specific bill;
> the final text of the bill, before it is introduced into Parliament; and
> any amendments to the bill after introduction.[31]

The Secretariat seeks to meet regularly with departmental bill teams to keep an eye on progress. In exercising these functions, the PBL institutions are not only attempting to ensure that the progress of the government's legislative programme through Parliament is as smooth as possible, without procedural hitches. They are also policing respect for the collective interest in the content of departmental bills. Clearly this represents a high level of central supervision of the way departments progress their bills. Extending it to the consideration of amendments may seem surprising, until account is taken of the extent to which bills may be modified in the course of their passage through Parliament and to the effectiveness of parliamentary challenge in inducing government-sponsored amendments.[32]

26 *Guide*, para 3.21, ch 18. More detail is provided in HM Treasury, *Managing Public Money* (March 2023) Annex 2.1: Treasury approval of legislation.

27 *Guide*, para 4.9; and see chapter 4, section 2.3.

28 *Guide*, para 3.9: required by Human Rights Act 1998, s 19. Detailed advice on these statements can be found in ch 11 of the *Guide*.

29 *Guide*, para 3.10.

30 *Guide*, para 4.12.

31 *Guide*, paras 3.5, 3.29.

32 For some statistics see Russell and Cowley (n 21) 129–30, showing that on a sample set of 12 bills presented by Labour and Coalition governments, 60% of the government's substantive amendments were traceable to influence from non-government parliamentarians, usually through prior amendments withdrawn when ministers promised to reconsider.

1.2.2 Legal issues and Law Officers' guidance

Every bill proposal must be accompanied by a Legal Issues Memorandum, to be presented along with the text to the PBL Committee. This has replaced the European Convention on Human Rights memorandum that formerly accompanied the bill, and while compatibility of the bill's provisions with obligations under the Convention will usually still be a significant concern of the Legal Issues Memorandum,[33] it has the broader purpose of ensuring

> that the Law Officers and all other members of the Parliamentary Business and Legislation (PBL) Committee are briefed by the responsible department on, and have the chance to consider fully, the key legal issues presented by a Bill, in good time.[34]

Before it reaches the PBL Committee the memorandum must be submitted to the Law Officers for their comments, and also for their consent to any retrospective provisions in the bill or any early commencement provisions.[35] The Attorney General's Office (AGO), along with that of the Advocate General for Scotland (LSAG), has circulated a document supplementary to the *Guide to Making Legislation*, which provides guidance on preparing the legal issues memorandum and on the Law Officers' approach to some of the legal issues that bills might raise. *Working with the Law Officers on Legislation: A Guide for Departments* identifies a number of types of provision that the Law Officers are unlikely to approve, and a second set of provisions that departments are advised to avoid if at all possible. In the first category are

> legislating in a way that is intended to have no legal effect;[36]
> the creation of broad duties for public bodies;
> legislative provision requiring one part of government to have the consent of another; legislating for a commitment to legislate in the future.

Such proposals are unlikely to be approved 'without compelling justification'.[37] Of the proposals to be avoided as far as possible, the most important are ouster clauses, requirements to make reports to Parliament, putting common law or prerogative powers on a statutory footing, putting targets into legislation, and wide or unjustified delegations of power.[38] Here the concerns of the Law Officers are based on 'maintaining the overall quality of legislation' and being made aware of 'points of constitutional interest'.[39] The possibility that proposed legislation might be in breach of the United

[33] For detailed discussion see *Guide*, ch 11.

[34] Attorney General's Office and Legal Secretariat of the Advocate General for Scotland, *Working with the Law Officers on Legislation: A Guide for Departments* (December 2019) para 98.

[35] *Guide*, para 3.10.

[36] For an analysis and classification of such legislation see David Feldman, 'Legislation that Bears no Law' (2016) 37 Statute Law Review 212.

[37] *Working with the Law Officers* (n 34) para 6.

[38] Law Officers are also concerned about any departmental plans (eg for spending in advance of obtaining royal assent for a bill) that may be seen as pre-empting Parliament, and that may create legal uncertainty or litigation risk if the Bill does not pass: para 39. On financial aspects of such pre-emption see chapter 8, sections 2.3, 3.2.

[39] *Working with the Law Officers* (n 34) para 7.

Kingdom's international legal obligations does not appear in either category, but the instructions for preparing the Legal Issues Memorandum assume compliance:

> Departments need to be in a position to reassure PBL committee that they have identified all of... international law obligations that are relevant to their legislation, that [the Bill] meets those obligations and that relevant procedural requirements (for example those set out in a treaty) have been satisfied.[40]

While the Law Officers invoke the rule of law as the key principle underlying their guidance, their attitude to it is strictly functional: the governing standard is 'whether legislation is effectively maintaining the Rule of Law', and this requires that proposed legislation be 'legally certain, effective, clear and accessible and that litigation risks are managed'.[41] Thus the advice to avoid wide delegations of power is not directed at preserving the ability of Parliament to debate and amend the policies underlying legislation, though we shall see in the next section that this is the main issue on which parliamentary committees have criticized the government's internal procedures for legislative preparation. Indeed the Law Officers present parliamentary influence as a possible threat to these rule of law standards, warning departments that pressures to make concessions during the passage of a bill must not result in their attenuation.[42]

There are two common threads in the Law Officers' concerns about the kinds of proposals mentioned in the two categories above. The first is their potential for creating legal uncertainty. A declaratory provision, for example, may be politically attractive, but 'the Court's starting assumption, reasonably, will be that a legislative provision is intended to have legal effect and it may interpret it accordingly'.[43] The second, which is closely associated with it, is the consequent risk of litigation, and in particular of judicial review proceedings, which may also follow from other proscribed items such as legislative requirements for intra-governmental consents, or to bring further legislation forward, or to pursue or achieve targets. *Working with the Law Officers* urges departments to discuss with OPC, as well as with AGO and LSAG, any proposals that fall into the above categories, and it may be assumed that if this is done, the Law Officers will also have the benefit of OPC advice when considering the need for such provisions.

One area in which there has clearly been recent change—though it is difficult to put a precise date on it—is that relating to 'legislative provision requiring one part of Government to have the consent of another'. Provisions of this sort requiring Treasury consent to expenditure and other decisions with financial implications, once extremely common, are now rare.[44] The relative absence of new permanent legislation authorizing spending schemes may account for a part of this decline, but the more important reason may be the adoption, as part of the working practice of OPC, and in the Law Officers' *Guidance*, of the notion that the internal regulation of the core

[40] *Working with the Law Officers* (n 34) 41 ('Things to include in your LIM').
[41] para 3.
[42] para 4.
[43] para 11.
[44] Chapter 8, section 2.4.2.

executive does not normally need, and should not normally receive, support from legislative stipulation. This was signalled in the Office's 2013 Good Law Initiative,[45] which proclaimed 'necessity' as one of the key features of good law.[46] Departments are advised that any such proposal must be brought to the attention of OPC, AGO, and LSAG at the earliest opportunity, and a drafter encountering such a consent requirement in departmental bill instructions would need to convince colleagues that there was a good reason for inserting it.[47] Apart from the case of the Treasury, provisions requiring the consent of another minister, including the Prime Minister, for the exercise of a minister's statutory power are all but unknown. Given the apparent weakness of the other levers through which the centre attempts to assert control over the exercise of departmental functions,[48] this distaste for legislative involvement (which is not shared by other 'Westminster' systems)[49] offers a striking demonstration of the high price the executive is prepared to pay for the maintenance of its autonomy. The increasing scope and penetration of judicial review, flagged by the *Guidance* as a possible consequence if a statutory consent requirement were ignored,[50] can only have operated to drive the price even higher.

It is not difficult to identify provisions in subsequent legislation that appear to transgress the rules and guidance laid down in *Working with the Law Officers*, though it is impossible to know if the Law Officers were persuaded by exceptional circumstances or if their advice was overridden. One can imagine, for example, that there was headshaking in the Attorney General's Office over the decision in *R (on the application of Friends of the Earth Ltd) v Secretary of State for the Business, Energy and Industrial Strategy*,[51] in which Mr Justice Holgate held that the government's Net Zero Strategy for responding to climate change did not satisfy the requirements of the Climate Change Act 2008. The Secretary of State had made decisions on whether the proposals and policies in the strategy would enable carbon budgets to be met without being briefed with crucial information about the contribution to reductions in greenhouse gas emissions from individual policies, and had also failed, in reporting to Parliament, to explain how his policies were intended to meet emissions targets. The Act mandates the preparation both of carbon budgets and of proposals and policies to meet them.[52] Such statutory targets and reporting obligations are classed in *Working with the Law Officers* among 'legislative policy proposals to avoid as far as possible': reasons given include the creation of uncertainty and of litigation risk, a risk that here materialized.

45 Office of Parliamentary Counsel, *When Laws Become Too Complex* (March 2013) s 5.2.

46 On this test of necessity see further Constitution Committee, *The Legislative Process: Preparing Legislation for Parliament* (HL 2017–19, 27) paras 1, 7–14.

47 *Working with the Law Officers* (n 34) paras 15–18; official interview, 21 February 2023.

48 Above, chapter 2, sections 2.2.1, 3.4.6, chapter 8, section 2.4.3.

49 See eg Australia's Public Governance, Accountability and Performance Act 2013 (C'th), which provides a comprehensive regime for the management of public funds and other resources.

50 *Working with the Law Officers* (n 34) para 16. No mention is made of the danger of adverse judicial review if a minister's exercise of legal powers turns out to be subject, as a matter of administrative practice, to the consent of another minister: *H Lavender & Son Ltd v Minister of Housing and Local Government* [1970] 1 WLR 1231 (QBD).

51 [2022] EWHC 1841 (Admin) (18 July 2022).

52 See 2008 Act, ss 4, 13, 14.

It is possible, however, that the risk of litigation might be viewed as a useful tool in the armoury of an institution trying to exercise control over departmental activity. We shall see that in 2015 the Coalition government promoted the passage of the Small Business, Enterprise and Employment Act. One of the purposes of the Act was to put certain elements of the government's 'better regulation' arrangements on a statutory footing. Alongside a formal requirement on the responsible minister to report annually to Parliament on reductions in regulatory cost burdens measured against a published target (ss 21–27—again, a type of provision to be avoided if at all possible, according to *Working with the Law Officers*), the Act also imposed a statutory duty on ministers to provide for regular post-enactment review of any subordinate legislation they made, and to publish reports on such reviews (ss 28–32). The reason for this, it appeared from evidence given to the Public Accounts Committee, was that departments were not respecting the administrative commitments they had given over the previous few years to provide for and carry out such reviews. After the passage of the Act, the Director of the Better Regulation Executive told the Committee,

> Q 89 We are chasing up the Departments concerned, emphasising that they have made a statutory commitment, it is a serious matter if they do not meet that statutory commitment and we will be on their backs.
> Q 90 Chair: You will be on their backs. What other penalty is there?
> Graham Turnock: If you have made a statutory commitment and failed to meet it, clearly there are consequences—judicial consequences, conceivably.[53]

1.3 Central control of legislative preparation: effectiveness

For constitutional lawyers, there is a temptation to assume that the crucial criterion for judging the effectiveness of the machinery and standards we have described is the quality of the legislative proposals that the government puts before Parliament. To focus too strongly on this would be to neglect the significance of Thring's maxim, 'Bills are made to pass, as razors are made to sell.'[54] If government can secure the legislative expression of its political commitments without the expenditure of excessive amounts of political capital, legislative quality may not be particularly high on its list of concerns, and the larger the majority it enjoys, the easier it may be to achieve this result. Clear criteria for judging the political success of the government's Parliamentary Business and Legislation machinery are however lacking, so we focus here on the legislative quality issue. Government professes to care deeply about this; the Law Officers' guidance, as we have seen, makes prominent reference to it. As for Parliamentary Counsel, we noted in 1999 that they 'act as the internal guardians of values customarily regarded as integral to the legal order such as those of non-retrospection, proper use of delegation, and respect for the liberties of the subject', and

[53] Public Accounts Committee, *Better Regulation* (HC 2016–17, 487) oral evidence (13 July 2016).

[54] See Sir George Engle, 'Bills are made to pass as razors are made to sell: practical constraints on the preparation of legislation' [1983] Statute Law Review 7.

that the concept of 'legal policy', as interpreted by Parliamentary Counsel, 'is as close as our system has traditionally come to a check on the "constitutionality" of legislation'.[55] Later commentators have reinforced our rather tentative allusion to the constitutional significance of OPC's work,[56] and First Parliamentary Counsel has recently agreed, in evidence to a House of Lords Committee, that OPC has a 'moral' and not merely a tactical responsibility to seek to produce 'good law'.[57]

Given all this executive apparatus devoted to ensuring that government bills are a quality product, one needs to ask why there appears to be chronic dissatisfaction outside government on this score, and in particular, increasing dissatisfaction in Parliament in recent years, provoked particularly by the excessively broad delegated powers that ministers seek for themselves in the bills they put forward. The grumbles are not new and are not confined to governments of a particular political stripe. Thus we find complaints in 2005 of lack of ministerial interest in bills or of concentrated thought about them, poorly drafted or unintelligible bills, and, where more than one department was involved in drafting a bill, failure to reconcile their different points of view before putting it into Parliament.[58] In the last few years the volume of critical comment has been greatly enlarged by the work of two House of Lords Committees whose remit covers subordinate legislation. The Delegated Powers and Regulatory Reform Committee (DPRRC) has since 1992 had the task of reporting whether the provisions of any bill inappropriately delegate legislative power, or subject the exercise of legislative power to an inappropriate degree of parliamentary scrutiny. The Secondary Legislation Scrutiny Committee (SLSC) was established in 2003 to draw instruments to the special attention of the House on grounds, *inter alia*, of their political or legal importance or their effectiveness, comprehensibility, or consultation processes. In their reports over recent years on individual bills and statutory instruments these Committees have returned again and again to themes of excessive delegation, inadequate preparation, and the link between them.

A warning had been sounded by way of complaints from another Lords Committee, the Constitution Committee, whose 2018 report, *The Legislative Process: The Delegation of Powers*[59] focused largely on practice prior to the passage of the European Union (Withdrawal) Act 2018. That Act's provisions permitting industrial-scale delegations were the subject of several further reports by the Committee.[60] Three years later the DPRRC and SLSC followed up with the simultaneous release of reports whose respective titles speak for themselves: *Democracy Denied? The urgent need to rebalance power between Parliament and the Executive*[61] and *Government by Diktat: A call to return power to Parliament*.[62] While the reports acknowledge that the process of

[55] Daintith and Page (n 3) 254.

[56] See Christopher Jones, 'Our Forgotten Constitutional Guardians: Preserving Respect for the Law' (2021) 42 Statute Law Review 1, 10–11 and authorities there cited.

[57] House of Lords Delegated Powers and Regulatory Reform Committee, *Democracy Denied? The Urgent Need to Rebalance Power between Parliament and the Executive* (HL 2021–22, 106) evidence (26 May 2021) q 5 (Dame Elizabeth Gardiner).

[58] Christopher Foster, *British Government in Crisis* (Hart Publishing 2005) 134–35.

[59] (HL 2017–19, 225).

[60] The 'Great Repeal Bill' and delegated powers (HL 2016–17, 123); European Union (Withdrawal) Bill: interim report (HL 2017–19, 19) and European Union (Withdrawal) Bill (HL 2017–19, 69).

[61] House of Lords Delegated Powers and Regulatory Reform Committee (HL 2021–22, 106).

[62] House of Lords Secondary Legislation Scrutiny Committee (HL 2021–22, 105).

managing departure from the European Union, followed immediately by the demands of effective response to the Covid pandemic, necessarily involved unprecedentedly wide conferment and vigorous application of delegated powers, the Committees attacked delegation practice across the whole span of legislative activity. Among their targets were broad or vaguely worded delegated powers and delegated powers for matters of policy significance, like creation of public bodies and imposition of criminal liability; presentation of 'skeleton bills' with little content beyond the conferment of powers; excessive use of 'Henry VIII' clauses empowering modification or repeal of primary legislation through delegated powers; and use of 'guidance' alongside or instead of formal legal rules, especially where such rules were explicitly provided for by legislation.[63] DPRRC was also highly exercised, in *Democracy Denied*, by the decline in the proportion of its recommendations accepted by government (down to only one in three in the 2019–21 session), and the disappearance, from the *Guide to Making Legislation*, of the statement that 'it is usual for the Government to accept most, if not all, of the DPRRC's recommendations'.[64]

What is striking about these complaints is they address matters on which government's internal guidance has long signalled the need for caution and explicit justification on the part of departmental proponents of legislation, and in particular, care in dealing with DPRRC.[65] On these matters central authorities like the Lord President, as Chair of PBL Committee, regularly express agreement in principle with the positions taken by the parliamentary scrutiny bodies. Indeed their responses proclaim an ever more stringent supervision on the part of the PBL Secretariat and Committee, exercised not just in formal Committee proceedings but also through early scrutiny and administrative contacts.[66] The ability of the central authorities to prevail in any argument with a well-prepared and determined minister is however weakened by the broad and qualified language of the government's legislative standards. Thus while DPRRC consistently attacks bills in which delegated powers cover the absence of a fully formulated policy, the *Guide* says only that the fact that 'the detailed policy has not been developed yet and there is not enough time to develop it' is, '*on [its] own, . . . unlikely* to be a sufficient justification for the inclusion of a delegated power in a bill'.[67] Recent practice indicates, however, that the PBL Committee tolerates rushing bills out quickly in the early days of a new Parliament, to show fidelity to manifesto promises, if necessary on the basis of half-baked policy.[68] How far PBL, or for that matter OPC or the Law Officers, are capable of putting the brakes on a technically bad proposal that has the prime-ministerial wind in its sails, or is the project

[63] See generally Constitution Committee (n 59) paras 41–81; DPRRC (n 61) paras 59–85, 89–100; SLSC (n 62) paras 30–41, 47–59.

[64] DPRRC (n 61) paras 143–46.

[65] *Guide to Making Legislation* (2022 revision) ch 15, esp paras 15.15–15.32.

[66] See the oral evidence given to DPRRC by successive Lord Presidents Jacob Rees-Mogg (12 May 2021) esp at q 9—early engagement by PNL secretariat with department on content of Bill, and Mark Spencer (20 July 2022) esp q 2—'some ministers . . . have literally been munched up and spat out in PBL'. The former Director of Legislative Affairs at No 10 confirmed that 'PBL, as a Cabinet Committee, had a reputation as a difficult committee for any Minister who was not up to speed on his/her legislative proposals'.

[67] *Guide*, para 15.4 (emphasis supplied).

[68] See DPRRC, oral evidence, 12 May 2021, q 6 (Childcare Bill). This may also happen with bills arriving in a later session: see DPRRC, oral evidence, 20 July 2022, q 3 (Schools Bill).

of a powerful minister (a 'big beast')[69] must also be open to doubt. Again, possession of a substantial Commons majority may make a department, or government as a whole, less anxious about the political handling costs of ill-prepared legislation. The decline in the acceptance of DPRRC recommendations coincided with the tenure of the Johnson government with its 80-seat majority.

For a compelling illustration of the pliability of executive procedures and standards for assuring the quality of legislation—notably the vital characteristic of clarity—we have only to look to the so-called 'Brexit freedoms bill', eventually enacted as the Retained EU Law (Revocation and Reform) Act 2023. Here the desire of the Johnson and then Truss governments to satisfy the appetite of their Brexiter members and supporters for some marks of signal progress on the uphill road out of the European Union produced a proposal to revoke all EU-derived law preserved by the European Union (Withdrawal) Act 2018 within the succeeding 15 months. In this space of time every EU-derived measure would need to be reviewed to see if it should be spared from this legislative massacre. If preserved, the bill provided very broad powers to modify or replace it. The effect was to create high levels of uncertainty about the legal regime governing large and important areas of economic and social life, including consumer safety, workers' rights, and environmental protection. It became clear, as the list of the measures that would be revoked under the terms of the bill steadily lengthened even as it was being discussed in Parliament,[70] that the government had introduced the provision without itself knowing what its effects on the law would be.[71] The standards embodied in the *Guide to Making Legislation* and in *Working with the Law Officers* were clearly displaced, in the internal consideration of this legislation, by perceived political imperatives. Any resistance offered by OPC in pursuit of its 'moral' obligation to produce good law was clearly vain,[72] and it would be unwise to assume that there was any resistance from the Attorney General then in office, a former chair of the European Research Group, the spearhead of the Conservative pro-Brexit tendency.

[69] See the discussion of the degree of influence that can be exercised by the Lord President and by OPC reported at Constitution Committee, *The Legislative Process: Preparing Legislation for Parliament* (HL 2017–19, 27) paras 154–65, and the comments of Daniel Greenberg, a former parliamentary draftsman, at q 54: 'If I do not care about the quality of legislation, I appoint a small beast as Leader of the House. If I care about it, I appoint a big beast.'

[70] The number of measures on the 'dashboard' created to provide information on the reform rose from some 2,400 in summer 2022 to more than 4,900 in May 2023: see Department for Business and Trade, *Retained EU Law Dashboard*.

[71] For the progress of the Bill and the eventual abandonment of the 'mass sunsetting' approach, see text at nn 96–100.

[72] For an unusual attack on OPC, prompted by the terms of the Bill, see HL Deb 6 February 2023, vol 827, cols 998–99 (Lord Rooker): '[OPC draftsmen] are following orders from Ministers in a way that their predecessors from a couple of decades ago would not recognise. Those who drafted Bills were a constraint on Ministers stepping over the line—not any more. Parliamentary counsel are wholly owned by the Government; they work for, and are accountable to, the Government and not Parliament.' Lord Rooker held a succession of junior ministerial posts between 1997 and 2008.

II Subordinate Legislation

2.1 Introduction

Writing in 1999, we treated subordinate legislation as a relatively uncontroversial topic, whose key interest lay in the need to manage the flow of EU law that could be implemented or applied through secondary legislation, and in the impact of policies of deregulation seeking to address a perceived problem of excessive regulatory burdens on business. The EU issue now presents itself in the form of the quite different question of how to manage the replacement of the massive volume of EU-generated law with law based purely on domestic legislative authority, and has been, and indeed continues to be, a highly controversial and politicized aspect of the Brexit process. Deregulation also continues to be an important policy area involving specialized executive machinery, and we deal with this in the next section. The two House of Lords Committee reports already discussed, *Democracy Denied? The urgent need to rebalance power between Parliament and the Executive* and *Government by Diktat: A call to return power to Parliament*, make it clear that concern about how the executive approaches the use of subordinate legislation as an instrument of government did not begin with Brexit and was, when it occurred, already on an upward path. That it should have continued in this direction since then is hardly surprising, given that the executive's sense of constitutional propriety has permitted it—in the interest, it claimed, of legal consistency—to introduce a statutory instrument (SI) under Henry VIII powers to reverse a legislative defeat in the House of Lords—with no acknowledgment of this manoeuvre in the accompanying Explanatory Memorandum.[73] This section supplements the preceding discussion of legislation creating delegated powers by examining how subordinate legislation has actually been used, particularly in response to the needs of Brexit policy and to the Covid emergency. In this part of the chapter, after setting out the formal structure for the making of subordinate legislation and the general concerns expressed by the Lords' Committees (section 2.2), we examine the use of subordinate legislation to effect the necessary legal changes consequent upon the Brexit referendum decision (section 2.3), and the use of such legislation, and other instruments of policy, in the fight against Covid-19 (section 2.4).

2.2 The formal structure

Parliament has not provided much in the way of a general structure within which decisions about subordinate legislation are to be taken. All that we have is the Statutory

[73] For discussion of this piece of 'constitutional chutzpah', as expressed in the making of the Public Order Act 1986 (Serious Disruption to the Life of the Community) Regulations 2023, SI 2023/665, see Tom Hickman and Gabriel Tan, 'Reversing Parliamentary Defeat by Delegated Legislation: The Case of the Public Order Act 1986 (Serious Disruption to the Life of the Community) Regulations 2023' (*UK Const L Blog*, 22 May 2023; House of Lords Secondary Legislation Scrutiny Committee, *38th Report of Session 2022–23* (HL 2022–23, 189) 4–7; HL Deb 13 June 2023, vol 830, cols 1910–42. The Regulations were held to be unlawful on grounds of excess of power and lack of adequate consultation in *R (National Council for Civil Liberties v Secretary of State for the Home Department* [2024] EWHC 1181 (Admin).

Instruments Act 1946, which makes general provision for the numbering, printing, publication, and citation of statutory instruments (ss 2, 3), for the laying of instruments before Parliament, and for the treatment of instruments expressed to be subject to annulment and instruments that are required to be laid in draft (ss 4-6). The application of the rules, however, is contingent upon the drafting of each individual Act by which powers to make subordinate legislation are conferred: it is for the draftsman to determine whether the legislation is to be identified as a statutory instrument,[74] and also whether it is to be laid before Parliament and if so, to what procedure it is to be subject. This will normally be either what is now normally termed negative resolution procedure, where the instrument is laid before Parliament and may be annulled within 40 days pursuant to a resolution of one of the Houses, or affirmative resolution, in which the instrument is laid before Parliament in draft and will only come into effect if approved by a resolution of each House within 40 days. The latter procedure entails the government's finding time for debate on the instrument (though Parliament cannot amend such statutory instruments) and hence is appropriate to instruments of greater importance. Some instruments of a routine or local character may not be laid at all, and there is ample scope for introducing variations to laying and approval procedures to reflect specific circumstances. Thus where it is important that a significant instrument should take immediate effect—for example to forestall evasion by those whose conduct it aims to control—it can be laid as made but with a stipulation that it should cease to have effect if affirmative resolutions have not been passed within a given period—normally 28 days.[75] A 2014 Hansard Society study identified no fewer than 16 variations in the scrutiny procedures set out in legislation,[76] and its working paper, *Proposals for a New System for Delegated Legislation*, published some 10 years later, has called for radical restructuring of the system.[77] This would provide a generally applicable procedure for the parliamentary scrutiny of delegated legislation, rather than leaving it to be determined by each piece of legislation conferring such powers.

2.3 Using subordinate legislation: Brexit

The unexpected 'leave' vote in the 2016 referendum on EU membership presented the government and its lawyers with a major problem. By the time the United Kingdom actually left the European Union, the whole of the large body of EU law operative in the United Kingdom, and of UK law dependent upon EU membership, would need

[74] s 1. All powers conferred on the government as a whole, rather than on an individual minister, ie on 'His Majesty in Council' are, so long as they are expressed to be exercisable 'by Order in Council', statutory instruments under the Act: s 1.

[75] For one among many examples see Sanctions and Anti-Money Laundering Act 2018, s 55(1)–(4). The section also identifies other instruments under the Act subject respectively to the ordinary negative and affirmative resolution procedures.

[76] Ruth Fox and Joel Blackwell, *The Devil is in The Detail: Parliament and Delegated Legislation* (Hansard Society 2014). For a more recent 'explainer' see Stephanie Pywell and Tom West, *Delegated Legislation: What Types Are There, and How Are They Made?* (Open University, December 2023).

[77] Hansard Society, *Proposals for a New System for Delegated Legislation: A Working Paper of the Hansard Society Delegated Legislation Review* (Hansard Society, February 2023).

to have been either replaced or validated as part of a post-EU domestic legal order. While departure was not imminent, depending as it did on the timing of the United Kingdom's declaration under Article 50 of the EU Treaty with its provision for a two-year period for settling the terms of withdrawal, the task was complicated by the fact that no policy had been developed to meet the eventuality of a 'leave' vote. The terms of withdrawal, and the future relationship, remained to be determined in their entirety. In consequence, at a very early stage, government lawyers concluded that whatever form those decisions took, there had to be a comprehensive statute to translate applicable EU law into UK law, and that that statute would have to make provision for a large number of adaptations that would be needed to make that law work in a post-EU context where, for example, many of the institutions applying it would no longer have any jurisdiction in the United Kingdom and would need to be replaced by local substitutes.[78] The necessary legislation, proclaimed by the government as the 'Great Repeal Bill'—highly misleading insofar as the bill's essential job was to preserve EU law, not repeal it—was introduced in July 2017. A White Paper presented a few months earlier had set out the main lines of the government's thinking, including the view that adaptations of what it termed EU-derived law should generally be made by subordinate legislation, and that some 800 to 1,000 statutory instruments would be needed to carry out this task.[79]

The government appears to have taken the view, from the moment the referendum result was known, that while Parliament should be given appropriate opportunities to discuss progress towards departure from the European Union, the fact of a referendum decision meant that despite the overwhelming constitutional, political, and economic significance of departure, routine procedures would suffice to support the necessary formal steps. There was, in consequence, no need to provide for any reinforcement of parliamentary scrutiny. The imprudence of this approach was demonstrated by the first *Miller* decision, to the effect that legislation, not just a prerogative-based executive decision, was necessary to provide constitutional authority for serving an Article 50 notice on the European Union.[80] The lesson was not picked up in the preparation of the Great Repeal Bill, which arrived in the Commons in July 2017 with numerous far-reaching powers to make subordinate legislation generally subject to negative resolution procedure—the effect of which would be severe constriction of parliamentary debate on these instruments as the process went forward. The range and width of the powers proposed to be conferred, including extensive powers to modify primary legislation (Henry VIII powers) attracted vigorous criticism from the Lords' Delegated Powers and Regulatory Reform Committee.[81] Only minor changes were made in the scope of powers as the bill proceeded through Parliament, but the complaints about the procedures chosen received an early response. At Commons committee stage, the government brought forward amendments, modelled on the suggestions of DPRRC,

[78] Jonathan Jones, Interview: UK in a Changing Europe (6 May 2021) 6–7. Jones was Treasury Solicitor at the time.

[79] Secretary of State, Department for Exiting the European Union, Legislating for the United Kingdom's withdrawal from the European Union (Cm 9446, March 2017) para 3.19; 1,156 instruments were eventually promulgated.

[80] *R (Miller) v Secretary of State for Exiting the European Union* [2017] UKSC 5, [2018] AC 61.

[81] *European Union (Withdrawal) Bill* (HL 2017–19, 22).

creating sifting mechanisms through which committees in both Commons and Lords would be able to review instruments designed to correct deficiencies in retained EU law, and certain other instruments, and ask for procedure to be upgraded to affirmative resolution if they thought it appropriate. These were accompanied by proposals to require ministers to lay statements before Parliament explaining the instruments being laid and justifying their appropriateness.[82] This responded to DPRRC's criticism of the use of 'appropriateness', as opposed to 'necessity', as the general test for instrument-making powers.

In the Commons, the sifting function was entrusted to a newly established committee, the European Statutory Instruments Committee, while in the Lords the task was added to the remit of the Secondary Legislation Scrutiny Committee. By October 2019 the Committees had considered over 240 instruments and the government had—according to the Lord President of the Council—accepted all its recommendations.[83] DPRRC recommended that the sifting procedure should be extended to cover instruments issued under the very wide power to make regulations for the purpose of implementing the Withdrawal Agreement concluded in late 2019,[84] but this proposal was successfully resisted by government. Further sweeping powers to make subordinate legislation, this time for the purpose of implementing the Trade and Cooperation Agreement settling the terms of the United Kingdom's post-withdrawal relationship with the European Union, were conferred by section 31 of the European Union (Future Relationship) Act 2020. On this occasion the bill, as introduced by the government, made provision for the sifting procedure to be used in cases where instruments exercising these powers could be presented under negative resolution procedure.[85]

One can feel a certain grudging sympathy for government's wish to keep parliamentary processes as undemanding as possible, given the massive rule-making task that it faced as it went through EU withdrawal procedures: a task that, moreover, had to be tackled in conditions of considerable uncertainty arising from the substantive negotiations proceeding in parallel, which might affect the content of the rules, and growing concerns about the possibility of breakdown of those negotiations and a consequent no-deal exit. Further complication was likely to arise from the fact that the framing of subordinate legislation had always been a task left very largely to departments. Significant differences might exist between the ways departments approached the task, in terms of division of labour between administrators and lawyers, drafting principles and procedure. Some departments with a substantial subordinate legislation load had developed their own guides for those involved.[86] Parliamentary

[82] For the eventual form of these requirements see European Union (Withdrawal) Act 2018, sch 7, paras 3, 17, 28. See also paras 30 and 32, requiring additional explanation where there is provision for sub-delegation of powers.

[83] Letter from Lord President of the Council (Jacob Rees-Mogg MP) to Chair of the European Statutory Instruments Committee, 2 October 2019.

[84] European Union (Withdrawal Agreement) Act 2020, s 18 (inserting a new s 8B into the European Union (Withdrawal) Act 2018): see Delegated Powers and Regulatory Reform Committee, *European Union (Withdrawal Agreement) Bill* (HL 2019–21, 3) para 16.

[85] European Union (Future Relationship) Act 2020, sch 5, paras 6 and 8. Instruments amending, repealing, or revoking primary legislation or retained direct principal EU legislation, or creating a power to legislate, are always subject to affirmative resolution procedure: para 6(1).

[86] See Daintith and Page (n 3) 258–60.

Counsel's involvement has traditionally been very limited: they draft certain orders of a cross-departmental nature, like transfer of functions orders, occasionally take on other work, and must be consulted on any subordinate legislation that amends primary legislation.[87] Guidance for departments on formal requirements for statutory instruments, and on procedures for validation, laying before Parliament, and publishing, is to be found in *Statutory Instrument Practice,* published by the National Archives and now in its fifth edition.[88]

Accordingly it was fortunate that in 2016, just a few weeks before the referendum, the newly created Government Legal Department (GLD) had established a central facility for work on subordinate legislation. The external trigger for this was a letter in late 2014 from SLSC to First Parliamentary Counsel and to the Treasury Solicitor complaining of the increasing numbers of defective statutory instruments being produced by departments. Their response was to establish the following year, on a pilot basis, an SI Hub.[89] Based on experience in this pilot phase, it was decided that, in addition to training and quality assurance roles, the Hub should take responsibility for drafting about 20% of statutory instruments, to be selected by departments in consultation with Hub managers. Today it numbers about 30 lawyers, including a secondee from OPC.[90] The Hub, operating alongside the legal team in the Department for Exiting the European Union, played a major role in ensuring that the massive task of adjusting retained EU law to the post-withdrawal situation was efficiently discharged. It provided comprehensive guidance to departments on the powers in the European Union (Withdrawal) Act, to ensure that the powers were used in a consistent way across government; issued drafting guidance to ensure consistency of approach (such as a requirement to include 'EU Exit' in the title of any SI which was made as part of the programme), and specific guidance on how to amend what were formerly EU Regulations, and which would become a new species of domestic legislation. To provide quality assurance, it created model checking guidance, which involves every SI being checked by two lawyers other than the drafter (a 'second' and 'third' pair of eyes check). The Hub also liaised with parliamentary authorities and committees to ensure as smooth and managed a flow of SIs as possible.

Such management was, however, primarily the job of new mechanisms created, both at the centre and in departments, in response to the Brexit challenge. Centrally the focus was the PBL secretariat, where a team was established to oversee new arrangements for governance of secondary legislation across government. PBL set up a

[87] Government Legal Service, *GLS Statutory Instrument Drafting Guidance* (August 2018) paras 1.6.3, 2.3.8–2.3.37.

[88] '[T]he functions of Her Majesty's Stationery Office (HMSO) are operated from within The National Archives, including official publishing and the management of Crown rights, for copyright and database rights. The Queen's Printer of Acts of Parliament (Controller of HMSO and an official in The National Archives) is therefore responsible, on behalf of the Crown, for registering, numbering and printing UK Statutory Instruments as they are first enacted or made.' National Archives, *Statutory Instrument Practice* (5th edn, 2017) para 1.1.2.

[89] Secondary Legislation Scrutiny Committee, *Number of Corrections to Statutory Instruments in 2014* (HL 2014–15, 93) paras 11–12 and app 1.

[90] See Government Legal Department, *Annual Report and Accounts 2015–16* (HC 2016–17, 6) 12; *Annual Report and Accounts 2017–18* (HC 2017–19, 989) 13; Susanna McGibbon, Letter to Chair, Regulatory Reform Committee (7 April 2021).

triage process to ensure that SIs were prioritized appropriately and brought forward in a timely manner in order to smooth the flow of SIs to Parliament. It also maintained central oversight of the whole SI programme throughout EU Exit and the transition period. At the departmental level SI ministers were appointed and trained, and the device of Senior Responsible Owners (SROs) was called into play, with the SRO in each department being responsible for oversight of their department's SIs, and for championing coordination of the SIs within that department. PBL has supported this process and coordinates regular SRO meetings.[91] These arrangements have attained permanent status.[92] They involve monthly scrutiny of proposed instruments by a group including the Chair of PBL Committee and the Whips, who check to see that they are achieving government policy, that they are what is wanted, that they are fair and proportionate, and that they will have the proper parliamentary mechanism.[93] The arrangements represent a substantial increase of central involvement and supervision in an area previously reserved to departments. Whether they work effectively is another matter. They have certainly not lowered the volume of parliamentary complaint about the subordinate legislation process in general,[94] and SLSC has again noted a rising trend in defective instruments that need to be withdrawn and re-laid.[95]

These changes represented a response to a problem—of legal continuity—that was an unavoidable consequence of terminating 40 years of membership of a law-making international organization. It is less easy to sympathize with the difficulties the government created for itself when it decided, in 2022, to attempt a massive acceleration of the process of reviewing and adapting the EU law preserved as part of the UK legal order by the Withdrawal Act. The scale of the delegation issues presented by that Act and its sequels was dwarfed by the proposals brought forward as the 'Brexit Freedoms Bill'.[96] The principal freedom involved was in fact the freedom for the government to remodel the corpus of retained EU law without the irritating necessity to obtain parliamentary consent for the specific changes and revocations to be made. As already noted, the initial proposal for achieving this was to revoke at the end of 2023 all EU-derived subordinate legislation and retained direct EU legislation (regulations and decisions) except instruments that had been preserved by express regulation. This 'move fast and break things' approach was abandoned at a late stage in the passage of the bill, after it had been taken over by a new Secretary of State, in favour of a listing of several hundred specific measures to be revoked at the end of 2023.[97] It had become clear, not least through the regular discovery of more and more retained EU law instruments that would need to be reviewed, that even with the help of the enhanced facilities just described the task set by the bill was an impossible one. As enacted, however, the bill

91 McGibbon (n 90) 4.

92 See the brief description in the *Guide to Making Legislation*, paras 15.37–15.41. Machinery of this sort had been suggested by the House of Lords Merits of Statutory Instruments Committee some years earlier: see *The Management of Secondary Legislation* (HL 2005–06, 149) paras 71–83; the government rejected the proposal at the time on the ground that it was for departments to manage their own programmes.

93 Rees-Mogg (n 66) q 10.

94 See eg Hansard Society (n 77).

95 *What Next? The Growing Imbalance between Parliament and the Executive: End of Session Report 2021–22* (HL 2021–22, 200) paras 60–64.

96 See text above at nn 70–72.

97 See now Retained EU Law (Revocation and Reform) Act 2023, s 1 and sch 1.

still provided that any retained EU secondary law might be amended, restated, revoked, or replaced, all by way of delegated legislation under powers available until 2026. Although this law covered sensitive areas like consumer safety, health and safety at work and other work-related rights, and environmental protection, the Act set few limits to executive discretion in modifying it. The powers it gave the government to replace revoked EU law with 'appropriate' provision 'to achieve the same or similar objectives', or simply to 'make such alternative provision as [it] considers appropriate', were restricted only by ruling out certain regulatory devices,[98] and requiring that the overall effect of changes made under this power should not increase the 'regulatory burden' relating to a 'subject area'.[99] Otherwise the government gave itself *carte blanche*, relying on the general argument that since the original EU instruments had been made without detailed parliamentary consideration, Parliament had no reason to complain if they were likewise revoked, modified, or replaced. The most it offered was a requirement for affirmative resolution procedure for certain instruments, notably those made under powers to achieve the same or similar objectives, or to make alternative provision; and a sifting procedure, of the type already described, for most other instruments.[100]

2.4 Using subordinate legislation: Covid

The new machinery that supported the EU exit programme of subordinate legislation was also pressed into service for the Covid pandemic emergency that followed—and indeed partly overlapped—the execution of that programme. Its needs, though, were different and more complex: harder to plan for, by reason of ignorance about the likely evolution of the pandemic; involving much greater time pressures, with quite draconian measures often needing to be prepared and introduced at very short notice; producing new problems of clarity of obligations, when government presented measures combining legally binding rules and formally advisory 'guidance'; and drawing on powers to legislate found in a range of different statutes—which limited the scope for cross-cutting Covid drafting guidance. The Treasury Solicitor has described the SI Hub as 'critical' to the delivery of this legislation.[101] Lawyers in the SI Hub drafted nearly all of the 'restrictions' SIs (those imposing business closures, social distancing, and other lockdown measures across England) as well as the original travel restrictions SI. They provided a flexible resource, taking on drafting for teams under particular pressure and working closely with the lawyers in GLD's Department of Health and Social Care legal team to deliver many projects to extremely challenging timescales. The Treasury Solicitor acknowledged that these pressures, maintained over a long period, may have caused declines in performance, as measured by the proportion of instruments reported by the Joint Committee on Statutory Instruments,

98 ie new delegated powers, criminal offences or monetary penalties, taxation, and creation of public bodies: see now Retained EU Law (Revocation and Reform) Act 2023, s 14(4).

99 On 'regulatory burden' see now Retained EU Law (Revocation and Reform) Act 2023, s 14(10).

100 Retained EU Law (Revocation and Reform) Act 2023, sch 5, paras 5 and 6.

101 McGibbon (n 90) 6.

and the percentage of instruments issued free of charge by way of correction. They also, of course, raised a number of important rule of law issues, such as the use of sub-delegation; lack of clarity in offences created; blurring of the lines between law and guidance; and issues of timing of commencement, laying, and publication. These were reviewed by the Joint Committee in a report published in mid-2021.[102]

III Regulation

3.1 Introduction

The executive practices and institutions we have described so far in this chapter can be seen as responding to familiar constitutional values of parliamentary control and the rule of law—to the extent, at least, of their compatibility with the demands of the government's political programme. Another set of institutions and practices, to which we now turn, articulates a different value: that of minimizing the burdens that regulation, in the public interest, imposes on the activities of business. Obviously the vehicle of such regulation will normally be the legislation and the subordinate legislation that was discussed in the first two sections of the chapter, along with the EU legislation which, until 2020, contained a substantial part of the rule-book to which UK business was subject, and which will continue, in the shape of retained (subsequently 'assimilated') EU law, to exercise a major if possibly dwindling influence for as long as its thousands of elements have not been extirpated, or replaced by authentically home-grown domestic law. The burden-reducing task that government has set itself has, since the arrival of the New Labour government in 1997, gone under the name of 'Better Regulation'. Repeated attempts to achieve this elusive goal have called forth a specialized apparatus of regulatory control, distinct from and additional to the mechanisms through which government pursues its general goal of making good law. In this section we examine the motley procession of intra-executive coordinating bodies, advisory bodies, and reviewing bodies charged from time to time with making regulation better, and the range of control instruments (of which regulatory impact assessment is the longest-lasting) provided for this purpose. We shall see that Parliament has been called upon to provide legislative support for this endeavour, not just by delegating powers to modify burdensome primary legislation, but also to provide stronger controls over the executive's appetite for regulation than it seems able to furnish from its own resources.

3.2 Deregulation under New Labour 1997–2010

The key elements of the deregulation programme that had been developed by Conservative governments since 1985 were retained, but renamed, by their Labour successors. Thus the tandem of an internal central coordinating body, and an external

102 Joint Committee on Statutory Instruments, *Rule of Law Themes from COVID-19 Regulations* (HL 2021–22, 57; HC 2021–22, 600).

advisory group attached to it, continued to operate as the Better Regulation Unit (located in the Cabinet Office) and Better Regulation Task Force (BRTF), and the principal control mechanism to restrain over-regulation continued to be the obligation to publish, alongside regulatory proposals and proposals for new legislation, a document now called a 'regulatory impact assessment' (RIA)—formerly a 'compliance cost assessment.' The RIA was described in 1998 as

> a short, structured document which is published with regulatory proposals and new legislation. It briefly describes the issue that has given rise to a need for regulation and compares various possible options for dealing with that issue. One or more non-regulatory options will normally be included. The costs and benefits of each option are identified—and quantified wherever possible—to assist informed public debate about regulation.[103]

The device of the RIA, despite being much criticized on a number of grounds, has been in continuous use ever since,[104] though the criteria for proposals to which an RIA needs to be attached have varied from time to time, as also have the procedures for vetting them. Responsibility for their preparation has always lain with the department promoting the regulatory proposal, whether this takes the form of primary or secondary legislation. Each department has its own Regulation Unit to advise on the process and liaise with the central institutions: the coordinating unit, in the Cabinet Office, was renamed the Regulatory Impact Unit in 1999, and since 2005, has been the Better Regulation Executive (BRE), now located in the Department for Business and Trade.

Under Labour the rule was that a regulatory proposal subject to RIA requirements could not go forward, through the legislative programming procedure already described or as a statutory instrument, unless it had been signed off by a departmental minister and approved by the internal coordinating unit. For a period this was further supported by a requirement to submit any new regulatory proposals likely to impose 'substantial' burdens on business to a Panel for Regulatory Accountability, a sub-committee of the ministerial Committee on Regulation, Bureaucracy and Risk, chaired by the Prime Minister. Government did not provide for any systematic independent or external assessment of RIAs, but, from 2002, following a Public Accounts Committee recommendation, the Comptroller and Auditor General was invited to undertake an annual evaluation of a sample of RIAs.[105] This process continued up to 2008, and demonstrated persistent wide variations in their quality.[106] Over this period, general performance improved, but despite the internal checks, a significant proportion of inadequate RIAs continued to appear, common defects being failure to analyse alternatives to the preferred option, and incomplete or dubious cost-benefit analysis. As an authoritative commentator has noted, this is hardly surprising:

103 Better Regulation Unit, *Guide to Good Regulation* (1998) 28.

104 It is now called simply an 'impact assessment'.

105 Comptroller and Auditor General, *Evaluation of Regulatory Impact Assessment Compendium Report 2004–05* (HC 2004–05, 341) para 3.

106 For the last report in the series see Comptroller and Auditor General, *Delivering High Quality Impact Assessments* (HC 2008–09, 128).

> Impact assessments must be drafted so as to be acceptable to Ministers who are often determined—for what seem to them good and strong reasons—to introduce the new burden, whatever it costs . . .;
>
> the costs and benefits are hard (or impossible) to quantify. (Departments' estimates of costs are bound to be optimistic, and by definition do not include unintended consequences, whilst it is very difficult to put a cost on a wide range of benefits, such as those associated with greater employment rights.)[107]

Under Labour governments there was substantial development of the legislative framework for better regulation. They inherited powers to amend or repeal by ministerial order primary legislation passed before the end of the 1993–94 session that imposed a burden on business, provided that necessary protection was not removed.[108] These powers were repealed and replaced by those in the Regulatory Reform Act 2001, which in turn were replaced by those in the Legislative and Regulatory Reform Act 2006, still in force today. The idea on each occasion was to obtain a broader and more flexible power of adjustment of regulation without the need for detailed amendment through primary legislation. On each occasion, however, parliamentary suspicion of government's motives in seeking wide delegated powers, and fears about the evasion of democratic debate on proposals of importance, led to the elaboration of substantive criteria for the exercise of the powers, coupled with procedural restrictions and enhanced opportunities for parliamentary scrutiny. We examine the 2006 Act in more detail later, but it is worth noting now that the rate of promulgation of orders has fallen from an average of more than nine per year under the 1994 Act to one of fewer than three per year under its 2006 successor. One explanation for this decline may of course be that the statute book is approaching regulatory perfection; another is that departments are increasingly reluctant to set out on the tortuous path through the substantive and procedural restrictions imposed by the Acts.

Authorizing administrative repeal of regulatory legislation was not, however, the only function of the 2001 and 2006 Acts. They also addressed the problems flowing from the fact that a large proportion of regulatory powers were in the hands of 'independent' regulators operating under statutory authority. According to the National Audit Office the United Kingdom has about 90 such regulators, among which one can find all the forms of arm's length body already discussed.[109] Bodies legally distinct from departments, like the Health and Safety Executive or Ofcom, could not simply be instructed, by ministers or by a body like the Regulatory Impact Unit, to diminish the burdens flowing from their regulatory practice. Accordingly, the 2001 Act allowed ministers to issue codes of practice with the aim of improving the practice of 'enforcement officers' 'so far as fairness, transparency and consistency are concerned'. The 2006 Act then gave broader statutory support to the regulatory principles that had

[107] Martin Stanley, *Deregulation 1948–2006*. This is part of a comprehensive website on regulation maintained by Stanley, a former chief executive of the Better Regulation Executive, the postal industry regulator Postcomm, and the Competition Commission.

[108] Deregulation and Contracting Out Act 1994, s 1; Daintith and Page (n 3) 278–79.

[109] House of Lords Industry and Regulators Committee, *Who Watches the Watchdogs? Improving the Performance, Independence and Accountability of UK Regulators* (HL 2023–24, 56) paras 1, 3, citing National Audit Office, *Regulation Overview 2019* (March 2020).

been laid down by the BRTF in 1998: that regulation should be transparent, accountable, proportionate, consistent, and targeted.[110] Section 21 required those performing regulatory functions (a term that has been defined, it should be noted, to include departmental regulators as well as 'independent' regulators)[111] to 'have regard' to these principles, and the Act also gave ministers a power to issue broader codes of practice to which regulators must have regard in determining any general policy or principles to govern the exercise of their functions (section 22).[112] The Act also conferred very wide powers to modify, by statutory instrument, the constitution of regulators or the mode of performance of their functions, or to transfer functions between them, where a minister considered that this would secure the performance of regulatory activities in accordance with the principles.[113]

A shift in better regulation policy was signalled by the Hampton Report, *Reducing Administrative Burdens: Effective Administration and Enforcement* (March 2005), which had been commissioned by Gordon Brown as Chancellor and shaped by the Treasury. The report's focus was on inspection and enforcement, but it also recommended the establishment of the Better Regulation Executive, which was set up in 2005, succeeding to the functions of the Regulatory Impact Unit, and reinforced by the appointment of a non-executive Chair recruited from outside the Civil Service. Since 2007 BRE has been located in the department responsible for trade and industry. In earlier years of the Labour governments, the Regulatory Impact Unit had devoted considerable attention to excessive regulatory burdens on public sector activity such as the National Health Service, but this disappeared with BRE's switch of departments, which signalled a more business-related focus. The external advisory body, BRTF, was briefly transformed into the Better Regulation Commission before being wound up in 2008, leaving the better regulation programme without the capacity for wider inquiry and reflection that the Commission and its predecessors had provided.[114]

BRE's early work was conducted against the background of one of the reports of BRTF, *Regulation—Less is More: Reducing Burdens, Improving Outcomes*, which was also presented in March 2005 and introduced the notion of measuring and then reducing the stock of regulation, beginning with the administrative burden it created, and subsequently moving on to a programme of regulatory simplification and reform, in part driven by suggestions from business. BRE did not find it easy to advance this policy, not least because of tensions with other functions of the department that housed it, such as employment and competition law, areas with a heavy regulatory content. A BRE proposal to equip departments with regulatory 'budgets', which would somehow cap the amount of regulation they could operate, failed to gain traction, as

[110] Better Regulation Task Force, *Principles of Good Regulation* (1998).

[111] Legislative and Regulatory Reform (Regulatory Functions) Order 2007, SI 2007/3544, sch.

[112] A Code was issued in 2008 and has been replaced by the Regulators' Code 2014, currently in force, issued by the Department for Business, Innovation and Skills, Better Regulation Delivery Office.

[113] s 2. The only use of this power appears to have been to abolish the Health and Safety Commission and to transfer its functions to a reconstituted Health and Safety Executive: see the Legislative Reform (Health and Safety Executive) Order 2008, SI 2008/960.

[114] For an excellent example the Commission's last report see *Risk, Responsibility and Regulation—Whose Risk Is It Anyway?* (October 2006).

had a similar 1996 proposal by the Deregulation Task Force for a control regime under which regulation would have been treated as a collective resource that could only be 'spent' with the approval of some kind of Ministry of Regulation, on lines similar to Treasury control of expenditure.

3.3 Deregulation under the Coalition government 2010–2015

Implementation of the BRTF's ideas about dealing with the stock of regulation thus had to await the arrival in power of the Coalition government. Policy on regulation figured in the Coalition Agreement (May 2010) between Conservatives and Liberal Democrats, under which the partners committed themselves to 'cut red tape by introducing a "one-in, one-out" rule whereby no new regulation is brought in without other regulation being cut by a greater amount', to achieve better targeting of inspection and enforcement, and to impose sunset clauses on new regulations and regulators to ensure that the need for each regulation is regularly reviewed. While BRE continued to provide the hub for regulatory reform, this programme engendered new rules and institutions. The 'one in, one out' (OIOO) rule was to be monitored by a new Cabinet sub-committee, the Reducing Regulation Committee, chaired by the Business Secretary, and supported by a body that had been set up by BRE in the last year of the Labour government, the Regulatory Policy Committee (RPC). RPC, which has survived until now, is a group of independent experts whose main task is to review departmental impact assessments. It was reconstituted as an advisory non-departmental public body in 2012. Government had already extended its remit to the review of each impact assessment that formed part of a departmental regulatory proposal to be considered by the Reducing Regulation Committee. At this stage, RPC opinions are confidential, but if the proposal moves forward, the impact assessment will in most cases be published by the department, and at that point RPC publishes its opinion. Under the OIOO system departments advancing a new regulatory proposal imposing a net burden on business or civil society organizations had to identify and remove existing regulations with an equivalent value in terms of net burden.[115] If these were not found the new regulation might be stalled. It is worth noting, in the light of the then recent experience of the banking crisis of 2007–09, that measures dealing with financial systemic risk issues were among the fairly lengthy list of instruments that fell outside the scope of the rule.[116]

While there were more dramatic elements in Coalition better regulation policy (the Deputy Prime Minister's 'Freedom Bill' announced in July 2010, and the 'Red Tape Challenge' launched by the Prime Minister in April 2011, each of which sought public input on what and how to deregulate and each of which foundered on inability to manage the response they received[117]), OIOO and the work of the associated

[115] HM Government, *One-In, One-Out (OIOO) Methodology* (July 2011).

[116] ibid para 16(xiv), which also notes that '[a]s a general principle where it is believed a crisis can be averted through introduction of a regulatory measure then there may be grounds to not apply the OIOO Rule to such a measure'.

[117] On these see Robin Ellison, *Red Tape: Managing Excess in Law, Regulation and the Courts* (CUP 2018) 295–98.

institutions (BRE, RPC, and the Reducing Regulation Committee) formed the core of the Coalition's programme, reinforced in January 2013 when 'one in, one out' became 'one in, two out' (OITO). Just how effective they were is open to question. In its survey of its work over the whole period of the 2010–15 Parliament, the RPC suggested that the rule had been a key factor in encouraging departments to bring forward deregulation, and to improve the quantification of the costs and benefits of any regulatory proposals.[118] The rule also encouraged them to keep their 'stock' of regulation under review in order to have 'out' measures available when they wanted to create new regulation. Only about half of the more than 1,200 regulatory proposals reviewed by RPC in 2010–15, however, fell within the scope of OIOO or OITO (para 1.1). Despite noting the continuing tendency of departments to underestimate costs and overestimate regulatory savings (para 2.6), RPC still concluded that the overall impact of the measures subject to the rule had been positive for business and civil society organizations, saving them £2.2bn per year (para 1.4). However, the RPC also estimated that there was a net *burden* imposed by *out-of-scope* measures of £2.8bn per year. Most of this derived from two EU measures that were introduced to protect against financial systemic risk (para 1.7 and table 1.1). The figure of £10bn in burden reduction claimed by the government for 2010–15[119] was thus, to say the least, optimistic.

3.4 Deregulation under Conservative governments 2015–2024

Though the Conservative government was able to cast off the shackles of coalition with the Liberal Democrats after winning the 2015 election, its policy in the field of better regulation was constrained by legislation passed very shortly before. This was the Small Business, Enterprise and Employment Act 2015. As well as containing a miscellany of measures designed to help small businesses, the Act, in its Part 2, furnished a statutory discipline for business regulation, in the shape of a 'business impact target', defined in terms of the net impact on business of new regulations, set against termination of regulations, measured over the life of a Parliament. The target, the methodology for assessing the impact of regulations, and the choice of which regulations were to count toward the target, were all for determination and publication by the Secretary of State, as were annual reports assessing the overall economic impact of qualifying regulatory measures year by year, and of the individual measures passed in the year. The effect of the Act was to constrain executive discretion only by requirements to publish the target, the methodology, the regulations in scope, and annual progress. The Act also required ministers to incorporate, into regulation effected through secondary legislation, provision for review at not less than five-yearly intervals, or to explain why such review was not appropriate.[120]

118 Regulatory Policy Committee, *Securing the Evidence Base for Regulation: Regulatory Policy Committee Scrutiny during the 2010 to 2015 Parliament* (March 2015) para 3.2.

119 Reported in Comptroller and Auditor General, *The Business Impact Target: Cutting the Cost of Regulation* (HC 2016–17, 236) para 1.5.

120 ss 28–32.

The Public Accounts Committee offered a rather bleak assessment of the new arrangements after a year or so of operation, noting that economies of less than £1bn out of a promised £10bn for the Parliament (2015–20) had so far been achieved, despite a ratcheting up of requirements from 'one in, two out' to 'one in, three out', and the setting for each department of a deregulatory 'budget', agreed with BRE. That any saving at all could be claimed was largely due to the fact that the business impact methodology made it possible to count a measure requiring retailers to charge for plastic bags as a deregulatory reduction of burden worth more than £1bn—because it would reduce the number of bags supplied and hence their cost to retailers.[121] This was because only direct costs to business were to be included in the calculation. As the Chairman of RPC, which validated the saving as compliant with the rules, admitted in evidence to the Committee, 'It's deregulation, but not as we know it.'[122] In addition, if account were also taken of measures in the 19 categories excluded from the business impact target calculation (a few in the Act—see s 22(4)—but most by ministerial decision, including EU measures), those implemented since May 2015 but not counted towards the target were estimated to have added costs to business in 2015–20 of £8.3bn.[123]

The subsequent attitude of government to its own better regulation efforts can be traced through the annual reports that have been its essential obligation under the 2015 Act.[124] After initially essaying some modest reforms, such as trying to quantify broader as well as direct business impacts of measures (2017–18, p 9), the May government had by 2019 come to the view that the current business impact target did not provide a full picture of the regulatory landscape in the United Kingdom, and undertook to brief its successor on possible reform options (2018–19, p 6). The Johnson government took the view from the beginning that the current methods of assessing regulatory impacts did not support its commitment to 'strive to achieve the right regulatory balance between supporting excellent business practice and protecting workers, consumers and the environment'. Accordingly it launched a review and meanwhile set an interim target of zero—no promise of burden reductions, but no increase either (2019–20, p 5). One area of business regulation that may surprise by its virtual absence from these reports is that which addressed the Covid pandemic with a range of restrictive measures bearing down particularly hard on the activities of the hospitality and transport industries.[125] The explanation is that the lockdown measures were imposed—initially at least—for periods less than one year, so that they did not count as 'regulatory provisions' for the purpose of the business impact target calculation.[126] Only two Covid-related regulations, out of several hundred, were referred to in the 2020–21 annual report: both are of indefinite duration.

[121] Public Accounts Committee (n 53) 6. For detailed background see Comptroller and Auditor General (n 119).

[122] Public Accounts Committee (n 53) 9.

[123] ibid 10.

[124] These are collected at <www.gov.uk/government/collections/business-impact-target-annual-reports> covering the period 2015–22.

[125] For the economic effects of the lockdowns in spring, autumn, and winter 2020, and in early 2021, see Daniel Harari and Matthew Keep, *Coronavirus: Economic Impact* (House of Commons Library, December 2021) ch 2.

[126] Small Business, Enterprise and Employment Act 2015, s 22(4).

New principles of regulation resulting from a consultation exercise in 2021 were rebadged as a 'Brexit opportunity', and organically linked with the process of review and revocation of retained EU law eventually provided for by the legislation already discussed.[127] There are five of these principles: a sovereign approach, 'leading from the front', proportionality, recognizing what works, and setting high standards.[128] It is apparent that these principles incorporate a much wider range of concerns about regulation than have animated deregulation and better regulation policies as they have been applied over most of the last few decades, though there is no obvious incompatibility between them and the BRTF's 1998 recipe for good regulation: that it should be transparent, accountable, proportionate, consistent, and targeted. There is plenty of scope for conflict among the new principles—where retained EU law is concerned, the sovereign approach may argue for UK-specific solutions, despite the fact that the inherited regulation works and, quite probably, entails less cost for business than home-grown replacements and variations—and their significance will not be apparent until the government completes, by mid-2026, the review of all retained EU law required by the Retained EU Law (Revocation and Reform) Act 2023.

The principles have been translated into a revised system of regulatory discipline by the Department for Business and Trade's *Better Regulation Framework Guidance*.[129] This comprehensive code for the making of 'regulatory provisions'—statutory provisions that relate to business activities—replaces existing rules including the business impact target, repealed by the Retained EU Law (Revocation and Reform) Act, and 'one in, two (or three) out' (OITO). The latter requirement was dropped following the Grenfell Tower fire disaster, and was strongly opposed, as being arbitrary, inflexible, and a threat to 'good' regulation, by respondents to the government's 2021 consultation.[130] Key changes in the new framework are the introduction of independent scrutiny, by RPC, earlier in the process, and a strong emphasis on post-implementation evaluation and review, reinforcing the obligations of this type still contained in the 2015 Act.[131] The list of exemptions has been shortened, but following the Grenfell disaster now includes the specific subject of building safety: an acknowledgment, perhaps, of the policy-distorting effect of mechanistic 'better regulation' procedures.

The new principles are also supposed to affect the way in which independent regulators go about their tasks. A policy paper and extensive programme of consultations about regulators' activities was launched by the Department of Business and Trade in 2023, and followed up, in May 2024, by a comprehensive White Paper covering the

[127] See text at nn 96–100.

[128] HM Government, *The Benefits of Brexit: How the UK is Taking Advantage of Leaving the EU* (January 2022) 22–29.

[129] Department for Business and Trade, *Better Regulation Framework Guidance* (September 2023).

[130] HM Government, *Reforming the Framework for Better Regulation* (January 2022) 23–25. For an analysis of how the revised Framework might bear on the performance of the Impact Assessment system, see Kate Ollerenshaw, 'Impact Assessment as an Accountability Mechanism: Past, Present and Future' (*UK Const L Blog*, 9 November 2023).

[131] Small Business, Enterprise and Employment Act 2015, ss 28–32. Current impact assessment procedure for legislative proposals can be found in the *Guide to Making Legislation* (rev edn, 2022) ch 13, which calls for adequately developed impact assessments to be presented when bidding for a slot in the legislative programme, when seeking collective approval of policy, and when PBL Committee approval is sought for introduction of a bill to Parliament: para 13.4.

work of both statutory regulators and departments and announcing further new regulatory principles.[132] The change of government three months later opens the way for yet further revisions.

IV The Interplay of Internal and External Control

In assessing the operation of executive controls in the field of public expenditure we drew attention to the interdependence between the Treasury, parliamentary select committees like the Public Accounts Committee and the Comptroller and Auditor General, developed through decades of practice since the passing of the Exchequer and Audit Departments Act 1866, and sustained by shared interests in regularity, propriety, and value for money in public expenditure. This chapter, we hope, will have shown that it would be vain to expect to find a similar degree of mutual support in the actions and reactions of executive and parliamentary instances relating to the use of legislative and regulatory powers. Despite regular invocations, by people like the Lord President of the Council as Chair of PBL, of the common executive and parliamentary interest in well-prepared legislative and regulatory proposals, and of the importance of 'good law', it is clear that the discussion of legislation, and of delegated legislation, takes place in a framework that is far more confrontational than that applying to financial procedure—doubtless because Parliament has retained, in relation to legislation, a power to stop or hinder executive progress that it has abandoned in the expenditure field, where it now contents itself with the less threatening, if sometimes inconvenient, function of calling the executive to account.

We also need to remember that getting legislative proposals before Parliament is an intensely competitive and political process within government. In this process there is no player with the institutional strength or interests of the Treasury to insist that the rules of the competition are respected by the departmental participants, and plenty of evidence to suggest that respect for the government's own legislative standards, which themselves exhibit little rigour, may be a function of the personal political standing of the Lord President, or the strength of the Law Officers' commitment to good legislation as a support for the rule of law. Political imperatives, whether shared by the executive as a whole or advanced by a powerful minister, often seem to push self-regulatory restrictions to one side. This is in itself a disturbing change from the position at the beginning of the century, when it was possible to assume that the standing of Parliamentary Counsel would offer some degree of protection against such ills as unformed legislative policy and its corollary of excessive delegation. It is not obvious that that is still the case. Complaints about bad legislation go back a long way and we are not in a position to say whether there is today less regard for legislative standards or whether the lapses that occur are made much more noticeable by the vigorous supervision offered by the specialist parliamentary committees, especially those of the House of Lords. There are certainly signs that despite the emollient language, there is a feeling within the executive that the House of Lords has become unduly assertive in its

[132] *Smarter Regulation to Grow the Economy* (May 2023); *Smarter Regulation: Delivering a Regulatory Environment for Innovation, Investment and Growth* (CP 1089, May 2024).

role of legislative reviewer.[133] A falling off in government acceptance of its committees' recommendations may be an echo of this sentiment.

It is also the case that in the legislative field, the values and preferences of internal and external controllers do not coincide to the extent apparent in relation to control of public expenditure. The standards of the *Guide to Making Legislation* and *Working with the Law Officers* are designed to produce legislation that is 'good' when seen from the executive standpoint. They are not designed as supports for representative democracy. The reader will look in vain in these documents for any suggestion that departmental bill teams should construct their proposals so as to allow the fullest opportunity for parliamentary discussion of the underlying policy and the means of its implementation.

Parliamentary pressure, Brexit, and Covid have together produced some centralization of the drafting and programming of delegated legislation, a field previously entrusted almost entirely to departments. Substantive central control over departments' rule-making proclivities is a different story. After a lengthy and unsuccessful experiment with quantitative restrictions, in which legislative discipline was ultimately invoked in support of internal control, guidance on criteria and procedures for regulation, reinforced by independent review, is once again the key instrument for securing government's goal of limiting the regulatory burden on business. Experience however warns that where the results of independent review are politically inconvenient, that review will simply be ignored. The Regulatory Policy Committee gave the 'Brexit Freedoms Bill' a red rating—not fit for purpose—which produced no discernible effect.[134]

[133] Thus Baroness Stowell of Beeston, Leader of the Lords 2014–16, claimed in 2023 that the Lords currently pursued an 'assertive approach' for which there was 'no precedent', citing the fact that since 2015, the government had lost more than half of all divisions in every parliamentary session, and nearly 70% in two of them: letter to the *Times*, reproduced in *The Week* (3 June 2023) 21. The significance of this statistic of course depends on the proportion of amendments that are pressed to a division.

[134] Regulatory Policy Committee, *Retained EU Law (Revocation and Reform) Bill*, 18 November 2022, RPC-CO-5223(1): 'The Department has not sufficiently considered, or sought to quantify, the full impacts of the Bill.'

PART F
THE RESOURCES OF THE EXECUTIVE: INFORMATION

11
Government Information: Privileges, Constraints, and Obligations

I Introduction: The Uses of Information

Information is an essential instrument of government. Good decision-making depends upon the possession by the decision-maker of information that is as reliable and comprehensive as possible. This is equally true whether the decision-maker forms part of the executive, the legislative, or the judicial branch of government. What information such decision-makers should gather, how they should test it, and how they should use it, are all potentially problematic issues. The legislative and judicial procedures with which we are familiar essentially represent our constitution's answers to these questions so far as Parliament and the courts are concerned; indeed the very notion of what 'judicial' decision-making is consists of rules about what information the decision-maker may take into account and how. The fact that most executive decision-making is not structured to the same degree and that its processes are less visible does not mean that such issues do not arise in that branch of government also. At various points in this book we have considered executive efforts in recent years to improve the informational basis for taking different kinds of decision, or for refining the methods through which that information is evaluated, in fields ranging from general policy analysis[1] or economic forecasting,[2] through investment appraisal[3] and regulatory impact assessment,[4] to evaluation of legal risk.[5]

In this chapter and the next, though, our concern is with the information that the executive communicates, or chooses not to communicate, to the public. This may be information that the executive generates itself—about its own policies, practices, decisions, and plans—or information that it collects. Public communication of information is an essential adjunct of coercive and financial tools of government, which will not work unless people are aware of the threats or advantages they are being offered, but it is also an important resource of government in its own right. Today 'communication' is recognized in official literature as 'one of the five main levers of government alongside legislation, regulation, taxation and spending'.[6] While coercion, in the form of legislative or regulatory prohibitions or restrictions, attempts to remove non-compliant behaviour choices from people's set of preferences, or to add to their

[1] Chapter 3, section 5.1.
[2] Chapter 7, section 2.2.1.
[3] Chapter 8, section 2.4.2.
[4] Chapter 10, section 3.1.
[5] Chapter 9, section 2.2.1.
[6] Government Communication Service, *Modern Communications Operating Model: A Blueprint for Government Communication: 2.0* (2020) 7.

Executive Self-Government and the Constitution. Terence Daintith and Alan Page, Oxford University Press.
 DOI: 10.1093/9780198937630.003.0011

costs, and while the offer of financial advantages seeks to reduce the costs of favoured choices, information may lead its recipients to re-order their preferences for themselves. Foreign Office information about disturbances, lack of personal security, and health risks in foreign countries is calculated to deter British subjects from taking unnecessary journeys to such destinations and doubtless has this effect in many cases. Other factual information, notably statistical and census information, may be disseminated with the sole aim of improving the knowledge base, and hence the performance, of enterprises, or of enabling individuals to make more informed, and hence more satisfactory, choices. Much of the time, however, government sees the release to the public of the information it holds as a means of advancing its policies. Its aims may be as narrow as persuading the public, or sections of it, to adopt specific patterns of behaviour—an approach with which we were all familiarized by varying iterations of Covid-19 guidance[7]—or as broad as attempting to ride the 24/7 news cycle by organizing an orderly flow of positive announcements from departments—where the behaviour that most interests the government is voting behaviour at the next election.[8]

The way the executive organizes itself to exploit this instrumental potential of information, and the rules and standards to which it subjects itself, are the subject of the next chapter. Before we reach those questions, though, we need to consider the more basic issue of executive autonomy in this area: how free is the executive to determine what part of the information it holds will be put into the public domain, or what part it will withhold? Automatic or even widespread dissemination of official information is not, it has to be said, the traditional posture of British governments. Over the centuries they have hewed closely to Guicciardini's maxim (1530) that

> [a] prince . . . ought not only to keep those things secret which it is better were not known, but must also accustom himself and his ministers to be silent about all things—even seemingly insignificant and unimportant matters—with the exception of those which it is advantageous to broadcast.[9]

Not all that long ago secrecy was still described as 'Whitehall's cardinal value and dominant characteristic'.[10] We shall see that even in the last century, that dominance was beginning to weaken, with the scope of legislation criminalizing the unauthorized disclosure of official information becoming much more tightly focused on specific defence and security threats, and increasing consciousness, within the executive, of the advantages, as opposed to the risks, flowing from openness about government decision-making; but it was not until the coming into force in 2005 of the Freedom of Information Act 2000, through which the executive abnegated its autonomy in this

[7] See also chapter 10, section 2.4, and on the failure adequately to distinguish persuasive guidance from legal obligation see Alison L Young, *Unchecked Power* (Bristol UP 2024) 72–76.

[8] On persuasion as a tool of government see generally JT Romans, 'Moral Suasion as an Instrument of Economic Policy' (1966) 56 American Economic Review 1220; Stephen Bell, Andrew Hindmoor, and Frank Bols, 'Persuasion as Governance: A State-Centric Relational Perspective' (2010) 88 Public Administration 851.

[9] Francesco Guicciardini, *Maxims and Reflections of a Renaissance Statesman* (Domandi tr, Peter Smith 1970) 63.

[10] Peter Hennessy, *Whitehall* (Fontana Press 1990) 345.

field, that there was a formal reversal of the preference for secrecy. Examination of the way the Act bears on executive decision-making and the conduct of government business forms the main subject of the chapter, but the Act needs to be viewed as part of a broader landscape of constraints and obligations to which the executive is subject in its handling of the information it receives and generates.

Unlike money, information does not lose its interest and value for the original holder when it is handed over to someone else, whether to a government department or public authority or to a private person or corporation. That continuing interest is reflected in the general law through the broad concept of confidentiality, through data protection legislation, and through more specialized arrangements like those supporting copyright and other intellectual property rights. All of these constrain the ways in which those in receipt of information, public actors no less than private ones, may use it. The application to government-held information of such legal rules may in some cases reflect particular powers and responsibilities of the government agencies involved.[11] Consensual transfers of information that might fall outside these categories are frequently also structured by agreements limiting such use. The executive may be subject in varying measure to all of these general constraints in dealing with the information it receives, but it is also subject to additional constraints that reflect its privileged position as a collector of information. Legal powers to demand information on pain of fine, imprisonment, or other sanctions for non-compliance are commonly—though not invariably[12]—associated with strong prohibitions on the unauthorized disclosure of such information, which may be supported by criminal penalties.[13] Such legislation may also specify in detail when and to whom disclosure is authorized and for what purposes.[14]

While these general and specific constraints form a significant part of the framework within which government information policy operates—for example, they may furnish, as we shall see, absolute exceptions to the disclosure obligations imposed on officials by the Freedom of Information Act—our focus in the remainder of this chapter is on the changes that have occurred in this century in the executive's obligations to disclose information. Such obligations may be essential to the operation of a constitution that embraces the rule of law and democratic decision-making. Legislative instruments and executive orders must be published; government must account for its activities to Parliament and to the electorate through appropriate and timely publication of information about what it has done and plans to do. Some of these publications are themselves mandated by legal provisions stipulating their timing, form, or content.[15] Others are, legally speaking, in the discretion of the executive, but are

[11] See eg the Copyright (Public Administration) Regulations 2014, SI 2014/1385, amending the Copyright, Designs and Patents Act 1988 so as to permit relevant public bodies to publish documents on the internet which are open to public inspection or on an official register, so that members of the public may access them online.

[12] See eg Energy Act 2016, s 61, forbidding disclosure of a wide range of information about petroleum operations that may have been collected by the Oil and Gas Authority, but providing no sanction for breach of this prohibition.

[13] For an example see Social Security Administration Act 1992, s 123, and for a (now-outdated) list of such provisions, Chancellor of the Duchy of Lancaster, *Open Government*, (Cm 2290, 1993) Annex 8, pt 1.

[14] See eg Energy Act 2016, ss 63–69(1), 75, listing numerous exceptions to the prohibition referred to at n 12 above.

[15] eg Statutory Instruments Act 1946, discussed in chapter 10, section 2.2.

sustained by basic and long-established constitutional relationships, such as that between a department and the parliamentary select committee that follows its work. Nonetheless, the preparation and presentation of such information may be subject to incremental change, and in section II of this chapter we examine developments in this century in the operation of internal controls over executive provision of information to Parliament: specifically, through departmental accounts and reports. Section III addresses the more fundamental shift from an assumption of confidentiality for government information to an assumption of a public 'right to know', and its impact on the internal operations of the executive. Finally, in section IV, we revisit the issue of how technological change may affect methods of communication within the executive, and what this may signify for executive accountability.

II Informing Parliament: Departmental Accounting and Reporting

2.1 Government accounts

The annual presentation to Parliament of independently audited accounts of departmental expenditure has a century and a half of history behind it and may fairly be regarded as one of the constitutional supports of our particular form of representative democracy. It takes place within an institutional structure which, by British governmental standards, is unusually clear, with responsibilities for the accounts allocated by the Exchequer and Audit Department Act 1866 and its successor legislation, the Government Resources and Accounts Act 2000. Under this legislation the department is responsible for preparing its accounts and the Comptroller and Auditor General for auditing them, but it is the Treasury that, by way of its *Financial Reporting Manual* and directions issued under section 5(2) of the Act, sets the standards for the presentation of accounts, by both departments and other public bodies, and oversees their presentation to Parliament. Up to 2000–01 departmental accounting for supply expenditure took the form of appropriation accounts prepared by each department but presented en bloc by the Treasury after audit by the Comptroller and Auditor General. With the switch to resource accounting and budgeting completed in 2001, accounts are now prepared, audited, and presented in accordance with the Government Resources and Accounts Act 2000. Each department's resource accounts, though formally still presented to Parliament by the Treasury as required by the Act, are now published by the department—normally by July—as part of its annual report, which is its principal vehicle of accountability for its activities over the year and contains extensive narrative discussion of performance and organization. We discuss in the next section the numerous changes that the form and content of departmental reports have undergone in this century.

The adoption of resource accounting required new legislation because resource accounts did not satisfy the definition of 'appropriation accounts' as required by the Exchequer and Audit Departments Act 1866.[16] In introducing the Act the government

[16] See s 24, as originally enacted.

intended to do only what was necessary to provide statutory authority for a change that enjoyed bipartisan support, while at the same time giving legislative recognition to a new accountability tool, Whole of Government Accounts, a consolidation of the accounts of over 9,000 public sector bodies, including central and local government and public corporations such as the Bank of England, designed to provide a complete picture of the United Kingdom's public finances.[17] (Further legislative adjustment of the departmental accounting regime occurred in 2010, when the government secured an amendment of the 2000 Act so that the Treasury could require departments to incorporate in their estimates and accounts the spending of their associated public bodies.)[18] In 2000, however, Parliament took the opportunity to introduce formal restrictions on the Treasury's long-established discretion as to the form of departmental accounts presented to Parliament,[19] and on its new power to determine the form of the new Whole of Government Accounts.[20]

In each case two constraints were imposed. First, the Treasury should not simply seek to ensure that the accounts presented a true and fair view and conformed so far as appropriate with generally accepted accounting practice—the government's initial proposal—but should also have regard to any relevant accounting standards guidance.[21] Second, it must consult an appropriate expert advisory group, and lay before the House of Commons a report from the group on the advice it gave.[22] Such a group was in existence before the passage of the Act, in the shape of the Financial Reporting Advisory Board (FRAB) set up in 1996 following the publication of the Treasury's July 1995 White Paper *Better Accounting for the Taxpayer's Money*.[23] The Board took over the new statutory role, and makes an annual report to Parliament; it also advises the devolved administrations under their own reporting regimes. An independent Chair, appointed by the head of the Government Finance Function,[24] presides over a mix of independent external experts, and representatives of accounts preparers and users; of professional auditors; and of bodies like the Treasury, the NHS, and the devolved administrations, as well as two 'parliamentary observers'.[25] In addition to its statutory role under the 2000 Act, FRAB gives advice on a wide range of public accounting matters. Currently the standards applied to public accounts under the 2000 Act are the International Financial Reporting Standards (IFRS) promulgated by the International Accounting Standards Board, part of the IFRS Foundation, a not-for-profit international organization, as originally adopted by the European Union.[26]

[17] ss 9–11.

[18] Constitutional Reform and Governance Act 2010, s 43, inserting a new s 4A into the 2000 Act. On accountability for arm's length bodies and other public bodies associated with departments see chapter 4, section III.

[19] This was previously provided for by Exchequer and Audit Departments Act 1868, s 22, repealed by Government Resources and Accounts Act 2000, s 5(9).

[20] For the key debates see HC Deb 6 December 1999, vol 340, col 572ff; HC Deb 24 July 2000, vol 354, col 825ff.

[21] Government Resources and Accounts Act 2000, ss 5(4), 9(5).

[22] Government Resources and Accounts Act 2000, s 24.

[23] Cm 2929 (July 1995). The creation of the Board was an element of the government's overall plans for the move to resource accounting and budgeting.

[24] On Government Functions, including the Finance Function, see chapter 2, section 3.4.6.

[25] HM Treasury, *Financial Reporting Advisory Board Terms of Reference* (November 2018).

[26] On leaving the European Union the United Kingdom established a UK Endorsement Board to decide whether new or revised IFR Standards will apply generally in the United Kingdom: see International

These were developed for commercial accounting purposes, and much of the work of FRAB consists in advising on how and to what extent the standards should be varied or departed from in public sector use. While the Treasury is under no statutory obligation to follow the advice of FRAB it has always done so. Going against that advice would create the risk that accounting standards might produce financial statements that did not show a true and fair view of the reporting entities' financial position and performance, leading to a qualified accounts opinion from the Comptroller and Auditor General.[27]

While the arrangements established by the Treasury in pursuance of these parliamentary requirements are almost certainly identical with those it would have adopted in their absence, the provisions represent an unusual example of a reduction of executive autonomy initiated by Parliament.

2.2 Departmental reporting

This long-established structure for departmental accounting does not extend to departmental reports. For decades it has been the practice, in legislation setting up statutory public bodies, to require them to present an annual report to the responsible minister, who in turn is to lay it before Parliament.[28] The idea that ministerial departments should themselves publish a written annual report on their doings is, however, on the British constitutional timescale, a very recent one. Annual reports began as part of the documentation of the Parliamentary Expenditure Survey system. From 1991, in substitution for the government's annual Public Expenditure White Paper, each department produced in the spring a document both reporting on its activity, particularly over the previous year and the year in progress, and presenting its expenditure plans for the next two to three years.[29] From the very beginning a tension was apparent between the need for departments to take responsibility for their own reports, and for accounting by reference to them to their departmental select committee, and the need for the reports, individually and in aggregate, to present an accurate and consistent picture of expenditure plans and performance. The Treasury tried to achieve this through the issuance of guidance on core elements to be included, and through oversight by the Treasury Officer of Accounts team. Since 1991 departmental reporting has taken a number of different forms, but the tension between departmental self-expression and cross-governmental consistency has never gone away.

The early reports, which were quite separate from the department's appropriation accounts, made little contribution to any assessment of departmental performance

Accounting Standards and European Public Limited-Liability Company (Amendment etc.) (EU Exit) Regulations 2019, SI 2019/685.

27 HM Treasury, *Simplifying and Streamlining Statutory Annual Report and Accounts*, (Cm 8905, July 2014) para 6.2.

28 For a century-old example see Electricity (Supply) Act 1926, s 25 (annual report of the Central Electricity Board).

29 For discussion and authorities on this phase of reporting, see Terence Daintith and Alan Page, *The Executive in the Constitution: Structure, Autonomy and Internal Control* (OUP 1999) 154–55.

in economy, efficiency, or effectiveness of expenditure, being concerned mostly with describing general developments in their areas of competence.[30] This changed with the introduction of the Spending Review (SR) system and the associated Public Service Agreements (PSAs). From 1998 to 2010 reporting was linked to PSA objectives and targets. Initially combined with departmental estimates, which produced unreadably lengthy documents, reports became freestanding from 2004 and were presented in the spring. While they reported on progress in relation to PSA objectives and targets, information on the resources attributed to pursuing given objectives was rarely included; departmental resource accounts were presented later in the year and were in any event structured by reference to estimates categories. The reporting approach changed with the Coalition government's abandonment of PSAs in 2010. Since then a combined annual report and resource accounts have been presented by each department in late summer or early autumn, in the form of a House of Commons paper. While presentation of the accounts is mandated by the Government Resources and Accounts Act 2000, the report is simply laid 'by command'.

In 2013 the Treasury set up the *Simplifying and Streamlining Accounts* project to produce better and more consistent reporting, as a follow-up to the introduction of resource accounting and other reforms. This was designed as a cooperative enterprise, steered by a group including participants from the National Audit Office (NAO), the Parliamentary Scrutiny Unit, the accountancy profession, and representatives of departments, presided over by the Treasury.[31] Its basis, said the Treasury, was 'HM Treasury's statutory powers under the Government Resources and Accounts Act 2000 to determine the reporting framework under which departments operate': an assertion of dubious validity, since the Treasury's power under section 5 of the Act extends only to the form of departmental *accounts*.

The *Streamlining* paper showed that since the introduction of resource accounting, the Treasury's approach had been one of applying private sector reporting requirements to public entities, with some adaptations made for the specific public sector context in which they operated, and with additional requirements included at the request of Parliament and other central government departments in an ad hoc manner. The result was departmental annual reports that effectively combined an annual report based on private sector Companies Act requirements (with a large number of additional mandatory disclosures) and a set of financial statements based on IFRS as adapted for the public sector context, with the addition of a statement to ensure accountability to Parliament: the Statement of Parliamentary Supply.[32] This was not thought to satisfy user needs, and the main idea of the project was to move to reporting via a threefold structure: a performance report, an accountability report, and financial statements. The project sought to identify key elements for each of these sections, while giving entities more scope to decide for themselves how they should report, so moving away from mechanically reproducing elements of commercial reporting

30 eg Secretary of State for Transport and the Chief Secretary to the Treasury, *Department of Transport Report 1991: The Government's Expenditure Plans 1991–92 to 1993–94* (Cm 1507, February 1991).

31 HM Treasury, *Simplifying and Streamlining Statutory Annual Report and Accounts* (Cm 8905, July 2014) para 1.9.

32 ibid para 2.2.

as mandated by the Companies Act.[33] Thus the accountability report should have a common structure in the form of a Corporate Governance Report, a Remuneration and Staff Report, and a Parliamentary Accountability and Audit Report, along with, normally, a section written by the departmental lead non-executive director framed in consultation with other non-executives and board members.[34] This remains the general format of annual reports and accounts.

The *Streamlining* paper noted that parliamentary users were the 'primary users' of reports and accounts and that it was their needs that should be met.[35] In some respects, however, its recommendations seemed to represent a relaxation of existing accountability requirements. Thus the obligation to report performance against a department's Business Plan priorities,[36] structural reform plans, and indicators was reframed to demand such reporting only to the extent that the department measured its performance against those criteria.[37] Unsurprisingly, perhaps, the Commons' Public Administration and Constitutional Affairs Committee (PACAC) subsequently complained, in a report published in April 2017,[38] that departments were failing, in the performance section of their reports, to relate their spending to their objectives, as set out in their Single Departmental Plans (SDPs), or to their programmes or the services they provided. Adequate data to show performance on major projects was also lacking. The Committee also noted that departmental planning and reporting continued to be bedevilled by excessive optimism and associated spin, and wanted to see departments held, in the performance sections of their annual reports, to higher objective standards such as those of frankness, impartiality, objectivity, and accessibility applied to governmental statistical information; and they asked for external audit of performance data that would go beyond the current check by NAO of consistency of the performance narrative with the accounts, and check for accuracy and fair use.[39] Its overriding demand was that 'Departments should report against their Single Departmental Plan in their Annual Report and Accounts in a consistent format throughout. Such reporting should provide a complete financial and performance picture of the Department's activity for the year.'[40]

Whether by reason of departmental resistance or other causes, the Treasury clearly did not find it easy to follow up on these requests. It took a year for it to provide a holding response and two years, and a further prod from the Committee,[41] for it to

33 Companies Act 2006, s 416 (directors' report requirements).

34 <IB>IIM Treasury, *Simplifying and Strcamlining Statutory Annual Report and Accounts* (n 31) para 5.3.

35 ibid para 1.11.

36 This was the form of planning instituted by the Coalition government after scrapping PSAs, and replaced by SDPs in 2015: chapter 3, section 4.2.1.

37 HM Treasury, *Simplifying and Streamlining Statutory Annual Report and Accounts* (n 31) paras 4.14, 4.15.

38 *Accounting for Democracy: Making Sure Parliament, the People and Ministers Know How and Why Public Money is Spent* (HC 2016–17, 95).

39 ibid paras 36–51, 140–49, 168–85. In later comments the Comptroller and Auditor General showed a marked lack of enthusiasm for undertaking this extended task: Public Administration and Constitutional Affairs Committee, *Accounting for Democracy Revisited: The Government Response and Proposed Review* (HC 2017–19, 1197) 84.

40 HC 2016–17, 95 (n 38) para 202.

41 In HC 2017–19, 1197 (n 39).

produce *The Government Financial Reporting Review*,[42] which promised a range of actions to improve reporting including a zero-based review of its guidance on producing annual reports and accounts, the *Financial Reporting Manual*.[43] In 2017 the PACAC had identified four purposes which it said reporting should serve and which drove its recommendations:

> supporting House of Commons' control of Government spending;
> informing public judgements about value for money and hence the effectiveness, efficiency, and economy of particular policies or programmes;
> providing a reliable, credible, and accurate record; and
> providing departmental Ministers and civil servants with the information that they require to run their department and its agencies efficiently and effectively.

While putting these purposes at the forefront of its own guidance,[44] the Treasury resisted or qualified some of the Committee's key substantive recommendations. Departments would be required to report by reference to policy areas, programmes, and major projects only where this was both relevant and material to the organization, and the Manual would support a 'comply or explain' approach where departments could choose to diverge from the best practice set out in the guidance, but must acknowledge and explain their divergence.[45] It likewise resisted the Committee's request that action on ministerial spending commitments outside Spending Review settlements should be specifically reported on in annual reports, arguing that they were not capable of containing all the necessary information, but acknowledging difficulties of tracking when, where, and how such promised spending was actually delivered.[46] The Review did, however, give some guarded endorsement to the Committee's complaints about spin and excessive optimism, noting that there was 'still scope for improvement' and promising further Treasury action to this end.[47] Yet on the Committee's key demand for alignment with SDPs, the response was still 'only when appropriate'.[48]

What is surprising in the light of the way this response tiptoes around departmental sensibilities is the extent to which the subsequent versions of the annually updated *Financial Reporting Manual* have taken on board the Committee's main demand for links between reports and SDPs (now Outcome Delivery Plans (ODPs)) and their objectives and indicators. While the minimum requirement set by the 2019–20 Manual was simply that

> the performance analysis . . . include information on how the entity measures performance i.e. what the entity sees as its key performance measures, how it checks

[42] HM Treasury, *The Government Financial Reporting Review* (CP 67, April 2019).

[43] The Manual is produced by a team which sits within one of the Groups reporting to the Director-General of Public Spending, who is also the Head of the Government Finance Function.

[44] They now appear in the *Government Financial Reporting Manual*: see HM Treasury, *Government Financial Reporting Manual 2023–24* (December 2023) para 2.4. They were stated somewhat more elaborately in HC 2016–17, 95 (n 38) para 2.

[45] HM Treasury, *The Government Financial Reporting Review* (n 42) 94–95.

[46] At 30–32 (esp para 4.93).

[47] At 102–03.

[48] At 109.

performance against those measures and narrative to explain the link between K[ey] P[erformance] I[ndicator]s, risk and uncertainty;[49]

from the 2020–21 version onward we find that departments, in the performance section of their annual report, must report against their priority outcomes with indicators using metrics agreed at the latest Spending Review and in a manner that they consider would best contribute to the understanding of performance and value for money, using quantitative or qualitative information, or both. They should provide outturn performance data against each of the indicators, with prior year comparative data (where data has been previously reported against a given outcome) and data for earlier years where available and relevant.[50] Annual reports for 2022–23, expressly identified by ministers as the vehicle of accountability on performance under unpublished ODPs, showed most departments respecting these requirements, though linkage between outcome metrics and financial resources remained weak or absent, with only feeble encouragement in this direction from the Treasury. Giving 'detail on outturn against Estimate by priority outcome agreed at the S(pending) R(eview), other strategic objective or other goal' is identified as best practice, but

it is recognised this reporting may be difficult to produce if objectives do not align to Estimate lines and if apportioning spend to objectives is highly judgemental.[51]

There is thus still some way to go to satisfy PACAC's desire that reporting should 'inform . . . public judgements about value for money and hence the effectiveness, efficiency and economy of particular policies or programmes'.[52]

III Informing the People: Freedom of Information

3.1 The background to the Freedom of Information Act 2000

Putting formerly autonomous executive action into a legislative framework may be an important symbolic step, but it does not necessarily change the way control is exercised.[53] One reform which certainly did make such a change was the Freedom of Information (FOI) Act 2000, whose core purpose was to overturn the long-standing presumption of confidentiality of government information by conferring legally enforceable rights on individuals to obtain it, replacing the non-binding disclosure policies previously in place. Despite the radical effects it might have been expected to produce on the internal handling of information, the Act said virtually nothing about how executive functions and organization were to be reshaped to manage the requirements it imposed; and it relied for its external enforcement on independent

[49] HM Treasury, *Government Financial Reporting Manual 2019–2020* (December 2019) para 5.2.10.

[50] See now HM Treasury, *Government Financial Reporting Manual 2023–24* (n 44) para 5.4.4.

[51] ibid para 5.4.6.c.iii.

[52] See text at n 44.

[53] See the discussion at chapter 6, section III, on the provision of a statutory framework for the Civil Service by the Constitutional Reform and Governance Act 2010.

institutions already in existence, the Data Protection Commissioner (previously Data Protection Registrar) and Tribunal.[54] These became the Information Commissioner and Tribunal under the 2000 Act; following the reform of the tribunal system in 2007 the tribunal functions were divided between the First-Tier and Upper Tribunals then established.[55]

By the time that the Labour government came to office in 1997 with a promise, initially made in 1992, that an FOI Act would be the first Home Office legislation that it would introduce, legislation and public opinion had moved a great distance from the original Official Secrets Act's criminalization[56] of any unauthorized communication of government information. Thinking within the executive generally had not. The first step in this direction was the issue in 1977 under the Labour government led by James Callaghan of the so-called Croham directive, telling Permanent Secretaries that they should reverse the hitherto operative assumption that background material relating to policy studies and reports would not be published unless the responsible minister decided otherwise, and assume instead that material would be published unless ministers decided that it should not be. This produced no lasting effect and had been forgotten within a year or so.

The Labour Party made a commitment to FOI in each general election from 1974 onwards, and in 1979 the Labour government published a Green Paper on Open Government, which however proposed not a Freedom of Information Act, but a non-statutory Code of Practice. It was not until 1994 that a Code was introduced, by the Conservative government, building on the commitment to greater transparency in the aims, performance and, delivery of public services contained in the government's Citizen's Charter.[57] The lesson of the Croham directive had been learned:

> 4.2 A general declaration in favour of openness is not enough. The vigilance with which it is observed may fade, and it may be bent to the convenience of holders of information, rather than those seeking it.
> 4.3 The essential requirements to make the intentions set out in this White Paper stick are:
>
> - a clear statement of principle on what kinds of information will be available:
> - a clear statement of the circumstances in which information can justifiably be withheld;
> - detached, authoritative and independent supervision.[58]

[54] Data Protection Act 1998, s 6, renaming the office originally created by the Data Protection Act 1984, s 3.

[55] Tribunals, Courts and Enforcement Act 2007, pt 1; Transfer of Tribunal Functions Order 2010, SI 2010/22, art 2(3).

[56] Official Secrets Act 1911, s 2. That provision had been repealed by the Official Secrets Act 1989, s 16(4) and sch 2, and replaced by a number of prohibitions focused on security, defence, and international relations.

[57] On the Charter see Daintith and Page (n 29) 349–66, and for details of the commitment to transparency, see Chancellor of the Duchy of Lancaster, *Open Government* (Cm 2290, July 1993).

[58] *Open Government* (n 57) paras 4.2, 4.3.

The Code contained all these elements, entrusting supervision to the Parliamentary Commissioner for Administration, but its impact was limited. Hopes that a flexible Code-based approach would be more effective than one that was statutory, and more likely to secure positive support from departments, were disappointed. The Parliamentary Commissioner reported in 1996 and 1998 that the tendency in some departments was to use every argument—legal, Code-based, or at times simply obstructive—to help justify non-disclosure; and he also reported in 1998 that others appeared not to have heard of the Code at all.[59] By this time the newly elected Labour government had announced with fanfare its intention to provide the people of this country, for the first time, with a general statutory right of access to the information held by public authorities. This, it said, was a step essential for moving beyond its predecessor's 'haphazard approach': non-statutory best practice arrangements (in particular the Code of Practice), with statutory requirements for openness applying only in certain areas such as environmental information[60] or limited to particular sectors of the public service, notably local authorities.[61]

3.2 From internal guidance to statutory duties: the innovations of the FOI Act

It took until 2000 for this right of access to government information to reach the statute book in the form of the FOI Act, and more than four further years for the Act to be brought fully into force, at the beginning of 2005. The scope of the Act, estimated to apply to some 100,000 public bodies, from the Cabinet Office to educational institutions, and to miscellaneous public bodies listed by name from the Administration of Radioactive Substances Advisory Committee down to the Zoos Forum,[62] was far wider than the Code, which had applied only to central government. The Act's duties were legally binding. Its enforcement was now in the hands of an expert regulator, with provision for ultimate resort to the courts. These were major changes, but the approach to achieving access to information was not fundamentally different from that followed in the Code. Both Code and Act contain a general obligation to *publish* certain kinds of information,[63] coupled with an obligation to *provide access* to information in response to specific requests.[64] The obligation to provide access is subject to a number of exemptions, some related to subject-matter (eg defence and security);

[59] Parliamentary Commissioner for Administration, *Annual Report for 1995* (HC 1995–96, 296) 51; *Annual Report 1997–98* (HC 1997–98, 845) paras 6.12–6.13, 6.29.

[60] Environmental Information Regulations 2004, SI 2004/3391, applying art 6 of Parliament and Council Directive 2003/4/EC.

[61] Chancellor of the Duchy of Lancaster, *Your Right to Know: The Government's Proposals for a Freedom of Information Act* (Cm 3818, December 1997) paras 1.3, 1.5.

[62] FOI Act, s 3(a)(i) and sch 1, as amended from time to time by orders under ss 4 and 5. The figure of 100,000 is from Robert Hazell and Mark Glover, 'The Impact of Freedom of Information on Whitehall' (2011) 89 Public Administration 1664, 1665.

[63] Cabinet Office, *Code of Practice on Access to Government Information* (1994, rev 1997) para 3(i)(ii)(iv); FOI Act 2000, s 19. The Code text is no longer accessible online. References here are drawn from *Code of Practice on Access to Government Information: Guidance on Interpretation* (2nd edn, 1997), republished by the Campaign for Freedom of Information.

[64] Cabinet Office, *Code of Practice* (n 63) para 3(iii)(v); FOI Act, s 1.

some to the type of information involved (eg personal data, formulation of policy, information intended for future publication); some to restrictions on disclosure (eg statutory prohibitions, breach of confidence).[65] Both Code and Act make provision for a charge to be imposed for the fulfilment of a request in certain circumstances.[66]

The FOI provisions designed to incentivize wider publication of information by public authorities have not been controversial and do not appear to have caused difficulties for government. This, it has been suggested, is because they mandate action that authorities would have wished to take anyway, or have been overtaken by the near-universal use of internet search engines and institution websites as the preferred approach to identifying useful information.[67] Under the Act this aspect of the policy takes the form of an obligation on every public authority to develop a 'publication scheme', which has to receive the approval of the Information Commissioner and to be kept under review (s 19). Though the Information Commissioner's Office has prepared 'definition documents' indicating, for different kinds of public body—including government departments—what kinds of information their publication schemes might be expected to contain,[68] practice as to what information is published and how it is organized varies significantly from department to department. The power (and the associated provision for the Commissioner to provide model publication schemes (s 20)) may be seen as elements—not necessarily the most important ones—of the more general push for greater transparency in government dating at least from the launch of the Citizen's Charter in 1991. We now take for granted the official provision of an incessant flow of performance standards and performance data—like NHS waiting lists and time spent in Accident and Emergency units—that would a few decades ago have been regarded as too sensitive to publish.

Greater transparency of executive action does not, however, necessarily diminish needs for access to specific information by way of FOI requests. Even with state-of-the-art websites, authorities may struggle to provide information in the forms and at the level of detail that people prove to want. Formulation and management of the right of access to specific information has proved to be much more problematic and controversial, and even at a distance of nearly two decades from the coming into force of the Act, there remains disagreement on the effectiveness of the right and on the balance between its positive and negative impacts on the way government is carried on. It did not take long for the new Labour government to discover that its trumpeted shift from the internal rules of the Code to a system of legal rights and obligations was going to demand a different kind of regime from that with which departments were familiar and comfortable. The draft bill presented by the Home Office for scrutiny and comment in May 1999 followed the traditional approach of leaving it to ministers and other authorities to decide whether, having regard to the public interest in freedom of information, they should exercise a discretion to disclose information covered by one

[65] *Code of Practice*, pt II; FOI Act, ss 2, 22–43.

[66] *Code of Practice*, para 7; FOI Act, s 9.

[67] Justice Committee, *Post-legislative Scrutiny of the Freedom of Information Act 2000* (HC 2012–13, 96-1) paras 19–32. On government arrangements for effective use of the internet see chapter 3, section 3.2, and chapter 12, text at nn 4–5.

[68] Information Commissioner's Office, *Definition Documents.*

of the exemptions listed in the bill.[69] This was generally seen as a step back from the access undertakings offered in the government's White Paper, and provoked widespread and vigorous protest.[70] The definitive bill introduced later in the year went some way towards meeting these complaints, and the duties were further strengthened by government acceptance of amendments during its passage. The result was an Act that is unusually restrictive of ministerial discretion as to the operation of its provisions.

Response to an access request under the Act is treated as having two elements: an indication of whether the relevant public authority holds the information requested, described in the Act as 'the duty to confirm or deny', and the communication (or withholding) of the information, if held (s 1(1)). If an appropriate statutory exemption is available, the authority may refuse to say whether it holds the information; or, having acknowledged that it does, may still refuse to disclose it. Exemptions themselves are divided into two categories: those that are 'absolute', and those whose operation depends on a judgement that the public interest in maintaining the exemption outweighs the public interest in disclosing whether the information is held, or in disclosing the information itself (s 2(1), 2(2)). Unlike the Code's *Guidance on Interpretation*, which stressed that decisions on disclosure would require 'judgement and discretion', and were to be made 'in accordance with the general policy and instructions of the Minister',[71] this public interest test is framed in objective terms, not in terms of subjective appreciation by the minister. While it must clearly be applied in the first instance by the department, it is subject to review and reversal by the Information Commissioner (s 50).[72]

Among the 10 classes of absolute exemptions are those for information certified as having been supplied by security agencies (s 23), court records (s 32), disclosures that would constitute an actionable breach of confidence (s 41), and information whose disclosure is prohibited by statute (s 44).[73] For 16 further classes of information exemption depends on the public interest test, but here too there are important differences in the formulation of the exemptions. While, for some, the test is automatically triggered by the nature or subject-matter of the information (information intended for future publication (s 22), information certified as required for the protection of national security (s 24),[74] information relating to the formulation of government policy (s 35), information protected by legal professional privilege (s 42)), most depend upon a showing that disclosure will prejudicially affect some interest, such as defence (s 26), international relations (s 27), the country's economic interests (s 29), or the effective

[69] Secretary of State for the Home Department, *Freedom of Information: Consultation on Draft Legislation* (Cm 4355, May 1999) paras 58–65.

[70] See House of Commons Select Committee on Public Administration, *Freedom of Information Draft Bill* (HC 1998–99, 570-I, 570-II); House of Lords, *Report from the Select Committee Appointed to Consider the Draft Freedom of Information Bill* (HL 1998–99, 97).

[71] *Code of Practice on Access to Government Information: Guidance on Interpretation* (n 63) pt II, para 0.2.

[72] The Commissioner's decision is subject to appeal by the applicant or the authority to the First-Tier and Upper Tribunals: ss 57–61.

[73] The Act provides a power to amend or repeal such prohibitions by order: s 75 and the Freedom of Information (Removal and Relaxation of Statutory Prohibitions on Disclosure of Information) Order 2004, SI 2004/3363.

[74] Though the issuance of such a certificate (and also of a certificate supplied under s 23) is subject to an appeal to the Tribunal: s 60.

conduct of public affairs (s 36, in cases where the 'formulation of public policy' tests of s 35 are not satisfied). Only once such prejudice is established does the public interest test come into play. Again, prejudicial effect is an objective criterion on which a departmental judgement may be overturned by the Information Commissioner or on appeal.

3.3 Policy formulation, the 'safe space', and the ministerial veto

There is an acute tension—some might say an irresolvable contradiction—between the need for a 'safe space' where ministers and senior officials can rely on being able to discuss sensitive matters in private without the fear of subsequent disclosure, and the legal 'right to know' promised by the Labour government's White Paper. Pressure to stick by this promise led the government, in the course of parliamentary discussion of the FOI Bill, to accept the idea that the Information Commissioner could override the decision of any public authority to withhold information on the balance of public interest, not excluding information on the formulation of public policy or information whose disclosure would be prejudicial to the conduct of public affairs: there is no reason, *prima facie*, why this power should not extend all the way up to the disclosure of Cabinet minutes. The government's price for going this far was the provision of a power of veto, in whose exercise a Cabinet minister or a Law Officer could substitute a 'no disclosure' decision for an order to disclose issued by the Commissioner or, on appeal, by the First-Tier or Upper Tribunal (s 53). 'Without the veto', the then Home Secretary later said, 'we would have dropped the Bill'.[75]

The veto became the subject of intense controversy when it was used in 2012 with the purpose of preventing publication of letters that the then heir to the throne, Prince Charles, had written to various government departments to express his views on a number of issues of public policy. The Information Commissioner had endorsed the relevant departments' refusal of disclosure, but the Upper Tribunal, to which—unusually—the case went directly on appeal, reversed this decision and ordered disclosure after a comprehensive reconsideration of the issues. It was at this point that the Attorney General issued the veto by certifying, under section 53(2), that he had on reasonable grounds formed the opinion that there was no duty to disclose. In *R (on the application of Evans) v Attorney General* the Supreme Court, by a majority, quashed this certificate.[76] The problem was that the Attorney was trying to apply his veto to a decision of the Upper Tribunal, a superior court of record. Given the detailed investigative processes by which a judicial decision is reached, the Supreme Court was not prepared to accept the Attorney's grounds as 'reasonable' where they simply involved disagreeing with the conclusions of a court or judicial tribunal on the same material as was before it.[77] While the decision is among those that have been paraded by ministers in support of claims of judicial overreach,[78] it is only a marginal note to the history of

[75] In evidence to the House of Commons Justice Committee (n 67) para 168.
[76] [2015] UKSC 21, [2015] AC 1787.
[77] [2015] AC 1787, 1789.
[78] See eg Suella Braverman (as Attorney General), 'Judicial Review Trends and Forecasts 2021: Accountability and the Constitution' (speech to Public Law Project Conference, 19 October).

FOI: its subject-matter lay outside the area of government policymaking, and the veto might well have been judicially sustained had it been imposed—as was apparently expected to be the normal course when the procedure was introduced[79]—in relation to the decision made by the Commissioner. The decision did, however, prompt the government to commission an 'independent review'

> to consider whether there is an appropriate public interest balance between transparency, accountability and the need for sensitive information to have robust protection, and whether the operation of the Act adequately recognises the need for a 'safe space' for policy development and implementation and frank advice.[80]

Given the composition of the Commission (a former Permanent Secretary to the Treasury, former Labour and Conservative Home Secretaries, the Chair of Ofcom, and a Liberal Democrat barrister and peer), its answering 'yes' to both questions, subject to some relatively minor suggestions for legislative reform of the policy exemptions, may have come as something of a surprise to government and FOI campaigners alike. No new legislation followed. On the point presented by the *Evans* case, the government simply announced that it would in future only deploy the veto after an Information Commissioner decision, as the Commission had recommended.[81]

It had always been the intention of government that the employment of the veto would be exceptional, and a policy statement issued in 2012 explained its approach in detail and undertook that it would only follow a collective Cabinet decision.[82] Use of the veto has in fact been extremely rare, with seven examples up to 2014 and (apparently) none since.[83] It would be a mistake, though, to interpret this absence as a sign that ministers and civil servants are now fully reconciled to the Act, and that early and vigorously expressed concerns about its 'chilling' effect on frank communication within government, and the risk that it would drive discussion into informal and unrecorded channels, have simply disappeared.[84] In explaining why a new government agency was to be kept outside the scope of the FOI Act, for example, an Industry Department minister in 2021 referred to it as 'a truly malign piece of legislation'.[85] Yet an extensive study of the operation of the Act reached the conclusion, in 2017, that while contributing to increased governmental transparency, it had 'not significantly affected the way British central government works', nor 'caused a "chilling effect" on frank advice and deliberation, or on the quality of government records'. Other factors,

[79] Independent Commission on Freedom of Information, *Report* (March 2016) 38–40.
[80] ibid 5.
[81] Matt Hancock, Minister for the Cabinet Office, Written Statement: Open and transparent government, HC Deb 1 March 2016, vol 606, cols 26–28WS.
[82] Justice Committee (n 67) para 171.
[83] Oonagh Gay and Ed Potton, *FoI and Ministerial Vetoes*, House of Commons Library Standard Note: SN/PC/05007 (last updated 19 March 2014).
[84] Documented in Justice Committee (n 67) paras 141–54, 180–90; and for subsequent research on the issue, Ben Worthy and Robert Hazell, 'Disruptive, Dynamic and Democratic? Ten Years of FOI in the UK' (2017) 70 Parliamentary Affairs 22, 31.
[85] Lord Callanan, Parliamentary Under-Secretary of State, Department of Business, Energy and Industrial Strategy, at HL Deb 22 November 2021, vol 816, col 147GC. He later added 'I genuinely do not think it achieves anything at all.'

like new communications technology (above), or deliberate leaking of information, may well be more important. The chilling effect was a 'pervasive myth', albeit one that 'may be self-fulfilling, leading to behaviour change and fear each time it is repeated'.[86] Departmental attitudes to the Act can be collected from Cabinet Office statistics indicating the proportion of requests to central government that were granted or refused, and the promptness—or lack of it—with which requests were processed.[87] Figures for complaints referred to the Information Commissioner, and how they were disposed of, do not distinguish between departments.[88]

3.4 Central coordination

In 2004, as part of preparation for bringing the Act into force, the responsible department—then the Department for Constitutional Affairs—established a Clearing House as an 'expert advice centre to which cases can be referred by central government departments for further assistance when assessing the duty to release or withhold information'. In the Act's first year of operation the Clearing House provided advice on over 3,100 cases, about 10% of the requests made to central government.[89] This coordination mechanism immediately engendered suspicion because of the department's uncommunicativeness about its operations, to the point of refusing FOI requests for information on the ground that this would prejudice the effective conduct of public affairs. The suspicion, particularly among journalists, that the Clearing House existed to block rather than facilitate the release of information, has persisted to the present day and has been reinforced by impressions that its procedures might function to identify and hinder particular requesters.

PACAC undertook a further inquiry into the Clearing House—currently lodged in the Cabinet Office, which has had policy responsibility for FOI since 2015—in 2022,[90] following a First-Tier Tribunal decision requiring the Cabinet Office to release its so-called 'Round Robin' list.[91] The list was at that time a daily circulation to departments listing requests identified as having been sent to a number of departments, with summary advice from the Clearing House on how they should be handled. A Cabinet Office notice also lists categories of 'sensitive' requests which should be referred to the Clearing House and on which it also circulates advice. Disclosure was resisted initially on grounds of formation of policy (s 35) later replaced by prejudice to the effective

86 Worthy and Hazell (n 84) 30, 31.

87 Cabinet Office, *Freedom of Information Statistics: Annual 2022 Bulletin* (May 2023), showing a range of full acceptance from 80% of requests at the Welsh Office down to 17% at the Treasury, and rates of late response ranging from zero at the Scottish Office and DEFRA to 34% at the Department for International Trade.

88 For overall complaints figures see Information Commissioner's Office, *Information Commissioner's Annual Report and Financial Statements 2022/23* (HC 2022–23, 1440) 59–66.

89 House of Commons Constitutional Affairs Committee, *Freedom of Information—One Year On* (HC 2005–06, 991) paras 86–92, evidence, 50, paras 5.14–5.20.

90 Public Administration and Constitutional Affairs Committee, *The Cabinet Office Freedom of Information Clearing House* (HC 2021–22, 505).

91 *Cabinet Office v Information Commissioner and Jenna Cordery* (First-tier Tribunal (General Regulatory Chamber)), Information Rights, Decision notice fs50841228 (19 May 2021).

conduct of public affairs (s 36), but eventually the Cabinet Office released a high proportion of the contents of the requested lists, and the Tribunal required most of the remaining entries, other than those related to security matters, to be released. Evidence before the Tribunal indicated that the Cabinet Office official in charge of the function did not correctly understand the content of the Round Robin list, that the minister required to support a section 36 exemption had likewise been incorrectly advised; that, contrary to usual practice, names of requesters were circulated with the list; that it took nearly a year for the Cabinet Office to reply to the original request after internal review; and that, when it did, the refusal did not satisfy the formal requirements of section 36.

While ministers, in correspondence with the Committee and others, indignantly rejected suggestions that the Round Robin procedure was used to identify and discriminate against 'difficult' requesters,[92] it was clear that Cabinet Office attitudes and practice on FOI were the opposite of exemplary. The possibility that the Clearing House might operate both as an additional source of delay in responses and as a further barrier to disclosure—the criteria for referral to it listed no less than 19 request areas,[93] and the Tribunal heard that departments were expected to 'explain' if they chose not to follow Clearing House advice[94]—was not displaced by any evidence to the Committee's inquiry. Having refused to accept the Information Commissioner's offer to conduct an audit of the process, Cabinet Office agreed to an internal inquiry, conducted by a former non-executive director at the Home Office. The inquiry recommended the abolition of the Clearing House function and its replacement within Cabinet Office by an FOI centre of excellence with purely advisory and educational functions.[95] In response, the government accepted 'that the title "FOI Clearing House" was confusing, suggesting a level of direction and control over other departments' FOI requests which in reality does not exist'. It promised to 'work to reconfigure the function to provide advice as efficiently to departments to enable them to meet their statutory obligations in a timely manner and to a high quality'.[96]

The attention paid to the Clearing House—a Tribunal decision, a parliamentary inquiry, an internal review—may well have exaggerated government's commitment to central control in this area. The Clearing House's staff consisted of only three Cabinet Office officials, who had other duties as well; referrals over the 2018–20 period were running at under 2% of requests, a fifth of the original percentage;[97] and in its reply to the PACAC inquiry, the government strongly asserted its view that

> departments are listed as public authorities in their own right [under the FOI Act] and it would be wrong for the Cabinet Office to intervene in another department's procedures and decisions. The Cabinet Office will continue to offer advice and

[92] Public Administration and Constitutional Affairs Committee (n 90) paras 12, 13.

[93] Cabinet Office, *FOI Referral Criteria* [nd].

[94] *Cabinet Office v Information Commissioner and Jenna Cordery* (n 91) para 22.

[95] Sue Langley, *Freedom of Information Clearing House Review* (Cabinet Office 2022) 10–12.

[96] ibid 4–5 (response of the Minister of State for the Cabinet Office).

[97] Letter from Michael Gove MP, Chancellor of the Duchy of Lancaster, to the Chair of PACAC, 9 March 2021: see PACAC (n 90) para 15.

guidance, but it is for individual departments to account for their compliance with the Act through the mechanisms set up by Parliament.[98]

If the views of Lord Callanan noted earlier[99] have any echo in other departments, FOI campaigners may end up wondering if a central advice function is a sufficient support for the openness they seek.

IV Ephemeral Information: Government by WhatsApp

Large and complex organizations like the executive depend totally for their effective operation on mechanisms for recording and preserving information. Such mechanisms also provide the essential underpinning for the discharge by the executive of its obligations of democratic accountability and compliance with legal constraints. These notions may be fundamental, but a combination of crisis conditions and rapid development in communications technique may render them unexpectedly fragile. A blog by Dominic Cummings, the former Chief Advisor to the Prime Minister, disclosed the extensive use of WhatsApp messaging by ministers, senior officials, and scientific advisers, as they worked to develop the government's responses to the Covid pandemic in 2020. Groups within which messages were exchanged were formed ad hoc and had no official existence. While Cabinet Office guidance made provision for preserving notes of such messages in more permanent form where necessary, it also encouraged the auto-deletion of such 'instant messages' after a few weeks. There was clearly a risk that under the stress of crisis conditions messages might not be permanently saved, and that the process of reaching key decisions would be imperfectly documented. The relevant internal rules and guidance were thus of constitutional significance—and have been modified as a result of the Covid experience.

In *R (on the application of All the Citizens and Good Law Project) v Secretary of State for Digital, Culture, Media and Sport and others*[100] the claimant organizations, concerned about the risks these information practices posed for public accountability, attacked the legality of use for government business of non-governmental ('private') communication systems (particularly WhatsApp, Signal and private email), as being both contrary to a statutory duty under the Public Records Act 1958 to select and preserve public records, and in breach of a number of internal policies regarding forms of communication within government and the preservation of records. The statutory claim was dismissed on the ground that the statutory duty did not extend to requiring the preservation of records prior to selection—or, for that matter, the making of records in the first place.[101] Instead the Act, in section 3, provided a flexible scheme, under which those responsible for public records were required to perform their duties under the guidance of the Keeper of Public Records, who was responsible for

[98] Public Administration and Constitutional Affairs Committee, *The Cabinet Office Freedom of Information Clearing House: Government Response to the Committee's Ninth Report of Session 2021–22* (HC 2021–22, 576) 4.

[99] Lord Callanan (n 85).

[100] [2022] EWHC 960 (Admin) (DC), [2022] EWCA Civ 1580 (CA).

[101] [2022] EWHC 960 (Admin) [53]–[61].

coordinating and supervising all action taken under the section. This enabled preservation and selection arrangements to keep up with changes to ways of working and communicating—such as those under consideration in the case.[102]

Such guidance, and other internal policies on ways of communication, thus moved to centre-stage in the litigation. More than 30 codes of practice, policies, guidance, advice, and notes that had an impact on the use of communication systems and the retention of information were disclosed in the proceedings at first instance. The Court reviewed 13 of these, starting with the statutory guidance—the National Archives' Records Collection Policy—issued by the Keeper of Records under the 1958 Act. It found that some of this material was irrelevant, that other guidance had not been breached by the messaging practices disclosed in the case, and that none of the policies was legally enforceable, so that if any breaches had occurred, no redress by way of judicial review was available. In an appeal brought by only one of the claimants, the Good Law Project, the Court of Appeal confirmed these findings in relation to the eight policies there in issue. Both courts discussed the case law governing the legal status of policies pursued by the executive, emphasizing the limited circumstances in which a legal obligation to follow a policy should be recognized. In this case, said the Court of Appeal,

> The proposition that the policies were enforceable by the Good Law Project on an application for judicial review does not sit easily with the fundamental principle of public law that guidance need not be slavishly followed. It is apparent that the eight policies were formulated at different times and cannot be read as a coherent whole. Any attempt to follow all these policies would lead to difficulty . . . It is for the executive to decide whether a greater degree of consistency between the policies would be helpful, and it is not the constitutional role of the courts to attempt to micromanage how the executive conducts its affairs in the selection and preservation of documents, or in the use of communications technology by ministers and officials.[103]

Though there would be no judicial intervention, there was a clear message here that there was work to be done within government to develop a coherent system of control of modern communication methods. The problem had already been flagged by the Information Commissioner, who launched an investigation under FOI Act powers in July 2021 based on complaints about practices of communication through instant messaging at the Department of Health and Social Care (DHSC) during the pandemic similar to those that prompted the litigation just discussed. The use by some DHSC ministers and non-executive directors of non-corporate, private correspondence and communication channels for conducting official business gave rise to genuine concerns that information which should form part of DHSC's official record might not have been retained or be accessible for the purposes of properly responding to legitimate FOI requests. These practices, which senior officials within DHSC were aware of, had the effect of undermining the concept of all official information being held and accessible via a single corporately controlled system. The result

[102] [2022] EWCA Civ 1580 [50]–[54].
[103] [2022] EWCA Civ 1580 [60].

was that DHSC committed numerous breaches of obligations under the Freedom of Information Code of Practice promulgated under section 45 of the FOI Act, in relation to requestors' rights to be informed whether or not the public authority held requested information, to time limits for response, and to the information to be provided. The Commissioner therefore issued a 'practice recommendation' under the Act setting out corrective steps to be taken by DHSC.[104] These did not exclude the continued use of devices like email and instant messaging, but recommended safeguards to ensure that their content was transferred to departmental systems, including a centrally held register of the individuals permitted to use private channels and devices, and a process for granting this permission that included confirmation of how, and with what frequency, official information will be transferred onto official systems.

By the time this recommendation emerged the Cabinet Office had already indicated that it would be updating its own guidance on the use of private correspondence channels: as well it might, given that some of the inconsistencies in guidance were to be found in its own policies. Thus while its Private Email Guidance of 2013 clearly contemplated the use of non-governmental electronic communication in the course of conducting government business, its Information and Records Management Policy (2021) stated that non-authorized repositories, including personal email, must not be used for the storage of information and records.[105] In March 2023 Cabinet Office issued its new guidance, which was expressed only to replace its Private Email Guidance of 2013 but which, by reason of its comprehensive character, should presumably prevail over any inconsistent advice in other earlier documents.[106] The new guidance, expressed to apply to 'all individuals in central government', not excluding ministers, distinguishes between government systems for communication and non-corporate communications channels (WhatsApp, private email, SMS etc) ('NCCCs'), and further discriminates between using NCCCs on corporately managed devices such as government-issued phones and laptops, and on privately owned devices. Appropriate modes of communication are also linked to the security classification of the relevant information, as set out in the Cabinet Office's *Government Security Classifications* last revised in 2018.[107] While information classified as 'secret' or 'top secret' must never be shared through NCCCs, other 'significant' information can be communicated through NCCCs on a corporately managed device if 'particular care' is used, but only in exceptional circumstances (and with subsequent reporting) on a privately owned device. More relaxed arrangements apply to logistical and other non-significant information. The guidance also updates existing requirements on transferring significant information in NCCCs into government systems to support accountability, emphasizing that use of NCCCs entails personal responsibility for ensuring that significant information gets on to the official record. Ministers and senior officials are asked to

[104] Information Commissioner, *Freedom of Information Act 2000 (Section 48) Practice Recommendation: Department of Health and Social Care* (11 July 2022). The Commissioner's decision to launch the investigation (though not the result) was noted by the Court of Appeal in the *Good Law Project* appeal ([2022] EWCA Civ 1580 [19]) but was not relied on by the claimants.

[105] As described by the Divisional Court at [2022] EWHC 960 (Admin) [77], [83].

[106] Cabinet Office, *Using Non-corporate Communication Channels (e.g. WhatsApp, Private E-mail, SMS) for Government Business* (30 March 2023).

[107] Cabinet Office, *Government Security Classifications* (May 2018).

consider including private office staff in communications groups and tasking them to undertake such transfer.

A former No 10 Director of Communications has stated that the UK government is 'largely run on WhatsApp' after the need to deal with Covid-19 'blurred the boundaries' between official communication and conversations on sites like WhatsApp.[108] It may not be the case, however, that this change has extended down to levels of government—day-to-day work in departments, for example—that are beyond the range of vision of No 10 Directors of Communication. The new guidance clearly represents an attempt to get some boundaries back, by strengthening the discipline imposed on the use of NCCCs in the interests of security and accountability, while still facilitating efficient day-to-day government discussions in a modern way. It takes the position that NCCCs are not the norm: 'Departments should, as far as reasonably practicable, enable approaches in their core systems that reduce the need for NCCCs' (para 4); 'In general, it is expected that you use government systems for government business' (para 8). How easy it will be to operate is another matter: trawling through WhatsApp messages to decide which should be held in official systems will be a time-consuming process.

While the guidance appears to be responsive to the recent judicial and other external concerns we have described, it is clear that Cabinet Office regards the management of the executive's internal communications as private territory where external bodies should have no right of entry. Cabinet Office failed in its attempt, via judicial review, to withhold from the Covid inquiry ministerial WhatsApp messages that it considered irrelevant to the inquiry's work, the Court holding that the inquiry could properly assert the right to be the judge of relevance.[109] The attempt clearly demonstrates the executive's acute sensitivity about such messages, whose 'instant' character means that their expression is likely to be far less guarded than the traditional documentary record. Cabinet Office had already supplied Cabinet minutes to the inquiry without redactions. The inquiry decided at an early stage that WhatsApp messaging was a matter of interest.[110] Records of the inquiry proceedings demonstrate the intensive use of such messaging, along with email messaging, in the process of managing the Covid crisis, and the significance of the material that was communicated.[111] While such occasional 'deep dives' into internal executive communications can produce spectacular results, the more important long-term consequence of this aspect of the Covid experience has been the assertion by the Information Commissioner—not challenged by the executive—of external standards for the management and preservation of internal communications based on the requirements of the FOI Act.

[108] Oscar Edwards, 'UK Government Largely Run on WhatsApp Says Ex-Comms Chief' *BBC News* (1 June 2023).

[109] *R (on the application of Cabinet Office) v Chair of the UK Covid-19 Inquiry* [2023] EWHC 1702 (Admin).

[110] ibid [9]–[10].

[111] See the witness statements, transcripts, and evidence from the inquiry's Module 2 (Core UK decision-making and political governance) at <https://covid19.public-inquiry.uk/>.

12

Government Communications: Persuasion with Propriety

I Introduction

A government that wants people to change their behaviour in line with its policy objectives does not necessarily have to resort to coercive legal measures or to providing financial incentives for compliance through the use of taxes and subsidies. Maybe it is enough to ensure that people are not left in ignorance about the benefits to them of the course of behaviour suggested by government policy. Thus while the provision of information is an essential adjunct to those other tools of government, which will not work unless people are aware of the threats or advantages they are being offered, it may also operate as an independent resource. Communication as a policy lever represents, however, only one area within the broad information landscape confronted by the executive. As we have seen, government also enjoys informational privileges—powers, granted in the public interest, to demand, acquire, and process information; is subject to general and specialized legal restrictions on the use of information; and bears specific obligations to disclose information responding to constitutional notions of political accountability and individual rights. While these powers and obligations are not irrelevant to the activity of government communicators as they set about their task of persuasion through information, the most important feature of that task, from the point of view of the legal and constitutional commentator, is that government does not enjoy a position of privilege in relation to the *dissemination* of information.

Any form of state monopoly or privilege in publishing could hardly be reconciled with the commitment to freedom of expression that the United Kingdom shares with other European democracies and that is now expressed in the Human Rights Act 1998.[1] In practical terms, the executive has always depended heavily on privately owned mass media for the purpose of communicating its messages to the public (as opposed to communicating with specific addressees). From time to time, as we shall see, it has equipped itself with its own publishing and propaganda facilities, notably in times of war: but since the winding up in 2011 of the Central Office of Information, which succeeded the wartime Ministry of Information as a provider of services across government in such fields as publishing; the preparation of public information in the form of pamphlets, broadcasts, and films, and the commissioning of advertising, departments have been left to secure these services from the private sector. Since 1996, when His Majesty's Stationery Office (HMSO) was privatized, the United Kingdom has relied on the private sector even for the publication of its core official documentation: legislation, parliamentary papers and proceedings, and the government's official

[1] European Convention of Human Rights, art 10(1), as applied by s 1 and sch 1.

Executive Self-Government and the Constitution. Terence Daintith and Alan Page, Oxford University Press.
 DOI: 10.1093/9780198937630.003.0012

journals of record, the London, Edinburgh, and Belfast Gazettes.[2] Publicly owned mass media are limited to the British Broadcasting Corporation, incorporated under Royal Charter; the Welsh-language channel S4C, now largely funded via the BBC from the television licence fee but governed by a separate statutory corporation; and Channel 4, which while commercially funded is owned by a statutory public corporation, Channel Four Television Corporation. Each of these operates at arm's length from government, and their regulation is increasingly assimilated to that of private broadcast media.

The coming of the digital age has, however, offered the government possibilities of mass communication that do not depend on access to privately owned or independent media. Like everyone else, the executive can be a self-publisher through the world wide web, and has devoted considerable efforts in recent decades to the creation of a comprehensive government website through which all departments and many other bodies present their communications.[3]

At the same time such departments and bodies seek to extend the reach of their digital communications by maintaining their own accounts on social media platforms like Facebook, Twitter (now X), and Instagram. More ambitious departmental initiatives have not always gone well. The Treasury's 2010 *Spending Challenge* website, inviting the public to submit and comment on ideas for public expenditure economies, survived as an interactive facility for only a week in the face of a flood of malicious attacks and inappropriate submissions that overwhelmed the site's slender moderating capacities.[4]

When the executive wants to communicate with the public, therefore, it is presented with the same media opportunities and constraints as any other would-be communicator; and it needs to compete via those media for the attention of the public with commercial advertisers and publicists, third-sector communicators, and political rivals. Like them, it is subject to general legal controls and restrictions: general and contractually based obligations of confidentiality, non-infringement of the intellectual property rights of others, avoidance of actionable misrepresentation, respect for defamation laws, and so on. The status of public authority may also entail subjection, in government communications, to disciplines from which private parties may be exempt, such as the duties imposed under the Human Rights Act 1998, notably in relation to the Convention right to respect for private and family life. In addition, as already noted, bodies and individuals within the executive are subject to the specific and

[2] The Stationery Office Ltd, the privatized successor of HMSO, was at one time a subsidiary of Deutsche Bundespost and was from 2017 to 2023 ultimately owned, via a chain of holding companies, by a private equity fund based in Boston, USA.

[3] The first online website for central government as a whole—open.gov.uk—was established by the Government Information Service in 1994. This was later replaced by uk.online and then by directgov, run as a cross-government internet interface by the Department of Work and Pensions. From 2011 the Government Digital Service (GDS), created by the merging of directgov with Cabinet Office digital teams, both ran the programme for bringing the many separate departmental internet interfaces onto the single site that is now gov.uk, and built common platforms to help departments improve their digital services. On the general management of digital services see further chapter 3, section 5.2.

[4] Christopher Hood and others, *The Way the Money Goes: The Fiscal Constitution and Public Spending in the UK* (OUP 2023) 89–91.

limited constraints on publication that form the corollary to its coercive information-gathering powers.

The sense that government is one among many actors on the information scene—albeit a powerful and ever-present actor—should not lead us to minimize the constitutional significance of the arrangements through which the executive organizes and controls its informational output. The quality and scope of the information that government places in the public domain provide an essential underpinning for political accountability, whether mediated through Parliament or operating directly through the ballot box. The requirements of truthfulness, accuracy, and completeness that flow from this underpinning role are in no way lessened or qualified by the fact that government may see its communications as a mechanism of persuasion, whether in relation to the advancement of particular policy aims or to the executive's overall reputation with the electorate. The tension that may undoubtedly exist between these two contrasting functions of government information and communications requires continuing management, and we examine below the executive's approaches to this task over this century, both generally and in relation to the particular, and sensitive, field of statistical information.

We start, therefore, by examining the ever-changing shape of the executive's organization of its communication functions, relating these to its professed objectives and standards in this field and to other developments such as the steady growth of the cohort of special advisers. We then consider the specialized controls to which the exercise of these functions is subject, both those operating within the executive itself and those wielded by external agencies: official regulators like the Statistics Authority and unofficial ones such as the Advertising Standards Authority.

II The Organization of the Communication Function

2.1 Before 1997

Ministers, as political animals, are peculiarly sensitive to the effectiveness of the information function in government, and it is perhaps for this reason that its organization has always been more volatile than that of other specialized services and has continued to be so over the period that interests us. Markers for this volatility include the fact that the function has had four different titles since Labour came to power in 1997,[5] and the wholesale culling of departmental directors of information and communications that took place both following Labour's return to power in 1997[6] and the arrival of the Coalition government in 2010.[7] And these were certainly not the first

[5] Government Information Service (1950s–97); Government Information and Communications Service (1997–2004); Government Communications Network (2004–13); Government Communications Service (2013–date).

[6] In the two years following the 1997 election, 17 of the 19 Departmental Heads of Information left office: see Anne Gregory, 'UK Government Communications: Full Circle in the 21st Century?' (2012) 38 Public Relations Review 367, 370.

[7] Of 20 Directors in post in 2010, only two remained in the same post in 2015: Ruth Garland, 'Between Media and Politics: Can Government Press Officers Hold the Line in the Age of "Political Spin"? The Case of the UK after 1997' (PhD thesis, London School of Economics 2016) app 8.

dramatic changes in the organization of the service. Twice during the 20th century, in each case in response to war, the government established a centralized information function, only to dismantle it when hostilities ended. A Department of Information was created in 1917, with the novelist and diplomat John Buchan as its Director, to be quickly replaced in 1918 by a Ministry of Information—which was immediately wound up once the Armistice was signed.[8] In the Second World War, a Ministry of Information came into being the day after war was declared. Again, it hardly outlasted the period of hostilities, and its abolition was under discussion in government as early as 1944.[9]

It would be a mistake to see these abrupt appearances and disappearances as reflections of the tension between centralized and departmental approaches to executive organization that has been evident in recent years. In 1917 hardly any departments had their own press or information function. The position only changed in the late 1930s, when departments (and also the Prime Minister's Office) began to establish their own information offices. By 1939 there were 'publicity divisions' in virtually all Whitehall departments.[10] The creation of the Ministry of Information did not eliminate the activity of these departments in mounting information campaigns in support of the war effort. The Ministry of Food's publicity on the best use of food, for example, was designed to boost morale by showing that a besieged nation could feed itself adequately and sometimes even pleasantly.[11] The Ministry of Information ran its own campaigns, supported those of departments, and from the end of 1941 was empowered to approve or block them. What caused its demise, like that of its predecessor in 1918, was the desire to make a clean break with the wartime regime of which it was an expression. This did not, however, mean the disappearance of the idea that there was value in having a government-wide information capability operating in support of departmental efforts. The post-war Labour government accordingly replaced the Ministry of Information with a Central Office of Information (COI). This was seen as essential to the effective explanation of the major changes in society projected by the new government, in particular the creation of the welfare state. While individual departments retained responsibility for their own publicity, the COI functioned as a common service agency, producing, and arranging procurement of, poster advertising, exhibitions, photographs, publications, and films, and providing a central channel for the distribution of government news provided by individual departments.[12] While COI's functions remained constant over its lifetime, it suffered regular changes of status and affiliation: founded as a non-ministerial department under the aegis of the Chancellor of the Exchequer, it became a vote-funded executive agency in 1990, and a year later a trading fund under the Central Office of Information Trading Fund Order 1991, financing its activities through the fees paid by the departments and other bodies for which it worked. Ministerial responsibility was transferred to the Cabinet Office in 1992.

[8] Alexander McKenna, *100 Years of Government Communication* (HM Government 2018) 24.
[9] McKenna (n 8) 55–56.
[10] ibid 38.
[11] Marjorie Ogilvy-Webb, *The Government Explains. A Study of the Information Services* (Royal Institute of Public Administration 1965) 59.
[12] On COI see generally McKenna (n 8) 59–60, 65–70, 77–80.

As well as operating this central service function, the centre of government interested itself in the coordination of departmental information activities. A Treasury-led review in 1947 addressed the duties of Information Officers, their pay, conditions, and recruitment.[13] This led to the creation of an 'Information Officer' class of civil servants constituting a Government Information Service (GIS), which like its legal and accountancy counterparts was essentially a professional grouping: a loose structure designed to promote coordination, improve career ladders and prospects, foster training, and create and sustain a sense of professionalism. At the end of Eden's Premiership, a review of overseas information services was accompanied by the establishment in 1957 of daily—soon to become weekly—meetings of departmental Chief Information Officers chaired by a coordinating minister.[14] The first occupant of this role, Dr Charles Hill, also advised ministerial colleagues (or at least, those among them who would listen) on the presentation of major policy initiatives, and attempted to provide for those in charge of information channels, on the basis of discussion in Cabinet, of which he was a member, a reasoned 'background of general policy'.[15]

The forerunner of the 'grid' introduced by Labour after 1997—a spreadsheet which laid out day by day the timing of policy announcements across government—may have appeared as early as 1972, when the Cabinet Office—at least for a while—compiled a weekly 'agenda of forthcoming attractions and ensure[d] there weren't clashes'.[16] The task of speaking for the government as a whole had however been lodged in the Prime Minister's Office since the creation of the office of Chief Press Secretary at 10 Downing Street in 1932, with the Downing Street Press Secretary, the Press Office, and the Parliamentary Lobby journalists forming 'a supreme nodal point'.[17] How much coordination and unity of voice this nodal point could produce was, however, very much a function of the strength of the Prime Minister vis-à-vis his or her colleagues, and of the personality and experience of the Downing Street Press Secretary.[18] Bernard Ingham, Margaret Thatcher's powerful and long-serving Press Secretary, was able to reinforce coordination among departmental press offices by cross-postings between them and his team at No 10, and by taking over the chair of the weekly information officers' meeting, but failed in his attempt to introduce a centralized computer system which would enable individual departments, and the Prime Minister's Office, to call up databases of other departments to check points crossing departmental boundaries, and to have access to the briefing lines being deployed within government. Such a system could have been used as a powerful instrument of central control.[19]

[13] Ogilvy-Webb (n 11) 73.
[14] ibid 89–90.
[15] Lord Hill of Luton, *Both Sides of the Hill* (Heinemann 1964) ch 10.
[16] McKenna (n 8) 77.
[17] ibid 61.
[18] ibid 61–62, 83–93.
[19] For Bernard Ingham's association with, and eventual position as head of GIS, see Bernard Ingham, *Kill the Messenger* (HarperCollins 1991) 367–78.

2.2 1997–2010: New Labour, new methods

When a Labour government returned to power in 1997 its approach to government communications contrasted dramatically with the caution and gradualism it displayed in other spheres like expenditure planning.[20] Experience in opposition had convinced Tony Blair of the central importance of effectively managing information about the government's activities, and he had already developed in opposition an active approach to media relations and news management that far outclassed the incumbent government's efforts.[21] This approach was carried over into government with the appointment of one of its architects, Alistair Campbell, as the Prime Minister's Chief Press Secretary, a post without constitutional precedent in that its holder was a special adviser, not subject to the Civil Service obligations of impartiality, but with the power, conferred by an Order in Council, to instruct civil servants in the performance of their duties.[22] The extent of Mr Campbell's powers over government communications under the Order only appears fully from his contract as a special adviser, whose Schedule states:

> In your role as Chief Press Secretary and the Prime Minister's official spokesman, you are required to brief the media on the Government's behalf and co-ordinate the Government's information activities. This involves 'on the record' briefing of Lobby journalists and others. You must make clear that the views expressed by you in this role are not your personal views but those of the Prime Minister and you must avoid entering into personal attacks. You will clear bids for major interviews and media appearances, and the policy content of all major speeches, press releases and new policy initiatives, in accordance with the procedures set out in the Ministerial Code.[23]

The incoming government also took the view that GIS had been underperforming.[24] A wide-ranging review by a working group (the Mountfield Report) recommended stronger central coordination of government's information activities, through such devices as a Strategic Communications Unit at No 10, planning and programming of policy announcements across government (what is now known as 'the grid'),[25] and a Media Monitoring Unit providing departments with daily, updated media

[20] Chapter 7, section I.

[21] Peter Oborne, *Alistair Campbell: New Labour and the Rise of the Media Class* (Aurum Press 1999) 133–45.

[22] Civil Service (Amendment) Order in Council 1997 (*London Gazette*, 16 May 1997) 5777, under which holders of up to three posts in the Prime Minister's Office which are designated by him are exempted from the prohibition in art 3(2) of the Civil Service Order 1995 on doing anything beyond giving advice. The Prime Minister's Chief of Staff occupied the second post, and the third exemption was never applied.

[23] Quoted in para 10 of the draft report prepared by Andrew Tyrie MP but rejected by majority vote of the Committee, in Public Administration Select Committee, *The Government Information and Communication Service* (HC 1997–98, 770) 'Proceedings of the Committee relating to the Report'. The detailed rules and guidance regarding ministerial statements in Tony Blair's 1997 Ministerial Code can be found in Amy Baker, *Prime Ministers and the Rule Book* (Politico's 2000) 160–62, 178–82.

[24] On the removal of most departmental Directors of Information in 1997–99 see Gregory, 'UK Government Communications' (n 6) and Bernard Ingham, *The Wages of Spin* (John Murray 2003) ch 21 ('The bloodletting').

[25] For an illustration see McKenna (n 8) 107.

summaries derived from the Unit's monitoring of all major broadcasting channels and the national newspapers. The GIS, whose character as a politically impartial service was stressed by the report, was renamed the Government Information and Communications Service (GICS), and headed by a permanent civil servant in the Cabinet Office. The Prime Minister's Chief Press Officer continued to preside over the weekly meetings of departmental heads of information. The dominance of Alistair Campbell in this and other aspects of his role[26] was notorious enough to be the subject of both theatrical (*Feelgood*, 2001) and television (*The Thick of It*, 2005–12) comedy.

The reforms did not, however, represent a centralization of the information function, which remained largely under departmental control. The attempt was to provide discipline and a coherent and forceful overall message. A sense of where that attempt had to start from can be gleaned from the remark in 1978 of Henry James, who had been Deputy Press Officer to Douglas-Home, Wilson, and Heath, and was to serve briefly as Mrs Thatcher's Chief Press Officer before Bernard Ingham's appointment, that 'the government itself has no policy of information. It is at the discretion of the individual minister.'[27] The distance travelled by the time Blair's government took office can be measured by the Cabinet Secretary's remark in 1998, to the House of Commons Public Administration Committee, that

> It is the duty of every government to communicate its policies and themes effectively to the public so that they understand it and so that the electoral process, the democratic process, can take place and that people can react.[28]

This looks like endorsement, from the highest level of the Civil Service, of the Campbellite view of government information as a support for a continuous campaign for re-election, and it is not surprising that over the next few years government information staff struggled to reconcile this approach with the political impartiality demanded by their Civil Service status. The solution widely adopted within departments was to enhance the communications role of special advisers, who were not subject to this constraint and whose numbers had greatly increased over Labour's tenure.[29] This was centrally endorsed by revision in 2001 of the Code of Conduct for Special Advisers to add 'representing the views of their Minister to the media' to 'the sorts of work a special adviser may do'. How special advisers might conceive of such media responsibilities was illustrated by the response of Jo Moore, a special adviser to the Department of Transport, to news of the September 11 World Trade Center attack, which took the form of an email to departmental communication staff suggesting that this was 'a

[26] It is worth noting that Bernard Ingham, in his account of the culling of departmental Chief Information Officers in 1997–99, directs his criticisms much more against ministers, special advisers, and Permanent Secretaries than against the Chief Press Officer, even remarking that 'there are those who were forced out who speak of Campbell's concern to retain them': n 24, 188.

[27] Henry James, 'The Role of the Central Office of Information' in Annabelle May and Kathryn Rowan (eds), *Inside Information: British Government and the Media* (Constable 1982) 186–88, at 186.

[28] Public Administration Select Committee, *The Government Information and Communication Service* (HC 1997–98, 770) evidence, q 237.

[29] From 37 immediately before the government took office to 73 in 2007–08: House of Lords Communications Committee, *Government Communications* (HL 2008–09, 7) para 87.

very good day to get out anything we want to bury'.[30] Reprimanded but not dismissed, just a few months later Ms Moore was reported to have reoffended by urging release of adverse rail statistics on the day of Princess Margaret's funeral: this led to her dismissal, to the departure of the department's Director of Communications, and to a further inquiry by the Public Administration Committee.[31] While the Committee (or at least its Labour members) had been relaxed in 1998 about government's approach to communications and the decapitation of GIS, by 2002 it saw the need for a 'radical external review of government communications', which was supplied by an inquiry commissioned by the Cabinet Office and conducted by a group including journalists and some government officials, and chaired by Robert Phillis, chief executive of the Guardian Media Group.[32]

The group's report, which government had committed itself in advance to accept, had as its central theme a 'three-way breakdown in trust between government and politicians, the media and the general public'. It asked for 'a sustained commitment to a long-term programme of radical change in the conduct, process and style of government communications', and called for steps to preserve and reinforce the tradition of Civil Service impartiality, as a key bulwark on which to rebuild trust.[33] The group was highly critical of the way the task of communication was viewed and organized both at the centre of government and in departments. Its main consequences were the replacement of GCIS, viewed by Phillis as ineffective and disconnected from the source of communications policy, with a Government Communications Network (GCN) under the leadership of a Permanent Secretary in the Cabinet Office, who would function as the leader of the communications profession within government and would work alongside a reconstructed No 10 media operation double-headed by a politically appointed Director of Communications and a 'Prime Minister's Official Spokesman' drawn from the Civil Service. Phillis recommended the termination of the special power to direct civil servants that had been enjoyed by Alastair Campbell as the Prime Minister's Chief Press Officer and, latterly, Director of Communications until his resignation in late 2003. Accordingly, Campbell's successors have not exercised this power, which was formally withdrawn in 2007.[34] The two posts envisaged by Phillis have sometimes been combined (as was the case during Gordon Brown's Premiership) but have generally been kept separate. In departments, Phillis asked for better integration between policy and communications functions, clearer relationships between special advisers and civil servants, and reinforcement of the impartiality and independence of departmental Directors of Communications.[35]

GCN had a wider reach than GICS, bringing press officers into the same professional grouping as other communications staff, but at the cost of abandoning rigorous

[30] On this incident, its background and consequences see in more detail Terence Daintith, '"A very good day to get out anything we want to bury"' [2002] Public Law 13.

[31] Public Administration Select Committee, *'These Unfortunate Events': Lessons of Recent Events at the Former DTLR* (HC 2001–02, 303).

[32] *An Independent Review of Government Communications (Chairman: Bob Phillis)* (presented to the Minister for the Cabinet Office, January 2004) ('Phillis Report').

[33] Phillis Report (n 32) 2.

[34] Civil Service (Amendment) (No 2) Order in Council 2007 (*London Gazette*, 6 July 2007) 2487.

[35] Phillis Report (n 32) 19–23.

GICS selection and promotion processes whose development had been initiated during Bernard Ingham's tenure. The new structure gave the Permanent Secretary in charge, profiting from the level of seniority attaching to the post, the opportunity to address concerns about propriety and impartiality (on which Phillis had laid heavy emphasis),[36] to improve relations with the media, to develop training initiatives for the use of departments, and to work on reshaping communications strategy generally to improve government's ability to lead behavioural change.[37]

The effects of the Phillis reforms were reviewed a few years later in broadly positive terms by the House of Lords Communications Committee. On organizational issues, the Committee simply repeated Phillis's suggestion that where possible the careers of high-flying civil servants should include a period of service in departmental press offices or communications generally.[38] Its report showed remarkable growth in the communications function over the previous 10 years.[39] The numbers of communications staff in central government departments rose from 793 in December 1998 to 1,376 in September 2008, with some striking increases in individual departments: fivefold at the Ministry of Justice, sixfold at Revenue and Customs. The Cabinet Office claimed that it could not be precise about these figures, because of the lack of a clear definition about what constituted a 'communications' post (which is suggestive of a failure of the GCN machinery). They certainly show however that communication was being taken more seriously across government, as Phillis had urged.

2.3 Coalition and Conservative governments

Cabinet Office was also unable to tell their Lordships in 2009 how much government communications were costing. Large advertising programmes were being undertaken and spending was also being driven by the need to deal with challenges like the 24-hour news cycle and the multiplication of digital and social media channels. When the Coalition government took office in 2010 on a deficit reduction and 'smaller government' manifesto, it immediately placed a freeze on government marketing and advertising activity, and announced the termination of the Permanent Secretary post, whose former occupant (only the second) was then tasked with conducting a review (the 'Tee Review') of the activities falling within the scope of the freeze, that is, all marketing and advertising products and services that were externally procured (as opposed to media relations—the work of press offices). Most of this procurement was conducted via COI, which suffered a massive reduction in its budget leading to a cut of 40% in staff numbers and 43% in operating costs. The review concluded for the winding up of COI, which took place at the end of 2011, with the transfer of all its remaining staff and assets to the Cabinet Office.[40] Given COI's function as a common service organization, this might seem an odd decision at a time when the Cabinet

[36] ibid 21–23.
[37] Gregory, 'UK Government Communications' (n 6) 371.
[38] House of Lords Communications Committee (n 29) paras 89–101.
[39] ibid paras 126–38.
[40] Central Office of Information, *Annual Report and Accounts for the Period Ended 30 December 2011* (HC 2011–12, 462).

Office was developing its commitment to Civil Service reform aimed at 'delivering efficiency savings through centralized service delivery and improving professional capability'.[41] What the review was suggesting, however, was essentially the continuation of at least some of COI's activity within a different, slimmed-down structure subject to greater central control.[42] The idea was that, ultimately, all direct communications professionals in government (that is, those concerned with marketing and advertising) should be employed directly by a Government Communications Centre established in the Cabinet Office, which would also operate newly introduced Cabinet Office spending controls applicable to advertising and marketing.

What actually followed the review was a further overhaul of government communications that was more broadly based, taking in all aspects of communications, not just advertising and marketing, but that did not go so far in the direction of centralization. In 2012 the service was renamed the Government Communication Service (GCS), under an Executive Director of Government Communication sitting in the Cabinet Office. Associated reform measures were the mandatory evaluation of all communication activity, formalized business planning for communication, the development of a corporate centre for communication, and a major push to integrate social and digital media in all communication functions. The service is now both a Civil Service profession and one of the 13 government functions, and in 2022 counted some 7,000 communications specialists across ministerial departments and other public bodies.[43] Earlier institutional divisions between groups like press officers and advertising specialists have disappeared, though the diverse needs of communicators in different functions and in different areas of government are recognized in GCS's training and developmental activities.[44]

Over the decade since the initiation of GCS, the idea of centralization floated by the Tee Review has been effectively abandoned. The model of a centrally employed and managed specialist staff, successfully carried through for the functions of law and internal audit, has been replaced by one of coordination of departmental activities, driven by a central unit located in the Cabinet Office. The unit enjoyed its moment of glory over the period of the Covid-19 pandemic, which made enormous demands on the government's communication capabilities and produced the largest spend ever on a government media campaign: £184m in 2020.[45] To deal with the crisis GCS created a central communications hub, which designed and delivered the main campaigns and also provided the research, behavioural insight, evaluation, and international communication coordination. Alongside staffing from the Civil Service, wider public service, and the armed forces the hub brought in outside experts from communications agencies and seasoned campaigners, including some who had worked on

[41] Civil Service, *Civil Service Reform Plan—Progress Report* (October 2014) 22–23. On the functions programme see further chapter 2, section 3.4.6.

[42] Matt Tee, *Review of Government Direct Communication and the Role of COI* (March 2011) 15–18.

[43] Government Communication Service, *What We Do* (October 2022).

[44] See generally Government Communication Service, *Modern Communications Operating Model: A Blueprint for Government Communication: 2.0* (2020?).

[45] Claire Forbes, 'The Changing Role and Status of Government Communication during the Covid-19 Crisis' (2021) 14 ESSACHESS—Journal for Communication Studies 33, 45. For a description of the early phases of the communication campaign see Jeremy Lee and Gideon Spanier, '"Single-minded and Unavoidable": How the Government Honed "Stay home" Message' *Campaign* (11 May 2020).

previous general election campaigns. Its work informed the main ministerial and official groups taking decisions throughout the crisis.[46]

The early success may perhaps have inspired a new centralization plan, which briefly broke surface in June 2020.[47] This would have brought government communications under the joint control of the No 10 Permanent Secretary and the Prime Minister's Director of Communications, with departmental communications teams stripped back to a maximum of 30 staff and reporting to four new Directors-General in the Cabinet Office. The plan did not survive the collapse—as an early casualty of the Downing Street Covid scandals—of the linked idea of a daily No 10 press conference. Instead the trend, in the 2020s, appears to have been towards the weakening, not strengthening, of central coordination. Central staffing has been reduced by 50% by way of the dismantling of the Covid Hub and other cross-government campaign facilities. Instead there is a new central Strategy and Campaigns team that coordinates cross-government strategy and campaigns, as well as providing expert marketing and brand advice.[48] Services to departments and ALBs in procuring commercial contracts for carrying out media campaigns are in the hands of the Crown Commercial Service, though GCS vets approved suppliers and derives part of its central funding from a 1% levy on central government media contracts.[49] Centralized commissioning of media channels, which was a key function of COI, is currently outsourced to a private contractor, whose services departments are recommended to use.

Central governance has also been downgraded. In 2011 GCS was equipped with a weighty Governing Board to oversee strategy, chaired by the Minister for the Cabinet Office and including other ministers and Permanent Secretaries, a number of Communication Directors from Departments and ALBs, and two independent external directors of communication. By 2021 the Board was being chaired by a junior Cabinet Office minister and run collectively by the Executive Director and departmental Directors of Communication. By 2022 ministers and Permanent Secretaries had disappeared altogether, but 'external communications directors' had joined the Board, whose remit is now described as 'direction and oversight of all elements of the GCS function'.[50] A small increment of prestige for the communications function has however been achieved through the appointment in 2021 of the Chief Executive and Head of Profession at Director-General level, one grade up from his predecessor. There are still voices in Whitehall calling for centralization of the function,[51] but little apparent appetite for yet further structural change.

[46] COVID-19 Communications Advisory Panel, *Report* (2020) 11.

[47] Richard Johnstone, 'Government Confirms Comms Reform Drive' *Civil Service World* (6 July 2020).

[48] Cabinet Office FOI response, ref TO2023/04377, 11 May 2023.

[49] Crown Commercial Service, *RM6125 Guide to Buying Marketing, Communication and Research Services through CCS*, and Government Communication Service, *Buying Communication Support* (January 2023).

[50] Cabinet Office FOI response (n 48).

[51] Lee Cain, *Modernising the Government Communication Service* (Institute for Government guest paper, September 2021) 5–7. Lee Cain was Downing Street's director of communications between July 2019 and December 2020 under Boris Johnson. The report by Lord Maude, *Review of the Cross-cutting Functions and the Operation of Spend Controls* (July 2021) 23–24, called for a central budget and unit for the delivery of major cross-government campaigns.

III Controlling Communications

3.1 In general

Our main concern in this section is with the executive's internal mechanisms for regulating and controlling its communications practice, as currently organized. In line with the government's position as one of myriad communicators to the public, however, its messages, like those emitted by others, are subject to external controls of general application: the laws relating to such subjects as copyright, defamation, data protection, privacy, and breach of confidence. In this section we limit our treatment of external controls to those that bear specifically on government communications addressed to the public generally through advertising and other forms of publicity campaign. These are controls that address the same sorts of issues of propriety as does the government's internal guidance.

3.2 Internal control: spending

When the Coalition government came into office in 2010 on a platform of reduction of public expenditure it took early aim at what it considered to be excessive spend by its predecessor on public information campaigns. There was an immediate moratorium on government marketing and advertising activity. This was followed by the subjection of paid advertising and marketing campaigns, along with other routine expenditures like commercial contracts, leases, facilities management, digital services, and consultancy, to a new and onerous set of requirements for prior consent, operated by the Cabinet Office under delegation from the Treasury.[52] Originally introduced as a temporary measure, the controls were put on a continuing basis in July 2012, and continue to operate in relation to advertising and marketing expenditure.

Introduced primarily with a view to cutting back unnecessary expenditure, over time the controls have been developed, in relation to the communications functions as elsewhere, as a mechanism for the exercise of central control and coordination of the activity of departments and arm's length bodies (ALBs). The control covers a very wide swathe of communications business, including not just advertising and marketing but also social, economic, and market research that informs communications activity, including polling; strategy, analysis, and evaluation; external campaign events; and public relations activity. Any campaign, programme, or project which involves expenditure on these activities of £100,000 or more within a financial year is subject to the control.[53] The control does not touch work by staff on the payroll, and in fact one of the broader objectives of the reshaping of communications activity endorsed by the Cabinet's Public Services and Public Expenditure Committee (PEX) sub-committee on efficiency and reform, following the Tee Report, was to shift

[52] On these Cabinet Office controls see generally chapter 8, section 2.4.3.

[53] Cabinet Office, *Advertising, Marketing and Communications Spending Controls* (April 2014, updated to January 2023) paras 3, 4.

the balance of activity towards the use of 'owned and earned' media before paid-for media.[54]

Criteria for approval of spending may be found in Cabinet Office guidance to departments. Over most of the period of operation of the control, it has been stated that advertising expenditure will only be approved in a limited range of cases:

> where government has a legal duty to provide people with information, such as changes to legislation or public services; where marketing and advertising is critical to the effective running of the government; and where there is robust evidence that marketing and advertising delivers measurable outcomes that meet government objectives.[55]

This text appeared in Cabinet Office guidance from the inception of spending control but was deleted in 2023. The test now appears to be 'that, where taxpayer money is being spent on government communications, it is cost-effective, coordinated and reflects functional standards and professional best practices'.[56] The government's functional standard for communications[57] incorporates a variety of general norms, ranging from high-level objectives of communication management, through desired characteristics of types of activities such as strategic communication (para 6.2), or marketing (para 6.3), down to criteria for the 'communications packages' that together make up a campaign (para 5.5.2). There is no lack of standards by which departmental work on communication might be judged, but the assumption underpinning the now abandoned test above, that advertising expenditure is something exceptional needing specific justification, appears to have been dropped.

The spending control procedure—which is referred to as 'professional assurance' in the functional standard—places a heavy emphasis on planning and coordination. Before the beginning of each financial year, departments and ALBs submit an overview of any campaigns and programmes of communications planned for that year. Each campaign or programme receives a rating from the central services at GCS, which determines whether it can go ahead without a detailed proposal (this 'light touch' arrangement took effect only from 2023–24), requires central approval at GCS on the basis of a detailed proposal, or requires approval by the Cabinet Office minister after central review by GCS. Campaigns not anticipated in the strategic planning exercise will only be accepted where the need for communications could not reasonably have been foreseen. GCS's *Strategy 2022–25* promised both to make professional assurance less cumbersome for departments, and to 'be more assertive in using spending controls to improve the quality of campaigns and join up with other departments'.[58]

An internal appraisal of Cabinet Office controls as a whole in 2015 suggested that 'the emphasis of the programme was shifting from spending controls to more positive

[54] Anne Gregory, 'UK Government Communication: The Cameron Years and Their Ongoing Legacy' (2019) 45 Public Relations Review 202, 208.

[55] HM Government, *Government Communications Plan 2013/14* (2013) 21.

[56] Cabinet Office (n 53) para 1.

[57] HM Government, *Government Functional Standard GovS 011: Communication 2.0* (July 2021).

[58] HM Government, *Performance with Purpose: Government Communication Service Strategy* (2022) 7.

standards and frameworks of delegation operating along a functional axis'.[59] The way 'professional assurance' has developed in the communications field can be seen as an illustration of this trend. But the appraisal also stated in 2015 that 'spending controls [would] remain in place until the government builds the necessary capability, standards, behaviours and governance within the functions'. Apparently this has yet to happen within GCS.

3.3 Internal control: propriety

Among the criteria referenced in *Government Functional Standard GovS 011: Communication 2.0* are four 'conventions of propriety' through which government has sought to strike and hold the delicate balance between the provision by government of information in the public interest and the use of government's information resources for party political advantage. Communication activities, says the standard, should

> be relevant to government responsibilities;
> be objective and explanatory, not biased or polemical;
> not be—and not liable to being misrepresented as—party political;
> be conducted in an economic and appropriate way, and should be able to justify the costs as expenditure of public funds.[60]

This wording, save for the insertion of 'biased' in place of 'tendentious', dates back at least to the redrafting by the Cabinet Office in 1997 of earlier guidance, originating in the 1970s, to form the publication *Guidance on the Work of the Government Information Service*, accompanied by practical *Guidance Notes*.[61] Today the conventions are presented as a basic element of a comprehensive set of *Government Communication Service Propriety Guidance*, which traverses a wide range of issues from 'Politicians and the Press Office', through such matters as the appointment of public relations consultancies, to rules about commercial confidentiality, reporting of legal proceedings, data protection, and the use of the Welsh language. The *Guidance* is, therefore, a mixture of executive self-regulation and reminders of the external regulation to which government, possibly in common with other communicators, may be subject. Breach of some of these external requirements may, as we shall see, call forth censure or sanctions from bodies like courts or external regulators like the Advertising Standards Authority.

So far as the purely internal rules are concerned, the institutional guarantees that support them are perhaps weaker than at the turn of the century. In 1997, the pathway for an internally generated concern about breach of the conventions or other rules led

[59] Cabinet Office, *The Functional Model: A Model for More Efficient and Effective Government* (March 2015).

[60] para 5.5.2. See also, with the same words in a slightly different arrangement, *Government Communication Service Propriety Guidance* (2014, rev 2021).

[61] Karen Yeung, 'Regulating Government Communications' (2006) 65 Cambridge Law Journal 53, 56–57.

from the department (via its Head of Information or directly) to the Head of GICS for advice or, if he thought fit, referral to the Propriety and Ethics Team within the Central Secretariat of the Cabinet Office or to the Cabinet Secretary.[62] Today any concerns raised by an individual follow a path explicitly traced only as far as the GCS Chief Operating Officer, with the promise that they 'will be treated with confidence and sensitivity', though the departmental Director of Communications may be consulted en route and 'can also advise if the matter needs further consideration from the Propriety and Ethics team at Cabinet Office'.[63] The National Audit Office noted in 2003 that the Head of GICS '[did] not, however, have formal authority to block government statements or information campaigns, occupying the position of standard setter, adviser and keeper of past precedents'.[64] The same would appear to be true of the GCS Chief Operating Officer. There is no published practice on the resolution of such issues. A rare exception is offered by a published Ministry of Defence inquiry into how its press office came to blacklist an online publication on political grounds, contrary to the Ministry's own guidance.[65]

Meanwhile, an internal check on adherence to the propriety conventions has disappeared by reason of the abolition of COI. The NAO's 2003 review pointed out that while responsibility for the propriety of government publicity ultimately belonged to the Accounting Officers of the departments or other government bodies that paid for it, the Chief Executive of COI, as its Accounting Officer, had responsibility for the propriety of the procurement services, including advice, that it supplied to government bodies. A former Head of GICS has described this role as 'pivotal'.[66] The NAO review offered several examples where COI functioned as a check on the propriety of campaigns departments were asking it to run, such as a campaign to publicize London mayoral elections, where red—remember this was the age of New Labour—was a dominant colour in some of the early poster proposals. COI considered this inappropriate and a more neutral colour was substituted. Another campaign in 2000–01 devised to inform the public about vehicle excise duty was deemed by COI to put too much emphasis on suggesting that motorists were getting a good deal. The Driver and Vehicle Licensing Agency did not agree with these objections and the campaign was referred to GICS, and revised when it supported COI's objection.[67] It seems much less likely that this kind of propriety concern would be raised by the private media buying organizations that have replaced COI. External controls may still operate (below, section 3.6), but only after the event.

The propriety conventions themselves are easy to state but their implementation remains problematic. The reason is simple. Government communications officers, it will be remembered, are civil servants bound by the general rule of impartiality of the Civil Service Code.[68] As the now withdrawn *GICS Handbook* so pithily put it:

[62] ibid 57.

[63] *Government Communication Service Propriety Guidance* (n 60), under the heading 'How to raise a concern'.

[64] National Audit Office, *Review of Government Advertising* (April 2003) para 3.3.

[65] Tom Kelly, Review of the Defence Communications Directorate's response to Declassified UK (7 December 2020). Kelly was the PM's official spokesperson 2001–07.

[66] Mike Granatt, private communication (2024).

[67] National Audit Office (n 64) paras 3.2, 3.5, 3.6.

[68] On the Code see further chapter 6, section 6.3.

> Ministers are political animals. Civil servants are not. Nowhere is this difference more likely to create difficulties than in the press office of a communication directorate.[69]

Official advice to government communicators has always implicitly acknowledged this situation by treating in detail the issues to which it may give rise. The 1997 *Guidance* covered such issues as how to deal with political material in ministerial speeches, and how to design different forms of publicity with due regard to how controversial their subject-matter might be, with further detailed practical advice in the *GICS Handbook*.[70] Today's *Guidance*, under the heading 'Politicians and the press office', offers government communicators a hotch-potch of advice, warnings, and hard to reconcile do's and don'ts. Thus they must 'present, describe and justify the thinking behind the policies of the minister'; 'be ready to promote the policies of the department and the Government as a whole' and 'make as positive a case as the facts warrant' but must not 'justify or defend policies in party political terms' or 'oversell policies, re-announce achievements or investments and claim them as new or otherwise attempt to mislead the public'. These fine lines must be trodden while working for ministers who may not 'always acknowledge the distinction between government communicators and their own party political spokespeople' and hence may ask for the dissemination of statements that 'cross the border of propriety', but who 'must be protected from accusations of using public resources for party political purposes'. Consolation is offered by way of the reminder that the Ministerial Code requires ministers to uphold the impartiality of the Civil Service.[71]

3.4 Internal control: special advisers

One way out of the inherent conflict between ministerial and Civil Service attitudes to communication is offered by the device of the special adviser. The overtly political nature of Alastair Campbell's position as the Prime Minister's Chief Press Secretary was proclaimed as a virtue by the Cabinet Secretary on the basis that 'everyone knows where he is coming from'.[72] The current propriety *Guidance* applies this rationale in much more general terms:

> Employing special advisers adds a political dimension to the advice and assistance available to ministers while reinforcing the political impartiality of the permanent Civil Service by distinguishing the source of political advice and support.[73]

[69] Mike Granatt, 'Politics and the Government Information Officer: A Note by the Head of Profession' in *GICS Handbook* (2001), cited in Terence Daintith, 'Spin: A Constitutional and Legal Analysis' (2001) 7 European Public Law 593, 605.

[70] For commentary see Yeung (n 61) 57–60; Daintith, 'Spin' (n 69) 618–22.

[71] *Government Communication Service Propriety Guidance* (n 60).

[72] Public Administration Select Committee (n 28) para 26.

[73] *Government Communication Service Propriety Guidance* (n 60), under the heading 'Propriety Guidance and Codes of Conduct'.

New Labour's entry into government in fact saw a very large increase in the involvement of special advisers in media roles and a much more aggressive and political approach to media than had been thought appropriate by most Directors of Information. Tension, dissension, and the early departure of a majority of Directors, already noted, were the results. In part this was due to a lack of clarity about advisers' roles, in particular the issue of how far they could properly involve themselves in the work of departmental press offices. The incidents that led to the departures of a special adviser and the Director of Communications at the Department of Transport in 2002 are the most notorious,[74] but attempts by special advisers to tell press officers how to do their work, or to do it for them, were clearly commonplace.[75] A positive contribution from special advisers to the balancing of ministerial desires and Civil Service constraints was eventually seen to depend upon clearer rules for activity by special advisers. The process of clarification began with the Code of Conduct for Special Advisers promulgated by government, after some foot-dragging, in July 2001.[76] The Code recognized for the first time the activity of special advisers in briefing the media on behalf of their minister, subject to authorization by the minister and keeping the departmental Head of Information informed of the adviser's media contacts. This function had not been mentioned in the advisers' Model Contract nor indeed was it authorized by the Civil Service Order in Council as then in force, under which special advisers could be appointed only for the purpose of giving advice.[77] Nonetheless, media briefing was a major activity of special advisers. The disparity between their authorized and their actual activity was one of the grounds on which the Committee on Standards in Public Life argued, in a 2003 report,[78] for statutory definition of activities that were off-limits to special advisers. This eventually arrived in the shape of a provision in the Constitutional Reform and Governance Act 2010, confirming an extension of the permissible activity of special advisers from 'advice' to 'assistance' made by Order in Council in 2005.[79]

While the arrival of the Coalition government saw a temporary reduction in the number of special advisers, there was no questioning of their utility. The current (2016) version of the Code in fact reinforces their position, empowering them to 'give assistance on any aspect of departmental business', and for this purpose to

> convey to officials Ministers' views, instructions and priorities, including on issues of presentation . . . ; request officials to prepare and provide information and data, including internal analyses and papers; hold meetings with officials to discuss the

[74] Daintith, '"A very good day . . ."' (n 30); Public Administration Select Committee, *"These Unfortunate Events"* (n 31).

[75] See eg the evidence of the departing Director of Information at the Department of Social Security to the Public Administration Select Committee (HC 1997–98, 770) app 5; Peter Waller, 'Special Advisers and Communications' in Hazell and Yong (eds), *Special Advisers: Who They Are, What They Do and Why They Matter* (Hart Publishing 2014) 111–28, 117–19.

[76] Daintith, '"A very good day . . ."' (n 30) 18–21; see for general discussion of the status and management of special advisers further chapter 6, section VII.

[77] Civil Service Order in Council 1995, ss 2(1), 3(2).

[78] Committee on Standards in Public Life, Ninth Report, *Defining the Boundaries within the Executive: Ministers, Special Advisers and the Permanent Civil Service* (Cm 5775, 2003) ch 7.

[79] For further details see chapter 6, section 7.1.

advice being put to Ministers; and review and comment on—but not suppress or supplant—advice being prepared for Ministers by civil servants.[80]

They can also give directions to the civil servants allocated by the department to provide them with 'non-political' support. Their contacts with the media must still be authorized by the minister and conducted in accordance with GCS's *Propriety Guidance*, but the requirement to keep the department's Director of Communications informed has been dropped.[81]

Overall it would seem that over this century the impact of special advisers with media responsibilities has been to diminish the role, and possibly also the status, of the professional staff of GCS, appropriating important elements of their work, at least in departmental press offices, and marginalizing their impact.[82] The positive corollary to this may have been a diminution of the tensions written into the relationship between politically driven ministers and their impartial Directors of Communication, relieved by the safety valve of political communication through special advisers. Use of this channel does not of course guarantee that government communication will not fall short of the standards of propriety set for GCS by its *Propriety Guidance*; probably the contrary is more likely to be true. While special advisers are bound by the *Guidance* (save insofar as it demands that communication not be 'party political'), they are not part of GCS, and though they are civil servants, their discipline is confided solely to the ministers who appointed them.[83] The record of apparent infractions of propriety rules by media special advisers, starting with the Jo Moore messages, and of the sanctions they attracted (or more often, failed to attract), suggests that ministerial discipline may be an unreliable guarantor of this particular set of internal executive rules.[84]

3.5 The special case of statistics

3.5.1 1941–1997: Institutional evolution and administrative self-regulation

By reason of their essential role both in underpinning government policy and in facilitating evaluation of its results, statistics have long been a type of information whose collection and use by departments have been seen to require central oversight. A Central Statistical Office (CSO) was established in 1941 in the Cabinet Office, with the task of handling the descriptive statistics required for the war effort and developing national income accounts. Winston Churchill, as Prime Minister, also envisaged that it would seek to ensure coherence of statistical information.[85] It was, however, given no explicit powers to control or coordinate the activity of statisticians within departments, who answered to their respective ministers through senior administrators.

[80] Cabinet Office, *Code of Conduct for Special Advisers* (2016) para 4.

[81] para 13. On the content of the Code see further chapter 6, section 7.2.

[82] A detailed general survey taking the story up to 2015 has been provided by Garland (n 7).

[83] See generally chapter 6, section 7.3.

[84] For a list of incidents, with a note of consequences, see *Research Note: Special Advisers and Public Allegations of Misconduct 1997–2013*.

[85] Economic Secretary to the Treasury, *Statistics: A Matter of Trust. A Consultation Document* (Cm 3382, 1998) Annex A, 26.

But when statistical functions were next the subject of comprehensive review, by the Estimates Committee in 1966, the Committee noted that

> the position of the CSO in the government machine, and its responsibility for ensuring that facts prepared for government committees are agreed between departments, have given it a considerable authority over the statistical work of departments,

enabling it to exercise a coordinating role throughout government, along with significant influence in relation to the recruitment and distribution of statisticians.[86] The Committee's recommendations led to the enlargement of central statistical functions through the creation of a Business Statistics Office and of a central Office of Population Censuses and Surveys headed by the Registrar-General, and also to the creation of a Government Statistical Service (GSS) as the professional grouping of statisticians across government, of which the Director of CSO became Head. After a period of expansion, the government cut back sharply on statistical provision in the 1980s following an inquiry by Sir Derek Rayner, which asserted that the primary purpose of statistical work should be to provide government with the information it needed, rather than to inform the public. There was, Rayner said, 'no more reason for Government to act as universal provider in the statistical field than in any other'.[87] This attitude downgrades the importance of integrity and accuracy in the public presentation of statistics. Along with the objectives of cost-cutting that drove the Rayner Review and the government's response, it was judged, by the Royal Statistical Society, to have had results that were 'harmful to quality'. This finding formed part of a major review by the Society in 1989–91 that expressed serious concern about the organizational framework in which UK official statistics were produced, the apparent lack of control which GSS had over its product, and the weak protection offered by statute and practice to the autonomy of the system. Contrary to Rayner, it saw the public as 'rightful consumers of the statistical product', and went on to propose, in the interests of quality and of rebuilding public trust, the centralization of statistical activities in the CSO, a national advisory body, and a statutory guarantee of the independence of the statistical function in the form of a UK Statistics Act.[88]

While it took the best part of two decades for that Act to arrive, administrative moves to reinstate resources for official statistics and to rebuild trust were already under way by the time of the Society's report; shortly thereafter, in November 1991, CSO was constituted as an executive agency.[89] This marked a turn away from the 'Rayner doctrine' by emphasizing the quality of service to be provided to users both within and outside government. Through CSO's Framework Document, agreed with the Chancellor of the Exchequer as responsible minister, the government provided a public statement of the arrangements to ensure the integrity and validity of UK official

[86] Estimates Committee, *Government Statistical Services* (HC 1966–67, 246) paras 13, 14.

[87] Lord President of the Council, *Government Statistical Services* (Cmnd 8236, 1981) Annex 2, paras 8, 17.1.

[88] Royal Statistical Society's Working Party on Official Statistics in the UK, 'Official Statistics: Counting with Confidence' (1991) 154 Journal of the Royal Statistical Society. Series A (Statistics in Society) 23, esp 26, 27, 31–34.

[89] On executive agencies generally see chapter 4, section I.

statistics. Important among these was acknowledgement that the form, coverage, and timing of CSO publications was a matter for decision by the Director of CSO, not ministers.[90] Nonetheless, when the Director reported on progress to the Royal Statistical Society in 1995, he acknowledged that although he was the government's Chief Advisor on Statistics and had particular concern for the reliability and integrity of government statistics and public confidence in them, was Head of Profession for statisticians and as such could exercise influence on the personnel side, and represented UK statistics in the European Union and the United Nations, in all these roles, without managerial responsibility, he could 'exercise influence only'. But he was firmly opposed to the centralization of statistical activity the Society had argued for. Though there had been a considerable increase in the previous few years in the proportion of statistical work undertaken by CSO,[91] full centralization was neither feasible nor desirable:

> It is not feasible because history and the way that the civil service operates are against it. It is not desirable because it is vital that the GSS builds on . . . the relevance to policy that the GSS enjoys by being decentralized.[92]

Just how decentralized was demonstrated by the staffing numbers he provided: of 624 professional statisticians employed by central government, 489 worked in departments, 135 in CSO and the Office of Population Censuses and Surveys. Of a total of 5,131 GSS staff in all grades and functions, 2,964 worked in departments.[93]

In the last years before the accession to power of the Labour government in 1997, there were two further developments of significance. The first was the promulgation, in April 1995, of an *Official Statistics Code of Practice,* to standardize and promote good practice throughout the GSS, and to engender trust among its users and contributors. It endorsed such principles as integrity, openness, consultation, placing no undue load on respondents, continuous professional improvement, and cost-effectiveness.[94] Addressed as it was to statisticians themselves, it could of course say nothing about the way statistics might be used or manipulated for political advantage. Eliminating that required measures of wider scope.

The second change, effected in April 1996, was the merger of CSO with the Office of Population Censuses and Surveys to form the Office of National Statistics (ONS), achieved as a purely administrative measure by appointing the Director of CSO as Registrar-General with the remit of integrating the work of the two organizations. ONS succeeded to the status of CSO as an executive agency reporting to Treasury Ministers but was also established as a non-ministerial department. This was accompanied by the centralization in the new Office of the main collection and primary analysis processes, while advice and assistance to policymakers and ministers remained decentralized in departments, thus combining (it was hoped) the advantages

[90] Bill McLennan, 'You Can Count on Us—with Confidence' (1995) 158 Journal of the Royal Statistical Society. Series A (Statistics in Society) 467, 471–73. McLennan was Director of CSO at this time.

[91] Cosmo Howard, *Government Statistical Agencies and the Politics of Credibility* (CUP 2021) 141.

[92] McLennan (n 90) 468, 474–75, 485, 486.

[93] ibid app A.

[94] These are listed in McLennan (n 90) 481.

of centralized and decentralized arrangements. Another hoped-for by-product was to make it easier for the Head of the GSS to influence standards, classifications, and practices across the service.[95]

3.5.2 The turn to statutory regulation

In its 1997 general election manifesto, the Labour Party committed itself to 'an independent National Statistical Service', alongside more open government via a Freedom of Information Act. Once in office, the government sought to address what it described as the popular perception that the reforms effected since the beginning of the decade had not gone far enough. It frankly acknowledged that

> [t]he root of most concerns is that the current system is regarded as lacking appropriate safeguards against political interference and as being insufficiently open, which serves to breed distrust of the figures.[96]

In launching a consultation in 1998 it suggested that much could be done without legislation, but that it would consider this if 'appropriate and necessary'.[97] Following that consultation, its initial decision was to try to get by without legislation, even though many voices, including the House of Commons Treasury Select Committee,[98] had recommended such a course. Its solution, presented in the White Paper *Building Trust in Statistics*,[99] was the administrative establishment of a new category of 'National Statistics' comprising the most important series, along with a 'Framework for National Statistics'. This incorporated a new office of National Statistician, in succession to the Director of ONS, with an enhanced role as government's professional adviser and the person responsible for the quality and integrity of National Statistics, whether these were produced by ONS or by departments. Heads of the statistical profession in departments would have professional responsibility to the National Statistician as Head of GSS in relation to such matters as release arrangements and professional standards for the National Statistics they produced. A Statistics Commission was established as an advisory non-departmental public body, keeping statistical activities under review and reporting annually to Parliament. A key role of the National Statistician would be to develop and maintain a Code of Practice for National Statistics building on the existing 1995 code. Implementation of a sound and consistent policy on the release of data was seen as particularly important, covering both the handling of, and access to, data within government and the release of statistics more widely. The White Paper promised that any ministerial comment on statistics would always be issued in separate news releases so that they were clearly distinguished from the National Statistics themselves.

[95] For background and details see John Pullinger, 'The Creation of the Office for National Statistics' (1997) 65 International Statistical Review 291, and for the initial responsibilities of ONS see Office for National Statistics, *Framework Document* (1996).

[96] Economic Secretary to the Treasury, *Statistics* (n 85) para 3.6.

[97] ibid para 1.13.

[98] Treasury Committee, *Office for National Statistics* (HC 1998–99, 43-I) para 51.

[99] Economic Secretary to the Treasury, *Building Trust in Statistics* (Cm 4412, 1999).

These arrangements were certainly not intended to preclude the possibility of the later adoption of a legislative framework, and the new Statistics Commission was invited to review the need for legislation after its first two years. Its review came down firmly in favour of legislation, carefully designed, in close collaboration with the Treasury Solicitor's Department, to avoid any interference with continuing ministerial responsibility for departmentally produced statistics.[100] Not only was a legislative framework the norm in organization of official statistics in other countries, but the need for it had been demonstrated by doubts about the commitment within government to the voluntary Code of Practice—which had taken a long time to emerge—and continuing suspicions about improper ministerial use and presentation of statistics.[101] The Chancellor's announcement, late in 2005, that he would introduce legislation

> to make the Office for National Statistics independent of government, making the governance and publication of official statistics the responsibility of a wholly separate body at arm's length from government and fully independent of it,[102]

nonetheless owed something to chance: according to an inside account

> the Chancellor ... needed credible new proposals to include in a speech about the government's economic reform credentials ... His officials floated the idea of statistical legislation without telling him how difficult it would be, and he announced—out of the blue—his intention to introduce legislation in due course.[103]

Government itself, it appeared, now accepted that a system relying on purely internal checks and controls, such as the existing Code of Practice, was incapable of providing the necessary assurance of integrity in the preparation and presentation of statistics. This did not, however, imply the abandonment of the strongly held belief in the value of a decentralized system of statistical provision, in which departments were major producers of important statistical series alongside ONS. Four-fifths of official statistics were estimated to be produced outside ONS at the time the legislation was adopted.[104] Accommodating this approach, however, meant that the legislation eventually proposed and adopted was a good deal more complex and nuanced than might have been expected purely on the basis of the simple statement above.

The legislative proposals were enacted as the Statistics and Registration Service Act 2007. This established a new non-ministerial department, the Statistics Board. The majority of the Board are independent non-executive members; executive members are the National Statistician and two other employees. The Act gave the Board responsibility both for providing statistics itself, through the ONS, which became its

[100] See Statistics Commission, *Legislation to Build Trust in Statistics*, Report No 18, May 2004.

[101] Statistics Commission, *Annual Report 2003–2004* (Cm 6250, July 2004) 20–23. Legislation was also recommended by the Treasury Committee, *National Statistics* (HC 2000–01, 137); by the Royal Statistical Society, *A Vision for National Statistics* (September 2002); and by the Phillis Report (n 32) 24–25. See also chapter 7, section 2.2.2 for the early experience of the Labour government with financial statistics.

[102] Treasury Committee, *Independence for Statistics* (HC 2005–06, 1111) para 1.

[103] Howard (n 91) 164, quoting an official at the Statistics Authority.

[104] Statistics Commission, *Annual Report 2007–2008* (Cm 7390, June 2008) 1.

executive office under the National Statistician, and for regulating the provision of official statistics by ONS and by others, through the framing and policing of a statutory Code of Practice. This latter function was to be managed by the holder of a new executive post, the Head of Assessment. To emphasize the separation of its two roles of provision and regulation, the Board adopted the title of United Kingdom Statistics Authority (UKSA) to cover its work as a whole, while its regulatory arm, under the Head of Assessment, is now described as the Office for Statistics Regulation (OSR). The Act, in section 6, defines as 'official statistics' any statistics produced by the Board itself (that is, by ONS), by a government department or devolved administration, or by any other person acting on behalf of the Crown, and provides that a minister or a devolved administration may by order specify other persons as producers of official statistics. The current ministerial order under this section lists 41 bodies for this purpose, running from the Arts Council to the Youth Justice Board for England and Wales.[105] Providers of official statistics are in fact considerably more numerous, since many others are covered by the rubric 'persons acting on behalf of the Crown'.[106] With the objective of 'promoting and safeguarding the production and publication of official statistics that serve the public good', the Authority has the statutory task of monitoring the production and publication of official statistics and reporting to the person responsible for them any concerns it has about their quality—which includes impartiality, accuracy and relevance, and coherence with other official statistics—and their comprehensiveness, and about good practice in relation to official statistics.[107] The express authorization to the Authority to publish such findings and reports provides it with a powerful instrument for stimulating good practice.

In addition to this general monitoring function, UKSA also has the task of assessing official statistics against the standards and requirements of the Code of Practice, when so requested by the authority responsible for those statistics—which might be a minister (for departmentally produced statistics), a devolved administration, or the National Statistician (for ONS statistics). Statistics that are compliant then receive the designation of 'National Statistics'. This designation, as we have seen, has been in use since 1999, and UKSA's initial activity in this field was to review the statistics already so designated: the size of this task is indicated by the fact that by 2011 it was reported as having published over 140 reports covering around 580 of the 1,059 National Statistics.[108] Designation provides an additional assurance of quality, but producer sovereignty is emphasized by the fact that it remains the decision of the producing authority (including ONS itself) as to whether statistics are submitted for assessment.[109] The Act has also been criticized for saying nothing about the relationship between UKSA and the statisticians in the various departments and ALBs who produce

[105] Official Statistics Order 2018, SI 2018/888. There is a separate list for Scotland, contained in a series of Official Statistics (Scotland) Orders.

[106] The total number of providers was reported to be more than 150 by the Public Administration and Constitutional Affairs Committee, *Governance of Statistics* (HC 2017–19, 1820) para 2.

[107] Statistics and Registration Service Act 2007, ss 7, 8.

[108] Cabinet Office, *Post-Legislative Scrutiny of the Statistics and Registration Service Act 2007* (Cm 8216, November 2011) para 23.

[109] Statistics and Registration Service Act 2007, s 12(1). UKSA may, however, require an authority to justify a failure to submit statistics for assessment: s 16.

their statistics under the leadership of each department's or body's Head of Statistical Profession. While Heads of Profession are appointed in consultation with the office of the National Statistician, to whom they are said to be accountable for professional issues, they remain responsible through Permanent Secretaries to their respective ministers. Professional accountability and departmental demands may not always be in perfect alignment. Nonetheless, departmental statisticians have noted greater respect for their professional status and authority since the passage of the Act.[110]

These relationships continue to be of central importance because statistical activity remains as decentralized as it was in 1995:[111] while the proportion of the total membership of the GSS employed at ONS has increased to well over half, this is because of growth in its personnel in other functions, like operational delivery. The number of professional statisticians working there is still only a fifth of the total, with the rest employed in departments and agencies.[112]

3.5.3 *Experience with the legislative regime*

The most recent external review of the operation of the UK statistics system, by the House of Commons Public Administration and Constitutional Affairs Committee, was strongly critical of the statutory structure within which UKSA works, of the limited resourcing and lack of institutional independence of its regulatory arm, the Office for Statistics Regulation (OSR), and of its performance in its regulatory role.[113] It asked for new legislation that would eliminate UKSA's dual role as provider and regulator of statistics, seen as the root of the system's limitations; but being dubious, as predecessor reviewers had been, of the likelihood of its early appearance, it also demanded non-legislative changes that would enhance the independence and resourcing of OSR. With only 29 staff, OSR is miniscule in comparison with ONS and the departmental statistical staffs it is required to regulate, and in the opinion of the Committee, relied too much on departments presenting their mistakes and failings to it, rather than actively seeking problems. It was 'not being sufficiently ambitious in its role and should be more proactive in safeguarding statistics for the public good'.[114] UKSA was praised for 'some tough public interventions that were unpopular with government' but had 'been too slow to act on serious statistical and methodological issues such as the classification of items on the national balance sheet and has seemed to have acted only when under pressure from others'.[115] Despite its interventions, however, ministers continue to misuse statistics for political advantage and to refuse to issue corrections when called out by UKSA.[116] The Ministerial Code requires them only to 'be mindful of' the statistics Code of Practice—whose first 'pillar' is 'honesty

[110] Howard (n 91) 142.

[111] See text at n 93.

[112] Cabinet Office, *Statistical* Tables—Civil *Service Statistics 2023*, Table 8: Civil Service employment; profession by government department, as at 31 March 2023.

[113] *Governance of Statistics* (n 106).

[114] ibid para 85.

[115] ibid para 67. On the specific issue of classification see chapter 7, section 2.2.2.

[116] See eg Response from Sir Robert Chote to Stephen Kinnock MP—Asylum Backlogs (23 March 2023) and 'Sunak Rebuked over Asylum Figures Claim' *The Times* (5 April 2023) 10.

and integrity'.[117] A subsequent independent review of UKSA, conducted within the framework of the Public Bodies Review Programme in 2023–24,[118] was satisfied as to the independence of OSR in practice, but urged that the 2007 Act should be updated so as to make this clear.[119]

The statistics story argues for a sceptical approach to the notion that a move to a legislatively based organization and control of government resources is of itself productive of enhanced accountability and democratic control, and hence of a real reduction in executive autonomy. It is at least arguable that the Statistics Commission, despite its lowlier status as an advisory NDPB and its short life, could with adequate resourcing have been no less effective as a statistical regulator than UKSA has been.[120] At this distance the commitment of the government to the legislative goal announced in 2005 of 'making the governance and publication of official statistics the responsibility of a wholly separate body at arm's length from government and fully independent of it' can be seen to have been less than half-hearted. Not only did the legislation confer no powers, beyond that of attaching or withdrawing the 'National Statistics' label, to regulate the four-fifths of statistical production it left in departmental hands, it also kept some specific key decisions in the hands of ministers: notably, the rules about pre-release of statistics to government bodies,[121] and authorization to modify the retail prices index.[122]

Pre-release issues are explicitly withdrawn from the Code of Practice and regulated by rules made under the Act, which restrict the period of pre-release access and require publication of who enjoys it in relation to particular statistics. Ministers, who are required by the Ministerial Code to 'have regard' to the rules, are understood to have delegated these decisions to their departmental Heads of Profession.[123] Pre-release remains an area of dispute. A Cabinet Office review of the issue in 2011 reported a virtually universal opposition across government to the idea of abolishing pre-release access altogether, because 'the public and media expects a considered government line to be ready at the time of publication and if no line was ready then a story would run anyway'.[124] In 2017, however, the National Statistician took precisely this step, banning pre-release access to ONS outputs.[125] The sky did not fall: but Cabinet Office has maintained its position. The recommendation of the independent review of UKSA that, to avoid the risk of undermining of trust, the regulations should be amended to bring practice across departments and the devolved administrations into line with

[117] Cabinet Office, *Ministerial Code* (2022) para 8.15; Office for Statistics Regulation and UK Statistics Authority, *Code of Practice for Statistics* (ed 2.1, May 2022) 14, 17.

[118] Discussed in chapter 4, section 3.3.

[119] Denise Lievesey, *Independent Review of the UK Statistics Authority* (March 2024) 29–33.

[120] For the Commission's vigorous approach to statistical independence and reform see Howard (n 91) 150–52.

[121] s 11. The rules and principles are to be found in the Pre-release Access to Official Statistics Order 2008, SI 2008/2998. Scotland has separate, more indulgent, regulation.

[122] s 21; see *Governance of Statistics* (n 106) paras 118–35 for the difficulties this has created.

[123] Cabinet Office, *Ministerial Code* (2022) para 8.16; Cabinet Office, *Review of Pre-Release Access to Official Statistics* [nd] 4.

[124] Cabinet Office, *Review of Pre-Release Access to Official Statistics* (n 123) 33.

[125] *Governance of Statistics* (n 106) para 61.

the ONS approach was the only one with which Cabinet Office expressed outright disagreement.[126]

At the beginning of the period we are chronicling the distribution of statistical work across government bore a strong resemblance to the distribution of legal work: a central service accompanied by the retention of substantial departmental provision. In statistics that position still obtains. Legal work, however, has been largely centralized—and without the need for legislation, to boot.

3.6 External control of government advertising

We saw earlier in this chapter that one of the areas of spending targeted by the Cabinet Office spending controls introduced by the Coalition government was paid advertising, whose costs were considered to have ballooned under its Labour predecessors. In the first years of this century government was spending on advertising in the media at a rate which made it one of the largest advertisers in the United Kingdom, in the same league as consumer giants like Unilever, Procter and Gamble, and British Telecom. Indeed, in February 2001, in rather depressed marketing conditions, the government was reported as spending more on advertising (£16.4m) than any of these corporations.[127] While central scrutiny controls have been relaxed so that they now catch only campaigns costing over £100,000, current departmental spending budgets dwarf earlier figures, and we have seen that, at £184m, the centralized 2020 Covid campaign was the costliest ever.[128]

Advertising is a largely self-regulated industry. At the centre of the system, policed by the Advertising Standards Authority (ASA), is the UK Code of Non-Broadcast Advertising and Direct and Promotional Marketing (the CAP Code). Broadcast advertising is covered by a different Code, the UK Code of Broadcast Advertising (the BCAP Code). A Committee of Advertising Practice is responsible for development of each of these Codes: again, these are industry bodies. The legal background to the two Codes is however different. While compliance and enforcement under the CAP Code are self-regulatory matters,[129] control of broadcast advertising has since 1955 been based on legislation, currently the Communications Act 2003.[130] The regulator, Ofcom, has however contracted out responsibility for broadcast (TV and radio) advertising to the ASA system in a co-regulatory partnership.[131] The CAP Code

[126] Lievesey (n 119) 34, 36; Cabinet Office, *Review of the UK Statistics Authority: Cabinet Office Response to the Recommendations* (12 March 2024) 3.

[127] Richard Tomkins, 'Media monitoring figures may fuel accusations of spin as government outstrips Unilever and Procter and Gamble' *Financial Times* (16 April 2001) quoting a survey by AC Nielsen MMS.

[128] Forbes (n 45).

[129] Since 1988, however, self-regulation has been backed up by legal prohibition of unfair or misleading advertising (see now the Consumer Protection from Unfair Trading Regulations 2008, SI 2008/1277, and the Business Protection from Misleading Marketing Regulations 2008, SI 2008/1276), enabling ASA to refer persistent infringers of the Codes to Trading Standards authorities. ASA says that 'this is a last resort and is rarely needed': see ASA, *Our History*.

[130] ss 319–28.

[131] Contracting Out (Functions Relating to Broadcast Advertising) and Specification of Relevant Functions Order 2004, SI 2004/1975.

incorporates the principle that all advertising should be 'legal, decent, honest and truthful' (rule 1.1), and sets up a mechanism of complaint and adjudication to enforce it. The BCAP Code, reflecting Ofcom's statutory obligations under section 319(2)(h) of the Communications Act, adopts as 'overarching principles . . . that advertisements should not mislead or cause serious or widespread offence or harm, especially to children or the vulnerable'.[132]

Among the few substantive exemptions from the CAP Code is one for political advertisements. Such an advertisement is defined as one 'whose principal function is to influence voters in local, regional, national or international elections or referendums' (rule 7.1). Until 1999, this was only a partial exemption: political advertisements had to meet general standards for taste and decency but were exempt from standards of honesty and fairness. ASA's explanation of the decision to extend the exemption was that trying to apply its rules to political advertising 'risked bringing advertising regulation in general into disrepute', because of

> the short, fixed timeframes over which elections run (i.e. the likelihood that complaints subject to ASA investigation would be ruled upon after an election has taken place);
>
> concerns that the independence of the system could be damaged by rulings for or against political parties;
>
> and the absence of consensus on the issue between the Labour, Conservative and Liberal Democrat Parties.[133]

ASA's approach was endorsed by the Electoral Commission in 2003. So far as broadcasting is concerned, the position is reversed: not exemption, but prohibition. Political advertising, defined in significantly wider terms, is prohibited by sections 321(2) and (3) of the Communications Act 2003, which are reproduced in the BCAP Code (rule 7). Despite its appearance in the Code, the enforcement of this prohibition is not delegated by Ofcom to ASA. Ofcom administers it directly.

The BCAP Code makes it clear that the 'political' prohibition does not apply to advertisements of a public service nature inserted by, or on behalf of, a government department (rule 7.2.3). Such advertisements must comply with BCAP rules and principles. Likewise, non-broadcast marketing communications by central or local government, as distinct from those concerning party policy, are subject to the CAP Code (rule 7.2). Of necessity, given the strict rules separating party and governmental activity, as applied in the field of information, publicly funded advertisements should present government policy on a non-political basis.[134] Respecting this principle does not, however, mean that they secure no political benefits for the party of government. The GCS *Propriety Guidance* recognizes the possibility of such incidental benefit, which may be a source of resentment for the government's opponents. Thus the Opposition did not scruple to characterize spending by the government in February 2001 on campaigns ranging from recruitment of nurses and encouragement

132 BCAP Code 8.
133 ASA News (26 April 2023).
134 *Government Communication Service Propriety Guidance* (n 60) under 'Paid publicity'.

of planning of sufficient pension provision to attacking benefit fraud—at a time when the calling of a general election was expected—as a 'propaganda stealth tax'.[135] GCS is certainly sensitive to the risk of being seen to milk public service information for political advantage. Its *Propriety Guidance*, for example, warns that such a risk can arise from many factors, including content, context, treatment, style, tone, and quality of presentation, and adds further internal restrictions to the legislative listing of 'political' advertisements, stipulating that information campaigns cannot be used to list the government's achievements or to provide balance to an argument or put the record straight (eg to counter biased or inaccurate media reporting).[136]

ASA publicly reports its adjudications on complaints of breaches of its Codes, and these reports give us some notion both of the frequency with which government communications contravene the Codes, and of the sort of propriety issues that are raised by paid government advertising.[137] Over the period 2007–23, some 64 advertisements or campaigns gave rise to complaints, of which 16 were subsequently held to have involved a breach of a provision of one of the Codes. Given the volume of government advertising, the fact that it may set out to deliver unpalatable messages like the adverse effects of smoking or drunk driving, and the political sensitivities of audiences, this suggests a high level of compliance with industry standards. Review of ASA adjudications over this century indicates that government breaches are for the most part of the same sorts as might be committed by any large advertiser. Examples are the inappropriate scheduling of broadcast advertisements unsuitable for children, and exaggerated or simplistic claims of the benefits provided by government action. Thus the Inland Revenue was censured in June 2000 for a leaflet suggesting that the Working Family Tax Credit might help people working from as little as 16 hours a week, when eligibility started at 35 hours; the Home Office was reproved in 2009 for claims about neighbourhood policing that were misleading in a number of respects, and the Department of Work and Pensions was called out in November 2019 for over-optimistic claims relating to the operation of Universal Credit.[138] Another common general complaint is the insertion in newspapers and websites of advertising material that is not clearly distinguishable from editorial matter—'advertorials'—a sin committed on several occasions by the Department for Levelling Up in 2022 when promoting local improvement programmes on a number of regional newspaper websites.[139]

Almost unknown, by contrast, is advertising that seeks to make controversial policies more acceptable by misrepresenting their real background and purpose. A Department of Trade and Industry press advertisement in April 1999 was censured as misleading for implying that the Working Time Regulations were primarily

[135] Richard Bennett and Richard Tomkins, 'Government advertising spending tops £30m', *Financial Times* (25 April 2001).

[136] *Government Communication Service Propriety Guidance* (n 60) under 'Paid publicity' and 'Ofcom guidance on advertising'.

[137] These are published online at ASA and CAP, *Rulings*, but are only available there for the last five years. Earlier examples are drawn from the author's archives.

[138] ASA, *Ruling on Department for Work and Pensions in Association with Associated Newspapers* (6 November 2019).

[139] ASA, *Ruling on Department for Levelling Up, Housing and Communities* (12 October 2022).

designed to help businesses be more productive, when their dominant purpose was to protect workers' safety and health. Since then there has apparently been no occasion for any comparable complaint. Departmental press releases, of course, are not subject to the same external discipline as departmental advertising, and it might be unwise to assume that internal control, in the shape of the *GCS Propriety Guidance*, has been equally effective in guaranteeing the integrity of their content.

PART G
CONCLUSION

13
The Impact of 21st-Century Challenges

I Introduction: Morbid Symptoms and Missed Opportunities

Two speeches, one given by the Minister for the Cabinet Office in the midst of the Covid-19 pandemic, the other by the Cabinet Secretary as the country emerged from it, carry important lessons for the interpretation of the processes of change in the executive documented in the preceding chapters. Michael Gove, in his Ditchley Annual Lecture delivered in June 2020,[1] argued that crises like that experienced by the financial system in 2007–09, and the Covid-19 pandemic that the country was traversing, might give rise to 'morbid symptoms' such as the withdrawal of popular support for the economic consensus which had underpinned globalization for at least three decades, or the desertion of broad-based national political movements in favour of a polarized identity politics. A part of the cure he suggested for dealing with this malaise was 'to change how Government itself works, to reorganise its institutions to become better at reform'. But why, his audience might have asked, had the 'tumultuous and difficult times' negotiated since 1997 and in the decade since Gove's party came to power not already produced such reorganization? Had no lessons been drawn from the Iraq war? from The Global Financial Crisis (GFC)? from The stumble into Brexit?

A part of the answer was offered a year or so later by the Cabinet Secretary's speech.[2] Envisaging the way government might develop after the pandemic, he warned of the 'Curse of the Missed Opportunity', exemplified by the decision, after the end of the Second World War, to disperse—as a sign of 'getting back to normal'—the scientists, engineers, mechanics, linguists, and others drafted in for the war effort, instead of retaining them to participate in the effort to rebuild the country. Case, naturally, emphasized in his speech the institutional changes that were being installed following Covid-19, but his reference to missed opportunities could be read as an implicit response to the question prompted by Gove's speech: how, if at all, experience of the crises weathered by British governments since 1997 had reshaped our institutions.

Reviewing the detailed analyses of change offered in this book, what we see is that successive crises certainly produced major changes in the context and content of substantive government policy, and we continue to feel the effects of these changes: public services, for example, still suffer from the spending constraints originally imposed to repair the damage wrought by the GFC and consolidated in response to Covid-19 costs and post-Brexit economic stagnation. The GFC also produced extensive change in the arrangements for supervision of banking and financial markets. The Ukraine War modified the government's approach to energy policy and reintroduced the issue of military conscription to the field of public debate after a lapse of

[1] Michael Gove, 'The Privilege of Public Service' (Ditchley Annual Lecture, 27 June 2020).
[2] Simon Case, Cabinet Secretary Lecture (13 October 2021).

Executive Self-Government and the Constitution. Terence Daintith and Alan Page, Oxford University Press.
 DOI: 10.1093/9780198937630.003.0013

50 years. Experience of crises may also have changed executive attitudes to the exercise of power and to the associated relationships with the other organs of the constitution: new cleavages, across the political spectrum and within parties, resulted from the Brexit referendum vote; unprecedented executive actions, and parliamentary and judicial reactions, were entailed by the process of implementing it; and the process of responding to Covid-19 further accustomed ministers and officials to the exercise of far-reaching controls over economic and social life.

Our core concern, however, is with institutional change. One of the lessons of the extensive political science and economics literature on the relationship between crisis and reform[3] is that while crisis may provoke reform—though whether it actually does so will depend upon multiple factors, notably its relationship with existing objectives of those holding power—such reform is much more likely at the level of substantive measures and policies than in arrangements that modify policy competences within government, and is very hard to introduce at the level of constitutional arrangements and general political practice. Our analysis supports this hypothesis. When we look at how the executive now operates, and how far its key characteristics—its autonomy, its structure, how it exercises internal control—have been modified when compared to their state in 1997, the general impression is one of continuity rather than rupture. Certainly, the executive has adjusted its methods of operation in times of crisis (not always efficiently, as Covid inquiry evidence has demonstrated), but practices and institutions called into being in crisis times have, generally, been dispensed with as soon as signs of a return to 'normality' appear: thus the Department for Exiting the European Union was wound up as soon as the EU Withdrawal Agreement was concluded, though needs for inter-departmental coordination did not thereby diminish; the Contingencies Fund, distended by the financial demands of the Covid pandemic, was swiftly shrunk to its normal size; the government's central Covid communications hub was likewise dismantled as the pandemic receded, despite several earlier proposals for centralization of the communications function.

Here and there, crisis-related measures have survived this tendency to regress to the established norm and have become entrenched as part of the system of internal control: most important are the Cabinet Office controls over certain routine items of departmental spending; a less familiar example is the process of central triage of departmental proposals for new delegated legislation, introduced to manage the tsunami of EU exit measures. Much more often, however, lasting institutional change comes from other directions. General elections may offer a 'window of opportunity'[4] for the successful introduction of significant reform, at least if the incoming government's victory is substantial enough: Gordon Brown's public expenditure and monetary

[3] For useful recent surveys see Arjen Boin and Paul T'Hart, 'From Crisis to Reform? Exploring Three Post-COVID Pathways' (2022) 41 Policy and Society 13; Mounir Mahmalat and Declan Curran, 'Do Crises Induce Reform? A Critical Review of Conception, Methodology and Empirical Evidence of the "Crisis Hypothesis"' (2018) 32 Journal of Economic Surveys 613; Mariano Tommasi, 'Crisis, political Institutions, and Policy Reform: It is not the Policy, it is the Polity, Stupid' (Paper presented at Annual World Bank Conference on Development Economics—Europe, June 2002).

[4] See John W Kingdon, *Agendas, Alternatives, and Public Policies* (Little, Brown 1984) 182–87, and the further development of the idea in John TS Keeler, 'Opening the Window for Reform: Mandates, Crisis, and Extraordinary Policy-making' (1993) 25 Comparative Political Studies 433.

policy reforms, along with some of Labour's constitutional initiatives—Freedom of Information (FOI), the Human Rights Act, devolution to Scotland and Wales—offer examples that have survived subsequent political changes. Longevity cannot however be guaranteed. Central direction of government communications did not even last out the lifetime of Labour governments; the novelty of fixed-term Parliaments had a short and inglorious life. And some windows of opportunity slam shut remarkably quickly: the rebalancing of the constitution promised by the victorious Johnson government in 2019 never happened. Instead that government and its successors chose to test to the limit (and sometimes beyond) the constraints they had failed to modify.[5]

Alongside the changes that can be traced to these moments of political renewal in the lives of successive governments are a larger number that reflect the steady advance of one or two long-term policies or trends. The most numerous policy-driven changes are those that have expressed executive governments' sempiternal quest for self-improvement, through better coordination, more economic and efficient organization, better evaluation of policy proposals and their results, greater professionalism and expertise, clearer lines of accountability, and other such betterments. While this quest has produced many incremental changes in institutions and in sustained practice, it is striking that despite the regular expression of a commitment to such reform at the very highest political and official levels of government, as exemplified in the Gove and Case speeches, it has no less regularly failed to provoke the degree of change in institutions or practice that it identifies as desirable. In our view this failure suggests both that the windows of opportunity for this kind of reform are not very wide, for the reason suggested by Lord Maude ('politicians have short attention spans and they get bored and move on to something else'),[6] and that there are structural obstacles to carrying it through that have not been adequately confronted by its proponents, as we shall argue later. Perhaps the most important contribution of recurrent 21st-century crises to executive development has been to 'consume the capacity' of senior officials who could otherwise be carrying forward the reforms ministers repeatedly initiated for this purpose.[7]

Constitutionally significant change in the executive can also be driven by changes in external expectations. Labour's freedom of information and 'right to know' policies gave harder edges to the idea of 'open government' advanced by the Major administration as part of its Citizens' Charter initiative,[8] but an increasingly open approach by the executive to information about its structure and operations has been steadily driven forward not just by these political initiatives but also by public expectations about the availability of knowledge, fed by the demands of the 24-hour news cycle and, more important still, the instant access promised by the world wide web—a promise that government has organized itself to satisfy through gov.uk. This opening up has occurred alongside a shift in the way government communicates internally,

5 See chapter 1, text at nn 47–49, and more generally Alison L Young, *Unchecked Power: How Recent Constitutional Reforms Are Threatening Democracy* (Bristol UP 2024).

6 See chapter 8, n 70.

7 Gareth Davies, 'Getting the Most from Every Public Pound—a Blueprint for Value for Money' (Speech in Parliament, 16 January 2024).

8 Terence Daintith and Alan Page, *The Executive in the Constitution: Structure, Autonomy and Internal Control* (OUP 1999) ch 11.

with a reliance, for steering actions and decisions across the executive, on formally expressed rules, standards, and guidance, to a much greater degree than was evident at the end of last century.

In this chapter we shall assess the changes over the period since 1997 in the executive's autonomy, its structure, and its internal system of control, by drawing on the detailed accounts we have provided of how the institutional profile of the executive has evolved and how its management of its key resources of people, money, laws, and information has developed. What this analysis will show (and what executive reaction to crises already hints at) is that there coexist in our constitutional structure both a high degree of flexibility, and elements that constrain executive responses to identifiable needs for change.

II Autonomy

2.1 Definition and measurement

Executive autonomy may be defined as—or denotes—the ability of government to determine for itself the rules that are to govern its actions and to decide for itself how those rules are to be interpreted and applied. In our time, obviously, autonomy is an exceptional state. The norm is empowerment and regulation of executive action by parliamentary legislation, and of authoritative interpretation of that legislation, and of the common law that also constrains executive action, by the courts. The content of this book bears witness, however, to the scope for rule-making and interpretation still possessed by the executive, and the constitutional significance of what goes on within it. In our predecessor (1999) volume we thought it necessary to argue at some length in support of the extent and importance of the executive's capacity to make rules for itself, rules that might also have a significant impact on its relations with citizens and with Parliament and the courts. While some of the developments on which we focused then—like the Citizen's Charter and its successor, Service First—have not survived in the same form, the lesson we drew remains sound. This is that the executive has the ability to modify its own approach to the discharge of its functions, and that such changes may in turn affect the operation of external controls such as those exercised through parliamentary accountability. The area over which this ability may be exercised is coterminous with the space occupied by the more familiar—to constitutional lawyers—notions of prerogative and the common law powers of the Crown. We continue to avoid, where we can, the language of prerogative because of its implication that the competences it covers are in some way exorbitant, representing anachronistic survivals in the hands of an executive whose proper constitutional role is confined to the carrying into effect of legislatively determined policies.[9] This choice follows from our view that the executive's functions in our polity are quite different in nature from those of Parliament and the courts, and rest on a distinct and independent constitutional basis: the obligation of seeing to it that government is carried on, and

[9] This has been graphically described as the 'stubborn stain' theory of executive power: Timothy Endicott, *The Stubborn Stain Theory of Executive Power: from Magna Carta to* Miller (Policy Exchange 2017).

in particular of assuring national security and public order. Parliament's own website expresses the idea with disarming simplicity: 'The Government are the people responsible for running the country . . . Parliament is there to represent our interests and make sure they are taken into account by the Government.'[10]

At one time it might have been plausible to characterize 'autonomy' as involving the ability to act not only independently of legislative authorization, but also outside the scope of judicial control. That freedom, already attenuated by the passage of the Crown Proceedings Act 1947, had been all but extinguished by the extension of judicial review to the exercise of non-statutory powers in the *GCHQ* case.[11] Even where the executive can make rules for itself without reference to Parliament, therefore, it may be exposed to judicial scrutiny of its own respect for them, if the matter is considered by the courts to fall within the proper scope of judicial review. Only if courts decide—or are thought likely to decide—that an issue falls outside that scope can the executive be said, in the context of executive-judiciary relations, to enjoy autonomy. Judicial decisions in this century, addressing high-profile exercises of prerogative power—treaty-making,[12] the Prime Minister's power to advise on prorogation of Parliament[13]—have made it clear that the extent of executive autonomy is subject to reconfiguration by the courts no less than by Parliament.

Here we first consider changes in autonomy in terms of the scope of legislation: specifically, by reference to the emergence of new legislation that structures or regulates executive functions previously performed on the basis of its prerogative or common law powers. Since the executive can ordinarily determine what legislation is presented for consideration by Parliament, and—in very large measure—the content of that legislation, reductions in autonomy are, with very few exceptions,[14] self-imposed. Why would a government want to constrain itself in this way? It is true that governments with clear majorities in the House of Commons are unlikely to suffer additional restraint from having to act under legislative rather than common law powers, but the passage of legislation in itself depletes the executive's scarce resource of parliamentary time, and translating competences into legislative form may eliminate areas of vagueness in the content and mode of operation of rules and standards that procure useful flexibilities, even when subject to the ever more penetrating gaze of judicial review.

2.2 Practice

Despite the potential drawbacks attaching to any reduction of executive autonomy, the period since 1997 has seen governments introducing a series of legislative initiatives

[10] UK Parliament, *Parliament and the Government*. Compare Endicott (n 9) 17: 'In the British constitution, the executive is the primary, general branch of government.'

[11] *Council of Civil Service Unions v Minister for the Civil Service* [1985] AC 374.

[12] *R (Miller) v Secretary of State for Exiting the European Union* [2017] UKSC 5, [2018] AC 61 ('*Miller no 1*').

[13] *R (Miller) v The Prime Minister; Cherry v Advocate General for Scotland* [2019] UKSC 41 ('*Miller no 2*').

[14] Among these, arguably, are the restrictions on Treasury discretion as to the form of government accounts introduced during the passage of the Government Resources and Accounts Act 2000: chapter 11, section 2.1.

that have had the effect of cutting it down. These range from legislatively based fiscal rules,[15] through freedom of information legislation,[16] to a statutory regime for statistics,[17] a statutory foundation for the Civil Service and parliamentary involvement in treaty-making,[18] restriction of executive power to dissolve Parliament,[19] and legislative reinforcement of policy to restrict regulatory burdens on business.[20] Some of these measures have the goal of increasing the credibility and predictability of economic decision-making by subjecting it to published rules and standards, sometimes with the added safeguard of putting decisions in the hands of expert non-political bodies like the Office for Budget Responsibility (OBR) or the Statistics Authority. An earlier transfer, with a similar objective, was the placing of interest rate decisions in the hands of a Monetary Policy Committee of the Bank of England (Bank of England Act 1998).

Another stream of legislation—Civil Service reform, treaty-making, human rights, freedom of information—responds to a more general concern to strengthen the democratic bases of UK government by fortifying the position of Parliament and individuals vis-à-vis the executive. This second stream can be seen as an employment of legislative ordering that is less instrumental and more principled than the first, and it is notable that its appearance coincides with the terms of office of the Blair and Brown Labour governments, and its disappearance with the return to power of the Conservative Party—initially in coalition with the Liberals. Indeed the Brown government announced constitutional reform as a key objective and placed restriction of its own autonomy at the centre of this project:

> For centuries the executive has, in certain areas, been able to exercise authority in the name of the Monarch without the people and their elected representatives in their Parliament being consulted. This is no longer appropriate in a modern democracy. The Government believes that the executive should draw its powers from the people, through Parliament.
>
> The Government believes that in general the prerogative powers should be put onto a statutory basis and brought under stronger parliamentary scrutiny and control.[21]

While the White Paper listed a number of prerogatives that the government proposed for conversion to statutory powers or for restriction by other means (such as parliamentary resolutions), it was only in the report of its subsequent detailed review of prerogative powers that it became clear that the programme would not impinge on the executive's common law powers and capacities, such as hiring and firing, concluding contracts, and generally managing its business.[22] The Brown government did not last

[15] Finance Act 1998; Budget Responsibility and National Audit Act 2011: see chapter 7, sections 2.1.1, 2.1.3.

[16] Freedom of Information Act 2000: see chapter 11, section III.

[17] Statistics and Registration Service Act 2007: see chapter 7, section 2.2.2 and chapter 12, section 3.5.2.

[18] Constitutional Reform and Governance Act 2010: see chapter 6, section III and chapter 1, section 3.1.

[19] Fixed-term Parliaments Act 2011—now repealed.

[20] Small Business, Enterprise and Employment Act 2015—now repealed: see chapter 10, section 3.4.

[21] Secretary of State for Justice and Lord Chancellor, *The Governance of Britain* (Cm 7170, July 2007) paras 14, 24.

[22] Ministry of Justice, *The Governance of Britain: Review of the Executive Royal Prerogative Powers: Final Report* (October 2009) para 29.

long enough to carry through its programme fully, but its attitude can be measured by the fact that in one area at least—that of the powers of the Attorney General over the prosecution process—it was prepared to go further in imposing more detailed legislative regulation than Parliament and the legal profession thought necessary.[23]

The process of chipping away at the government's non-statutory powers did not come to a total halt with the arrival of the Coalition government. The inclusion, in the Coalition Agreement, of the Liberal Democrats' commitment to introduce fixed-term Parliaments led to the replacement of the prime-ministerial power to request a dissolution by a legislatively determined timetable (Fixed-Term Parliaments Act 2011), and the Coalition did not reverse, but reinforced, Labour's legislative structure for budget decision-making with the enactment of the Budget Responsibility and National Audit Act 2011. By contrast, the various Conservative governments installed after 2015 energetically asserted their executive autonomy, removing legislative restrictions,[24] restoring prerogative powers (Dissolution and Calling of Parliament Act 2022), and exercising them without much reflection as to alternatives (as with the United Kingdom's Article 50 notice to leave the European Union)[25] or with careless exuberance (as with the Prime Minister's 2019 prorogation advice).[26]

When calls are made for some additional area of its activity to be placed on a legislative footing, the default posture of the executive has been one of reluctance, varying in expression from foot-dragging to firm resistance. Among prominent examples of such resistance are the repeated governmental refusals to move to provide a statutory foundation for 'integrity' bodies like the Committee on Standards in Public Life, the Advisory Committee on Business Appointments, the Commissioner for Public Appointments, and the Independent Adviser on Ministerial Interests.[27] At the core of its resistance in this area is the idea that these bodies deal with matters that are part of the internal business of the executive, so that putting them on a legislative basis would upset a carefully constructed balance between the executive and Parliament, and would risk 'drawing the Courts into political matters that are the sole purview of the Government'.[28] Quite generally, in any case where departments are ready to move common law functions onto a statutory footing, the Law Officers warn them against it. They advise that such moves should where possible be avoided, suggesting that departments satisfy themselves that legislation is clearly 'necessary', and warning of the risk that existing common law and prerogative powers will be curtailed as a result.[29] The commitment to autonomy is most clearly expressed in the Law Officers' further statement that 'legislation should not be used to deal with what is essentially

[23] See chapter 9, text at nn 118–22.

[24] eg through the provisions of the Retained EU Law (Revocation and Reform) Act 2023, s 18, abolishing the statutory business impact target introduced by the Small Business, Enterprise and Employment Act 2015.

[25] See *Miller no 1* (n 12).

[26] See *Miller no 2* (n 13).

[27] See generally Robert Hazell and Peter Riddell, *Trust in Public Life: Restoring the Role of Constitutional Watchdogs* (UCL Constitution Unit 2024), and above, chapter 2, sections 3.2–3.3, and chapter 4, section IV.

[28] Cabinet Office, *Strengthening Ethics and Integrity in Central Government* (CP 900, July 2023) 25.

[29] Attorney General's Office and Legal Secretariat to the Advocate General for Scotland, *Working with the Law Officers on Legislation: A Guide for Departments* (December 2019) para 29.

an internal matter within the UK Government'.[30] We shall argue at the end of this chapter that unthinking adherence to this position has been a serious obstacle to rational consideration of executive reform.

2.3 Significance

Positions in the debate about executive autonomy correspond broadly not only with political differences—the Labour Party's 2024 general election manifesto, for example, promised an independent Ethics and Integrity Commission[31]—but also with the general divide between the 'legal constitutionalists' who favour a stronger formal structure for our constitution and the supporters of maintaining a 'political' constitution relying more heavily on executive accountability to Parliament than on legal ordering.[32] The issue may have more importance as a contest of principles than as a determinant of the extent of real constraints on executive behaviour. In some cases the change has appeared to be purely formal, as with the institution by the Constitutional Reform and Governance Act 2010 of a statutory basis for the Civil Service, which preserved intact the Prime Minister's powers of management. At the other extreme legal constraints on previously purely internal functions like budget preparation can be sensitive enough to bring down a government if it looks as though they are being ignored or devalued: if you legislate to secure market trust in your budget forecasts by outsourcing them to an independent statutory body in the shape of the OBR, you should not be surprised by adverse market reactions if you try—as did the Truss government—to sideline your forecaster.[33]

Between these extremes the provision of new legislative frameworks for executive action appears to have highly varied consequences. There are areas like freedom of information where the extent of change mandated by legislation looks dramatic but where the results, in terms of the extent of difference in official behaviour, are still contested. In other areas, such as the subjection of budgetary decision-making to legislatively supported fiscal rules, it is clear that the existence of the rules does modify behaviour: the Chancellor does not want to be seen to be breaching his own rules. Some of the consequent budgetary choices have however been criticized as economically irrational; the rules themselves have proved to be unstable; and the rules might, perhaps, have been no less effective had the government simply announced them formally as a matter of internal financial discipline, following the precedent of John Major's publication of the Ministerial Code in 1992.

While the need for legislative underpinning of fiscal rules is debatable, legislation was certainly necessary to support their reinforcement through the creation of independent forecasting capability in the shape of the OBR, a statutory non-departmental public body (NDPB). Legislation was likewise necessary to transfer the government's

[30] ibid paras 15-18; and see above, chapter 8, section 2.4.2, and chapter 10, text at nn 44–50, for practice in relation to this guidance.

[31] Labour Party, *Change: Labour Party Manifesto 2024* (June 2024): 'Serving the country'.

[32] For a comprehensive recent treatment of this debate see the contributions collected in Graham Gee and Chris McCorkindale (eds), 'The Political Constitution at Forty' (2019) 30 King's Law Journal 1.

[33] See chapter 7, text at nn 59–62.

central (but not departmental) statistical functions, and responsibility for statistical integrity, to an independent body, the Statistics Authority, this time in the shape of a non-ministerial department (NMD). Just how much difference such legislation makes will obviously depend upon the extent of the powers it confers on such bodies. Less obviously, but no less importantly, the independence it confers will also be relative, in that while legislation may guarantee operational autonomy, these bodies' finance and resourcing, and hence their overall capacity for action, is dependent on negotiation and agreement either with their sponsor department (in the case of an NDPB) or the Treasury (through the Estimates process, for NMDs having their own Vote).

III Structure

3.1 Stable core, unstable periphery

A consistent refrain of the official and unofficial programmes of executive reform proposed since 1997 has been the need to 'strengthen the centre', with the evocation of a range of possible institutional changes: the creation of a Prime Minister's Department, or the splitting of the Cabinet Office or the Treasury or both, or the redistribution of responsibilities between these bodies. Yet for all the talk, the core executive in 2024 looks—in broad outline at least—very much the way it did in 1997. The number of ministerial departments is about the same (24 as against 20); their central coordination and control remain in the hands of Prime Minister, Cabinet Office, and Treasury. The balance of legal power between centre and departments has not been touched: when the UK government receives new powers from Parliament, legislation continues to allot them to departments through their individual Secretaries of State, not to the executive as a whole or to its 'centre'. The balance of political power continues to vary with the personal prestige and popularity of the Prime Minister. The constitutional upheaval represented by devolution might have been expected to produce a new 'great office of state', a Secretary of State for Intergovernmental and Constitutional Affairs, with a status akin to the Chancellor of the Exchequer, Foreign Secretary, or Home Secretary: it did not.[34]

This seeming immobility of the basic structure in the face of repeated calls for change may, however, be deceptive. If one stands back a little to take in the many public bodies that cluster round the core ministerial departments, one kind of body that dominated the scene in 1997 can be seen to have shrunk into insignificance: the executive agencies introduced with such fanfare in the 1990s, whose near-demise we noted in chapter 4. To the extent that their functions have been reabsorbed into the operations of their parent departments, which is how the existence of some large and prominent agencies has ended, this development may signal a revival of the modes of management and accountability traditionally associated with individual ministerial responsibility. More generally, the shrinkage of this kind of institution suggests that it has come to be seen in government as an unstable compromise between demands

[34] See chapter 5, section II.

for accountability for politically sensitive decisions and for efficiency and a degree of independence in the performance of specialized tasks. The push to develop more 'business-like' ways of running core departmental functions (departmental boards, chief operating officers, senior responsible owners) may have reinforced doubt about the utility of the agency model.

3.2 Growth at the centre

Evidence of change is also visible if one gets closer to the executive and condescends to look not for big shifts in institutional characteristics and competences that might obviously be of constitutional salience, but at the movement of indicators like staff numbers. The number of civil servants employed in the central departments gives a sense of the balance between centre and departments. While total Civil Service numbers were about the same in 2022 as in 1997, the proportion employed in the Cabinet Office substantially increased, from 0.54% in 1997 to 2.27% in 2022, reflecting the growth of the Office's headcount from 2,569 FTE in 1997 to 10,840 in 2022.[35] Discounting Brexit and pandemic effects, what has produced this remarkable growth is the steady accretion to the Cabinet Office of specialized units and groups. We have encountered some of these, such as the Public Bodies team and the central group of the Government Communication Service, in the course of our detailed analysis. There are plenty of others: 'offices' like the Offices of Government Property or the Office for Veterans Affairs; 'units' such as the Borders Unit or the Public Inquiry Response Unit; and a collection of task forces, hubs, commissions, and authorities. While the Gershon Report, recommending the grouping of departmental 'back office' functions like payroll management in a number of shared service centres,[36] perhaps marked the beginning of this movement, the most important driver for the creation of these centrally located, usually small, groups of civil servants has been the functional programme formally initiated in 2015. The majority of the 13 specialist functions created under this programme, whose membership is spread across the Civil Service, are led by such units in the Cabinet Office, acting in concert with function leaders within departments. Essentially therefore the functions programme represents an attempt at reinforcement of central control,[37] rather than a change in the balance between central and departmental responsibilities, but there are exceptions. Cabinet Office gets involved in the day-to-day management of certain cross-government activities, through two executive agencies: the Government Property Agency and the Crown Commercial Service. Its Infrastructure Projects Authority, a joint venture with the Treasury, both leads the Project Delivery Function and scrutinizes and advises on departmental infrastructure projects. The Government Commercial Function, led from the Cabinet

[35] For further statistics see chapter 6, section I, and for the less dramatic rate of Treasury expansion, chapter 2, section 4.3.

[36] Sir Peter Gershon, *Releasing Resources to the Front Line: Independent Review of Public Sector Efficiency* (2004) 38, 42–43. Coordination of these services across departments is now in the hands of a Cabinet Office unit, Government Business Services.

[37] See further section IV of this chapter.

Office, also directly employs, through the Government Commercial Organisation, senior commercial personnel operating in departments across government.

These new cross-government responsibilities for specialist functions do not always end up in the Cabinet Office. We have seen how lawyers from across government have been assembled in what was the Treasury Solicitor's Office and is now the Government Legal Department (though for reasons that are obscure legal services are not now treated as a function within the functions programme), while departmental internal auditors ended up in a Treasury executive agency. When the Office for National Statistics, which leads the government-wide analysis function, was detached from the Treasury, ownership by an independent NMD (the Statistics Authority) was thought more appropriate than Cabinet Office status.

Taken together these changes have produced a more complex structure for the core executive, in which senior specialists in departments have reporting responsibilities both within the department and across departmental boundaries, and where departmental ministers and senior managers may sometimes—though still not very often—need to rely on services provided elsewhere in government. The loss to departments of a measure of autonomy, and of capacity for comprehensive self-organization and self-management, may—we are not in a position to judge—be justified by improvements in quality of performance of relevant functions and economies in the use of resources, but it is not obvious that there has been a commensurate increase in the ability of the central authorities to shape the behaviour of the executive as a whole, because of the distribution of central control, influence, and service provision across numerous separate teams within Cabinet Office, and indeed beyond. External blueprints for reform have consequently emphasized the need for more coherent direction and management of these Cabinet Office functions, for example by way of moving them into a department of the Civil Service under a First Secretary of State who would also have primary responsibility for delivering the government's priorities.[38] By itself, however, such a move would not address the underlying problem posed by the principle of allocation of legal powers not to the Cabinet Office, but to ministers and, through them, Permanent Secretaries. This, as we argue later, may require a different kind of solution.

IV Internal Control

4.1 The coming of New Labour: evolution not revolution

At the end of last century, it remained the case that the principal components of the executive's system of internal control were the legal authority of each minister over their department's use of the resources with which it was endowed, and over the activities of the public bodies associated with the department; and the political authority of Prime Minister and Cabinet through which general lines of policy could be laid down and issues retained for central determination or identified for collective

[38] See Commission on the Centre of Government, *Power with Purpose: Final Report* (Institute for Government 2024) 72–73, 98–100.

disposition. As a result, coordination of policy and harmonization of administrative practice across the executive needed to be achieved through the formulation of policies, rules, standards, or guidance by authorities at the centre of government, and their dissemination to departments and other bodies, or by the provision of ad hoc instructions or advice by those authorities. Given the legal authority of ministers over the action of their departments, acceptance and application of these centrally developed norms and advice depended upon the political authority of those promulgating them, and their addressees' acceptance that they represented a legitimate exercise of such authority. The exception was and remains the sphere of public finance, where the Treasury's 'ancient authority' and specific statutory powers mean that it, not departmental ministers, disposes of legal authority over departmental finances; but the Treasury's practice of delegation and consent has meant that the management of public expenditure depends as heavily upon departmental respect for central norms and advice as do other areas of activity. The difference is that the Treasury's requirements and suggestions enjoy a formal authority (and practical sanction) that other rules, standards, and guidance lack—though they may still be displaced, in individual cases, by collective political decision at Cabinet level.

It would be a mistake to view the arrival of New Labour in office in 1997 as marking a radical change in the objectives and manner of exercise of internal control. Certainly, Tony Blair and Gordon Brown seemed to have a more ambitious vision than their predecessors of how they might steer, from No 10 Downing Street, activity across the full span of executive competence. This could be seen, for example, in the use of Public Service Agreements to reinforce departmental commitment to central priorities, or the placing, at the Prime Minister's right hand, of a special adviser with extraordinary powers over communications activity across government. These moves were controversial and certainly modified existing relationships, but the trend towards a more pervasive central interest in steering departmental activity was already clearly visible under earlier governments, notably in John Major's Citizen's Charter programme, which aimed to raise the standard of public service provision across all departments and agencies, and in its Code of Practice on Access to Government Information, the forerunner of the Freedom of Information Act.[39] Not all movement was in the direction of greater central involvement. Towards the end of the century the scope of central control was substantially narrowed, to the benefit of departments, by the gradual dismantling of central management of Civil Service recruitment, pay, and conditions, once a Treasury monopoly but by 1996 a departmental responsibility exercised subject to a degree of central supervision.[40] Central guidance, and central advisory resources, had however been developed by 1997 in most of the areas covered by this book, from ministerial conduct (chapter 2) to contacts with the media and paid publicity (chapter 12). Concern for the preservation of executive autonomy meant that these initiatives relied on internal control, exercised through Cabinet Office units and Cabinet Office and Treasury guidance to departments.[41]

[39] Daintith and Page (n 8) ch 11.

[40] For the process through which this was brought about see Daintith and Page (n 8) 59–78.

[41] For a reasonably comprehensive list and summary of guidance applicable to the work of civil servants in 2000 see Cabinet Office, *Directory of Civil Service Guidance* (2000), containing short summaries of

4.2 The style of central control: formalization, compulsion, publicity

4.2.1 Formalization

Developments since 1997 thus represent not the adoption of a new approach to internal control but rather the intensification of several features of the existing approach. One element in this has been more systematic and detailed provision of central documentation, reflecting greater attention to harmonizing departmental approaches through central articulation of standards and structures that departments are advised, requested, or required to apply. This was the objective of the 'functional model' developed by the Coalition government to provide 'strong central leadership of cross-departmental corporate functions' to support Civil Service professionalization, improved public services, and financial savings.[42] The general standards of organization and behaviour developed by the lead bodies for each of the 13 functions have been filled out by numerous more detailed guidance documents. As an example of this expansion of central effort, guidance on combating risks of fraud, in 2000 contained in a single Treasury document, was by 2021 the concern of the Government Counter-Fraud Function, whose Counter-Fraud Standard was supported by eight further guidance documents, including separate treatments of fraud risk assessment; fraud investigation; fraud leadership, management, and strategy; fraud loss reporting; and anti-corruption strategy.[43]

While the functional standards collect together a large body of guidance material, making reference to some 300 guidance documents, there remains a great deal of other material linked to activities or issues outside their scope. Much of it originates from the Treasury (though *Managing Public Money (MPM)* is a basic reference in all the standards), and Cabinet Office units have also produced extensive guidance on matters such as arm's length bodies, relations with Parliament, appointments, and other propriety and integrity issues. Some responsibilities for maintaining and implementing government-wide rules and standards have been farmed out to other departments. The Better Regulation Executive went from the Cabinet Office to what was then the Department for Business, Enterprise and Regulatory Reform (now the Department for Business and Trade) in 2007. In 2022 the team overseeing the culling and conversion of retained EU law—a task involving all departments—followed the same path, apparently simply because the responsible minister moved from the Cabinet Office to become Secretary of State at the department. Developments of this kind continued under the Labour government that took office in July 2024, with the transfer of the Central Digital and Data Office from Cabinet Office to the Department for Science, Innovation and Technology, along with the Government Digital Service.

In the 1990s, this process of formalization seemed to respond to developments like the need to ensure that administrative practice reflected public sector and

guidance and/or contact details for (further) information (vol 1), and statements of hitherto unpublished guidance on selected matters (vol 2). Much Treasury guidance does not appear in these volumes.

42 Cabinet Office, *The Functional Model: A Model for More Efficient and Effective Government* [nd].

43 HM Government, *Government Functional Standard GovS 013: Counter-Fraud* (August 2021) 13, and compare Cabinet Office (n 41) vol 1, 29.

constitutional reforms, the fragmentation of the public service through the multiplication of public bodies of different kinds, and fears about the breakdown of established mechanisms of professional socialization within the service, a breakdown compounded by the then growth in recruitment from the private sector. To this last concern we may now add the sense that civil servants need formal guidance in order to know how to do their jobs properly. Increasingly rapid internal turnover, as civil servants move between jobs within and across departments in search of promotion and the higher pay that comes with it,[44] diminishes the capacity to learn on the job. The continuing proliferation of written guidance documents can be seen as an attempt to provide a substitute for the shrinking corpus of experience and knowledge held by existing staff: what is 'in their heads'.[45]

4.2.2 Compulsion

What distinguishes the functional standards, as a vehicle of internal control, from the mass of other guidance, is their presentation as elements of a coherent system of central regulation of departmental and arm's length body behaviour. The substance of the standards themselves is presented in a common format, moving from overall strategies and structures to delivery mechanisms and practice, and each standard commences with a handy glossary explaining the significance of expressions such as 'shall' and 'should'. In thus explicitly identifying some of their provisions as mandatory, and others as mere guidance, the functional standards break new ground in the design of 'guidance' originating in the Cabinet Office. Treasury documentation like *MPM* and its forerunners has long included many mandatory provisions, the obligation of compliance being grounded in the Treasury's 'ancient authority' and statutory powers.[46] Cabinet Office, however, does not possess any powers of this sort that can be turned to coercive purposes: even the exercise of leadership through persuasion represents, as we have explained, a modern addition to its traditional function of coordination.[47] Permanent Secretaries may therefore have been surprised to see, on publication of the standards, that Cabinet Office was telling them not only what their department 'should' be doing in the performance of the relevant functions, but also that it was subject to the requirements indicated by the use of the word 'shall'. For the most part, it is true, the mandatory provisions of the standards refer to obligations of a very general nature that a department is unlikely to fail to satisfy in some way, but this is not always the case: for example, the *Human Resources* standard requires that senior officers 'regularly assess workforce and human resource related risks';[48] the *Communications* standard requires that '[t]he government and each organisation shall have a media relations operation which shall maintain a media planning schedule and forward look

44 Tom Sasse and Emma Norris, *Moving On: The Costs of High Staff Turnover in the Civil Service* (Institute for Government January 2019).

45 Christopher Pollitt, 'Bureaucracies Remember, Post-Bureaucratic Organisations Forget?' (2009) 87 Public Administration 198, 202–03.

46 Such as its most basic provision: 'Departments must have Treasury consent before undertaking expenditure or making commitments which could lead to expenditure, or have other fiscal implications' (para 2.3.1).

47 See chapter 2, section 3.4.2.

48 HM Government, *Government Functional Standard GovS 003: Human Resources* (July 2021) para 4.3.3.

(in some organisations, referred to as the "grid")'.[49] Issuing commands without sanctions to back them up is a risky business, and we should not be surprised that a review conducted by Lord Maude in 2020 found that departmental compliance with the standards was less then perfect. Rather than give central units any power to enforce the mandatory standards for which they were responsible, government preferred to respond by making compliance an obligation of Accounting Officers under the public expenditure regime of *MPM*.[50] How—if at all—this obligation might be enforced by the Treasury is open to question.

The Coalition government and its Conservative successors also applied this more muscular approach to 'guidance' outside the areas covered by functions, for example stipulating in 2018 that formal approval for setting up a new arm's length body (ALB) be sought and received from Cabinet Office ministers and the Chief Secretary to the Treasury, but mandatory language does not seem to have spread into areas where Cabinet Office guidance is unsupported by Treasury authority.

4.2.3 Publicity

At one time most of the working of the system of internal control—both the central elements which we have emphasized in the previous paragraphs and the operation of departmental self-discipline—would have been hidden from public view. Only a minority of the items of guidance listed in the *Directory of Civil Service Guidance* in 2000 were framed as publicly available documents. Since then the practice at the centre of government has been to put an ever-increasing proportion of the rules, requirements, standards, and guidance it addresses to departments and other executive bodies into the public domain. Departments have been less forthcoming. Despite the listing by the Information Commissioner, in a *Definition document for government departments*,[51] of 'Internal communications guidance, criteria used for decision-making, internal instructions, manuals and guidelines' among the kinds of information that should normally be included in a department's publication scheme under the Freedom of Information Act,[52] their publications policies for such guidance are inconsistent and restrictive. Some have perhaps taken advantage of the caveat that such publication is expected only 'if this would help the public understand how decisions are made and would not risk damaging the department's operations'.[53]

The presentation of centrally promulgated internal norms has also become more clearly structured. The government's comprehensive website, www.gov.uk, seeks to provide effective public access through a rational and consistent ordering of material on different subjects, and offers an increasing number of 'collections' pages making it possible to survey both central guidance on particular topics and departments' and

[49] HM Government, *Government Functional Standard GovS 011: Communication 2.0* (July 2021) para. 6.4.

[50] *MPM*, para 4.2.1, box A4.1A, and paras A.4.5.6, A5.1.8. See further chapter 2, section 3.4.6, and chapter 3, section 3.3.2.

[51] Information Commissioner's Office, *Definition Document for Government Departments* (version 3.1) 5–6.

[52] Freedom of Information Act 2000, s 19. For the obligation to develop such a scheme and get it approved by the Commissioner see chapter 11, section 3.2.

[53] Information Commissioner's Office (n 51).

other institutions' responses to it. The effect of these developments has been to make the inner workings of the executive far more visible than in the last century. Where once we would speculate about what advice on good legislative practice Parliamentary Counsel might be giving departments, and how far it would be backed up by the Law Officers,[54] we can now point to the detailed prescriptions in *Working with the Law Officers on Legislation*.[55] Where information about drawings on the Contingencies Fund was once limited to numbers buried in departmental annual accounts, we can now find the details of individual departmental requests, with reasons, on line.[56]

We need of course to define the precise gains in accountability that flow from greater openness about the executive's control system. Its effect is to add, to the accountability deriving from the obligation of ministers to answer generally for the activity of their departments, a more focused accountability resulting from the ability of agents outside government—Parliament and its committees and other institutions, the media, interest groups—to test individual executive decisions against published norms (whether presented as rules, standards, or just guidance) and challenge apparent disparities. Publication of guidance does not guarantee that the relevant decision-makers will choose to follow it—as the record of the Johnson administration in relation to the use of delegated legislation amply demonstrates—nor that those entrusted with its enforcement will be conscientious in applying it—as the Cabinet Office's performance in a number of spheres, from controlling creation of ALB's to supervising public appointments, has shown. Its contribution is to enhance the capacity of the external supervisors of the executive to call government to account.

4.3 Judicial review

Greater transparency for internal control norms may also have helped interest groups to challenge executive practice through judicial review. Decisions in this century by the Supreme Court and the Appellate Committee of the House of Lords as its predecessor have put beyond doubt the ability—and the readiness—of the courts to review departmental policies, especially those that provide guidance to other public bodies. Review may address both the legality of a policy and the relationship between the policy and individual decisions.[57] Mechanistic compliance with a policy may be censured as a failure to exercise discretion; departure from a policy may (sometimes) disappoint legitimate expectations. In 1999 we speculated that if initiatives like the Citizen's Charter programme were successful in raising standards of public service and promoting the provision of adequate systems of administrative complaint and redress, there might be less resort to judicial review for the resolution of individual complaints, and that as a corollary

[54] Daintith and Page (n 8) 254–58.
[55] See chapter 10, section 1.2.
[56] See chapter 8, section 2.3.
[57] See eg *R (A) v Secretary of State for the Home Department* [2021] UKSC 37; *R (BAPIO Action Ltd) v Secretary of State for the Home Department* [2008] UKHL 27.

> it is people who want to make a point, about the legality of administrative action, who will continue to go to the courts. Whatever the rhetoric of administrative action, policy rather than administration may become the primary concern of judicial review.[58]

There are indeed signs of this change of emphasis. If immigration cases, whose numbers have grown enormously, are set to one side, judicial reviews on civil matters—hence on issues to which public service standards and complaints might be relevant, like housing and homelessness—came down by some 10% between 2000 and 2019.[59] At the same time, policy-related reviews brought or supported by interest groups of many kinds have proliferated, to the great annoyance of some ministers. They are offered as the principal evidence for dangers of undemocratic overreach by courts and the substitution of tendentious legal judgment for healthy political debate.[60] The subject of such litigation is normally the exercise of statutory powers, but the opening up of prerogative and common law powers to review, coupled with the greater visibility of internal control, has meant that judges have occasionally been asked to consider and interpret the internal rules and guidance emanating from the centre of government.

Hitherto the general judicial attitude to such requests has been one of considerable caution. Cases like *R (People and Planet) v HM Treasury* (2009)[61] and *R (All the Citizens and Good Law Project) v Secretary of State for Digital, Culture, Media and Sport* (2022)[62] suggested that the courts were ready to consider the significance of this kind of material, but unlikely to move on to find that it constrains the decisions complained of. It is not possible, however, for the executive to be sure that this further step will never be taken. This happened in *R (FDA) v Prime Minister and Minister for the Civil Service*,[63] where the Divisional Court reviewed the Prime Minister's finding, following a complaint against the Home Secretary, that there had been no breach of the Ministerial Code. The court rejected the government's argument that the whole of the Ministerial Code, being 'a political document issued in a political context [that] did not set legal standards enforceable by a court',[64] was non-justiciable. The Code's use, in its provisions forbidding ministerial bullying, of concepts familiar from employment law contexts led the court to conclude that it could properly review their application by the Prime Minister, even if much or most of the Code might fall outside judicial competence.[65] While one obvious danger of such judicial assertiveness is the comfort it gives to those who would happily impose radical restrictions on judicial review, there is—so far at least—no evidence that it has prompted any reconsideration,

[58] Daintith and Page (n 8) 397.

[59] Calculated from data in Independent Review of Administrative Law (CP 407, March 2021) paras D13, D14. See also paras D17–D19 for data on subjects on which cases were brought.

[60] See Suella Braverman, 'Judicial Review Trends and Forecasts 2021: Accountability and the Constitution' (Speech to Public Law Project Conference, 19 October 2021); Richard Ekins, *The Case for Reforming Judicial Review* (Policy Exchange, December 2020). See also chapter 9, section 1.2.

[61] See chapter 8, text at nn 174–76.

[62] See chapter 11, text at nn 100–03.

[63] [2021] EWHC 3279 (Admin).

[64] Sir James Eadie KC, for the government [28].

[65] For strong criticism see Michael Gordon, '*R (on the application of FDA) v Prime Minister*: The Ministerial Code, Justiciability, and the Limits of Judicial Review' [2023] Public Law 1, 8.

in Cabinet Office or Treasury, of their operation of internal control through formulating and publishing general standards, guidance, and rules, as opposed to reliance on less visible negotiation and ad hoc decision-making.

4.4 Discretion and accountability

Whatever the extent of their exposure to judicial review, internal regulatory processes continue to be significantly different from controls directly founded on legislative ordering. In particular, accountability for individual decisions under the latter type of regime is likely to be much more formal. Bodies implementing statute-based regulation usually have reporting obligations from which their approach to their enforcement tasks, and their success in performing those tasks, may become apparent. Independent bodies charged with the supervision of executive action under prerogative or common law powers may offer a similar degree of accountability through annual or other reporting processes. This is far less likely where supervision or monitoring is the responsibility of Cabinet Office or Treasury. Individual cases of their operation (or failure to operate) may be brought into public view by the occasional litigation we have mentioned, or as a result of the enquiries of parliamentary select committees. Much of what we know about the way the Treasury operates its controls over departmental expenditure, for example, has emerged over decades of enquiries and reports by the Public Accounts Committee, often prompted by specific spending decisions and supported by the unusually penetrating investigative powers of the Comptroller and Auditor General. How much of these decision-making processes nonetheless normally remains in the dark only becomes apparent when government—as part of a reform process, or under external pressure—publishes a more general review,[66] or opens its files to academic researchers.[67]

Despite the steadily increasing visibility of the rules and standards on which they are based, such internal control procedures may continue to operate in a highly discretionary environment in which political considerations can readily, and regularly, come into play. When an individual decision taken within the executive appears to be inconsistent with the applicable internal control, how is this to be explained: as a weakness in the control system, or as a sign of its political elasticity? Take the case where internal rules or guidance subject a departmental decision to the consent of another authority within the executive—typically Treasury consent. When a proposal that appears not to satisfy the requirements for such consent, enunciated in *MPM* or elsewhere, is nonetheless carried through, was this because the Treasury in fact waved it through on the basis of a relaxed interpretation of its own rules, or perhaps offered a negotiated consent in exchange for constraints elsewhere? Or does it reflect a ruling at the centre, whether by Cabinet or No 10, accepting the departmental case at the expense of respect for the Treasury position? Similar questions arise when

[66] For an example see Sue Langley, *Freedom of Information Clearing House Review* (Cabinet Office 2022) in chapter 11, section 3.4.

[67] As did the Treasury when supporting the research reported in Christopher Hood and others, *The Way the Money Goes: The Fiscal Constitution and Public Spending in the UK* (OUP 2023).

legislative proposals that contravene the principles enunciated in the *Guide to Making Legislation* or *Working with the Law Officers on Legislation* come forward with the *imprimatur* of the Parliamentary Business and Legislation Committee. Were these cases where the Law Officers were persuaded of a 'compelling justification', or did they find themselves in a minority on the Committee? Greater transparency regarding the internal control norms may, in other words, tell us where the norms are not working, but is unlikely—in the absence of further inquiry—to tell us why.

4.5 Effectiveness and obstacles

The flexibility exemplified by the different ways in which even the best-established and supported internal controls—like the Treasury controls just described—may be made to yield to political expediency has been seen within government as essential to the effective—and politically responsive—conduct of executive business. Maintaining the degree of flexibility inherent in the current system would be all but impossible in relation to controls transferred to a statutory basis. From the outside, however, this flexibility looks like an expression of weakness, which is compounded by the fact that most centrally generated control measures do not even have the sort of support that established Treasury powers provide. The functional programme, the most ambitious central control programme over the period of our study, has never secured sufficient departmental compliance on the basis of Cabinet Office persuasion alone, but has had to be propped up by reliance on pre-existing Treasury delegations of spending control powers, and latterly, by treating the whole enterprise as an outgrowth of public expenditure control. Other departments charged with tasks of cross-government control or coordination seem to experience even more difficulty in securing compliance because, as one Permanent Secretary put it, 'Putting responsibilities in a line Department signals to the rest of Whitehall that this set of issues is a lower order priority than the things that the centre wants to concentrate on.'[68] Thus the Secretary of State for Business and Trade had to tell members of the Commons European Scrutiny Committee impatient to see departments revoking their EU-derived regulations, 'I can give dashboards and have metrics, but I cannot make Departments do things that they do not want to do, . . . unless it is escalated and a different decision is made by the centre or by No. 10.'[69]

Even where the control system puts final decisions in the hands of a central authority, as with access to finance for new policies and programmes and to the legislation to support them, the testing involved in the relevant processes may be far less demanding than the official literature suggests. Lack of experience and expertise in departments is replicated in a Treasury whose spending teams have the highest rate of turnover anywhere in central government, and in any case Treasury concern with new programmes focuses strongly—and perhaps not unreasonably—on their financial

[68] See chapter 5, n 43.

[69] European Scrutiny Committee, *Oral Evidence: Retained EU Law: The Progress and Mechanics of Reform* (13 March 2024, HC 2023–24, 376) q 76. For how the Secretary of State came to have these responsibilities see q 65.

implications. As for legislation, the gateway to a place in the legislative programme is policed by a committee of ministers for whom the quality of proposals may be less important than their hoped-for political impact—and if existing legislation is worded loosely enough, radical policy changes may not even need new law.[70] Elsewhere, lack of sustained commitment to internal control initiatives has been dramatized by the seeming inability of the controllers to operate them even in their own departments.[71]

The regularity with which we have drawn attention, in the preceding chapters, to failings of central control over departmental activity prompts the question of why the leaders of successive governments over more than a quarter of a century have tolerated a situation that they regularly profess themselves to be committed to rectify. One reason, surely, is that administrative reforms do not win votes, and as Lord Maude has remarked, ministers quickly lose interest in such matters. The electorate is assumed to be interested in results—levels of public service, successful and coherent delivery of policies of which it approves—not in the machinery through which these things are achieved. This sort of ministerial thinking is exemplified by the reason given by the Sunak government in 2023 for cancelling the expected updating of departments' outline Outcome Delivery Plans, already in draft.[72] They were all, apparently, too busy advancing the Prime Minister's five policy priorities—whether these were relevant to their mission or not.

Internal control also suffers, politically, from the fact that the perception of its impact, on the part of the electorate and interest groups, may often be negative. This is most obviously the case in relation to Treasury controls that stifle exciting infrastructure projects, deny extra-statutory payments to distressed claimants, and drive up hospital waiting lists through restriction of funding. Other controls, like those designed to rein in departmental appetites for regulation, may be attractive to some groups in society while removing valued protections from other groups like employees and consumers, who carry greater political weight. The exercise of 'integrity' controls—over appointments, official and ministerial behaviour, and the funding of the Prime Minister's wallpaper—is most likely, perhaps, to attract the interest and sympathy of the voters, but this may be the field in which the demands of political expediency impose the most powerful restraints on the conscientious application of controls.

This sort of public perception provides a reason why ministers and their departments might resist the application or extension of central controls, but it is not the only one. Most fundamental is the fact that ministers and departments prize their autonomy and may, indeed, as we explained in chapter 3, cherish the features that set them apart from other departments. Central controls tend to have the effect of eroding such differences—even though acknowledgment is routinely made of the varied shapes and sizes of the bodies to which they are designed to apply—and may frequently have this as their purpose as well. Where controls go beyond guidance and incorporate consent mechanisms, they impinge further upon freedom of departmental

[70] As was the case with the disastrous partial privatization of the probation service in 2013: see Ian Dunt, *How Westminster Works... and Why it Doesn't* (Weidenfeld & Nicholson 2023) 1–25.

[71] As illustrated by Cabinet Office non-compliance with the Public Appointments Code (chapter 4, section 4.4) or Treasury practice in relation to departmental board meetings (chapter 3, section 3.5).

[72] See chapter 3, section 4.2.2.

choice by seeking to determine what departments may do, as well as how they should do it. This of course cuts across both the legal structure of the executive, whose ruling principle is the allocation of legal powers and functions to individual ministers and their departments. Likewise it cuts across the resulting accountability structure in which, as a triumvirate of senior Permanent Secretaries pointed out to the Public Accounts Committee in 2014,

> Secretaries of State [are] each responsible for areas of policy where he or she enjoys considerable autonomy subject to collective responsibility. This is complementary to the century old model of the Accounting Officer, who is personally responsible for the activity the organisation he or she leads. On this is founded our system of accountability to Parliament, notably to your committee and to other select committees too.[73]

There is no reason to think that the consensus of opinion among Permanent Secretaries on this point has changed much in the last 10 years. The 2021 *Declaration of Government Reform*, jointly agreed by the Cabinet and Permanent Secretaries, in no way challenged this received wisdom. Indeed, 'reinvigorate the principle of departmental accountability' appeared ahead of 'improve cross-government functions' among the actions to which Cabinet and Permanent Secretaries committed themselves.[74] Cross-government working has been a problem at least since New Labour flagged cross-departmental objectives as a concern of its Public Service Agreements programme in 1998, elevating them in 2007 to become its sole object.[75] Disappointment with the results of cross-government initiatives has been a note regularly struck in reports from the National Audit Office and the Public Accounts Committee ever since. It is striking that while a wide variety of incentives, guidance, and controls are being deployed to advance successful work on policies that do not fit within the competence of single departments, all of the six models of cross-government working provided, for departmental guidance, in the 2023 version of *MPM* envisage the location of leadership of the programme in a single department.[76] This doubtless minimizes the risk of dilution of Accounting Officer responsibility, and preserves individual ministerial responsibility, but it suggests that there is no appetite for approaches to managing cross-government policies that would depart to any significant degree from the model of placing legal powers in the hands of individual Secretaries of State.

Ministers, for their part, have to balance their legal autonomy against their collective responsibility and loyalty to Prime Minister and party. The uncertainty of

[73] Sir Bob Kerslake, Sir Nicholas Macpherson, and Richard Heaton, 'Treasury Minutes on Civil Service Reform, etc' Letter of 24 March 2014 to Chair of Public Accounts Committee.

[74] HM Government, *Declaration on Government Reform* (June 2021) 6.

[75] See chapter 3, section 4.1. As Jack Straw, who headed three major departments between 1997 and 2010, put it: 'a critical part of the constitutional architecture of our system is that individual secretaries of state are responsible for what happens in their department . . . These things are done in your name. That makes the departments very strong but trying to work across government much more difficult, and that of course is compounded by inherent rivalry between ministers': Jack Straw, *Ministers Reflect* (Institute for Government May 2016) 12.

[76] *MPM*, s 7.6, box 7.4.

ministerial tenure, with the pressure it brings to 'make one's mark' on the activity of the department at the earliest possible moment, militates against the easy acceptance of centrally imposed constraints that might retard the progress of ministerial schemes. It also gives ministers every incentive to rush the development and implementation of policies, in a frantic race to get some achievement on record before being moved on. The risk that these might be bad policies, which will nonetheless get through, has been amplified in recent years by loss of expertise and institutional memory in departments caused by rapid staff turnover at upper levels,[77] and perhaps also by increasing nervousness among Permanent Secretaries, as Accounting Officers, about being seen to obstruct ministerial wishes.[78] Their own increased mobility, and reduced expectations of tenure at the head of any given department that followed the Coalition's imposition of five-year tenure periods for the Senior Civil Service, may reinforce this tendency. A remarkable articulation of the tensions between central and departmental ministerial standpoints can be found in Michael Gove's Ditchley speech, with which we began this chapter. As Cabinet Office Minister, Gove held political responsibility for all the Office's centralizing, guidance, and harmonization activities. Yet some of his most impassioned language was reserved for an attack on the attitudes and institutions that act as a drag on innovation and experimentation in government. Citing initiatives of his own as Education Secretary which he admitted were 'flawed' or 'a fiasco' but to which he nonetheless attributed—ultimately—major benefits, he complained:

> Sadly far too often, innovation in Government is treated as though it were a mischief rather than a model. The default mechanism of the National Audit Office, Public Accounts Committee, other select committees and various commentators is that any departure from the status quo must be assumed to be more downside than upside . . . The whole culture of Government, and the wider world of political commentary, is hostile to risk, adventure, experimentation and novelty.[79]

How this culture was to be changed, while other steps he recommended—like rigorous and fearless evaluation of policy and projects, and the extension of Treasury scrutiny to take account of social value as well as cost—might work to reinforce it, he did not say.

V The Constitution Within the Executive: Bringing the Law Back In?

Crises and reform notwithstanding, the UK executive, in 2024, looks and acts much as it did at the beginning of the century. Its work continues to be carried out by a congeries of departments supervising a large and unstable mass of other public bodies, with little centralization of functions and an unreliable system of internal control and

[77] Sasse and Norris (n 44).
[78] See chapter 7, section V.
[79] Gove (n 1).

coordination. This system, it is widely agreed, fails to provide the standard of executive performance that is required and expected.

> Reform is necessary . . . as a means of delivering the better Britain that the public demands and deserves.[80]
>
> The arrangements for governance and accountability of the Civil Service are unclear, opaque and incomplete . . . The centre is . . . unwieldy, with confusion about where responsibilities lie and a lack of clear lines of accountability.[81]
>
> No.10 Downing Street, the Cabinet Office and the Treasury are not capable of meeting the challenges facing the United Kingdom in the 2020s and beyond. The centre of government must become more strategic, better able to set direction and hold the rest of government accountable for delivery.[82]

These diagnoses have been accompanied by comprehensive prescriptions for reform. Remarkably, in the eyes of a constitutional lawyer, they ignore totally, or set to one side, the possibility that the legal structure of the executive might in some way be contributing to the problem, or that legal change might be a means of addressing it. So far as official documentation is concerned, this presumably reflects the belief, most clearly articulated in the Law Officers' guidance on legislation, that 'legislation should not be used to deal with what is essentially an internal matter within the UK Government'.[83] Because of this principle—brandished in defence of executive autonomy—it is not 'necessary or appropriate' to provide by legislation for one part of the executive to obtain the consent of another before it acts. While the Law Officers' statement carries the implication that this is a law-free area where only political and bureaucratic norms hold sway, the organization of the executive is in fact comprehensively ordered by statute insofar as legislation determines who, within the executive, gets to exercise the powers that it confers. As the powers of government over the lives of citizens have extended and multiplied, we have experienced a century or more of legislative practice under which individual ministers, rather than any agency at the centre of government, or government as a whole, hold statutory powers. Taken in conjunction with the Prime Minister's prerogative powers (as the Monarch's adviser on the organization of the executive and the choice of ministers), this produces the paradoxical result that, *in law*, the Prime Minister enjoys unfettered power over the structure of the government but no power at all over most of what it does.[84]

Proclaiming, in this situation, that legislative stipulation of intra-executive controls or consents cannot be 'necessary or appropriate' shows a remarkable, and excessive, faith in the political and financial instruments of internal control and

[80] HM Government, *Declaration on Government Reform* (n 74) 3.

[81] Lord Maude, *Independent Review of Governance and Accountability in the Civil Service* (13 November 2023) 5.

[82] Commission on the Centre of Government, *Power with Purpose* (Institute for Government March 2024) 7.

[83] Attorney General's Office and Legal Secretariat of the Advocate-General for Scotland, *Working with the Law Officers on Legislation: A Guide for Departments* (December 2019) para 15.

[84] Prerogative and (some) common law powers, and powers vested by statute in His Majesty or 'His Majesty in Council' provide the exception.

coordination whose operations we have documented in this book and whose limitations we have summarized in this chapter. This position also ignores the fact that the Treasury controls on which governments today rely when political leverage fails are themselves grounded in legislation—prerogative originally, parliamentary today. External commentators have not been so sanguine. In 2022 a report by the Institute for Government put forward the idea of a statute for the Civil Service that would make officials explicitly responsible for maintaining the capability of the service over the longer term while not impinging on ministerial responsibility for policy.[85] One proposed support for this responsibility was direct statutory authority for the Cabinet Secretary to set benchmarks for shared practices across government, and to enforce them where needed—in other words, to move the basis for compliance with the government functional standards and other similar guidance from departmental consent to legal obligation.[86]

The government, as we have seen, preferred to respond to Lord Maude's demonstration of lack of compliance with the functional standards by seeking reinforcement from Treasury control, obliging Accounting Officers, through a 2023 amendment to *Managing Public Money*, to 'comply with the functional standards'.[87] Failure to comply would in consequence be 'irregular', but it might be difficult to link such non-compliance with specific financial transactions, essential if the issue was to be the subject of report by the Comptroller and Auditor General. Reinforcement might thus be purely cosmetic; and in any event, the move offers no support for central guidance outside the functions programme.

Lord Maude, despite his complaints about the operation of functional standards, was not prepared to contemplate the kind of legislative solution proposed by the Institute for Government. Introducing a statutory basis for what he called the 'stewardship' obligation of the Civil Service

> would represent a major constitutional reform, with all the attendant controversy and delay. It would set up significant potential conflict between the [Head of the Civil Service](HoCS) and the Prime Minister, when, for example, the HoCS felt obliged to disobey a Prime Minister's instruction on the basis that it conflicted with the statutory obligation to pursue reform . . . Of course that conflict can occur with the arrangements proposed in this review. I am clear that if that conflict were to arise, the will of the government of the day must prevail. The remedy lies not in statutory law, but in transparency.[88]

Maude's proposal, in his 2023 *Independent Review of Governance and Accountability in the Civil Service*, was that a similar result could be achieved through the delegation by the Prime Minister to the Head of the Civil Service (a new post,

[85] Alex Thomas and others, *A New Statutory Role for the Civil Service* (Institute for Government March 2022).

[86] Thomas (n 42) 34–35, 41. See also Commission on the Centre of Government, *Power with Purpose: Final Report* (Institute for Government March 2024) 100–01.

[87] *MPM* (May 2023) para 4.2.1.

[88] Lord Maude, *Independent Review of Governance and Accountability in the Civil Service* (13 November 2023) paras 4.53, 4.54

separated from that of Cabinet Secretary) of responsibility to implement an agreed programme of Civil Service reform, based on the Prime Minister's statutory power, as Minister for the Civil Service, to manage the service under the Constitutional Reform and Governance Act 2010.[89] In fact, of course, this remedy, no less than the Institute for Government's, does lie in statutory law, but with the reassuring wrapping of prime-ministerial discretion under an established statute. What we should also notice, though, is that there is nothing in the 2010 Act to restrict the subject-matter of prime-ministerial delegations to the Head of the Civil Service to specific programmes of reform. Functional standards, and much other central guidance, clearly fall within the rubric of 'management of the civil service'. Maude's proposals for strengthening cross-government working in fact went further: each function, he thought, should be led by a Chief Officer, appointed at Permanent Secretary level, who should be directly accountable to parliamentary select committees in certain circumstances, to ensure that 'horizontal' accountability (across departments) gets the same scrutiny as 'vertical' accountability within them.

Maude's report received the briefest of acknowledgments from the government that commissioned his inquiry, and his specific recommendations may be destined for the well-populated graveyard of unimplemented reform proposals, but this proposal is significant as evoking the possibility of a direct central control, emanating from the Prime Minister and grounded in legislation, of the activity of civil servants. The device of delegation may reduce the risk of undesirable judicial review that would, according to the Law Officers, arise from legislation subjecting one minister's activity to the consent of another. The omission of the departmental minister from the envisaged line of command offers a protection against claims of a resurgence of 'presidentialization' that would be evoked by any proposal to enlarge the legal powers of the Prime Minister vis-à-vis ministers, such as the sample Prime Minister (Office, Role and Functions) Bill published by the House of Commons Political and Constitutional Reform Committee in 2014;[90] but it risks transposing, to the arena of departmental management, the potential conflicts for which Maude criticized the Institute for Government proposal. A Permanent Secretary required to manage their department in a way unacceptable to its minister would not be in a comfortable position.

Maude's proposal, and those of the Institute for Government, nonetheless deserve the scrutiny and criticism of constitutional lawyers, alongside the consideration they receive from political scientists and public administration specialists. Along with earlier initiatives like the Political and Constitutional Reform Committee's proposal above and Jack Straw's idea of a Cabinet Government Act,[91] they should be at the centre of a more far-reaching constitutional debate about the executive than Maude was prepared to contemplate, one that does not take for granted the existing legal framework through which the powers of the executive are allocated and exercised. We do not need to look far for alternatives. Even the identity of ministerial responsibilities

[89] ibid Annexes 5 and 5A.

[90] House of Commons Political and Constitutional Reform Committee, *Role and Powers of the Prime Minister* (HC 2014–15, 351) app 3. This went so far as to provide, in cl 7, that, '[f]or the avoidance of doubt, any power under statue *[sic]* which may be exercised by a Secretary of State may be exercised by the Prime Minister'.

[91] ibid para 23.

with departmental functions, assumed in all these reform discussions, is not an inevitable feature of 'Westminster-model' constitutions. Devolution legislation confers statutory powers on the Scottish (or Welsh) Ministers collectively, with the consequence that statutory functions may legally be exercisable by any minister and that the First Minister may determine administratively which minister is to exercise any particular statutory function by allocating the relevant ministerial portfolio. This enabled the Scottish Government, in 2007, to abolish the system of departments inherited upon devolution and instead to give the Directors-General who previously ran them a collective responsibility for carrying forward overall governmental priorities, transferring to Directors, at the next level below, responsibility for policy and operational oversight of the distinct functions of the Scottish Government.[92] In Australia, too, the system of 'Administrative Arrangements Orders' makes for a looser and more flexible relationship between ministerial portfolios and departmental boundaries.[93] While these alternatives may carry their own risks,[94] they at least demonstrate that existing legal arrangements need pose no barrier to reform.

The general election of July 2024 opened a new window of opportunity for this sort of discussion, which this book has sought to support and inform by documenting a quarter of a century of experience of executive operation, demonstrating the flexibility of which it is capable and identifying the constraints that limit its effectiveness.

[92] Sir John Elvidge, *Northern Exposure: Lessons from the First Twelve Years of Devolved Government in Scotland* (Institute for Government 2011) 31. Since 2000 the Scottish Government has had a single Permanent Secretary and 'Accountable Officer': Public Finance and Accountability (Scotland) Act 2000, s 14.

[93] See further chapter 3, n 25.

[94] In Australia, for example, prime-ministerial abuse of these arrangements was documented in Hon Virginia Bell, *Report of the Inquiry into the Appointment of the Former Prime Minister to Administer Multiple Departments* (Commonwealth of Australia, 25 November 2022).

Bibliography

1 Books, articles, and other unofficial publications

Allen G, *The Last Prime Minister* (Andrews UK 2003, rev edn 2017)

Anderson Sir J, 'The Machinery of Government' (1946) 30 Public Administration 147

Anthony S, *Public Relations and the Making of Modern Britain* (Manchester UP 2012)

ASA, *Our History* <www.asa.org.uk/about-asa-and-cap/our-history.html>

—— *Ruling on Department for Work and Pensions in Association with Associated Newspapers* (6 November 2019) <www.asa.org.uk/rulings/department-for-work-and-pensions-G19-1021769.html>

—— *Ruling on Department for Levelling Up, Housing and Communities* (12 October 2022) <www.asa.org.uk/rulings/department-for-levelling-up--housing-and-communities-a22-1154358-departm ent-for-levelling-up--housing-and-communities.html>

—— *News* (26 April 2023) <www.asa.org.uk/news/why-we-don-t-regulate-political-ads.html>

—— and CAP, *Rulings* <www.asa.org.uk/codes-and-rulings/rulings.html>

Baker A, *Prime Ministers and the Rule Book* (Politico's 2000)

Barber M, *Instruction to Deliver: Tony Blair, Public Services and the Challenge of Achieving Targets* (Politico's 2007)

Barnard B, *Open, Meritocratic and Transparent: Reforming Civil Service Appointments* (Policy Exchange November 2021)

Barwell G, *Chief of Staff: Notes from Downing Street* (Atlantic Books 2021)

Bateman W, *Public Finance and Parliamentary Constitutionalism* (CUP 2020)

Bell S, Hindmoor A, and Bols F, 'Persuasion as Governance: A State-Centric Relational Perspective' (2010) 88 Public Administration 851

Bell V, *Report of the Inquiry into the Appointment of the Former Prime Minister to Administer Multiple Departments* (Commonwealth of Australia, 25 November 2022) <www.smh.com.au/interactive/hub/media/tearout-excerpt/11872/ministries-inquiry-report.pdf>

Benn T, *Against the Tide: Diaries 1973–76* (Arrow Books 1990)

Bennett R and Tomkins R, 'Government advertising spending tops £30m' *Financial Times* (25 April 2001)

Black J, 'The Credit Crisis and the Constitution' in Dawn Oliver, Tony Prosser, and Richard Rawlings (eds), *The Regulatory State: Constitutional Implications* (OUP 2010)

Blick A and Jones G, *Premiership: the Development, Nature and Power of the British Prime Minister* (Imprint Academic 2010)

Boin A and T'Hart P, 'From Crisis to Reform? Exploring Three Post-COVID Pathways' (2022) 41 Policy and Society 13

Bridges Sir E, *The Treasury* (2nd edn, Allen and Unwin 1966)

Buckland R, Lord Chancellor Speaks at UCL Conference on the Constitution <www.gov.uk/government/speeches/lord-chancellor-speaks-at-ucl-conference-on-the-constitution>

Burch M and Holliday I, *The British Cabinet System* (Prentice Hall 1996)

—— 'The Prime Minister's and Cabinet Offices: An Executive Office in All But Name' (1999) 52 Parliamentary Affairs 32

Cain L, *Modernising the Government Communication Service*, guest paper (Institute for Government September 2021)

Chapman R, *Ethics in the British Civil Service* (Routledge 1988)

Chester N, *The English Administrative System 1780–1870* (Clarendon Press 1981)

Chote R and others, 'The IFS Green Budget: January 2007' (Institute for Fiscal Studies 2007) <www.ifs.org.uk/green-budget/2007>

——'The IFS Green Budget: January 2009' <www.ifs.org.uk/green-budget/2009>

Clyne R and Davies N, *Outcome Delivery Plans: The Case for Keeping and Improving the Government's Performance Framework* (Institute for Government September 2022)

Commission on the Centre of Government, *Power with Purpose: Final Report* (Institute for Government March 2024)

Commission for Smarter Government, *Departmental Boards: Boosting Reform* (April 2021)

Conservative Party (Great Britain), *The Conservative Manifesto 2010, Invitation to Join the Government of Britain* (2010)

——*The Conservative Party Manifesto 2015* (2015)

—— *Get Brexit Done: Unleash Britain's Potential: The Conservative Party and Unionist Party Manifesto 2019* (2019)

Costello M, 'Northern Rock blows a hole in government's debt pledge' *The Times* (7 February 2008) <www.thetimes.co.uk/article/northern-rock-blows-a-hole-in-chancellors-debt-pledge-wswrz0fbb7v>

Da Costa N, 'The Proposed Restructuring of Number Ten Risks Mistaking a Personnel Problem for a Structural One' (*conservativehome*, 21 March 2022)

Daintith T, 'Between Domestic Democracy and an Alien Rule of Law? Some Thoughts on the "Independence" of the Bank of England' [1995] Public Law 118

——'The Legal Effects of the Appropriation Act' [1998] Public Law 552

——'Spin: A Constitutional and Legal Analysis' (2001) 7 European Public Law 593

——'"A very good day to get out anything we want to bury"' [2002] Public Law 13

——'Government Companies as Regulators' (2019) 82 Modern Law Review 397

——and Ng Y-F, 'Executives' in Cheryl Saunders and Adrienne Stone (eds), *The Oxford Handbook of the Australian Constitution* (OUP 2018)

Darling A, *Back from the Brink: 1000 Days at Number 11* (Atlantic Books 2011)

Dennis AH, 'The Legal Departments of the Crown' (1926) 4 Public Administration 141

Dewar D and Funnell W, *A History of British National Audit: The Pursuit of Accountability* (OUP 2017)

Dunt I, *How Westminster Works . . . and Why it Doesn't* (Weidenfeld & Nicolson 2023)

Dyson (Lord), 'Criticising Judges: Fair Game or Off-Limits' (Third Annual BAILI Lecture, 27 November 2014) <www.judiciary.uk/wp-content/uploads/2014/11/bailli-critising-judges.pdf>

Edwards JLlJ, *The Law Officers of the Crown* (Sweet and Maxwell 1964)

——*The Attorney-General, Politics and the Public Interest* (Sweet and Maxwell 1984)

Edwards O, 'UK Government Largely Run on WhatsApp Says Ex-Comms Chief' *BBC News* (1 June 2023) <www.bbc.co.uk/news/uk-wales-65776560>

Ekins R, *The Case for Reforming Judicial Review* (Policy Exchange December 2020)

——Laws S, and Casey C, *Government Lawyers, the Civil Service Code and the Rule of Law* (Policy Exchange 2023)

Ellison R, *Red Tape: Managing Excess in Law, Regulation and the Courts* (CUP 2018)

Elston T, 'Principles Meet Practicalities: Challenges of Accountability Reform in the British Civil Service' in Tom Christensen and Per Lægreid (eds), *The Routledge Handbook to Accountability and Welfare State Reforms in Europe* (Routledge 2017)

Elvidge Sir J, *Northern Exposure: Lessons from the First Twelve Years of Devolved Government in Scotland* (Institute for Government 2011)

Emmerson C, Frayne C, and Love S, *Updating the UK's Code for Fiscal Stability* (WP04/29) (Institute for Fiscal Studies 2004)

Endicott T, *The Stubborn Stain Theory of Executive Power: from Magna Carta to Miller* (Policy Exchange 2017)

Engle Sir G, 'Bills are made to pass as razors are made to sell: practical constraints on the preparation of legislation' [1983] Statute Law Review 7

Fawcett P and Rhodes RAW, 'Central Government' in Anthony Seldon (ed), *Blair's Britain 1997–2007* (CUP 2007)

Fearon P, 'Energy Safety Regulation: Prescriptive versus Goal-based Approaches' (Presentation, University of Melbourne, 21 March 2016, on file with author)
Feldman D, 'Legislation that Bears no Law' (2016) 37 Statute Law Review 212
Flinders M, *Delegated Governance and the British State: Walking without Order* (OUP 2008)
—— and Kelso A, 'Mind the Gap: Political Analysis, Public Expectations and the Parliamentary Decline Thesis' (2011) 13 British Journal of Politics and International Relations 249
Foley M, *The Rise of the British Presidency* (Manchester UP 1993)
Forbes C, 'The Changing Role and Status of Government Communication during the Covid-19 Crisis' (2021) 14 ESSACHESS—Journal for Communication Studies 33
Foster C, *British Government in Crisis* (Hart Publishing 2005)
Foster CD and Plowden FJ, *The State under Stress: Can the Hollow State be Good Government?* (Open UP 1996)
Foster M, 'Existing extended ministerial offices "to be dismantled", Cabinet Office confirms' *Civil Service World* (17 January 2017) <www.civilserviceworld.com/professions/article/existing-extended-ministerial-offices-to-be-dismantled-cabinet-office-confirms>
Fox R and Blackwell J, *The Devil is in The Detail: Parliament and Delegated Legislation* (Hansard Society 2014)
Gallagher J, 'Intergovernmental Relations: Two Decades of Co-operation, Competition and Constitutional Change' in Michael Keating (ed), *The Oxford Handbook of Scottish Politics* (OUP 2020)
Garland R, 'Between Media and Politics: Can Government Press Officers Hold the Line in the Age of "Political Spin"? The Case of the UK After 1997' (PhD thesis, London School of Economics 2016)
Gee G and McCorkindale C (eds), 'The Political Constitution at Forty' (2019) 30 King's Law Journal 1
Gill M and Dalton G, *Reforming Public Appointments* (Institute for Government August 2022)
Gordon M, '*R (on the application of FDA) v Prime Minister*: The Ministerial Code, Justiciability, and the Limits of Judicial Review' [2023] Public Law 1
—— and Tucker A (eds), *The New Labour Constitution: Twenty Years On* (Hart Publishing 2022)
Gould P, *The Unfinished Revolution: How the Modernisers Saved the Labour Party* (Little, Brown 1998)
Greaves HRG, 'The Structure of the Civil Service' in William A Robson (ed), *The Civil Service in Britain and France* (The Hogarth Press 1956)
Gregory A, 'UK Government Communications: Full Circle in the 21st Century?' (2012) 38 Public Relations Review 367
—— 'UK Government Communication: The Cameron Years and Their Ongoing Legacy' (2019) 45 Public Relations Review 202
Guerin B, McCrae J, and Shepheard M, *Accountability in Modern Government: What Are the Issues?* (Institute for Government 2018)
Guicciardini F, *Maxims and Reflections of a Renaissance Statesman* (M Domandi tr, Peter Smith 1970)
Haddon C, Hogarth R, and Nice A, *Judicial Review and Policy-Making: The Role of Legal Advice in Government* (Institute for Government April 2021)
Haggard S and Kaufman R, *Backsliding: Democratic Regress in the Contemporary World* (CUP 2021)
Hailsham (Lord), 'Elective Dictatorship' *The Listener* (21 October 1976) 496–500
Haldane Viscount Haldane of Cloan, 'An Organised Civil Service' (1923) 1 The Journal of Public Administration 8
Hamilton I, 'Sir Warren Fisher and the Public Service' (1951) 29 Public Administration 3
Hansard Society, 'Proposals for a New System for Delegated Legislation' A Working Paper of the Hansard Society Delegated Legislation Review (Hansard Society February 2023)
Harris J, *Following the Pound: The Accounting Officer in Central Government* (Institute for Government [nd])
Hazell R and Glover M, 'The Impact of Freedom of Information on Whitehall' (2011) 89 Public Administration 1664
—— and Riddell P, *Trust in Public Life: Restoring the Role of Constitutional Watchdogs* (UCL Constitution Unit 2024)
—— and others, *Critical Friends? The Role of Non Executives on Whitehall Boards* (UCL Constitution Unit January 2018)

Hennessy P, *Whitehall* (Fontana Press 1990)
—— *The Prime Minister: The Office and its Holders since 1945* (Allen Lane The Penguin Press 2000)
—— *Land of Shame and Glory: Britain 2021–2022* (Haus Publishing 2023)
Heywood S, *What Does Jeremy Think? Jeremy Heywood and the Making of Modern Britain* (William Collins 2021)
Hickman T and Tan G, 'Reversing Parliamentary Defeat by Delegated Legislation: The Case of the Public Order Act 1986 (Serious Disruption to the Life of the Community) Regulations 2023' (*UK Const L Blog*, 22 May 2023) <https://ukconstitutionallaw.org/>
Hill (Lord) of Luton, *Both Sides of the Hill* (Heinemann 1964)
Holt R, *Second Among Equals: Chancellors of the Exchequer and the British Economy* (Profile Books 2001)
Hood C and others, *The Way the Money Goes: The Fiscal Constitution and Public Spending in the UK* (OUP 2023)
Hooper HJ, 'Delegated Legislation in an Unprincipled Constitution' in Richard Johnson and Yuan Yi Zhu (eds), *Sceptical Perspectives on the Changing Constitution of the United Kingdom* (Bloomsbury Publishing 2023)
Howard C, *Government Statistical Agencies and the Politics of Credibility* (CUP 2021)
Ilbert C, *Legislative Methods and Forms* (Clarendon Press 1901)
Ingham B, *Kill the Messenger* (HarperCollins 1991)
—— *The Wages of Spin* (John Murray 2003)
James H, 'The Role of the Central Office of Information' in Annabelle May and Kathryn Rowan (eds), *Inside Information: British Government and the Media* (Constable 1982)
Jennings I, *Cabinet Government* (3rd edn, CUP 1959)
John S, Roberts M, and Weeken O, 'The Bank of England's Special Liquidity Scheme' (2012) Q1 Bank of England Quarterly Bulletin <www.bankofengland.co.uk/quarterly-bulletin/2012/q1/the-bank-of-englands-special-liquidity-scheme>
Johnstone R, 'Government confirms comms reform drive' *Civil Service World* (6 July 2020) <www.civilserviceworld.com/professions/article/government-confirms-comms-reform-drive>
Jones C, 'Our Forgotten Constitutional Guardians: Preserving Respect for the Law' (2021) 42 Statute Law Review 1
Jones GW, 'The United Kingdom' in William Plowden (ed), *Advising the Rulers* (Basil Blackwell 1987)
Jones J, 'UK in a Changing Europe' (Interview, 6 May 2021) <https://ukandeu.ac.uk/interview-pdf/?personid = 44845>
Keegan W, *The Prudence of Mr Gordon Brown* (Wiley 2003)
Keeler JTS, 'Opening the Window for Reform: Mandates, Crisis, and Extraordinary Policy-making' (1993) 25 Comparative Political Studies 433
Kell M, 'An Assessment of Fiscal Rules in the United Kingdom' (2005) IMF Working Paper WP/01/91
Kenny M, Rycroft P, and Sheldon J, *Union at the Crossroads. Can the British State Handle the Challenges of Devolution?* (The Constitution Society 2021)
Kerry M, 'Administrative Law and the Administrator' (1983) 38 Management in Government 168
—— 'Administrative Law and Judicial Review—The Practical Effects of Developments over the Last 25 Years on Administration in Central Government' (1986) 64 Public Administration 163
King A, *The British Constitution* (OUP 2007)
—— and Crewe I, *The Blunders of Our Governments* (Oneworld 2013)
Kingdon JW, *Agendas, Alternatives, and Public Policies* (Little, Brown 1984)
Kreppel A, 'Typologies and Classifications' in Shane Martin, Thomas Saalfeld, and Kaare Strom (eds), *Oxford Handbook of Legislative Studies* (OUP 2014)
Labour Party, *New Labour: Because Britain Deserves Better* (1996)
—— *Report of the Joint Consultative Committee on Constitutional Reform* (March 1997)
—— *Change: Labour Party Manifesto 2024* (June 2024)
Laws S, *The Treasury Devil and the Scandal that Never Was* (Policy Exchange 20 June 2022)
Lee J and Spanier G, '"Single-minded and unavoidable": how the government honed "Stay Home" message' *Campaign* (11 May 2020) <www.campaignlive.co.uk/article/single-minded-unavoidable-government-honed-stay-home-message/1682448>

Lee JM, *Reviewing the Machinery of Government 1942–1952. An Essay on the Anderson Committee and its Successors* (Birkbeck College 1977)
—— Jones GW, and Burnham J, *At the Centre of Whitehall: Advising the Prime Minister and Cabinet* (Macmillan 1998)
Le Sueur A, 'The Judicial Review Debate: From Partnership to Friction' [1996] Government and Opposition 8
Letwin O, *Hearts and Minds: The Battle for the Conservative Party from Thatcher to the Present* (Biteback 2017)
Lewis P and Mulcahy L, 'Government Lawyers: Technicians, Policy Shapers and Organisational Brakes' (2021) 28 International Journal of the Legal Profession 23
LGC contributor, 'Cabinet Reshuffle: Briefing from No 10 and Summary' *Local Government Chronicle* (13 June 2003) <www.lgcplus.com/archive/cabinet-reshuffle-briefing-from-number-10-and-summary-13-06-2003>
Lienert I, 'Who Controls the Budget: The Legislature or the Executive?' (2005) IMF Working Paper WP/05/15
—— 'Should Advanced Countries Adopt a Fiscal Responsibility Law?' (2010) IMF Working Paper WP/10/254
Lipsey D, *The Secret Treasury: How Britain's Economy is Really Run* (Viking 2000)
Lodge G and Rogers B, *Whitehall's Black Box: Accountability and Performance in the Senior Civil Service* (Institute for Public Policy Research 2006)
Ludlow J, 'The Queen's Speech 2005: How Government Laws Are Initiated in the United Kingdom' (2005) 31 Commonwealth Law Bulletin 61
Lowe R, *The Official History of the British Civil Service*, vol I: *The Fulton Years, 1966–81* (Routledge 2011)
—— and Pemberton H, *The Official History of the British Civil Service. Reforming the Civil Service*, vol II: *The Thatcher and Major Revolutions, 1982–97* (Routledge 2020)
McCormick C, *The Constitutional Legitimacy of Law Officers in the United Kingdom* (Hart Publishing 2022)
McCrae J and Gold J, *Professionalising Whitehall* (Institute for Government 2017)
McDonald A (ed), *Reinventing Britain: Constitutional Change under New Labour* (Politico's 2007)
McDonald A, *Changing States, Changing Nations: Constitutional Reform and National Identity in the Late Twentieth Century* (Bloomsbury Publishing 2021)
McEldowney JF, 'The Contingencies Fund and the Parliamentary Scrutiny of Public Finance' [1988] Public Law 232
McKenna A, *100 Years of Government Communication* (HM Government 2018)
Mackenzie K, 'How the Reforms Came About' in Andrew McDonald (ed), *Reinventing Britain: Constitutional Change and New Labour* (Politico's 2007)
Mackenzie WJM and Grove JW, *Central Administration in Britain* (Longmans 1957)
McLennan B, 'You Can Count on Us—with Confidence' (1995) 158 Journal of the Royal Statistical Society. Series A (Statistics in Society) 467
Mahmalat M and Curran D, 'Do Crises Induce Reform? A Critical Review of Conception, Methodology and Empirical Evidence of the "Crisis Hypothesis"' (2018) 32 Journal of Economic Surveys 613
Major Sir John, 'In Democracy we Trust? A Keynote Speech by the Rt Hon Sir John Major' (Institute for Government 10 February 2022)
Mandelson P and Liddle R, *The Blair Revolution: Can New Labour Deliver?* (Faber & Faber 1996)
Markson T, 'Attorney General accuses "overcautious" government lawyers of "hampering ministers"' *Civil Service World* (2 August 2022) <www.civilserviceworld.com/news/article/government-lawyers-too-cautious-says-attorney-general>
Marsh D, Richards D, and Smith M, *Changing Patterns of Governance in the United Kingdom: Reinventing Whitehall* (Palgrave 2001)
Martin C, Kan H, and Fink M, *Crisis Preparation in the Age of Long Emergencies. What Covid-19 Teaches us About the Capacity, Capability and Coordination Governments Need for Cross-cutting Crises* (Blavatnik School of Government 2023)

Maude F, 'I stress that I became disillusioned with the Service, not with Civil Servants' (Speaker's Lecture) (*conservativehome*, 13 September 2017)
Mitchell C, 'Recovery of Ultra Vires Payments by Public Bodies' [2010] Public Law 747
Moosavian R, 'Power/Knowledge Dynamics in the Attorney-General's Iraq War Advice' [2020] Public Law 72
Morrison H (Lord), *Government and Parliament: A Survey from the Inside* (OUP 1964)
Mount F, *The British Constitution Now: Recovery or Decline?* (William Heinemann 1992)
—— *Big Caesars and Little Caesars. How They Rise and How They Fall—from Julius Caesar to Boris Johnson* (Bloomsbury 2023)
Normington Sir D, 'The five reasons I'm concerned about plans to overhaul the public appointments process' *Civil Service World* (21 March 2016) <www.civilserviceworld.com/news/article/sir-david-normington-the-five-reasons-im-concerned-about-plans-to-overhaul-the-public-appointments-process>
Oborne P, *Alistair Campbell: New Labour and the Rise of the Media Class* (Aurum Press 1999)
O'Cinneide C, 'The UK's Post-Brexit "Constitutional Unsettlement"' (*Verfassungsblog*, 16 April 2021) <https://verfassungsblog.de/the-uks-post-brexit-constitutional-unsettlement/>
Ogilvy-Webb M, *The Government Explains. A Study of the Information Services* (Royal Institute of Public Administration 1965)
O'Halpin E, *Head of the Civil Service: A Study of Sir Warren Fisher* (Routledge 1989)
Ollerenshaw K, 'Impact Assessment as an Accountability Mechanism: Past, Present and Future' (*UK Const L Blog*, 9 November 2023) <https://ukconstitutionallaw.org/>
Padmore Sir T, 'Civil Service Establishments and the Treasury' in William A Robson (ed), *The Civil Service in Britain and France* (The Hogarth Press 1956)
Page J and others, *Leading Change in the Civil Service* (Institute for Government 2014)
Panchamia N and Thomas P, *Civil Service Reform in the Real World: Patterns of Success in UK Civil Service Reform* (Institute for Government March 2014)
—— *Capability Reviews* (Institute for Government [nd]) <www.instituteforgovernment.org.uk/sites/default/files/case study capabilities.pdf>
—— *Public Service Agreements and the Prime Minister's Delivery Unit* (Institute for Government [nd])
Parker S and others, *Shaping Up: A Whitehall for the Future* (Institute for Government 2010)
Parris H, *Constitutional Bureaucracy: The Development of British Central Administration since the Eighteenth Century* (Allen and Unwin 1969)
Paun A, *Supporting Ministers to Lead: Rethinking the Minister's Private Office* (Institute for Government March 2013)
—— and Harris J, *Accountability at the Top: Supporting Effective Leadership in Whitehall* (Institute for Government 2013)
—— and Munro R, *Governing in an Ever Looser Union* (Institute for Government 2015)
—— and others, *Sewel Convention* (Institute for Government February 2022)
Payne S, *The Fall of Boris Johnson: The Full Story* (Macmillan 2022)
Pearson J, Gash T, and Rutter R, *Out of the Ashes: Priorities for Reforming Arm's-length Government in the UK* (Institute for Government 2015)
Poirier J, *The Functions of Intergovernmental Agreements: Post-Devolution Concordats in a Comparative Perspective* (The Constitution Unit, UCL 2001)
—— and Saunders C, 'Conclusion' in Johanne Poirier, Cheryl Saunders, and John Kincaid (eds), *Intergovernmental Relations in Federal Systems. Comparative Structures and Dynamics* (OUP 2015)
Pollitt C, 'Bureaucracies Remember, Post-bureaucratic Organisations Forget?' (2009) 87 Public Administration 198
Powell J, *The New Machiavelli. How to Wield Power in the Modern World* (Vintage 2011)
Prosser T, '"An Opportunity to Take a More Fundamental Look at the Role of Government in Society": The Spending Review as Regulation' [2011] Public Law 596
—— *The Economic Constitution* (OUP 2014)
Pullinger J, 'The Creation of the Office for National Statistics' (1997) 65 International Statistical Review 291

Pywell S and West T, *Delegated Legislation: What Types Are There, and How Are They Made?* (Open University December 2023) <www.hansardsociety.org.uk/publications/delegated-legislation-what-types-are-there-and-how-are-they-made>
Rawlings HF, 'Judicial Review and the "Control of Government"' (1986) 64 Public Administration 135
Reid G, *The Politics of Financial Control: The Role of the House of Commons* (Hutchinson 1966)
Research Note: Special Advisers and Public Allegations of Misconduct 1997–2013 <www.ucl.ac.uk/constitution-unit/sites/constitution-unit/files/special_advisers_and_public_allegations_of_misconduct_1997_-_2013.pdf>
Riddell P, 'Blair as Prime Minister' in Anthony Seldon (ed), *The Blair Effect: The Blair Government 1997–2001* (Little, Brown and Company 2001)
—— 'The Coalition and the Executive' in Anthony Seldon and Mike Finn (eds), *The Coalition Effect 2010–2015* (CUP 2015)
Riley-Smith B, *The Right To Rule: Thirteen Years, Five Prime Ministers and the Implosion of the Tories* (John Murray 2023)
Romans JT, 'Moral Suasion as an Instrument of Economic Policy' (1966) 56 American Economic Review 1220
Roseveare H, *The Treasury 1660–1870* (Allen and Unwin 1973)
Royal Statistical Society, *A Vision for National Statistics* (September 2002)
Royal Statistical Society's Working Party on Official Statistics in the UK, 'Official Statistics: Counting with Confidence' (1991) 154 Journal of the Royal Statistical Society. Series A (Statistics in Society) 23
Russell M and Cowley P, 'The Policy Power of the Westminster Parliament: The "Parliamentary State" and the Empirical Evidence' (2016) 29 Governance 121
—— and Gover D, *Legislation at Westminster: Parliamentary Actors and Influence in the Making of British Law* (OUP 2017)
—— Gover D, and Wollter K, 'Does the Executive Dominate the Westminster Legislative Process?: Six Reasons for Doubt' (2016) 69 Parliamentary Affairs 286
Rutter J, *The Strange Case of Non-Ministerial Departments* (Institute for Government 2013)
Ryan M, 'The Constitutional Reform and Governance Act 2010: The Evolution and Development of a Constitutional Act' (2014) 35 Liverpool Law Review 233
Sasse T and Norris E, *Moving On: The Costs of High Staff Turnover in the Civil Service* (Institute for Government January 2019) <www.instituteforgovernment.org.uk/sites/default/files/publications/IfG_staff_turnover_WEB.pdf>
Sedley S, 'The Sound of Silence: Constitutional Law without a Constitution' (1994) 110 Law Quarterly Review 270
Seldon A and Lodge G, *Brown at 10* (Biteback Publishing 2010)
—— with Meakin J, *Blair Unbound* (Simon and Schuster 2007)
—— and Meakin J, *The Cabinet Office 1916–2016. The Birth of Modern Government* (Biteback Publishing 2016)
—— and Newell R, *Johnson At 10: The Inside Story* (Atlantic Books 2023)
Simcock AJC, 'One and Many—the Office of Secretary of State' (1992) 70 Public Administration 535
Smellie KB, *A Hundred Years of English Government* (Duckworth 1937)
Smith M, *The Core Executive in Britain* (Palgrave MacMillan 1998)
Stanley M, *Deregulation 1948–2006* <www.regulation.org.uk/deregulation-1948_to_2006.html>
—— *Special Advisers: Statistics* <www.civilservant.org.uk/spads-statistics.html>
—— *Permanent Secretaries' Objectives* <www.civilservant.org.uk/csr-permanent_secretaries_objectives.html>
—— *Key Facts* (June 2024) <www.civilservant.org.uk/information-numbers.html>
Steinbeis M, 'Right-Wing Crits' (*Verfassungsblog*, 15 November 2019) <https://verfassungsblog.de/right-wing-crits/>
Stephen, Sir James, letter in *Papers relating to the Re-organisation of the Civil Service*, Parl Pap (1854–55) vol 20
Stevens R, *The Independence of the Judiciary: The View from the Lord Chancellor's Office* (Clarendon Press 1993)
Straw J, *Last Man Standing: Memoirs of a Political Survivor* (Pan Books 2012)

—— *Ministers Reflect* (Institute for Government May 2016) <www.instituteforgovernment.org.uk/sites/default/files/2022-11/jack-straw-ministers-reflect.pdf>

Talbot C and Talbot C, 'One step forward, two steps back? The rise and fall of government's Next Steps agencies' *Civil Service World* (23 September 2019) <www.civilserviceworld.com/news/article/one-step-forward-two-steps-back-the-rise-and-fall-of-governments-next-steps-agencies>

Thain C, 'A Very Peculiar British Crisis?: Institutions, Ideas and Policy Responses to the Credit Crunch' (2009) 4 British Politics 434

Thomas A, *The Heart of the Problem. A Weak Centre is Undermining the UK Government* (Institute for Government January 2021)

—— and others, *A New Statutory Role for the Civil Service* (Institute for Government March 2022)

Thomas RM, *The British Philosophy of Administration: A Comparison of British and American Ideas 1900–1939* (Longmans 1978)

Tomkins R, 'Media monitoring figures may fuel accusations of spin as government outstrips Unilever and Procter and Gamble' *Financial Times* (16 April 2001)

Tomlinson J, Coakley N, and Gambroudes R, 'It's a Trap! The Changing Dynamics of Executive Engagement with Judicial Review' (*UK Const L Blog*, 28 July 2022) <https://ukconstitutionallaw.org/>

Tommasi M, 'Crisis, Political Institutions, and Policy Reform: It is not the Policy, it is the Polity, Stupid' (Paper presented at Annual World Bank Conference on Development Economics—Europe, June 2002) <https://cdi.mecon.gob.ar/bases/doc/cedi/dt73.pdf> and in slightly different form at <www.files.ethz.ch/isn/30248/2003-01.pdf>

Trench T, 'Washing Dirty Linen in Private: The Processes of Intergovernmental Relations and the Resolution of Disputes' in Alan Trench (ed), *Devolution and Power in the United Kingdom* (Manchester UP 2007)

Viney C and Poole T, 'Independent Fiscal Institutions' in Roger Masterman and Robert Schütze (eds), *The Cambridge Companion to Comparative Constitutional Law* (CUP 2019)

Waller P, 'Special Advisers and Communications' in Robert Hazell and Ben Yong (eds), *Special Advisers: Who They Are, What They Do and Why They Matter* (Hart Publishing 2014)

Wallis N, *The Great Post Office Scandal* (Bath Publishing 2021)

Warner J, 'The OBR has been a triumph of transparency—little wonder Truss wants rid' *The Telegraph* (24 August 2022) <www.telegraph.co.uk/business/2022/08/24/obr-has-triumph-transparency-little-wonder-truss-wants-rid/>

White A and Dunleavy P, *Making and Breaking Whitehall Departments: A Guide to Machinery of Government Changes* (Institute for Government 2010)

White H, *Held in Contempt: What's Wrong with the House of Commons?* (Manchester UP 2022)

Wilks S, 'Boardization and Corporate Governance in the UK as a Response to Depoliticization and Failing Accountability' (2007) 44 Public Policy and Administration 652

Willetts D, 'The Perils of Political Power' *Financial Times* (30 January 1997)

Wilson H, *The Governance of Britain* (Weidenfeld & Nicolson and Michael Joseph 1976)

Wilson JQ and Rachal P, 'Can Government Regulate Itself' (1977) 46 Public Interest 12

Wilson Sir R, 'Portrait of a Profession Revisited' (Speech, 26 March 2002) <www.civilservant.org.uk/library/2002_Portrait_of_a_Profession_Revisited.pdf>

Worthy B and Hazell R, 'Disruptive, Dynamic and Democratic? Ten Years of FOI in the UK' (2017) 70 Parliamentary Affairs 22

Wright M, *Treasury Control of the Civil Service 1854–1874* (Clarendon Press 1969)

Yeung K, 'Regulating Government Communications' (2006) 65 Cambridge Law Journal 53

Yong B, *Risk Management: Government Lawyers and the Provision of Legal Advice within Whitehall* (Constitution Society 2013)

—— and Hazell R, *Special Advisers: Who They Are, What They Do and Why They Matter* (Bloomsbury Publishing 2014)

Young AL, *Unchecked Power: How Recent Constitutional Reforms Are Threatening Democracy* (Bristol UP 2024)

2 Parliamentary, governmental, and other official publications

Andrew R, *Review of Government Legal Services* (Cabinet Office 1989)

The Andrew Review of Government Legal Services—Lawyers' Pay, National Archives file PO-CH/NL/0207, Part A (1988)

Attorney General, *Use of the Private Sector for Government Legal Work: Guidance* (mimeo, 1991)

—— *Guidance on Legal Risk* (2 August 2022) <www.gov.uk/government/publications/attorney-generals-guidance-on-legal-risk>

—— Attorney General's Guidance on Legal Risk (November 2024) <www.gov.uk/government/publications/guidance-attorney-generals-guidance-on-legal-risk>

Attorney General's Office, *AGO Business Plan 2020–21*

—— and Crown Prosecution Service, *Framework Agreement between the Law Officers and the Director of Public Prosecutions* (18 December 2020) <https://assets.publishing.service.gov.uk/government/uploads/system/uploads/attachment_data/file/965815/Framework_agreement_between_the_Law_Officers_and_the_Director_of_Public_Prosecutions__CPS.pdf>

—— and Legal Secretariat of the Advocate-General for Scotland, *Working with the Law Officers on Legislation: A Guide for Departments* (December 2019)

—— and Serious Fraud Office, *Framework Agreement between the Law Officers and the Director of the Serious Fraud Office* (21 January 2019) <https://assets.publishing.service.gov.uk/government/uploads/system/uploads/attachment_data/file/772685/SFO_Framework_Agreement.pdf>

Better Regulation Commission, *Risk, Responsibility and Regulation—Whose Risk Is It Anyway?* (October 2006) <www.regulation.org.uk/library/2006_risk_responsbillity_regulation.pdf>

Better Regulation Task Force, *Regulation—Less is More: Reducing Burdens, Improving Outcomes* (March 2005) <www.regulation.org.uk/library/2005_less_is_more.pdf>

Blair T, Speech given by the Prime Minister on the subject of Civil Service Reform (24 February 2024) <www.civilservant.org.uk/library/2004_PM_CSR_Delivery_Speech.pdf>

Board of Enquiry, *Report of the Board of Enquiry appointed by the Prime Minister to investigate certain Statements affecting Civil Servants* (Cmd 3037, 1928)

Braverman S, 'Judicial Review Trends and Forecasts 2021: Accountability and the Constitution' (Speech to Public Law Project Conference, 19 October 2021) <www.gov.uk/government/speeches/judicial-review-trends-and-forecasts-2021-accountability-and-the-constitution>

Cabinet Office, *The Civil Service: Continuity and Change* (Cm 2627, 1994)

—— *Responsibilities for Recruitment to the Civil Service* (1994)

—— *The Civil Service: Taking Forward Continuity and Change* (Cm 2748, 1995)

—— *Guidance on Guidance* (1996)

—— *Cabinet Committee Business: A Guide for Departments* (1997)

—— *Code of Practice on Access to Government Information* (1994, rev 1997)

—— *Code of Practice on Access to Government Information: Guidance on Interpretation* (2nd edn, 1997) <www.cfoi.org.uk/wp-content/uploads/2014/01/copguidance.pdf>

—— *Ministerial Code: A Code of Conduct and Guidance on Procedures for Ministers* (1997)

—— *Directory of Civil Service Guidance*, vols 1 and 2 (2000)

—— *Ministerial Code: A Code of Conduct and Guidance on Procedures for Ministers* (July 2001)

—— *Civil Service Reform: Delivery and Values* (2004)

—— *A Draft Civil Service Bill: A Consultation Document* (Cm 6373, 2004)

—— *Public Bodies: A Guide for Departments* (June 2006) <www.gov.uk/government/publications/public-bodies-a-guide-for-departments>

—— *Annual Report and Accounts 2008–09* (July 2009)

—— *Civil Service Code* (2010, revd 2015)

—— *Draft Structural Reform Plan* (June 2010) <https://assets.publishing.service.gov.uk/media/5a790b5c40f0b676f4a7d6e3/srp-cabinet-office_3.pdf>

—— *Review of Pre-Release Access to Official Statistics* [nd – 2011?] <https://assets.publishing.service.gov.uk/government/uploads/system/uploads/attachment_data/file/62084/pre-release-stats.pdf>

—— *The Cabinet Manual: A Guide to Laws, Conventions and Rules on the Operation of Government* (October 2011)

—— *Post-legislative scrutiny of the Statistics and Registration Service Act 2007* (Cm 8216, November 2011)
—— *Public Bodies Reform—Proposals for Change* (14 December 2011) <www.gov.uk/government/publications/public-bodies-reform-reports>
—— *Memorandum of Understanding and Supplementary Agreements between the United Kingdom Government, the Scottish Ministers, the Welsh Ministers and the Northern Ireland Executive Committee* (October 2013)
—— *Extended Ministerial Offices—Guidance for Departments* (2013, rev June 2015) <https://assets.publishing.service.gov.uk/media/5a807a3c40f0b62305b8b627/EMOguidance01062015.docx.pdf>
—— *Giving Evidence to Select Committees: Guidance for Civil Servants* (October 2014) <https://assets.publishing.service.gov.uk/government/uploads/system/uploads/attachment_data/file/364600/Osmotherly_Rules_October_2014.pdf>
—— *A Better Civil Service: Triennial Review of the Civil Service Commission* (December 2014)
—— *The Functional Model: A Model for More Efficient and Effective Government* (March 2015) <www.gov.uk/government/publications/functional-model-for-more-efficient-and-effective-government>
—— SRO appointment letter (April 2015) <https://assets.publishing.service.gov.uk/government/uploads/system/uploads/attachment_data/file/434057/SRO_letter_next_generation_shared_services_programme.pdf>
—— *Machinery of Government Changes: Guidance* (October 2015) <www.gov.uk/government/publications/machinery-of-government-changes-information#full-publication-update-history>
—— *Civil Service Management Code* (November 2016)
—— *Governance Code on Public Appointments* (December 2016, rev July 2024)
—— *Report on the Outcome of the Classification Review* [nd but 2016] <www.gov.uk/government/publications/classification-review-of-public-bodies-outcome-report>
—— *Better Public Appointments: A Review of the Public Appointments Process* (March 2016)
—— *Tailored Reviews of Public Bodies: Guidance* (March 2016) <www.gov.uk/government/publications/tailored-reviews-of-public-bodies-guidance>
—— *Classification of Public Bodies: Guidance for Departments* (Public Bodies Handbook—Part 1) (April 2016)
—— *Business Appointment Rules for Ministers* (December 2016)
—— *Code of Conduct for Special Advisers* (December 2016)
—— *Guide to Making Legislation* (July 2017, rev 2022)
—— *Government Security Classifications* (May 2018) <https://assets.publishing.service.gov.uk/government/uploads/system/uploads/attachment_data/file/715778/May-2018_Government-Security-Classifications-2.pdf>
—— *The Approvals Process for the Creation of New Arm's-Length Bodies: Guidance for Departments* (Public Bodies Handbook—Part 2) (2018)
—— *Executive Agencies: A Guide for Departments* (2018) <https://assets.publishing.service.gov.uk/government/uploads/system/uploads/attachment_data/file/690636/Executive_Agencies_Guidance.PDF>
—— *Annual Report and Accounts 2017–18* (July 2018)
—— *Agreement on Joint Working* (July 2019) <www.gov.uk/government/publications/draft-principles-for-intergovernmental-relations>
—— *Review of UK Government Union Capability* (November 2019)
—— *Shared Services Strategy for Government* (March 2021)
—— *Public Bodies 2020* (15 July 2021) <www.gov.uk/government/publications/public-bodies-2020>
—— *Cabinet Office Outcome Delivery Plan: 2021 to 2022* (July 2021)
—— *Annual Report and Accounts 2020–21* (July 2021)
—— *Review into the Development and Use of Supply Chain Finance (and Associated Schemes) in Government Part 2: Recommendations and Suggestions* (August 2021)
—— *Statement of Government Policy: Standards in Public Life* (27 May 2022)
—— *Ministerial Code* (August 2019)
—— *Ministerial Code* (May 2022)

——*Ministerial Code* (December 2022)
——*Ministerial Code* (November 2024)
—— *Arm's Length Body Sponsorship Code of Good Practice* (May 2022) <https://assets.publishing.service.gov.uk/media/628cb378e90e071f5d4f1d20/alb-sponsorship-code-of-practice.pdf>
——*Annual Report and 2021–22* (December 2022)
——*Annual Report and Accounts 2022–23* (September 2023)
——*Advertising, Marketing and Communications Spending Controls* (April 2014, updated to January 2023) <https://assets.publishing.service.gov.uk/government/uploads/system/uploads/attachment_data/file/1121909/Advertising__marketing_and_communications_controls.pdf>
—— *Using Non-corporate Communication Channels (e.g. WhatsApp, Private e-mail, SMS) for Government Business* (30 March 2023) <https://assets.publishing.service.gov.uk/government/uploads/system/uploads/attachment_data/file/1147629/2023-03-30_Non-corporate_communications_channels_guidance.pdf.>
——*Freedom of Information Statistics: Annual 2022 Bulletin* (May 2023) <www.gov.uk/government/statistics/freedom-of-information-statistics-annual-2022/freedom-of-information-statistics-annual-2022-bulletin#overview>
——*Annual Report on Special Advisers 2023* (July 2023)
—— *FOI Referral Criteria* [nd] <www.gov.uk/government/publications/cabinet-office-and-freedom-of-information>
——*Statistical* Tables—Civil Ser*vice Statistics 2023* (August 2023) <www.gov.uk/government/statistics/civil-service-statistics-2023>
——*Public Bodies Review Programme* (2022, updated to October 2024) <www.gov.uk/government/publications/public-bodies-review-programme>
——*Commercial Spend Controls (version 7)* (1 February 2023) <www.gov.uk/guidance/commercial-spend-controls-version-5>
——*Guidance: Digital and Technology Spend Controls (version 5)* (21 July 2023) <www.gov.uk/guidance/digital-and-technology-spend-controls-version-5>
——*Strengthening Ethics and Integrity in Central Government* (CP 900, 2023)
——*A Modern Civil Service: The Next Steps on Our Journey* (July 2023)
——*List of Cabinet Committees and their Membership* (December 2023) <www.gov.uk/government/publications/the-cabinet-committees-system-and-list-of-cabinet-committees>
——*About Us* <www.gov.uk/government/organisations/cabinet-office/about>
——*Review of the UK Statistics Authority: Cabinet Office Response to the Recommendations* (12 March 2024) <https://assets.publishing.service.gov.uk/media/65ef2f855b6524420bf21b15/UKSA_REVIEW_Government_Response.pdf>
——Code of Conduct for Special Advisers (September 2024)
—— *Investigation into Alleged Gatherings on Government Premises During Covid Restrictions—Update* (31 January 2022)
——and Civil Service Commission, *Memorandum of Understanding between the Cabinet Office and the Civil Service Commission* (11 November 2010) <https://civilservicecommission. independent.gov.uk/wp-content/uploads/2019/03/01b_Memorandum-of-Understanding.pdf>
——and Department for Levelling Up, Housing and Communities, *The Review of Intergovernmental Relations* (January 2022)
——and HM Treasury, *Spending Public Money: Governance and Audit Issues* (Cm 3179, March 1996)
—— and HM Treasury, Letter to the Chair of the Public Accounts Committee, 'Outcome Delivery Plans' (16 March 2021) <https://committees.parliament.uk/publications/5187/documents/52040/default/>
—— and UK Statistics Authority, Memorandum of Understanding between Cabinet Office and the UK Statistics Authority (April 2020) <https://assets.publishing.service.gov.uk/media/5eaa997dd3bf7f6523c81c1a/MoU_-_Cabinet_Office_UK_Statistics_Authority.pdf>
——Central Digital and Data Office, and Office for Artificial Intelligence, *Ethics, Transparency and Accountability Framework for Automated Decision-Making* (2021, updated 29 November 2023) <www.gov.uk/government/publications/ethics-transparency-and-accountability-framework-for-automated-decision-making/ethics-transparency-and-accountability-framework-for-automated-decision-making>

—— Performance and Innovation Unit, *Wiring it up: Whitehall's Management of Cross-cutting Policies and Services* (2000)
Cabinet Secretary: Individual Performance Objectives 2015/16 <https://assets.publishing.service.gov.uk/media/5a80c8aced915d74e62306bc/Jeremy-Heywood-objectives-2015-16.pdf>
Cameron D, PM's Speech on Business Plans (8 November 2010) <www.gov.uk/government/speeches/pms-speech-on-business-plans>
Case S, Cabinet Secretary Lecture (13 October 2021) <www.gov.uk/government/speeches/cabinet-secretary-lecture-wednesday-13-october-2021--2>
Central Digital and Data Office, *Transforming for a Digital Future: 2022 to 2025 Roadmap for Digital and Data* (updated September 2023) <www.gov.uk/government/publications/roadmap-for-digital-and-data-2022-to-2025/transforming-for-a-digital-future-2022-to-2025-roadmap-for-digital-and-data>
—— *Government Functional Standard GovS 005: Digital* (November 2023) <www.gov.uk/government/publications/government-functional-standard-govs-005-digital>
Chancellor of the Duchy of Lancaster, *Open Government* (Cm 2290, July 1993)
—— *The Government's Response to the First Report from the Committee on Standards in Public Life* (Cm 2931, 1995)
—— *Your Right To Know: The Government's Proposals for a Freedom of Information Act* (Cm 3818, December 1997)
Chancellor of the Exchequer, *Financial Statement and Budget Report 1997–98* (HC 1996–97, 90)
—— *Budget 1998: The Code for Fiscal Stability* (March 1998)
—— *Stability and Investment for the Long Term: Economic and Fiscal Strategy 1998* (Cm 3978, June 1998)
—— *Modern Public Services for Britain: Investing in Reform* (Cm 4011, July 1998)
—— *The Code for Fiscal Stability* (December 1998)
—— *Budget 2020* (HC 2019–20, 121)
—— *Budget 2021* (HC 2019–21, 1226)
—— *Autumn Budget and Spending Review 2021: A Stronger Economy for the British People* (HC 2021–22, 822)
—— *The Growth Plan 2022* (CP 743, September 2022)
Chief Secretary to the Treasury and the Minister for the Cabinet Office, Letter to the Chair of the Public Administration and Constitutional Affairs Committee (6 July 2023) <https://committees.parliament.uk/publications/40934/documents/199435/default/>
Chisholm A, Civil Service Chief Operating Officer and Cabinet Office Permanent Secretary, Letter to Chair of Public Accounts Committee (23 June 2021) <https://committees.parliament.uk/publications/6525/documents/70818/default/>
Chote R, Response to Stephen Kinnock MP—Asylum Backlogs (23 March 2023) <https://uksa.statisticsauthority.gov.uk/correspondence/response-from-sir-robert-chote-to-stephen-kinnock-mp-asylum-backlogs/>
Civil Service Reform: Report to the Prime Minister from Sir Richard Wilson (October 1999) <www.civilservant.org.uk/library/1999-SRW's_report _to_PM.pdf>
Cabinet Office, *Civil Service Reform Plan: One Year On Report* (July 2013) <https://assets.publishing.service.gov.uk/media/5a7c71dd40f0b62aff6c1b6e/CSR_OYO_LOW_RES_PDF.pdf>
—— *Civil Service Reform Plan—Progress Report* (October 2014) <https://assets.publishing.service.gov.uk/government/uploads/system/uploads/attachment_data/file/360637/Civil_Service_Reform_Plan_-_Progress_Report__web_.pdf>
Civil Service Commission, *Annual Report and Accounts 2014–15* (HC 251)
—— *Recruitment Principles* (April 2018)
—— *Annual Report and Accounts 2018–19* (HC 2414)
—— *Annual Report and Accounts 2019–20* (HC 455)
—— *Annual Report and Accounts 2020–21* (HC 465)
—— *Annual Report and Accounts 2021–22* (HC 525)
—— *Annual Report and Accounts 2022–23* (HC 95)
Civil Service Commissioners, *Annual Report 1994–95*
—— *Annual Report 2002–03*
—— *Annual Report 2003–04*

——*Recruitment Code* (5th edn, 2004)
——*Annual Report 2007–08*
Commission on Devolution in Wales, *Empowerment and Responsibility: Financial Powers to Strengthen Wales* (November 2012)
——*Empowerment and Responsibility: Legislative Powers to Strengthen Wales* (March 2014)
Commission on Scottish Devolution, *The Future of Scottish Devolution within the Union: A First Report* (December 2008)
——*Serving Scotland Better: Scotland and the United Kingdom in the 21st Century* (June 2009)
Commissioner for Public Appointments, *Annual Report 2020–21* <https://publicappointmentscommissioner.independent.gov.uk/wp-content/uploads/2021/10/OCPA-20-21-Annual-Report.pdf>
——*Annual Report 2022–23*
Committee on the Civil Service, *The Civil Service: Report of the Committee 1966–68* (Cmnd 3638, 1968)
Committee on Standards in Public Life, *Standards in Public Life: First Report* (Cm 2850, 1995)
——*Reinforcing Standards: Review of the First Report of the Committee on Standards in Public Life* (Cm 4557, 2000)
——Ninth Report, *Defining the Boundaries within the Executive: Ministers, Special Advisers and the Permanent Civil Service* (Cm 5775, 2003)
——*Getting the Balance Right: Implementing Standards of Conduct in Public Life* (Cm 6407, 2005)
——*Standards Matter: A Review of Best Practice in Promoting Good Behaviour in Public Life* (Cm 8519, 2013)
Comptroller and Auditor General, *Evaluation of Regulatory Impact Assessment Compendium Report 2004–05* (HC 2004–05, 341)
——*Delivering High Quality Impact Assessments* (HC 2008–09, 128)
——*HM Treasury: Maintaining the Financial Stability of UK Banks: Update on the Support Schemes* (HC 2010–11, 676)
——*Progress on Public Bodies Reform* (HC 2013–14, 1048)
——*Delivering Major Projects in Government: A Briefing for the Committee of Public Accounts* (HC 2015–16, 713)
——*Accountability to Parliament for Taxpayers' Money* (HC 2015–16, 849)
——*The Business Impact Target: Cutting the Cost of Regulation* (HC 2016–17, 236)
——*Government's Management of its Performance: Progress with Single Departmental Plans* (HC 2016–17, 872)
——*Investigation into Government's Management of the Business Appointment Rules* (HC 2017–19, 245)
——*Improving Government's Planning and Spending Framework* (HC 2017–19, 1679)
——*Central Oversight of Arm's Length Bodies* (HC 2021–22, 297)
——*The Challenges in Implementing Digital Change* (HC 2021–22, 575)
——*Managing Government Borrowing* (HC 2022–23, 1658)
——*Lessons Learned: Cross-Government Working* (HC 2022–23, 1659)
Correspondence between the Prime Minister and Lord Evans on the Independent Adviser on Ministers' Interests <https://www.gov.uk/government/publications/correspondence-between-the-prime-minister-and-lord-evans-on-the-independent-adviser-on-ministers-interests>
——*Standards Matter 2—Committee Findings* (June 2021)
——*Upholding Standards in Public Life: Final Report of the Standards Matter 2 Review* (November 2021)
COVID-19 Communications Advisory Panel, *Report* (2020) <https://gcs.civilservice.gov.uk/publications/covid-19-communications-advisory-panel-report/>
Crown Commercial Service, *General Legal Advice Services* <www.crowncommercial.gov.uk/agreements/RM3786>
——*RM6125 Guide to Buying Marketing, Communication and Research Services through CCS* and *Customer Guide* [nd] <www.crowncommercial.gov.uk/agreements/RM6125>
Crown Prosecution Service, *Prosecuting Welfare and Health Fraud Cases* (September 2019) <www.cps.gov.uk/legal-guidance/prosecuting-welfare-and-health-fraud-cases>

—— *Termination of Proceedings (including Discontinuance)* (November 2019) <www.cps.gov.uk/legal-guidance/termination-proceedings-including-discontinuance>

—— *Relations with other Prosecuting Agencies and the Prosecutors Convention* (updated to October 2023) <www.cps.gov.uk/legal-guidance/relations-other-prosecuting-agencies-and-prosecutors-convention>

Davies G, 'Getting the Most from Every Public Pound—a Blueprint for Value for Money' (Speech in Parliament, 16 January 2024) <www.nao.org.uk/insights/improving-productivity-could-release-tens-of-billions-for-government-priorities/>

Department for Business, Energy and Industrial Strategy, *Post Office Limited: Shareholder Relationship Framework Document* (March 2020) <https://assets.publishing.service.gov.uk/media/5e74fe04e90e073e313755cc/post-office-limited-shareholder-relationship-framework-part-1.pdf>

Department for Business, Innovation and Skills, Better Regulation Delivery Office, *Regulators Code* (2014) <www.gov.uk/government/publications/regulators-code>

Department for Business and Trade, *Retained EU Law Dashboard* <www.gov.uk/government/publications/retained-eu-law-dashboard>

—— *Smarter Regulation to Grow the Economy* (May 2023) <https://assets.publishing.service.gov.uk/government/uploads/system/uploads/attachment_data/file/1155774/smarter_regulation_to_grow_economy-may_2023.pdf>

—— *Better Regulation Framework Guidance* (September 2023) <https://assets.publishing.service.gov.uk/media/65420ee8d36c91000d935b58/Better_Regulation_Framework_guidance.pdf>

—— *Smarter Regulation: Delivering a Regulatory Environment for Innovation, Investment and Growth* (CP 1089, May 2024)

Department for Communities and Local Government, *Accountability: Adapting to Decentralisation* (September 2011) <www.gov.uk/government/publications/accountability-adapting-to-decentralisation--2>

Department for Constitutional Affairs, Government response to the Public Administration Select Committee's Fourth Report of Session 2003-04, *Taming the Prerogative: Strengthening Ministerial Accountability to Parliament* (Cm 6187, 2004)

Department for Environment, Food and Rural Affairs, *Enforcement Policy Statement 2015* <https://assets.publishing.service.gov.uk/government/uploads/system/uploads/attachment_data/file/470454/defra-enforcement-policy-statement-2015.pdf>

Department of Health and Social Care, *Annual Report and Accounts 2019–20* (HC 2019–21, 1077)

Department for Levelling Up, Housing and Communities, *Intergovernmental Relations Annual Report 2022* (CP 826, 2023)

—— *Intergovernmental Relations Annual Report 2023* (CP 1064, 2024)

Department of Work and Pensions, *Treatment of Historical Institutional Abuse Payments in Means-Tested Benefits* (December 2021) <www.gov.uk/government/publications/treatment-of-historical-institutional-abuse-payments-in-means-tested-benefits>

Departmental Committee to Inquire into the System under which the Legal Business of Government is Conducted, *First, Second and Third Reports* (Sir George Jessel, MR, Chairman) (HC 1876–77, 199), 1877 Parl Pap XVIII (folio)

Deputy Prime Minister, Lord Chancellor and Secretary of State for Justice, *Human Rights Act Reform: A Modern Bill of Rights: A Consultation to Reform the Human Rights Act 1998*, CP 588 (December 2021)

Devolution Guidance Note 1 *Common Working Arrangements. Devolution: Guidance for Civil Servants* <www.gov.uk/government/publications/devolution-guidance-for-civil-servants/devolution-guidance-for-civil-servants>

Digital Economy Council, *Organising for Digital Delivery* (9 September 2020) <www.gov.uk/government/publications/organising-for-digital-delivery/organising-for-digital-delivery>

Economic Secretary to the Treasury, *Statistics: A Matter of Trust. A Consultation Document* (Cm 3382, 1998)

—— *Building Trust in Statistics* (Cm 4412, 1999)

Efficiency Unit, *Improving Management in Government: the Next Steps. A Report to the Prime Minister* (1988)

Equality and Human Rights Commission, *Making Fair Financial Decisions: An Assessment of HM Treasury's 2010 Spending Review conducted under Section 31 of the 2006 Equality Act* (May 2012)

—— *Future Fair Financial Decision-Making* (February 2015) <www.equalityhumanrights.com/sites/default/files/future_fair_financial_decision-making.pdf>

Estimates Committee, *Government Statistical Services* (HC 1966–67, 246)

European Scrutiny Committee, *Oral evidence: Retained EU Law: The Progress and Mechanics of Reform* (HC 2023–24, 376) (13 March 2024) <https://committees.parliament.uk/oralevidence/14479/pdf/>

Eurostat, *ESA 2010* (Publications Office of the European Union 2013)

—— *Manual on Government Deficit and Debt* (2016)

Evans (Lord), Speech on Upholding Standards in Public Life <www.gov.uk/government/speeches/upholding-standards-in-public-life-speech-by-lord-evans>

—— Response to Lord True <https://assets.publishing.service.gov.uk/media/6294dce2e90e07039f799f2a/Lord_Evans_Response_to_Lord_True.pdf>

Food Standards Agency, *Manual for Official Controls: Legal Requirements and Standards for Approved Meat Establishments* (January 2022)

Gay O and Potton E, *FoI and Ministerial Vetoes*, House of Commons Library Standard Note: SN/PC/05007 (last updated 19 March 2014)

Geidt, Lord, email to the chair of the Public Administration and Constitutional Affairs Committee <committees.parliament.uk/publications/22732/documents/167114/default>

Gershon Sir P, *Releasing Resources to the Front Line: Independent Review of Public Sector Efficiency* (2004)

Gove M, 'The Privilege of Public Service' (Ditchley Annual Lecture, 27 June 2020) <www.gov.uk/government/speeches/the-privilege-of-public-service-given-as-the-ditchley-annual-lecture>

—— Letter to Lord Dunlop 24 March 2021 <https://covid19.public-inquiry.uk/wp-content/uploads/2023/07/21173033/INQ000221630-1.pdf>

Government Communication Service, *Modern Communications Operating Model: A Blueprint for Government Communication: 2.0* (2020?) <https://gcs.civilservice.gov.uk/wp-content/uploads/2020/03/GCS-MCOM_Blueprint_for_government_communications.pdf>

—— *Government Communication Service Propriety Guidance* (2014, rev 2021) <https://gcs.civilservice.gov.uk/publications/propriety-guidance/>

—— *What We Do* (October 2022) <https://gcs.civilservice.gov.uk/about-us/what-we-do/>

—— *Buying Communication Support* (January 2023) <https://gcs.civilservice.gov.uk/guidance/marketing/delivering-government-campaigns/buying-communication-support/>

Government Lead Non-Executive, *Annual Report 2021–22* <https://assets.publishing.service.gov.uk/media/645b8b10c6e89700l2a0fc7f/2023-05-10_Final-GovtLeadNEDAnnualReport2021-22.pdf>

Government Legal Department, *Guidance Note on Legal Risk* (2015) <https://assets.publishing.service.gov.uk/government/uploads/system/uploads/attachment_data/file/736503/Legal_Risk_Guidance_-_Amended_July_2015.pdf>

—— *Annual Report and Accounts 2015–16* (HC 2016–17, 6)

—— *Annual Report and Accounts 2017–18* (HC 2017–19, 989)

—— *Annual Report and Accounts 2019–20* (HC 2019–21, 310)

—— *Annual Report and Accounts 2022–23* (HC 2022–23, 1279)

Government Legal Service, *GLS Statutory Instrument Drafting Guidance* (August 2018) paras 1.6.3, 2.3.8–2.3.37 <www.whatdotheyknow.com/request/gls_statutory_instrument_draftin/response/1540344/attach/3/FOI 28 20 Greenhill GLS drafting guidance.pdf>

Granatt M, 'Politics and the Government Information Officer: A Note by the Head of Profession' in *GICS Handbook* (2001)

Heywood Sir J, 'The Role of the Modern Cabinet Secretary' (April 2015) <www.instituteforgovernment.org.uk/article/comment/role-modern-cabinet-secretary>

—— 'How the Civil Service is Preparing for Brexit' (*Civil Service Blog*, 11 July 2017) <https://civilservice.blog.gov.uk/2017/07/11/how-the-civil-service-is-preparing-for-brexit/>

HM Government, *The Coalition: Our Programme for Government* (May 2010)

—— *One-In, One-Out (OIOO) Methodology* (July 2011) <www.regulation.org.uk/library/2011_oioo_methodology.pdf>
—— *The Civil Service Reform Plan* (June 2012) <https://assets.publishing.service.gov.uk/government/uploads/system/uploads/attachment_data/file/305148/Civil-Service-Reform-Plan-final.pdf>
—— *Government Communications Plan 2013/14* (2013) <https://communication-plan.gcs.civilservice.gov.uk/wp-content/uploads/2019/04/https-gcn.civilservice...nicationsPlan201314.pdf>
—— *Scotland in the United Kingdom: An Enduring Settlement* (Cm 8890, 2015)
—— *Declaration on Government Reform* (June 2021: jointly signed by the Prime Minister on behalf of Cabinet and the Cabinet Secretary on behalf of Permanent Secretaries) <https://assets.publishing.service.gov.uk/media/60c88586d3bf7f4bd53453b1/FINAL_Declaration_on_Government_Reform.pdf>
—— *Government Functional Standard GovS 003: Human Resources* 2.0 (July 2021) <https://assets.publishing.service.gov.uk/media/6109bbd68fa8f50433efa936/2356GOV_HR003_Standards_Digital_v3-2.pdf>
—— *Government Functional Standard GovS 002: Project Delivery: Portfolio, Programme and Project Management* 2.0 (15 July 2021) <https://assets.publishing.service.gov.uk/government/uploads/system/uploads/attachment_data/file/1002673/1195-APS-CCS0521656700-001-Project-Delivery-standard_Web.pdf>
—— *Government Functional Standard GovS015: Grants* 2.0 (July 2021) <https://assets.publishing.service.gov.uk/media/60f7fc0c8fa8f50c716bcd62/Final-CO_Govt_Functional_Std_GovS015_WEB.pdf>
—— *Government Functional Standard GovS 013: Counter-Fraud* (August 2021) <https://assets.publishing.service.gov.uk/media/612e5a8ce90e0705355a552b/6.7628_CO_Govt-Functional-Std_GovS013-Counter-Fraud_v4.pdf>
—— *Net Zero Strategy: Build Back Greener* (October 2021)
—— *The Benefits of Brexit: How the UK is Taking Advantage of Leaving the EU* (January 2022)
—— *Government Functional Standard GovS001: Government Functions* (15 June 2022) <https://assets.publishing.service.gov.uk/media/62d67f0de90e071e8021344d/GovS-001-government-functions-WEB-version.pdf>
—— *Performance with Purpose: Government Communication Service Strategy* (2022) <https://strategy.gcs.civilservice.gov.uk/wp-content/uploads/2022/05/gcs-strategy-2022-25.pdf>
—— *Reforming the Framework for Better Regulation* (January 2022) <https://assets.publishing.service.gov.uk/government/uploads/system/uploads/attachment_data/file/1050947/reforming-framework-for-better-regulation-summary-responses.pdf>
—— *Government Functional Standard GovS 011: Communication 2.1* (October 2023) <www.gov.uk/government/publications/government-functional-standard-govs-011-communication>
HM Procurator General and Treasury Solicitor, *Annual Report and Accounts 2021–22* (HC 2021–22, 189)
—— *Annual Report and Accounts 2022–23* (HC 2022–23, 1320)
HM Treasury, *Notes for the Use of Accounts Branches of Government Departments* (4th edn, HMSO 1929)
—— *Better Accounting for the Taxpayer's Money: Resource Accounting and Budgeting in Government* (Cm 2626, July 1994)
—— *Better Accounting for the Taxpayer's Money, The Government's Proposals: Resource Accounting and Budgeting in Government* (Cm 2929, July 1995)
—— *Modern Public Services in Britain: Investing for Reform. Comprehensive Spending Review: New Public Spending Plans 1999-2002* (Cm 4011, July 1998)
—— *Public Services for the Future: Modernisation, Reform, Accountability Comprehensive Spending Review: Public Service Agreements 1999–2002* (Cm 4181, December 1998)
—— *2000 Spending Review: Public Service Agreements* (Cm 4808, July 2000)
—— *Reforming Britain's Economic and Financial Policy: Towards Greater Economic Stability* (Palgrave 2002)

—— *Corporate Governance in Central Government Departments: Code of Good Practice* (July 2005, updated 2011, 2017)
—— *Meeting the Aspirations of the British People: 2007 Pre-Budget Report and Comprehensive Spending Review* (Cm 7227, October 2007)
—— *Contingencies Fund Account 2008–2009* (HC 2008–09, 892)
—— *Alignment (Clear Line of Sight) Project* (Cm 7567, March 2009)
—— *Reforming Arm's-Length Bodies* (March 2010)
—— *The Spending Review Framework* (Cm 7872, June 2010)
—— *Spending Review 2010* (Cm 7942, October 2010)
—— *Charter for Budget Responsibility 2011* (April 2011)
—— *Supply Estimates: A Guidance Manual* (July 2011)
—— *Review of HM Treasury's Management Response to the Financial Crisis* (March 2012) <https://assets.publishing.service.gov.uk/government/uploads/system/uploads/attachment_data/file/220506/review_fincrisis_response_290312.pdf>
—— *Spending Round 2013* (Cm 8639, June 2013)
—— *Class (2013) 1: Sector Classification* (August 2013) <https://assets.publishing.service.gov.uk/media/5a7c18e0e5274a25a91406dc/PU1547_final.pdf>
—— *Review of Financial Management in Government* (December 2013)
—— *Charter for Budget Responsibility, March 2014 Update* (March 2014)
—— *Simplifying and Streamlining Statutory Annual Report and Accounts* (Cm 8905, July 2014)
—— *The Aqua Book: Guidance on Producing Quality Analysis for Government* (2015)
—— *Spending Review and Autumn Statement 2015* (Cm 9162, November 2015)
—— *Treasury Minute on Public Accounts Committee Report 39 of 2015–16* (Cm 9389, December 2016)
—— *Charter for Budget Responsibility Autumn 2016 Update* (2017)
—— *Accounting Officer System Statements: Guidance* (April 2017) <https://assets.publishing.service.gov.uk/government/uploads/system/uploads/attachment_data/file/626226/pu2074_accounting_officer_guidance_2017.pdf>
—— *Delivering Better Outcomes for Citizens: Practical Steps for Unlocking Public Value* (17 November 2017) <www.gov.uk/government/publications/delivering-better-outcomes-for-citizens-practical-steps-for-unlocking-public-value>
—— *Guidance for Publishing Spend over £25000* (November 2017) <https://assets.publishing.service.gov.uk/government/uploads/system/uploads/attachment_data/file/662332/guidance_for_publishing_spend.pdf>
—— *Financial Reporting Advisory Board terms of reference* (November 2018) <www.gov.uk/government/publications/financial-reporting-advisory-board-terms-of-reference>
—— *The Government Financial Reporting Review* (CP 67, April 2019)
—— *Spending Round 2019* (CP 170, September 2019)
—— *Government Financial Reporting Manual 2019–2020*
—— *Central Government Supply Estimates 2020–21: Main Supply Estimates* (HC 2019–21, 293)
—— *Annual Report and Accounts 2019–20* (HC 2019–21, 746)
—— *Contingencies Fund Account 2019–20* (HC 2019–21, 764)
—— *Debt Management Report 2020–21* (March 2020) 15–16 <https://assets.publishing.service.gov.uk/government/uploads/system/uploads/attachment_data/file/871876/03032020_DMR_off-sen_v2_FINAL_with_jpegs_v2.pdf>
—— *Magenta Book: Central Government Guidance on Evaluation* (March 2020)
—— DAO letter, 'Revision of Target Dates for Implementing Public Accounts Committee Recommendations' (12 June 2020) <https://assets.publishing.service.gov.uk/media/5ee35fd2d3bf7f1eb2043f4e/DAO_0220.pdf>
—— *Spending Review 2020* (CP 330, November 2020)
—— *Outcome Delivery Plan 2021 to 2022* (15 July 2021) <www.gov.uk/government/publications/hm-treasury-outcome-delivery-plan/hm-treasury-outcome-delivery-plan-2021-to-2022>
—— *Autumn Budget and Spending Review 2021* (HC 2021–22, 822)
—— DAO letter, 'Mandating Functional Standards from end September 2021' (DAO 05/21) (30 September 2021) <https://assets.publishing.service.gov.uk/media/6154921f8fa8f5297b643e0f/05-21_DAO_Letter_-_functional_standards_for_pub_with_amends_LLJ.pdf>

—— *Spending Review 2021: Priority Outcomes and Metrics* (October 2021) <https://assets.publishing.service.gov.uk/government/uploads/system/uploads/attachment_data/file/1029277/Supplementary_Document_on_Outcomes_Metrics.pdf>
—— *Charter for Budget Responsibility, Autumn 2021 Update* (January 2022)
—— *Treasury Approvals Process for Programmes and Projects* (March 2022) <https://assets.publishing.service.gov.uk/government/uploads/system/uploads/attachment_data/file/567908/Treasury_approvals_process_guidance_final.pdf>
—— *Managing Public Money: Framework Documents* (July 2022) <www.gov.uk/government/publications/managing-public-money-framework-documents>
—— *Accounting Officer Standard Appointment Letter* <https://assets.publishing.service.gov.uk/government/uploads/system/uploads/attachment_data/file/1123168/AO_appointment_-_standard_template_-_December_2022__1_.pdf>
—— *Contingencies Fund Account 2021–22* (HC 2022–23, 329)
—— *Charter for Budget Responsibility: Autumn 2022 Update* (January 2023) <https://assets.publishing.service.gov.uk/government/uploads/system/uploads/attachment_data/file/1131729/Charter_for_Budget_Responsibility_-_AS22_-_FINAL_as_published_in_draft.pdf>
—— *Debt management report 2023–24* (March 2023) <https://assets.publishing.service.gov.uk/media/6502e166702634000d89b835/M5237_Debt_Management_Report_2023-24_FINAL_corrected.pdf>
—— *Consolidated Budgeting Guidance 2023–24* (March 2023) <https://assets.publishing.service.gov.uk/government/uploads/system/uploads/attachment_data/file/1141848/CBG_2023-24_final.pdf>
—— *Managing Public Money* (May 2023) <https://assets.publishing.service.gov.uk/government/uploads/system/uploads/attachment_data/file/1174979/Managing_Public_Money_-_May_2023_.pdf>
—— *Template Delegated Authority Letter* (2023) <www.gov.uk/government/publications/managing-public-money>
—— *Accounting Officer Assessments: Guidance* (2017, rev May 2023) <https://assets.publishing.service.gov.uk/media/646632530b72d3000c34478a/AOA_guidance_May_2023__3_.pdf>
—— Framework Document: Government Internal Audit Agency (May 2023) <https://assets.publishing.service.gov.uk/media/646b863c382a5100139fc53b/GIAA_Framework_Document.pdf>
—— *Annual Report and Accounts 2022–23* (HC 2022–23, 1467)
—— *The Green Book: Central Government Guidance on Appraisal and Evaluation* (October 2023)
—— *Government Financial Reporting Manual 2023–24* (December 2023) <https://assets.publishing.service.gov.uk/media/657b03c8095987000d95e120/MASTER_FINAL_2023-24_FReM___1_.pdf>
—— *Framework Documents: Collection* <www.gov.uk/government/collections/framework-documents-collection>
—— and Cabinet Office, *Corporate Governance in Central Government Departments: Code of Good Practice* (July 2011, rev 2017)
Hampton P, *Reducing Administrative Burdens: Effective Administration and Enforcement* (HM Treasury March 2005) <www.regulation.org.uk/library/2005_hampton_report.pdf>
Harari D and Keep M, *Coronavirus: Economic Impact* (House of Commons Library, December 2021)
House of Commons, *House of Commons Standing Orders as at 6 November 2019* (HC 2019–20, 314)
House of Commons Committee of Privileges, *Matter Referred on 21 April 2022 (Conduct of Rt Hon Boris Johnson): Final Report* (HC 2022–23, 564)
House of Commons Constitutional Affairs Committee, *Freedom of Information—One Year On* (HC 2005–06, 991)
—— *The Constitutional Role of the Attorney-General* (HC 2006–07, 306)
House of Commons European Scrutiny Committee, *Oral Evidence: Retained EU Law: The Progress and Mechanics of Reform* (HC 2023–24, 376) (13 March 2024)
House of Commons Justice Committee, *Devolution: A Decade On* (HC 2008–09, 529)
House of Commons Political and Constitutional Reform Committee, *Role and Powers of the Prime Minister* (HC 2014–15, 351)

House of Commons Scottish Affairs Committee, *The Relationship between the UK and Scottish Governments* (HC 2017–19, 1586)
—— *Coronavirus and Scotland: Interim Report on Intergovernmental Working* (HC 2019–21, 314)
House of Commons Library, Research Paper 03/49, *Whither the Civil Service?* (May 2003) <https://commonslibrary.parliament.uk/research-briefings/rp03-49/>
House of Commons Scrutiny Unit webpage <www.parliament.uk/mps-lords-and-offices/offices/commons/scrutinyunit/>
House of Lords, *Report from the Select Committee Appointed to Consider the Draft Freedom of Information Bill* (HL 1998–99, 97)
House of Lords Communications Committee, *Government Communications* (HL 2008–09, 7)
House of Lords Constitution Committee, *Devolution: Inter-Institutional Relations in the United Kingdom* (HL 2002–03, 28)
—— *The Cabinet Office and the Centre of Government* (HL 2009–10, 30)
—— *The Accountability of Civil Servants* (HL 2012–13, 61)
—— *The Pre-emption of Parliament* (HL 2012–13, 183) evidence <www.parliament.uk/globalassets/documents/lords-committees/constitution/preemption/PPEvidence.pdf>
—— *Proposals for the Devolution of Further Powers to Scotland* (HL 2014–15, 145)
—— *Inter-governmental Relations in the United Kingdom* (HL 2014–15, 146)
—— *The Union and Devolution* (HL 2015–16, 149)
—— *The 'Great Repeal Bill' and Delegated Powers* (HL 2016–17, 123)
—— *European Union (Withdrawal) Bill: Interim Report* (HL 2017–19, 19)
—— *The Legislative Process: Preparing Legislation for Parliament* (HL 2017–19, 27)
—— *European Union (Withdrawal) Bill* (HL 2017–19, 69)
—— *The Legislative Process: The Delegation of Powers* (HL 2017–19, 225)
—— *Respect and Cooperation: Building a Stronger Union for the 21st Century* (HL 2021–22, 142)
—— *Permanent Secretaries: Their Appointment and Removal* (HL 2022–23, 258) Cabinet Office written evidence (SCS0003) <https://committees.parliament.uk/work/7319/the-appointment-and-dismissal-of-permanent-secretaries-and-other-senior-civil-servants/publications/>
—— *The Governance of the Union: Consultation, Cooperation and Legislative Consent* (HL 2024–25, 13)
House of Lords Delegated Powers and Regulatory Reform Committee, *Inquiry into Delegated Powers Memoranda* (HL 2014–15, 39)
—— *European Union (Withdrawal Agreement) Bill* (HL 2019–21, 3)
—— *Democracy Denied? The Urgent Need to Rebalance Power between Parliament and the Executive* (HL 2021–22, 106), and Evidence, 12 and 26 May 2021 and 20 July 2022 <https://committees.parliament.uk/oralevidence/2269/html/>, <https://committees.parliament.uk/oralevidence/2175/html/>, <https://committees.parliament.uk/oralevidence/10623/html/>
House of Lords Industry and Regulators Committee, *Who Watches the Watchdogs? Improving the Performance, Independence and Accountability of UK Regulators* (HL 2023–24, 56)
House of Lords Merits of Statutory Instruments Committee, *The Management of Secondary Legislation* (HL 2005–06, 149)
House of Lords Secondary Legislation Scrutiny Committee, *Number of Corrections to Statutory Instruments in 2014* (HL 2014–15, 93)
—— *Government by Diktat: A Call to Return Power to Parliament* (HL 2021–22, 105)
—— *What Next? The Growing Imbalance between Parliament and the Executive: End of Session Report 2021–22* (HL 2021–22, 200)
—— *38th Report of Session 2022–23* (HL 2022–23, 189)
Independent Adviser on Ministers' Interests, *Annual Report 2021–22*
Independent Commission on Freedom of Information, *Report* (March 2016) <https://assets.publishing.service.gov.uk/government/uploads/system/uploads/attachment_data/file/504139/Independent_Freedom_of_Information_Commission_Report.pdf>
Independent Review of Administrative Law (CP 407, March 2021)
Information Commissioner, *Freedom of Information Act 2000 (Section 48) Practice Recommendation: Department of Health and Social Care* (11 July 2022) <https://ico.org.uk/

media/action-weve-taken/practice-recommendations/4020918/dhsc-practice-recommendation.pdf>

Information Commissioner's Office, *Definition Documents* [nd] <https://ico.org.uk/for-organisations/foi/publication-schemes-a-guide/definition-documents/>

—— *Definition Document for Government Departments* (version 3.1) <https://ico.org.uk/media/for-organisations/documents/1246/definition_document_for_government_departments.pdf>

—— *Rights relating to Automated Decision Making Including Profiling* [nd] <https://ico.org.uk/for-organisations/uk-gdpr-guidance-and-resources/individual-rights/individual-rights/rights-related-to-automated-decision-making-including-profiling/>

—— *Information Commissioner's Annual Report and Financial Statements 2022/23* (HC 2022–23, 1440)

Infrastructure and Projects Authority, *Mandate* (January 2021) <www.gov.uk/government/publications/infrastructure-and-projects-authority-mandate>

—— *Project Delivery: Guidance. The Role of the Senior Responsible Owner* (version 2.0, April 2023) <https://assets.publishing.service.gov.uk/government/uploads/system/uploads/attachment_data/file/1158010/2023-04-11-V2-AFIGT-The-role-of-the-senior-responsible-owner-2.pdf>

—— *Annual Report on Major Projects 2022–23* (2023) <https://assets.publishing.service.gov.uk/government/uploads/system/uploads/attachment_data/file/1175756/IPA-Annual-report-2022-2023.pdf.pdf>

Insolvency Legal Services Directorate webpage <www.gov.uk/government/groups/insolvency-service-legal-services-directorate>

Institute for Public Policy Research, *Accountability and Responsiveness in the Senior Civil Service: Lessons from Overseas* (Cabinet Office 2013) <www.civilservant.org.uk/library/2013_ippr_Accountability_and_Responsiveness_in_the_SCS.pdf>

Iraq Inquiry (Chilcot Inquiry), oral evidence (26 January 2010) <https://webarchive.nationalarchives.gov.uk/ukgwa/20160512093814/http://www.iraqinquiry.org.uk/transcripts/oralevidence-bydate/100126.aspx>

Joint Committee on the Draft Constitutional Renewal Bill, vol I: *Report* (HL 2007–08, 166-I; HC 2007–08, 551-I)

Joint Committee on Statutory Instruments, *Rule of Law Themes from COVID-19 Regulations* (HL 2021–22, 57; HC 2021–22, 600)

Justice Committee, *Post-legislative Scrutiny of the Freedom of Information Act 2000* (HC 2012–13, 96-1)

—— *The Work of the Attorney-General* (HC 2015–16, 409)

—— *The Work of the Attorney-General* (HC 2017–19, 1887)

—— *The Work of the Attorney-General* (HC 2019–21, 462)

—— *Private Prosecutions: Safeguards* (HC 2019–21, 497)

—— *Private Prosecutions: Safeguards: Government Response* (HC 2019–21, 1238)

—— *The Work of the Attorney-General* (HC 2021–22, 962)

Keep M, *The 17 October 2022 Fiscal Statement: Summary and Background* (House of Commons Library 17 October 2022) <https://commonslibrary.parliament.uk/research-briefings/cbp-9643/>

Kellaway M, *Public Sector Interventions in the Financial Crisis—Statistical Classification Decisions* (Office for National Statistics 2009)

Kelly R, *Pre-legislative Scrutiny under the Coalition Government: 2010–2015* (House of Commons Library Briefing Paper no 05859, 13 August 2015)

Kelly T, Review of the Defence Communications Directorate's Response to Declassified UK (7 December 2020) <www.gov.uk/government/publications/review-of-the-defence-communications-directorates-response-to-declassified-uk/review-of-the-defence-communications-directorates-response-to-declassified-uk>

Kerslake Sir B, Macpherson Sir N, and Heaton R, Letter to Margaret Hodge, Chair, Public Accounts Committee (24 March 2014) <https://old.parliament.uk/documents/commons-committees/public-accounts/Correspondence-from-Cabinet-Office-and-HM-Treasury-to-Chair-relating-to-Treasury-Minutes-on-civil-service-reform.pdf>

Langley S, *Freedom of Information Clearing House Review* (Cabinet Office 2022)

Liaison Committee, *Annual Report for 2004* (HC 2004–05, 419)

—— *Parliament and Government Finance: Recreating Financial Scrutiny* (HC 2007–08, 426)

Lievesey D, *Independent Review of the UK Statistics Authority* (March 2024) <https://assets.publishing.service.gov.uk/media/65ef2f733649a23451ed63a9/UKSA_Review.pdf>

Lord Chancellor and Secretary of State for Justice, *Judicial Review Reform: The Government Response to the Independent Review of Administrative Law* (CP 408, March 2021)

—— *Judicial Review Reform Consultation: The Government Response* (CP 477, July 2021)

Lord Chancellor's and Law Officers' Departments, *Departmental Report: The Government's Expenditure Plans 1996–97 to 1998–99* (Cm 3209, March 1996)

Lord President of the Council, *Government Statistical Services* (Cmnd 8236, 1981)

Lord President of the Council (Jacob Rees-Mogg MP), letter to Chair of the European Statutory Instruments Committee (2 October 2019) <https://old.parliament.uk/documents/commons-committees/european-statutory-instruments/Leader-to-Sir-Patrick-McLoughlin--Use-of-Urgent-Made-Affirmative-Procedure-for-EU-Exit-SIs.pdf>

McCormick C and Cowie G, *The Law Officers: A Constitutional and Functional Overview* (House of Commons Library Briefing Paper, May 2020)

McGibbon S, Letter to Chair, Regulatory Reform Committee (7 April 2021) <https://committees.parliament.uk/publications/5988/documents/67864/default/>

Macpherson Sir N, 'The Origins of Treasury Control' (January 2013) <www.gov.uk/government/speeches/speech-by-the-permanent-secretary-to-the-treasury-sir-nicholas-macpherson-the-origins-of-treasury-control>

Magnus, Sir Laurie, *Investigation Report to the Prime Minister* <https://assets.publishing.service.gov.uk/government/uploads/system/uploads/ttachment_data/file/1152026/2023.04.20_Investigation_Report_to_the_Prime_Minister.pdf>

Mair L and McGuinness F, *Public Bodies Bill (HL)* (House of Commons Library Research Paper 11/50)

Maritime and Coastguard Agency, *Guidance: MCA Enforcement Policy Statement* (16 November 2021) <www.gov.uk/government/publications/mca-enforcement-policy-statement/mca-enforcement-policy-statement>

Maude F, 'Ministers and Mandarins: Speaking Truth unto Power' (Lecture, 4 June 2013) <www.gov.uk/government/speeches/ministers-and-mandarins-speaking-truth-unto-power>

—— and Alexander D, Letter to Margaret Hodge, Chair, Public Accounts Committee (13 May 2014) <www.parliament.uk/globalassets/documents/commons-committees/public-accounts/Correspondence-from-Francis-Maude-MP-Danny-Alexander-MP-to-Chair-on-Corporate-Centre.pdf>

Maude (Lord), *Review of the Cross-cutting Functions and the Operation of Spend Controls* (July 2021) <www.gov.uk/government/publications/review-of-the-cross-cutting-functions-and-the-operation-of-spend-controls>

—— *Independent Review of Governance and Accountability in the Civil Service* (13 November 2023) <https://assets.publishing.service.gov.uk/media/6552350b8a2ed40013720d82/Independent-Review-of-Governance-and-Accountability-in-the-Civil-Service-The-Rt-Hon-Lord-Maude-of-Horsham-Final-3.pdf>

Ministry of Justice, *The Governance of Britain—Constitutional Renewal* (Cm 7342, 2008)

—— *The Governance of Britain: Review of the Executive Royal Prerogative Powers: Final Report* (October 2009)

Ministry of Reconstruction, *Report of the Machinery of Government Committee (Haldane)* (Cd 9230, 1918)

Modernising Government (Cm 4310, 1999)

National Archives, *Statutory Instrument Practice* (5th edn, 2017)

National Audit Office, *Review of Government Advertising* (April 2003) <https://webarchive.nationalarchives.gov.uk/ukgwa/20170207052351/https://www.nao.org.uk/wp-content/uploads/2003/04/gov_advertising.pdf>

—— *The Debt Management Office—Borrowing on Behalf of Government* (January 2007) <www.nao.org.uk/wp-content/uploads/2012/11/debt_management_office.pdf>

—— *Over-optimism in Government Projects* (December 2013) <www.nao.org.uk/wp-content/uploads/2013/12/10320-001-Over-optimism-in-government-projects.pdf>

——*Departmental Overview; the Performance of the Cabinet Office 2013–14* (November 2014)

——*The Centre of Government* (HC 2014–15, 171)

——*The Centre of Government: An Update* (HC 2014–15, 1031)

—— *The Art of Spending Public Money Wisely* (September–October 2015) <www.nao.org.uk/wp-content/uploads/2015/10/The-art-of-spending-public-money-wisely1.pdf>

——*Capability in the Civil Service* (March 2017)

——*A Short Guide to the Cabinet Office* (September 2017)

—— *Survival Guide to Challenging Costs in Major Projects* (June 2018) <www.nao.org.uk/insights/survival-guide-to-challenging-costs-in-major-projects-2/>

—— *Regulation Overview 2019* (March 2020) <www.nao.org.uk/wp-content/uploads/2020/03/Overview-Regulation-2019.pdf>

—— *Code of Practice dealing with the Relationship between the National Audit Office and the Comptroller and Auditor General* (HC 2021–22, 1230)

——*Annual Report and Accounts 2022–23* (HC 2022–23, 1515)

——*Covid-19 Cost Tracker* <www.nao.org.uk/overviews/covid-19-cost-tracker/>

——*Cabinet Office Functional Savings* (HC 2022–23, 1865)

Northcote S and Trevelyan CE, *The Organisation of the Permanent Civil Service*, Parl Pap, Vol XXVII, 1854

O'Donnell G, *Financing Britain's Future: Review of the Revenue Departments* (Cm 6163, 2004)

Office for Budget Responsibility, *Economic and Fiscal Outlook* (CP 230, March 2020)

——*Economic and Fiscal Outlook* (CP 545, October 2021)

——*Economic and Fiscal Outlook* (CP 804, March 2023)

——and HM Treasury, *Framework Document* (7 March 2019) <https://obr.uk/docs/dlm_uploads/OBR_HMT_framework_document_2019_update_web.pdf>

—— HM Treasury, the Department for Work and Pensions and HM Revenue and Customs, *Memorandum of Understanding* (8 March 2017) <https://obr.uk/docs/dlm_uploads/MoU_2017_updateWebPDF.pdf>

Office for National Statistics, *Framework Document* (1996) <https://uksa.statisticsauthority.gov.uk/wp-content/uploads/2015/12/images-onsframework_tcm97-18283.pdf>

——*Clarifying How Public Sector Finances Classification Decisions Are Made* (July 2016 <www.ons.gov.uk/economy/governmentpublicsectorandtaxes/publicsectorfinance/methodologies/clarifyinghowpublicsectorfinancesclassificationdecisionsaremade>

——*UK Economic Statistics Sector and Transaction Classifications: The Classification Process* (28 June 2018) <www.ons.gov.uk/methodology/classificationsandstandards/economicstatisticsclassifications/ukeconomicstatisticssectorandtransactionclassificationstheclassificationprocess>

—— *New Treatment of Student Loans in the Public Sector Finances and National Accounts* (17 December 2018) <www.ons.gov.uk/economy/governmentpublicsectorandtaxes/publicsectorfinance/articles/newtreatmentofstudentloansinthepublicsectorfinancesandnationalaccounts/2018-12-17>

—— *Public Sector Employment* (March 2020) <www.ons.gov.uk/employmentandlabourmarket/peopleinwork/publicsectorpersonnel/datasets/publicsectoremploymentreferencetable>

——*Public Sector Classification Guide* (November 2022) <www.ons.gov.uk/economy/nationalaccounts/uksectoraccounts/articles/economicstatisticssectorclassificationclassificationupdateandforwardworkplan/november2022>

—— *Public Sector Classification Guide and Forward Work Plan* (29 February 2024) <www.ons.gov.uk/methodology/classificationsandstandards/economicstatisticsclassifications/introductiontoeconomicstatisticsclassifications>

—— *UK Economic Statistics Sector and Transaction Classifications: The Classification Process* [nd] <www.ons.gov.uk/methodology/classificationsandstandards/economicstatisticsclassifications/ukeconomicstatisticssectorandtransactionclassificationstheclassificationprocess>

Office of Parliamentary Counsel, *When Laws Become Too Complex* (March 2013) <www.gov.uk/government/publications/when-laws-become-too-complex>

Office for Product Safety and Standards, *Regulators Code* <www.gov.uk/government/publications/regulators-code>

Office of Public Service, *Guide to Legislative Procedures* (4th edn, 1996)
Office for Statistics Regulation and UK Statistics Authority, *Code of Practice for Statistics* (edn 2.1, May 2022)
Organisation for Economic Co-operation and Development, *OECD Independent Fiscal Institutions Review, Office for Budget Responsibility (OBR) of the United Kingdom* (OECD 24 September 2020)
Parliamentary Commissioner for Administration, *Annual Report for 1995* (HC 1995–96, 296)
——*Annual Report 1997–98* (HC 1997–98, 845)
Permanent Secretary, Department of Transport, Letter to Secretary of State (7 February 2018) <https://assets.publishing.service.gov.uk/government/uploads/system/uploads/attachment_data/file/842456/letter1-eu-exit-direction.pdf>
Phillis B, *An Independent Review of Government Communications (Chairman: Bob Phillis)* (January 2004) <https://universityofleeds.github.io/philtaylorpapers/pmt/exhibits/1967/Phillis.pdf>
Post Office Horizon IT Inquiry, *Terms of Reference* <www.postofficehorizoninquiry.org.uk/publications/terms-reference>
—— *Completed List of Issues 17-11-21,* Governance and Oversight, nos 206–10 <www.postofficehorizoninquiry.org.uk/publications/completed-list-issues>
Prime Minister, Letter to Lord Geidt (31 May 2022) <www.gov.uk/government/publications/letter-from-the-prime-minister-to-the-independent-adviser-on-ministers-interests-31-may-2022--2>
Procedure Committee, *Resource Accounting and Budgeting* (HC 1997–98, 438)
——*Estimates and Appropriations Procedure* (HC 2003–04, 393)
——*Authorising Government Expenditure: Steps to More Effective Scrutiny* (HC 2016–17, 190)
—— *Review of Estimates Memoranda by the House of Commons Scrutiny Unit: Response to the Committee's Fifth Report of Session 2016–17* (HC 2017–19, 1156)
Public Accounts Committee, *Epitome of the Reports from the Committee of Public Accounts 1857–1937* (HC 1937–38, 154) (Epitome I)
—— *Epitome of Reports from the Committees of Public Accounts 1938 to 1969* (HC 1969–70, 187) (Epitome II)
——*The Proper Conduct of Public Business* (HC 1993–94, 154)
——*Pergau Hydro-Electric Project* (HC 1993–94, 155)
——*Treasury Controls* (HC 1998–99, 157)
——*Accountability for Public Money* (HC 2010–12, 740)
——*Accountability for Public Money—Progress Report* (HC 2010–12, 1503)
——*Managing Budgeting in Government* (HC 2012–13, 661)
——*Civil Service Reform* (HC 2013–14, 473)
——*Accountability to Parliament for Taxpayers' Money* (HC 2015–16, 732)
——*Better Regulation* (HC 2016–17, 487)
——*Managing Government Spending and Performance* (HC 2016–17, 710)
——*Improving Government Planning and Spending* (HC 2017–19, 1556)
——*Government's Delivery through Arm's-Length Bodies* (HC 2021–22, 181)
——*Improving the Accounting Officer Assessment Process* (HC 2022–23, 43)
——*Government Shared Services* (HC 2022–23, 734)
——*Cross-Government Working* (HC 2023–24, 75)
Public Administration Select Committee, *The Government Information and Communication Service* (HC 1997–98, 770)
——*Freedom of Information Draft Bill* (HC 1998–99, 570-I, 570-II)
——*Making Government Work: The Emerging Issues* (HC 2000–01, 94)
——*'These Unfortunate Events': Lessons of Recent Events at the Former DTLR* (HC 2001–02, 303)
——*A Draft Civil Service Bill: Completing the Reform* (HC (2003–04, 128)
—— *Taming the Prerogative: Strengthening Ministerial Accountability to Parliament* (HC 2003–04, 422)
——*The Ministerial Code: The Case for Independent Investigation* (HC 2005–06, 1457)
——*Machinery of Government Changes* (HC 2006–07, 672)
—— *The Ministerial Code: The Case for Independent Investigation: Government Response to the Committee's Seventh Report of Session 2005–06* (HC 2006–07, 1088)

—— *Machinery of Government Changes: Government Response to the Committee's Seventh Report of Session 2006–07* (HC 2007–08, 90)
—— *Propriety and Peerages* (HC 2007–08, 153)
—— *Machinery of Government Changes: A Follow-up Report* (HC 2007–08, 160)
—— *Machinery of Government Changes: Further Report with the Government Response to the Committee's First Report of Session 2007–08* (HC 2007–08, 514)
—— *Change in Government: The Agenda for Leadership* (HC 2010–12, 714)
—— *Business Appointment Rules* (HC 2012–13, 404)
—— *The Prime Minister's Adviser on Ministers' Interests: Independent or Not? Government Response to the Committee's Twenty Second Report of Session 2010–12* (HC 2012–13, 976)
—— *Truth to Power: How Civil Service Reform Can Succeed: Government Response* (HC 2013–14, 955)
—— *Latest Proposals for Ministerial Involvement in Permanent Secretary Appointments: PASC's Recommendations* (HC 2013–14, 1041)
Public Administration and Constitutional Affairs Committee, *Accounting for Democracy: Making Sure Parliament, the People and Ministers Know How and Why Public Money is Spent* (HC 2016–17, 95)
—— *Managing Ministers' and Officials' Conflicts of Interest: Time for Clearer Values, Principles and Action* (HC 2016–17, 252)
—— *The Future of the Union, Part Two: Inter-institutional Relations in the UK* (HC 2016–17, 839)
—— *Better Public Appointments? Follow-up and the Government Response to the Committee's Third Report, Better Public Appointments?: The Grimstone Review on Public Appointments* (HC 2016–17, 1062)
—— *The Minister and the Official: The Fulcrum of Whitehall Effectiveness* (HC 2017–19, 497)
—— *Accounting for Democracy Revisited: The Government Response and Proposed Review* (HC 2017–19, 1197)
—— *Devolution and Exiting the EU: Reconciling Differences and Building Strong Relationships* (HC 2017–19, 1485)
—— *Governance of Statistics* (HC 2017–19, 1820)
—— *Delivering the Government's Infrastructure Commitments through Major Projects* (HC 2019–21, 125)
—— *The Role and Status of the Prime Minister's Office* (HC 2021–22, 67)
—— *The Cabinet Office Freedom of Information Clearing House* (HC 2021–22, 505)
—— *The Cabinet Office Freedom of Information Clearing House: Government Response to the Committee's Ninth Report of Session 2021–22* (HC 2021–22, 576)
—— *The Role and Status of the Prime Minister's Office: Government's Response to the Committee's First Report* (HC 2021–22, 710)
—— *The Role of Non-Executive Directors in Government* (HC 2022–23, 318)
—— *Propriety of Governance in Light of Greensill* (HC 2022–23, 888)
—— *The Work of the Cabinet Office* (HC 2022–23, 950) evidence (12 July 2023)
Regulatory Policy Committee, *Securing the Evidence Base for Regulation: Regulatory Policy Committee Scrutiny during the 2010 to 2015 Parliament* (March 2015)
Report of the Royal Commission on Standards of Conduct in Government (Cmnd 6524, 1976)
Revenue and Customs Prosecutions Office, *Annual Report and Resource Accounts* 2008/09 (HC 2008–09, 658)
Riddell P, Pre-Valedictory Speech to the UCL Constitution Unit on Public Appointments (April 2021) <https://publicappointmentscommissioner.independent.gov.uk/pre-valedictory-speech-to-the-ucl-constitution-unit-on-public-appointments/>
Royal Commission on the Civil Service, *Report* (Cm 7748, 1914)
Royal Commission on Standards of Conduct in Government 1974–76 (Cmnd 6524, 1976)
Rycroft P and Barnes R, 'Getting to Grips with the Devolution Challenge' (5 February 2016) <https://civilservice.blog.gov.uk/2016/02/05/getting-to-grips-with-the-devolution-challenge/>
Scott E and Evennett H, *Strathclyde Review and the Primacy of the House of Commons* (House of Lords Library, December 2015)

Scott Sir R, *Report of the Inquiry into the Export of Defence Equipment and Dual-Use Goods to Iraq and Related Prosecutions* (HC 1995–96, 115)
Scottish Government, *Choosing Scotland's Future: A National Conversation* (August 2007)
Secretary of State, Department for Exiting the European Union, *Legislating for the United Kingdom's withdrawal from the European Union* (Cm 9446, March 2017)
Secretary of State for the Home Department, *Freedom of Information: Consultation on Draft Legislation* (Cm 4355, May 1999)
Secretary of State for Justice and Lord Chancellor, *The Governance of Britain* (Cm 7170, July 2007)
Secretary of State for Transport and the Chief Secretary to the Treasury, *Department of Transport Report 1991: The Government's Expenditure Plans 1991–92 to 1993–94* (Cm 1507, February 1991)
Smith Commission, *Report of the Smith Commission for Further Devolution of Powers to the Scottish Parliament* (November 2014)
Statistics Commission, *Legislation to Build Trust in Statistics*, Report No 18 (May 2004) <https://uksa.statisticsauthority.gov.uk/wp-content/uploads/tempdocs/report-18--legislation-to-build-trust-in-statistics--may-2004-.pdf>
——*Annual Report 2003–04* (Cm 6250, July 2004)
Tee M, *Review of Government Direct Communication and the Role of COI* (March 2011)
Tolley A, *Investigation Report to the Prime Minister* <www.google.com/search?client=firefox-b-d&q=2023.04.20_Investigation_Report_to_the_Prime_Minister.pdf>
Trade and Industry Committee, *Exports to Iraq* (HC 1991–92, 86)
Treasury Committee, *The New Fiscal Framework and the Comprehensive Spending Review* (HC 1997–98, 960)
——*Office for National Statistics* (HC 1998–99, 43-I)
——*Spending Review 2000* (HC 1999–2000, 485)
——*Spending Review 2000: The Government's Response to the Committee's Ninth Report of Session 1999–2000* (HC 1999–2000, 941)
——*National Statistics* (HC 2000–01, 137)
——*Government's Cash and Debt Management* (HC 2000–01, 154)
——*The 2006 Pre-Budget Report* (HC 2006–07, 115)
——*The 2007 Comprehensive Spending Review: Prospects and Processes* (HC 2006–07, 279)
——*Financial Reporting and the National Accounts*, oral evidence (4 March 2008) (HC 2007–08, 397-I)
——*Pre-Budget Report 2008* (HC 2008–09, 27)
——*Office for Budget Responsibility* (HC 2010–12, 385)
——*Spending Review 2010* (HC 2010–12, 544)
——*Reviewing the Office for Budget Responsibility* (HC 2015–16, 514)
——*Spending Review and Autumn Statement 2015* (HC 2015–16, 638)
——*Spending Review and Autumn Statement 2015: Government and Office for Budgetary Responsibility Responses to the Sixth Report from the Committee, 2016–17* (HC 2016–17, 683)
——*Oral evidence: The work of the Debt Management Office* (HC 2017–19, 2082)
——*Oral evidence: Work of the Treasury* (HC 2022–23, 137)
Treasury and Civil Service Committee, *Civil Servants and Ministers: Duties and Responsibilities* (HC 1985–86, 92)
——*The Role of the Civil Service* (HC 1993–94, 27)
——*Simplified Estimates and Resource Accounting* (HC 1994–95, 212)
Treasury Officer of Accounts, *Regularity, Propriety and Value for Money* (November 2004)
——*The Accounting Officer's Survival Guide* (December 2015)
Treasury Solicitor, *Annual Report and Accounts 2001–02* (HC 2002–03, 252)
——*Annual Report and Accounts 2010–11* (HC 2010–12, 1053)
Treasury Solicitor's Department, *The Judge over Your Shoulder* (Cabinet Office 1987)
Turnbull, Sir A, Civil Service Reform Event—24 February 2004, Opening remarks <https://www.civilservant.org.uk/library/2004-CSR_Conference_Opening_Remarks.pdf>
UK Covid-19 Inquiry, *Module 1: The Resilience and Preparedness of the United Kingdom* (July 2024) <https://covid19.public-inquiry.uk/>

UK Government, *The Orange Book: Management of Risk—Principles and Concepts* (2023)
UK Parliament, *Parliament and the Government* <www.parliament.uk/about/how/role/relations-with-other-institutions/parliament-government/>
Wilson Sir R, *Report to the Prime Minister on Civil Service Reform* (December 1999) <www.civilservant.org.uk/library/1999-SRW's_report _to_PM.pdf>

Index

For the benefit of digital users, indexed terms that span two pages (e.g., 52–53) may, on occasion, appear on only one of those pages.